SCHOOL PROGRAM • TEACHER EDITION

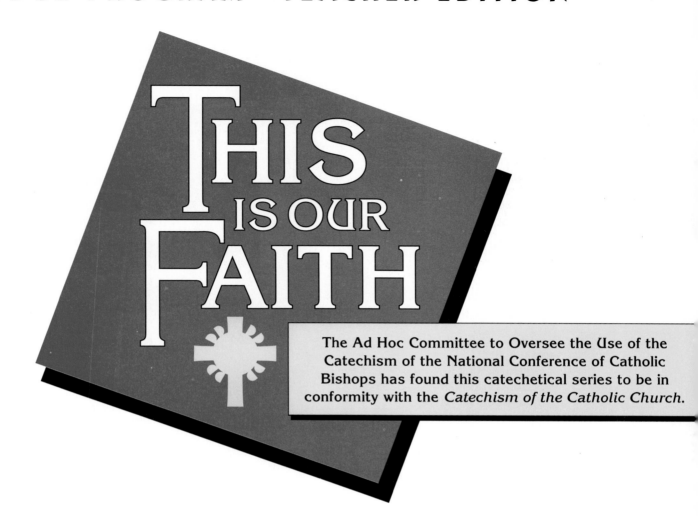

THIS IS OUR FAITH

The Ad Hoc Committee to Oversee the Use of the Catechism of the National Conference of Catholic Bishops has found this catechetical series to be in conformity with the *Catechism of the Catholic Church.*

Series Authors: Janaan Manternach
Carl J. Pfeifer

Teacher Edition Authors: Dolores Ready
Kate Sweeney Ristow
Judene Leon

Contributing Authors: Susan G. Keys   Maureen Shaughnessy, S.C.
Paula Lenz   Barbara Carol Vasiloff

Student Edition Authors: Dolores Ready   Maureen Gallagher
Joan R. DeMerchant   Jean Marie Weber

SILVER BURDETT GINN
PARSIPPANY, NJ

Contents . . . . ● ● ●

Consultants

Linda Blanchette; Anita Bridge; Fred Brown; Rod
Brownfield; Sister Mary Michael Burns, S.C.;
Patricia Burns; Bernadine Carroll; Mary Ellen
Cocks; Sister Peggy Conlon, R.S.M.; Mary Ann
Crowley; Pamela Danni; Sister Jamesetta
DeFelice, O.S.U.; Sister Mary Elizabeth Duke,
S.N.D., Mary M. Gibbons; Yolanda Gremillion;
Sister Angela Hallahan, C.H.F.; Alice J. Heard;
Sister Michele O'Connoll, P.B.V.M.; Sister Angela
O'Mahoney, P.B.V.M.; Sister Ruthann O'Mara,
S.S.J.; Sandra Okulicz-Hulme; Judy Papandria;
Rachel Pasano; Sallie Ann Phelan; Sister Geraldine
M. Rogers, S.S.J.; Mary Lou Schlosser; Patricia
Ann Sibilia; Margaret E. Skelly; Lisa Ann Sorlie;
Sister Victorine Stoltz, O.S.B.; Sister Nancy Jean
Turner, S.H.C.J.; Christine Ward; Judith Reidel
Weber; Kay White; Elizabeth M. Williams;
Catherine R. Wolf; Florence Bambrick Yarney;
Kathryn K. Zapcic

Advisory Board

Rev. Louis J. Cameli; Philip J. Cunningham; Sister
Clare E. Fitzgerald; William J. Freburger; Greer G.
Gordon; Sister Veronica R. Grover, S.H.C.J.; Rev.
Thomas Guarino; Rev. Robert E. Harahan; Rev.
Eugene LaVerdieré, S.S.S.; Rev. Frank J. McNulty;
Rev. Msgr. John J. Strynkowski

National Catechetical Advisor

Kathleen Hendricks

Nihil Obstat

Kathleen Flanagan, S.C., Ph.D.
Censor Librorum
Ellen Joyce, S.C., Ph.D.
Censor Librorum

Imprimatur

Most Reverend
Frank J. Rodimer
Bishop of Paterson
November 8, 1996

The *nihil obstat* and *imprimatur* are official
declarations that a book or pamphlet is free of
doctrinal and moral error. No implication is
contained therein that those who have granted the
nihil obstat and *imprimatur* agree with the
contents, opinions, or statements expressed.

ACKNOWLEDGMENTS

Excerpts from the English translation of the
memorial acclamation from *The Roman Missal*
© 1973, International Committee on English in
the Liturgy, Inc. All rights reserved.

All adaptations of Scripture are based on the *Saint
Joseph Edition of the New American Bible.*

English translation of the *Catechism of the
Catholic Church* for the United States of America
copyright © 1994, United States Catholic
Conference, Inc. - Libreria Editrice Vaticana. Used
with permission.

©1998 Silver Burdett Ginn Inc.
All rights reserved. Printed in the United States of
America. This publication, or parts thereof, may
not be reproduced in any form by photographic,
electrostatic, mechanical, or any other method, for
any use, including information storage and
retrieval, without written permission from the
publisher.   ISBN 0-382-30502-7

2345678910–0504030201009998

Dear Catholic School Teacher,

The teaching of religion is an important responsibility for all Catholic School teachers. We commend you for assuming this responsibility and are proud to be your partner in sharing the Catholic faith with children.

We are especially pleased to announce that the National Conference of Catholic Bishops' Ad Hoc Committee to Oversee the Use of the Catechism has found this new edition of *This Is Our Faith* to be in conformity with the *Catechism of the Catholic Church*. This means that *This Is Our Faith* has a breadth and depth of content wherein the presentation of Catholic doctrine is authentic and therefore suitable for catechetical instruction.

This sharing of faith includes many dimensions: the instruction in doctrine, Scripture, and morality; the experience of prayer and liturgy; the building of a value system; the ability to relate teaching to life; the knowledge of the rich heritage we share in time, place, and people; and the profound respect for and love of the Catholic Church. *This Is Our Faith* addresses each of these dimensions.

We take our responsibility to Catholic education seriously and once again we have consulted you, the classroom teacher, at every step along the way of the development of this revision. The next few pages will give you an overview of the new *This Is Our Faith*. We know that you will find in this program everything that a publisher can provide to support you in your important work.

Your commitment to Catholic education and to the children whom you teach is one that we share. This program has been created to be the best for you and for your class. It is to you that we dedicate this edition of *This Is Our Faith*.

Sincerely,

Raymond T. Latour

Raymond T. Latour
Vice President & Director
Religion Division

Content is important to Catholic identity.

What content is included?

THIS IS OUR FAITH is a developmental program, based on Scripture and rooted in the teachings of the *Catechism of the Catholic Church*. While the content for each year centers on one particular theme, strands on Church, Sacraments, Trinity, and Morality are interwoven throughout the program. The presentation of doctrine has been increased in each chapter of this new edition.

Plus—chapter reviews and **expanded unit reviews** help you to evaluate student progress as you teach!!

The chart to the right outlines the doctrinal content of Grade 1.

TRINITY — THREE PERSONS ONE GOD

CREATOR/FATHER	JESUS
God is the creator of all things.	Jesus is God's most special gift to us.
God loves and cares for each one of us.	Jesus is the Son of God.
God wants us to be happy and always forgives us.	Jesus is our Savior.
The people of God are the Church.	Jesus is our friend and brother.
	Jesus is always with us.
	Jesus teaches us about God.
	Jesus brings us God's forgiveness.
	Followers of Jesus are called Christians. Jesus is a person like us. He grew up in a family with Mary and Joseph.

THE BIBLE	PRAYER AND PRECEPTS
The Bible is a special book about God's love for us.	Sign Of The Cross
Each book in the Bible was written by someone especially chosen by God.	The Lord's Prayer
God speaks to us at Mass through readings from the Bible.	Hail Mary
	Glory Be To The Father
	Grace Before Meals
	Grace After Meals
	Morning Prayer
	Evening Prayer
	Prayers and precepts of the Church are used in lessons throughout the texts. Selected traditional prayers and precepts also appear in a special end-of-text section designed to encourage their memorization.

Our Amen Section of Saints, Feasts and Seasons is still conveniently located in the back of the student book and has been expanded just as you requested. Every year your students will have the opportunity to celebrate the holy seasons of Advent, Lent, Christmas, and Easter in addition to other special feasts.

THE HOLY SPIRIT

The Holy Spirit is the spirit of God.

The Holy Spirit gives us strength and joy.

The Holy Spirit helps us live together in peace.

The Holy Spirit helps us forgive and be forgiven.

The Holy Spirit gives us special gifts to help us live good lives.

The Holy Spirit gives us strength.

SACRAMENTS

At Baptism, the family of Jesus welcomes us as new members.

At Baptism, we celebrate our new life in Jesus.

At Mass, Jesus shares a meal with us.

At Mass, Jesus gives us himself in the form of the Eucharist–the bread of life.

In the Eucharist, we remember what Jesus did and said at the Last Supper.

About the Mass

About Forgiveness

A complete chapter reviewing the basics of these sacraments.

CHURCH

The Church is a group of Christians.

We belong to the Catholic Church.

We are Catholic Christians.

A church is a special place.

A church is home for the family of Jesus.

Celebrations and the receiving of God's special gifts are a part of the church.

MORALITY

We love our family.

We care for all things.

We care for others and for our world, as Jesus did.

We live good lives with the help of the Holy Spirit.

We try to be like Jesus and do what he would do.

RELIGIOUS VOCABULARY

Angel
Baptism
Bible
Catholic Church
Christ
Christian Church
Create

Creator
Eucharist
Forgive
Galilee
God
Godparents
Good Samaritan

Gospel
Hallowed
Heaven
Holy Family
Holy Spirit
Jesus
Mass

Peter and Andrew
Prayer
Rabbi
Temple
Trespass
Trust

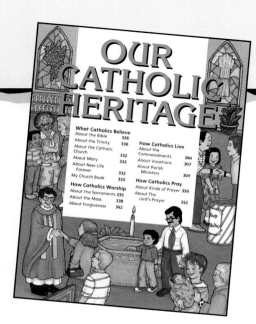

OUR CATHOLIC HERITAGE

Our Catholic Heritage, a special doctrinal section organized according to the four pillars of the *Catechism of the Catholic Church,* is included in each grade-level student book, to provide you with the opportunity and resources necessary to teach and review basic Catholic teachings every year.

What about prayer?

THIS IS OUR FAITH emphasizes prayer in all forms from traditional to spontaneous, from music to meditation, from the spoken word and formal liturgical prayer to the psalms and prayers of the heart. Children learn not only prayers, but how to pray alone, in a small group, within the classroom or school or in the church assembly. **Among other resources within THIS IS OUR FAITH, you will find the following:**

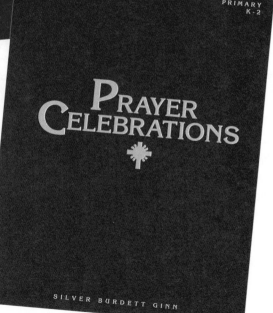

Praying with a Play
There are many ways to think over the stories from the Bible.
We can act out the story.
Putting on a play helps us remember the story.
We can imagine what happened and what people said.

You might want to put on a play about the Good Samaritan.

140   Prayer

▲ Prayer pages in each chapter of the student book provide instruction on and an experience of prayer each week.

PRIMARY
K-2

PRAYERS
FOR
EVERY DAY

SILVER BURDETT GINN

▲
Prayers for Every Day is a wonderful resource for you. In it you will find prayers for every day of the year, as well as additional prayers to be said during special times and seasons.

PRIMARY
K-2

PRAYER
CELEBRATIONS

SILVER BURDETT GINN

◄
Prayer Celebrations are resource books full of complete grade-level-specific prayer services ready to use with your class. Everything is done for you. All you need to do is read the special preparation page, duplicate the master sheet, and begin the celebration!

What about Sunday?

This brand-new supplemental program helps prepare children to better understand the Sunday readings. It provides ways to help children participate more fully in the Sunday liturgy—a need expressed by many teachers. Here's how to do it!

Each week, perhaps on Friday, distribute the student leaflets for Sunday. Then together, listen to the Word of God and follow the specific activities that will help the Word take on real meaning for children. They will be ready to listen and pray on Sunday!

This is indeed a true liturgical-year program! Each leaflet is brand-new and developed for each liturgical cycle!

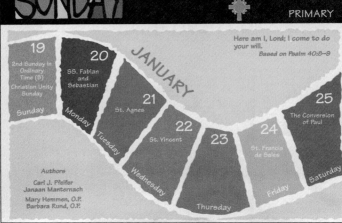

◀ Background for the Teacher and a session outline are clearly and simply presented on each teacher folder—which also provides a handy storage unit for the student leaflets.

THIS IS OUR FAITH has always provided the best in Teacher Editions.

What's new in this one?

Chapter Organizers keep you on target and make planning quick and easy.

All content is correlated with the *Catechism of the Catholic Church*

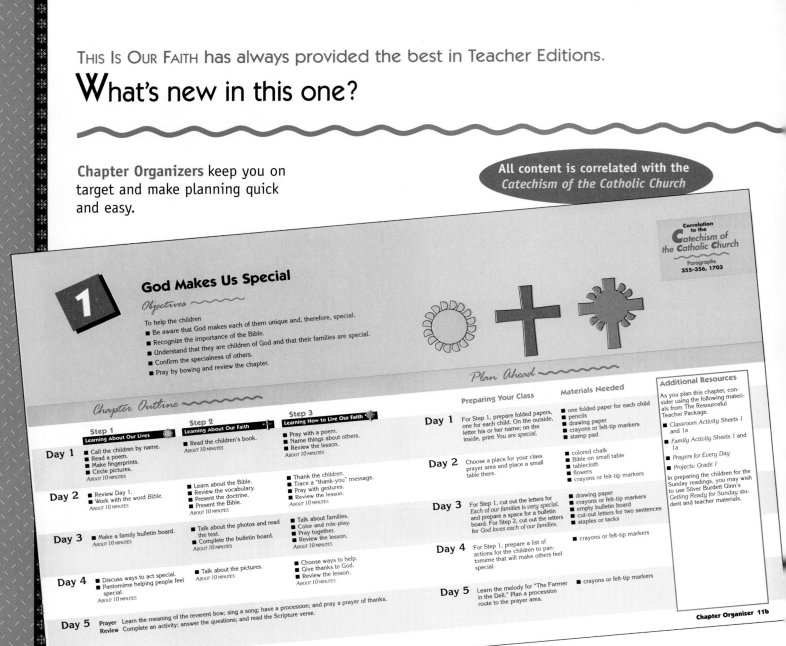

Correlation to the Catechism of the Catholic Church
Paragraphs 355–356, 1703

1 God Makes Us Special

Objectives

To help the children
■ Be aware that God makes each of them unique and, therefore, special.
■ Recognize the importance of the Bible.
■ Understand that they are children of God and that their families are special.
■ Confirm the specialness of others.
■ Pray by bowing and review the chapter.

Chapter Outline

	Step 1 Learning About Our Lives	Step 2 Learning About Our Faith	Step 3 Learning How to Live Our Faith
Day 1	■ Call the children by name. ■ Read a poem. ■ Make fingerprints. ■ Circle pictures. *ABOUT 10 MINUTES*	■ Read the children's book. *ABOUT 10 MINUTES*	■ Pray with a poem. ■ Name things about others. ■ Review the lesson. *ABOUT 10 MINUTES*
Day 2	■ Review Day 1. ■ Work with the word *Bible.* *ABOUT 10 MINUTES*	■ Learn about the Bible. ■ Review the vocabulary. ■ Present the doctrine. ■ Present the Bible. *ABOUT 10 MINUTES*	■ Thank the children. ■ Trace a "thank-you" message. ■ Pray with gestures. ■ Review the lesson. *ABOUT 10 MINUTES*
Day 3	■ Make a family bulletin board. *ABOUT 10 MINUTES*	■ Talk about the photos and read the text. ■ Complete the bulletin board. *ABOUT 10 MINUTES*	■ Talk about families. ■ Color and role-play. ■ Pray together. ■ Review the lesson. *ABOUT 10 MINUTES*
Day 4	■ Discuss ways to act special. ■ Pantomime helping people feel special. *ABOUT 10 MINUTES*	■ Talk about the pictures. *ABOUT 10 MINUTES*	■ Choose ways to help. ■ Give thanks to God. ■ Review the lesson. *ABOUT 10 MINUTES*
Day 5	**Prayer** Learn the meaning of the reverent bow; sing a song; have a procession; and pray a prayer of thanks. **Review** Complete an activity; answer the questions; and read the Scripture verse.		

Plan Ahead

	Preparing Your Class	Materials Needed
Day 1	For Step 1, prepare folded papers, one for each child. On the outside, letter his or her name; on the inside, print *You are special.*	■ one folded paper for each child ■ pencils ■ drawing paper ■ crayons or felt-tip markers ■ stamp pad
Day 2	Choose a place for your class prayer area and place a small table there.	■ colored chalk ■ Bible on small table ■ tablecloth ■ flowers ■ crayons or felt-tip markers
Day 3	For Step 1, cut out the letters for *Each of our families is very special,* and prepare a space for a bulletin board. For Step 2, cut out the letters for *God loves each of our families.*	■ drawing paper ■ crayons or felt-tip markers ■ empty bulletin board ■ cut-out letters for two sentences ■ staples or tacks
Day 4	For Step 1, prepare a list of actions for the children to pantomime that will make others feel special.	■ crayons or felt-tip markers
Day 5	Learn the melody for "The Farmer in the Dell." Plan a procession route to the prayer area.	■ crayons or felt-tip markers

Additional Resources

As you plan this chapter, consider using the following materials from The Resourceful Teacher Package.

■ *Classroom Activity Sheets 1 and 1a*
■ *Family Activity Sheets 1 and 1a*
■ *Prayers for Every Day*
■ *Projects: Grade 1*

In preparing the children for the Sunday readings, you may wish to use Silver Burdett Ginn's *Getting Ready for Sunday* student and teacher materials.

Chapter Organizer 11b

11a Chapter Organizer

Also in each chapter you will find special feature boxes, giving you additional tips where you need them.

 **CURRICULUM CONNECTION**

 **Enriching the Lesson**

Focus On
provides background information for you on specific topics.

Curriculum Connection
helps you tie in what is being taught in Religion with other content areas.

Enriching the Lesson
includes extras—additional ideas to expand and enrich the lesson.

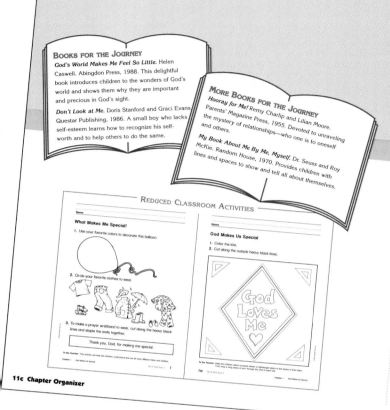

BOOKS FOR THE JOURNEY

God's World Makes Me Feel So Little. Helen Caswell. Abingdon Press, 1988. This delightful book introduces children to the wonders of God's world and shows them why they are important and precious in God's sight.

Don't Look at Me. Doris Stanford and Graci Evans. Questar Publishing, 1986. A small boy who lacks self-esteem learns how to recognize his self-worth and to help others to do the same.

MORE BOOKS FOR THE JOURNEY

Hooray for Me! Remy Charlip and Lilian Moore. Parents' Magazine Press, 1955. Devoted to unraveling the mystery of relationships—who one is to oneself and others.

My Book About Me By Me, Myself. Dr. Seuss and Roy McKie. Random House, 1970. Provides children with lines and spaces to show and tell all about themselves.

REDUCED CLASSROOM ACTIVITIES

What Makes Me Special!

1. Use your favorite colors to decorate this balloon.

2. Circle your favorite clothes to wear.

3. To make a prayer wristband to wear, cut along the heavy black lines and staple the ends together.

Thank you, God, for making me special.

To the Teacher: This activity will help the children understand that we all have different likes and dislikes.

Chapter 1 God Makes Us Special

God Makes Us Special

1. Color the kite.
2. Cut along the outside heavy black lines.

God Loves Me

To the Teacher: Help the children attach crossed straws in lightweight sticks to the backs of their kites. Then tape a long piece of yarn through the end of each kite.

Chapter 1 God Makes Us Special

11c Chapter Organizer

Background for the Teacher

THE PARADOXICAL SIX-YEAR-OLD

In their classic book on child development *Your Six-Year-Old: Loving and Defiant*, Ames and Ilg demonstrate that there can be a contradiction between the behavior of the six-year-old and the need for approval the child wants so badly. For example, at the end of a very bad day, a child can ask blissfully, "Have I been good today?" It is an interesting fact that often the less praise and credit a child deserves the more the six-year-old seems to want love and praise. Any failure is very hard at this age, and severe criticism is most painful.

This paradoxical behavior of six-year-olds may be a challenge to you, but the theme of Chapter 1 will do much to make the children feel loved and acclaimed. The lessons will focus on God's love for them and how special God made them.

THE SIX-YEAR-OLD IS WONDROUSLY MADE

Thousands of years ago, the psalmist, captured by the mystery of a God who made us so wonderfully, prayed:

Truly you have formed my inmost being;
     you knit me in my mother's womb.
I give you thanks that I am fearfully, wonderfully made;
     wonderful are your works.

Psalm 139:13–14

Not only the Scriptures but also the teachings of the Church respect the uniqueness of each individual as created by God. As a catechetical instrument, THIS IS OUR FAITH continues this tradition and celebrates the specialness of each of God's children.

The youngsters with whom you will share this lesson are loved by God. Unceasingly, God calls them to wholeness and holiness. But they can respond to God's love only if they find themselves worthy of love, if they find themselves lovely and lovable.

Children need to know that their God delights in their creation. God loves each of them—tall or short, stout or lean, clumsy or graceful. Whatever their limitations—the need to use a wheelchair, the inability to see or to hear well—God is helping them to be their best selves. Whatever their dispositions—happy or disgruntled, hyperactive or passive, moody or sunny—God is present to them.

This lesson enables you to help the children appreciate themselves. By helping them know that they exist because of God's love for them, you can create an atmosphere of love and acceptance in which each child feels appreciated for being the unique person that God has loved into existence.

Chapter Organizer 11d

Background for teachers provides excellent information for you on what is to be taught as well as insights into how to teach it.

Cultural Awareness
gives you needed information to aid students in their appreciation of other cultures.

Teaching Tips
provides just what you need—an extra idea, project, or help - just when you need it.

These new features plus our new size and easier to use format, along with our proven method of teaching—our three-step lesson plan—and a complete lesson every day makes this the best teacher edition ever!

You've always had great additional teacher resources.

What's new in this edition?

We've already told you about the *new* **Prayer Celebrations Book,** the *new* **Prayers for Every Day,** and the *new* **Getting Ready for Sunday** program.

Here's more!

NEW!

► **Project Books**
One per grade give ideas and opportunities to enhance and expand learning.

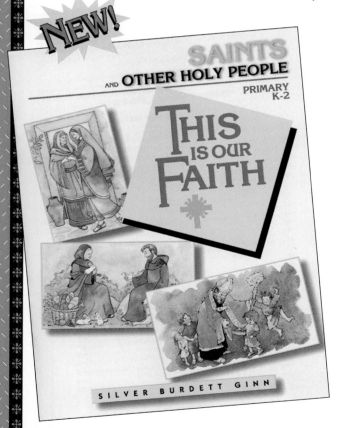

NEW!

▲
Saints and Other Holy People
provide excellent role models
for students.

NEW!

Mary's Visit with Elizabeth

Saint Francis Xavier

Saint Vincent de Paul

► **Saints Cards**
(32 of 6 Saints for each year)
Take-home cards for
each child to treasure.

Teacher Resource Package
Includes Project Booklet, Classroom Activities, Family Activities and Letters in English and Spanish, and Tests as well as a handy tote to keep all your resources together.

▲

◄ **Videos**
One per grade, correlated to each unit!
(Ready in 1998)

Familiar Resources Designed Especially for the 1998 Edition!

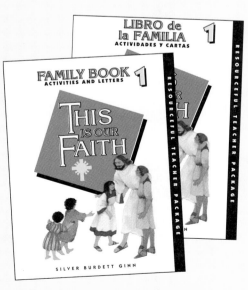

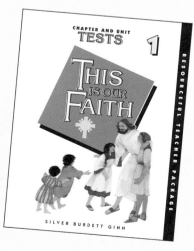

▲ **Classroom Activities**
two sheets for every chapter!

▲ **Family Activities and Letters**
(in English and in Spanish)
Ready to duplicate and send home!

Tests
Both Chapter and Unit
▲

And, as your students would say,

"What does THIS IS OUR FAITH have to do with real life?"

DAY TO DAY SKILLS FOR CHRISTIAN LIVING

BECOMING A FEELINGS DETECTIVE
We can discover how others feel. We can look and listen.

Activity
Each picture below shows a different feeling.
Look for the clues in the pictures that tell how
Boots and Zip are feeling.
Match the "feeling" words to the correct pictures.

1. Happy
2. Shy
3. Angry
4. Proud

and pictures to match.

3. Embarrassed

to care.

Day to Day   105

Living our faith goes well beyond the classroom experience into the everyday challenges and opportunities faced by each of our children every day. Each class begins with a life experience and ends with an integration of what has been learned into the child's life.

◀ **Day to Day: Skills for Christian Living**
At the end of each unit, two pages focus on the development of personal and moral skills in a sensitive and constructive way consistent with our Gospel values and Christian life. This is an infinitely practical feature that will help the faith and life to emerge as one.

God loves me.
I love God.
I want to learn more about God this year.

◀ For each grade-level the **gatefold** invites students to journey together as a school community through faith and life!

THIS IS OUR FAITH provides a complete and comprehensive coverage of Doctrine, Scripture, Morality, Prayer and Review, all taught in age-appropriate and proven ways.

Including all of the resources you've used and loved—and many new ones that you've wanted.

Written with you in mind and backed by the very best service in publishing for Catholic schools.

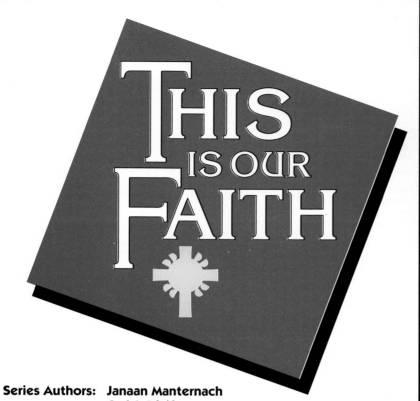

THIS IS OUR FAITH

Series Authors: Janaan Manternach
Carl J. Pfeifer

Authors: Dolores Ready
Joan R. DeMerchant
Maureen Gallagher
Jean Marie Weber

Contributing Author: Kate Sweeney Ristow

SILVER BURDETT GINN
PARSIPPANY, NJ

THIS IS OUR FAITH
SCHOOL PROGRAM

Contributing Authors: James Bitney, Robert Hamma, Paula A. Lenz, Judene Leon, Yvette Nelson, Sister Carolyn Puccio, C.S.J., Anna Ready, Kate Sweeney Ristow, Barbara Carol Vasiloff, Sister Maureen Shaughnessy, S.C., Sister Cecilia Maureen Cromwell, I.H.M., Patricia Frevert, Mary Lou Ihrig, Sister Arlene Pomije, C.S.J., Sister Mary Agnes Ryan, I.H.M., Brother Michael Sheerin, F.M.S.

Opening Doors: A Take-Home Magazine: Peter H.M. Demkovitz, Janie Gustafson, Margaret Savitskas

Day to Day: Skills for Christian Living: Susan G. Keys

Advisory Board:

Rev. Louis J. Cameli

Philip J. Cunningham

Sister Clare E. Fitzgerald

William J. Freburger

Greer J. Gordon

Sister Veronica R. Grover, S.H.C.J.

Rev. Thomas Guarino

Rev. Robert E. Harahan

Kathleen Hendricks

Rev. Eugene LaVerdieré, S.S.S.

Rev. Frank J. McNulty

Rev. Msgr. John J. Strynkowski

Consultants: Linda Blanchette, Anita Bridge, Fred Brown, Rod Brownfield, Sister Mary Michael Burns, S.C., Pat Burns, Bernadine Carroll, Mary Ellen Cocks, Sister Peggy Conlon, R.S.M., Mary Ann Crowley, Pamela Danni, Sister Jamesetta DeFelice, O.S.U., Sister Mary Elizabeth Duke, S.N.D., Mary M. Gibbons, Yolando Gremillion, Sister Angela Hallahan, C.H.F., Alice T. Heard, Sister Michele O'Connoll, P.B.V.M., Sister Angela O'Mahoney, P.B.V.M., Sister Ruthann O'Mara, S.S.J., Sandra Okulicz-Hulme, Judy Papandria, Rachel Pasano, Sallie Ann Phelan, Sister Geraldine M. Rogers, S.S.J., Mary Lou Schlosser, Patricia Ann Sibilia, Margaret E. Skelly, Lisa Ann Sorlie, Sister Victorine Stoltz, O.S.B., Sister Nancy Jean Turner, S.H.C.J., Christine Ward, Judith Reidel Weber, Kay White, Elizabeth M. Williams, Catherine R. Wolf, Florence Bambrick Yarney, Kathryn K. Zapcic

Nihil Obstat

Kathleen Flanagan, S.C., Ph.D.
Censor Librorum

Ellen Joyce, S.C. Ph.D.
Censor Librorum

Imprimatur

✠ Most Reverend Frank J. Rodimer
  Bishop of Paterson

November 8, 1996

The *nihil obstat* and *imprimatur* are official declarations that a book or pamphlet is free of doctrinal and moral error. No implication is contained therein that those who have granted the *nihil obstat* and *imprimatur* agree with the contents, opinions, or statements expressed.

ACKNOWLEDGMENTS

Scripture selections are taken from *The New American Bible* © 1986, 1970 Confraternity of Christian Doctrine, Washington, DC. Used with permission.

Scripture texts used in this work are taken from *The New American Bible with Revised New Testament* ©1986 by the Confraternity of Christian Doctrine, Washington, D.C., and are used with permission of copyright owner. All rights reserved.

Excerpts from the English translation of *The Roman Missal* © 1973, International Committee on English in the Liturgy, Inc. (ICEL); excerpts from the English translation of *The Rite of Baptism for Children* © 1969, International Committee on English in the Liturgy, Inc. (ICEL); excerpts from the English translation of *Book of Blessings* © 1988, ICEL.
All rights reserved.

Contents ~~~~~~~~

Unit 1 **God Gives Us Many Gifts**

Unit 2 **Jesus Learned About Life**

Unit 3 **Jesus Teaches Us to Love**

Catechism of the Catholic Church

Since its publication in June 1994, the English translation of the Catechism of the Catholic Church has enjoyed a wide readership among Catholics throughout the United States. Parents and teachers will want to know how the chapter themes in This Is Our Faith relate to the content of the Catechism. As a service, we have included a Catechism Reference Box at the beginning of each chapter in the Teacher Edition. We suggest that in preparing to teach the chapter, teachers first read the section "Background for the Teacher." For additional enrichment, you may wish to refer to the paragraphs in the Catechism that are indicated in the Reference Box.

Although the Catechism of the Catholic Church is not the only source of enrichment regarding doctrine, it can be most helpful in broadening our understanding of faith. We are encouraged to use it as a reference in our ongoing study of our Catholic tradition.

Learning Prayers

The children at this age probably have learned some of the prayers on this page. You may want to review these prayers by discussing the meaning of each line of every prayer and the meaning of each prayer in our daily lives.

Introducing the Prayers

Ask the children to look at the prayers on page 1. They are placed here as an easy-to-find reference for the children. You might use one or more of these prayers to open and close each class session.

Challenge the children to commit these prayers to memory and to pray them often. Suggest that they pray one or more of these prayers each night before falling asleep. Ask the children to suggest other times when they might say the prayers on this page.

Let Us Pray

Sign of the Cross
In the Name of the Father,
   and of the Son,
   and of the Holy Spirit.
Amen.

2

The Lord's Prayer

Our Father, who art in heaven,
    hallowed be thy name;
thy kingdom come;
thy will be done on earth
    as it is in heaven.
Give us this day our daily bread;
and forgive us our trespasses
    as we forgive those
    who trespass against us;
and lead us not into temptation,
    but deliver us from evil.
Amen.

3

Let Us Pray

Hail Mary

Hail Mary, full of grace,
the Lord is with you.
Blessed are you among women,
and blessed is the fruit
of your womb, Jesus.
Holy Mary, Mother of God,
pray for us sinners, now,
and at the hour of our death.
Amen.

Glory Be to the Father

Glory be to the Father,
and to the Son,
and to the Holy Spirit.
As it was in the beginning,
is now, and ever shall be,
world without end.
Amen.

Grace Before Meals

Bless us, O Lord,
   and these your gifts,
   which we are about to receive
   from your goodness,
   through Christ our Lord.
Amen.

Grace After Meals

We give you thanks
   for all your gifts,
   almighty God,
   living and reigning
   now and forever.
Amen.

5

Let Us Pray

A Morning Prayer

My God, I offer you today
   all I think and do and say,
   uniting it with what was
   done on earth,
   by Jesus Christ,
   your Son.
Amen.

Evening Prayer

Dear God, before I sleep
   I want to thank you
   for this day so full
   of your kindness and
   your joy.
I close my eyes to rest
   safe in your loving care.
Amen.

Beginning the Journey

Introductory Lesson

Objectives

To help the children

- Experience a sense of welcome.
- Make a commitment to the journey of faith.
- Want to learn more about God.

Lesson Outline

- Welcome the children.
- Get acquainted.
- Introduce the student text.
- Pray together.
- Make a commitment to the faith journey.
- Conclude the lesson.

Plan Ahead

If possible, contact the children's parents prior to the session to introduce yourself and to learn something about each of the children.

Before the session, make a name tag for each child and one for yourself.

Prepare a special area for prayer in your room. This area need not be elaborate. Cover a table or desk with a cloth and place a Bible stand and a candle on the table. You might also add flowers to decorate the table.

Materials Needed

- a chalkboard or posterboard
- pencils
- a Bible
- a Bible stand
- a candle and matches (if permitted)
- flowers
- *Parent Preview Magazine*

Background for the Teacher

Becoming a Community

An ancient Chinese proverb tells us that "A journey of a thousand miles must begin with a single step." You and your first graders are about to begin an exciting journey together. Your goals for the year should be not only to introduce the children to the Three Persons of the Trinity, but also to help them become part of a community of faith. Helping the children get acquainted, learn one another's names, and feel comfortable with one another and their surroundings will help to ensure that your group is on the way to becoming a community.

At this session, invite the children to participate in the journey of faith. As Catholic Christians, we are like pilgrims on a long journey. Our ultimate destination, of course, is everlasting life and happiness with God and all those who have tried to love God in this life. While this concept is beyond the understanding of six- and seven-year-old children, you can help them appreciate that they are called to grow closer to God, Jesus, and the Holy Spirit as they learn more about the beliefs and traditions of our faith.

Jesus Is with Us

The journey theme is meant to help focus the attention of the children and illustrate in a memorable way this fact: The loving Jesus they meet in their studies is with them in all their life experiences. The world they find so interesting, so demanding, and sometimes so thrilling is God's world, which has been made a new, grace-filled creation for them through Jesus and the Spirit.

The session concludes with a prayer experience in which the children dedicate themselves to the challenging faith journey. They are invited to sign their names on the commitment page located on the inside front cover panel of the student text. They will also hear encouraging words from the book of God's word, the Bible. These promises from Scripture will assure the children that Jesus' presence and care will continue as they journey through life.

Starting the Year Right

A successful year begins long before the children arrive for the first session. To help you succeed, The Resourceful Teacher section of this book, beginning on page 363, includes

- notes on catechesis, faith, the role of the teacher, the *National Catechetical Directory*, and the *Catechism of the Catholic Church*
- a profile of the first-grade child
- tips on creating a healthy classroom environment
- suggestions for helping the children develop social skills
- tips on good planning strategies
- ideas on using learning activities
- suggestions for assessing learning
- ideas for using prayer within the sessions
- tips on involving the community

Refer to The Resourceful Teacher section before planning your first session and whenever you need help throughout the year.

Beginning the Journey

We are on our way to learn more about God.
What do you already know about God?

Here is a picture of me.

This is my teacher's name.

Here is my family.

We are on a journey together to learn more about God.

7

Beginning the Journey

Welcoming the Children

Greet the children warmly and tell them how happy you are to have them in your class. Help the children put on their name tags.

or...

Have a variety of colorful stickers on hand for the children to decorate their own name tags. Allow them to choose stickers and to place them on their name tags. Then ask the children to tell why they chose their stickers.

Getting Acquainted

Tell the group something about yourself. You may want to name a favorite food, hobby, or pet. Invite the children to tell something about themselves. Be sensitive to the children who may feel shy about sharing. Affirm those who participate.

Introducing the Student Text

Distribute the student texts to the children. Give them the opportunity to look through them and to comment on their religion books that they will be using this year.

Ask the children to turn to page 7. Read the session title aloud. Ask the children what the word *journey* means. Clarify that a journey is a trip, or the act of going from one place to another. Tell them that they can learn more about their journey by listening as you read the session-focus statement aloud. Then read aloud the question that follows and discuss with the children what they know about God.

Distribute crayons or felt-tip markers. Ask the children to draw a picture of themselves in the space provided in the student text. As they work, move about the room, speaking with the children about their drawings.

Print your name on the chalkboard. Instruct the children to use pencils to copy your name on the line in the student text. Then have them draw a picture of their families in the space provided. Allow time for the children to share their drawings.

When the children have completed these tasks, invite them to repeat after you the sentence at the bottom of the page.

Praying Together

Ask the children to form a line behind you. Tell them to bring their books and pencils with them. Hold the Bible at shoulder height in front of you and process with the children to the prayer area. When they are quiet, ask them to open their books to page 8.

Read aloud the introduction to the Scripture story. Then read aloud the story and the final words from Matthew 28:20. Raise the Bible and say, "The word of the Lord!" Teach the children this response and ask them to recite it with you.

Invite the children to hold up their books to be blessed. Read the blessing prayer aloud and ask the children to respond, "Amen!"

Making a Commitment

Direct the children to turn to the front inside cover panel. Tell them to repeat each line after you. Then instruct them to sign their names on the line provided.

Concluding the Session

Tell the children how happy you are that they have begun this year's journey with you. Remind them of their promises to learn more about God. Remember to send the *Parent Preview Magazine,* from the student text, home with the children.

Prayer for the Journey

Leader This is the Bible, the book of God's word.
Let us listen to Jesus' promise to be with us on our journey.
Wherever we are, he is with us.
Here are his words.
"Behold, I am with you always" (Matthew 28:20).
The word of the Lord!

All Thanks be to God.

Leader May God bless each of us as we begin our journey.
May he bless these books, which we will use as our map along the way.

All Amen!

8

Enriching the Lesson

Distribute to the children heart shapes you have drawn on construction paper prior to the session. Have printed on each heart the words, *I will learn about God.* Read the words aloud to the children and invite them to repeat the words after you. Instruct the children to trace over the words with their crayons and cut out their hearts. Encourage the children to display their hearts at home.

THIS IS OUR FAITH ✦ A Preview of Grade 1

OPENING DOORS
A Take-Home Magazine ™

SILVER BURDETT GINN • SCHOOL PROGRAM 1

THIS IS OUR FAITH ✦

You are cordially invited . . .

A Profile of the First-Grade Child

No one knows your first grader better than you! It may be helpful and interesting to you as a parent or guardian, however, to explore some of the characteristics of the first grader.

First graders

- learn that they are unique and lovable through your words and actions
- depend upon their families to care for their needs
- have a natural curiosity
- are self-centered and may have difficulty sharing
- have short emotional fuses
- have short attention spans
- need concrete experiences
- are responsive to religious practices that convey a sense of mystery
- are beginning to understand that their actions have consequences
- can begin to express their own simple prayers
- have experienced being hurt and have experienced forgiveness

Take Time You may want to make a special effort this week to notice the unique personality and giftedness of your first grader. Be sure to affirm him or her often. Cherish the great gift your child is to you and your family!

4

© Silver Burdett Ginn Inc.

A Preview of Grade 1

The purpose of the *Parent Preview Magazine* is to introduce the parents of your children to THIS IS OUR FAITH, Grade 1. This preview invites the family to join their child on this year's journey of faith, while providing a brief summary of the material taught in Grade 1. Special emphasis is given to describing *Opening Doors: A Take-Home Magazine,* as well as to profiling the first-grade child.

Sending the Magazine Home

At the end of the first lesson, help the children carefully remove the *Parent Preview Magazine* from their texts. Explain to the children that this preview magazine will introduce their families to THIS IS OUR FAITH, Grade 1. Demonstrate how to fold the magazine. Encourage the children to bring the preview magazine home and to share it with their families.

My Prayer Book ~

This booklet is intended to be taken home so that during the year family members may help the children learn some of the basic Catholic prayers. You will find some of these same prayers in the Let Us Pray section on pages 1–6 in the front of the student text.

Encourage the children to decorate their booklets at home. As you introduce new prayers, remind the children to pray the prayers in the booklet. You may begin by asking the children to have their parents help them learn the Sign of the Cross. Remind the children about the booklet after teaching the Hail Mary in Chapter 6, The Lord's Prayer in Chapter 12, and the Glory Be in Chapter 20. Although the prayers before and after meals are in the Prayers section in the front of the book, they are not in this booklet, since family mealtime is often used for a variety of rituals. However, you will probably want to teach the children traditional Catholic grace before and after meals.

---

to continue in faith the same journey you first embarked on when you presented your son or daughter for Baptism. Throughout the years you have been—and continue to be—the most important person of faith for your child. As your first-grader commits to this year's faith journey, you are invited as the primary educator in faith to journey along with your child, in whatever way is most comfortable for you. This Is Our Faith is privileged to assist you in this important task.

This Year In Grade 1

This year your first grader will be introduced to some of the basic teachings that the Catholic Church teaches about the Blessed Trinity. He or she will discover much about God the Father, Son, and Holy Spirit.

The first unit introduces God as creator. Your child will also be presented with a picture of God as a loving parent. God blesses us with a multitude of gifts. In order to recognize something of the goodness and blessings that fill God's creation, your child will consider all the wonderful gifts God has given him or her. Chief among these gifts will be Jesus, God's most special gift to us.

As your child completes each unit of This Is Our Faith, you will receive a take-home magazine entitled *Opening Doors: A Take-Home Magazine.* Each magazine will include the following features to help you grow in your faith and to help you share that faith with your child.

A Closer Look

includes an article relating the unit theme to a particular aspect of the Mass and family interactive pages for you and your child to enjoy together.

Being Catholic

highlights a particular aspect of our Catholic heritage.

Growing Closer

suggests activities to help you and your family integrate your faith into everyday life.

And also . . .

Looking Ahead
previews the next unit of This Is Our Faith.

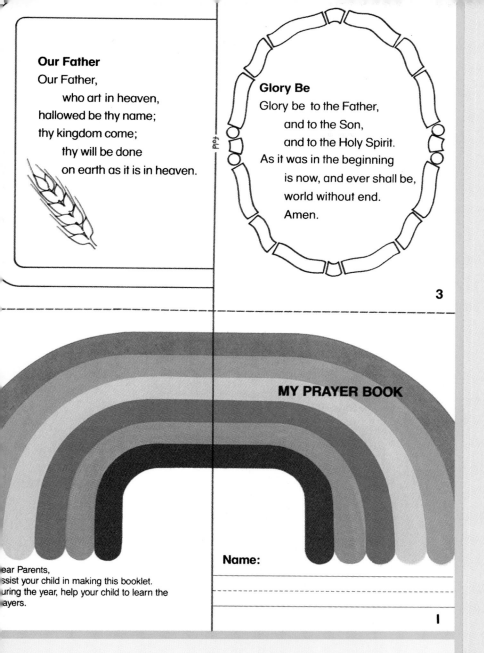

Our Father

Our Father,

  who art in heaven,

hallowed be thy name;

thy kingdom come;

  thy will be done

  on earth as it is in heaven.

Fold

Glory Be

Glory be to the Father,

  and to the Son,

  and to the Holy Spirit.

As it was in the beginning

  is now, and ever shall be,

  world without end.

  Amen.

3

MY PRAYER BOOK

Name:

ear Parents,
ssist your child in making this booklet.
uring the year, help your child to learn the
ayers.

I

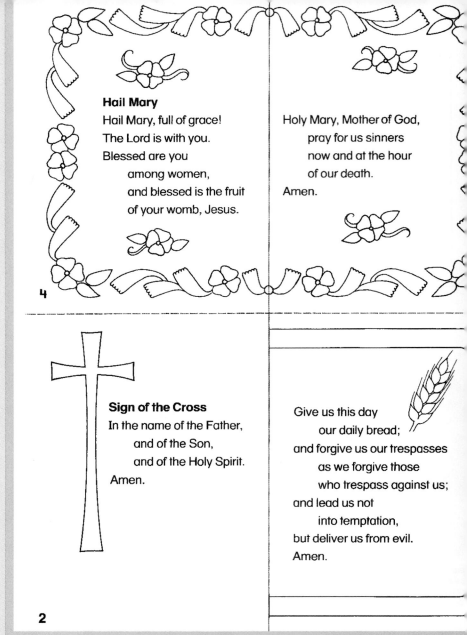

Hail Mary

Hail Mary, full of grace!
The Lord is with you.
Blessed are you
    among women,
    and blessed is the fruit
    of your womb, Jesus.

Holy Mary, Mother of God,
    pray for us sinners
    now and at the hour
    of our death.
Amen.

4

Sign of the Cross
In the name of the Father,
    and of the Son,
    and of the Holy Spirit.
Amen.

Give us this day
    our daily bread;
and forgive us our trespasses
    as we forgive those
    who trespass against us;
and lead us not
    into temptation,
but deliver us from evil.
Amen.

2

God Gives Us Many Gifts

What kinds of gifts do you like to receive?

Unit Aim

To help the children know God as loving Creator and give thanks to God for all the gifts of creation, especially for God's Son, Jesus.

Doctrinal Summaries

CHAPTER 1
God makes us special because God loves us.

CHAPTER 2
God creates all things for us because God loves us.

CHAPTER 3
God gives us special people to love and care for us.

CHAPTER 4
Jesus is the Son of God and our friend. He is God's most special gift to us.

Note:

As you prepare to teach this unit, you may wish to refer to the reference section, *Our Catholic Heritage,* beginning on page 327.

Additional resources for Unit 1 include a Unit Test and a Family Letter as well as a video and selections from THIS IS OUR FAITH Music Program. You might also find it helpful to preview *Saints and Other Holy People* and *Prayer Celebrations* for possibilities to enhance the unit.

Introducing the UNIT

Invite the children to study the photograph on page 11 and tell a story about the picture. Read aloud the focus question and invite the children's responses. Help the children appreciate that everyone enjoys receiving gifts. Read aloud the unit title. Explain that in Unit 1, they will learn about the many gifts God gives to all people.

New Words

Bible
create
Creator
Jesus
Savior

1 God Makes Us Special

Objectives ～～～

To help the children

- Be aware that God makes each of them unique and, therefore, special.
- Recognize the importance of the Bible.
- Understand that they are children of God and that their families are special.
- Confirm the specialness of others.
- Pray by bowing and review the chapter.

Chapter Outline ～～～～

	Step 1 Learning About Our Lives	Step 2 Learning About Our Faith	Step 3 Learning How to Live Our Faith
Day 1	■ Call the children by name. ■ Read a poem. ■ Make fingerprints. ■ Circle pictures. *ABOUT 10 MINUTES*	■ Read the children's book. *ABOUT 10 MINUTES*	■ Pray with a poem. ■ Name things about others. ■ Review the lesson. *ABOUT 10 MINUTES*
Day 2	■ Review Day 1. ■ Work with the word *Bible*. *ABOUT 10 MINUTES*	■ Learn about the Bible. ■ Review the vocabulary. ■ Present the doctrine. ■ Present the Bible. *ABOUT 10 MINUTES*	■ Thank the children. ■ Trace a "thank-you" message. ■ Pray with gestures. ■ Review the lesson. *ABOUT 10 MINUTES*
Day 3	■ Make a family bulletin board. *ABOUT 10 MINUTES*	■ Talk about the photos and read the text. ■ Complete the bulletin board. *ABOUT 10 MINUTES*	■ Talk about families. ■ Color and role-play. ■ Pray together. ■ Review the lesson. *ABOUT 10 MINUTES*
Day 4	■ Discuss ways to act special. ■ Pantomime helping people feel special. *ABOUT 10 MINUTES*	■ Talk about the pictures. *ABOUT 10 MINUTES*	■ Choose ways to help. ■ Give thanks to God. ■ Review the lesson. *ABOUT 10 MINUTES*
Day 5	**Prayer** Learn the meaning of the reverent bow; sing a song; have a procession; and pray a prayer of thanks. **Review** Complete an activity; answer the questions; and read the Scripture verse.		

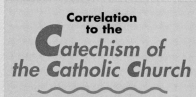

Plan Ahead

	Preparing Your Class	**Materials Needed**	**Additional Resources**
Day 1	For Step 1, prepare folded papers, one for each child. On the outside, letter his or her name; on the inside, print *You are special.*	■ one folded paper for each child ■ pencils ■ drawing paper ■ crayons or felt-tip markers ■ stamp pad	As you plan this chapter, consider using the following materials from The Resourceful Teacher Package. ■ *Classroom Activity Sheets 1 and 1a* ■ *Family Activity Sheets 1 and 1a* ■ *Chapter 1 Test* ■ *Prayers for Every Day* ■ *Projects: Grade 1* In preparing the children for the Sunday readings, you may wish to use Silver Burdett Ginn's *Getting Ready for Sunday* student and teacher materials.
Day 2	Choose a place for your class prayer area and place a small table there.	■ colored chalk ■ Bible on small table ■ tablecloth ■ flowers ■ crayons or felt-tip markers	
Day 3	For Step 1, cut out the letters for *Each of our families is very special,* and prepare a space for a bulletin board. For Step 2, cut out the letters for *God loves each of our families.*	■ drawing paper ■ crayons or felt-tip markers ■ empty bulletin board ■ cut-out letters for two sentences ■ staples or tacks	
Day 4	For Step 1, prepare a list of actions for the children to pantomime that will make others feel special.	■ crayons or felt-tip markers	
Day 5	Learn the melody for "The Farmer in the Dell." Plan a procession route to the prayer area.	■ crayons or felt-tip markers	

BOOKS FOR THE JOURNEY

God's World Makes Me Feel So Little. Helen Caswell. Abingdon Press, 1988. This delightful book introduces children to the wonders of God's world and shows them why they are important and precious in God's sight.

Don't Look at Me. Doris Stanford and Graci Evans. Questar Publishing, 1986. A small boy who lacks self-esteem learns how to recognize his self-worth and to help others to do the same.

MORE BOOKS FOR THE JOURNEY

Hooray for Me! Remy Charlip and Lilian Moore. Parents' Magazine Press, 1955. Devoted to unraveling the mystery of relationships—who one is to oneself and others.

My Book About Me By Me, Myself. Dr. Seuss and Roy McKie. Random House, 1970. Provides children with lines and spaces to show and tell all about themselves.

REDUCED CLASSROOM ACTIVITIES

Name

What Makes Me Special!

1. Use your favorite colors to decorate this balloon.

2. Circle your favorite clothes to wear.

3. To make a prayer wristband to wear, cut along the heavy black lines and staple the ends together.

> Thank you, God, for making me special.

To the Teacher: This activity will help the children understand that we all have different likes and dislikes.

Chapter 1   God Makes Us Special   THIS IS OUR FAITH 1   **1**

Name

God Makes Us Special

1. Color the kite.
2. Cut along the outside heavy black lines.

To the Teacher: Help the children attach crossed straws or lightweight sticks to the backs of their kites. Then loop a long piece of yarn through the end of each kite.

1a   THIS IS OUR FAITH 1   Chapter 1   God Makes Us Special

Background for the Teacher 〰️

THE PARADOXICAL SIX-YEAR-OLD

In their classic book on child development *Your Six-Year-Old: Loving and Defiant,* Ames and Ilg demonstrate that there can be a contradiction between the behavior of the six-year-old and the need for approval the child wants so badly. For example, at the end of a very bad day, a child can ask blissfully, "Have I been good today?" It is an interesting fact that often the less praise and credit a child deserves the more the six-year-old seems to want love and praise. Any failure is very hard at this age, and severe criticism is most painful.

This paradoxical behavior of six-year-olds may be a challenge to you, but the theme of Chapter 1 will do much to make the children feel loved and acclaimed. The lessons will focus on God's love for them and how special God made them.

THE SIX-YEAR-OLD IS WONDROUSLY MADE

Thousands of years ago, the psalmist, captured by the mystery of a God who made us so wonderfully, prayed:

Truly you have formed my inmost being;
     you knit me in my mother's womb.
I give you thanks that I am fearfully, wonderfully made;
     wonderful are your works.

Psalm 139:13–14

Not only the Scriptures but also the teachings of the Church respect the uniqueness of each individual as created by God. As a catechetical instrument, THIS IS OUR FAITH continues this tradition and celebrates the specialness of each of God's children.

The youngsters with whom you will share this lesson are loved by God. Unceasingly, God calls them to wholeness and holiness. But they can respond to God's love only if they find themselves worthy of love, if they find themselves lovely and lovable.

Children need to know that their God delights in their creation. God loves each of them—tall or short, stout or lean, clumsy or graceful. Whatever their limitations—the need to use a wheelchair, the inability to see or to hear well—God is helping them to be their best selves. Whatever their dispositions—happy or disgruntled, hyperactive or passive, moody or sunny—God is present to them.

This lesson enables you to help the children appreciate themselves. By helping them know that they exist because of God's love for them, you can create an atmosphere of love and acceptance in which each child feels appreciated for being the unique person that God has loved into existence.

Objective

This lesson helps the children know that God makes each of them unique and, therefore, special.

Step 1/INTRODUCTION

Learning About Our Lives

Calling the Children by Name

Begin this class with an acceptance ritual. Have prepared folded paper with each child's name clearly visible on the outside. Folded inside is the message "You are special."

Ask the group if anyone knows what the word *special* means. Help the children understand that special means "important" or "not like anyone or anything else."

Call each name as you hand out the folded paper. Tell the children there is an important message written inside, but they cannot open the paper yet.

When all the children have received their papers, have the children unfold their slips and read the message on them—"You are special." Tell the children that you are happy each of them is in the class because each of them is so special.

Reading a Poem

Invite the children to open their books to page 12. Read the poem to the children and help them enjoy the illustrations. Call out some special thing about each child pictured. Point out that the children are not all doing the same things; rather, they are doing different things. Help the children understand that not being exactly the same is one way we are all special.

Making Fingerprints

Tell the children that something special about each of us is that our fingerprints are not like anyone else's. Circulate with a stamp pad and have the children press two of their fingerprints in the boxes provided on page 13. Allow time for the children to compare fingerprints.

Circling Favorite Activities

Remind the children that they are also special because they each have certain things they

12

God Makes Us Special

I Am Special

My face is my own
And so is my name.
I am like many others,
But not just the same.

I am glad that I am.
I am happy to be
Like so many others,
Yet special, that's ME!

Everyone is special. Name two things that make you special.

12   Scripture

Teaching Tips

Be as specific as possible when you work with ideas about uniqueness. For example, ask the children about the illustrations on page 12 by having them find the following.
The boy who can do something special—he can stand on his head.
The girl who is having fun dressing in grown-up clothes.
Three special children who formed a pyramid.
Help the children realize that some children enjoy doing one thing; others, another.

Cultural Awareness

Call attention to the last two lines in the first verse of the poem "I Am Special." Ask the children to identify how they are "like many others." Emphasize ways in which each person is the same. Then ask them to give examples of being "not just the same." Help the children begin to value the uniqueness and specialness of each person.

Activity

1. Show how you are special.
   Put your fingerprints here.

2. Circle three things you can do. Tell about them.

God Knows Us

God tells us that we are special.

God says, "You are precious and I love you."

Based on Isaiah 43:4

really enjoy doing. Ask the children to circle the things they like to do from among those pictured in the activity on page 13. Invite the children to share what they like to do.

Step 2/DEVELOPMENT

Learning About Our Faith

Reading the Children's Book

Ask the children who made them so special. Print the word *God* on the chalkboard.

Then read the section "God Knows Us" on page 13. Call the children, one by one, by name. Invite them to gather around you, perhaps on the reading chairs or the carpet. Tell them that God says each of them is important, and precious. If your class is not too large, address each child in a reverent way, saying, "(*Name*), you are precious and I love you."

Step 3/CONCLUSION

Learning How to Live Our Faith

Praying with a Poem

Encourage the children to thank God for making them special. Teach them the following response: *Thank you, God.* Then turn to page 12 and use the poem "I Am Special" once more, this time as a prayer. Read one sentence (not one line) at a time, pause, and invite the children to pray their response. Continue with the next sentence, repeating this procedure.

Naming Special Things About Others

Tell the children that God knows exactly what is special about each person, both inside and outside. Invite volunteers to name something special about their moms and dads or friends.

or . . .

Distribute paper and help the children fold it twice to make four sections. Have them draw their moms, dads, and other family members doing things that make them special.

Reviewing the Lesson

To review the lesson, ask the following.

- What have we learned about everyone in our class? (*We are special.*)
- Who has made each of us special? (*God*)
- What are some things that make you special? (*Answers will vary.*)

13

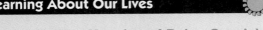
Objective

This lesson helps the children recognize and understand the importance of the Bible.

Step 1/INTRODUCTION

Learning About Our Lives

Reviewing the Meaning of Being Special

With the children, think about the meaning of being special—that is, important, not like anyone or anything else.

Working with the Word *Bible*

Ask the children to name their favorite stories and to talk about some of their favorite characters in them. Then tell the children that they will learn about a book called the Bible that has many stories, full of many wonderful characters. Explain that the Bible is special because it is God's book. There is no other book like it, and it is very important. Then print the word *Bible* on the chalkboard and ask the children to repeat it.

Step 2/DEVELOPMENT

Learning About Our Faith

Learning About the Bible

Invite the children to look at the picture on page 14. Talk about the father reading a story from the Bible to his daughter. Then read the children's text.

Print the following on the chalkboard:
   In the Bible, God says, "I made you because
   – – – – – – – –."

Tell the children they can fill in the blank letters by finding this sentence on page 14. Elicit from them the reason God says he made us. Then print the words *I love you* in colored chalk in the blank spaces. After filling in the spaces, read the first section to the children and have a child finish reading the part in color. Read this several times.

Reviewing the Vocabulary

Point to the New Word section on page 15. Ask the children to repeat the word *Bible* and its definition after you.

Our Special Book

The **Bible** is a special book about God's love for us.
In the Bible, God says,
"I made you because I love you."
God's love makes each of us special.

Based on Wisdom 11:24

14   Scripture

CURRICULUM CONNECTION

Language Arts Invite the children to compose a story about a special person in their lives. Show the children how to fold lined paper in half to create a four-page booklet. Help them number the pages 1 through 4, directing them to use the first page as a cover and title page. Then ask the children to draw a sequence of events showing what happened first, next, and last. Encourage them to write a sentence or more for each picture and to title the story. They may share the booklets with classmates.

Teaching Tips

Throughout THIS IS OUR FAITH, Grade 1, you will find references to a prayer area. Establish a place in your classroom to gather for prayer. At least designate a special place for the Bible. The ideal location for the Bible stand or table would be in the prayer area. If you have space restrictions, train the children to prepare the prayer area before you gather for daily prayer. Assign "servers" to move the Bible to the prayer area.

14

Thank You, God

God made me very special,
And so I smile and say,
"O God, I want to thank you
For making me this way."

Activity

It is good to thank God for making us so special.
Trace the letters to complete the prayer. Then pray it.

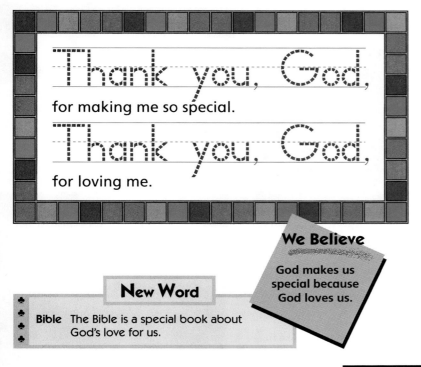

Thank you, God,
for making me so special.
Thank you, God,
for loving me.

We Believe

God makes us special because God loves us.

New Word

♣ **Bible** The Bible is a special book about God's love for us.

Doctrine 15

Teaching Tips

For your classroom you may want two Bibles—an adult version and a child's picture Bible. Both translations may be displayed in the prayer corner and placed on the table. Explain the difference between the Bibles and let the children examine them both.

You may want to establish a procedure for the children to use the prayer corner and the Bible.

CURRICULUM CONNECTION

Music Using the melody for "Frère Jacques" ("Are You Sleeping, Brother John?"), teach the children the following words.

Here's our Bible.
Here's our Bible.
God's great love,
God's great love.
We can read about God.
We can read about God.
Every day,
Every day.

Presenting the Doctrine

Read aloud the We Believe section on page 15, which summarizes the chapter's doctrine. Ask the children to repeat the sentence after you.

Presenting the Bible

Invite the children to gather in the prayer area. Reverently hold up the Bible and tell them that this year they will find out from the Bible how much God loves them. Then carefully place it on a table with a tablecloth and a vase of flowers. Tell the children that this will be their special place for the Bible and that they will pray here together often. Offer a brief prayer of thanks for God's special book.

Step 3/CONCLUSION

Learning How to Live Our Faith

Thanking the Children

Ask for volunteers to bring you something from around the room, such as a book, an eraser, and so on. As each child does so, say "Thank you." Ask the children why they like you to say *thank you* to them. Tell them that God also likes to hear *thank you*. Invite volunteers to share ideas of what they might thank God for.

Tracing a Thank-you Message

Have the children trace the letters on page 15. Afterward, read aloud the message and invite the children to read it with you.

Praying with Gestures

Read aloud the poem "Thank You, God" on page 15. Help the children choose an appropriate gesture for each line. For example, they might raise their arms, palms up when they say, "Thank you, God." When they have selected the gestures, practice them with the group. Direct the children to stand in the prayer area and to make their gestures prayerfully as you read the poem prayer out loud.

Reviewing the Lesson

■ What is the Bible? (*A special book about God's love*)

■ Why did God make us? (*Because God loves us*)

■ Why are we special? (*Because God made us*)

15

Objective

This lesson helps the children understand that they are children of God and that their families are special.

Step 1/INTRODUCTION

Learning About Our Lives

Making a Bulletin Board

Distribute drawing paper and crayons or felt-tip markers to the children, and invite them to draw pictures of their families doing things together. Invite the children to talk about their families and what makes their families special (unique).

Pin all the children's pictures on a bulletin board. Have these thirty letters cut out for the following sentence: *Each of our families is very special.* Give each child a letter to hold, and then ask the children to hand them to you as you tack this sentence to the bulletin board. Talk about how the sentence applies to their drawings.

Step 2/DEVELOPMENT

Learning About Our Faith

Talking About the Photos

Using the captions for the pictures on page 16, talk with the children about the special things we can do with families.

Afterward, read the text. Then call each child by name and say "You are a beloved child of God." Ask the children who else they know who is a child of God. Help them understand that everyone they know is a child of God because God makes everyone.

Completing a Bulletin Board

Gather the children around the bulletin board. Have twenty-five letters cut out for the following sentence: *God loves each of our families.* Give each child a letter to hold and ask the children to help you pin this sentence to the bulletin board. Talk about how the sentence applies to their drawings.

God Loves Our Family

The Bible tells us that God made everyone. So all of us are the children of God. God loves each of us. And God loves each of our families. Each of our families is very special.

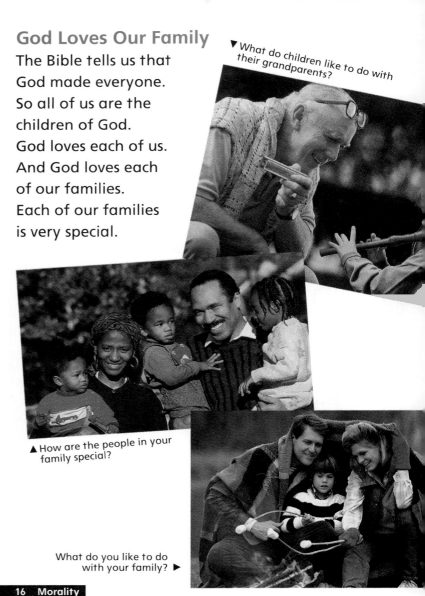

▼ What do children like to do with their grandparents?

▲ How are the people in your family special?

What do you like to do with your family? ▶

CURRICULUM CONNECTION

Math   Help the children make a graph that represents the colors that people are wearing in the illustration on page 17. Ask the children to find and count the number of people wearing red. Record their answers on the graph by drawing, in one line, the correct number of stick figures representing people wearing red. Follow through with blue, green, gold, and purple. Have the children distinguish which color was worn the most and which was worn the least.

Enjoy this poem with your teacher.

Berta and her family
Like to juggle balls.
Timmy and his family
Like to see waterfalls.

Miki and her family
Like to take long hikes.
Jacy and his family
Like to ride red bikes.

Families are special
In all that they do.
Families are special.
Your family is too.

Activity

Color each object that the families are using as they do special things together.

What are some things you do with your family?

Teaching Tips

This is the first time the children discuss families in this grade level. The children's book shows a variety of common family configurations: two-parent, single parent, and intergenerational. Be aware of the different kinds of family structures that exist and are represented in this book; show respect for each.

Teaching Tips

Some of the children in your classroom may be part of families who are unhappy and even abusive. When you have activities during which you and the children talk about their families, be sensitive to the children's experiences of love and acceptance. Be careful not to make them feel unacceptable because their families may fall short of what you would wish for all the children you teach. Children are very protective of even the worst in their families, so exercise courtesy and tact.

Step 3/CONCLUSION

Learning How to Live Our Faith

Talk About What Families Can Do Together

Ask the children to look at the bulletin board and to comment on any activities the families pictured there are doing together. Then read the poem on page 17. Discuss the illustrations on the page and invite the children to find in the illustrations each of the four families mentioned in the poem. Point out the magnifying glasses in the pictures. Ask the children what these tools do and what the people are looking at through these glasses.

Coloring Objects to Distinguish Specialness

Distribute crayons or felt-tip markers. Read the directions at the bottom of the page and invite the children to color the objects each family is using as they do special things together. Then discuss what special things the children's families do together.

Role-Playing

Reread the poem on page 17. Invite volunteers to act out what the four families in the poem do together.

Praying a Litany of Thanks

Gather the children in their prayer area and invite them to join you in prayer. Teach them the following response: *We thank you, God.* Then lead the following litany and invite the children to respond after each line.

- For making each of us so special . . .
- For giving us the Bible, which tells us how much you love us . . .
- For all the special things we do with our families . . .

Reviewing the Lesson

To review the lesson, ask the following.

- Which of us is a child of God? (*All of us*)
- Why are we children of God? (*Because God made us*)
- Who does God love? (*All of us*)

17

Objective

This lesson helps the children realize that they can help others feel special by their actions.

Step 1/INTRODUCTION

Learning About Our Lives

Discussing Ways of Acting Special

Tell the children something that they do for you that helps make you feel special. Then ask them what others do that helps them feel special. Ask questions like the following to get the children thinking.

- How do you feel when someone says *thank you* to you? (*Proud—Answers will vary.*)

- How do you feel when someone helps you do something hard? (*Thankful—Answers will vary.*)

- How do you feel when someone is nice to you? (*Happy—Answers will vary.*)

- How do you feel when someone treats you as if you are very special—valuable, important, and precious? (Important—*Answers will vary.*)

Emphasize that all these events help make the children feel both happy and special. Explain that everyone feels special when people do special things for them.

Pantomiming Helping People Feel Special

Ask for volunteers to pantomime an action that shows them doing something to help people feel special and important. You might use some of the following actions.

- Picking up someone's books
- Taking out the trash
- Erasing the chalkboard
- Clearing the table
- Throwing litter in the wastepaper basket
- Giving a hug
- Telling a joke

Invite the children to guess what is being pantomimed. Discuss how each action can help people feel special and important.

Being Special, Acting Special

God made us all special,
so we can act in special ways.
We can love others.
We can help our family and friends.
When we show love to others,
we act like God.
That is very special!

▲ How do you help others?

▲ How do you help other people feel happy?

▼ How do you show that you are special?

18   Morality

Focus on

Feeling Special   In this lesson, focus on how the children, through their actions, can help make other people feel special. Talk about how you feel special when people are kind to you, thoughtful, generous with their time, and so on. Help the children realize that others help them feel special and that they have this same ability. Children can also help their friends and families and neighbors to feel special.

CURRICULUM CONNECTION

Art   Distribute drawing paper and crayons or felt-tip markers. Invite the children to draw pictures of themselves helping someone feel happy and special. Afterward, invite the children to share their drawings with their classmates.

Activity

Look at the pictures.
Tell how these people are helping.
Circle one special way you will help.

Morality 19

Learning About Our Faith

Telling Stories About Pictures

Read aloud page 18. Help the children appreciate that they can thank God for making them special and that they can care about others by helping those people feel special. Discuss the pictures inviting the children to tell a story about each one. Use the captions to help the discussion and to give the children ideas about a possible story line.

Step 3/CONCLUSION

Learning How to Live Our Faith

Choosing Ways to Help

Read the text on page 19. Ask the children questions like the following about each illustration.

- What is happening in this picture?
- Who needs help?
- Who is helping someone else feel special?

Distribute crayons or felt-tip markers and ask the children to circle the ways they help others feel special. Discuss their choices.

Giving Thanks to God

Gather the children in the prayer area. Ask them what they are thankful for today. Then invite them to say with you the following prayer.

O God, we are special.
You made us this way.

Reviewing the Lesson

To review the lesson ask the following.

- How does God want us to treat others? (*God wants us to help other people feel special.*)
- What special things can you do for others to help them feel special? (*Answers will vary.*)
- How do you show that God makes you special? (*Answers will vary.*)

CURRICULUM CONNECTION

Music Using the melody for "Frère Jacques" ("Are You Sleeping, Brother John?"), teach the children the following.

We act special.
We act special.
Yes, we do.
Yes, we do.
Thank you very much, God.
Thank you very much, God.
You love us.
You love us.

Objective

This lesson helps the children use a reverent bow to honor the Bible and to remember that their specialness is a gift of God's love.

Learning a Reverent Bow

Invite the children to look at the illustration on page 20 and then ask the following questions.

- Which of these children have you seen before? (*Four were pictured on page 17.*)
- What is happening in this picture? (*Bowing*)
- What book is on the table? (*The Bible*)
- Why is the child bowing before the Bible? (*Answers will vary.*)

Discuss with the children that people bow to show respect for someone or something. Explain to the children that they will show reverence for God's special book, the Bible, by bowing toward it. Demonstrate a bow and provide time to practice.

Learning a Song of Thanksgiving

Teach the children the song "Celebrate God," page 12 of *Young People's Glory and Praise*, OCP. Or teach the following words to the melody "The Farmer in the Dell."

Verse 1: Oh, thank you, God, so much.
(Repeat.)

We are your special friends.
(Repeat first line.)

Verse 2: You love us all so much.
(Repeat.)

We are your special friends.
(Repeat first line of Verse 1.)

Verse 3: Oh, thank you for your love.
(Repeat.)

We are your special friends.
(Repeat first line of Verse 1.)

Bowing

Line up the children for a procession around the room. Explain to them that they can sing their song as they process and that when they come to the Bible, they will want to bow reverently and stand in a semicircle around the Bible. Pray the prayer at the bottom of page 20. Ask the children to repeat the prayer after you.

20

Praying By Bowing

All: Thank you, God, for the Bible, our special book about your love for us. Amen.

Focus on

Body Prayers The children will learn the bow as a way of praying with their bodies. It is a gesture of reverence and respect and is used throughout the world to show submission and honor. Other ways of praying with the body are by making gestures and movements. Of course, using the body to pray is an excellent way of focusing the children. Perhaps the most important gesture is the Sign of the Cross, which they will use throughout their lives. It is a prayer of the Christian community and a reminder of Jesus.

CURRICULUM CONNECTION

Language Arts Divide the class into pairs. Then give each pair a magnifying glass. Ask the children to use this tool to look at their partner's fingernails, knuckles, thumbs, eyebrows, and hair. Encourage them to share with their partners what they discover about each other. Then help each pair write a story about their specialness, as it is revealed by the magnifying glass.

Chapter Review

God makes each of us special.
Color the pictures to show what
is special about each child.

1. Who makes you so special? God

2. What is the name of the special
book about God's love for us?

   the Bible

3. Tell what is special
about you.

God says,
"You are precious
and I love you."
Based on Isaiah 43:4

Completing an Activity

Use the activity on page 21 to review the
learning of Chapter 1. Point to the illustrations
at the top of page 21. Ask the children the
following questions.

- Have you ever seen these four children
  before? (*On pages 17 and 20*)
- What do you know about these children?
  (*Answers will vary.*)
- What makes them special? (*Answers will
  vary.*)
- What can you see in these pictures?
  (*Answers will vary.*)

Read the copy at the top of page 21. Distribute
crayons or felt-tip markers and invite the
children to color what each child in the pictures
likes to do with his or her family (*juggle, see
water falls, hike, ride a bike*). Then invite the
children's responses to the question "What is
special about you?"

Answering the Questions

Read aloud the first two questions and ask
volunteers to respond. Direct the children to
print the answers in their texts. Encourage all
the children to participate in the discussion of
the third question. Be supportive of each child
who responds.

Using the Scripture Verse

Ask the children to read the Scripture verse
after you. It is a good way to end the lesson by
reflecting on the word of God. If you wish you
may have the children memorize this verse.

Enriching the Lesson

Put an empty vase on the Bible
table in the prayer area. Show the
children how to make simple paper
flowers. Prepare a calendar on
which you print a child's name on
one of the days of the school week,
and invite that child to make a
flower for that particular day. Assign
each child a day. Each morning,
you might sing a song, say a thank-
you prayer, and have the child who
made the flower for that day put it in
the vase.

2 God Gives Us Special Gifts

Objectives

To help the children
- Know that God created the whole world.
- Enjoy, share, care, and make things from God's gifts.
- Care for the world as God asks.
- Use God's gifts to create wonderful things.
- Express thanks for God's gifts of creation.

Chapter Outline

	Step 1 Learning About Our Lives	Step 2 Learning About Our Faith	Step 3 Learning How to Live Our Faith
Day 1	■ Introduce Chapter 2. ■ Identify God's gifts of nature. *ABOUT 10 MINUTES*	■ Work with a rebus story. ■ Talk about God who creates. ■ Review the vocabulary. ■ Present the doctrine. *ABOUT 10 MINUTES*	■ Talk about caring for God's gifts. ■ Say "Thank you" to God. *ABOUT 10 MINUTES*
Day 2	■ Pantomime God's gifts. ■ Talk about God's gifts. *ABOUT 10 MINUTES*	■ Talk about God's world. ■ Role-play a response. *ABOUT 10 MINUTES*	■ Color to make a choice. ■ Thank God for creation. ■ Review the lesson. *ABOUT 10 MINUTES*
Day 3	■ Compose a cooperative chart. ■ Sing a song about caring. *ABOUT 14 MINUTES*	■ Discuss caring for God's world. ■ Review the word *create*. *ABOUT 4 MINUTES*	■ Complete picture stories. ■ Tell stories about caring. ■ Pray a prayer of thanks. *ABOUT 12 MINUTES*
Day 4	■ Talk about how things are made. ■ Make things from God's creation. *ABOUT 8 MINUTES*	■ Read the story of making cotton cloth. ■ Post the children's art work. *ABOUT 12 MINUTES*	■ Praise others for using God's gifts well. ■ Thank God. *ABOUT 10 MINUTES*
Day 5	**Prayer**	Think about God's creation; re-examine the meaning of the bow; learn a song; process; and pray a thank you prayer.	
	Review	Complete an activity; answer the questions; and read the Scripture verse.	

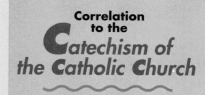

**Correlation
to the
Catechism of
the Catholic Church**

Paragraph
353, 358

Plan Ahead

	Preparing Your Class	**Materials Needed**	**Additional Resources**
Day 1	For Step 1, decide whether you will take the children on a nature walk, or collect some natural objects, or pictures to use in the classroom.	■ natural objects (stones, leaves, flowers, fruit, vegetables, pets) or pictures of natural objects	As you plan this chapter, consider using the following materials from The Resourceful Teacher Package.
Day 2	Collect an array of natural objects for the children to hold during the prayer in Step 3.	■ crayons or red felt-tip markers ■ natural objects (stones, leaves, flowers, pieces of bark, bugs, fruit, vegetables)	■ *Classroom Activity Sheets 2 and 2a* ■ *Family Activity Sheets 2 and 2a* ■ *Chapter 2 Test* ■ *Prayers for Every Day* ■ *Projects: Grade 1*
Day 3	For Step 1, decide whether you will take the children on a nature walk. Learn the melody for "If You're Happy and You Know It."	■ classroom plants ■ crayons (not felt-tip markers)	In preparing the children for the Sunday readings, you may wish to use Silver Burdett Ginn's *Getting Ready for Sunday* student and teacher materials.
Day 4	For Step 1, collect pictures showing things made from wood. Make sure to have a bulletin board available for Step 2.	■ pictures of things made from wood: furniture, houses, toys ■ drawing paper, crayons ■ empty bulletin board	
Day 5	Learn the melody for "This Old Man." Plan a procession route to the prayer area.	■ crayons or felt-tip markers	

BOOKS FOR THE JOURNEY

All God's Creatures. Susan Swanson Swartz. Augsburg, 1994. A poetic and beautifully illustrated creation book.

Clap! Clap! Mary Claire Heldorfer. Viking, 1993. This beautiful book celebrates the beauty and majesty of life, capturing all the promise and joy of each unique day.

MORE BOOKS FOR THE JOURNEY

God Cares When I'm Thankful. Elspeth Campbell Murphy. David C. Cook, 1983. Gives an appreciation for what it means to be thankful in bad times as well as in good.

The World God Made. Alice Bergey. Concordia, 1965. Encourages an understanding of creation from the perspective of God's intention for it.

REDUCED CLASSROOM ACTIVITIES

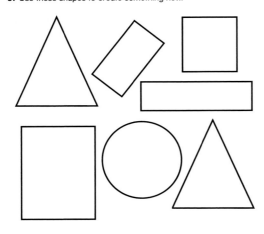

Name

We Can Make Things from God's Gifts

1. Color the shapes.
2. Cut along the heavy black lines.
3. Use these shapes to create something new.

To the Teacher: This activity will help the children understand that they are involved in ongoing creation. After the children have cut the shapes, help them arrange the shapes on a large piece of colored paper. Then help them paste the shapes to the paper.

Chapter 2   God Gives Us Special Gifts   THIS IS OUR FAITH 1   **2**

Name

God Created the World

1. Listen to the poem in the box.
2. To finish the poem, draw a picture of your favorite season.

God covered the world
With many pretty things.
I've drawn a picture
Of what one season brings.

To the Teacher: This activity will help the children notice the beauty in nature. Before the children begin to draw, discuss the change of seasons.

2a   THIS IS OUR FAITH 1   Chapter 2   God Gives Us Special Gifts

Background for the Teacher

CHILDREN, NATURAL WONDERERS

According to Ilg and Ames in their book *Your Six-Year-Old: Loving and Defiant,* one of the most endearing qualities of children this age is their extreme enthusiasm. They are eager learners, who will respond spontaneously as you introduce God's gifts of creation to them. They will enjoy naming the gifts of creation, from dinosaurs to lightning bugs.

Nearly 2,500 years ago, the psalmist delighted in God's gifts.

> Praise the LORD from the heavens . . .
> Praise him, sun and moon;
>   praise him, all you shining stars.
> Praise the LORD from the earth . . .
> You mountains and all you hills,
>   you fruit trees and all you cedars;
> You wild beasts and all tame animals,
>   you creeping things and you winged fowl.
>
>   Psalm 148:1, 3, 7, 9–10

Like the psalmist who gazed up at the night sky, the children naturally "oooh" and "ahhh" at the wonders of creation. The psalmist felt a kinship with the heavens and the earth and praised God. As the children explore more and more of God's world, they long to raise their voices in praise and thanksgiving. With Lesson 2, you provide the six-year-olds with an opportunity to praise and give thanks and to rejoice in the love of God.

THE GOODNESS OF GOD'S CREATION

In this lesson you help the children see the goodness of God's creation, as set forth in Genesis, Chapter 1. After God creates each element of our world, God looks and sees that creation is good: the sky with its sun, moon, and stars and its winged birds that fly; the earth with its waters teeming with life and its dry land that knows the tread of cattle, elephant, and giraffe; and the beauty of fall foliage, winter snow, and spring blossoms. All creation is good.

TAKING CARE OF GOD'S GIFTS

As God's people the children have been called to take care of their world and to share the gifts of God with others. As you help the children become more caring of their own universe, start with little things.

Chapter 2 encourages the children to care for animals. Children often imagine that animals—real or stuffed—are their best friends. By caring for animals, children frequently learn to care for others. They learn gentleness as they brush a cat's fur or hug a dog. Help the children learn an important truth: Animals are part of God's goodness, and God wants all of us to love and care for them.

SCRIPTURE/DOCTRINE

Objective

This lesson helps the children know that God created the whole world.

Step 1/INTRODUCTION

Learning About Our Lives

Introducing Chapter 2

Read aloud the chapter title on page 22. Call attention to the focus question. Ask the children to name some things they like in God's world.

Identifying God's Gifts of Nature

If possible, take the children outside to admire nature. Or show the children the natural objects you brought to class or pictures of these objects: stones, leaves, flowers, fruit, vegetables, a pet cat, a dog, a gerbil, or fish. As the children talk about each of these gifts from God, tell them that God made each gift and gives it to them with love.

Step 2/DEVELOPMENT

Learning About Our Faith

Reading About God's Creation

Direct the children to follow along as you read the story on pages 22 and 23. Pause at each picture and encourage the children to supply the word for the rebus symbol.

After you have read the story, ask the children questions like the following.

- With what did God fill the sea? (*Fish*)
- What did God send up into the sky? (*Birds*)
- What did God put all over the land? (*Animals, flowers, trees*)
- How did God feel about everything God created? (*God loved it all.*)
- To whom did God give the earth that is full of all wonderful things? (*People*)

Acting Out a Rebus Story

Invite the children to stand. Reread the rebus story on pages 22 and 23. Each time you come to a picture, invite one or more of the children to show how the pictured gift from God walks, flies, swims, and so on. Then allow time for

---

2 God Gives Us Special Gifts

God Created a Wonderful World

God made the and the .

God covered the empty land with

and  .

God filled the seas with .

God sent  up into the sky.

All over the land, God put animals,

 and  .

> **What are some things in God's world that you like?**

Cultural Awareness

Tell the children that God gives us the earth as our home and wants us to share the good things we have with those who may need help. Assist the children in identifying people who may need help: hungry people, homeless people, or sick people. Discuss with the children realistic ways they can help these people, such as beginning a toy collection for homeless and poor children or making get-well cards for sick people in the parish (often announced in the parish bulletin).

CURRICULUM CONNECTION

Science Divide the children into groups of three. Give each group one of the following categories to research: trees, flowers, animals, birds, fish, bugs, fruit, vegetables, and nuts. Provide an array of magazines and ask the children to find pictures that fit their category and to make a poster out of their pictures. Afterward, display the posters and invite the children to comment on their posters.

God saw how very good everything was.

God loved it all. Then God made .

God gave them the full of special

Based on Genesis 1:1–31

God's Gift of the World

God wanted to **create** the world for us.
God made the whole world out of nothing.
God loves the world and all the people in it.
God loves the animals, the plants,
and all the things in it.
The world is a special gift from God to us.

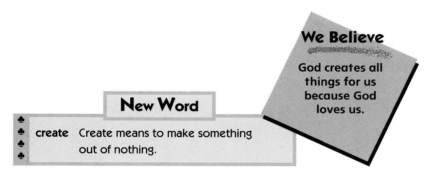

We Believe

God creates all things for us because God loves us.

New Word

♣ create Create means to make something
♣ out of nothing.

Doctrine 23

---

everyone to imitate the creature. Be sure each child has enough room to move.

Reading from the Bible

Pause to show the children the Bible citation. Read the phrase *Based on Genesis 1:1–31*. Simply tell them that this means the story comes from the Bible.

Discovering that God Created the World

Read out loud "God's Gift of the World," on page 23. Afterward, display once again the natural objects you brought to class or hold up the pictures.

or...

Hand out clay to the children and ask them to model one thing God made. Go around and admire the children's work, encouraging them to tell God how wonderful creation is.

Reviewing the Vocabulary

Point to the New Word section on page 23. Ask the children to repeat the word *create* and its definition.

Presenting the Doctrine

Read aloud the We Believe section on page 23, which summarizes the chapter's doctrine. Ask the children to repeat the sentence after you.

Step 3/CONCLUSION

Learning How to Live Our Faith

Talking About Caring for God's Gifts

Tell the children that they can show God their appreciation for the gifts of creation by taking care of them. Show the children gifts of nature, pictures, or their clay objects. As you display each gift, ask the children to name concrete ways they can take care of it.

Saying "Thank You" to God

Gather the children in the prayer area. Invite volunteers, one by one, to use creative movements to imitate one of God's gifts. (For instance, the children might demonstrate a flower blooming, a tree leafing out, a puppy doing tricks, or a carrot growing up through the earth.) After each imitation, invite the children to thank God for that gift.

Focus on

Begin to gradually introduce the children to Bible citations. Show the children the phrase after each Bible story, such as *Based on Genesis 1:1–31*. Tell them that this means the story is from one of the books of the Bible. This is meant as a simple readiness technique. Surely the children do not need to know the names of these books, but by seeing the phrase, they will begin to identify quotes as coming from the Bible.

Teaching Tips

Children like ritual. To gather the children into the prayer area, teach them to form a procession. In the beginning you can have them fold their hands in prayer. Eventually, you might add leaders who carry simple paper banners with the theme of the prayer, or one of the children might hold the cross up high to lead the procession. Singing is another feature of a procession and suggestions for song appear throughout this teacher edition.

DAY 2
MORALITY

Objective

This lesson helps the children realize that they can enjoy God's natural gifts, care for the world, share God's natural gifts with others, and make new things out of God's creation.

Step 1/INTRODUCTION

Learning About Our Lives

Pantomiming God's Gifts

Invite the children, one by one, to choose one of God's natural gifts for which they are thankful (animals, fish, birds, flowers, trees, bugs, fruit, vegetables) and to pantomime how this natural gift does something: walks, swims, gallops, flies, grows, blooms. Encourage the other children to guess what is being pantomimed.

Talking About God's Gifts

To help the children understand that God's gift of the world can call forth many responses from them, ask volunteers questions like the following.

- What do you enjoy in God's wonderful world? (*Answers will vary.*)
- Name one gift of the world that you can share with others. With whom do you want to share this gift? (*Answers will vary.*)
- How can you take care of God's world? (*Answers will vary.*)

As you respond to the children's answers, emphasize the words *enjoy, share,* and *care.*

Step 2/DEVELOPMENT

Learning About Our Faith

Talking About Loving God's Wonderful World

Direct the children's attention to page 24. Encourage them to talk about each picture and what they think is happening. Then read the caption beneath each picture, and discuss how the young boy is *enjoying* God's world, how the two children are *sharing* the wooden blocks, how the girl is *caring* for God's gift of a kitten, and how the two children are *making* a sand castle from God's gift of sand. Emphasize the

24

God's Wonderful World

We can enjoy God's world.

We can care for all that God has made.

We can share God's gifts with others.

We can make things from the things God has made.

24 Morality

Focus on

God's Plan The *Catechism of the Catholic Church* states, "God willed the diversity of his creatures and their own particular goodness, their interdependence, and their order. He destined all material creatures for the good of the human race. Man, and through him all creation, is destined for the glory of God" (#353).

God's Wonderful Colors

God uses many colors to create our wonderful world.
Which color is your favorite?

ctivity

What would our world look like if God had used only one color to create the world?
Let's find out! Color everything in the first box with only your favorite color.
Then color the next box with many of the colors God made.

Which picture do you like best?
Why do you think God used many colors to create our wonderful world?

Role-Playing a Response to God's World

Invite volunteers to choose one of the illustrations on page 24 to role-play. Talk to the children before they do their presentations and help them think up a story to accompany each picture. (Involve as many of the children as you can in the role-play.) After each role-play, invite the children to tell God how much they enjoy God's wonderful world.

Step 3/CONCLUSION

Learning How to Live Our Faith

Coloring to Make a Choice

Read the text at the top of the page 25. Distribute crayons or felt-tip markers and instruct the children to color the first picture with their favorite color. Tell the children they may use *only* that color. After the children have finished coloring the first picture, have them color the second one, but this time instruct them to use many colors. Afterward, ask the children the questions at the bottom of the page.

Thanking God for Creation

If possible, give each child a natural gift from God to hold (stone, leaf, flower, piece of bark, a piece of fruit, a vegetable). Gather the children in the prayer area. Teach them the following response: *Thank you, God, for this wonderful gift.* Invite the children, one by one, to tell God about the gift of nature they are holding. After each child prays, encourage the children to repeat in unison the following prayer after you. *Thank you, God, for your wonderful world. Help us enjoy it, care for it, share it, and use it to make things from.*

Reviewing the Lesson

To review the lesson ask the following.

■ What do you enjoy in God's world? (*Answers will vary.*)

■ Whom can you share God's gifts with? (*Answers will vary.*)

■ How can you care for God's world? (*Answers will vary.*)

■ What can you make from one of God's gifts? (*Answers will vary.*)

CURRICULUM CONNECTION

Language Arts Provide the children with pieces of see-through colored plastic or plastic wrap. Invite each child to view the classroom through the colored sheet. Then have the children create stories about the world in only one color. Story themes might focus on humorous bumpings into things or center on good relationships among people who all are the same color. To stimulate the imagination of the children, ask them how people might act differently in an all one-colored world than they do in ours.

Enriching the Lesson

Use magnifying glasses to examine the various natural gifts God has given us: the bark of a tree, the veins of a leaf, the petals and stamen of a flower, the color of a puddle, the wings of a bug, the sheen of a tomato on the vine. Encourage the children to look at each item, to touch it, and even, if appropriate, to smell it. Help them marvel at the beauty of God's created world.

Objective

This lesson helps the children realize that God asks them to take care of the world.

Step 1/INTRODUCTION

Learning About Our Lives

Composing a Cooperative Chart

Help the children write a cooperative chart that details ways of caring for the classroom plants. Organize the chart around plant needs. Guide the children in making up rules for each need listed. For example, one rule might be the following: Give the plant enough light.

To begin getting the children to think about caring for plants, ask the following questions.

- What do plants need? (*Sun, water, plant food*)
- How do we know when the plant needs water? (*Test the soil with your finger.*)
- What would happen if we put the plant near the heating vent? (*It would dry out.*)
- What rules should we make about plants? (*Answers will vary.*)

Write the rules on a chart. When the chart is completed, hang it in the classroom and assign children to care for the plants. (*You will want to supervise this activity.*)

Singing a Song About Caring

Using the word *caring* instead of *happy*, sing "If You're Happy and You Know It" on page 13 of this Teacher Edition.

Step 2/DEVELOPMENT

Learning About Our Faith

Learning More About Caring for God's World

Direct the children's attention to the text at the top of page 26. Read the first three lines. Then ask the children questions like the following.

- All of you know many special people. Who is someone special you know? (*Answers will vary.*)
- How do you show that you care for this special person? (*Answers will vary.*)

Caring for God's Wonderful World

God made our wonderful world.

God made people, animals, plants, and things.

We can care for God's world and everything in it.

ctivity

Finish each of the five picture stories.

Draw what you think will happen next in each story.

CURRICULUM CONNECTION

Language Arts   Give each child three pieces of drawing paper and some crayons or felt-tip markers. Encourage the children to create a story about ways they can care for God's world. Ask them to divide their stories into a series of three pictures, drawing one picture on each sheet of paper. Afterward, staple the three-page storybooks together and put them in the library for the other children to read. Or, for the next few days, ask two or three children each day to tell their caring stories at the end of each religion lesson.

Tell a story about how you care for God's world.

- All of you know many special animals. What is the name of one of the animals you know? (*Answers will vary.*)
- How can you show you care for this animal? (*Feed it; shelter it.*)
- All of you love plants and flowers. What is the name of a special plant or flower you like? (*Answers will vary.*)
- How can you show you care for this plant? (*Answers will vary.*)
- Who made all these wonderful people and animals and plants and gave them to you with love? (*God*)

Reviewing the Word *Create*

Ask the children what *create* means. Help them remember that God created everything—people, animals, plants, and things—out of nothing. Ask volunteers to name three animals, birds, flowers, trees, fruits, bugs, vegetables.

Step 3/CONCLUSION

Learning How to Live Our Faith

Completing Caring Picture Stories

Direct the children to the five picture stories on pages 26 and 27, and read the directions for the activity. As a group, work on the first picture story of a plant. Discuss with the children what is happening in boxes one and two. Invite the children to draw a picture in the third box to show how they could help the plant.

Ask volunteers to tell what is happening in each of the four remaining picture stories. After discussing the happenings in the first two pictures of each story, provide time for the children to independently draw in the third box how they could show they care. Invite them to share their pictures.

Telling Stories About Caring

Read the copy at the bottom of page 27. Invite volunteers to tell their favorite stories about how they care for God's wonderful world.

Praying a Prayer of Thanks

Gather the children in the prayer area. Teach the following response: *Thank you, God, for helping us care.* Ask volunteers to tell how they have cared for God's world. After each story, invite the children to pray their response.

Teaching Tips

You will note that in Step 3 of this lesson, the children are asked at two different times to tell about how they care for God's creation. Both times children volunteer to tell their experiences. This is done with a purpose. The shared stories will give more reticent children an idea for what they might talk about. Also, hearing volunteers tell stories before assembling in the prayer area will help those children who are shy to be able to tell a story when they pray.

DAY 4
MORALITY

Objective

This lesson helps the children realize that they can use God's wonderful world to make many wonderful things.

Step 1/INTRODUCTION

Learning About Our Lives

Talking About How to Make Things

Show the children pictures of things humans make from wood: furniture, houses, boats, blocks, pull toys, and so on. Ask volunteers questions like the following.

- What is this made of? (*Wood*)
- Who gave us this wonderful gift of wood? (*God*)
- Where did the person who made this get the wood? (*From the lumber yard or from the forest*)
- Where does lumber come from? (*Trees*)
- Which of you wants to tell a story about how trees become a house?

Encourage the children to be creative with their stories. Help them out with words and concepts.

Making Things from God's Creation

Provide the children with drawing paper and crayons (not felt-tip markers). Tell them that people make crayons from God's gift of oil. Then invite the children to draw a picture of one of God's wonderful gifts of creation that people use to create things. Afterward, invite the children to share their drawings. Praise them for their work. Tell the children that their ability to make things is a special gift from God to them. Put the pictures aside for use in Step 2.

Step 2/DEVELOPMENT

Learning About Our Faith

Reading a Story About Making Cotton Cloth

Direct the children's attention to pages 28 and 29. Read the text at the top of page 28. Read the caption under each picture, and invite the children's comments and questions. Emphasize

28

Using God's Wonderful World

God made many wonderful things.
We can use them to make other things.
People use wheat to make bread
and wood to make houses.
People can use cotton to make cloth.
Here is the story of cotton.

From Cotton to Clothes

God gives us cotton plants.

Farmers pick the cotton with big machines.

The cotton is spun into yarn at the factory.

An artist draws colored flowers for the new cloth.

28   Morality

Cultural Awareness

If possible, take the children on a field trip to a local art gallery or museum that has artifacts in it made by people throughout the world. Talk about these artifacts (paintings, clothing, bowls, jewelry, boats, masks, and so on) and how people from all over the world use God's wonderfully created gifts to make things.

A woman weaves the pattern into the cloth.

Workers sew the cloth into clothes for us.

At the store, a salesperson hangs up the new clothes.

We shop at the store and try on the new clothes.

Our Prayer Today

Thank you, God, for letting people help to make nice things.

CURRICULUM CONNECTION

Encourage the children to bring in things made from wood to make a classroom collection. For example, the children might bring in blocks, pencils, small figurines, boxes, toys, and Christmas ornaments. After examining the display, help the children to compose an experience about wood. Encourage them to express the idea that God gave us wood, and we have made many things from it.

Enriching the Lesson

Help the children find out how a book is made—from the tree being cut and made into wood pulp and then paper, to an author writing a story and an artist drawing pictures, to printing the words and art on the paper, to binding the book together and putting a cover on it. Then invite the children to draw a picture story of this process, modeled on pages 28 and 29 of the children's book. Make their pictures into a book and place it in your classroom library.

---

that people make cotton clothes from God's gift of cotton.

Posting the Children's Artwork

Display on a bulletin board the pictures the children made in Step 1. As you post each picture, ask the child who made it to stand. Then praise the child for using God's special gift, the gift of making things.

Step 3/CONCLUSION

Learning How to Live Our Faith

Praising Others for Using God's Gifts Well

Show the children the Step 1 pictures of things made from wood. Teach them the following names of the people who used God's gift of trees to make the things: *builder, furniture maker, cabinet maker, toy maker,* and so on.

Ask the children how they feel when someone praises them for something they have made or done. Tell them that other people also feel good when they hear praise. Ask the children what words of praise they would say to the persons who made each of the pictured items. Encourage the children to be specific in their praise. For instance, they might praise the builder for the big porch or the blue door.

Recall for the children the fact that each of these people is using a special gift from God— the gift of making things from God's creation.

Thanking God for Helping Us Make Things

Gather the children in the prayer area. When they are ready to pray, invite volunteers, one by one, to thank God for helping them make something. Encourage the children to name specific things they have made in their lives. At the end of the children's responses, invite the children to say aloud with you the prayer at the bottom of page 29: *Thank you, God, for letting people help to make nice things.*

PRAYER/REVIEW

Objective

This lesson helps the children express thanks in their own words.

Thinking of God's Wonderful Creation

Read the top of page 30 with the children. Have them draw a picture of a gift from God. When they have finished ask the following questions. (*Answers will vary.*)

■ Why do you *enjoy* this?

■ Whom can you *share* this with?

■ How can you *care* for this?

■ What can you *make* with this?

■ Who created these wonderful gifts? (*God*)

Preparing to Pray

Recall for the children the bow they made to show reverence to the Bible. Tell them that today they are going to have a procession and again show reverence for God's special book.

Teach the children the melody to "This Old Man." Use the following words.

Thank you, God, for your gifts.
For your love in all we do.
With a knick knack paddy whack,
    thank you for our world.
Thank you for the sky so blue.

Processing to the Prayer Area

Line up the children for a procession to the prayer area. Ask the children to bring their religion books with them. Explain that they can sing their song as they process and that when they come to the Bible, they will bow reverently.

Thanking God for Creation

Invite the children to open their books to page 30. Encourage each child, one by one, to say *for the gift of* and then to name the gift he or she has drawn. The other children should all say, *Thank you, God.* Before ending the prayer, ask the children if they want to thank God for anything else today. Encourage their responses. After each response, invite the rest of the children to pray *Thank you, God.*

Praying in Our Own Words

We can make up our own prayers.
We can make up a prayer to thank God.

Activity

Draw a picture of something you want to thank God for.

For . . .

Thank You, God

Look at your picture.
Pray the prayer you made up.
The other children can help you.
They can pray, "Thank you, God."

30 Prayer

CURRICULUM CONNECTION

Art Help the children make mobiles that show God's created gifts. Provide magazine pictures of trees, flowers, bugs, animals, fish, birds, bushes, vegetables, and fruit. Direct the children to choose one or two pictures to paste on heavy paper. Using varied lengths of yarn, help the children attach the pictures to a plastic hanger. Display the mobiles in class or encourage the children to take them home and display them.

Teaching Tips

You might promote two actions: (1) encourage the children to pick up litter, (2) help the children plant small gardens. In these ways children can beautify the world and proclaim the goodness of God, who creates the flowers. You could begin to plan these gardens now with the children. Perhaps, you would like to start by gathering dirt, flowerpots, and seeds. Gather an array of seed catalogs for the children to look at and wonder over.

Chapter Review

We can use the things God created.
God makes peanuts.
We can make other things from peanuts.
Put the pictures in order.
Write **1**, **2**, **3**, and **4** in the correct box.

1. Who made the world?

God

2. What word means to make something out of nothing?

create

3. Talk about what you can thank God for.

Give thanks to God because God is good.
Based on Psalm 13

Review   31

Completing an Activity

Use the activity on page 31 to review Chapter 2. Direct the children's attention to the four pictures. Then ask the following questions.

- Which of you likes to eat peanut butter and jelly sandwiches? (*Answers will vary.*)
- How do you make a peanut butter and jelly sandwich? (*Put peanut butter and jelly on bread.*)
- Where do we get the peanut butter from? (*The store*)

Read the copy at the top of page 31. Distribute crayons or felt-tip markers and invite the children to put the pictures in order by printing the correct number under each picture. Afterward, discuss their work. Emphasize that peanut butter comes from God's gift of the peanut.

Answering the Questions

Read aloud the first two questions and ask volunteers to respond. Direct the children to print the answers in their texts. Encourage all the children to participate in the discussion of the third question. Be supportive of each child who responds.

Praying with the Scriptural Verse

Point out the scriptural verse at the bottom of the page. Explain that the verse is a thank-you prayer. Read it and ask the children to pray it after you. You may wish to have the children memorize it.

CURRICULUM CONNECTION

Science Play "science bingo." Draw five boxes on a piece of 8 1/2" × 11" paper. Duplicate one sheet per child. In each box on each sheet, print one category from the following: *fruit, tree, flower, animal, fish, bird, body of water, universe, vegetable.* (Make each sheet different.) Give each child five buttons or five small pieces of colored paper to cover the boxes. Call out items belonging to each category, such as apple for *fruit.* Players must cover all their category boxes to win.

Enriching the Lesson

Invite a Daisy, Brownie, or Cub Scout leader to come and talk to your class about their organization and what it does to help children take better care of our world. Ask the speaker to make practical suggestions about what first graders can do to take care of their world.

3 God Gives Us Special People

Objectives

To help the children

■ Recognize God's love through the love of people.

■ Understand that God created people.

■ Recognize God's law of love in action.

■ Choose to act unselfishly.

■ Express thanks for special people.

Chapter Outline

	Step 1 Learning About Our Lives	Step 2 Learning About Our Faith	Step 3 Learning How to Live Our Faith
Day 1	■ Introduce Chapter 3. ■ Read a poem. ■ Act out the poem. *ABOUT 10 MINUTES*	■ Present the doctrine. ■ Thank God for special people. *ABOUT 10 MINUTES*	■ Tell a story about special people. ■ Say "thank you" to God for special people. *ABOUT 10 MINUTES*
Day 2	■ Discuss a garden with no people in it. ■ Make clay people. *ABOUT 10 MINUTES*	■ Read a Bible story. ■ Understand the message. ■ Review the vocabulary. ■ Discuss the Bible story. *ABOUT 10 MINUTES*	■ Pretend to be alone in God's world. ■ Thank God for creating people. *ABOUT 10 MINUTES*
Day 3	■ Examine pictures of the law of love. *ABOUT 8 MINUTES*	■ Read about God's law of love. ■ Role-play selfish and unselfish actions. *ABOUT 12 MINUTES*	■ Play a game. ■ Thank God for the law of love. ■ Review the lesson. *ABOUT 10 MINUTES*
Day 4	■ Review the learning of Day 3. ■ Share decisions to follow God's law of love. *ABOUT 10 MINUTES*	■ Choose ways to act unselfishly. ■ Find caring pictures. *ABOUT 10 MINUTES*	■ Choose to follow God's law. ■ Thank God for people who love and help us. ■ Review the lesson. *ABOUT 10 MINUTES*
Day 5	**Prayer** Draw pictures of people the children love; learn a song; have a procession; and pray a prayer of thanks. **Review** Complete an activity; answer the questions; and read the Scripture verse.		

Correlation
to the
**Catechism of
the Catholic Church**

Paragraphs
2203–2207, 2209

Plan Ahead

	Preparing Your Class	Materials Needed	Additional Resources
Day 1	Read the poem on page 32 and think of gestures or body movements for the children to use as you read the poem.	■ drawing paper	As you plan this chapter, consider using the following materials from The Resourceful Teacher Package. ■ *Classroom Activity Sheets 3* and *3a* ■ *Family Activity Sheets 3* and *3a* ■ *Chapter 3 Test* ■ *Prayers for Every Day* ■ *Projects: Grade 1*
Day 2	Prepare the clay to be used in Step 1. Divide it into equal portions for each child.	■ a colorful magazine picture of a flower ■ garden without people in it ■ clay	You may also wish to refer to the following Big Book. ■ *We Celebrate God's Word,* page 3
Day 3	For Step 1, collect pictures of children playing happily together and children quarreling or fighting. For Step 2, prepare role-plays of being selfish/unselfish.	■ pictures of children playing happily and unhappily together ■ coins ■ buttons	In preparing the children for the Sunday readings, you may wish to use Silver Burdett Ginn's *Getting Ready for Sunday* student and teacher materials.
Day 4	Read the poem on page 39 and consider gestures or body movements for the children to use as you read the poem aloud.		
Day 5	Learn the melody for "Here We Go 'Round the Mulberry Bush." Or plan to play some quiet background music while the children process and pray.		

BOOKS FOR THE JOURNEY

Fly Away Home. Eve Bunting. Houghton Mifflin, 1991. A story of a homeless child and his father caring for each other and doing what they can to have shelter, food, a sense of belonging, and hope.

My Father's Hands. Sheila McGraw and Paul Cline. Green Tiger Press, 1992. A poignant chronicle of a young boy's childhood as he comes to appreciate how his strengths and values are reflected in his father's hands.

MORE BOOKS FOR THE JOURNEY

Now One Foot, Now The Other. Tomie de Paola. G. P. Putnam's Sons, 1992. Just as the child needs his grandfather, the grandfather needs the child.

People. Peter Spier. Doubleday, 1980. A book that helps children see and know other people and appreciate them.

REDUCED CLASSROOM ACTIVITIES

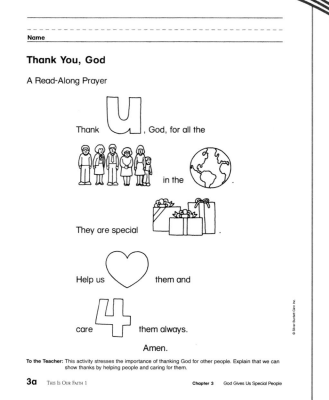

Name

God Gives Us Special People

1. Draw a line to match the pictures.
2. Tell a partner how each person is a helper.

To the Teacher: Extend this activity to help the children understand that community workers also help us. After the picture discussion, ask the children to name other people who help them.

Chapter 3   God Gives Us Special People   This Is Our Faith 1   **3**

Name

Thank You, God

A Read-Along Prayer

Thank **U**, God, for all the [people] in the [world]

They are special [gifts].

Help us [♥] them and

care **4** them always.

Amen.

To the Teacher: This activity stresses the importance of thanking God for other people. Explain that we can show thanks by helping people and caring for them.

3a   This Is Our Faith 1   Chapter 3   God Gives Us Special People

Background for the Teacher ～～～～～

THE LAW OF LOVE

In the Gospel of Luke, a lawyer questions Jesus: "And who is my neighbor?" In response, Jesus tells the story of the Good Samaritan (Luke 10:30–37). Jesus answers more than the "who" of the question. He also tells us "how" we must choose to love.

This call to love of neighbor that is epitomized in the story of the Good Samaritan is part of the Great Commandment: Love God with your whole heart, mind, and soul; love your neighbor as yourself. Here you see that if the children are to follow Jesus' command and love their neighbors as themselves, then the children must first love themselves. This is why the religion text stresses in Chapter 1 that the children are lovely and lovable. And if they are to love others, then they must first love themselves.

WHO IS OUR NEIGHBOR?

The question comes to mind as we try to love others: "How can I be a good neighbor?" After telling the parable of the Good Samaritan, Jesus asked the lawyer to identify the person who had acted like a good neighbor to the wounded man. The lawyer answered, "The one who treated him with mercy." Here Jesus teaches us that to be a neighbor is to show compassion.

CHILDREN'S ABILITY TO LOVE

Six-year-olds are developing their abilities to reason and to get along with other people. You can help the children understand that what they do affects not only themselves but also their relationships with others. To help you do this, Chapter 3 distinguishes between loving/unselfish actions and unloving/selfish actions.

Chapter 3 also helps the children know that they can choose between selfishness or unselfishness. They learn that their actions have consequences that are the result of their choices. The activities are designed to help the children understand that they can change their selfish actions and decide to be loving.

The world of six-year-old children expands daily, as they gain new experiences and meet new people. In Chapter 3, you will explore with the children many of their relationships with people they meet in their expanding world. You will help the children realize that many of these people help them and show them God's love and that God will also help them show love to their grown-up friends.

By caring for their newfound friends and neighbors in the ways that are open to them as six-year-olds, the children in your classroom can begin the journey of becoming compassionate like Jesus. They can follow the law of love.

Objective

This lesson helps the children recognize God's love in their experiences with people.

Step 1/INTRODUCTION

Learning About Our Lives

Introducing Chapter 3

Ask the children to open their books to page 32. Read aloud the chapter title and the focus question in the border. Encourage each child to name someone special in his or her life. Remind the children that they are special and that God loves them very much. Recall for the children that God has given each of them special gifts. Explain that today they will learn about another of God's gifts—special people who love them.

Reading a Poem About Special People

Explain to the children that the poem on page 32 is about people whom God gives them to help them. Read the poem; then ask the following questions.

■ What helpers did we read about? (*Answers will vary.*)

■ How did people like this help you when you needed someone to care for you? (*Answers will vary.*)

Acting Out the Poem

Reread the last two lines of the poem on page 32. Then decide on a rhythmic gesture or body movement the children can do as a group for these two lines. Next, divide the class into six groups for the six types of people mentioned in the first four lines of the poem. Encourage each group to stand together and to come up with a gesture or body movement to illustrate their type of person. Then reread lines 5 through 10 of the poem, and assign each group one of these lines. Provide time for the groups to work out rhythmic gestures or body movements.

When the groups are ready, reread the poem and invite the groups to add their gestures and body movements to your reading. Praise the children for their work.

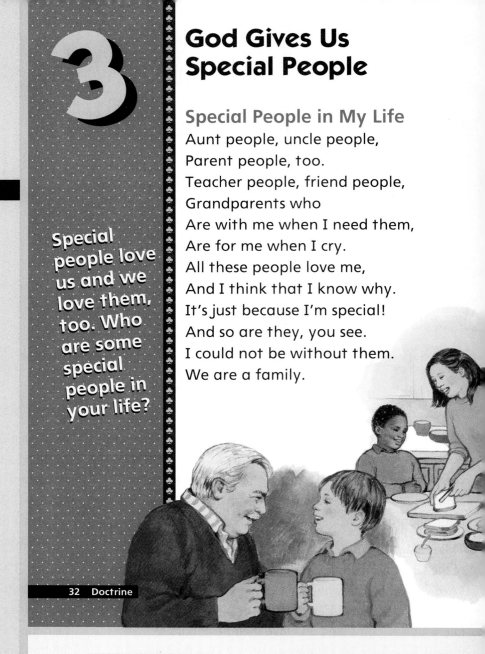

3

God Gives Us Special People

Special people love us and we love them, too. Who are some special people in your life?

Special People in My Life

Aunt people, uncle people,
Parent people, too.
Teacher people, friend people,
Grandparents who
Are with me when I need them,
Are for me when I cry.
All these people love me,
And I think that I know why.
It's just because I'm special!
And so are they, you see.
I could not be without them.
We are a family.

32 Doctrine

Teaching Tips

The poem "Special People in My Life" is very rhythmic. The children will find it natural to do gestures with this poem. Some rhythmic movements to suggest to get the children started in creating their own gestures might be clapping, foot tapping, and holding arms close to the body and opening them at the elbows, bringing them back with a soft clap. There are many other movements the children might suggest.

CURRICULUM CONNECTION

Language Arts Give each child a sheet of 8 1/2" × 11" paper and crayons or markers. Direct the children to fold their papers in half and to write thank-you notes to anyone they would like to thank for helping them. Encourage the children to decorate their notes. Ask the children to deliver their notes, to watch how the person reacts, and to report on this in the next class. Or provide envelopes and stamps, and help the children address and mail their notes. Perhaps you can take the children to the mailbox to mail the notes.

God Cares for Us

God gives us people to love us and help us.
God takes care of us through these people.

Activity

Look at the pictures on both pages.
Choose a picture that reminds you
of someone who loves you.
Tell a story about that special person.

We Believe

God gives us
special people
to love and care
for us.

Doctrine 33

Enriching the Lesson

With the children, compile a list of helpers on the chalkboard: doctors, nurses, trash collectors, janitors, teachers, telephone workers, firefighters, postal carriers. (Make sure the number of helpers equals or exceeds the number of children.) Display pictures and objects associated with helpers to expand the children's concept of each occupation. Then discuss the helpers. Using butcher paper, children will create a "Special Helpers" mural. Each child may choose one of the helpers to draw.

Step 2/DEVELOPMENT

Learning About Our Faith

Presenting the Doctrine

Read to the children the We Believe statement on page 33. Print the words *special people* on the chalkboard. Ask for volunteers to print the names of some special people.

Thanking God for Special People

Read aloud "God Cares for Us" on page 33. Ask the children who gave them these special people to love them (*God*). Spend a few moments talking about the love God has shown the children by creating each of them special, by creating a wonderful world for them, and by giving them special people. Help the children to express their thanksgiving for God's love.

Step 3/CONCLUSION

Learning How to Live Our Faith

Telling a Story About Special People

Encourage the children to talk about the people illustrated on pages 32 and 33, one at a time. Then ask the following questions.

- Who do you think this person is?
- What special thing is this person doing for the child? (*Answers will vary.*)
- Do you know a special person like this one? (*Answers will vary.*)
- Name a person who is special to you. (*Answers will vary.*)

Read the text at the bottom of page 33. Distribute drawing paper and crayons or felt-tip markers, and invite the children to draw a picture to illustrate a story about the special people in their lives. Afterward, encourage volunteers to share their drawings and stories.

Saying Thank You to God for Special People

Gather the children to pray and invite them to sing one of their favorite songs. Encourage them to thank God for a special person in their lives.

God Gives Us People

God scooped up some clay.
God formed a man from the
clay of the earth.

God gave him a garden full of
flowers and fruit.
The man liked them all, but he
felt very lonely.

So God made dogs and cats,
tigers and giraffes, birds and
butterflies for the man.
He liked them all, but still the
man felt lonely.

"The man needs a friend," God
thought.
So God made a woman to be
with the man.

Objective

This lesson helps the children understand why and how God created people.

Step 1/INTRODUCTION

Learning About Our Lives

Discussing a Garden with No People in It

Show the children a colorful magazine picture of a flower garden without people in it. Encourage the children to name the gifts from God in the picture. Ask the following questions.

- What colors do you see in this garden? What shapes? (*Answers will vary.*)
- What do you think you would smell in this garden? (*Answers will vary.*)
- What could you touch in this garden? (*Answers will vary.*)
- What do you like best about this garden? (*Answers will vary.*)
- What special gift is missing from this garden?

Help the children to see that there is no person in the garden to enjoy God's gifts.

Making Clay People

Give some clay to each child. Invite the children to shape their clay into persons. Ask what the clay persons can do. Can they move? speak? laugh? Why not? Point out that none of us can give life to a clay person.

Step 2/DEVELOPMENT

Learning About Our Faith

Reading a Bible Story About Creation

Read the children a story from the Bible on pages 34–35. Suggest that they look at the pictures as you read "The Creator Gives Us People." Relate the Creation story to the children's making of clay persons. Point out the difference between God's act and theirs. Emphasize the wonderful power of God to create life.

Focus on

Genesis Help the children respect the message of the biblical story of creation as profoundly true, even though it is not a scientific explanation. The Bible was not written to affirm nor deny the scientific theories of evolution, but rather teach that all that is good comes from our loving God. Its message about creation is true whether the universe began with a big bang or whether humanity gradually evolved from lesser forms of life. When teaching this lesson, focus on God's immense, unconditional, unequivocal, irrevocable love for us.

CURRICULUM CONNECTION

Art Provide each child with many colors of modeling clay and an empty shoe box. Invite each child to make a garden in the box. Encourage the children to use the modeling clay to add flowers, fruit trees, animals, and the first man and the first woman to their garden. Afterward, invite the children to talk to the class about their work. If possible, display these dioramas where others can enjoy them.

34

"At last," the man said, "God has created a woman so I am no longer alone.
Her mind and heart are like mine.
We can love each other and share God's gifts."

Based on Genesis 2:4–24

God Knows We Need People

God, our loving **Creator**, gives us special people to love and care for us.
These people are gifts from God to us.

New Word

♣
♣ **Creator**   Our Creator is God, who makes
♣   everything in the world out of nothing.

Scripture 35

Understanding the Message of the Bible Story

Read "God Knows We Need People" on page 35. Ask the children whom God has created to love and care for them.

Reviewing the Vocabulary

Point to the New Word on page 35. Ask the children to repeat the word *Creator* and the definition after you.

Discussing the Bible Story

Reread the story on pages 34 and 35. Encourage the children to talk about the illustrations. Then ask these questions.

■ What did God use to form and create the first man? (*Clay*)

■ What do we call God, who made the world from nothing? (*The Creator*)

■ Where did God put the man? (*In a garden*)

■ What else did God create and put in the garden? (*Flowers and fruit and animals*)

■ How did the man feel? (*Lonely*)

■ What did God know the man needed? (*A friend*)

■ So whom did God make? (*A woman*)

■ What did the man say he and the woman would do? (*Love each other and share God's gifts*)

Praise the children for their responses.

Step 3/CONCLUSION

Learning How to Live Our Faith

Pretending to Be Alone in God's World

Tell the children to close their eyes and imagine that God has created no one else but them. Then ask how they would feel. Help them realize how much everyone needs family and friends. Ask them to open their eyes and encourage each child to turn to the person next to him or her, shake hands, and thank that person for being a classmate. If there is an extra child, you can be that child's partner.

Thanking God for Creating People

Invite the children to walk to the prayer area with the children whose hands they shook and to stand side by side as partners. Reread the last sentence of the story of Creation. Invite volunteers to thank God for their partners.

Focus on

Genesis   This lesson presents the second Creation story as found in Genesis. In the first account (Genesis 1), God's creative activity is structured by the six-day theme. The second account (Genesis 2) is chiefly concerned with the creation of human beings and the relationship of friendship and partnership between Adam and Eve.

35

DAY 3
MORALITY

Objective
This lesson helps the children recognize God's law of love in action.

Step 1/INTRODUCTION

Learning About Our Lives

Examining Pictures of the Law of Love
Display two types of pictures: children playing happily together and children quarreling or fighting. Ask the children which picture they would rather be in and why. Tell them that God gave them people to help make their lives happier but that each person must do his or her part by loving, helping, and caring for others.

or...

Using a picture of children in a harmonious situation, tell a story about one of the children getting angry and refusing to play with the others. Cut the picture so that one child (the angry one) is separated from the others. Move the portion of the picture with the angry child some distance from the harmonious group.

Discuss the feelings the distanced child might be feeling and the emotions of the other children who were playing happily, only to have their good mood interrupted.

Then discuss that God wants everyone to love, help, and care for others. Invite the children to suggest a simple way for the child who forgot to be loving, caring, or helpful to reunite with the others. Then tape the picture back together.

Step 2/DEVELOPMENT

Learning About Our Faith

Reading About God's Law of Love
Read with the children the text "God's Law of Love" on page 36. Encourage the children to talk about the difference between doing good, unselfish things for others and doing selfish things. Ask the children to give examples of selfish actions and unselfish actions.

God's Law of Love
God creates us to be friends.
We can be friends with God, our Creator.
We can be friends with each other.
We can be friends with ourselves, too.

We can love God.
We can love others.
We can love ourselves.
When we love, we do good things.
When we love, we do unselfish things.

You helped around the house. Move ahead one.

BLAST OFF

36 Morality

CURRICULUM CONNECTION
Music Use the melody to "London Bridge." **Verse 1:** God wants us to love and share/ love and share, love and share./ God wants us to love and share with all people. **Verse 2:** God wants us to love the world,/ love the world, love the world./ God wants us to love the world, and we love it. **Verse 3:** God wants us to love our friends,/ love our friends, love our friends./ God wants us to love our friends,/ and we love them. **Verse 4:** God is always loving us/ loving us, loving us./ God is always loving us. We are thankful.

Focus on
God's Law Days 3 and 4 of Chapter 3 are interconnected. Day 3 introduces God's law of love: to love God, others, and self. In addition, the children meet the words *selfish* and *unselfish*. On Day 4, the children go deeper into God's law of love and explore the concept of choice: They can choose to be loving and unselfish or unloving and selfish. Thus, on Day 3, you focus on God's law of love and selfish and unselfish actions. On Day 4, you focus on how the children can choose to follow God's law of love.

Activity

Try to get to the people walking in space.

1. You will need a coin and a button.
2. Flip the coin to see how many spaces to move the button.

   Heads = 1 space
   Tails = 2 spaces

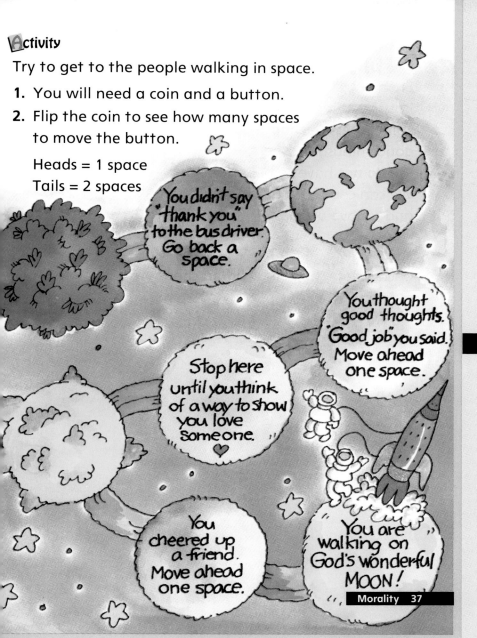

You didn't say "thank you" to the bus driver. Go back a space.

You thought good thoughts. "Good job" you said. Move ahead one space.

Stop here until you think of a way to show you love someone. ♥

You cheered up a friend. Move ahead one space.

You are walking on God's wonderful MOON!

Morality 37

Call on volunteers to role-play stories of selfish or unselfish actions. Call on two or more volunteers at a time to give each group a scene to role-play. Select scenes like the following: a parent telling a child to help clean the dinner table and the child refusing; a child giving a flower to a special friend; a child refusing to share a toy; a child pushing in ahead of another at the water fountain. Encourage the children's comments after each role-play. After each role-play, tell the children that God wants them to practice the law of love and to do unselfish things for others.

Step 3/CONCLUSION

Learning How to Live Our Faith

Playing a Game About the Law of Love

Direct the children's attention to the game board on pages 36 and 37. Spend a few moments discussing the illustrations there. Read through the steps of the game.

Next, divide the class into groups of two or three. Give each group one coin and a button for each player. Invite each group to play the game.

Thanking God for the Law of Love

Have the groups that played the game together go to the prayer area and stand together. Teach the children the following response: *Thank you, God, for your law of love.* Then say the following litany and invite the children's response after each line.

- For showing us how to love others . . .
- For showing us how to love creation . . .
- For showing us how to love ourselves . . .
- For showing us how to love you . . .
  Amen.

Reviewing the Lesson

To review the lesson ask the following.

- What is God's law of love? (*Answers will vary.*)
- What does being unselfish mean? (*Answers will vary.*)
- What unselfish things can we do for others? (*Answers will vary.*)

37

Objective

This lesson helps the children understand that they can choose to act unselfishly.

Step 1/INTRODUCTION

Learning About Our Lives

Reviewing the Learning of Day 3

Review the words *God's law of love, selfish,* and *unselfish* with the children. Stress that when the children follow God's law of love, they love God, others, and themselves, therefore showing unselfish love.

Sharing Decisions to Follow God's Law of Love

Print the word *choose* on the chalkboard and talk about this word. Then ask the children the following questions.

- Which of you has chosen to do something unselfish for someone recently?
- What did you do? (*Answers will vary.*)
- How did you feel when you chose to be unselfish? (*Answers will vary.*)
- How did the person for whom you showed love feel? (*Answers will vary.*)
- What made you decide to choose to follow God's law of love? (*Answers will vary.*)

or...

Make two simple animal stick-puppets from heavy construction paper, with a large face on both the front and back sides of the puppets. One side should be smiling and the other frowning.

Tell a story about the two animals playing together. They might be building a castle of snap-on blocks. The castle is growing larger and larger, and the animals are more and more excited about their creation. There are several blocks left, and one of the puppets decides to grab them all. As the puppet pulls them forward, the castle crashes. Explore the feelings the children think each animal feels. Invite the children to choose which puppet face best suits each animal's feelings.

38

We Can Choose to Be Unselfish

Everything God created is good.
Each of us is good.
But sometimes we can be selfish.
Sometimes we choose not to do
good things for others.
We do not have to be selfish.
We can choose to be unselfish
and to love others.

Activity

Circle the pictures of children choosing to love.

Focus on

Choices   Days 3 and 4 are connected. In today's lesson, review the learning of Day 3 about God's law of love, unselfish/loving actions, and selfish/unloving actions. Then help the children realize that they can choose how they will act. When angry, some children are apt to lash out. Talking about how they feel when they lash out, when they get in trouble, when they choose to be peacemakers, and so on, can help the children learn to choose the path of God's law of love.

Choose to Love

Ann sets a butterfly free.
Sam won't share his apple tree.
Flo won't share her ball or truck.
Gan lets others pet his duck.
Carl has to win each game.
Lani treats us all the same.

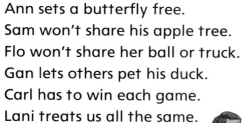

Activity

Draw a circle around the pictures of the children
who are choosing not to show love.
Then tell how they can become loving and unselfish.

Morality 39

Enriching the Lesson

Help the children make buttons to give to the special people in their lives. Duplicate a worksheet for each child on which you have drawn three circles, each about 3 1/2" in diameter. In the center of each circle, print *I choose to care*. Then cut three 3 1/2" construction-paper circles for each child. Distribute the worksheet and tell the children to trace over the letters and to decorate the buttons. Help the children cut out the buttons and paste them on the construction-paper circles. The children can present their buttons to their loved ones.

Step 2/DEVELOPMENT

Learning About Our Faith

Choosing Ways to Act Unselfishly

Read page 38 with the children. Ask them to name ways they can show caring. To help the children get started, offer the following examples: picking up toys, giving mom a hug, thanking the art teacher. List the children's ideas on the chalkboard or on posterboard. Encourage the children to choose one thing that they will do for someone today.

Finding Caring Pictures

Read aloud the directions to the activity on page 38, and instruct the children to complete the activity by circling the pictures of children who have chosen to love others and to act unselfishly.

Step 3/CONCLUSION

Learning How to Live Our Faith

Choosing to Follow God's Law of Love

Direct the children's attention to the poem on page 39. Encourage them to talk about the children in the pictures and help the class identify which children are following God's law of love. Then read the poem.

Read the instructions for the activity on page 39. Encourage the children to find the children mentioned in the poem and to circle the ones who are loving.

Then ask the children to identify which of the pictured children are not following God's law of love. Discuss the loving actions each of these children could choose.

Thanking God for People Who Love and Help Us

Quiet the children for prayer and encourage them to pray in their own words (spontaneously) for the people who love them.

Reviewing the Lesson

To review the lesson ask the following.

- What is the difference between being selfish and unselfish? (*Showing love or not.*)
- Why does God want us to choose to be loving? (*Answers will vary.*)
- How do you feel when you choose to follow God's law of love? (*Answers will vary.*)

39

Objective

This lesson helps the children express their thanks for special people and remember that God has given them these people.

Drawing Pictures to Thank God for Special People

Direct the children's attention to page 40. Tell them that they are going to use this page in their prayer celebration today. Distribute crayons or felt-tip markers. Then read the page to the children, and invite them to draw in the hearts pictures of the special people they want to thank God for.

Learning a Song About Choosing to Love

Using the melody to "Here We Go 'Round the Mulberry Bush," teach the children the following words.

> God wants us all to choose to love,
> To choose to love, to choose to love.
> God wants us all to choose to love
> And make our actions caring.

or...

Have available a record or tape player and some quiet background music to play while the children process.

Processing to the Prayer Area

Ask the children to bring their books with them and to line up for a procession to the prayer area. Encourage them to sing their song as they process and to bow to the Bible when they arrive at the prayer area. They can stand in a semicircle around the Bible.

Thanking God for Special People

Provide a few moments for the children to reflect quietly. Begin the prayer by thanking God for helping the children choose to follow the law of love and do loving actions. Then pray the prayer on page 40. Pray out loud the first two lines, and then call on the children to display their drawings and to thank God for these special people by name. At the end of the prayer, invite the children to sing their song again.

Praying a Prayer of Thanks

In the hearts, draw pictures of the special people you want to thank God for.

Thank you, God, for the special people who love me.

Thank you, God, for . . .

Thank you, God, for . . .

Thank you, God, for . . .

Thank you, God, for loving me.
Amen.

40 Prayer

Focus on

Praying by Giving Thanks The prayer skill in this lesson encourages the children to express thanks for people who are special to them. It is age-appropriate prayer because children indeed do focus on their own experiences of being loved. Children need to be guided to appreciate that God gave them special people to love them and that God should be thanked for the gift of love in their lives. This prayer skill builds on last week's that introduced the prayer of thanks.

Chapter Review

God wants us to show love for others.
The picture shows children being selfish.
In the heart below, draw them
being unselfish.

1. Who is our Creator? God

2. Who gives us special people?

   God

3. Talk about what you can do
   for the people you love.

God says,
"People need
other people."
Based on
Genesis 2:18

Enriching the Lesson

Brainstorm with the children the names of the special people in their lives (mom, dad, sister, brother, grandpa, uncle, grandma, friend, aunt, firefighter, teacher, bus driver, and so on). Print their responses on the chalkboard. Then ask the children to brainstorm words to describe each person. (For instance, the children might say the following: *smiling* mom, *storytelling* grandpa, *pizza-making* uncle, *bingo-playing* grandma, and so on.) Invite the children to choose one of these special people and to tell or draw a story about them.

Completing an Activity

Use the activity on page 41 to review the learning of Chapter 3. Direct the children's attention to the picture. Then ask the children questions like the following.

- What is happening in this picture? (*A boy is left out.*)
- How do you know that these children are not following God's law of love? (*They are not inviting someone to play.*)
- What could they choose to do so that they could follow God's law of love? (*Answers will vary.*)

Read the copy at the top of page 41. Distribute crayons or felt-tip markers, and invite the children to draw in the heart a way that the children can choose to be loving and unselfish.

Answering the Questions

Read aloud the first two questions on page 41 and ask volunteers to respond. Direct the children to print the answers in their texts. Encourage all the children to participate in the discussion of the third question. Be supportive of each child who responds.

Reading the Scripture Verse

Ask the children to read the Scripture verse after you. It is a good way to end the lesson by reflecting on the word of God. If you wish, you may have the children memorize this verse.

God Gives Us Jesus

Objectives

To help the children

■ Recognize Jesus as God's Son and their greatest gift from God.

■ Rejoice in Jesus their friend who loves them.

■ Discover that the Bible contains stories about what Jesus *said* and *did*.

■ Be aware that Jesus is their Savior who helps them remember God's love for them.

■ Learn and pray the Sign of the Cross.

Chapter Outline

	Step 1 Learning About Our Lives	Step 2 Learning About Our Faith	Step 3 Learning How to Live Our Faith
Day 1	■ Review God's gifts. *ABOUT 10 MINUTES*	■ Enjoy a rebus. ■ Discover God's best gift. *ABOUT 10 MINUTES*	■ Meet Jesus as a baby. ■ Pray with Jesus' name. *ABOUT 10 MINUTES*
Day 2	■ Find out about friendship. ■ Create a friendship bulletin board. *ABOUT 10 MINUTES*	■ Read a Bible story. ■ Role-play the Bible story. ■ Review the vocabulary. ■ Present the doctrine. *ABOUT 10 MINUTES*	■ Add Jesus to the friendship bulletin board. ■ Thank God for Jesus' friendship. *ABOUT 10 MINUTES*
Day 3	■ Develop a deeper understanding of friendship. *ABOUT 10 MINUTES*	■ Talk about Jesus' friendship. ■ Read Bible stories about Jesus. ■ Act out two Bible stories. *ABOUT 10 MINUTES*	■ Finish a story about friendship. ■ Thank God for the gift of Jesus. ■ Review the lesson. *ABOUT 10 MINUTES*
Day 4	■ Review Day 3. ■ Discuss the photos. ■ Share stories about being saved. *ABOUT 10 MINUTES*	■ Discover that Jesus is our savior. ■ Brainstorm the signs of God's love. ■ Review the vocabulary. *ABOUT 10 MINUTES*	■ Write a note about God's love. ■ Pray with a song. *ABOUT 10 MINUTES*
Day 5	**Prayer** Learn the Sign of the Cross; think about Jesus; learn a song; process; and thank God. **Review** Complete the activity; answer the questions; and read the Scripture verse.		

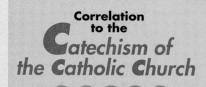

Correlation
to the
Catechism of
the **C**atholic **C**hurch

Paragraphs
454, 469, 604, 2009

Plan Ahead ~~~~~~~

	Preparing Your Class	**Materials Needed**	**Additional Resources**
Day 1	For Step 1, prepare gaily wrapped packages. Add gift tags to these that say "*From God, who loves you.*" Make one box bigger and more elaborate than the others.	■ array of wrapped boxes ■ ribbons ■ tags ■ pencils ■ crayons or felt-tip markers	As you plan this chapter, consider using the following materials from The Resourceful Teacher Package. ■ *Classroom Activity Sheets 4* and *4a* ■ *Family Activity Sheets 4* and *4a* ■ *Chapter 4 Test* ■ *Prayers for Every Day* ■ *Projects: Grade 1* You may also wish to refer to the following Big Book. ■ *We Celebrate God's Word,* pages 9 and 11 In preparing the children for the Sunday readings, you may wish to use Silver Burdett Ginn's *Getting Ready for Sunday* student and teacher materials.
Day 2	For Step 1, collect magazine pictures that illustrate friendship, cut out letters for *These are our special friends,* and prepare a bulletin-board space for a display.	■ magazine pictures illustrating friendship ■ drawing paper, crayons ■ empty bulletin board, letters ■ staples or tacks	
Day 3	For Step 3, prepare an uncompleted friendship story. Think of some body movements to use for the prayer.	■ friendship bulletin board from Day 2	
Day 4	Read over the entire lesson plan for this session.	■ note paper ■ pencils ■ crayons or felt-tip markers	
Day 5	Learn the melody for "Frère Jacques." Have available quiet background music. Plan a procession route to the prayer area.	■ Jesus' gift box from Day 1 (the biggest one) ■ pencils	

BOOKS FOR THE JOURNEY

The Beginner's Bible. As told by Karyn Henley. Questar Publishing, 1989. A book that tells the story of God and Jesus in short, simple sentences that young children can understand and embrace.

The Life of Jesus. The Liturgical Press, 1993. The story of Jesus, narrated and illustrated.

MORE BOOKS FOR THE JOURNEY

A Christmas Story. Brian Wildsmith. Knopf, 1989. An exquisitely illustrated story of the birth of Jesus, God's greatest gift to us.

Sunday's Children. "Sunday Is a Thanksgiving Day," page 27; "Promises to Keep," pages 88–89. James Bitney. Resource Publications, 1986. Two poems of thanks and recognition of Jesus as God's gift to us.

REDUCED CLASSROOM ACTIVITIES

Name

God Gives Us Jesus

1. Color the picture.
2. Trace the letters.

Jesus is God's Son and our friend.

To the Teacher: This activity reinforces the Scripture story "Jesus and the Children." Emphasize the fact that Jesus is always with us.

Chapter 4 God Gives Us Jesus   THIS IS OUR FAITH 1 **4**

Name

Our Special Sign

1. Connect the dots.
2. Start and finish at number 1.
3. Color the picture.

To the Teacher: This activity will help the children visualize the cross.

4a THIS IS OUR FAITH 1   Chapter 4 God Gives Us Jesus

GIFTS OF A LOVING GOD

Throughout Unit 1, the children have explored the gifts lavished upon them by a loving God. They have learned that they themselves are lovely and lovable gifts, that creation sings of God's goodness, and that their lives are enriched by the people who love them. Now, in Chapter 4, the children meet God's greatest gift to them—Jesus.

JESUS—GOODNESS INCARNATED

Jesus is the center and culmination of all creation. Through Jesus, God is revealed to us and experienced as the God of forgiveness, peace, compassion, and unending love.

The goodness that is Jesus reaches out to the children and makes known to them who they can be before God. Jesus tells them stories about God his father's love and demonstrates that love through his actions. Jesus shows them the way to live fully by living wholeheartedly.

Jesus is presented as the Son of God and the children's friend, the one who will remain with them throughout their lives. Jesus' promise, "I am always with you" (based on Matthew 28:20), is a basic concept found in Grade 1.

This year you have the opportunity to live out the charge given the disciples: "Let the little children come to me" (based on Mark 10:14–16). Under your guidance the children will come to Jesus. He will show them the way to live fully by living wholeheartedly. One of the primary ways your children will draw nearer to Jesus is through Scripture stories. They will make real the love and the actions of the children's new friend, Jesus.

KNOWING JESUS THROUGH BIBLE STORIES

Almost nothing captures the human heart, fires the human imagination, or inspires the human spirit so much as a story well told. And the stories in Scripture are well told by storytellers who talked to those who had known Jesus throughout his life and by those who had actually walked the dusty roads of Galilee with him. In the Gospels we find these stories about Jesus. (You will tell the children two such stories this week.) And we also find stories that Jesus told. (Chapter 4 shares one such story with the children.) In addition, the children learn that through his actions and his stories, Jesus reminds them that God loves them, right now and forever.

In Jesus Christ we find God's master storyteller; we find the Word made flesh, the story in action. In the Gospel stories, we discover the good news that God's favorite story is a love story. Down through the years the Church has passed on the stories of Jesus that we might make them our own, that we might better love God and the world.

Objective

This lesson helps the children recognize Jesus as God's Son and their greatest gift from God.

Step 1/INTRODUCTION

Learning About Our Lives

Reviewing God's Gifts

Show the children a series of wrapped and ribboned gift boxes, and read the tags on them, which say *From God, who loves you.* Tell the children that these presents represent the many gifts God has given them.

Recall Chapter 2 and God's gift of the world with its stars, moon, sun, fruits, vegetables, flowers, trees, animals, birds, and fish. Then talk about Chapter 3 and God's gift of loving people, and ask the following questions.

- What gifts did God give us in our world? (*Answers will vary.*)
- What special people did God give us as gifts? (*Answers will vary.*)

Finally, show the children the largest and most lavishly decorated present. Read the tag, which says, *This is my best gift to you. From God, who loves you.* Ask them what gift they think this present represents.

or...

Have drawn on the chalkboard a series of gift boxes with the same tags as described above. Use the bulleted questions above to stimulate thinking. Then ask for volunteers to draw a gift in each box as you point to it. Have the children name their gifts before going to the chalkboard so that what they draw will not be duplicated by another child.

Then point to the most elaborate box representing our best gift from God, Jesus. Ask a volunteer to draw Jesus' picture in the box.

Step 2/DEVELOPMENT

Learning About Our Faith

Enjoying a Rebus

Direct the children's attention to page 42. Read "God's Best Gift," pausing at each rebus

What do you think is the best gift God gives us?

God Gives Us Jesus

God's Best Gift

What do you think is the best gift God gives us?

God loved all .

But some forgot about God.

They forgot God loved all

and promised to be with them always.

The came for God to help

them remember.

God chose to give

the best 🎁 of all.

CURRICULUM CONNECTION

Art Provide materials for the children to make a class mosaic that says *Thank you, God, for Jesus.* Display the newsprint with the outlined letters and distribute small pieces of colored construction paper. Have the class work in groups to paste the paper on the letters. If possible, post the mosaic in your classroom. Each day during this week, ask the children once or twice a day to read the message out loud.

God's best gift to us is

Jesus
_____

Doctrine 43

Activity

Color the part of the picture that shows the best gift God has ever given to us.

In this chapter you introduce the children to three stories about God. These stories are from the Bible, God's own storybook. As you teach, make a special effort to help the children realize the joy of the stories of Jesus. Use expression in your voice; show delight on your face. Realize that you are introducing the children to the greatest stories ever told—the stories of God's greatest gift, Jesus.

Honoring Jesus' Name Explain that one way to show God that they are grateful for the gift of Jesus is to speak his name with respect. Recall for the children the reverent bow they use when they bow before the Bible in their prayer services. Tell them that when they pray with Jesus' name they can show respect by bowing their heads. Explain that they bow their heads because Jesus is God's best gift to us. Ask the children to repeat Jesus' name after you and to bow their heads to show their respect.

---

symbol for the children to say the word. After reading the selection, ask the following questions.

■ What did some people do? (*Forgot about God*)

■ What did the people forget? (*That God loved them and promised to be with them always*)

■ Why did God choose to give us a gift? (*To help us remember God's love*)

Discovering God's Best Gift

Read aloud the question on the top of page 43, and encourage the children to respond. Hold up the large gift-wrapped box from Step 1, and tell the children that now they know that Jesus is God's best gift to them. Ask the children to use pencils to trace Jesus' name in the space provided.

Step 3/CONCLUSION

Learning How to Live Our Faith

Meeting Jesus as an Infant

Ask the children to look at the drawing on page 43. Point to the picture of the infant Jesus. Ask the children what they know about Jesus and the Christmas story. Then invite the children to color the picture of the infant Jesus.

Praying with Jesus' Name

Gather the children in the prayer area. Bring the gift box that represents Jesus to the prayer table and ask the children who is God's best gift to them. (*Jesus*) Then place the gift box next to the Bible on the table. (Keep the box there all week.)

Tell the children that they will thank God for Jesus and reverently bow their heads when they use Jesus' name in prayer. Say the following litany and invite the children to respond with the name of Jesus.

■ Thank you, God, for giving us your best gift. The name of this gift is . . .

■ Thank you, God, for giving us someone to help us remember your love for us. The one who helps us remember is . . .

■ Thank you, God, for promising to be with us always. The one who reminds us that you are with us always is . . .

Objective

This lesson helps the children rejoice that Jesus is their friend and that Jesus loves them.

Step 1/INTRODUCTION

Learning About Our Lives

Finding Out About Friendship

Show the children magazine pictures that illustrate friendship, encouraging the children to tell stories about each picture. To stimulate their imaginations, ask the following questions.

- What are these friends doing together?
- How do you know that they are friends?
- What do you think they are saying to one another?

Creating a Friendship Bulletin Board

Invite the children to draw pictures of their favorite friends. Afterward, encourage the children to talk about their friends.

Pin all the children's pictures in a circle on a bulletin board, with a space in the middle. Have 25 letters cut out for the following sentence: *These are our special friends.* Give each child a letter to hold and then ask the children to help you tack the letters above the circle of drawings. Talk about how the sentence applies to their drawings.

Step 2/DEVELOPMENT

Learning About Our Faith

Reading a Bible Story About Jesus' Friendship

Direct the children to look at the illustration on pages 44 and 45. Invite them to tell what is happening in the picture. Then read aloud "Jesus Is Our Friend." Afterward, ask the following questions.

- Who brought the children to see Jesus? (*Their parents*)
- Why do you think the mothers and fathers wanted their children to meet Jesus? (*Answers will vary.*)
- What did Jesus' friends say to the parents? (*"Leave Jesus alone."*)

44

Jesus Is Our Friend

God gives us **Jesus** to be our friend.
Jesus is the Son of God.
Jesus, our friend, loves us very much.
This story from the Bible shows how much Jesus loves children.

Jesus and the Children

One day Jesus felt tired.
He wanted to sit down and rest.
But some mothers, fathers, and children came to meet Jesus.
Some friends of Jesus
told the people to go away.
"Leave Jesus alone," they said.
"He is tired."
But Jesus said, "I am never too tired to talk to children.
Let them come to me!
I love them very much."

  **Cultural Awareness**

Bring in artistic representations of Jesus during his infancy, childhood, and adulthood. If possible, include pictures that portray Jesus as belonging to a variety of ethnic groups. (You may be able to find prayer cards with African or Asian images of Jesus.) Avoid pictures that show Jesus' passion and death at this time. Discuss the similarities and differences the children notice in the pictures. Explain that artists draw Jesus in different ways to help people all over the world understand that Jesus is everyone's friend.

 **CURRICULUM CONNECTION**

Language Arts At the top of sheets of 8 1/2" x 11" paper, print the words *I am a good friend just like Jesus because I . . . .* Then encourage the children to think of ways in which they are good friends. Distribute crayons or felt-tip markers and invite the children to draw their endings to the sentence or to write stories to finish the statement. Afterward, invite children to share their stories with the class.

Then Jesus hugged the children.
He held them on his lap and
blessed them.
Jesus and the children were happy.
They were friends.

Based on Mark 10:13–16

New Word

♣ **Jesus** Jesus is the Son of God and our friend.

We Believe

Jesus is God's most special gift to us. Jesus is the Son of God.

Doctrine 45

Teaching Tips

To encourage children to enter into a role-play, change roles and repeat the dramatization. When changing roles, the teacher can take a child's role. This allows the children to observe the teacher and gives them ideas about dialogue and body language. The next time, the teacher can be someone else. Continue until several children have had turns and the role-play becomes fluent, without a lot of painful coaching.

■ What did Jesus say to his friends? (*"I am never too tired to talk to children."*)
■ What did Jesus do to show how much he loved the children? (*Hugged them, held them on his lap, blessed them*)
■ How do you know that Jesus and the children were friends? (*Answers will vary.*)

Role-Playing the Bible Story

Invite the children to role-play the Bible story on pages 44–45. You be Jesus and have the children play the parents, the disciples, and the children who became Jesus' friends. Then exchange roles. Encourage the children to get into the spirit of the role-play and to talk to Jesus and to share their lives.

Reviewing the Vocabulary

Point to the New Word section on page 45 of the children's book. Ask them to repeat the word *Jesus* and its definition.

Presenting the Doctrine

Read aloud the We Believe section on page 45 of the children's book, which summarizes what this chapter teaches about Jesus. Ask the children to repeat the two sentences after you.

Step 3/CONCLUSION

Learning How to Live Our Faith

Adding Jesus to the Friendship Bulletin Board

Show the children a picture of Jesus and recall that Jesus is their friend. Then gather the children around the friendship bulletin board from Step 1. Ask a volunteer to read the words there—*These are our special friends.* Then ask the children if they want to add Jesus' picture to the bulletin board. If the children would like to do this, put the picture in the space at the center of their circle of pictures.

Thanking God for Jesus' Friendship

Gather the children into the prayer area. Then tell them that today they can thank God for Jesus' friendship by singing a song. Then, using the word *friendly* instead of *happy,* sing "If You're Happy and You Know It."

45

SCRIPTURE/DOCTRINE

Objective

This lesson helps the children discover that the Bible contains stories about what Jesus *said* and *did*.

Step 1/INTRODUCTION

Learning About Our Lives

Experiencing a Deeper Understanding of Friendship

Gather the children around the friendship bulletin board they made on Day 2. Invite a volunteer to read the title: *These are our special friends.* Encourage the children to talk about the friendly things the people pictured there do and say. To help the children begin their sharing, invite a few children to point to their drawings from Day 2 and then ask the following questions.

■ What does your special friend say to you that helps make you feel happy? (*Answers will vary.*)

■ What does your special friend do for you that helps make you feel special and loved? (*Answers will vary.*)

Step 2/DEVELOPMENT

Learning About Our Faith

Talking About Jesus' Friendship

While the children are still gathered around the friendship bulletin board, point to the picture of Jesus and ask the children to answer the following questions.

■ What does your friend Jesus say to you that helps make you feel happy? (*Answers will vary.*)

■ What does your friend Jesus do for you that helps make you feel special and loved? (*Answers will vary.*)

Reading Bible Stories

After reading the story ask the following questions.

■ What do you think happened to the young man when he left home? (*Answers will vary.*)

46

Jesus and the Bible

In the Bible, there are stories that Jesus told about God, his Father. Jesus told the story below. Listen to it to hear about the great love a father has for his son. It is like God's great love for us.

A Father Loves His Son

One day, a son left home and got into trouble. Then the son remembered his father's love and came home. His father was so happy! He gave a party for his son. The father said, "Let us celebrate! My son has come home."

Based on Luke 15:11–32

46   Scripture

Cultural Awareness

Prepare a large sheet of newsprint with the outlined words *Jesus Loves Everyone in the World.* Then collect pictures of people from different countries. As you show these pictures to the children, note the variety and, if possible, identify the nationalities of the persons pictured. Then have the children paste these pictures on the prepared newsprint. Distribute crayons or felt-tip markers and ask each child to color a letter of the sentence. Tell the children that Jesus wants them to treat everyone with friendship.

Besides stories about his Father's love, there are stories about Jesus' love in the Bible.
Here is one.

A Crippled Woman

One day Jesus saw a woman
who was bent over.
She could not stand up straight.
Jesus said to her,
"You are healed."
Jesus touched her and
she stood up straight.

How happy she was that
Jesus loved and cared for her.
Now she knew what God is like.
God is full of love for us.

Based on Luke 13:10–13

Scripture 47

Enriching the Lesson

Have the children draw a picture of Jesus and label it *Jesus is my friend*. Encourage the children to take their pictures home to hang in their rooms. Suggest that they look at their drawings each night before they go to sleep, talking to their friend Jesus about happy and sad occurrences of their day.

■ What did the young man suddenly remember about his father? (*His love*)

■ Why was the father happy that his son came home? (*He loved his son.*)

Then read the story "A Crippled Woman" on page 47 and ask the following questions.

■ Why did the woman in the Bible story need help? (*She could not stand up straight.*)

■ How did Jesus show her God's love? (*He healed her.*)

Acting Out the Bible Stories

Role-play each of the Bible stories. Take a part yourself to stimulate dialogue and enliven the role-play with voice expression and body language that the children can easily imitate. Then repeat the role-play, changing roles.

Step 3/CONCLUSION

Learning How to Live Our Faith

Finishing a Story About Friendship

Tell a friendship story without an ending and ask the children to complete the story. For example, use the following story.

> Sandy asked her mother if she could go to Barbara's house to play. Her mother said, "Yes, but be home by 5:00 because we are having an early supper." Sandy played with Barbara in her back yard for a long time. When she went inside Barbara's house to get a drink of water, Sandy saw that the kitchen clock said 5:30.

Thanking God for the Gift of Jesus

Gather the children into the prayer area. Invite them to add gestures and body movements to the following prayer. Make suggestions as necessary.

> Thank you, God, for the wonderful gift of Jesus. He is your best gift to us.

When the children are ready, pray this short prayer with their agreed-upon gestures.

Reviewing the Lesson

Ask the following questions for review.

■ In what special book do we find stories about Jesus? (*The Bible*)

■ What does Jesus tell us about? (*Jesus and God, his Father's, love for us*)

■ How does Jesus treat his friends? (*Answers will vary.*)

Objective

This lesson helps the children recognize Jesus as their Savior, who helps them remember God's love for them.

Step 1/INTRODUCTION

Learning About Our Lives

Reviewing the Learning of Day 3

Recall the two Bible stories of Day 3. Ask volunteers to retell the story of the young man who got into trouble. Then ask the following questions.

- What did the son remember when he was away from home and in trouble? (*He remembered his father's love.*)
- Why did he come home? (*Answers will vary.*)
- How did his father show that he loved his son who needed help? (*He gave a party.*)
- How would you feel if you needed help? (*Answers will vary.*)
- Whose love would you remember? (*Answers will vary.*)
- Who would save you if you needed help? (*Answers will vary.*)

Encourage the children to respond to these questions.

Discussing the Photos

Direct the children's attention to page 48. Invite comments on the photos there. Read the text and talk about why the child in each situation needs to be saved.

Sharing Stories About Being Saved

Invite the children to talk about times when they needed to be saved. Use the three situations on page 48 to prompt their stories. Encourage the children to say who helped them.

Needing to "Be Saved"

Activity

Tell what kind of help each child above needs. How could you help save each child?

48 Doctrine

Focus on

Jesus the Savior The concept of "savior" is not an easy one for children. Note that on Day 4, you help the children understand this concept by stressing that Jesus saves them when they forget God's love. The children need to hear again and again, that God loves them. Help them understand that Jesus has come to show them God's deep, everlasting, and unconditional love. Emphasize that Jesus does this through his healing and forgiving actions. In this lesson, focus on God's love.

Jesus Saves Us

The Bible says that Jesus saves us.
How does he save us?
Jesus helps us remember that God
loves us and that we are very special.

We call Jesus our **Savior** because he
saves us when we forget God's love.

Jesus says, "I am always with you."
So we can always ask Jesus to save us.
We can always say, "Save me, Jesus!
Help me remember that God loves me."

I am always with you.

New Word

♣ **Savior** Our Savior is Jesus, the Son of God and
our friend. He saves us and helps us.

Doctrine 49

Teaching Tips

Divide the class into pairs. Ask each child to face his or her partner and to say something nice about that person. Give examples if necessary. Afterward, talk about how the children feel when someone praises them. Encourage the children to often tell their classmates what they like about them and to praise their classmates for doing well.

Step 2/DEVELOPMENT

Learning About Our Faith

Discovering That Jesus Is Our Savior

Direct the children's attention to page 49 of the text. Read aloud "Jesus Saves Us." Then point to the illustration on page 49. Then read the Scripture verse in the talking balloon.

Ask volunteers questions like the following to be sure the children understand the message of "Jesus Saves Us," the illustration, and the Scripture verse in the balloon.

■ How does Jesus save us? (*He helps us remember that God loves us and that we are special.*)

■ Why do we call Jesus our Savior? (*Because he helps us even when we forget God's love*)

■ How long will Jesus be with us? (*Always*)

Brainstorming Signs of God's Love

Invite the children to brainstorm all the signs of love God has given them (*Jesus, themselves, parents, special friends, the universe, trees, flowers, animals, fish, birds, and so on*). Print their responses on the chalkboard.

Reviewing the Vocabulary

Point to the New Word section of the children's book, page 49. Ask the children to repeat the word *Savior* and the definition after you.

Step 3/CONCLUSION

Learning How to Live Our Faith

Writing a Note About God's Love

Talk with the children about how Jesus helps them remember God's love. Ask the following questions.

■ What does Jesus want us to remember about God's love? (*Answers will vary.*)

■ Whom does God love? (*Everyone*)

■ Whom does God want us to love? (*Everyone*)

Praying with a Song

Gather the children in the prayer area and teach them to chant the following response.

God, I remember your love for me.

Then ask the children to recall signs of God's love. As individual children name a sign, the others answer with the chant.

49

Objective

This lesson helps the children learn and pray the Sign of the Cross.

Making the Sign of the Cross

Direct the children's attention to "Praying the Sign of the Cross" on page 50, and read the Sign of the Cross with the children. Then demonstrate this basic Christian sign by blessing yourself with exaggerated motions. Use the photographs in the text to walk the children though the Sign of the Cross, step by step. Allow time for the children to practice this prayer.

Thinking About Jesus

Play background music and tell the children that you would like them to be still for a few minutes. Then read to the children the Bible story on pages 44 and 45 and the two Bible stories on pages 46 and 47. Finally, read the last paragraph of "Jesus Saves Us" on page 49.

Teaching a Song About Jesus

Using the melody for "Frère Jacques" ("Are You Sleeping, Brother John?"), teach the children the following words.

Save me, Jesus;
Save me, Jesus.
Help me now;
Help me now.
Help me to remember;
Help me to remember,
God's great love;
God's great love.

Processing to the Prayer Area

Process to the prayer area. Invite the children to sing their song as they process and to bow reverently before the Bible and the gift package that symbolizes Jesus.

Thanking God for Creation

Lead the children in praying the Sign of the Cross. Then pick up the gift package symbolizing Jesus and hand it to the children, one by one. Ask each child what he or she wants to thank God for. Close with the Sign of the Cross.

50

Praying the Sign of the Cross

Friends of Jesus pray a prayer called
The Sign of the Cross.
It helps us remember that God loves us.
This special prayer helps us remember
that Jesus is God's best gift to us.

In the name of the Father,

and of the Son,

and of the Holy Spirit.

Amen.

Focus on

Praying the Sign of the Cross
The prayer skill for this chapter introduces the children to the Sign of the Cross. It is one of the traditional prayers of the Church and one that the children need to know early on so that they may use it frequently at times of prayer throughout the school day. The Sign of the Cross is introduced as a special sign that Jesus' friends make to remind themselves that God the Father sent Jesus to be with us always.

Teaching Tips

If the children are puzzled by the word *sign* in the phrase *Sign of the Cross*, discuss common signs that tell us something, such as a red stop sign that tells cars to stop. Or talk about the signs on fast-food restaurants and other stores. Discuss seasonal signs: new leaves proclaim spring, swimming declares summer, buying new school clothes defines fall, snow may announce winter. When the children are comfortable with signs telling them things, remind them that the Sign of the Cross tells them that God is with us.

Chapter Review

Cross out all the **B** letters to find a message.

BBJESUSBBISBMYBBFRIENDBB

Copy the message below.

Jesus is my friend.

1. Who is God's Son and our friend?

Jesus

2. What does Jesus, our Savior, help us to remember?

God loves us.

Jesus says,
"I am always
with you."
Matthew 28:20

3. Tell what you know and like about Jesus.

Completing an Activity

Use the activity on page 51 to review the learning of Chapter 4. Distribute pencils and instruct the children to cross out the B's in the boxes on page 51. Then have the children read the special message. Encourage the children to print the message on the lines provided.

Answering the Questions

Read aloud the first two questions and ask volunteers to respond. Direct the children to print the answers in their texts. Encourage all the children to participate in the discussion of the third question. Be supportive of each child who responds.

Reading the Scripture Verse

Ask the children to read the Scripture verse after you. It is a good way to end the lesson by reflecting on the word of God. If you wish, you may have the children memorize this verse.

🍎 Teaching Tips

Remember that when you are making the Sign of the Cross in front of the children, they may get confused about which hand to use and which shoulder to touch first. Be sure that they use their right hands and touch their left shoulders first and then their right shoulders.

Using the Unit Organizer

Completing a graphic organizer such as a chart or table can help students to organize the information that has been presented in the unit. Organizers can enable students to visualize their thinking and recognize relationships among ideas. This will give students the opportunity to understand more completely the material they have been studying.

Drawing God's Gifts

To help the children think about this unit, ask them to read the unit theme: God's Gifts to Us. Then invite them to read the tags on the gift boxes and draw one of God's gifts of the world, themselves, their family, and their friends. Finally they should draw the greatest of all gifts, Jesus. These gifts represent the main ideas of the chapters and summarize the unit for the children.

Looking Back: Self-Assessment

The questions below give the children an opportunity to look back through this unit to help them recall such things as stories, ideas, and activities they found most interesting or enjoyable. Invite the students to share their responses with one another.

- What was your favorite Scripture story? What did you like most about it?

- What activity did you most enjoy doing? Do you want to do more things like it?

- Name one important thing about God you want to remember.

Unit 1 Organizer

Draw
God's Gifts to Us

ME

THE WORLD

MY FAMILY

MY FRIENDS

JESUS

Unit 1 Review

Look at the words in the box.
Choose a word to finish each sentence.
Write the word below the sentence.

loves	God	thank	share

1. _____created you to be special.

God

2. God made us because God_____us.

loves

3. We say_____you for God's gifts.

thank

4. We can_____God's gifts with others.

share

Reviewing the Unit

The purpose of the Unit Review is to reinforce concepts presented in the preceding four chapters and to check how well the children understand these concepts. After explaining the directions, give the children sufficient time to complete the review. Answer any questions the children might have.

Optional Testing

After the children have completed the Unit Review, you may wish to distribute copies of the Unit 1 Test from the Test Booklet in The Resourceful Teacher Package.

Optional Unit Project

If time permits, you may wish to do the following project with the children.

Before the session, draw an outline of a tree on a large piece of art paper. If the group is large, you may need to draw two or three trees. Cut from construction paper one large leaf for each child. Explain to the children that they will make a family tree of the whole class. Distribute crayons or felt-tip markers and the leaf shapes. Tell the children to draw on their leaves pictures of themselves with their families. Invite the children, one at a time, to introduce the members of their families and to paste their leaves on the family trees. Point out that each of us belongs to a special family, and all of us belong to God's family.

Unit **1** Review

Draw a line to the word that ends each sentence.

1. Our Creator is _ _ _ _ _ _ _ •   • Jesus

2. The special book about
   God's love is the _ _ _ _ _ _ •   • God

3. God's most special gift is _ _ •   • Bible

Circle the correct answer.

1. Each person is special and God loves us all.

   (Yes)   No

2. Jesus is never with us.

   Yes   (No)

3. Jesus is our Savior.

   (Yes)   No

4. Jesus is God's brother.

   Yes   (No)

5. "Create" means to make something out
   of nothing.

   (Yes)   No

6. God gives us special people to love and care for us.

   (Yes)   No

FEELINGS, GIFTS FROM GOD

Boots and Zip are
good friends.
They are happy
to see each other.

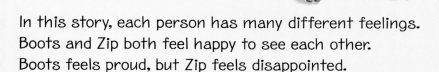

"Boots, let's play ball when
we get home," Zip said.
"Oh, not today.
I get to help my dad wash
the car," Boots said proudly.
Zip was disappointed.

In this story, each person has many different feelings.
Boots and Zip both feel happy to see each other.
Boots feels proud, but Zip feels disappointed.

Day to Day   55

🍎 Teaching Tips

When working with feelings on page 55, the children are asked to identify how Boots felt about helping his dad wash the car. Children will usually answer either *proud* or *happy*. *Proud* is the better choice, but the children will name *happy* more easily. Help them see that *proud* describes Boots's feelings better because having someone depend on you and feeling able to do something well contribute to feeling *proud*.

Introducing Day to Day: Skills for Christian Living

Lessons for Grade 1 of the Day to Day: Skills for Christian Living facilitate the children's awareness of feelings in themselves and others. Through the lives of two friends, Boots and Zip, the children learn in Lesson 1 that their feelings are part of what makes them special and that their feelings are a gift from God. Lesson 2 focuses on looking and listening as the means to discover how others feel. Expressing feelings is addressed in Lessons 3 and 4. Skills for coping with sadness are discussed in Lesson 5. This exploration of feelings is a necessary foundation for work in later grades on communication and problem solving.

Objective

This lesson helps the children increase their awareness that feelings are a special gift from God, that each person has many different feelings, and that feelings can change.

Looking at the Illustrations

Invite the children to look on page 55 at the pictures that show Boots and Zip walking home from school. Ask the children how the two friends feel in the first picture. Point out that Zip seems to be feeling differently in the second picture. Before reading the story aloud, ask the children to listen for the reason that Zip's feelings changed.

Discussing the Story

To discuss the story, ask the following questions.

■ How does Zip feel when he sees Boots? (*Happy*)

■ What does Zip want Boots to do? (*Play ball with him after school*)

■ What does Boots say to Zip when Zip asks him to play? (*Oh, not today. I get to help my dad wash the car.*)

■ How does Boots feel about helping dad wash the car? (*Proud, happy*)

Lesson continues on page 56. ➡

55

- How does Zip feel about not getting to play with Boots? (*Disappointed, sad*)

- What happened in the story to change Zip from feeling happy to feeling disappointed? (*Boots tells Zip that he can't play with him after school.*)

- Has anyone had an experience like Zip, when you start out feeling one way and then something happens and your feelings change? (*Answers will vary.*)

- How many of you have had more than one feeling already today? Tell us about your different feelings. (*Answers will vary.*)

Completing the Activity

Read aloud the directions to the activity on page 56. Be sure to read each of the "feeling" words listed. Encourage the children to draw pictures of themselves experiencing the feelings they circled. Allow time for students to share their pictures and experiences.

Concluding the Lesson

Reinforce the lesson content by having the children read aloud the Following Jesus section. Invite the children to pray together a brief prayer of thanks to God for giving them the gift of feelings.

Follow-Up Activities

Use children's literature to enhance awareness of different feelings. Many fine books are available from your local library.

56

Activity

Circle one of the words below.

Draw a picture of a time you felt like the word you circled.

Happy   Proud   Disappointed

Following Jesus

Our feelings are a gift from God.

Each of us has many different feelings.

Our feelings are a part of what makes us special.

Teaching Tips

The following books discuss feelings. ***I Have Feelings.*** Terry Berger. Behavioral Publications (General) ***Feelings.*** Aliki. Greenwillow Books (General). ***Feelings.*** Phoebe and Trish Dunn. Creative Educational Society (General). ***Brunus and the New Bear.*** Ellen Stoll Walsh. Doubleday & Company (Jealous). ***Timothy Goes to School.*** Rosemary Wells. The Dial Press (Jealous). ***The Lonely Prince.*** Max Bollinger. Atheneum (Lonely). ***Sam.*** Ann Herbert Scott. McGraw-Hill (Lonely). ***I Never Win.*** Judy Delton. Carolrhoda Books (Sad).

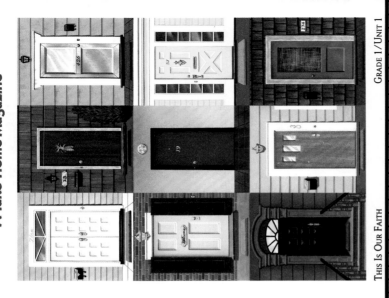

OPENING DOORS
A Take-Home Magazine™

Growing Closer

BEDTIME offers family members an opportunity to spend a few quiet moments together. A good way to share your love with your children at this time is to call down God's blessing on each of them. Touch your child's head while simply saying, "God bless you," or use your own words. Allow your child to bless you, too!

ALL OF US have been gifted by a gracious and generous God. Set this week aside as "Gratitude Week" in your family. Make a family list of all of the gifts, blessings, and talents your family has enjoyed. Use this list as part of your family meal prayer or bedtime prayer. Be sure to make a special effort to thank one another, too!

Looking Ahead

Unit 2 will focus on Jesus, the Son of God, who came to live among us. By appreciating Jesus, your child can begin to know him as a friend. As your child grows older, he or she will come to recognize Jesus as a leader whose unparalleled courage, sensitivity, and compassion to others bear witness to who Jesus is.

© Silver Burdett Ginn Inc.

8

Opening Doors ~

A Take-Home Magazine

The five removable, family-directed supplements entitled *Opening Doors: A Take-Home Magazine* provide you, the teacher, with a unique opportunity to involve parents or guardians more fully in their child's religion program. Each magazine will include the following features.

A Closer Look

An article relating the unit theme in the text to a particular aspect of the Mass

Being Catholic

An article explaining a particular aspect of our Catholic heritage

Growing Closer

Suggested activities to help the family integrate faith into everyday life

Looking Ahead

A preview of the next unit in THIS IS OUR FAITH, Grade 1

Sending the Magazine Home

As you complete Unit 1 with your class, assist the children in carefully removing *Opening Doors: A Take-Home Magazine* (two pages) from their texts by separating the magazine from the book along the perforations. Demonstrate how to fold the two pages to form an eight-page booklet.

When the magazines are folded, take time to explain each section of the magazine to the children. Allow the children to ask any questions they may have. Ask the children to take their magazines home and encourage their families to read them together and participate in the suggested activities. You may wish to attach a letter of your own, encouraging the families to use the magazines each time their children bring them home.

Follow the same procedure in sending home the remaining magazines for Units 2, 3, 4, and 5.

Thank You!

We live in a time when we supposedly never "get something for nothing." When we find ourselves echoing this jaded attitude, it is time to remember that generosity still exists. God's generosity toward us never diminishes.

Catholics have a way of expressing their gratitude to God by celebrating the Eucharist, or Mass. The word *eucharist* means "thanksgiving" and the Mass is our prayer of thanksgiving.

During the Liturgy of the Word, we hear the good news that God loves us. Each Sunday, we listen to stories of divine interaction in the individual lives and in the community life of God's people, and we know that God is equally concerned for us today. God's generosity is unbounded. To this graciousness we respond,

"Thanks be to God."

At the beginning of the eucharistic prayer, we pray,

"It is right to give him thanks and praise."

Grazie

Thank you

Arigato

Gracias

hands in prayer carries a strong message—I am united with a group of people who repeatedly thank God for their blessings. I understand that this is important because we do it over and over. Both repetition and community are essential to ritual, a corporate symbolic action that we do over and over again.

Another way of praying can be introduced gently to children — that of meditating. Children love stories, especially those that touch the heart, and none do this better than the stories of Jesus. The scripture accounts not only relate events in the life of Jesus but also develop a relationship with him. After reading a biblical selection, help your child produce standup cutouts of the characters. Keep the cutouts in a place accessible to the children. During play, they will recall the details of the story and relive the emotions. In this way their imaginations and hearts are engaged with the person of Jesus — a kind of mental prayer.

Sources of help for family prayer are listed below:

Catholic Household Blessings and Prayers published by The United States Catholic Conference offers table prayers, bedside prayers, blessings, and simple rituals.

This Is Our Faith Family Prayer Book published by Silver Burdett and Ginn contains traditional Church prayers in addition to a wide variety of prayers for everyday use in family life.

Thank You

Obrigado

Dank U zeer MERCI

Tark

Thank you

During the eucharistic prayer, fleeting thoughts cross our minds as we thank God for all of creation. We express our gratitude for our own humanity; for the diversity of nature: "male and female he created them" (Genesis 1:27), of every race and color; for varieties of landscapes, climate, and cultures. We acknowledge God as the source of all goodness.

As we pray the eucharistic prayer, we do not pray alone. Re-enacting the Lord's supper, we know that Jesus is with us, and we unite our prayers with his. Praising Jesus for his passion, death, and resurrection, we thank God for our salvation. No more fitting prayer of thanksgiving could be offered.

As we are dismissed to love and serve the Lord, we respond, "Thanks be to God."

Leaving the church, we are thankful that God goes with us as we work with Jesus to continue the building of the kingdom.

3

Being Catholic

Family Prayer

"Prayer begins very early in childhood by hearing others pray; even small children can learn to call upon the Father, Jesus, and the Holy Spirit. In time, the child will become familiar with the various prayers . . . and make them part of his or her life" (Sharing the Light of Faith: National Catechetical Directory for Catholics of the United States #145).

Many families find mealtimes convenient to introduce different types of prayer. Young children respond well to simple rituals such as holding hands during grace. This may seem like a very simple thing to do, but when you think about it, this ceremony has much significance.

What exactly is a ritual? It is an action that conveys meaning. The fact that it is practiced by a group of people makes it even more meaningful. Take for example the childhood ritual, superstitious though it is, of avoiding cracks in sidewalks. This is not a mere game; it conveys the conventional wisdom of the group that stepping on a crack will "break your mother's back." So, too, the joining of

6

Thank You!

Your child knows the joy of both giving and receiving gifts. Use this understanding to introduce these concepts as they relate to the Mass. Reading the rebus story below with your child will help you identify some of the gifts for which we thank God and the gifts we offer.

4

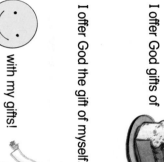

At I say, "Thank You," for

the gifts God has given me. I give

to God, too.

I offer God gifts of 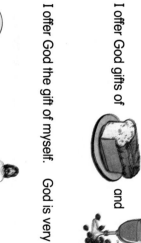 and .

I offer God the gift of myself. God is very

 with my gifts! gives

himself to us as the Bread of Life. Jesus is

God's best !

Remember to offer your gifts to God the next time you go to Mass. Thank God for the gifts that have been given you.

5

60

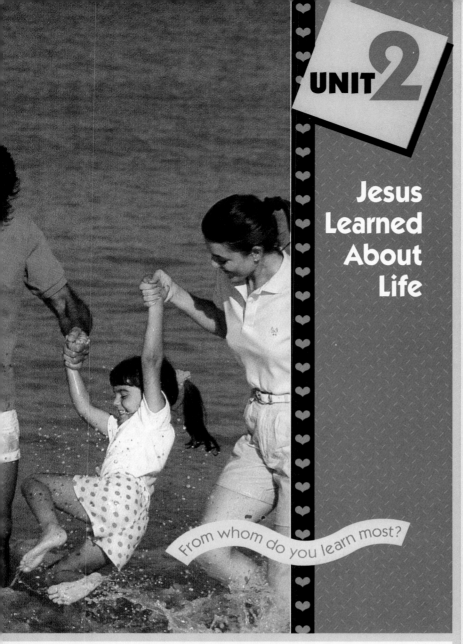

UNIT 2

Jesus Learned About Life

From whom do you learn most?

To help the children come to a deeper personal knowledge of Jesus by appreciating the fact that he grew and learned.

Doctrinal Summaries

CHAPTER 5
Jesus is the true God and true man. We call Jesus and his family the Holy Family.

CHAPTER 6
Mary is the mother of Jesus, God's son. Mary is our Mother, too.

CHAPTER 7
Jesus listened and learned.

CHAPTER 8
We can grow closer to God by praying. We can pray anytime, anywhere, and about everything.

Note:

As you prepare to teach this unit, you might wish to refer to the reference section *Our Catholic Heritage,* beginning on page 327.

Additional resources for Unit 2 include: a Unit Test and a Family Letter as well as a video and selections from the THIS IS OUR FAITH Music Program. You might also find it helpful to preview *Saints and Other Holy People* and *Prayer Celebrations* for possibilities to enhance the unit.

Introducing the UNIT

Invite the children to study the photograph on page 61 and tell a story about the picture. Read aloud the unit-focus question and elicit the children's responses. Help the children appreciate that we can learn much from our families, who love and care for us.

New Words

Holy Family
Nazareth
Temple
angel
rabbi
prayer

5 Jesus Grew Up in a Family

Objectives

To help the children

- Recognize that Jesus lived a human life with his family.
- Value being part of a family.
- Appreciate the members of their families.
- Appreciate how family members help one another.
- Express thanks for their families and for the Holy Family and review the chapter.

Chapter Outline

	Step 1 Learning About Our Lives	**Step 2** Learning About Our Faith	**Step 3** Learning How to Live Our Faith
Day 1	■ Study the photographs. ■ Read a poem. *ABOUT 8 MINUTES*	■ Learn about the Holy Family. ■ Present the doctrine. ■ Review the vocabulary. *ABOUT 10 MINUTES*	■ Compare Jesus' life to ours. ■ Create a bulletin board. ■ Thank God for families. *ABOUT 12 MINUTES*
Day 2	■ Talk about families. ■ Use the bulletin board. *ABOUT 10 MINUTES*	■ Examine a picture. ■ Listen to a story. ■ Review the vocabulary. *ABOUT 10 MINUTES*	■ Discover what holy families do. ■ Pray a litany of thanksgiving. ■ Review the lesson. *ABOUT 10 MINUTES*
Day 3	■ Draw portraits of family members. *ABOUT 10 MINUTES*	■ Learn about Jesus' family. *ABOUT 10 MINUTES*	■ Discuss the meaning of names. ■ Treasure names. ■ Gather for prayer. *ABOUT 10 MINUTES*
Day 4	■ Discuss ways to help. ■ Pantomime ways of helping family members. *ABOUT 11 MINUTES*	■ Read the children's book. ■ Create dialogue for a dramatization. *ABOUT 11 MINUTES*	■ Discover ways to help. ■ Thank God for the children. ■ Review the lesson. *ABOUT 8 MINUTES*
Day 5	**Prayer** Read a psalm; learn a song; have a procession; and pray a prayer of thanksgiving. **Review** Dismantle the bulletin board; complete an activity; answer the questions; and read the Scripture verse.		

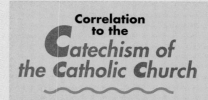

Correlation
to the
Catechism of
the Catholic Church

Paragraphs
531–533

Plan Ahead ~~~~~~~~

	Preparing Your Class	**Materials Needed**
Day 1	For Step 3, cut out the letters: *These are our holy families* for a bulletin board.	■ drawing paper, crayons ■ empty bulletin board ■ cut out letters for a sentence ■ thumbtacks/staples
Day 2	Ask the children to bring in pictures of their families for use in Step 1.	
Day 3	For Step 3, prepare a list of positive qualities about yourself and each child.	■ drawing paper
Day 4	Read through the lesson plan. If you plan to use any Teaching Option, make preparations and collect materials.	
Day 5	Use the drawings from Day 1 during prayer. Learn a song. Plan a procession route to the prayer area.	

Additional Resources

As you plan this chapter, consider using the following materials from The Resourceful Teacher Package.

■ *Classroom Activity Sheets 5 and 5a*

■ *Family Activity Sheets 5 and 5a*

■ *Chapter 5 Test*

■ *Prayers for Every Day*

■ *Projects: Grade 1*

In preparing the children for the Sunday readings, you may wish to use Silver Burdett Ginn's *Getting Ready for Sunday* student and teacher materials.

BOOKS FOR THE JOURNEY

A Chair for My Mother. Vera B. Williams. William Morrow, 1988. Words affectionately describe a family saving money and buying a chair after all their furniture is lost in a fire. (BIG BOOK EDITION, 1993)

Cinco de Mayo. Janet Riehecky. Children's Press, 1993. The story of a family preparing for a special holiday and helping the youngest to participate in a winning way.

MORE BOOKS FOR THE JOURNEY

Fathers, Mothers, Sisters, Brothers. Mary Ann Hoberman. Puffin Books, 1993. A collection of family poems that reveals what families are and do and how everyone in them makes families unique and special.

The Hummingbirds' Gift. Stefan Czernecki. Hyperion Books for Children, 1994. A family shares its gifts and, in turn, learns how to creatively use gifts that are part of the earth's bounty.

REDUCED CLASSROOM ACTIVITIES

Name _____

Jesus Grew Up in a Family

1. Trace the words.
2. Draw a picture of an adult you know who reminds you of Mary or Joseph.
3. Cut around the heart and deliver it to your special person.

My family is holy, too.

To the Teacher: This activity follows the story "The Holy Family."

Chapter 5   Jesus Grew Up in a Family   THIS IS OUR FAITH 1   **5**

Name _____

We Show Love

1. Color the pictures about family members helping each other.
2. Tell why you did not color the other picture.

To the Teacher: This activity stresses that it is the responsibility of all family members to contribute to peace and unity.

5a   THIS IS OUR FAITH 1   Chapter 5   Jesus Grew Up in a Family

GROWING WITHIN A FAMILY

It was in the context of the Holy Family that God's love became incarnate. The Gospels provide us with few details of the life of the Holy Family, in the small town of Nazareth, in first-century Palestine. However, Mary and Joseph must have raised Jesus to be a God-fearing and compassionate man, for we see these qualities in him when he grows to manhood.

JESUS' RESPONSE TO FAMILY

Several times in the gospels we see that Jesus was sensitive to the life that family members shared. Examples of his concern are given in the story of the centurion's slave who was a member of his master's household (Luke 7:1–10); in the raising to new life of the widow's son (Luke 7:11–15); and in the healing of the twelve-year-old daughter of Jairus (Luke 8:40–42, 49–56). These stories reveal a man of great compassion who knew the love of parents for their child.

Jesus learned compassion from his own family, who helped him grow in wisdom, age, and grace (Luke 2:52). From Mary and Joseph, Jesus learned to respond to people seeking justice and healing, love and understanding, forgiveness and new life. They taught him to respond to others with love; he followed their example all his life.

As you introduce Jesus' family to the children, impart an understanding of him that includes both familiarity and a sense of mystery. Jesus is like us but not just like us. However, many of the human experiences of Jesus as a child were probably similar to the experiences of children today.

TEACHING ABOUT FAMILIES

The teacher should be sensitive to the problems of modern family life, which is often varied, complex, and strained. Nearly one third of school-age children are not living with both natural parents. Do emphasize that there are many different kinds of families and that a family is made up of people who love, care for, and respect one another.

Be very aware that each child in your classroom has a deep need to accept the members of his or her own family. Be very careful not to look surprised by any stories the children may tell about their families. Children do not understand what their innocent sharings might tell an adult. Be grateful for their openness and assure them repeatedly that God loves them and that you love them too.

With Jesus as model and guide, the children can grow as responsible, loving, and caring family members. They can learn to pray to the Holy Family to help their own family members become closer to one another and to God.

Objective

This lesson helps the children recognize that Jesus lived a human life with his family.

Step 1/INTRODUCTION

Learning About Our Lives

Studying the Photographs

Explain that a family is made up of people who love and care for one another. Then invite volunteers to tell how many members there are in their families. Write the numbers and names on the chalkboard. Afterward, emphasize that there are many different sizes of families and that each family is special. Direct the children to look at the pictures on page 62. For each picture, ask questions such as the following.

- How are these family members showing love for one another? (*Having fun by building a snowman; playing and caring for one another in a pool; various other answers.*)
- Have you ever done something like this with your family? (*Answers will vary.*)
- How did you feel then? (*Answers will vary.*)

Reading a Poem

Read with the children the poem "Families Are Special" on page 62. Make sure the children understand the words *family tree.* Afterward, reread the poem and invite the children to underline the words they think are important. Make this a game by asking which important word begins with *F, P, T,* and so on. Among the important words, include *family, people, together, need, young, old, sister, brother, you, playing, working, kindness,* and *care.*

Step 2/DEVELOPMENT

Learning About Our Faith

Learning About the Holy Family

Read "The Family of Jesus" on page 63. Ask what the word *holy* means. Help the children understand that holy means "to live the way God calls us to live." Explain that families do this when they show each other love and help each other grow. So all families trying to

5

Jesus Grew Up in a Family

Who are the people you belong with?

A family is a group of people who belong together.

Families Are Special

A family is people
Like you and like me,
Who are all together
On one family tree.

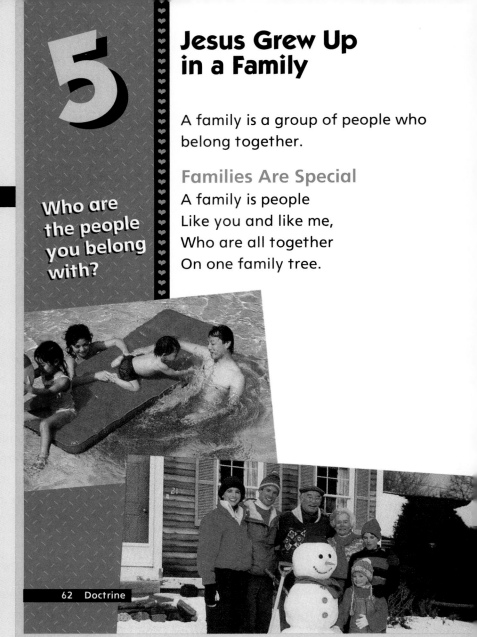

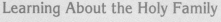
62   Doctrine

Cultural Awareness

Have the children examine the illustration and note that the Holy Family is sitting on pillows to eat a meal. Call the children's attention to the fact that there are few dishes and no silverware. They probably scooped up their food with bread. Explore the foods the Holy Family is eating: figs, bread, and a common dish, possibly mashed beans. Also note the family's pleasant expressions and attention to each other.

Focus on

Family Life   Each of us has been accepted and loved by God from our creation. The family is meant to echo the love and acceptance of God and to teach selfless love. To expand the children's love of their own families, provide the first graders with occasions to introduce their families through art, discussion, and, whenever possible, in person to the class. Help the children discover their own special contributions to their families.

The Family of Jesus

Jesus, God's own Son, grew up
in a family, just as we do.
He lived with Mary and Joseph.
Jesus' family is the **Holy Family**.

New Word

❤
❤ **Holy Family**   Mary, Joseph, and Jesus are
❤   the Holy Family.

We Believe

Jesus is the Son
of God and human,
too. We call
Jesus and his
family the
Holy Family.

Doctrine   63

bring life and love into our world can be called
holy families.

Presenting the Doctrine

Read aloud the We Believe section on page 63,
which summarizes the chapter's doctrine.

Reviewing the Vocabulary

Point to the New Word section on page 63. Ask
the children to repeat *Holy Family* and its
definition after you.

Step 3/CONCLUSION

Learning How to Live Our Faith

Comparing Jesus' Life to Ours

Ask the children in what ways the child Jesus
was like them. Emphasize that Jesus ate, slept,
learned, and worked. Stress that he felt happy,
sad, lonely, and frustrated at times. Point out
that he needed a family to take care of him, just
as all children do.

Creating a Bulletin Board

Discuss some happy times the Holy Family
might have had together. Then ask the children
to draw pictures of their families doing
something happy together.

Afterward, gather the children around an empty
bulletin board. Pin their pictures on the board.
Have 23 letters cut out for the following
sentence: *These are our holy families.* Give
each child a letter to hold and then ask the
children to help you tack up the letters.
Afterward, talk about how the sentence applies
to their drawings.

Thanking God for Their Families

As you and the children are gathered around
the bulletin board, teach them this prayer:
Thank you, God, for this holy family. Invite the
children, one by one, to point to their pictures
and explain them. After each sharing,
encourage all the children to pray the short
prayer they just learned.

CURRICULUM CONNECTION

Music Teach the children the fol-
lowing words to the melody for
"Frère Jacques" ("Are You Sleep-
ing, Brother John?").
   Holy Family, Holy Family.
   Just like mine. Just like mine.
   Loving, caring, helping.
   Loving, caring, helping.
   Every day. Every day.

Enriching the Lesson

If possible, show the children some
food that the Holy Family may have
eaten. The foods available during
Jesus' time include Bread; dried,
salted fish; boiled chicken; eggs;
goat's milk and cheese; yogurt; nuts;
honey; beans; lentils; cucumbers;
leeks; olives; onions; figs; melons;
grapes; pomegranates; cornmeal;
wheat flour; ground barley; wine;
olive oil; salt; mint; cumin; and cinnamon. You might want to have the
children taste some of these foods.

Objective

This lesson helps the children to value being part of a family.

Step 1/INTRODUCTION

Learning About Our Lives

Talking About Families

Recall that Jesus lived in a family just as the children do. Then encourage the children to talk about their families. Ask the names of their family members, where they live, or what kind of work their parents do. Any of the children who brought in pictures of their families may show them to the class.

or...

Help the children make a family tree. Draw a simple tree outline on the board. Add the names of your immediate family members and grandparents. When the children understand the concept, tell them to copy the tree and write in the names of their family members, including their own.

Using the Bulletin Board

Gather the children around the bulletin board from Day 1 that shows their families. Encourage the children to talk about their pictures and to tell the class what happy things their families are doing together. Afterward, emphasize that when families show they love and care, they are acting like the Holy Family.

Step 2/DEVELOPMENT

Learning About Our Faith

Examining a Picture

Invite the children to look at the illustration on pages 64 and 65 and ask the following questions.

- What is Mary doing for her family? (*Making bread*)
- What is Joseph doing for the family? (*Making something from wood*)
- What is Jesus doing? (*Helping Joseph*)

The Holy Family

The Holy Family lived in **Nazareth.**
Most people there lived in houses
made from stone and mud.
The Holy Family probably did, too.

In their house, Joseph had a workplace.
He was a carpenter.
With his hammer and nails, he could
build chests and stools.
With his saw and ax, Joseph cut wood.

Cultural Awareness

Help the children compare and contrast Joseph's work as a carpenter and Mary's as a homemaker with their parent(s) jobs. Elicit from the children what their caregivers do for a living. Ask the children what kind of tools or machinery their mom and dad use in their jobs. Then invite the children to draw pictures contrasting Mary and Joseph working with the children's parents at work.

Focus on

Life in Jesus' Time   In biblical times many houses were only one room with a raised platform on which the family slept at night. The beds were narrow mattresses that were rolled up each morning. At night, the animals (donkeys, goats, and chickens) were brought in and tethered by the manger, where they could eat. The household goods were very few: a chest for clothes and treasures; earthenware pots for oil, grain, and water; millstones to grind corn; an oil lamp; stools; rugs; shelves; and cubbyholes.

Mary and Joseph cared for Jesus
and for each other.
She and Joseph taught Jesus that
members of a family love each other.

Jesus loved his family.
They cried together in sad times.
They laughed together in happy times.
They thanked God for each other.

New Word

❤
❤ **Nazareth**   Nazareth is the town where Jesus
❤   lived with Mary and Joseph.
❤

Focus on

Games of Biblical Times For their games, children of biblical times often used pebbles. For one game, called "Gap," they threw twelve pebbles in the air and tried to catch them in one hand. They also played hop-scotch by drawing and numbering squares on the flat roofs of their homes and then throwing pebbles into the squares.

Enriching the Lesson

Have the children plan and present dramatizations about family life and how family members show their love and care. Make suggestions such as the following.

Mom and several children are watching TV after supper. Each of them wants to watch a different show.

Tell the children to give names to their characters and then act out the situation. Remind them to try to act toward their imaginary family members as Jesus, Mary, and Joseph might have acted toward one another.

- What do you see in this picture that you might see in your own home? (*Answers will vary.*)
- What is different from your home? (*Answers will vary.*)

Listening to a Story

Read pages 64 and 65. Afterward, print the words *Nazareth*, *Jesus*, *Mary*, and *Joseph* on the chalkboard. Ask the children to underline these words in their books.

Reviewing the Vocabulary

Point to the New Word section on page 65. Ask the children to repeat the word *Nazareth* and its definition.

Step 3/CONCLUSION

Learning How to Live Our Faith

Discovering What Holy Families Do

Reread the story on pages 64 and 65 and ask the children to listen carefully and to circle the words in the story that tell about what holy families do. (*Care, love, cry, laugh, thank God*)

Praying a Litany of Thanksgiving

Gathering the children in the prayer area, teach them the following response: *We thank you, God, for our holy families.* Invite the children to respond after each phrase.

Because our families help us . . .
Because our families laugh together . . .
Because our families teach us . . .
Because our families love us . . .
Amen.

Reviewing the Lesson

To review the lesson ask the following questions.

- What did Joseph do for his family? (*Answers will vary.*)
- What did Mary do for her family? (*Answers will vary.*)
- What did Jesus do for his family? (*Answers will vary.*)
- Where did the Holy Family live? (*In Nazareth*)

DAY 3
DOCTRINE/MORALITY

Objective

This lesson helps the children appreciate the members of their families.

Step 1/INTRODUCTION

Learning About Our Lives

Drawing Portraits of Family Members

Direct the children's attention to the picture frame on page 66. Encourage the children to draw the faces of their family members. Help them complete the page by using pencils to print the names of their family members.

After the children have completed their work, invite them to share with the class the names of their family members and the pictures they have drawn.

Step 2/DEVELOPMENT

Learning About Our Faith

Learning About Jesus' Extended Family

Direct the children's attention to page 67. Read the text "Jesus' Family" aloud. Then discuss the meaning of the biblical names in the chart.

- Mary's name means "excellence" or "the very best." God loved Mary. Why do you think God loved her? (*Answers will vary.*)

- Joseph's name means "God gives more than I can ever think of asking for." What wonderful things did God do for Joseph? (*He lived his life with Jesus and Mary.*)

- Jesus' name means "God saves and helps us." How does Jesus help us? (*He helps us remember God's love.*)

(NOTE: The above answer reflects the learning from Chapter 4.)

 Activity

In the space below, draw the faces of the people in your family.
Write their names under their pictures.

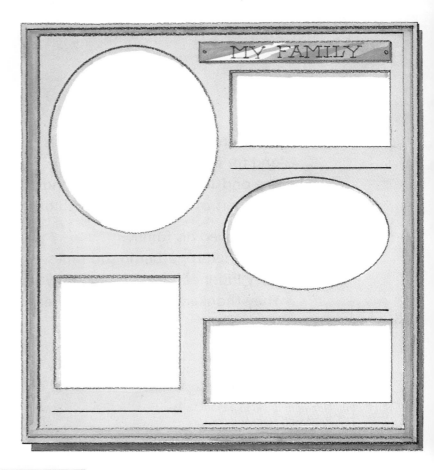

CURRICULUM CONNECTION

Art Invite the children to decorate a name of one of their family members. First, have the children decide on whose name to decorate. Then encourage the children to name good qualities about that person. Write the qualities on the chalkboard as the children enumerate them. Then have the children print their chosen names on a piece of drawing paper. Instruct the children to turn the paper over and print the qualities of that person, copying the qualities from the chalkboard. Finally, have them decorate it with glitter and glue.

Jesus' Family

Jesus was part of a family.
He had relatives named Zechariah,
Elizabeth, and their son, John.
Zechariah led the people in prayer.
He helped them to remember God's love.

Jesus' family did many things to remember God's love.
Even their names reminded them that God was
always with them.

Mary
The very best

Elizabeth
God makes
me happy.

Jesus
God saves
and helps us.

John
God has
blessed me.

Joseph
God gives more
than I can even
think of asking for.

Zechariah
God is always
thinking of me
and helping me.

Doctrine 67

Teaching Tips

Before the children take their own decorated name home, post their names around the room. Throughout the next several days, read the names and the qualities, and assure the children that you will indeed remember these wonderful things about them. Throughout each day, stress these qualities about the children when you respond to their answers, their work, and their activities in the classroom.

Learning How to Live Our Faith

Discussing the Meaning of Names

Recall that the names of Jesus, Mary, Joseph and Jesus' family members have special meanings. Ask the children what they would like their names to mean. To begin, mention what you would like your name to mean. Stress some quality for which you personally would like to be remembered by the children.

Next, help the children find qualities that they wish their names would mean and that they wish people would remember about them. If the children hesitate to share, say the name of one child and tell that child what his or her name means to you. (For instance: John is funny or helpful or a good artist.)

Tell the children that these qualities about them help make them important and wonderful persons.

Treasuring Our Names

Provide the children with drawing paper and crayons or felt-tip markers and encourage them to make gifts of their names for their families.

Have the children print their names on the paper. Then go around the room and ask the children, one by one, what qualities they wish their names would mean and what qualities they wish people would remember about them. After each child's name, print the words *wants to be remembered for* and then print the qualities the child has picked.

or . . .

Obtain several names books and tell each child what his or her name means. Then when the children decorate their names, instruct them to write the meaning of their names on the back of the papers.

Gathering for Prayer

Ask the children to bring their decorated names to the prayer area. When they are quiet, ask the children, one by one, to step in front of the Bible, to say the qualities they chose to represent their names, and to lay their drawings on the prayer table as a thank-you to God for the gift of themselves. After each child does this, say *Thank you, God, for,* and add the child's name.

Objective

This lesson helps the children appreciate how family members love and care for one another.

Step 1/INTRODUCTION

Learning About Our Lives

Discussing Ways to Help One Another

Gather the children around the bulletin board they assembled on Day 1. Ask a few volunteers to use their posted drawings to talk about how family members help one another and help make one another happy.

Pantomiming Ways of Helping the Family

Invite the children to pantomime ways in which members of their families help them: cooking a meal, setting the table, using the vacuum sweeper, snow blowing, helping to build a snow fort, playing baseball, or making a bed. After each pantomime, compliment the children on their creative expression.

Step 2/DEVELOPMENT

Learning About Our Faith

Reading the Children's Book

Direct the children's attention to page 68 of the children's book and read "The Holy Family Helps and Cares." Invite the children to comment on what they think might be happening in the illustration, using the following questions to guide the discussion.

- Where are Jesus and Joseph going? (*Answers will vary.*)

- What might they be talking about? (*Answers will vary.*)

- What places do you go with your dad, grandfather, uncle, or friend? (*Answers will vary.*)

- What would you like to talk over with them? (*Answers will vary.*)

Then direct the children to the activity on page 68. Ask them what surprise Joseph and Jesus might have planned for Mary. After several ideas have been suggested, have the children write on the lines provided a possible surprise

68   Morality

The Holy Family Helps and Cares

Mary and Joseph brought up Jesus to be a caring person.

Joseph and Jesus often walked together to evening prayer. On the way, they might have talked over their day. Maybe, they chatted about what Jesus and Joseph built. They might even have thought of ways to surprise Mary.

The Holy Family loved and cared for each other. They showed their love by helping one another.

Activity

What surprise might Joseph and Jesus have planned for Mary?

_____

_____

_____

_____

Focus on

Chores   To help the children appreciate ways in which Jesus might have helped his family, point out family chores that needed to be done in biblical times: washing up the serving dishes, sweeping the earthen floor, grinding grain; heating the oven and helping to make bread; filling, cleaning, and lighting the evening lamps; and running errands. Stress that Joseph taught Jesus to be a carpenter, so Jesus must have helped him build houses, make furniture for the home, and farm implements for the farmers.

Enriching the Lesson

Give each child two sheets of writing paper, a piece of construction paper, and crayons or felt-tip markers. Have the children fold the sheets in half to make a four-page booklet with a construction-paper cover. Ask them to print *My Family Book* on the cover. Encourage the children to draw on each page a picture that shows a family member helping someone else and to print that family member's name on the page. Afterward, invite the children to share their booklets.

We Help Our Families

Jesus helped Mary and Joseph.
God wants us to be like Jesus.
God wants us to help our families, too.

ctivity

Draw lines to match the pictures that show family members helping one another and showing love.

To help the children better understand the pictures, study the illustrations on page 69 with the children and invite comments on the facial expressions of the people who need help. Also explore the actions these people are doing (their body language). For example, the overheated grandfather is mopping his brow. Have the children mop their brows as if they were very hot and needed water. Invite them to dramatize the actions and expressions of the other needy people.

Enriching the Lesson

Caring for others helps to build children's self-esteem. Create "helping" coupons for each child. Before the lesson, draw four coupons on a sheet of paper and print a description of a loving act on each, such as *Pick up my toys* or *Care for my pet*. Distribute the coupons and tell the children to color and cut them out. Explain that the children can give these coupons to family members. Emphasize that when a family member redeems a coupon, the child can show love to that person by doing what is written on the coupon.

---

for Mary that they think would have been nice for Jesus and Joseph to plan for her.

Creating Dialogue for a Dramatization

Reread the second paragraph to revisit the possible topics that Jesus and Joseph might have talked about. Divide the class into small groups of twos and threes. Invite the groups to demonstrate how Jesus helped Joseph. Encourage each set of partners to talk to one another just as Joseph and Jesus must have talked as they helped one another.

Invite the groups to demonstrate how Jesus and Joseph might have surprised Mary. Encourage the children to talk to one another just as Jesus and Joseph might have talked if they were preparing a surprise. Encourage the children to show how Mary reacted to the surprise.

Step 3/CONCLUSION

Learning How to Live Our Faith

Discovering Ways to Help the Family

Read aloud "We Help Our Families" at the top of page 69. Then point to the activity on page 69. Point out that each of these people needs help. Read the directions aloud and encourage the children to use pencils to draw lines to the pictures that match. When the children have finished, discuss their choices.

Thanking God for the Children

In the prayer area, gather the children in a semicircle. Invite them to hold hands. When the children are quiet, stand in front of the first child in the semicircle. Lay your hands on the child's head and thank God for how helpful this child can be to his or her family. Repeat this action and prayer over each child.

Reviewing the Lesson

To review the lesson ask the following questions.

- How did Jesus help his family? (*Answers will vary.*)
- Why did the Holy Family help each other? (*Because they loved one another*)
- In what way does God want us to be like Jesus? (*God wants us to help our families.*)

Objective

This lesson invites the children to pray a psalm.

Discovering a Psalm About Families

Ask the children what the children in the picture on page 70 are holding (*their religion books opened to page 66*). Have the children turn back to page 66. Encourage volunteers to say the names of the family members they printed and drew on that page.

Next read aloud the text "Praying with a Psalm" on page 70. After reading the psalm, ask the following questions.

■ What did the Holy Family do for each other so that they could live together in peace and love? (*Answers will vary.*)

■ What does the word *pleasant* mean? (*Pleasing, delightful, peaceful*)

■ What is wonderful and pleasant about living with a happy family? (*Answers will vary.*)

Learning a Thanksgiving Song

Teach the children the following words to the melody "Mary Had a Little Lamb."
    Thank you for my family,
    Family, family.
    Thank you for my family,
    They help me love and care.

Thanking God for Families

Encourage the children to hold their pictures in front of them as they process into the prayer area. When the children are quiet, invite them to sing their song. Then pray the psalm on page 70 and ask the children to repeat each line. Conclude the prayer by singing the song again.

Encourage the children to take their drawings home to share with their families.

Praying with the Psalms

When Jesus was growing up,
he learned some prayers in the Bible.
These prayers are called psalms.
We can pray this psalm with Jesus
and his Holy Family.

How wonderful it is,
and how pleasant,
for the family of God
to live together
in peace and love.

Based on Psalm 133:1

70   Prayer

CURRICULUM CONNECTION

Music Play the following song about families for the children: "Five People in My Family" from *The Sesame Street Book and Record* Original Cast Album. (New York: Columbia Records, 1970). Afterward, discuss the lyrics.

Focus on

Praying the Psalms Throughout this book the children will pray the psalms from time to time. This lesson introduces the children to the psalms as a form of prayer that the Holy Family prayed often. The psalms are one type of prayer found in the Bible and are used frequently in Jewish prayer.

Chapter Review

Jesus, Mary, and Joseph cared for one another.
Draw a line between the things each member of the
Holy Family used to help the others. *Accept all reasonable answers.*

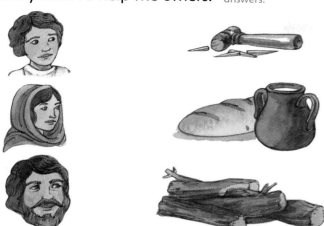

Name the people in Jesus' family.

Jesus, Mary, Joseph

Where did Jesus grow up?

Nazareth

Talk about how Jesus is like us.

> Children,
> love and help
> your parents.
> Parents, be good
> to your children.
> **Based on**
> **Ephesians 6:1,4**

Review 71

★ ★ ★ ★ ★
**Enriching
the Lesson**

Show a filmstrip that illustrates
how children can contribute to family living. Consider using "Me First"
(from Kindle Filmstrips, Scholastic).
Note that this filmstrip deals with
the concept of taking turns and
allowing others a chance to be first
in doing what they wish.

6 Mary, the Mother of Jesus

Objectives ～～～

To help the children
- Learn the story of the annunciation.
- Recognize Mary as their Mother.
- Recognize that Mary loves all people.
- Discover ways Catholics honor Mary.
- Learn the Hail Mary and review the chapter.

Chapter Outline ～～～～～～～

	Step 1 Learning About Our Lives	**Step 2** Learning About Our Faith	**Step 3** Learning How to Live Our Faith
Day 1	■ Talk about mothers. ■ Read a picture story. *ABOUT 8 MINUTES*	■ Tell a Bible story. ■ Review the vocabulary. ■ Dramatize the story. *ABOUT 12 MINUTES*	■ Learn from Mary. ■ Prepare to pray. ■ Pray with movement. *ABOUT 10 MINUTES*
Day 2	■ Review Day 1. ■ Dramatize how to be a messenger. *ABOUT 8 MINUTES*	■ Discover Mary our Mother. ■ Present the doctrine. *ABOUT 10 MINUTES*	■ Share with Mary and pray. ■ Affirm that Mary loves us. ■ Make a bulletin board. *ABOUT 12 MINUTES*
Day 3	■ Discuss the bulletin board from Day 2. ■ Dramatize ways to love. *ABOUT 8 MINUTES*	■ Discover Mary's love for everyone. ■ Share thoughts on pictures of Mary. *ABOUT 12 MINUTES*	■ Draw a picture of Mary. ■ Use the bulletin board for prayer. *ABOUT 10 MINUTES*
Day 4	■ Discover the meaning of birthdays. *ABOUT 10 MINUTES*	■ Remember Mary's special days. ■ Honor Mary in special ways. *ABOUT 10 MINUTES*	■ Choose a way to honor Mary. ■ Thank God for Mary. *ABOUT 10 MINUTES*

Day 5 **Prayer** Learn the Hail Mary; have a procession; crown a statue of Mary; give flowers to Mary; and pray the Hail Mary.

Review Complete the activity; answer the questions; and read the Scripture verse.

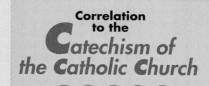

Correlation
to the
Catechism of
the **C**atholic **C**hurch

Paragraphs
509, 723, 963, 2677

Plan Ahead ∼∼∼∼∼∼∼∼∼∼∼

	Preparing Your Class	**Materials Needed**
Day 1	For Step 2, practice reading "A Message for Mary" on page 73. Select soft background music. For Step 3, think of body movements and rhythmic gestures.	■ record or cassette of soft instrumental music ■ phonograph or cassette player
Day 2	For Step 3, collect magazine pictures of caring people. Cut out letters for *Like Mary, many people love children.* Prepare a space for a bulletin board.	■ pictures of people caring for children ■ scissors ■ empty bulletin board ■ cut-out letters for one sentence
Day 3	For Step 1, prepare stories that show love.	
Day 4	For Step 1, be prepared to name positive things about each child. For Step 3, consider ways you and the children can honor Mary.	■ materials for honoring Mary
Day 5	Practice the song. Place a statue of Mary and a vase on the prayer table. Cut out one construction-paper flower for each child and a small crown to fit the statue.	■ construction-paper crown ■ construction-paper flowers ■ statue of Mary ■ vase

Additional Resources

As you plan this chapter, consider using the following materials from The Resourceful Teacher Package.

■ *Classroom Activity Sheets 6 and 6a*

■ *Family Activity Sheets 6 and 6a*

■ *Chapter 6 Test*

■ *Prayers for Every Day*

■ *Projects: Grade 1*

You may also wish to refer to the following Big Book.

■ *We Celebrate God's Word,* page 6

In preparing the children for the Sunday readings, you may wish to use Silver Burdett Ginn's *Getting Ready for Sunday* student and teacher materials.

BOOKS FOR THE JOURNEY

Even If I Did Something Awful. Barbara Shook Hazen. Atheneum, 1984. A child learns that a mother is someone who loves you no matter what you do.

Love You Forever. Robert Munch. Firefly Books, 1989. This story describes a mother's love as unconditional and never-ending.

MORE BOOKS FOR THE JOURNEY

Mama One, Mama Two. Patricia Maclachlan. Harper & Row, 1982. This story tells what mothers—natural and foster—are like.

The Runaway Bunny. Margaret Wise Brown. Harper & Row, 1977. A mother bunny's love is so great that no matter where her little bunny goes, she will be with him.

REDUCED CLASSROOM ACTIVITIES

Name

Mary, the Mother of Jesus

1. Color the picture of Jesus' mother.
2. Cut along the heavy black outside lines.
3. Draw a circle behind Mary and glue A to B.

Mary shares her love with us.

To the Teacher: This activity follows the Scripture story "A Message for Mary."

Chapter 6   Mary, the Mother of Jesus   THIS IS OUR FAITH 1   **6**

Name

Mary Is Our Mother, Too

1. Color the pictures in boxes 1 and 2.
2. In box 3, draw yourself doing something at school that shows your love for Mary.

1	2	3
"Yes," Mary told the angel, "I will do what God wants."	Mary loved Jesus and took good care of him.	This is how I show my love for Mary at school.

To the Teacher: This activity follows the review.

6a   THIS IS OUR FAITH 1   Chapter 6   Mary, the Mother of Jesus

Background for the Teacher ~~~~~~

MOTHER OF GOD

Exalted by God above all creation, Mary is the most honored member of the Church. In the litany in her honor, we Catholics address Mary as "Mother of Good Counsel," "Mystical Rose," "Help of Christians," "Queen of Martyrs," and "Queen of Peace."

Two of Mary's most beloved titles, "Blessed Mother" and "Mother of God," point to the central mystery of the incarnation. The incarnation occurred at the annunciation when Mary said yes to God's request that she become the mother of Jesus. At the moment she embraced God's love, the Word of God became flesh in her womb, forever joining human nature to God's nature.

As Mary grew up in the town of Nazareth, God's Spirit enveloped Mary and reached her deepest center. There God dwelt, prompting Mary to assent to her place in God's plan for her life. She replied, "I am the handmaid of the Lord. May it be done to me according to your word" (Luke 1:38).

MARY, OUR MOTHER

As Jesus neared his death on the cross, he bequeathed Mary to us. Looking down upon John, Jesus said to his mother, "Woman, behold, your son." Then Jesus gazed at John and said, "Behold, your mother" (John 19:26–27).

When Jesus entrusted Mary to John, he entrusted her to all of us. She is ours to love; from her we receive the love that she lavished on Jesus. During her life in Palestine, Mary showed how to grow in faith and hope and love. She showed what saying yes to God can mean. Because she is the model of all virtues, she encourages us to follow Jesus.

THE HAIL MARY

Chapter 6 introduces the children to the Hail Mary. Catholics greet Mary by saying, "Hail Mary—hello!" They recall that significant moment of her life when she said yes to God's life in her. Recalling this incarnational moment, they proclaim: "The Lord is with you," as they acknowledge the fruit of her womb, Jesus. They beg her to ask God, whose Word took flesh in her womb, to grace their lives.

THE CHILDREN AND MARY

In Chapter 6, the children in your classroom explore their relationship with Mary. This relationship can be a great source of comfort to the children. In any discussion of the mother-child bond, you must be sensitive to situations in today's families. Some children may not live with their mothers; some may not even know their mothers. Therefore, you need to help the children appreciate "mothering"—those nurturing virtues of loving caregivers.

SCRIPTURE

Objective

This lesson helps the children appreciate Mary's response to God.

Step 1/INTRODUCTION

Learning About Our Lives

Talking About Mothers

Direct the children's attention to the chapter-focus question. Invite them to respond by naming the things they think make a mother special. List these qualities on the chalkboard. Emphasize that other relatives, male as well as female, can also show love in these ways.

Reading a Picture Story

Ask the children to study the picture story on page 72 and tell a story about it. Afterward, ask the children the following questions.

- How do you think Suzy felt when she fell? (*Answers will vary.*)
- How do you think she felt when her mother comforted her? (*Answers will vary.*)
- How do you feel when someone comforts you? (*Answers will vary.*)

Invite volunteers to make up dialogue to accompany each picture.

Step 2/DEVELOPMENT

Learning About Our Faith

Telling the Story of the Annunciation

Read with expression "A Message for Mary" on page 73. (Try to read the story as if you do not know what Mary will answer. Read with expectation.) Afterward, ask the following questions.

- Who was the special messenger God sent to Mary? (*The angel Gabriel*)
- What message from God did the angel Gabriel have for Mary? (*God wanted Mary to be the mother of Jesus, the Son of God.*)
- What was Mary's answer to God? (*Yes*)

Conclude the story by telling the children that Mary is special because God chose her to be the mother of Jesus and she said yes.

---

6 Mary, the Mother of Jesus

Suzy and Her Mother

Look at the pictures of this mother with her child, Suzy.
What are three things the mother does that make her special to Suzy?

What are some things that you think make a mother special?

 **Teaching Tips**

Be especially sensitive to children who may be without a mother's support. Throughout your discussion, talk about all the other caregivers in the children's lives. In this lesson, teach from the children's understanding of the qualities of mothers in general and then of Mary in particular. Stress that not only can mothers display these qualities but also that fathers, guardians, and all their caregivers can say yes to God and be loving and caring.

 **Teaching Tips**

Some children learn better when they can relate the words of a story to its illustrations. To better connect the words and pictures of "A Message for Mary," invite the children to add talking balloons to the page. Encourage the children to write a conversation between Mary and Gabriel. Or help them concentrate on either Mary's response or the angel's message. For instance, focusing on Mary, they might choose to write *Yes*, or *I will be Jesus' mother.*

A Message for Mary

One day, God sent an angel to give
a message to Mary.
She was a young woman who
lived in Nazareth.
The angel's name was Gabriel.

"Hail Mary," the angel said.
"God wants you to be the mother
of a special baby boy.
You will name the baby Jesus.
He will be called the Son of God."

Mary loved God,
so she said to Gabriel,
"Yes, I will be the mother of Jesus.
I will do what God asks of me."

Then the angel left Mary.
She prayed about the baby
who was coming.

Based on Luke 1:26–38

New Word

❤
❤ **angel**   An angel is a messenger and helper
❤   from God.
❤

Scripture   73

CURRICULUM CONNECTION

Language Arts Distribute crayons or felt-tip markers and a sheet of drawing paper to each child. Show the children how to fold the paper into four sections. Then ask the children to think of a story about a mother (a caregiver) who is special. Invite the children to tell their stories in four pictures. While the children are working, go around the room and talk to each child about his or her story, becoming more familiar with each one's home situation. Ask any child who wishes to share a story with the group.

Reviewing the Vocabulary

Point to the New Word section on page 73. Ask the children to repeat the word *angel* and its definition.

Dramatizing the Story

Select volunteers to dramatize the story of the annunciation. You will need to choose a narrator, an angel, and Mary. Provide a few minutes for the children to rethink the story and to discuss what can be done in a dramatization. Have the class members suggest possible dialogue. Assure the children that they can use their own words as they role-play the story.

Repeat the role-play to give other children the opportunity to make the story their own. If you wish, enter into it to stimulate natural dialogue.

or...

Select one half of the class to read Mary's words and ask the other half to read Gabriel's words. Take the narrator's part yourself. Ask for two volunteers, one from each group, to pantomime the roles of Mary and Gabriel as the rest of the children read the words.

Step 3/CONCLUSION

Learning How to Live Our Faith

Learning from Mary

Reread Mary's response to the angel Gabriel in paragraph 3 of the story on page 73. Point out that through her response, Mary showed that she loved God. Ask the children to suggest ways they can follow Mary's example and show God their love.

Preparing to Pray

Teach the children the following response: *Mary said yes. Please, God, help us to say yes, too.* Then divide the class into two groups. Assign the first sentence of the response to one group. Assign the second sentence to the second group. Ask the children to brainstorm body movements and gestures to use when they pray their response. Tell the children that they will use their gestures and response to pray today.

Praying with Movement

Gather the children in the prayer area. Reread the story on page 73. After each paragraph is read, invite each group to pray its response.

73

Objective

This lesson helps the children recognize Mary as their Mother.

Step 1/INTRODUCTION

Learning About Our Lives

Reviewing Day 1

Recall that an angel is a messenger and helper from God. Ask the children to name the messenger God sent to Mary (Gabriel). Discuss the story of the annunciation, emphasizing Mary's response to God's request.

Dramatizing How to Be a Messenger

Invite the children to think of possible messages they might bring to people. Call on volunteers who will each choose another child to deliver the message to. Then, one by one, invite the "messengers" to knock at an imaginary door. The receiver of the message answers the door, listens to the message, and responds. Talk about how we feel when people give us different kinds of messages.

Step 2/DEVELOPMENT

Learning About Our Faith

Discovering that Mary Is Our Mother

Read aloud the first two paragraphs of "Mary Is Our Mother, Too." Ask the following questions.

■ What did Mary remember about God? (*That God loves her*)

■ What did Mary teach her son, Jesus? (*Many things: among them—how to pray, and how to love others*)

■ What did Mary help her son, Jesus, remember? (*God's love*)

Pause here to discuss the illustration. Elicit ideas of what Jesus and Mary might be talking about. Then continue reading the last paragraph and ask the following questions.

■ Why does Jesus share his mother with us? (*Because he loves us*)

■ What does Mary want for us? (*To be happy*)

As you conclude the discussion, emphasize that Mary is the children's Mother, too.

74

Mary Is Our Mother, Too

When God asked Mary to be
Jesus' mother, she said, "Yes!"
She remembered that God loved her.
Mary trusted God's love.

As Jesus grew up, he saw how much
Mary trusted God.
Mary also showed Jesus how to love others.
She helped him remember God's love.

Because Jesus loves us, he shares his
mother with us.
Our Mother Mary loves us and wants us
to be happy.

🍎 Teaching Tips

Children can carry messages. They enjoy making deliveries to the school office. Most have brought memos home from school. These are usually the more formal, written type of message. At home, children can be asked by a parent to convey a message to other family members: "Turn down the TV"; "Dinner is ready"; "There's a surprise in the family room"; "The phone's for you, Dad." Discuss possible feelings and verbal and physical expressions connected with delivering or receiving these messages.

Focus on

Mary, Our Mother According to the *Catechism of the Catholic Church* "Mary is truly 'Mother of God' since she is the mother of the eternal Son of God made man, who is God himself." (#509) "Because she gives us Jesus, her son, Mary is Mother of God and our mother . . . ." (#2677)

Mary Loves Us

❤ Mary taught Jesus to be kind.
She can teach us to be like Jesus.

❤ Mary likes to hear our stories.
She knows about being happy,
and she knows about being sad.

❤ Mary is a mother to us.
She wants to hear our troubles.
Mary will ask God to help us.

ctivity

Trace the letters. Then complete the prayer.

Dear God,
Thank you for

M̶a̶r̶y̶ w̶h̶o̶

l̶o̶v̶e̶s̶ u̶s̶.

Amen.

We Believe

Mary is the
mother of Jesus,
God's Son.
Mary is our
Mother, too.

Doctrine 75

Teaching Tips

Place a statue or picture of Mary in the prayer area and remind the children that Mary can teach them how to pray and that Mary will pray to God for them.

Enriching the Lesson

Cut out one flower petal for each child. Print a question on each petal. If necessary, repeat some questions. *Who is the mother of Jesus? Who gives us his mother to love us? What is the name of God's messenger to Mary? What was Mary's answer to God? What did Mary teach Jesus?* On a posterboard, draw several flower stems. Direct the children to choose a petal and answer its question. When a child responds correctly, help him or her tape the petal to the flower stem. Several petals will form a flower.

Read aloud the We Believe section on page 75, which summarizes the chapter's doctrine. Ask the children to repeat the sentences after you.

Step 3/CONCLUSION

Learning How to Live Our Faith

Affirming that Mary Loves the Children

Direct the children's attention to "Mary Loves Us" on page 75. Read the text out loud. Then ask the following questions.

■ What can Mary teach us? (*How to be like Jesus*)

■ What does Mary like us to tell her? (*The stories of our happiness and sadness*)

Sharing with Mary and Praying

Recall that Jesus has given the children Mary, his mother, to be their Mother too. Invite the children to look at the picture on page 74 again. Note that in the picture, Jesus is talking to Mary. Invite volunteers to share with the class what they would tell Mary today. Stress that the children can share their joys, their sorrows, and their troubles with Mary, their Mother.

Affirming that Mary Loves Us

Then direct the children's attention to the activity on page 75. Read the directions and ask the children to trace the words *Mary, who loves us*. When they are finished tracing the prayer, encourage the children to share their thoughts and feelings with Mary.

Making a Bulletin Board About Mothering

Distribute magazines, calendars, newspapers, and scissors. Have the children find and cut out pictures of people caring for children. After each child has a picture, invite the children to tell stories about their selections.

Have the children bring their pictures and gather around an empty bulletin board. Pin the children's pictures in a circle. Have 30 letters cut out for the following sentence: *Like Mary, many people love children.* Give each child a letter to hold and then ask the children to hand them to you as you tack the letters to the board. Afterward, talk about how the sentence applies to their pictures.

75

DAY 3
DOCTRINE/PRAYER

Objective
This lesson helps the children recognize that Mary loves all the people in the world.

Step 1/INTRODUCTION

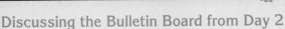
Learning About Our Lives

Discussing the Bulletin Board from Day 2
Gather the children around the bulletin board they assembled on Day 2. Read the bulletin board's message: *Like Mary, many people love children.* Then ask the children to talk about the love they see in the pictures on the bulletin board. Discuss the loving actions displayed in each picture. Ask the children to talk about other ways they like to be loved by their mothers or other caregivers.

Dramatizing Ways to Love
Divide the class into pairs and invite each set of partners to think up a story that shows love or to use one of the pictures on the bulletin board for a story about love. Encourage volunteer partners to role-play a story for the class. Invite the children's comments on the love each skit shows.

Step 2/DEVELOPMENT

Learning About Our Faith

Discovering Mary's Love for Everyone
Direct the children's attention to pages 76 and 77. Encourage their comments on the pictures there. Then read "Mary Loves All People" on page 76. Afterward, ask the following questions.

- Whom does Jesus love? (*Everyone*)
- Whom does Mary love? (*Everyone*)
- Why do people make statues and pictures of Mary? (*Because they want to remember Mary and Jesus and Mary's love for Jesus and them*)

Sharing Thoughts on Pictures of Mary
Encourage the children to talk about what each picture on pages 76 and 77 tells them about Mary, their Mother. Note that some pictures and statues show Mary with Jesus.

76

Our Lady of Guadalupe

Korean, "Virgin and Child"

Our Lady of Fatima

76   Doctrine

Mary Loves All People
Jesus loves all the people in the world.
Mary loves them, too.

People make beautiful pictures and statues of her. Statues can help us remember that Mary loves us.
Which picture or statue do you like best?

Cultural Awareness
Invite the children to bring to school some pictures or statues of Mary from home. Obtain prior permission from parents and arrange for the delivery and the return home at an agreed-upon time.

When the items arrive, discuss why artists make so many different representations of Jesus and Mary, explaining that artists help people all over the world understand that Mary loves them and will help them love Jesus as she does.

"Mother of the Streets" by Robert Lentz.
Courtesy of Bridge Building Images, Inc.

"Cheyenne Virgin and Child" by Father John Giuliani.
Courtesy of Bridge Building Images, Inc.

Activity

Show your love for
Mary with a drawing.
In the space below,
draw a picture of
Mary.

Courtesy of S.M.A. Fathers

Explain that when we think of Mary, we also think of Jesus, whom she loved.

Next, remind the children that Jesus shares his mother with people all over the world. So artists often like to paint her and her son to look like the people in their own lands.

Afterward, ask the children which picture or statues they like best of those on the two pages. Encourage the children to share the reasons for their choices.

Step 3/CONCLUSION

Learning How to Live Our Faith

Drawing a Picture of Mary

Direct the children's attention to the activity on page 77. Read aloud the directions. Then provide crayons or felt-tip markers and encourage the children to show their love for Mary by drawing a picture of her. Afterward, invite the children to talk about their artwork.

Using the Bulletin Board for Prayer

Gather the children around the bulletin board they assembled on Day 2. Teach the children the following response: *Thank you, God, for Mary and for all those people who love children.* Then invite the children to point to their pictures and to say something about them. After each sharing, invite the children to pray their response.

CURRICULUM CONNECTION

Music Allow the children to listen to a song about Mary. You might play "Hail Mary: Gentle Woman," by Carey Landry, *Young People's Glory and Praise* (OCP, 1984) or "Mother of God," by Douglas P. Crotty, Silver Burdett Ginn's *THIS IS OUR FAITH Music Program*, Program Director's Manual, p.122.

Enriching the Lesson

If possible, take the children to visit your church. Point out the statues, pictures, or stained glass windows of Mary. Explain that the Church honors and loves Mary because she is the mother of Jesus and because she always did what God called her to do. Emphasize that Catholics do not honor the pictures or statues but that we do honor Mary, the person whom these images represent.

SCRIPTURE/DOCTRINE

Objective

This lesson helps the children remember Mary's love for them and discover ways to honor her.

Step 1/INTRODUCTION

Learning About Our Lives

Discovering the Meaning of Birthdays

Encourage the children to talk about their birthdays. Tell them that on their birthdays, people celebrate their birth and remember special things about them. Ask questions like the following to help the children understand.

- What do we celebrate and remember on a birthday? (*Someone's birth*)

- When is your birthday?

- How do people show they remember you and love you on your birthday? (*Answers will vary.*)

- What do you think people remember about you on your birthday? (*Answers will vary but might include such things as they remember you can read, so they bring you a good book; they remember you are big enough to care for things, so they might get you a puppy.*)

Help the children name positive and wonderful things about themselves.

Step 2/DEVELOPMENT

Learning About Our Faith

Remembering Mary's Special Days

Tell the children that we celebrate and remember special days in the life of Mary, the mother of Jesus. Encourage the children to talk about any special days in Mary's life that they remember. Direct their attention to the artwork on page 78. Talk about why Christmas is a special day and discuss Mary's part in it as the mother of Jesus. While discussing Christmas you may wish to refer to Silver Burdett Ginn's *We Celebrate God's Word* (a Big Book), page 6.

Read aloud "Remembering Mary's Love" on page 78. Encourage the children to talk about these great events in Mary's life and ask them what they will always remember about her. In

78

Remembering Mary's Love

When someone loves us, we often remember special things that they do and say.

We remember that the angel
Gabriel visited Mary in Nazareth.
Mary said yes to God's messenger.

We remember that Mary rode
a donkey all the way to Bethlehem.
She gave birth to Jesus.

We remember that Mary loves Jesus
and that she loves us, too.

78 Scripture

Teaching Tips

With the children, plan a way to honor Mary. Consider some of the following options: (1) making paper flowers, taking them to church, and placing them before her statue; (2) gathering in a circle, holding hands, and then having the children say, one by one, something like *Mary, pray for us to God;* or (3) preparing a dramatization about Mary for another class. Encourage the children to find a way that suits the class.

Teaching Tips

You might want to use the story of Joachim and Anne whom tradition names as the parents of Mary. This story is found on page 312 of the children's book under the title "The Birth of Mary." You may tell the children that the Church celebrates Mary's birthday on September 8.

We Honor Mary

To show that we love Mary, we do special things.

▲ We name churches after Mary.

▲ We pray the Rosary and think of Mary and her son, Jesus.

▲ We walk and sing songs about Mary.

Activity

Circle the way you would like to honor Mary.

Prayer 79

---

this discussion, return again and again to the love Mary has for all God's people.

Honoring Mary in Special Ways

Direct the children's attention to page 79. Encourage them to comment on the illustrations. Point out the church with the name of Mary, the procession, and the person saying the Rosary. Point to the word *honor* in the title and ask the children if they know the meaning of this word. Explain that when we honor someone, we show them that they are special to us.

Read aloud "We Honor Mary." Afterward, ask questions like the following.

- Why do we honor Mary? (*Because we love her*)
- What are some ways we honor her? (*We name churches after her, have processions, and pray the Rosary.*)
- What is a procession? (*A procession is a line of people walking. In processions held in church, the people are thinking about God. In the procession on page 79, people are thinking of Mary.*)

Step 3/CONCLUSION

Learning How to Live Our Faith

Choose a Way to Honor Mary

Direct the children to the activity on page 79. Read the directions aloud for the children to follow.

Thanking God for Mary

Gather the children in the prayer area. Tell them that one of the things they can always remember about Mary is that she loves them. Explain that when someone loves them, they remember the special things that person does and says.

When the children are quiet, teach them the following response: *Thank you, God, for Mary.* Then invite volunteers to tell God about the special things Mary has done and said. After each volunteer shares, pray the response with the children.

DAY 5
PRAYER/REVIEW

Objective

This lesson helps the children express their love for Mary by learning the Hail Mary.

Learning the Hail Mary

Read the text on page 80. Before teaching the children the Hail Mary, encourage them to recall the visit the angel Gabriel made to Mary.

Help the children understand that the first part of the prayer (the first 5 lines)comes from the story of Mary and Gabriel. Read aloud each line of the first part of the prayer and explain the vocabulary.

- *Hail* means "hello."
- *Grace* means "God's life and presence."
- *Blessed* means "special and holy."
- *Fruit of your womb* means "Jesus, Mary's son."

After explaining the vocabulary, read the first part of the prayer aloud again.

Next, explain that in the second part of the prayer (the last 3 lines and Amen), they ask Mary to pray to God for them. Read aloud the second part of the prayer. Then ask the children if they have any questions about the prayer. Have the children practice saying the prayer aloud together several times.

Honoring Mary

Show the children the construction-paper crown you prepared before class and let the children hold it and examine it. Explain to them that this is the crown with which they will honor Mary. Then give each child one of the construction-paper flowers you prepared before class.

Have the children process around the classroom. Holding the crown, lead the children to the prayer area.

After the children reach the prayer area, encourage them to quiet themselves. Place the crown on the statue of Mary. Then have each child place his or her flower in the vase in front of the statue of Mary. Invite the children to hold one another's hands and pray out loud the lines of the Hail Mary after you.

Praying The Hail Mary

We can say a special prayer.
In this prayer, we remember
one of Mary's stories.
We remember that the angel Gabriel
came from God to ask Mary to be Jesus' mother.

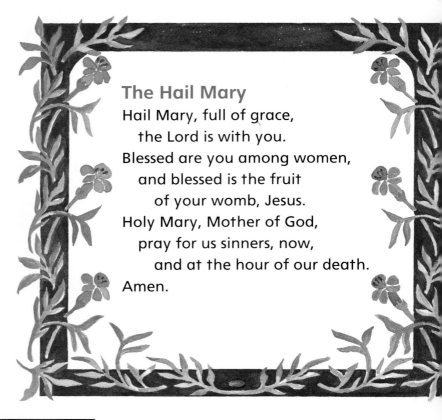

The Hail Mary
Hail Mary, full of grace,
　　the Lord is with you.
Blessed are you among women,
　　and blessed is the fruit
　　　　of your womb, Jesus.
Holy Mary, Mother of God,
　　pray for us sinners, now,
　　　　and at the hour of our death.
Amen.

80   Prayer

The Hail Mary   The prayer skill in this chapter consists of beginning to understand the Hail Mary. The children may also begin to memorize it. The Hail Mary is traditionally divided into two parts: The first part incorporates the words of Gabriel addressed to Mary and the words of Elizabeth, Mary's kinswoman at the visitation. In addition is a petition asking Mary to pray to God for us.

CURRICULUM CONNECTION

Music   Using the melody to "Twinkle, Twinkle, Little Star," teach the following words.
　　Mary, Mary, Mother mine,
　　Thank you for your love
　　　　so kind.
　　Pray for me to God each day,
　　Help me when I work and play.
　　Mary, Mary, Mother mine,
　　Thank you for your love
　　　　so kind.

80

Chapter Review

The angel Gabriel brought a message
from God to Mary.
God asked Mary to be the mother of Jesus.
Mary said yes!
Color Mary's answer to show how happy
God, Mary, and the angel Gabriel were.

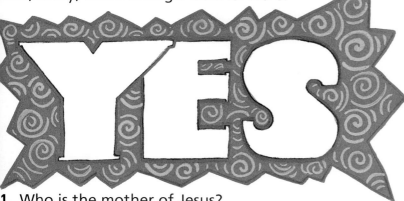

1. Who is the mother of Jesus?

   Mary

2. With whom does Jesus share
   his mother?

   Us

3. Talk about how you can show
   your love for Mary.

Jesus says,
"My mother is
your Mother,
too."
Based on John 19:27

Completing an Activity

Use the activity on page 81 to review Chapter 6. Read the copy at the top of page 81. Talk about how great and how important Mary's response was. Then invite the children to use brilliant colors and creative designs to decorate Mary's response to God's message.

Answering the Questions

Read aloud the first two questions and ask volunteers to respond. Direct the children to print the answers in their texts. Encourage all the children to participate in the discussion of the third question. Be supportive of each child who responds.

Reading the Scripture Verse

Ask the children to read the Scripture verse after you. It is a good way to end the lesson by reflecting on Scripture. If you wish, you may have the children memorize this verse.

Cultural Awareness

If possible, bring to the children's attention versions of the Hail Mary in other languages. Explain that people all over the world pray to Mary in their own languages. Ask if any of the children knows any prayers in languages other than English.

Enriching the Lesson

To help the children learn the words to the Hail Mary, consider playing the song "Hail Mary: Gentle Woman" by Reverend Carey Landry on the album *Young People's Glory and Praise* (OCP, 1984).

Jesus Learned Many Things

Objectives ~~~~~~

To help the children

■ Recognize that Jesus learned as a child much as they learn.

■ Discover that Jesus liked to learn about God.

■ Discover ways in which Jesus learned about the everyday world he lived in.

■ Discover that some signs tell them about God's love.

■ Ask God to help them learn and review the chapter.

Chapter Outline ~~~~~~~~~~

	Step 1 **Learning About Our Lives**	**Step 2** **Learning About Our Faith**	**Step 3** **Learning How to Live Our Faith**
Day 1	■ Introduce the chapter. ■ Complete a checklist. *ABOUT 10 MINUTES*	■ Discover that Jesus learned. ■ Study the text. ■ Present the doctrine. *ABOUT 10 MINUTES*	■ Discover who helps us learn. ■ Write a thank-you note. ■ Share curiosity with God. *ABOUT 10 MINUTES*
Day 2	■ Wonder about life. *ABOUT 10 MINUTES*	■ Discuss a Bible story. ■ Discover how we learn about God. ■ Review the new words. *ABOUT 10 MINUTES*	■ Ask questions about God. ■ Create a bulletin board. ■ Use the bulletin board for prayer *ABOUT 10 MINUTES*
Day 3	■ Ask questions about pictures. *ABOUT 10 MINUTES*	■ Discover ways Jesus learned. ■ Dramatize the story. *ABOUT 10 MINUTES*	■ Discover ways to learn. ■ Complete a learning activity. ■ Thank God. ■ Review the lesson. *ABOUT 10 MINUTES*
Day 4	■ Learn about signs. ■ Listen to a story about signs. ■ Dramatize the story. *ABOUT 10 MINUTES*	■ Learn about signs of God's care. *ABOUT 10 MINUTES*	■ Look for signs of God's love. ■ Complete an activity on signs. ■ Pray with signs of love. *ABOUT 10 MINUTES*

Day 5 **Prayer** Discover that God helps us learn; learn a prayer gesture; learn a song about learning; have a procession, and pray a psalm.

Review Complete an activity; answer the questions; and read the Scripture verse.

Correlation
to the
Catechism of
the Catholic Church

Paragraphs
533–534; 2204;
2712; 2564–2602

Plan Ahead

	Preparing Your Class	Materials Needed
Day 1	For Step 3, prepare ways to help the children name the people who help them learn.	■ pencils ■ writing paper ■ envelopes
Day 2	For Step 1, formulate questions about the things in your world. For Step 3, cut out: *Our Questions about God* and prepare a bulletin board.	■ drawing paper ■ empty bulletin board ■ cut-out letters for a sentence ■ thumbtacks or staples
Day 3	For Step 1 find magazine pictures of people, places, and animals that the children can ask questions about. Frame these pictures with construction paper.	■ colorful magazine pictures ■ construction-paper frames
Day 4	For Step 1, think of what children do that tell things about themselves. For Step 2, have pictures that speak to you of God's love.	■ pictures of people and items that are signs of God's love
Day 5	Learn the melody for "Frère Jacques" or "London Bridge." Plan a procession route to the prayer area.	■ Bible

Additional Resources

As you plan this chapter, consider using the following materials from The Resourceful Teacher Package.

■ *Classroom Activity Sheets* 7 and *7a*

■ *Family Activity Sheets* 7 and *7a*

■ *Chapter 7 Test*

■ *Prayers for Every Day*

■ *Projects: Grade 1*

You may also wish to refer to the following Big Book.

■ *We Celebrate God's Word*, page 7

In preparing the children for the Sunday readings, you may wish to use Silver Burdett Ginn's *Getting Ready for Sunday* student and teacher materials.

BOOKS FOR THE JOURNEY

A Child's First Catholic Dictionary. Richard W. Dyches & Richard Mustachio. Ave Maria Press, 1994. In this book, children can learn many things about God, Jesus, and their Catholic Christian tradition.

God's Love Is for Sharing. Helen Caswell. Abingdon Press, 1987. This delightfully simple book shows us the love God has for the world.

MORE BOOKS FOR THE JOURNEY

It Must Hurt A Lot. Doris Sanford and Graci Evans. Questar Publishers, 1985. When Joshua's puppy is accidentally killed, Joshua discovers some very special secrets that help him cope with death.

The Bee Tree. Patricia Polacco. Putnam, 1993. A child learns from Grandfather that books contain knowledge and wisdom.

REDUCED CLASSROOM ACTIVITIES

Name _____

Jesus Learned Many Things

1. Number the pictures in the right order.
2. Use the numbers 1 through 4.
3. Cut along the heavy black lines.
4. Glue the pictures in the right order on another piece of paper.
5. Tell the story to a friend.

To the Teacher: This activity follows the Scripture story "Jesus Liked to Learn."

Chapter 7   Jesus Learned Many Things   THIS IS OUR FAITH 1   **7**

Name _____

I Can Learn About God

Finish the lists.

1. Where can I learn about God?

_____   _____
_____   _____
_____   _____

2. Who teaches me about God?

_____   _____
_____   _____
_____   _____

To the Teacher: Brainstorm one question at a time with the children and write their ideas on the chalkboard.

7a   THIS IS OUR FAITH 1   Chapter 7   Jesus Learned Many Things

Like Us in All Things but Sin

Jesus was man as well as God and, therefore, had human experiences. Because God entered our flesh and feels our pain and joy, the events of human life are sanctified. We can see and hear God in Jesus.

A chapter in Luke's Gospel records the story of Mary and Joseph finding the twelve-year-old Jesus in the Temple of Jerusalem. The boy Jesus, the Word of God, who communicated to us and shared with us, is depicted as questioning, sharing, eager to learn about God, and just as eager to teach about God. We read ". . . they found him in the temple, sitting in the midst of the teachers, listening to them and asking questions, and all . . . were astounded at his understanding and his answers" (Luke 2:46–47).

Then Jesus journeyed home with Mary and Joseph. He left the Temple behind, for he was still a child, part of a holy family. He had much to learn about life. Mary, Joseph, and people in Jesus' village and in the surrounding countryside would teach him.

As he grew to manhood, Jesus must have questioned and listened to shepherds, farmers, fishermen, weavers, potters, and servants. Later, when he began his public life he had stored in his heart all that he had seen and learned. This learning was a treasure-trove from which he drew forth his parables. Because Jesus had learned about and understood the everyday life of the people, he was able to speak in metaphors familiar to the people and established in their culture.

Childhood is Curiosity

Children by nature have a wondering attitude. Assure the children that their curiosity, their creativity, their boundless energy are gifts from a loving God and that Jesus, too, was once a curious, creative, energetic child.

The stories of Jesus learning in the Temple and being guided by his parents help the children become aware that he, too, was curious and learned about life around him. Encourage an inquisitive attitude in the children, for it lies at the heart of the learning process and can shape a child's future quest for knowledge about God. God invites us to seek meaningful religious answers in our lives. The natural curiosity of children assists them in this quest.

God often speaks to us when we are willing to look at the world through the eyes of a child. Religion classes, liturgical celebrations, the beauty and wonders of nature, the word of God in Scripture, interacting with others, and our thoughts and feelings—all are ways in which God's presence is communicated to us. In your own teaching, help the children find within themselves the boundless beauty of the God who loves them.

DAY 1
DOCTRINE

Objective

This lesson helps the children recognize that Jesus learned as a child in ways similar to the ways they learn.

Step 1/INTRODUCTION

Learning About Our Lives

Introducing the Chapter

Read aloud the chapter title and the focus question on page 82. Stimulate the children's imaginations by sharing some things you wonder about.

Completing a Checklist

Invite the children to study the picture on page 82. Briefly discuss birds and bird-watching.

Read the directions to the activity on page 82 and ask the children to complete it. Afterward, encourage them to share their answers to the checklist. For the last item (*I like to learn about God*), ask the following questions.

- What are some of the things you wonder about God? (*Answers will vary.*)

- What would you like to ask God? (*Answers will vary.*)

Step 2/DEVELOPMENT

Learning About Our Faith

Discovering That Jesus Learned

Encourage the children's comments about the drawing at the top of page 83. Help them realize that this is a drawing of the Holy Family. Then ask the following questions.

- When you look up at the sky at night, what questions do you have? To stimulate discussion, talk about astronomical things you wondered about, such as why the moon has so many shapes.

- What questions do you think Jesus might have had? (*Answers will vary.*)

- How do you get answers to your questions? (*Answers will vary.*)

82

Jesus Learned Many Things

Children wonder and learn all the time. What is one thing you would like to learn

What is one thing you wonder about?

82 Doctrine

Here are some things that many children like to learn.
Print **YES** on the line before each thing you like to learn.

_____ I like to learn how to play games.

_____ I like to learn how to make things.

_____ I like to learn about animals.

_____ I like to learn new songs.

_____ I like to learn about God.

 Teaching Tips

As the children are discussing learning new things, spend time allowing them to volunteer to show each other things they have learned. Or if a child expresses a desire to learn something (for example, how to whistle or to play checkers) any child who knows how can offer to teach the inquisitive child. Suggest the children bring in games they know how to play and teach others when the weather keeps the children indoors at recess.

When Jesus Was a Boy

▲ When you look up at the night sky, what questions do you have?

Jesus listened and asked questions.
Jesus learned about God
and the world around him.
Like Jesus, we can listen and
ask questions.

We Believe

Jesus learned
and so can we.
We can learn about
life and about God.
We can ask Jesus to
help us learn
more about
God.

Focus on

Roofs of Homes Note that in the drawing on page 83, the Holy Family is standing on the roof of their home. Explain to the children that the roofs of the homes in Nazareth were usually flat and the family did many things there: They enjoyed the cool of the evening; the children played games; sometimes they slept there when the temperature became too hot for comfort in the house below. Note that the parapet surrounded the roof and explain that this kept the family members from falling off.

Enriching the Lesson

Talk with the children about the television programs they enjoy watching. Ask what they learn about life or about God by watching these programs. Encourage them to choose two programs that they watch frequently and to pay special attention during the coming week to discover what they learn from these two programs. After the week is over, invite the children to share what they've learned with their classmates and you.

- How do you think Jesus got answers to his questions? (*From Mary and Joseph and other sources, too.*)
- What is one question Jesus might have asked Mary or Joseph? (*Answers will vary.*)

Studying the Text

Read aloud "When Jesus Was a Boy" on page 83. Stress that Jesus learned by being curious, by listening, and by asking questions. Help the children appreciate their own curiosity.

Presenting the Doctrine

Read aloud the We Believe section on page 83, which summarizes the chapter's doctrine. Ask the children to repeat the sentences after you.

Step 3/CONCLUSION

Learning How to Live Our Faith

Discovering Who Helps the Children Learn

Talk with the children about the people who help them learn. *Elicit from the children that they learn from parents, friends, teachers, Scout leaders, grandparents, siblings, and others.* To begin the discussion, ask the following questions.

- Who answers your questions about God?
- Who answers your questions about school?
- Who answers your questions about life?
- Who answers your questions about games?
- Who answers your questions about animals?

Writing a Thank-You Note

Encourage the children to think about one special person who helps them learn and who answers their questions. Distribute writing paper and envelopes and ask each child to write a note thanking that person for his or her help.

Sharing Curiosity with God

Gather the children in the prayer area. When they are quiet, teach them the following response. *Thank you, God, for our curiosity.* Invite volunteers to tell God one thing they are curious about. After each one shares what he or she wonders about, the children should pray their response.

Objective

This lesson helps the children discover that Jesus liked to learn about God.

Step 1/INTRODUCTION

Learning About Our Lives

Wondering About Life

Ask the children to talk about some of their questions and share some of your own with them. Recall Day 1 and the questions the children shared during that lesson. Help them understand that Jesus had many of the same questions.

Emphasize that it is good to ask questions when we want to learn new things and when we don't understand something.

Step 2/DEVELOPMENT

Learning About Our Faith

Discussing a Bible Story

Direct the children's attention to the story "Jesus Liked Learning About God" on page 84. Read the story aloud with expression. Afterward, ask the following questions.

- How old was Jesus when he visited the Temple in Jerusalem? (*Twelve*)
- Whom did Jesus meet at the Temple? (*Rabbis*)
- What are rabbis? (*Teachers*)
- What did they teach Jesus? (*They taught him about life, the Bible, and God.*)
- How did Jesus amaze the rabbis? (*He asked wonderful questions.*)
- Why was Jesus happy? (*He was learning.*)
- Why do you think Jesus wanted to learn more about life, the Bible, and God? (*Answers will vary.*)

Discovering How People Learn About God

Read aloud the text "We Like to Learn About God" on page 85. Invite the children to examine the pictures and to talk about the ways the people in them are learning about God. Finally, ask the children to share their favorite way of learning about God's love for them.

84

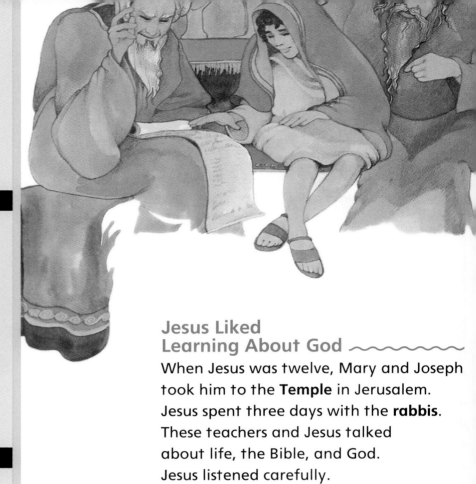

Jesus Liked Learning About God

When Jesus was twelve, Mary and Joseph took him to the **Temple** in Jerusalem.
Jesus spent three days with the **rabbis**.
These teachers and Jesus talked about life, the Bible, and God.
Jesus listened carefully.
He amazed the rabbis with his questions.
How happy he was to learn more!

Based on Luke 2: 41–47

84   Scripture

Enriching the Lesson

Ask the children what they can remember learning about God thus far this year. To jog their memories, use their religion books. Go through Chapters 1–6, pointing out pictures, reading snippets of materials, and helping the children remember all they have learned about God's love for them. Encourage the children to tell stories about themselves and God's love.

Cultural Awareness

Ask the children if they know of different kinds of schools where children might go to learn. Point out that some children go to the public schools, some to Catholic schools, and some to Yeshivas; others attend Amish schools or Christian schools directed by other churches. Tell the children that in some cultures, the children learn by being apprenticed to someone who is a master at a trade or craft.

We Like to Learn About God

Look at each picture.

How are the people learning about God?

What is your favorite way to learn about God's love for you?

New Words

rabbi When Jesus was a boy, a rabbi was someone who taught about God and about life.

Temple The Temple was a holy place in the city of Jerusalem where people prayed and learned about God.

Doctrine 85

DAY 3
SCRIPTURE/DOCTRINE

Objective

This lesson helps the children discover ways in which Jesus learned about his world and about God.

Step 1/INTRODUCTION

Learning About Our Lives

Asking Questions About Pictures

Show the children several colorful magazine pictures framed on construction paper that show life in their world today: the city, the countryside, animals, fish, birds, reptiles, people, and so on.

Invite volunteers to come up with at least one question about each picture. For each picture, print the children's question(s) on the frame surrounding the picture. Then post the pictures somewhere in the classroom.

Step 2/DEVELOPMENT

Learning About Our Faith

Discovering Ways Jesus Learned

Read aloud the text "Jesus Liked to Learn" on page 86. Then ask the following questions.

- What are some things Jesus did? (*Answers will vary.*)
- What did Jesus learn when he watched the birds? (*That God loves the world, cares for birds, and so on*)
- What have you learned when you watched birds? (*Answers will vary.*)
- What did Jesus learn when he picked olives? (*That vegetables and fruit need good soil to grow in*)
- What have you learned when you worked in gardens? (*Answers will vary.*)
- What did Jesus learn when he helped the fishermen? (*A lot about fishing*)
- What have you learned when you fished? (*Answers will vary.*)
- When Jesus looked at his world, what might he have wondered? (*He wondered why.*)
- Where did Jesus find his answers? (*Answers will vary.*)

86

Jesus Liked to Learn

Jesus spent time outside in
God's wonderful world.
He studied things around him.

Jesus looked up in the sky
and watched the birds fly.
He saw that God cares
for them.

Jesus picked olives from trees.
He learned that the best fruit came
from trees planted in good soil.

He saw the fishermen pull in
nets stuffed full of fish.
He liked fishermen.
He chose some of them as special friends.

When Jesus grew up, he told stories
about birds, olives, soil, and fish.
He had enjoyed learning about these things.

Focus on

The view from Nazareth's Hills
From atop the hills surrounding Nazareth, Jesus could have seen the snow covered peaks of Mount Hermon and the Roman road linking Jerusalem to Damascus. Roman soldiers clad in armor marched down this road. Camels and mules carried merchants' wares, the poor people begged for alms, and caravans of Jewish pilgrims traveled to the Temple in Jerusalem.

We Like to Learn About Our World

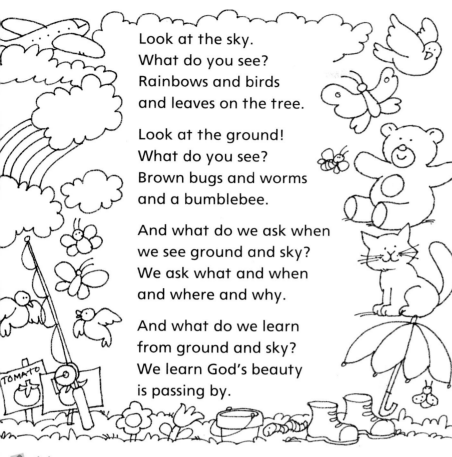

Look at the sky.
What do you see?
Rainbows and birds
and leaves on the tree.

Look at the ground!
What do you see?
Brown bugs and worms
and a bumblebee.

And what do we ask when
we see ground and sky?
We ask what and when
and where and why.

And what do we learn
from ground and sky?
We learn God's beauty
is passing by.

Color all God's gifts you have learned something about.
Circle all God's gifts you have questions about.

Doctrine   87

Dramatizing the Story

Invite volunteers to choose a paragraph to act out from "Jesus Liked to Learn" on page 86. Compliment the children on their creativity.

Step 3/CONCLUSION

Learning How to Live Our Faith

Discovering Ways the Children Learn

Direct the children's attention to "We Like to Learn About Our World" on page 87. Invite their comments on the border around the poem. Then read the poem aloud. Afterward, discuss the questions in the first and second stanzas and invite the children's responses. Discuss what the children can learn when they look at the sky and the ground.

Next, reread Stanza 3. Ask the children to come up with questions that begin with the words *what, when, where,* and *why*. Finally, reread the fourth stanza and encourage the children to talk about God's beauty in their world.

Completing a Learning Activity

Read the directions for the activity at the bottom of page 87. Provide crayons and encourage the children to look at the border of the poem on that page and to do two things: 1) Color all God's gifts they can answer questions about. 2) Circle all God's gifts they have questions about. Afterward, discuss their questions and answers.

Thanking God for Questions and Answers

Gather the children around the magazine pictures they asked questions about in Step 1. When they are quiet, teach them the following response: *Thank you, God, for our questions and our answers.* Read aloud the question on each picture. Then invite volunteers to tell God their answers to these questions. After each volunteer shares, encourage the children to pray their response.

Reviewing the Lesson

To review the lesson ask the following questions.

■ Where did Jesus find answers to his questions? (*Answers will vary.*)

■ What did Jesus learn about God? (*Answers will vary.*)

■ What did Jesus learn about his world when he asked questions? (*Answers will vary.*)

CURRICULUM CONNECTION

Music   The song "When Jesus Was My Age" from Silver Burdett Ginn's THIS IS OUR FAITH Music Program, Grade 1 correlates well with this unit. Perhaps, you would like to introduce it here.

Enriching the Lesson

Print the captions *We Learn from People, We Learn from the World,* and *We Learn from Books* on three large sheets of newsprint. Then tape each sheet to the wall or chalkboard. Recalling the children's wonderful ability to learn, ask volunteers to think of things they have learned from each of these three sources and to print them on the newsprint.

87

DAY 4
DOCTRINE/MORALITY

Objective

This lesson helps the children discover that they can learn from signs and that some signs tell them about God's love.

Step 1/INTRODUCTION

Learning About Our Lives

Learning About Signs

Raise your hand and wave at the children. Then ask them what the gesture means. Next, shake hands with the children and ask them what that gesture means. Finally, smile a big smile and ask them what that facial expression means. Afterward, tell the children that the hand waving, the handshake, and the smile are signs.

Print the word *sign* on the chalkboard and invite the children to show signs of happiness. (*They might smile, dance, clap their hands, raise their arms over their heads, sing, whistle, and so on.*)

Finally, ask the children if they know any more signs that tell people things about them and their world.

Listening to a Story About Signs

Read "We Learn from Signs" on page 88. Afterward ask the following questions.

■ What sign did Sarah use to say goodbye to her mother? (*She waved her hand.*)

■ What did Sarah do in the lunchroom that was a sign of friendship? (*She saved a seat for Stephen.*)

■ When Stephen sat with someone else, what was he telling Sarah? (*Answers will vary.*)

■ What sign of sadness did Sarah show her mother when she got home? (*She cried.*)

■ What sign could Sarah's mother give to help her daughter feel better? (*Answers will vary.*)

■ What sign could Stephen give to Sarah to say, "I'm sorry"? (*Answers will vary.*)

Dramatizing the Story

Invite volunteers to act out the story on page 88. Have the volunteers work in groups of three to tell the story of Sarah, Stephen, and Sarah's mother. Encourage them to use their bodies as signs of how the characters feel. After each

88

We Learn From Signs

When Sarah got on the school bus, she waved to her mother.
That was a good-bye sign.

At lunch time, Sarah saved a seat for Stephen.
That was a sign that they were friends.
But Stephen sat with someone else.
What was that a sign of?

Activity

When Sarah got home from school, she cried.
That was a sign that Sarah was sad about Stephen.

What sign could Sarah's mother give to help her daughter feel better?
What sign could Stephen give to say, "I'm sorry"?

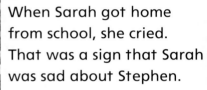

88   Doctrine

CURRICULUM CONNECTION

Social Studies Talk about commonly seen signs—billboards, advertisements, business, highway, and safety signs. Introduce the idea of sign booklets. Give the children the next few days to examine their homes and neighborhoods for signs. Then give each child several pieces of paper. Instruct the children to draw a different sign on each page. Display the booklets in the classroom library.

Signs of God

All around us everywhere
Are signs of life
That show God's care.

Activity

Circle the pictures that show signs of God's care.

1.

2.

3.

4.

5.

6.

Doctrine **89**

CURRICULUM CONNECTION

Music In the THIS IS OUR FAITH Music Program, there are several songs that have accompanying sign language instructions worked out in the *Program Director's Manual*. You might want to sing one such song with the children.

---

presentation, invite the children to applaud as a sign that they liked the dramatization.

Step 2/DEVELOPMENT

Learning About Our Faith

Learning About Signs of God's Care

Tell the children that they can see signs of God's care in their world, too. Share with them some signs that speak to you of God's love and then invite the children to share anything at school, at home, in church, or in nature that speaks to them of God's love.

Step 3/CONCLUSION

Learning How to Live Our Faith

Looking for Signs of God's Love

If possible, take the children outside for a short walk. Have them name things that show God's care and love for them.

Completing an Activity About Signs

Direct the children's attention to the activity on page 89. Read the directions and then have the children circle the pictures that show signs of God's love and care. Afterward, invite the children to share their choices and to talk about what each sign tells them.

Praying with Signs of Love

Gather the children in the prayer area. When they are quiet, teach them the following response: *This is a sign of my love for you, God.* Then invite volunteers to use their bodies to give God a sign of love. (Note that the children might smile, dance, shake hands, clap their hands, raise their arms over their heads, sing, whistle, and so on.) After each child shares a sign, encourage the children to pray the response.

Objective

This lesson helps the children beseech God to help them learn.

Discovering That God Helps Us Learn

Direct the children's attention to page 90. Read the first three lines of "Praying an Asking Prayer" aloud. Open the Bible in your prayer area to the psalms and encourage the children to look at these pages and see that the Old Testament contains 150 psalms.

Reread "Praying an Asking Prayer" aloud, emphasizing the last line, that the children can ask God to help them learn.

Learning a Prayer Gesture

Teach the children a prayer gesture. Have them look at the picture on page 90 and notice the way the children are holding their hands. Explain to them that the children are asking God for help in their prayer. They are holding their hands in such a way that they could receive a gift in them. This is a sign that we trust God will give us what we need and we are ready to receive it. Tell the children they will use this gesture in their prayer today.

Learning a Song About Learning

Teach the children the following song, using the melody "Frère Jacques."

> I am learning;
> I am learning,
> Everyday, everyday.
> I am learning my world.
> I am learning God's love.
> Thank you, God.
> Thank you, God.

Praying an Asking Prayer

Invite the children to sing the song as they process to the prayer area. When they have finished, read the psalm on page 90, having the children repeat each sentence after you. As they pray, encourage them to hold their arms out in front of them with their hands slightly cupped as shown in the picture. End the prayer by singing the song again.

90

Praying an Asking Prayer

Jesus sometimes used the psalms to pray.
Like Jesus, we can use the psalms to pray.
We can ask God to help us learn.

> Teach me, God, what you want me to know.
> Show me your special love.
> Help me to learn what you ask of me.
>
> Based on Psalm 119: 33, 41, 73

90   Prayer

Focus on

Praying by Asking The children are introduced to asking as a kind of prayer. This skill provides readiness for the prayer of petition. Confidence in asking for God's help rests on the children's trust in God. In this session, they will ask God to help them learn, but the concept of asking him for help can be extended to all their needs.

Chapter Review

Draw a line from Jesus to all the gifts that
helped him learn about God and the world.
Put an X by the gifts that help you learn.

1. Name one thing Jesus learned about.

   _____

   The children may name any of the things pictured above or on page 86.

2. At the Temple, who helped Jesus
   learn about life and about God?

   the rabbis

   > Teach me, God,
   > what you want
   > me to know.
   > **Based on
   > Psalm 119:33**

3. Talk about ways that you are
   like Jesus.

Cultural Awareness

Point out that in our Church, many people teach us about God and life. Emphasize that priests do this in a special way by leading our parishes. Tell the children that in the Jewish religion rabbis lead the people in their places of worship called synagogues.

Enriching the Lesson

Make construction-paper stars with a question on each: *Who were Jesus' teachers? Who teaches us about God and life? What book answers questions about God? What Bible prayers did Jesus pray?* Form two teams. Use one side of the chalkboard for each team. As the teams take turns, tape correctly-answered stars to the board. A team can claim a star the other team could not answer by responding correctly. The team with the most stars wins.

Completing an Activity

Use the activity on page 91 of the children's book to review the learning of Chapter 7. Direct the children's attention to the picture of Jesus at the top of page 91. Then read the three lines at the top of the page. Provide the children with crayons and encourage them to draw a line from Jesus to all the gifts that helped him learn about God and the world. Next, have them put an X by the gifts that help them learn, too.

Answering Questions

Read aloud the first two questions and ask volunteers to respond. Direct the children to print the answers in their texts. Encourage all the children to participate in the discussion of the third question. Be supportive of each child who responds.

Reading the Scripture Verse

Ask the children to read the Scripture verse after you. It is a good way to end the lesson by reflecting on Scripture. If you wish, you may have the children memorize this verse.

8 Jesus Prayed

Objectives

To help the children

- Value prayer in their life.
- Learn how Jesus prayed.
- Recognize that, like Jesus, they can pray the psalms.
- Discover ways to get ready to pray.
- Center themselves with one of God's gifts and review the chapter.

Chapter Outline

	Step 1 Learning About Our Lives	**Step 2** Learning About Our Faith	**Step 3** Learning How to Live Our Faith
Day 1	■ Introduce the chapter. ■ Listen and talk. ■ Read a poem. ■ Brainstorm gestures for a poem. *ABOUT 10 MINUTES*	■ Learn more about prayer. ■ Discuss the reasons for prayer. ■ Review the vocabulary. ■ Present the doctrine. *ABOUT 10 MINUTES*	■ Complete an activity on prayer. *ABOUT 10 MINUTES*
Day 2	■ Review the learning from Day 1. ■ Discuss pictures and prayers. ■ Tell stories about the pictures. *ABOUT 12 MINUTES*	■ Learn about Jesus and prayer. ■ Extend the learning about Jesus and prayer. *ABOUT 10 MINUTES*	■ Complete an activity on prayer. ■ Learn how to pray from a picture. ■ Pray with closed eyes. *ABOUT 8 MINUTES*
Day 3	■ Review the learning from Day 2. ■ Complete an activity on prayer. *ABOUT 10 MINUTES*	■ Discover the prayers Jesus used. ■ Learn selections from four psalms. *ABOUT 10 MINUTES*	■ Make prayer cards. ■ Thank God for prayer. *ABOUT 10 MINUTES*
Day 4	■ Review the learning from Day 3. ■ Discuss prayer. ■ Tell a story about getting ready. *ABOUT 5 MINUTES*	■ Learn how to get ready to pray. *ABOUT 10 MINUTES*	■ Share ways the children pray. ■ Draw themselves at prayer. ■ Sing a prayer. *ABOUT 15 MINUTES*
Day 5	**Prayer** Put ourselves in God's presence; learn a prayer technique; choose gifts from nature; and pray in quiet. **Review** Complete the activity; answer the questions; use the children's books; and read the Scripture verse.		

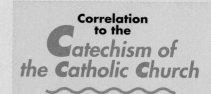

Plan Ahead

	Preparing Your Class	**Materials Needed**
Day 1	For Step 1, be ready to suggest gestures and body movements the children might use as you read the poem on page 92.	
Day 2	For Step 1, collect magazine pictures that show people in a variety of situations. Be prepared to use these pictures to discuss when and where people pray.	■ colorful magazine pictures
Day 3	For Step 3, be prepared to suggest sample prayers for the children to use when they make their prayer cards.	■ index cards
Day 4	Be ready to suggest a song for prayer.	■ drawing paper ■ thumbtacks or staples
Day 5	Learn the song "Kum Ba Yah." Collect an array of stones, flowers, ribbons, leaves, feathers, and pieces of grass.	■ stones, flowers, ribbons, leaves, feathers, and pieces of grass

Additional Resources

As you plan this chapter, consider using the following materials from The Resourceful Teacher Package.

■ *Classroom Activity Sheets 8* and *8a*

■ *Family Activity Sheets 8* and *8a*

■ *Chapter 8 Test*

■ *Prayers for Every Day*

■ *Projects: Grade 1*

You may also wish to refer to the following Big Book.

■ *We Celebrate God's Word,* page 13

In preparing the children for the Sunday readings, you may wish to use Silver Burdett Ginn's *Getting Ready for Sunday* student and teacher materials.

Books for the Journey

A Little Book of Poems and Prayers. Joan Walsh Anglund. Simon & Schuster, 1989. Use this book to show the many ways of praying and the many kinds of prayer.

If You Listen. Charlotte Zolotow. Harper & Row, 1980. Listening is described through a mother helping her child hold onto the love of someone she misses.

More Books for the Journey

Poems and Prayers for the Very Young. Martha Alexander. Random House, 1973. Exquisite prayer–poems by a variety of poets

Sunday's Children. "Signs and Wonders," pp. 8–9; "A Person Who Shares," p. 40. James Bitney and Suzanne Schaffhausen. Resource Publications, 1986. Two prayer–poems that express trust in prayer and hope that God hears us.

Reduced Classroom Activities

Name _____

Jesus Prayed

Draw a picture in each box to finish the prayer.

Thank you, God, for this gift I can see.

Thank you, God, for this gift I can hear.

To the Teacher: Before the children begin this activity you may want to take them on a "five senses" walk. When they return they will be better prepared to draw pictures for this page and page 8a.

Chapter 8   Jesus Prayed   THIS IS OUR FAITH 1   **8**

Name _____

Thank you, God, for this gift I can smell.

Thank you, God, for this gift I can feel.

Thank you, God, for this gift I can taste.

8a   THIS IS OUR FAITH 1   Chapter 8   Jesus Prayed

Background for the Teacher

JESUS LEARNED TO PRAY FROM OTHERS

Mary and Joseph surely taught the boy Jesus to turn prayerfully to God in all the experiences of his life—when he was sad, happy, lonely, grateful, or in need of God's help. Jesus learned the prayers of his people. At the synagogue he would have learned the ancient psalms of praise, love, thanksgiving, repentance, and petition. The daily rituals that culminated in the Sabbath immersed the boy Jesus in a prayerful atmosphere in which his awareness of his unique relationship with God grew ever more intimate.

JESUS PRAYED THROUGHOUT HIS LIFE

The Gospel of Luke depicts Jesus in prayer often, searching out the will of his Father. In Chapter 4 of Luke's Gospel, we find Jesus praying when faced with the temptation to seek earthly power and control. After he began his public life, the tensions of the day, the clamor of the people needing help, and the snide remarks of those who denounced him brought forth in Jesus a great need for prayer. Luke 5:16 tells us that Jesus withdrew "to a deserted place to pray."

Before Jesus chose his Apostles, he "departed to the mountain to pray, and he spent the night in prayer to God" (Luke 6:12). And while praying to God one day on a mountain, Jesus was transfigured, so that the glory of his life in God shone through (Luke 9:28–29).

At the Last Supper, Jesus told Peter that he had prayed that his apostle's faith would not fail. Later that same night at the Mount of Olives, Jesus prayed. There he asked God to deliver him from the horror that was to come. Jesus was able to read the signs of the time and he knew that crucifixion lay before him. And so he asked his Father to take "this cup" from him. Then he accepted whatever was for the good of the universe (Luke 22:41–42).

At the moment of his death, Jesus entrusted himself to God with the words "Father, into your hands I commend my spirit" (Luke 23:46). Having trusted God's love all his life, Jesus trusted God to the end.

EARLY PRAYER EXPERIENCE

Children love to talk and listen, expressing themselves in joy and wonder. Many six-year-olds talk with God without naming what they are doing. In this chapter, you introduce the children to ways in which Jesus prayed. The children can identify with the prayerful experiences of Jesus.

Use every opportunity you can to teach the children that they can pray anywhere and any time. Assure them with perfect confidence that their God is ever-present to them, and that their God enfolds their prayers in love and grace.

Objective

This lesson helps the children value prayer in their lives.

Step 1/INTRODUCTION

Learning About Our Lives

Introducing the Chapter

Read aloud the chapter title and the focus question on page 92. Invite the children to quickly call out what they know about prayer while you list their ideas on the chalkboard.

Listening and Talking

Read "Listening and Talking" on page 92 and invite the children to answer the questions.

Next, divide the class into pairs and invite each set of partners to "talk on the phone" with a friend. Brainstorm some topics they might want to share with their phone partners.

- What they like best about school
- What they like to do on Saturdays
- What their favorite games or hobbies are

Allow a few minutes for the conversations. Ask volunteers to recall what their partners said. Then, explain to the children that in a conversation, they need to talk and to listen.

Reading a Poem

Invite the children's comments on the photograph on page 92. Read the poem with the children. Explain that when they pray, they talk and listen to God just as they did with their partners when they had a "telephone conversation." Discuss the following points.

- Friends like to talk and listen to one another.
- We are God's special friends. God wants to talk to us and is always ready to listen.
- Evening is a good time to be quiet and think over our day. Encourage the children to take a few moments each night to talk to God.

Brainstorming Gestures for a Poem

Brainstorm with the children gestures they might use with each line of the poem on page 92. Provide time to practice the gestures.

Jesus Prayed

What two things do you know about prayer?

Listening and Talking

Whom do you like to talk to?
Whom do you like to listen to?
What do you like to talk about?

Prayer

I said a prayer
And went to bed.
I know God heard
The prayer I said.
My dad told me,
And it is true,
God knows my prayer
Before I do!

92   Prayer

Teaching Tips

In *Your Six-Year-Old: Loving and Defiant*, Louise Bates Ames and Frances L. Ilg maintain that most first graders delight in talking and love to share their thoughts. Nearly all children naturally want to talk to anyone who is interested in them. Your task is to help them realize that no one is more interested in them than God. Emphasize that God delights in talking and in listening to them. Assure the children that they can bring to God all the events of their days and all their feelings.

CURRICULUM CONNECTION

Music   Using the melody to "London Bridge," sing the following words with the children.

I can pray both day and night,
Day and night,
Day and night.
I can pray both day and night.
My God loves me.

Listening and Talking to God

We can talk to God about anything and everything.
God always listens to us.
Talking and listening to God is called **prayer**.

ctivity

Look at each picture and answer the question.

▲ What would you say to God about a baby?

▲ What do you want to say to God about your feelings?

▲ What can you tell God about school?

We Believe

Prayer is talking and listening to God. We grow closer to God when we pray.

New Word

prayer Prayer is listening and talking to God.

Prayer 93

Teaching Tips

Children need concrete examples of experiences they can talk over with God. You may want to encourage them to pray about the wondrous things they saw on a trip; the excitement of a visit to the circus; or their first experience at swimming, dance class, or Little League. Encourage the children to tell God not only what they saw, but also how they felt about their experiences.

Enriching the Lesson

To stress the importance of listening attentively, engage the children in a game of "telephone." Sit the children in a circle, and whisper a sentence in one child's ear. Ask him or her to pass the message along by whispering it to the next child, and so on. Often the message changes during the course of the game, thus teaching the children the importance of careful listening.

Step 2/DEVELOPMENT

Learning About Our Faith

Learning More About Prayer

Read aloud the text "Listening and Talking to God" on page 93. Invite the children to underline the words they think are important. Make this a game by asking which important word begins with G, A, L, P, E, T and so on. Among the important words include *God, anything, listening, prayer, everything, talk.*

Discussing the Reasons for Prayer

Encourage the children to talk about praying. Ask the following questions.

- Why do you like to talk and listen to friends? (*Answers will vary.*)
- What are some things you can tell God, who is your friend? (*How you feel, that you love God, and so on*)
- What are some things you think God might want to say to you? (*Answers will vary.*)
- Where and when do you pray? (*Anytime, everywhere. Children may name specific times and places.*)

Reviewing the Vocabulary

Point to the New Word section on page 93. Ask the children to repeat the word *prayer* and its definition.

Presenting the Doctrine

Read aloud the We Believe section. Ask the children to repeat the sentences after you.

Step 3/CONCLUSION

Learning How to Live Our Faith

Completing a Prayer Activity

Direct the children's attention to the activity on page 93. Encourage them to examine each picture and the accompanying question. Invite the children to close their eyes for a moment and talk to God about the situation. Allow time for quiet personal prayer.

Afterward, emphasize to the children that they can pray to God about anything and everything and that they can pray anywhere and any time.

Objective

This lesson helps the children learn how Jesus prayed.

Step 1/INTRODUCTION

Learning About Our Lives

Reviewing the Learning from Day 1

Recall the gestures the children brainstormed for the poem on Day 1. Then reread the poem on page 92 and invite the children to demonstrate their movements as you read. Invite the children to share what this poem says to them.

Discussing Pictures and Prayers

Have available an array of colorful magazine pictures that show people in a variety of situations. Show the pictures, one by one. Ask the following questions.

- What might the person in this picture say to God? (*Answers will vary.*)
- What might God say to this person? (*The people might be sure that God loves them.*)
- When could the person in this picture pray? (*Answers will vary.*)
- Where could the person in this picture pray? (*Answers will vary.*)

Emphasize that people always and everywhere can ask God for help, praise God, and thank God.

Telling Stories About Pictures

Invite volunteers to tell stories about the pictures and about prayer. Praise the children's creative storytelling.

Step 2/DEVELOPMENT

Learning About Our Faith

Learning About Jesus and Prayer

Direct the children's attention to the drawing on page 94. Invite them to talk about what Jesus is doing (*Sitting in a quiet place talking to God*).

Read aloud the text "Jesus Prayed" on page 94. Connect the story with the illustration on that page. Then ask the following questions.

94

Jesus Prayed

Jesus prayed at home with
Mary and Joseph.
He prayed in the morning.
He prayed in the evening.
He always prayed at meals.
He prayed with others
and alone.

Jesus prayed anytime and
everywhere.
Because he loved God, his
Father, Jesus liked to pray .

94   Scripture

Teaching Tips

Most children are not used to periods of silence when they are with others. In the home there are usually conversations going on, or television or music is playing in the background. Select peaceful instrumental music to play during quiet times and times of prayer. It will help the children feel "at home."

Activity

Like Jesus, we are called to love God.
We, too, can talk and listen to God.
Put an **X** next to each time and
place you like to pray.

☐ outside

☐ inside

☐ in the morning

☐ in the evening

☐ at meals

☐ in church

Prayer 95

- When did Jesus pray? (*In the morning, at meals, in the evening*)
- With whom did Jesus pray? (*With Mary and Joseph, with others, by himself*)
- Where did Jesus pray? (*Everywhere*)
- Why did Jesus like to talk and listen to God? (*Because he loved God*)

Extending the Learning About Jesus and Prayer

Invite the children to think about places where Jesus might have prayed. Help them understand that Jesus could pray anywhere— outside in the hills around Nazareth, by the Sea of Galilee, in the Temple, or in his home.

Ask the children what Jesus might have prayed about. Emphasize that Jesus prayed when he was happy or sad, when he needed help, and when he felt lonely. List on the chalkboard things Jesus might have talked to God about.

Step 3/CONCLUSION

Learning How to Live Our Faith

Completing an Activity on Prayer

Tell the children that the people in the drawings on page 95 are all doing the same thing. Ask the children if they can guess what it is (*praying*). Invite the children to put an **X** next to each time and place they like to pray.

Invite volunteers to choose one of the six pictures and to pretend to be the child in the picture.

or...

Encourage the volunteers to think about and then to share a short prayer that the person in the picture might be saying. Do this for each picture.

Learning How to Pray from a Picture

Direct the children's attention to the illustration on page 94. Talk about prayer. Tell the children that people often like to sit quietly and close their eyes when they pray. Explain that thinking about God may be easier this way.

Praying with Closed Eyes

Gather the children in the prayer area. Invite the children to sit on the floor in a semicircle and to close their eyes and breathe deeply. As the children sit with their eyes closed, read them the text on page 94.

Teaching Tips

To help the children discuss the possibilities of what the boy Jesus might have talked to God about, invite the children to look over the illustrations in Chapter 5. This artwork may help the children recall daily occurrences of life in the time of Jesus, such as household tasks, outdoor activities, and things learned. Remind the children that Jesus would have told God about his feelings, too.

Enriching the Lesson

Talk with the children about the custom of praying before and after meals. Explain that meals are special times when the family gathers to share some of God's gifts of food. Encourage the children to remind their families to pray before and/or after meals. Help the children make up a simple prayer they and their families might use when praying at meals. For instance, you might suggest the following prayer: *Dear God, Bless this food we are sharing together. Help everyone in the world to get enough food to eat.*

95

Objective

This lesson helps the children extend the concept that, like Jesus, they can pray the psalms.

Step 1/INTRODUCTION

Learning About Our Lives

Reviewing the Learning from Day 2

Recall the children's discussion on Day 2 about what Jesus might have prayed about. Ask the children what Jesus might have said to God when Jesus was happy, when he was sad, when he needed help, or when he was scared. You might want to list some of their ideas on the chalkboard.

Completing an Activity on Prayer

Direct the children's attention to the activity on page 96. Read aloud the text at the top of the page and within the speech balloons. Encourage the children to think of a time when they were feeling thankful, scared, sorry, happy, or in need of help. Distribute crayons and invite the children to draw a picture of that time and then to draw a line to connect the appropriate speech balloons to the picture.

When the children have completed their drawings, invite volunteers to share their work and to talk about what prompted their prayers.

Step 2/DEVELOPMENT

Learning About Our Faith

Discovering the Prayers Jesus Used

Encourage the children's comments about the illustrations on page 97. Then read aloud the text "Kinds of Prayer." Talk about the psalms and help the children recall that they prayed a psalm in Chapter 7.

Ask the children to turn to page 70. Read aloud the psalm on that page and recall the children's learning on page 90. Read aloud the psalm on that page and recall the children's learning on that day. Invite their comments on the psalm.

96

Talking to God

We can talk to God about many things.

Activity

Below are some things that people tell God when they pray.
Think of a time you said one of these things to God.

Draw a picture of that time.
Then draw a line to connect the prayer to your picture.

"Thank you, God!"

"I'm sorry, God!"

"God, I'm scared!"

"God, help me!"

"God, I love you!"

Focus on

The Psalms   Explain to the children that the Book of Psalms is one of the oldest books of prayer the Jewish people and Christians have. Tell the children that many people composed these prayers over a long period of time and that the Jewish people finally collected the hymns in one book. Stress that Jesus and all the Jewish people he knew learned psalms by heart and prayed some of them daily.

CURRICULUM CONNECTION

Handwriting   After completing "Reviewing the Learning from Day 2," have each child choose one of the prayers listed on the board. Encourage each child to choose one that he or she identifies with, such as one Jesus prayed when he was happy or worried. After copying and proofreading their work, the children can decorate it with a drawing of themselves saying the prayer.

Kinds of Prayer

Jesus talked to God about many things.
Jesus often used his own words to pray.
Sometimes Jesus prayed the psalms
that are from the Bible.
Here are some kinds of prayers he said.

O Lord, my God,
you are great and good.

Based on Psalm 104:1

 Praise

I will give thanks to you,
O Lord, with all my heart.

Based on Psalm 9:2

 Thanks

Listen to me, O Lord,
and be my helper.

Based on Psalm 30:11

 Help

I love you, O Lord.
You keep me safe.

Based on Psalm 18:2, 4

 Love

Scripture   97

★★★★★
Enriching the Lesson
★★★★★

Help the children memorize the four psalms on page 97 by reading them over from time to time and by finding key words that will help with the memorization. Encourage the children to use these psalms often. You might use these four psalms on a rotating basis as morning prayer for a while.

Learning Selections from Four Psalms

Direct the children to the four psalms on page 97. Encourage them to look at each illustration and to say what feeling the picture is illustrating. Read aloud each psalm and ask the children to repeat it after you. Discuss situations in which a child might say each prayer. (For example: A child might say a prayer of praise on a sunny day or a prayer of thanksgiving because she or he got to spend the day with a special person, such as Grandma or Uncle Joe. A child might ask God for help when someone is ill or say "I love you, God" when he or she thinks of God.)

Finally, ask the children: Which psalm from the Bible do you want to pray? Encourage volunteers to reply and to share the reasons for their choices.

Step 3/CONCLUSION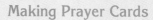

Learning How to Live Our Faith

Making Prayer Cards

On page 97, reread the types of prayer Jesus learned. Ask the children to choose one of these four types and to make up a short prayer following the same pattern. If necessary, suggest the following sample prayers.

- Praise—*Lord, I think you are wonderful because you made such a beautiful world for us. Amen.*
- Thanksgiving—*Dear God, Thank you for all your loving gifts. Amen.*
- Help—*God, help me to always do the best I can in everything. Amen.*
- Love—*Oh God, I love you with all my heart because you are so good. Amen.*

Distribute index cards and ask the children to print and decorate their prayers on the cards. Encourage the children to take their prayer cards home, keep them in a special place, and use them to pray.

Thanking God for Prayer

Gather the children in the prayer area. Teach them the response: *Thank you, God, for listening and talking to us.* Invite volunteers, in turn, to pray prayers of praise, thanks, help and love. After each volunteer prays, encourage the children to pray their response.

DAY 4
PRAYER

Objective

This lesson helps the children discover ways to get ready to pray.

Step 1/INTRODUCTION

Learning About Our Lives

Reviewing the Learning from Day 3

Help the children recall what they know about the psalms. Recall that by praying the psalms, the children can praise and love God, thank God, and ask God for help. Encourage them to recite any of the psalms they remember.

Discussing Prayer

To sum up the learning of the last few days, read aloud the definition of prayer on page 93. Then ask the following questions.

■ What do you talk to God about? (*Answers will vary.*)

■ Do you ever listen to God? (*Answers will vary.*)

Help the children remember that God is always listening to them and loving them.

Telling a Story About Getting Ready

Read page 98. Ask the children what they do to get ready for school each day and have them mark an **X** next to each thing they do to get ready.

Step 2/DEVELOPMENT

Learning About Our Faith

Learning How to Get Ready to Pray

Explain that when the children pray, they also need to get ready to talk and listen to God. Read "Getting Ready to Pray" on page 99.

As you read aloud each of the preparations Winona made for prayer, invite the children's comments. Ask the following questions.

■ In what quiet place can you pray? (*Answers will vary.*)

■ When can you go to this quiet place to pray? (*Answers will vary.*)

98

ctivity

Roberto gets ready for school each day.
Look at all the things he does.
Put an **X** next to each thing you do
to get ready for school.

☐ Check on the weather report.

☐ Comb your hair.

☐ Pack your books.

☐ Put out your clothes.

Focus on

A Jewish Prayer Custom   One Jewish custom is associated with the doorpost of the Jews' homes. The Book of Deuteronomy 6:7–9 instructed the people to write God's Great Commandment on their doorposts. This was called the Mezuzah. Today, these words are placed in a small box. Upon entering or leaving the house, people reach up, touch the Mezuzah, and kiss the hand that caressed the holy text. They say, "May God keep my going out and my coming in" (Psalm 121:8).

Getting Ready to Pray

Winona wants to pray.
She gets ready to talk and listen to God.

She finds a quiet place
to pray.

Winona makes the Sign
of the Cross.

She tries to think only
about God.

Winona talks to God about
the beautiful world.

Prayer 99

- Which of you wants to show us how to make the Sign of the Cross? (*Children demonstrate*)
- What could you tell God about your day today? (*Answers will vary.*)

Step 3/CONCLUSION

Learning How to Live Our Faith

Sharing Ways the Children Pray

Invite the children to talk about the ways they prepare to pray. Talk about special times and places, or special prayers they use. In this discussion, stress that the children can use their own words, the psalms, or the Hail Mary; that they can pray any time and anywhere; that they can pray aloud or silently; that they can use their bodies and their minds and hearts; and that they can tell God anything. Ask the following questions to have children discuss ways of using their bodies to pray and demonstrate the procedure.

- Which of you likes to raise your arms up when you pray?
- Who likes to fold his or her hands to pray?
- Who likes to kneel to pray?
- Who likes to sit comfortably and quietly?
- Who likes to close his or her eyes to pray?

Drawing Themselves at Prayer

Distribute drawing paper and crayons or felt-tip markers. Invite the children to draw pictures of themselves when they are praying.

Singing a Prayer

Gather the children in the prayer area and invite them to sing one of the songs they have learned this year. Assure them that God likes to hear their singing and that God is happy to see them singing and moving to the music.

or...

With the help of teacher's aides who will be with the children, allow the children to choose one of several sites to pray: the church, outdoors, the prayer area. They may use any prayerful posture they wish.

99

Objective

This lesson helps the children to concentrate on one of God's gifts of nature, by praying as they hold that gift.

Putting Ourselves in God's Presence

Explain to the children that before praying, it is always good to stop and remind ourselves that God is always with us. That means that God is with us right now.

or...

Teach the children the song "Kum Ba Yah." Explain that the phrase *kum ba yah* means "Come by me." Explain that when the children sing this song, they are asking God to be with them.

Learning a Prayer Technique

Tell the children that today they will get ready to pray in a new way. Explain that holding one of God's beautiful gifts of nature can sometimes help them think only of that thing and then they can talk to God about it. Remind them of Winona doing this on page 99.

Using the Children's Book

Read aloud the text "Praying with God's Gifts" on page 100. Discuss how praying with one of God's gifts can quiet the children and help them concentrate, thinking of one thing to pray about.

Show the children the selection of stones, flowers, ribbons, leaves, feathers, and pieces of grass that you have brought to class. Invite the children, one by one, to choose one of these gifts from God to hold while they pray today.

Praying with an Object

Invite the children to carry their objects to the prayer area. Have them sit quietly and remind them that God is always with them. Ask them to greet God quietly in their own way. Or if you taught "Kum Ba Yah," sing it now. Tell the children the words ask God to "Come by me."

Invite the children to silently talk to God about the objects they are holding—where it came from, what it does, its color, shape or weight, how much they like it, and so on.

100

Praying with God's Gifts

God loves us and give us many gifts.
When we pray, we can hold one of God's gifts.
The gift will remind us of God's love.
The gift will help us to be quiet inside.

Activity

Circle one of the gifts you would like to hold as you talk to God.

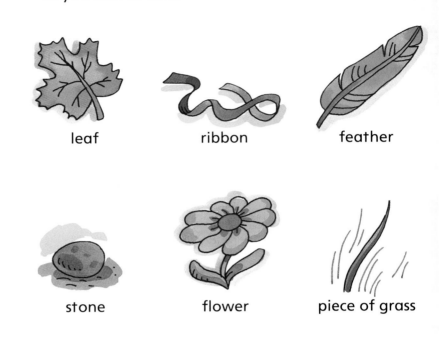

leaf   ribbon   feather

stone   flower   piece of grass

Focus on

Praying with an Object Help the children pray by concentrating on a single interesting object. They may choose this object from a variety of objects you have ready for them. This is, of course, an excellent centering technique, but the children do not have to be taught this term. Simply, give them the opportunity to talk to God about a wonderful gift of God.

Chapter Review

Cross out all the **R** letters.

`RR I RRCANRRTALKRRTORRGODRR`

What message can you read?
Copy the message below.

I can talk to God.

1. What do we call listening and talking to God?

   prayer

2. Where can we pray?

   any place

3. Talk about when, why, and where you pray.

Always
remember
to pray.

Based on
Colossians 4:2

Completing an Activity

Use the activity on page 101 to review Chapter 8. Read the directions to the children and then invite them to use pencils or crayons to cross out all the *R*s and find the message. Encourage them to copy the message on the lines provided.

Answering the Questions

Read aloud the first two questions on page 101 and ask volunteers to respond. Direct the children to print the answers in their texts. Encourage all the children to participate in the discussion of the third question. Be supportive of each child who responds.

Reviewing by Circling

Ask the children to circle the gifts pictured on page 100 that they chose to hold as they prayed. Stress that the gift can help them remember the wonderful things God made. If they choose things not pictured, ask them to draw these on the page.

Reading the Scripture Verse

Ask the children to read the Scripture verse after you. It is a good way to end the lesson by reflecting on Scripture. If you wish, you may have the children memorize this verse.

Enriching the Lesson

Reviewing the Chapter Invite the children to flip through the chapter and play a game with the illustrations. Ask the children to find a picture of a child saying night prayers (*pages 92 and 95*); of a child praying in church (*page 95*); of someone telling God about how he or she feels (*pages 92, 93, 96, and 99*) and; of Jesus praying (*page 94*). As the game progresses, a child could call out the clues and the others find the pictures.

101

Using the Unit Organizer

Completing a graphic organizer such as a chart or table can help students to organize the information that has been presented in the unit. Organizers can enable students to visualize their thinking and recognize relationships among ideas. This will give students the opportunity to understand more completely the materials they have been studying.

Completing the Organizer

The theme of Unit 2 is that Jesus learned about life. The child Jesus learned about life and God mainly within the context of the Holy Family. Therefore, the Unit 2 Organizer has been designed against the background of their home in Nazareth.

With the children, look at each picture of the Holy Family and have the children identify what the members are doing. Then direct the children's attention to the phrase directly under the picture. Look at the first word and alert the children that only the first letter is given. Direct them to complete the word. When all have finished, call on volunteers to read all the phrases, summarizing the unit.

Looking Back: Self Assessment

To help the children assess what they have learned ask these or similar questions.

- What story in this unit did you most enjoy? Why?

- Which picture in this unit did you like best? Why?

- Which person in this unit would you like to learn more about?

Unit **2** Organizer

Finish the words.

W<u>orked</u> together   P<u>rayed</u> together

The Holy Family

L<u>earned</u> from one another   L<u>oved</u> each other

Unit 2 Review

Draw a line to match the words with their meanings.

1. The Holy Family •   • messenger from God

2. Angel   •   • Jesus' hometown

3. Nazareth   •   • Jesus' family

Circle the correct word to complete each sentence.

1. Joseph was a _____.
   doctor   (carpenter)

2. _____ is the mother of Jesus.
   (Mary)   Gabriel

3. Jesus' teachers were called _____.
   holy men   (rabbis)

4. The _____ is a place where people pray.
   hall   (Temple)

5. Jesus learned to pray _____ and everywhere.
   sometimes   (anytime)

6. _____ is listening and praying to God.
   Baptism   (Prayer)

Unit **2** Review

Look at the pictures below.
Fill in the first letter of each word.

1.  _m_ oon   4.  _h_ ouse

2. _o_ wl   5.  _e_ lephant

3. _t_ ree   6.  _r_ ainbow

The first letters form a new word.
Write the new word.

Mary is our _Mother_ .

SKILLS FOR CHRISTIAN LIVING

DAY TO DAY

BECOMING A FEELINGS DETECTIVE

We can discover how others feel. We can look and listen.

◢Activity

Each picture below shows a different feeling.
Look for the clues in the pictures that tell how
Boots and Zip are feeling.
Match the "feeling" words to the correct pictures.

1. Happy   2. Shy   3. Angry   4. Proud

Day to Day   105

🍎 Teaching Tips

Your "Feelings Detectives" can use both voice and body clues to detect feelings. Voice clues include both tone and content—what is said as well as how it is said. For example, the person in the picture on page 105 is showing anger. Ask your "detectives" if they can recognize a speaking clue in the picture. (The person looks to be yelling.) Emphasize that what we say as well as how we say it are important clues in detecting feelings.

Day to Day

Objective

This lesson helps the children recognize verbal and nonverbal clues that signal how another person might be feeling.

Looking for Clues

Write the words *detective* and *clue* on the board. Ask the children if they know what these words mean. Explain that a detective is someone who looks for evidence (or clues) to help solve a mystery. Invite the children to become detectives. Tell them that they must look for clues that tell how people feel. Two types of clues are especially important: body clues, or how someone looks, and voice clues, or what someone says and the tone of voice the person uses when saying it. Demonstrate feeling happy and feeling angry by using your body and voice (in an exaggerated form). Or, use popsicle-stick puppets or hand puppets, combined with your voice, to show the emotions. If the children find it difficult to determine the feeling, repeat the demonstration, this time freezing in motion the exaggerated form and emphasizing even more the tone of voice.

Completing the Activity

Read aloud the directions to the activity on page 105. Read the feelings aloud and ask volunteers to share examples of times they experienced these feelings. Have the children write the number of the feeling in the box of the picture that best illustrates the emotion. Invite the children to share their responses. When they have finished this page they may continue with the activity on page 106.

Lesson continues on page 106.

Concluding the Lesson

Help the children understand that there are many reasons that it is important to be able to recognize how other people are feeling. Among them are the following.

- To help the other person if they are sad
- To share their joy if they are happy and their friendship if someone feels lonely
- To know to wait to ask for help if the other person is upset or mad

Tell the children that by recognizing how someone feels we can do as Jesus asks. We can care for others who need our help and friendship.

Read with the children the concluding statements in the Following Jesus section.

Follow-Up Activities

Provide a grab bag full of folded papers with "feeling" words printed on them. Invite the children to take turns selecting a "feeling" word and dramatizing the feeling. Have the children try to guess what feelings are being enacted. Then have a follow-up discussion to identify the clues the detective uncovered.

Ask the children to play detective during the day to discover how many different "feelings" they observe. Provide a space on the chalkboard or on a bulletin board entitled *On the Lookout for Feelings*. The children may write on the board the names of any feelings they have observed. Stickers or stars could be added under a particular feeling word to mark each time the feeling was observed.

106

Activity

Here are more "feeling" words and pictures to match. Be a good Feelings Detective!

1. Worried   2. Sad   3. Embarrassed

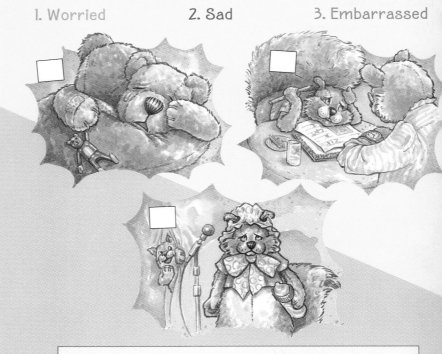

Following Jesus

Jesus asks us to care about people.
Knowing how someone feels helps us to care.
We can tell how someone feels by
LOOKING and **LISTENING**.

★ Enriching the Lesson

Have volunteers act out these feelings. The others may guess what the feelings are.

Happy: A smile, straight body posture, skipping

Sad: A frown, slouched body posture, hands in pocket

Angry: Closed eyes, clenched fists or jaw, yelling mouth

Worried: Crinkled lips, raised eyebrow, tight body posture, biting nails

Shy: Head down and cocked, downcast eyes, slumped body posture

Embarrassed: Blushing face, hunched shoulders

OPENING DOORS

A Take-Home Magazine™

Growing Closer

FIND THE BOOK OF PSALMS in the Old Testament section of the Bible. Read a few psalms, either alone or to your family. Then, write your own family "psalms." Psalms can express praise, thanks, sorrow, or petition. Use your "psalms" as meal prayers or bedtime prayers.

I will give You thanks, O God, with all my heart.

AS A FAMILY, discover one way you can all learn more about God. Try reading the Scriptures together, discussing a topic such as prayer, or joining Bible classes for children and adults in your parish.

Looking Ahead

To help your child realize the importance of caring for ourselves and others, Unit 3 focuses on Jesus' teaching and example. Your child will learn that prayer is one expression of caring that Jesus lived and taught. He or she will also learn the Our Father and will consider the meaning of this prayer in our daily lives.

8

Opening Doors ~~~

Sending the Magazine Home

As you complete Unit 2 with your class, assist the children in carefully removing *Opening Doors: A Take-Home Magazine* (two pages) from their texts by separating the magazines from the book along the perforations. Demonstrate how to fold the two magazine pages to form an eight-page booklet. Ask the children to take the magazines home and encourage their families to read them and participate in the suggested activities.

Praise the Word of the Lord!

When we were young, we were taught to be respectful. Standing when introduced to a dignitary, offering our seat on the bus to an elderly person, or holding the door open were ways we learned to show deference. Catholics have always esteemed certain people, places, and things because they are of God. One of those things that we hold sacred is the Bible. Over the centuries, we honored God's word and developed traditions to show reverence for the Scriptures, especially when they are read at Sunday Mass. These rituals are described below.

The Scripture readings are in the Lectionary. The book called a Lectionary contains all the Scripture readings for Mass. It is sometimes covered elaborately to show the regard we have for God's word.

The Lectionary has a special place. Believing that the Lectionary contains the message of Jesus, we carry it in procession to the lectern. In many parishes, the book is displayed on the front ledge of the lectern where it can be reverenced throughout the week.

We sing "Alleluia." To prepare ourselves to hear the message of Jesus, we sing Alleluia, which means "Praise the Lord."

Ordinarily, the opinion of women was unsolicited, but Luke includes the responses of three women to highlight Jesus' sense of the importance of women. Mary, the faithful handmaiden, becomes the mother of the Savior. Elizabeth, her cousin and John the Baptizer's mother, acknowledges the presence of Jesus in Mary's womb. Anna, the aged prophetess in the Temple, is together with Simeon the symbol of the faithful Jewish people who longed for the Messiah.

You can see from these examples that Luke brought together many stories and Old Testament prophecies to help the early Christians better understand Jesus. Matthew, too, used the infancy narratives to interpret the meaning of Jesus. Writing for the many Christian Jews that existed in his time, Matthew opens his gospel with a genealogy of Jesus. Designating Jesus as "the son of David," the author establishes the newborn infant as the anticipated royal Messiah. Matthew highlights the childhood suffering of Jesus—the persecution by Herod and the subsequent flight into Egypt. For Jesus' Jewish audience, these stories depict Jesus as reliving the experiences of the People of Israel. The Holy Family takes refuge in Egypt as their ancestors did many generations ago, and like Moses, Jesus is called out of Egypt to save the people.

Although we do not discover many facts about the childhood of Jesus from the infancy narratives, we can learn much about Jesus.

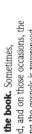

We incense the book. Sometimes, incense is used, and on those occasions, the book containing the gospels is reverenced.

A special minister proclaims the gospel. To emphasize the importance of the gospel, a special minister—the deacon—reads the gospel. When no deacon is available, the priest proclaims the gospel.

We have an "honor guard." At times ministers, often servers, stand with lighted candles to honor the words of Jesus. You have probably seen this on festive days such as Christmas.

We stand for the reading of the gospel. Standing has long been considered a sign of respect. While we sit for the other readings during the Liturgy of the Word, we stand to hear Jesus' message.

God's word is praised. At the end of the gospel, the deacon or priest says,
"The word of the Lord."
We respond,
"Praise to you, Lord Jesus Christ."

We venerate the gospel book. At Mass both the altar and the gospel book are kissed by the priest. This action is a sign that both the table and the word are signs of the presence of Jesus.

The Childhood of Jesus

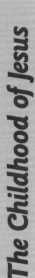

Christians have always been curious about the childhood of Jesus. We love to imagine Jesus helping Joseph in the carpenter shop or drawing water for Mary at the well. Actually the Bible tells us nothing of these kinds of facts. Even such familiar things as the manger scene imprinted on our Christmas cards have much more meaning than meets the eye.

Why are details about Jesus' early life so noticeably absent from the gospels? The reason is that the authors did not intend to draft biographies of the baby Jesus but rather to answer questions such as "Is Jesus really the Messiah?" or "Can Jesus really be God if he was born here on earth? Two gospels tell of the event surrounding the birth and early childhood of Jesus in stories that we call infancy narratives: Matthew 1:1–2:23 and Luke 1:5–2:52.

Addressing the question, "Who is Jesus Christ?" Luke portrays the joy and peace associated with the Savior's coming to earth. "On earth peace to those on whom his favor rests," proclaims the heavenly host the first Christmas night (Luke 2:14).

Luke also shows Jesus' concern for the poor and the lowly in the infancy narratives. It was no accident that the lowly shepherds were the first to behold the newborn Savior. They are signs for us all that God favors the poor and the lowly.

Learning More About God

The Liturgy of the Word contains several distinct yet related parts. These pages will focus on two of these parts: the responsorial psalm and the homily. Read these pages with your child and talk about the illustrations. Help your child complete the activity.

Read Along

When Jesus was about my age, Mary and Joseph took him to the Temple to pray. Jesus probably prayed special prayers called psalms.

When I go to Mass with my family, I pray the psalms, too. Sometimes I say the psalm aloud. Sometimes I sing it.

4

At the Temple, the rabbis and Jesus talked about God. Together, they read stories from the Bible. Then the rabbis and Jesus discussed what those stories meant.

At Mass I hear stories from the Bible, too. The priest or deacon helps me understand what the stories mean. This is called the homily.

I try to listen carefully. I want to learn more about God, just as Jesus did!

Circle the pictures of people who help you learn more about God.

Pray the responsorial psalm with the priest and people the next time you go to Mass. Listen carefully to the homily.

5

110

How do you show you love someone?

UNIT 3

Jesus Teaches Us To Love

To help the children learn that Jesus teaches us about God's love for us and how we should respond to that love.

Doctrinal Summaries

CHAPTER 9

Jesus teaches us that God his Father cares for all living things and for people most of all.

CHAPTER 10

Jesus loves and cares for everyone. One way Jesus cares for people today is through the actions of caring people, including each one of us.

CHAPTER 11

Jesus teaches us to care for people who need help.

CHAPTER 12

Jesus prayed and teaches us to pray.

Note:

As you prepare to teach this unit, you might wish to consult the reference section, *Our Catholic Heritage,* beginning on page 327.

Additional resources for Unit 3 include a Unit Test and a Family Letter as well as a video and selections from THIS IS OUR FAITH Music Program. You might also find it helpful to preview *Saints and Other Holy People* and *Prayer Celebrations* for possibilities to enhance the unit.

Introducing the UNIT

Direct attention to the photograph on page 111 and ask the children to tell a story about what is happening in the picture. Help the children recognize that the parent and the child are showing love for each other. Read aloud the unit-focus question and invite the children's responses. Emphasize that we can show love for others in many different ways. Tell the children that in Unit 3, they will learn how Jesus wants us to love others.

Vocabulary

trust
Peter
Andrew
Good Samaritan
hallowed
heaven
trespass

Jesus Teaches Us That God Cares

Objectives

To help the children

■ Recognize that people and all living things need care.

■ Understand that God provides care for all living things.

■ Discover ways in which God cares for all creation and for them.

■ Plan ways they can help God care for the world.

■ Express praise for God and review the chapter.

Chapter Outline

	Step 1 **Learning About Our Lives**	Step 2 **Learning About Our Faith**	Step 3 **Learning How to Live Our Faith**
Day 1	■ Introduce Chapter 9. ■ Use a picture story to learn about caring. ■ Extend the concept of care. *ABOUT 7 MINUTES*	■ Learn about God's care. ■ Draw a picture about needs. *ABOUT 10 MINUTES*	■ Find ways the children care. ■ Create a bulletin board. ■ Use the bulletin board for prayer. *ABOUT 13 MINUTES*
Day 2	■ Draw how God cares for God's creation. *ABOUT 10 MINUTES*	■ Listen to a Bible story. ■ Discuss an illustration. ■ Act out the story. ■ Review vocabulary and doctrine. *ABOUT 12 MINUTES*	■ Choose ways to care. ■ Use the Bible story for prayer. *ABOUT 8 MINUTES*
Day 3	■ Find ways to care for God's creation. *ABOUT 5 MINUTES*	■ Discuss God's creation. ■ Learn how God cares for all creation. *ABOUT 12 MINUTES*	■ Complete an activity. ■ Find ways to care. ■ Gather for prayer. *ABOUT 13 MINUTES*
Day 4	■ Use the bulletin board. *ABOUT 7 MINUTES*	■ Discover ways to care for creation. ■ Learn from pictures. *ABOUT 8 MINUTES*	■ Plan ways to care for creation. ■ Draw caring for creation. ■ Pray for help in caring. *ABOUT 15 MINUTES*
Day 5	**Prayer** Read the children's book; have a procession; and praise God for all of creation. **Review** Use the children's drawings to review; complete an activity; answer the questions; and read the Scripture verse.		

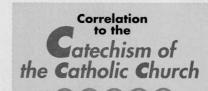

Correlation
to the
**Catechism of
the Catholic Church**

Paragraphs
340, 342–343

Plan Ahead

	Preparing Your Class	**Materials Needed**
Day 1	For Step 3, collect magazine pictures that show people and things the children can care for. Cut out: *We help God care for all creation.*	■ crayons, paper, paste, colorful magazine pictures ■ empty bulletin board ■ cut-out letters
Day 2	For Step 2, practice reading the Bible story with enthusiasm.	■ drawing paper
Day 3	For Step 1, collect at least seven colorful pictures that show God's creation. Select a place to display them after the children finish their work.	■ pictures of each of the following categories: bugs, vegetables, flowers, birds, animals, trees, and people
Day 4	For Step 3, consider things the children could do to care for God's world. Select a place to display the children's drawings.	■ drawing paper
Day 5	Be prepared to use the children's drawings from Day 4. Obtain an instrumental music piece and collect musical instruments for the procession.	■ drawings from Day 4 ■ musical instruments (cymbals, drums, whistles, spoons)

Additional Resources

As you plan this chapter, consider using the following materials from The Resourceful Teacher Package.

■ *Classroom Activity Sheets 9 and 9a*

■ *Family Activity Sheets 9 and 9a*

■ *Chapter 9 Test*

■ *Prayers for Every Day*

■ *Projects: Grade 1*

In preparing the students for the Sunday readings, you may wish to use Silver Burdett Ginn's *Getting Ready For Sunday* student and teacher materials.

BOOKS FOR THE JOURNEY

Sunday's Children. "Nervous Eyes," p. 32. James Bitney. Resource Publications, 1986. This is a prayer poem that expresses belief that God cares for all things.

The Velveteen Rabbit. Margaret Williams. Simon and Schuster Trade, 1994. Caring makes people and things real.

MORE BOOKS FOR THE JOURNEY

A Thousand Pails of Water. Ronald Roy. Alfred A. Knopf, 1978. A child's care for a beached whale inspires a whole village to care.

All the Places to Love. Patricia MacLachlan. Harper Collins, 1994. A book that sensitively shares the experience of a family's love for each other and the living things that surround them.

REDUCED CLASSROOM ACTIVITIES

Name

Jesus Teaches Us That God Cares

1. Use a green crayon to color all the spaces with an X.
2. Use the word to finish the sentence below the puzzle.

God cares for ___people___ most of all.

To the Teacher: This activity follows the Scripture story "Jesus Teaches Us About God."

Name

Sharing Our Love

Flowers are gifts from God.
They show us that God loves us.

1. Color the flower.
2. Cut along the heavy black line.
3. Write your name or initials on the flowerpot.
4. Glue a craft stick to the back of the flowerpot.
5. "Plant" a class garden in your special prayer place and continue to care for each other.

To the Teacher: This activity explains that we are called to care for others as God cares for us. Flowers can be "planted" in clay or posted on the bulletin board.

GOD'S LOVING CARE

In the Book of Genesis, we read the account of creation and learn that all creation is good, for it reflects the goodness and beauty of the Creator. Flowers, trees, vegetables, bugs, animals, birds, fish, people—all are filled with God's glory.

Following this short account, the Bible expands into the centuries-long story of God's love for creation as expressed through God's providential care of the Chosen People. Providence and creation are both expressions of God's love.

In the covenant with the Chosen People, the Israelites, are graced with the presence of the Creator, who said, "Ever present in your midst, I will be your God, and you will be my people" (Leviticus 26:12). The divine love for the Chosen People is unconditional. God loves them freely, generously, unequivocally, and irreversibly.

JESUS TEACHES US ABOUT GOD'S LOVE

In Jesus, who is the Word of God, we encounter God made flesh. Jesus came as part of the covenant God ratified with the Chosen People to invite us into a new covenant. Jesus fully reveals God's love for us.

Does God weep over us? Yes, for Jesus wept at the tomb of his friend Lazarus. Does God rejoice in our celebrations? Yes, for Jesus ate and drank with the newly married couple at Cana. Does God grieve over our pain? Yes, for Jesus grieved when the lepers and the blind and the lame came to him and when those torn by doubt, like Nicodemus, approached him. In Jesus we discover God's love.

In the Bible teaching of Chapter 9 (Matthew 6:26–30), Jesus reveals God's loving care for all creation. Jesus asks us to consider the birds of the air and the lilies of the field that God clothes in beauty and dignity. Through this story, Jesus proclaims that God cares for all of creation and for each of us. It is a story that invites first graders to deepen their level of trust in God's love for them. Trust in this love—this is Jesus' message. Ask God to help us care for our world so that beauty and goodness (God's beauty and goodness and our own beauty and goodness, which reflects our Creator's) can flourish.

FINDING WAYS FOR THE CHILDREN TO CARE

In Chapter 9, the children approach creation from the point of view of the care God lavishes on it and from the realization that they, too, can care for creation. Most children have experienced being cared for. They know that plants, animals, and people need attention and nurturing. This chapter begins to examine the children's part in caring for creation.

Objective

This lesson helps the children recognize that people and all living things need care.

Step 1/INTRODUCTION

Learning About Our Lives

Introducing Chapter 9

Read aloud the question in the margin of page 112. Invite the children to name some people and things that might need care—pets, plants, and people, such as senior citizens and people with disabilities.

Using a Picture Story to Learn About Caring

Ask volunteers to study the picture story on page 112 to tell a story. Then read aloud "All Things Need Care." Talk about how plants need dirt, water, sunshine, and care to grow.

Extending the Concept of Care

Read the directions to the activity at the top of page 113. Invite volunteers to tell how the children in the illustrations are caring for the pictured animals. Talk about animals' needs for love, food, warmth, and gentleness.

Step 2/DEVELOPMENT

Learning About Our Faith

Learning About God's Care for All Things

Read "God Cares for All Things." Ask the children the following questions.

■ What do plants need? animals? (*Answers might include sunshine, water, food, space to grow.*)

■ How does God care for plants? animals? (*God gives plants sunshine and water and gives animals the desire to find food and shelter.*)

■ What do people need to be happy and healthy? (*Answers will vary.*)

■ How does God care for us? (*Answers will vary.*)

---

9 Jesus Teaches Us That God Cares

All Things Need Care

People, animals, and plants need care.

1. Mike planted a seed. He covered it with dirt.

2. Joan watered the seed. Soon she saw a tiny plant.

3. Mike put the tiny plant in the sun. He watched and waited.

4. The plant grew and grew. One day a flower bloomed.

What are the names of some people and things that need care?

Cultural Awareness

Provide pictures of children from various nations, including some with disabilities. Ask your class what these children need to be healthy and happy. Help your class appreciate that all people have the same basic needs—to be fed, clothed, sheltered, and loved. Remind the children that while all of us have basic needs each is specially created by God. Each of us is special.

Focus on

Caring According to the *Catechism of the Catholic Church*, "God wills the *interdependence of creatures*. The sun and the moon, the cedar and the little flower, the eagle and the sparrow: the spectacle of their countless diversities and inequalities tells us that no creature is self-sufficient. Creatures exist only in dependence on each other, to complete each other, in the service of each other." (#340)

Activity

Circle the ways you can care for animals.

God Cares for All Things

God knows what plants and animals need.
God knows what we need, too.

Activity

Draw something that you need to be healthy.

CURRICULUM CONNECTION

Music Teach the following words to "London Bridge."

We can care for
  everyone,
Everyone, everyone,
We can care for
  everyone,
Just like God does.

Enriching the Lesson

Science Make "caring charts." Provide three posterboards with one of the following printed at the top: plants, animals, or people. Elicit from the children the kinds of care each group needs *(Plants—sun, good soil, water, and weeding; Animals—food, water, exercise, being kept clean, and love; People—food, drink, exercise, sleep, warmth, love).* Have the children illustrate the charts.

In your discussion, help the children realize that one very important way God cares for plants, animals, and people is through people. Tell the class that they can care, too.

Drawing a Picture About Needs

Direct the children's attention to the activity at the bottom of page 113. Invite the children to draw something they need to be healthy. When they have completed their drawings, invite volunteers to tell about ways God helps them to stay healthy.

Step 3/CONCLUSION

Learning How to Live Our Faith

Finding Ways the Children Care

Ask the children to share ways in which they care for people, animals, plants, and things. Assure the children that God helps them care for others.

Creating a Bulletin Board About Caring

Invite the children to choose a magazine picture that shows someone or something they might be able to care for. Provide each child with paste and writing paper. Invite the children to paste their pictures to the paper and to print on the paper something they can do to show how they might care for this person, animal, plant, or thing. Circulate around the room to offer the children help with spelling.

When the children are finished, have them bring their pictures and gather around an empty bulletin board. Pin up the children's pictures. Have twenty-seven letters cut out for the following sentence: *We help God care for all creation.* Give each child a letter to hold as you tack up the letters.

Using the Bulletin Board for Prayer

As the children are gathered around the bulletin board, teach this response: *Thank you, God, for helping us care.* Using the pictures on the bulletin board, the children may talk to God about what they can do for people, animals, plants, and things. After each volunteer speaks about a picture, invite the other children to pray the above response.

DAY 2
SCRIPTURE/DOCTRINE

Objective
This lesson helps the children understand that God provides the care needed by all living things.

Step 1/INTRODUCTION

Learning About Our Lives

Drawing
Recall that all creatures are signs of God's love and care. Invite each child to draw his or her favorite bird, animal, or flower. Call on volunteers to talk about their pictures. Ask a child who chose to draw a bird to tell where it lives, and where it sleeps, to show what it eats, and so on. Tell the children that today they will be learning more about God's care for all creation.

Step 2/DEVELOPMENT

Learning About Our Faith

Listening to a Bible Story
Read aloud "Jesus Teaches Us About God his Father" on pages 114–115. Invite the children to retell the story in their own words. Conclude this section by emphasizing that the children can trust God to love and care for them. Call their attention to the words of Jesus: *God, your Father.* Point out that Jesus speaks of his Father as their caring heavenly Father, too.

Discussing an Illustration
Invite the children to study the illustration on pages 114–115 and ask the following questions.

■ Why do you think all these people are gathering together? (*To be with Jesus*)

■ Which person is Jesus? (*Jesus is in front in white.*)

■ Why do you think these people wanted to hear Jesus speak? (*Answers will vary.*)

Explain to the children that Jesus, God's Son, often spoke to people about God his Father's love for them and encouraged the people to trust God.

Acting Out the Story
Invite volunteers to act out the Bible story. Parts for Jesus, the listeners, and even the birds and

114

Jesus Teaches Us About God, His Father

One sunny day many people sat
on a hillside with Jesus.
Jesus pointed to birds in the sky.
He said, "Look at the birds!
God cares for them and feeds them.
But you are more important
than the birds.
God, your Father, cares even more about you."

Focus on

Plants The "lilies of the field" probably consisted of a wide range of flowers; among them may have been scarlet, white, purple, and blue anemones, which bloom in the Holy Land even today. Rose, iris, jasmine, daffodil, almond blossom, and lily of the valley were known in Jesus' time. Each January, white and pink almond blossoms appeared to announce that spring was near.

CURRICULUM CONNECTION

Music Teach the children the following words to the melody for "The Farmer in the Dell."

God cares for all of us;
God cares for all of us.
Hi ho, the derry oh,
God cares for all of us.

Then Jesus said, "Look at the flowers.
How beautiful they are!
But you are more beautiful than
these flowers.
God, your Father, cares much more for each
of you."

Based on Matthew 6:26-30

Jesus tells us that God cares for everyone.
We **trust** God to care for us and
for all creation.
We are most like God when we care
for each other and all creation.

We Believe

Jesus teaches us that God the Father cares for all living things. God cares for people most of all.

New Word

trust   Trust means to believe in someone's love for us.

Doctrine   115

the flowers of the field may be given to the children. Encourage the volunteers to develop dialogue that shows how everyone felt about Jesus' message.

or...

Reread the story and ask the children to imagine themselves listening to Jesus. When you read that Jesus says that God the Father cares for them even more than the birds and that they are more important than the flowers, have the children act out their feelings with facial expressions and body movements.

Reviewing the Vocabulary

Read the New Word section on page 115. Ask the children to repeat the word *trust* and its definition.

Presenting the Doctrine

Read aloud the We Believe section on page 115, which summarizes the chapter's doctrine. Ask the children to repeat the sentences.

Step 3/CONCLUSION

Learning How to Live Our Faith

Choosing Ways to Care

Discuss with the children how they feel when they hear that God, their loving Father, cares so much for them. Encourage them to share ways in which they will help care for creation—plants, animals, and people.

Using the Bible Story for Prayer

Gather the children in a semicircle in the prayer area. Ask them to close their eyes and to pretend that they are sitting on a hillside, listening to Jesus. Tell the children to imagine the beautiful flowers, the birds, and the gentle voice of Jesus.

Reread the story on pages 114–115 as the children sit with their eyes closed. Encourage the children to sit for a moment in silence while they think about Jesus' message.

Finally, invite the children to open their eyes. Lead the children in the following prayer: *Thank you, God, for loving me so very much.*

Focus on

Animals of Jesus' Time   The people avoided dogs, viewing them as scavengers and therefore unclean. Shepherds did use dogs to herd and watch sheep but did not treat them as pets.
Among these ancient people, goats were highly valued for their milk and hair. People wove tents, curtains, shepherds' cloaks, and other garments from goat hair. They made sacks to hold wine, milk, and water from goat skin.

Enriching the Lesson

Bring in some seed catalogs to show pictures of the many "lilies of the field." (See "Focus On Plants" in this lesson.) Discuss the many colors of these flowers. If possible, plant bulbs and flower seeds that grow into these flowers. Or provide materials for the children to paint a huge mural of the flowers.

115

Objective

This lesson helps the children discover ways in which God the Father cares for all creation and for them.

Step 1/INTRODUCTION

Learning About Our Lives

Finding Ways to Care for God's Creation

Show the children colorful pictures of God's creation. (Have at least seven pictures—each emphasizing one of the following categories: bugs, vegetables, flowers, birds, animals, trees, and people.) Divide the class into seven groups. Assign each group one picture and ask the children to suggest ways to care for the gift of God represented in their picture. Then invite the group members to share their discussion with the class. Print their suggestions on a sheet of paper and post them together with the picture in a prominent place.

Step 2/DEVELOPMENT

Learning About Our Faith

Discussing a Border of God's Creation

Direct the children's attention to the border on pages 116–117. Read aloud what the children pictured in the border are saying. Ask the class what they might like to say to God about all the wonderful things in creation. Connect this border with the work the children did in Step 1.

Learning How God Cares for All Creation

Read aloud "God Cares for All Creation" on pages 116–117. Ask questions about it to be sure the children understand that as God takes care of the earth, plants, animals, and all creation, God is taking care of human beings, too. For instance, for paragraph 1, you might ask the following questions.

■ Who created bugs? (*God*)

■ What do worms do in the ground? (*Wiggle and make good dirt*)

■ What grows out of the good dirt? (*Roses and other plants*)

■ What is so wonderful about flowers? (*They smell good and are beautiful.*)

116

Wow! God is wonderful!

God Cares for All Creation

God takes good care of the earth.
God creates bugs.
Worms wiggle to make good dirt.
Then roses bloom for us to enjoy.

God takes good care of plants.
God's sun shines in the sky.
God's rain falls on the ground.
Then carrots and other food grow
for us to eat.

Thank you, God!

116 Doctrine

Teaching Tips

While teaching this lesson, bring in wildflowers (daisies, violets, dandelions, and so on). Explain that people do not usually take special care of wildflowers but that God provides for them through the sun and the rain. Remind the children that Jesus said that people are even more beautiful than the flowers. Then call each child by name and tell the child that God loves him or her more than the most beautiful flower.

Teaching Tips

To help the children appreciate ways that God cares for them, encourage the children to think each evening of all the loving things God did for them that day. Remind them that God often cares for them through the people and things that happen in their lives. Give the following examples: *Mom and Dad worked today to care for the family. God sent rain today to water the flowers to make our world beautiful. I fell down today, but my friend helped me up.*

God takes good care of animals.
God clothes the animals with fur.
Then the cats and dogs can stay
warm in the winter.

God takes good care of all of us.
God dresses the mountains with trees.
Then maples and evergreen trees
clean the air for us to breathe.
God takes good care of us.

Activity

Make a chart of some of the things
in God's creation.
Count the things that God cares for.

3 Bugs	34 Fruits & Vegetables	25 Flowers
7 Birds	8 Animals	3 People

God is so great!

Doctrine 117

When God takes care of the ground/earth/dirt, how does God take care of us? (*Answers will vary.*)

Step 3/CONCLUSION

Learning How to Live Our Faith

Completing an Activity on God's Creation

Direct the children's attention to the activity at the bottom of 117. Invite volunteers to count the number of bugs, vegetables, flowers, birds, animals, trees, and people in the border. Encourage the children to use their pencils to fill in their chart of God's creation on page 117.

Using a Border to Find Ways to Care

Discuss the varied things in the border on pages 116–117 and invite the children to talk about how God cares for these creations and how the children can care for them and respect their specialness, too. For example, if they find a bug on them, they can put it back in nature, rather than kill it.

Gathering for Prayer

Invite the children to bring their textbooks and to gather around the display of posted pictures from Step 1. Encourage a member of each of the seven groups from Step 1 to talk about the group's suggestions for ways to care for nature. Then direct the children's attention to the border on pages 116–117. Help them to find the children in the border who are praising God our Creator. Use the words in the speech balloons as today's prayer.

Focus on

Spontaneous Prayer As part of this lesson, the children will examine the border of the pages on which there are children expressing their feelings to God spontaneously. Considering the wonders and beauty of nature may foster spontaneous prayers of praise. Invite the children to respond spontaneously in prayer to the wonders of God's creation that they are discussing today.

Enriching the Lesson

Art Pass out drawing paper, paste, and seeds. Instruct the children to draw a horizontal line across the bottom of the page for the ground. Have them paste seeds beneath the line and then draw roots to the seeds. Above the ground the children may draw stems shooting up from each seed into leaves and flowers. They may paste on other natural materials.

Objective

This lesson helps the children plan ways they can help God care for the world.

Step 1/INTRODUCTION

Learning About Our Lives

Using the Bulletin Board from Day 1

Gather the children around the bulletin board from Day 1 that shows people, animals, pets, and things they can care for. Encourage the children to talk about their pictures and to tell their classmates two things: (1) how God cares for these gifts of creation and (2) how they can help God care for these gifts of creation.

Step 2/DEVELOPMENT

Learning About Our Faith

Discovering Ways to Help Care for God's Creation

Read aloud "Caring for God's Creation" on pages 118–119. Afterward, invite volunteers to retell the story in their own words. If you think the children may not understand the message of the story (that children can help care for creation), ask the following questions.

- What did the three first graders see that made them want to take care of the world? (*A city dump*)

- Why do you think they wanted to help God take care of the world? (*Answers will vary.*)

- How did Brian help take care of the world? (*He recycled his toys and created less garbage.*)

- How did Luis help take care of the world? (*He made sure garbage did not hurt animals.*)

- How did Kate help take care of the world? (*She made a bird feeder and, by doing so, did not create any garbage.*)

Learning from Pictures

Have the children look at each picture and ask them to enter into the meaning of the pictures by making the following gestures and expressions.

Caring for God's Creation

One day three first graders saw the city dump filled with garbage.
"Some of this junk can harm our earth. Let's do something about it," Luis said.
"Let's help God take care of the world."

Brian said. "I'll take care of my toys so they won't break."
When he grew too old for his toys, Brian gave them to other children to use.

118   Morality

Kate drank lots of milk.
Then she had a wonderful idea.
"I could make a bird feeder," she said.
She cut an opening in a milk bottle
and hung the bird feeder from
a tree limb.
Kate did not make garbage.
Instead, she made a feeder
for God's birds.

At the beach, Luis saw a piece of
plastic with six rings to hold cans.
"A little fish could get caught
in the rings and die," Luis said.
So he snipped the rings with scissors.
That way the garbage could not
hurt any fish or animals.

Activity

Look at the pictures and
think about the stories.
Circle what you will do.

Focus on

The Environment   Instead of discarding outgrown toys, the children might start a toy collection for younger children, such as preschoolers. Make this a voluntary project since parents may be saving the toys for younger siblings. If possible, bring the children with you to present the toys to the preschoolers and their teacher.

- The dump: Have the children make facial expressions that say, "What a mess!" Encourage them to react to seeing usable things thrown away. Ask them to demonstrate their feelings with gestures.

- Giving out-grown toys to a younger child: Invite the children to make facial expressions and body movements, such as pulling the toy or jumping up and down to depict the joy of the younger child receiving the new toy.

- Cutting plastic: Invite the children to use their fingers as scissors to cut the plastic.

- The bird house: Invite the children to pantomime filling the bird house with seeds and hanging it up. Encourage them to imitate a bird flying toward it. (The children may flap extended arms.)

Encourage the children to think of their own gestures, body movements, and facial expressions.

Step 3/CONCLUSION

Learning How to Live Our Faith

Planning Ways to Care for the World

Discuss with the children ways they can make less garbage to put in the city dump. Talk about the recycling their families do. Encourage them to talk about ways they can be like Brian, Luis, and Kate (the characters in the story).

Drawing a Picture of How to Care

Pass out drawing paper and invite the children to draw what they plan to do during the following week to help care for God's world. Afterward, invite the children to share their plans and post their work in a prominent place in the classroom.

Praying for Help in Caring for Creation

Gather the children in the prayer area in a semicircle. Teach them the following response: *We trust that you will help us, God.* Invite the children to hold hands. When they are quiet, stand in front of the first child in the semicircle. Lay your hands on the child's head, speak the child's name, and ask God to help him or her care for all creation. Then invite the children to pray the response.

119

Objective

This lesson helps the children express praise to God, who cares for all of creation.

Reading the Text

Direct the children's attention to page 120. Read the text under the title "Praying a Prayer of Praise." Ask the children what the word *praise* means. Talk about times when people have praised them. Ask them how they feel when someone praises them. Help the children understand that when they praise their heavenly Father, they express admiration for God's great goodness and love.

Preparing to Process to the Prayer Area

Tell the children that today they are going to praise God just as the children in the illustration on page 120 are doing. Provide the children with musical instruments, such as cymbals, drums, whistles, and spoons. Explain to them that they can play their musical instruments as they process. Or encourage the children to dance, clap their hands, or raise their arms in praise as they process. You may wish to play a very lively instrument or "All for the Glory of God" by Jack Miffleton, from the record *Wake Up the Earth* (OCP Resources).

Praising God for Caring

Process with the children. After they have all gathered in the prayer area, encourage them to raise their arms in praise. Small instruments can be held in their hands and large ones should be laid down in front of them. Then pray the psalm on page 120 by asking the children to pray each line after you. Conclude the prayer by playing the music again while the children play their musical instruments, dance, or clap their praise.

Praying a Prayer of Praise

God created the world and all that is in it.
We can praise our good God.
We can sing, dance, and play instruments.

Praise God in the heavens!
Praise God for creation!
Praise God with the trumpet!
Praise God with the harp!
Praise God with song and dance!
Praise God with cymbals!
Let all creation praise God!

Based on Psalm 150

120 Prayer

CURRICULUM CONNECTION

Science and Language Arts Use the book 50 *Simple Things Kids Can Do to Save the Earth* by the Earth Works Group (Andrews and McMeel, a Universal Press Syndicate Company). Plan a classroom environmental project. After the children have completed their project (in a day or week or month), invite them to write a story about their efforts and to make a "We Care for the Earth" booklet.

Chapter Review

CHAPTER REVIEW

Activity

God cares for all creation.

Show how you can care for God's creation, too.

Put the pictures below in 1, 2, 3 order.

 **2**  **3**  **1**

1. Who cares for all creation?

God

2. What word means to believe in someone's love for us?

trust

Jesus says, "Put your trust in God."
Based on Mark 11:22

3. Talk about how God cares for people and all creation.

Review 121

Using the Drawings from Day 4 to Review

Use the children's drawings from Day 4 to review the week by talking about how God cares for all creation and about how the children can care, too. Invite the children to talk about how they can trust that God loves them and will help them care for their world.

Finally, give each child his or her drawing and encourage the children to take their drawings home, post them in a place they will be noticed each day, and follow through on their plans to care for God's creation.

Completing the Activity

Read the text at the top of page 121. Then direct the children's attention to the three photos. Instruct the children to put them in order. Talk about how the pictures show how we can help care for God's creation.

Answering the Questions

Read aloud the first two questions and ask volunteers to respond. Direct the children to print the answers in their texts. Encourage all the children to participate in the discussion.

Using the Scripture Verse

End the session by reading the Scripture verse and asking the children to repeat it after you. If you wish, the children may memorize the verse.

Focus on

Praying a Prayer of Praise The prayer skill centers on praise of God. This chapter's lessons build toward this culmination. The Bible story of the lilies of the fields created a wonderment at God's great love of us. Amazement at God's great care of all creation bursts forth in the prayers on pages 116–117. To celebrate God's greatness, the children are invited to praise God with music and dance.

Teaching Tips

It is easier to introduce children to the use of instruments when they do not have to concentrate on anything else, such as singing words. For this reason, use highly rhythmic instrumental music when first introducing the children to rhythm instruments, or, if you really want the children to sing, use a song that is so familiar to them that it is practically second nature.

10 Jesus Cares for Us

Objectives ～～～～

To help the children

- Recognize ways in which Jesus cared for people.
- Trust that they can count on Jesus to care for them.
- Learn that Jesus wants us to care for others and bring love to the world.
- Discover ways in which other people care for them as Jesus did.
- Dance, pantomime, or draw pictures to reflect on the Scripture and review the chapter.

Chapter Outline ～～～～

	Step 1 Learning About Our Lives	**Step 2** Learning About Our Faith	**Step 3** Learning How to Live Our Faith
Day 1	■ Review Chapter 9. ■ Tell stories about pictures. *ABOUT 6 MINUTES*	■ Respond to a Bible illustration. ■ Read a Bible story. ■ Dramatize the Bible story. ■ Review the vocabulary. *ABOUT 15 MINUTES*	■ Find ways to care for others. ■ Prepare to pray. ■ Pray with movement. *ABOUT 9 MINUTES*
Day 2	■ Choose people to trust. ■ Read about counting on people. *ABOUT 8 MINUTES*	■ Discover that we can trust Jesus. ■ Recall the Bible story about trust. *ABOUT 7 MINUTES*	■ Predict a Bible story outcome. ■ Discuss predictions. ■ Pantomime the predictions. ■ Pray the Hail Mary. *ABOUT 15 MINUTES*
Day 3	■ Read a poem. ■ Memorize a poem about caring. *ABOUT 5 MINUTES*	■ Discover the ways Jesus cares. ■ Read a play about caring. ■ Do a dramatic reading. ■ Present the doctrine. *ABOUT 20 MINUTES*	■ Complete an activity on caring. ■ Prepare to pray. ■ Pray with gestures. *ABOUT 5 MINUTES*
Day 4	■ Review the learning of Days 1–3. *ABOUT 5 MINUTES*	■ Discover ways Jesus cares. ■ Discuss an illustration. ■ Act out caring stories. *ABOUT 18 MINUTES*	■ Complete an activity on caring. ■ Act out caring actions. ■ Gather for prayer. *ABOUT 7 MINUTES*

Day 5　　**Prayer**　Discuss ways to pray; choose a way to retell a story; learn a song; and pray by retelling a Bible story.

Review　Complete an activity; answer the questions; and read a Scripture verse.

Plan Ahead ~~~~~~~

	Preparing Your Class	**Materials Needed**
Day 1	For Step 1, plan on using the bulletin board made on Day 1 of Chapter 9.	■ soft background music and tape player
Day 2	If you plan to use any Teaching Option, make preparations and collect materials.	
Day 3	For Steps 1 and 3, have ready some suggestions for body movements the children might add to their poem. For Step 2, collect props for the dramatic reading.	■ props for play: blanket, books, food or milk
Day 4	If you plan to use the Teaching Option, make preparations and collect materials.	
Day 5	Consider how to help the children pantomime, dance, or draw Bible stories. Learn the melody for "Mary Had a Little Lamb."	■ drawing paper (optional)

Additional Resources

As you plan this chapter, consider using the following materials from The Resourceful Teacher Package.

■ *Classroom Activity Sheets 10* and *10a*

■ *Family Activity Sheets 10* and *10a*

■ *Chapter 10 Test*

■ *Prayers for Every Day*

■ *Projects: Grade 1*

In preparing the students for the Sunday readings, you may wish to use Silver Burdett Ginn's *Getting Ready For Sunday* student and teacher materials.

BOOKS FOR THE JOURNEY

Louie. Ezra Jack Keats. Greenwillow, 1983. This book shows children sensitively caring for another child.

A Special Trade. Sally Wittman. Harper Collins, 1985. The person who gives care changes hands after Bartholomew—Nelly's friend—falls, is hospitalized, and is unable to do things that they had enjoyed together.

MORE BOOKS FOR THE JOURNEY

An Angel for Solomon Singer. Cynthia Rylant. Orchard Books, 1992. A caring waiter in a restaurant changes the life of a lonely man.

The Paper Crane. Molly Bang. Morrow, 1987. A restaurant owner treats a visitor with generosity and respect and is rewarded in a mysterious and wonderful way.

REDUCED CLASSROOM ACTIVITIES

Name

Jesus Cares for Us

1. Cut out the large letter **J**.
2. With a pencil, punch a hole through the black dot.
3. Thread yarn through the hole to make a neck chain. Tie together the two ends of the yarn.

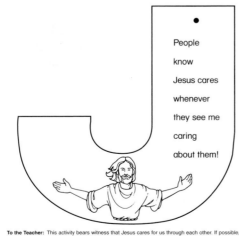

People
know
Jesus cares
whenever
they see me
caring
about them!

To the Teacher: This activity bears witness that Jesus cares for us through each other. If possible, use heavyweight paper for the large **J** and 36" of yarn per child.

Chapter 10   Jesus Cares for Us   THIS IS OUR FAITH 1   **10**

Name

Others Care for Us

1. Put an **X** by each helper in the picture.
2. Color the picture.

To the Teacher: This activity reinforces the concept that Jesus cares for us through other people.

10a   THIS IS OUR FAITH 1   Chapter 10   Jesus Cares for Us

Background for the Teacher

THE LOVE OF GOD

Jesus, the Word made flesh, enables us to turn from self toward God, the source of love. When the light of God's love shines through us, we can turn to others and let the light shine on them. The love we give is the love we are given. The Godhead does not dwell in self-centeredness. The very nature of the Trinity is to pour out life, love, beauty, and goodness. To be God is to give life. And this life is love, enriching every aspect of our humanity. In Jesus, we see this love, as he lived among us.

In the Epistle to the Romans, St. Paul urges us to "put on the Lord" (Romans 13:14) by loving, forgiving, healing, and reconciling. Jesus said, "If you live according to my teaching, you are truly my disciples; then you will know the truth and the truth will set you free" (Based on John 8:31–32). The hope of Jesus is that we will become free to face God in simplicity and honesty and to embrace the love God wants to shine through us and in us.

Chapter 10 explores the mystery of God's infinite love manifested in flesh. Faith in Jesus Christ is the basis of this week's lesson. The concepts introduced in Chapters 3 and 4 are further developed in the teaching that the children experience the love of Jesus through those who care for them as Jesus has shown us.

Jesus lived for others. His caring was deeply personal. He healed the blind, the deaf, the lepers. He miraculously fed the hungry. He embraced the outcast. He even raised the dead to life. Through the miracles, Jesus proclaimed the power and love of God; through these miracles, Jesus announced God's kingdom of peace. In Jesus' touch, people experienced conversion and faith.

EXPERIENCING JESUS' LOVE

In Chapter 10, the children in your classroom will learn more about the love of God as revealed in Jesus. The love of Jesus is the healing power that mends body and soul. In this lesson, the children learn that they experience Jesus' love for them in the care they receive from others. God's love, manifested in Jesus, touches their lives daily through the caring actions of others.

By providing a consistently caring attitude toward each child in your classroom, you communicate in action the love that Jesus has for each child. Your constancy tells the children in concrete terms that they can always count on receiving the love of Jesus. Because the children are experiencing your care, they may begin to look for signs of Jesus' love in all the loving people they meet.

Objective

This lesson helps the children recognize ways in which Jesus cared for people.

Step 1/INTRODUCTION

Learning About Our Lives

Reviewing Chapter 9

Gather the children around the bulletin board made on Day 1 of Chapter 9. Connect the heading *We help God care for all creation* with the pictures. Then recall that God cares for all creation but that God loves people most of all.

or...

Tell the children that today they are going to learn about how Jesus, God's Son, cares for everyone.

Telling Stories About Pictures

Read and discuss the focus question in the margin. Then read the text under "Caring People" on page 122. Divide the class into three groups and assign each group one of the pictures. Have the groups make up stories about the pictures. Tell the children that their stories should tell what the people in the pictures are doing to show that they care. As the children create their stories, encourage them to think about the feelings of the pictured people.

Step 2/DEVELOPMENT

Learning About Our Faith

Responding to a Bible Illustration

Direct the children's attention to the illustration on page 123. Tell them that the woman has been sick. Then ask the following questions.

- How do you feel when you are sick? (*Answers will vary.*)
- How do you think this woman feels? (*Answers will vary.*)
- Who takes care of you when you are sick? (*Parents, grandparents, baby-sitters, others.*)
- Who do you think took care of this woman? (*Answers will vary. Of course, the children may recognize Jesus and name him.*)

122

Jesus Cares for Us

Caring People

Tell a story about each picture.
Look at the people being cared for.
How do they feel?

What are some ways that people show you they care about you?

CURRICULUM CONNECTION

Art Invite each child to print on a slip of paper someone's name who is sick or lonely. Collect the slips and draw a name. Ask the class to make "care cards" for the person whose name they wrote. Encourage the children to tell the person that they care for him or her and that Jesus does, too. Collect the cards and ask someone to deliver them. Allow the children to make more cards in their free time.

Focus on

The Caring Jesus According to the *Catechism of the Catholic Church,* "All Christ's riches 'are for every individual and are everybody's property.' Christ did not live his life for himself but *for us,* from his Incarnation 'for us men and for our salvation' to his death 'for our sins' and Resurrection 'for our justification.' He is still 'our advocate with the Father,' who 'always lives to make intercession' for us" (#519).

Jesus Cares for a Sick Woman

One day Jesus went to visit
his friends Peter and Andrew.
They were brothers and fishermen.
How happy they were to see Jesus!

"My wife's mother is very sick with a
high fever," Peter told his friend.
"I don't know how to help her."

"I will help her," Jesus said.
Holding the woman's hand,
he helped her sit up.
At once her fever went away.

"Thank you, Jesus," she said.
"Let me get you some food."
Then she made everyone a meal.

Based on Mark 1: 29-31

New Words

Peter and Andrew Peter and Andrew were brothers.
They were good friends of Jesus.

Scripture   123

Teaching Tips

When teaching the story "Jesus Cares for a Sick Woman," emphasize that she became completely well at once. As a matter of fact, she felt so well that she wanted to cook a meal. Contrast this with the children's experiences of becoming totally well only gradually.

Focus on

Fishing Peter and Andrew were fishermen who fished in the Sea of Galilee, through which the River Jordan flowed. The Sea of Galilee teemed with fish, and tiny fishing villages dotted the shore. The fishermen waded out into the shallow water to cast small circular nets. They also strung dragnets between two boats or between a boat and fishermen who walked along the shore.

Reading a Bible Story

As the children look at the illustration, read "Jesus Cares for a Sick Woman." Discuss Jesus' friendship with Peter and Andrew. Make sure that the children understand that the woman is the mother of Peter's wife and that she was very sick. Discuss how the woman may have felt because Jesus cured her.

Dramatizing the Bible Story

Invite the children to dramatize the story "Jesus Cares for a Sick Woman." Assign the following parts to volunteers: Andrew, Peter, Peter's wife, Peter's mother-in-law, Jesus. Provide a few minutes for the volunteers to consider what they will do in their dramatization.

Reviewing the Vocabulary

Point to the New Words section on page 123. Ask the children to repeat *Peter* and *Andrew* and the definition.

Step 3/CONCLUSION

Learning How to Live Our Faith

Finding Ways to Care for Others

Recall that God cares for everyone and that the children can care for others, too. Ask what the children might do for people who are sick or lonely. Make the point that the children can lift a person's spirits. Encourage the children to visit sick friends or elderly neighbors who may be lonely. (Stress that the children should ask their parents' permission to do this.)

Preparing to Pray

Teach the children the following response: *Jesus, you are great and holy.* Ask the children to brainstorm gestures they can use to pray their praise response.

Praying with Movement

Gather the children in the prayer area. Say the following prayer. After each sentence, pause and invite the children to pray their responses, using their gestures and body movements to praise God.

> Dear Jesus, you care for everyone.
> You care for all of us, too, just as you cared for Peter's mother-in-law.
> Thank you, Jesus, for letting us help you care for others.

123

DAY 2
SCRIPTURE

Objective
This lesson helps the children trust that they can count on Jesus to care for them.

Step 1/INTRODUCTION

Learning About Our Lives

Choosing People to Trust
Read the text at the top of page 124. Help the children remember that they learned the word *trust* in Chapter 9. Have the children brainstorm other words that come to mind when the word *trust* is mentioned. Stress that to trust someone means to believe in that person's love and care.

Reading About Counting on People
Invite the children to read "Counting on Someone" on page 124. Read aloud the first paragraph, and then have the children look at the pictures as you read the conversation accompanying them. After discussing the section, ask the children whom they trust to love and care for them.

Step 2/DEVELOPMENT

Learning About Our Faith

Discovering That We Can Trust Jesus
Ask the children if they think they can trust Jesus. Elicit reasons for their responses. Then read "We Can Trust Jesus" at the bottom of page 124.

Recalling a Bible Story About Trust
Ask volunteers to retell the story of Jesus and Peter's mother-in-law. To help the children connect this story with today's learning, ask questions like the following.

■ Did Peter's mother-in-law trust Jesus? (*Yes*)

■ What did Jesus do that showed her that she could trust him? (*He cured her.*)

■ Who else do you think trusted Jesus? (*Peter and Andrew*)

■ Can you trust Jesus, too? (*Answers will vary.*)

Emphasize that Jesus is always with the children and that Jesus loves them very much.

124

Counting on Someone
We can trust some people
to do their best to help us.
They try to keep their promises to us.
They often know what is good for us.

Read the stories below.

"Daddy, thank you for keeping your promise and taking me to the zoo." ▶

◀ "I will put a bandage on your cut."
"I am glad I was here to help you."

We Can Trust Jesus
We can count on Jesus to love and help us.
Remember, Jesus is always with us.

CURRICULUM CONNECTION

Music   Teach the children the following words to the melody for "London Bridge Is Falling Down."

Jesus cares for all of us,
All of us,
All of us.
Jesus cares for all of us.
Jesus loves us.

Activity

This story is about Jesus and a man who trusted him.
One day Jesus and his friend went walking.
They met a man who was blind.

The blind man trusted Jesus.
"Help me see, Jesus," he said.

Based on Mark 10:46

Draw what you think happened.

Scripture 125

Focus on

Physical Ailments In biblical times, eye diseases resulting from climate, infection, heredity, and senility were common. Trachoma was widespread, producing bleary, itchy, or painful eyes. (This infection is still prevalent in developing countries today.) Paralysis, no doubt caused by polio and stroke, was also prevalent. However, it is not known why so much deafness existed.

🍎 Teaching Tips

In this lesson the children engage in predicting. To do this well, they need clues that suggest the possible outcome. The children have grown in appreciation of Jesus as the one who loves all people. They know that he can heal from the story of Peter's mother-in-law. Without much difficulty, they should be able to predict that Jesus can and will cure the blind man.

Predicting a Bible Story Outcome

Read the first line of text at the top of page 125. Direct the children to the two pictures and read the text. Encourage the children to draw a picture to show what they think happened next in the story.

Discussing the Predictions

After the children have completed their drawings, invite volunteers to tell what they think happened next in the Bible story. To stimulate discussion, ask the following questions.

■ What made you think that this would happen next? (*Answers will vary.*)

■ Why do you think Jesus would do that? (*Answers will vary.*)

■ How do you think the man who was blind felt after Jesus healed him? (*Answers will vary.*)

■ Could the man who could not see trust Jesus? (*Answers will vary.*)

After all the children who want to share their predictions are finished, read Mark 10:46–52 to the class so that they can see what actually happened—Jesus cured the blind man.

Pantomiming the Predictions

If time permits, invite volunteers to pantomime the story, adding the outcomes they predicted. Encourage the other children to applaud the creativity of the volunteers.

Praying the Hail Mary

Gather the children in the prayer area. Remind them that Jesus' mother, Mary, taught him to care for others and to be kind. Then pray the Hail Mary with the children.

125

Objective

This lesson helps the children learn that when they care for others, they are helping Jesus bring love to the world around them.

Step 1/INTRODUCTION

Learning About Our Lives

Reading a Poem

Have the following poem printed on the chalkboard or on posterboard. Read the poem to the children.

> You help me,
> And I'll help you.
> It works both ways, you see.
> We need to share
> Ourselves each day.
> We need to show we care.

Then ask the children to close their eyes and think of a time when they really needed someone to care. Ask for volunteers to share their personal experiences of needing care and receiving it.

Memorizing a Poem About Caring

Have the children repeat the poem after you line by line. Then invite them to brainstorm a gesture or body movement for each line or stanza. Have them use the gestures as they repeat the poem after you again. Tell the children that they will use their poem during prayer today.

Step 2/DEVELOPMENT

Learning About Our Faith

Discovering the Way Jesus Cares for Us

Read aloud "Jesus Cares for Us" on page 126. Emphasize the last line of the text and tell the children that today they will read a play that shows how Jesus cares for people through the loving actions of others.

Reading a Play About Caring

Read aloud the introduction to the play "A Caring Woman" on pages 126–127. Stress that when Mother Seton cared for people, she was helping spread God's love. Next, read the play

126

Jesus Cares for Us

Jesus cared for Andrew, Peter, and Peter's mother-in-law. He cared for the blind man.

Jesus cares for everyone. He loves us and is always with us. One way Jesus cares for us is through the loving care of others.

A Caring Woman

This play is about Elizabeth Seton, who cared for many children.

We have no home, no place to live.

Come with me, I will make a home for you.

We want to learn to read, but we have no schools.

Focus on

Mother Seton Tell the children that Mother Seton was a real person named Elizabeth Ann Bailey. She married William Seton, but after he died, she had to support her children alone. The bishop, who was her friend, suggested she open a school for poor children. She did, with the aid of some other young women. Together they started many schools and brought Jesus' love to many children.

My sisters and I will teach you. Come with us.

We are hungry, but we have no money for food and milk.

I will ask Jesus to help me, and I will find food and milk for you.

Jesus never forgets us. Elizabeth Seton's love shows Jesus' love.

Activity

These are the names of people who care for me.

_____

_____

_____

We Believe

Jesus loves and cares for everyone. One way Jesus cares for people today is through caring people. We must care for others also.

Doctrine 127

★ ★ ★ ★
Enriching the Lesson
★ ★ ★

Language Arts Act out "A Caring Woman" for the children's parents or another class. Set a date for the play and help the children make invitations or decorate ones you have duplicated. Help the children memorize their parts. After the play, provide simple treats and beverages as refreshments. Explain to the class that offering guests food and drink is a way of showing care for them.

aloud. Talk about the children, explaining that those who had no homes were homeless (perhaps, they were orphans) and those who wanted to learn to read had no schools. Discuss how Mother Seton helped each group. Emphasize that when Mother Seton helped the children, she was doing as Jesus asked, bringing his love to others.

Doing a Dramatic Reading

Divide the class into three groups. Assign each group one of the following roles: the homeless children, the children who wanted to learn to read, and the hungry children. Explain that each group has one speaking part in the play plus the final part that everyone recites. Have the three groups practice their lines several times. Provide props for Mother Seton's use. (For example, she might have a blanket for the homeless children, books for those who want to learn to read, and food or milk for the hungry children.)

Direct the children to bring their books to an open area in the classroom. Tell them that you will read the part of Mother Seton. Then, together, perform a dramatic reading of the play.

Presenting the Doctrine

Read aloud the We Believe section on page 127, which summarizes the chapter's doctrine. Ask the children to repeat it after you, sentence by sentence.

Step 3/CONCLUSION

Learning How to Live Our Faith

Completing an Activity on Caring

Direct the children to the activity at the bottom of page 127. Discuss the people who care for them and ways they are cared for. Invite the children to print the names of these people on the lines provided.

Preparing to Pray

Go over the poem the children memorized in Step 1, encouraging them to add the gestures they prepared.

Praying with Gestures

Gather the children in their prayer area. Pray the three stanzas of the poem, using the gestures and body movements.

DAY 4
MORALITY

Objective

This lesson helps the children discover ways in which other people care for them as Jesus wants his friends to do.

Step 1/INTRODUCTION

Learning About Our Lives

Reviewing the Learning of Days 1–3

Help the children recall that God gives them special people to love and care for them. In your discussion, ask the following questions.

■ What are some things that people do that make you feel loved? (*Answers will vary.*)

■ How do you feel when you know that Jesus loves you and cares for you through other people? (*Answers will vary.*)

Step 2/DEVELOPMENT

Learning About Our Faith

Discovering Ways Jesus Cares Through Other People

Read aloud "People Can Show Jesus' Love" on page 128. After reading the question that ends each paragraph, pause and encourage the children to respond.

Discussing an Illustration of Caring

Direct the children to the illustration on page 128. Talk about how the grown-ups could use these items in the collage to show caring for the children. Encourage volunteers to tell how someone used one of these items to care for them.

Acting Out Caring Stories

Invite volunteers to act out the four stories contained in "People Can Show Jesus' Love." Provide time for the volunteers to develop a beginning, middle, and end to each story and to make up dialogue. When each group of volunteers is ready, have them present their skit. After each skit, tell the children that when the adult character in the skit (name the character) cared, he or she was acting the way Jesus showed us to act.

128

People Can Show Jesus' Love

Emily plays games with Tim.
He knows that Jesus is loving him
through Emily.
How does Tim feel when his sister
cares for him as Jesus showed us?

Grandpa O'Mara takes Tara fishing.
Tara knows that Jesus is loving
her through Grandpa.
How does Tara feel when Grandpa
cares for her just as Jesus calls us to?

Aunt Ramona bakes cookies for Carlos.
Carlos knows that Jesus is loving
him through Aunt Ramona.
How does Carlos feel when his aunt
cares for him as Jesus wants?

Mr. Ling bandages Chun's knee.
Chun knows that Jesus is caring
for him through Mr. Ling.
How does Chun feel when her
neighbor cares for her as
Jesus showed us?

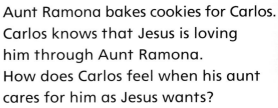

128 Morality

🍎 Teaching Tips

It might be fun to bring in common household items, such as a wrench, a teapot, bandages, a broom, or a rake. Divide the class into as many groups as you have objects. Blindfold a child from each group and let him or her pick an object. Then the group should role-play a situation in which the object is used to help someone.

★ Enriching the Lesson ★

Invite people who care for children to the class. You might ask a nurse to tell how she helps keep children healthy, the cafeteria workers to share how much they enjoy preparing the children's lunches, or the crossing guard to express pleasure in protecting the children each day. The principal and the maintenance personnel might make good guests, too.

Activity

Draw lines to match the pictures that go together. Then tell what you think the children might say to the people who care for them.

Learning How to Live Our Faith

Completing an Activity on Caring

Read the directions for the activity on page 129 and provide time for the children to match the pictures. After the activity has been completed, ask the children to tell how they determined which pictures went together. Encourage the children to use appropriate language to show appreciation for the help they received.

or...

Have the children draw pictures of what happened and who helped. Instruct the children to use speech balloons to show the dialogue.

Acting Out Caring Actions

Encourage volunteers to make up and perform a play in which someone helps a child. Before beginning, give the volunteers a few minutes to think of a situation, talk about what they will do, and develop their dialogue. When the play is finished, ask the rest of the children to name the helping action. Whoever gives the correct answer first can choose a partner and put on another play for the class.

Gathering for Prayer

Gather the children in the prayer corner and invite them to close their eyes. Ask the children to think of some caring action someone did for them recently. Invite the children to remember how they felt. Remind them that the person who helped them was spreading love, as Jesus wanted us to do. Encourage the children to say a silent prayer for the person who cared for them.

🍎 Teaching Tips

In this session the children are asked to create appropriate dialogue that shows appreciation for being helped. Many children cannot articulate the correct social response that a situation warrants because they do not have the necessary skills. Introduce appropriate responses such as "Thank you," "I'm glad you helped me," and so forth. Role-play the responses.

Enriching the Lesson

Duplicate a drawing of two large boxes with a heart between them. The heart should touch both boxes. Distribute the papers and invite the children to draw a picture of Jesus in the first box and a grown-up who cares for them in the second one. Have the children draw themselves in the heart to show how they feel when they are loved by Jesus and other people.

129

PRAYER/REVIEW

Objective

This lesson helps the children retell a Bible story by dancing, pantomiming, or drawing.

Discovering Many Ways to Pray

Read "Praying with Bible Stories" on page 130. Encourage the children to tell what the children in the picture are doing as they pray.

Choosing Ways to Retell a Bible Story

Encourage the children to think about a favorite Bible story about Jesus caring for someone. There are two in this chapter: the cures of the sick woman and the blind man. Tell the children that each child can decide how he or she wants to retell a Bible story by getting a group together to pantomime it, drawing a picture about it, or doing a dance that retells the story. Provide time for the children to prepare their stories.

Learning a Song About Caring

Tell the children that today they are going to learn a song about Jesus and caring, which they can sing as they process. Use the melody to "Mary Had a Little Lamb" and teach the following words.

Jesus always cares for us;
Cares for us; cares for us.
Jesus always cares for us,
Each and every day.

Praying by Retelling Bible Stories

Form the children into a line for the procession and encourage them to sing their song as they process around the room into the prayer area. After the children reach the prayer area, encourage them to quiet themselves. Then invite the volunteers to pantomime a Bible story. Afterwards allow a few moments of silence for the children to close their eyes and quietly think about the story. Encourage spontaneous prayers in praise of Jesus. Conclude the prayer service by inviting the children to sing their song a final time.

Praying With Bible Stories

When we gather to pray, we can remember Jesus' love. To help us, we can retell some Bible stories we know about Jesus. Here are some different ways to tell a story we know.

• We can pantomime it.
• We can draw pictures of it.
• We can make up a dance that retells the story.

Choose one of these ways to tell a story of Jesus' love.

130   Prayer

Teaching Tips

When grouping the children to perform a task, it is best to place some self-starters in each group. At other times you will want to challenge the more advanced students by placing them all in the same group so that they can stimulate one another. Occasionally put the less-verbal children all in the same group. Someone among them then takes the responsibility of calling the group to action.

hapter Review

ctivity

any special people love us and care for us.
o discover who loves us the most, color the
aces that have an X in them. Jesus

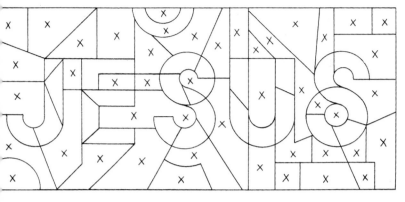

Which two brothers were friends of Jesus?

Andrew and Peter

Who cured the woman in the
Bible story?

Jesus

Talk about ways that Jesus
cares for you through caring people.

Jesus loves
me.
Based on
Galatians 2:20

Review   131

Completing an Activity

Use the activity on page 131 to review the
learning of Chapter 10. Read the text at the top
of page 131. Then invite the children to color
the spaces that have an X in them to discover
who loves them. Ask the children to raise their
hands when they are finished and can read the
word.

When everyone is ready, read the word *Jesus*
together. Invite the children to tell you as many
things as they can remember that they have
learned about Jesus in this chapter. Try to lead
them to an appreciation of the great love Jesus
has for them and for all people. Once again,
emphasize that Jesus wants people to love and
to care for them, as he showed us.

Answering the Questions

Read aloud the first two questions and ask
volunteers to respond. Direct the children to
print the answers in their texts. Encourage all
the children to participate in the discussion of
the third question. Be supportive of each child
who responds.

Reading the Scripture Verse

Ask the children to read the Scripture verse with
you. It is good to end the lesson by reflecting on
the word of God. If you wish you may have the
children memorize this verse.

Focus on

Praying by Retelling Bible Stories
The prayer skill for this lesson helps
the children reflect on Bible stories.
The children put a great deal of emotion into the retelling of a story. They
relive not only the events as they
know them, but the feelings the story
conjures up within them. This is a
form of meditation that helps children integrate the message of the
story into their hearts and minds.

Jesus Teaches Us to Care

Objectives

To help the children

- Identify some of the caring actions of others.
- Understand what Jesus means by being a good neighbor.
- Practice being good neighbors as Jesus taught them to be.
- Recognize that many people are Good Samaritans.
- Reflect on the Scripture by putting on a play and review the chapter.

Chapter Outline

	Step 1 **Learning About Our Lives**	**Step 2** **Learning About Our Faith**	**Step 3** **Learning How to Live Our Faith**
Day 1	■ Review Chapter 10. ■ Read a poem. ■ Add gestures to the poem. *ABOUT 10 MINUTES*	■ Learn what Jesus wants. ■ Present the doctrine. *ABOUT 10 MINUTES*	■ Discover ways people care for God's creation. ■ Use a poem to pray. *ABOUT 10 MINUTES*
Day 2	■ Imagine needing the help of a neighbor. *ABOUT 10 MINUTES*	■ Read a Bible story. ■ Discuss the Bible story. ■ Act out the Bible story. ■ Review the vocabulary. *ABOUT 15 MINUTES*	■ Answer Jesus' question. ■ Pray for our good neighbors. *ABOUT 5 MINUTES*
Day 3	■ Brainstorm ways of being good neighbors. *ABOUT 7 MINUTES*	■ Discover what Jesus wants. ■ Play a game about caring. *ABOUT 15 MINUTES*	■ Learn to be good neighbors. ■ Complete an activity. ■ Pray an echo prayer. *ABOUT 8 MINUTES*
Day 4	■ Learn about neighbors. *ABOUT 10 MINUTES*	■ Examine a border of Good Samaritans. ■ Read about Good Samaritans. *ABOUT 12 MINUTES*	■ Pantomime caring. ■ Think about other Good Samaritans. ■ Pray for our Good Samaritans. *ABOUT 8 MINUTES*
Day 5	**Prayer** Discuss the prayer skill; sing a song about Good Samaritans; and reflect on the Good Samaritan by putting on a play. **Review** Complete an activity; answer the questions; and read a Scripture verse.		

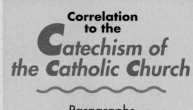

Correlation
to the
Catechism of
the **C**atholic **C**hurch

Paragraphs
1911–1913, 2013

Plan Ahead ~~~~~~~~

	Preparing Your Class	**Materials Needed**
Day 1	For Step 1, consider gestures for the poem.	
Day 2	For Step 2, help the children enact the story of the Good Samaritan.	
Day 3	For Step 1, select a prominent place in the classroom to display the children's list. If time permits, allow the children who will put on the play on Day 5 to practice.	■ newsprint ■ coins ■ buttons
Day 4	For Step 1, consider telling the children a story about someone who acted like a Good Samaritan to you. Give the children time to practice the play for Day 5.	■ map of your state
Day 5	Learn the melody for "Jingle Bells." Be sure the children have all the props needed for the play.	

Additional Resources

As you plan this chapter, consider using the following materials from The Resourceful Teacher Package.

■ *Classroom Activity Sheets 11* and *11a*

■ *Family Activity Sheets 11* and *11a*

■ *Chapter 11 Test*

■ *Prayers for Every Day*

■ *Projects: Grade 1*

In preparing the students for the Sunday readings, you may wish to use Silver Burdett Ginn's *Getting Ready For Sunday* student and teacher materials.

BOOKS FOR THE JOURNEY

Flap Your Wings. P. D. Eastman. Random House, 1991. This story reveals how parents care for their children, no matter what.

Parable of the Good Samaritan. Helen Caswell. Abingdon Press, 1992. This is a beautiful retelling of this parable and what it means.

MORE BOOKS FOR THE JOURNEY

Wilfred Gordon. McDonald Partridge. Mem Fox. Kane/Miller, 1989. A small boy cares so much for an elderly friend that he tries to restore something that she's lost—her memory.

The Jewel Heart. Barbara Helen Berger. Philomel Books, 1994. This wondrous story is about the healing and transforming power of love.

REDUCED CLASSROOM ACTIVITIES

Name _____

Jesus Teaches Us to Care

1. Think of ways you can help care for God's world at home or in your neighborhood.
2. In each box, draw a picture or write one thing you will do. Tell your family what you're doing and invite them to help.

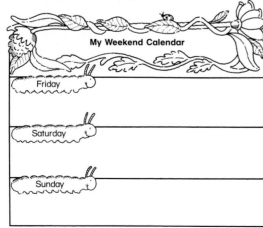

My Weekend Calendar

Friday

Saturday

Sunday

To the Teacher: This activity will help the children accept the responsibility of caring for God's gifts of creation.

Chapter 11   Jesus Teaches Us to Care   THIS IS OUR FAITH 1   **11**

Name _____

The Good Samaritan

1. Color each figure.
2. Cut along the heavy black lines.
3. Glue each figure onto a cardboard stand made from an empty tube.
4. Use the figures to tell the story of the Good Samaritan.

To the Teacher: This activity follows the Scripture story "The Good Samaritan." For stands, cut one bathroom tissue roll per child into five rings.

11a   THIS IS OUR FAITH 1   Chapter 11   Jesus Teaches Us to Care

Background for the Teacher

A PARABLE OF LOVING SERVICE

"Love your neighbor as yourself" is the mandate of the New Testament. In the Gospel story (Luke 10:25–26) used in Chapter 11, a man whom the Jews considered not part of God's people helped a Jewish traveler who had been attacked and battered by a group of robbers.

A priest of the Temple (one who was devoted to the service of God) came up the road from Jericho to Jerusalem and ignored the wounded man. A Levite (a servant of the Temple priests) ignored him, too. Then a Samaritan saw the distressed man at the side of the road and took pity on him.

When Jesus concluded his story, he asked the scribe to whom he was speaking, "Who acted like a good neighbor?" The scribe answered that the good neighbor was the one who had treated the wounded man with compassion.

In this parable, the priest and the Levite were probably hurrying to Jerusalem to participate in the Temple service. To them, serving in God's Temple was much more important than helping the wounded man. How often do we hasten past those in need by hiding among our chores and responsibilities?

And what was the teaching that Jesus offered to the scribe? Love your enemies; do good to those who hate you; love all as you would love yourself. Jesus is saying here that God's love embraces all, as should our love. While some did not interpret the Jewish law this way, it was the heart of the law in Jesus' view. The fictional priest and Levite had embraced the law, but had missed its point.

THE CHRISTIAN CALL

Jesus calls us to meet other's human needs of food, clothing, shelter, consolation, education, prayer, forgiveness, and healing. Jesus has said that as often as we provide these for the least of our brothers and sisters, we provide them for him (Based on Matthew 25:40).

We are called to let Jesus' justice and peace be formed in us and radiate outward in service to others. As he once walked the streets of Jerusalem, he will now walk our streets, as we Christians serve one another.

First graders can easily recognize their need for love. They need reassurance that they are loved in your classroom as well as at home. Children learn best to give love when they grow up in a loving environment. At their age they are somewhat aware that others have needs. However, they may require help in naming the needs and emotions of others and in knowing how best to respond to them.

In Chapter 11, the children in your classroom will become more aware of the call to meet the needs of others. They will also consider the many Good Samaritans who love and help them each day.

DAY 1

DOCTRINE/MORALITY

Objective

This lesson helps the children identify some of the caring actions of others.

Step 1/INTRODUCTION

Learning About Our Lives

Reviewing Chapter 10

Spend a few moments with the children, recalling how God cares for all creation and how Jesus cares. In the discussion, stress that God wants us to care, too. Then discuss the question in the margin of page 132.

Reading a Poem

Direct the children's attention to the poem "Who Cares?" on page 132. Read aloud the first verse and then discuss with the children how a mother can show care when she hears her baby cry. Suggest that the children study the illustration to discover the answer. Follow this same procedure with verses 2 and 3, which refer to a gardener and a teacher. Finally, read aloud the fourth verse and ask the children to tell you who the Creator is (God). Ask the children to use their pencils to underline the words that tell what God cares for.

Adding Gestures to the Poem

Invite the children to brainstorm a gesture to accompany each verse of the poem. (For example, they might make a rocking gesture for the first verse and act as if they are watering a plant for the second verse.) After they decide on the gestures they want to use, direct the children to stand and act out the poem as you read it aloud.

Step 2/DEVELOPMENT

Learning About Our Faith

Learning What Jesus Wants

Read aloud "Jesus Asks Us to Help" on page 133. Then ask the following questions to help the children think of ways they might care for their world.

- Who created the world and all that is in it? (*God*)

132

Jesus Teaches Us to Care

Who Cares?

"I care!"
The mother says,
When she hears
A baby cry.

"I care!"
The gardener says,
When he sees
The plants are dry.

"I care!"
The teacher says,
When a student
Doesn't know.

"I care!"
The Creator says,
"For all that
Lives and grows."

What is one thing that you do for someone that shows you care?

132 Doctrine

CURRICULUM CONNECTION

Music Teach the children the following words to the melody of "The More We Get Together."

The more we care for others,
For others, for others,
The more we care for others,
The happier we'll be.

Like Jesus we're caring;
Like Jesus we're caring.
The more we care for others,
The happier we'll be.

Focus on

Holiness The *Catechism of the Catholic Church* states, "'All Christians in any state or walk of life are called to the fullness of Christian life and to the perfection of charity.' All are called to holiness: 'Be perfect, as your heavenly Father is perfect'" (#2013).

Jesus Asks Us to Help

Jesus wants us to care for the world. Jesus teaches us to care for people who need help.

Activity

Jesus teaches us to take care of God's world.
Circle all the people in the picture who are caring for God's creation.

We Believe

Jesus teaches us to care for people who need help.

- The poem said that God cares for all that lives and grows. How can we help God care for living and growing things? (*Answers will vary.*)
- Who are some people in our world who need help? (*Answers will vary.*)
- What kind of help can you give to these people? (*Answers will vary.*)

or . . .

After reading "Jesus Asks Us to Help," show the children several pictures that illustrate people in need of help. Help the children consider what Jesus might do in each situation and what they could do to show that they care. Encourage each child to contribute to the discussion.

Presenting the Doctrine

Read aloud the We Believe section on page 133, which summarizes the chapter's doctrine, and ask the children to repeat the sentence.

Step 3/CONCLUSION

Learning How to Live Our Faith

Discovering Ways People Can Care for Creation

Direct the children's attention to the activity on page 133. Read the directions and then invite the children to circle all the people in the illustration who are caring for God's creation. When the children complete their work, invite volunteers to talk about how the people in the drawing are caring. Encourage the children to make up stories about the people in the illustration and the care they are showing.

Using a Poem to Pray

Gather the children in the prayer area. Teach them the following response: *Dear God, help us to care, too.* Again read aloud the poem on page 132 and invite the children to use the gestures they brainstormed in Step 1. After each verse of the poem, invite the children's response.

★ Enriching the Lesson ★

Before class, decorate a box with the words *I Care*. Ask the children to think of ways they can care at home, at school, and in their neighborhoods. Then have the children print their suggestions on slips of paper and put them in the box. Once a week throughout the rest of the year, invite a child to draw a slip from the box and have the class follow the suggestion listed.

DAY 2
SCRIPTURE

Objective

This lesson helps the children understand what Jesus means by being a good neighbor.

Step 1/INTRODUCTION

Learning About Our Lives

Imagining Needing the Help of a Neighbor

Invite the children to think of a time when they needed help. Have the children close their eyes and picture the time. Ask them to think about where they were, what they were doing, and how they felt. Then tell them to imagine that someone whom they think will help them approaches. Describe the person coming near, looking at the child, and passing by. Next have them think about a second neighbor who is going by. Finally, encourage them to imagine that a third neighbor is walking toward them. Tell them to picture this person helping them. Ask the children to "see" what the person does and to "hear" what the person says.

Then ask the children to open their eyes and to share how they felt when they were passed by and when the third person helped them.

Step 2/DEVELOPMENT

Learning About Our Faith

Reading a Bible Story

Tell the children that you are going to read aloud the story on pages 134–135. Explain that this story is from the Bible, and that Jesus told this story to a group of people because someone asked Jesus a question. Read aloud the first paragraph on page 134 and ask the children what the question was. Then read "The Good Samaritan." Ask volunteers to retell the story by using the illustrations.

Discussing the Bible Story

Using the following questions, discuss the story on pages 134–135.

■ Why did Jesus tell this story? (*Someone asked, "Who is my neighbor?"*)

■ What happened to the man in the story? (*He was beaten by robbers.*)

134

The Good Samaritan

One day someone said to Jesus,
"God says we must love our neighbor.
But who is my neighbor?"
Jesus answered by telling this story
about the **Good Samaritan**.

A man was walking down a road.
Some robbers jumped out of the bushes
They stole his money and clothes.
Then they beat him up.

A leader of the people passed by.
He saw the man but did not stop.

Next, a helper from the Temple came by.
He too saw the man but did not stop.

134   Scripture

Cultural Awareness

Most Jews of Jesus' time disliked the Samaritans. Although the Samaritans worshipped Yahweh and observed the Law of Moses, to the Jewish way of thinking they had corrupted both their practices and beliefs. Yet Jesus chose to make a hero of a Samaritan. For his Jewish listeners, no more inclusive answer could have been given to the question, "Who is my neighbor?"

Focus on

The Two Who Passed By   The men who passed by the wounded stranger in "The Good Samaritan" might have had culturally acceptable reasons: (1) The wounded man might be dead, and to touch him would defile a Temple priest or Levite. A long purification ritual was required to participate in worship again. (2) The robbers might be waiting to attack. (3) Suffering may have been seen as punishment for sin. Better not interfere!

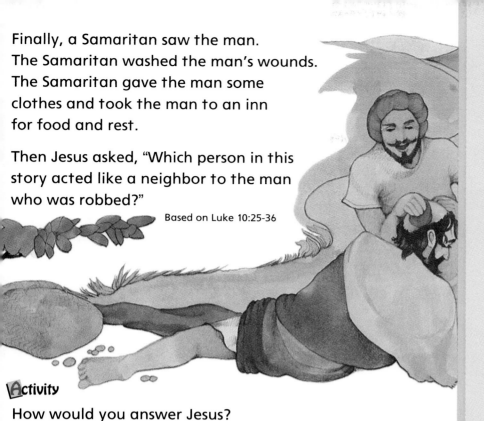

Finally, a Samaritan saw the man.
The Samaritan washed the man's wounds.
The Samaritan gave the man some
clothes and took the man to an inn
for food and rest.

Then Jesus asked, "Which person in this
story acted like a neighbor to the man
who was robbed?"

Based on Luke 10:25-36

How would you answer Jesus?

The Good Samaritan

New Word

Good Samaritan The Good Samaritan was
a person who cared for
someone who needed help.

Scripture 135

Focus on

Dangerous Travel Most people in Jesus' time traveled in caravans because the roads were dangerous. The road in the story of the Good Samaritan was well known, for it connected Jericho to Jerusalem. It wound through barren and wild hills. Robbers hid in caves and jumped from behind giant boulders to attack travelers. So many bloody incidents occurred there that it was called the red road.

🍎 Teaching Tips

A presentation of the play of the Good Samaritan is scheduled for Day 5. As the children reenact the story on Day 2, observe who does it with ease and select a cast for Day 5. Have these children bring in costumes (robes, towels, some twine or roping, perhaps an old tie to secure the towel as a head dress) and other simple props, such as oil, a thermos for water, and money.

- What did the first man do when he saw the man who was hurt? (*He walked by.*)
- What did the second man do when he saw the man who was hurt? (*He walked by.*)
- Who finally stopped to help the man? (*The Good Samaritan*)
- How did the Samaritan take care of the man? (*He washed the man's wounds and took him to an inn.*)

Print the words *Good Samaritan* on the chalkboard and ask the children to tell the class what they think of the Good Samaritan.

Acting Out the Scripture Story

Invite the children to act out the story of the Good Samaritan. Choose volunteers to portray the wounded man, the robbers, the priest, the Temple helper, the Good Samaritan, and the innkeeper. Provide time for the children to decide what they will say in their play. When the actors are ready, invite them to present their play. Repeat this play with different actors.

Reviewing the Vocabulary

Point to the New Word section on page 135. Ask the children to repeat the phrase *Good Samaritan* and its definition.

Step 3/CONCLUSION

Learning How to Live Our Faith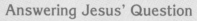

Answering Jesus' Question

Reread the last paragraph of "The Good Samaritan" on page 135. Then read the directions for the activity at the bottom of the page and encourage the children to print their answers on the line provided.

Praying for Our Good Neighbors

Gather the children to pray. Invite them to close their eyes and think of someone who recently helped them. Tell the children that we sometimes call people who come to our aid "Good Samaritans" because they offer help when we need it. Ask for volunteers to tell about being helped. When they have finished, the class may pray the following response: *Thank you, God, for this Good Samaritan.*

135

Objective

This lesson helps the children practice being good neighbors as Jesus taught us to be.

Step 1/INTRODUCTION

Learning About Our Lives

Brainstorming Ways to Be Good Neighbors

Recall the Good Samaritan story from Day 2. Explain that Jesus wants all people to be good neighbors and to act as the Good Samaritan did. Ask the children to brainstorm ways that they can be good neighbors, too. Print these suggestions on newsprint and post the sheet in a prominent place in the classroom.

Step 2/DEVELOPMENT

Learning About Our Faith

Discovering What Jesus Wants

Talk about how the Good Samaritan was a good neighbor to the wounded man. Then direct the children to the top of page 136. Read the text under "Being Good Samaritans." Tell the children that today they are going to play a game about being good neighbors.

Playing a Game About Caring

Divide the class into groups of two or three. Give each group one coin and a button or small piece of construction paper for each player. Read the directions for the game on page 136 and invite the children to play it. Point out that the way they play the game together will be an example of how they can have fun while acting as good neighbors.

As the children play the game, go around the room and offer help with reading when needed. When the groups finish their games, invite the children to comment on the different ways they learned to care while playing the game.

Being Good Samaritans

Jesus wants us to care for others.
We can care for plants, animals, and people.
We can find many ways to care for others.

Activity

Play the game that follows.

1. You will need a coin and a button.
2. Flip the coin to see how many spaces to move the button.

Heads=1 space
Tails=2 spaces

6 You brought flowers to che someone up.

Climb the ste to the next space.

5 Who teache us to care ?

Fill in the blank

1 Your mom needed help today.
You said, YES
Move ahead 1 space.

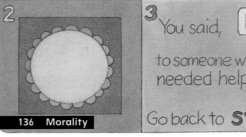

2

3 You said, NO to someone who needed help.
Go back to **START**.

4

Teaching Tips

Bulletin boards, as they are used throughout this Teacher Edition, aim at helping the children focus on an important idea being taught. If you wish to impress upon the children the concept that we can be good neighbors, too, have them draw pictures of themselves being Good Samaritans and display the pictures on the bulletin board with an appropriate concept as a caption.

ou visited a
riend who was
ck.

e ahead 1 space.

esus says,
CARE FOR OTHERS.

or the letters.

END

12 Stay here until you flip Heads.

11

10 You got angry. You hit your friend.

Go back **3** spaces.

Activity

Choose a word to complete each sentence.

1. A good neighbor is kind and

helps _____ people.

2. Jesus wants me to be a

good _____ neighbor.

Enriching the Lesson

Print these words on the chalkboard for the children to copy:
Because I love you _____,
I promise to _____.
Love, _____.
Ask each child to choose someone he or she loves and to think of something to do to be a Good Samaritan to the chosen person. Have the children fill in the blanks. Suggest that they deliver their promises personally.

Step 3/CONCLUSION

Learning How to Live Our Faith

Learning to Be Good Neighbors

After the children finish playing the game, have them look at the game board and find the number of each square in which people acted like good neighbors—Good Samaritans (1, 6, 8). Then ask them to find the number of each square in which people did not act like Good Samaritans (3, 10).

Completing an Activity

Direct the children's attention to the activity at the bottom of page 137. Read the sentences with the children and encourage them to choose a word to complete each sentence.

Praying an Echo Prayer

Ask the children if any of them know what an echo is. Make sure that everyone understands that an echo is a call-and-repeat pattern. Tell the children that today they are going to pray a poem about caring. One group will echo the other. Then print the following poem on the chalkboard in letters large enough for the children to read from a distance.

Dear God of all,
Help me to care.
When things go wrong,
Teach me your way to share.

Dear God of all,
Help me to care
And spread your love
Here, there, and everywhere.

Divide the class into two groups. The first group stands in a line on the left side of the room and the second group stands on the right side. Ask the children to close their eyes and think about their neighbors and what caring things they can do for them. Then have the children open their eyes and read the poem line by line, with Group 2 echoing what Group 1 says.

Objective

This lesson helps the children recognize that many people in their lives are Good Samaritans.

Step 1/INTRODUCTION

Learning About Our Lives

Learning About Neighbors

Print the words *neighbor* and *Good Samaritan* on the chalkboard. Ask the children what these words mean to them. Explain to the children that in addition to the people who live near their homes, they have many other neighbors who are Good Samaritans to them.

Share a story about someone who did not live next door to you and yet acted as a good neighbor to you. Ask the children to comment on how this person was a Good Samaritan to you.

Step 2/DEVELOPMENT

Learning About Our Faith

Examining a Border of Good Samaritans

Direct the children's attention to the border around the text on pages 138–139. Look at the various items pictured in the border and ask the children who would use these items. Then point out the words in the border: *artist, astronaut, barber,* and so on. Tell the children that the items in the border are symbols that stand for the names of people who can be Good Samaritans. Point out several symbols and ask the children to name the person each symbol stands for. (For example, the brush and palette stand for an artist.)

Reading About Good Samaritans

Point out the stories on pages 138–139. Tell the children that as you read each story, you will pause at each symbol, give them time to find it in the border, and then invite them to say aloud the name of the occupation represented by the symbol.

Then read "Many Good Neighbors" on pages 138–139. When you come to the symbol in the first story—the one about Mr. Martin—pause to

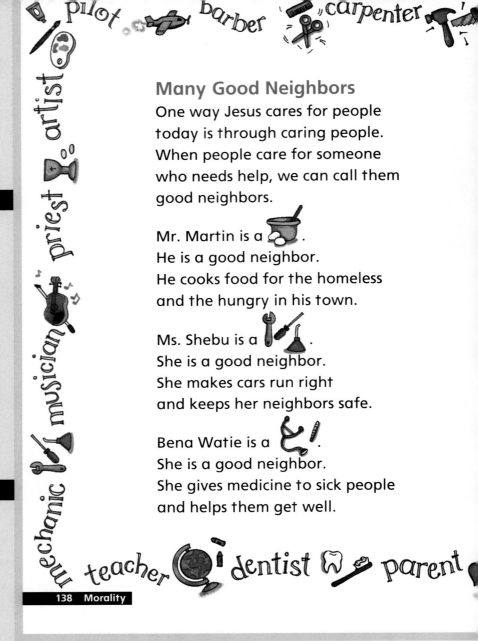

Many Good Neighbors

One way Jesus cares for people today is through caring people. When people care for someone who needs help, we can call them good neighbors.

Mr. Martin is a .
He is a good neighbor.
He cooks food for the homeless and the hungry in his town.

Ms. Shebu is a .
She is a good neighbor.
She makes cars run right and keeps her neighbors safe.

Bena Watie is a .
She is a good neighbor.
She gives medicine to sick people and helps them get well.

CURRICULUM CONNECTION

Language Arts Invite volunteers to add a beginning, middle and end to each of the descriptions of neighborly people in "Many Good Neighbors" on pages 138–139. Ask the children to elaborate how each person is a Good Samaritan. Then provide drawing paper for the children to make booklets of their Good Samaritan stories to put in the classroom library.

Taro Uno is a 🌐.
He is a good neighbor.
He teaches children about God's world and helps them learn to read and write.

Mrs. Ming is a ❤.
She is a good neighbor.
She loves her two children and listens to their stories.

Mr. Johnson is a 🚜.
He is a good neighbor.
He raises food for us to eat and is kind to animals.

When these people care,
they are being good neighbors.

give the children time to find the symbol and the occupation it stands for in the border.

Continue reading the description of Mr. Martin and ask the children to tell how he was a Good Samaritan. Repeat this procedure for each of the good neighbors.

Step 3/CONCLUSION

Learning How to Live Our Faith

Pantomiming Caring

Invite volunteers to pantomime how each person in each story cares for others. The children may choose partners to help them pantomime the story.

Thinking About Other Good Samaritans

Recall that in today's stories the children learned about Good Samaritans who cooked, fixed cars, took care of sick people, taught school, cared for the family, and raised crops for food. Then return to the border on pages 138–139 and discuss the occupations and their symbols that do not have stories in "Many Good Neighbors." Discuss how people having these occupations can be Good Samaritans.

Praying for the Good Samaritans

Gather the children in the prayer corner. When they are quiet, encourage them to close their eyes. Then invite them to say a silent prayer of thanksgiving to God for all the Good Samaritans in their lives.

Teaching Tips

Collect from the library some books on various occupations. You might display them with the clay symbols suggested in Enriching the Lesson on this page. Children can make simple reports on books they like by telling the name of the book and the author and by showing some of the pictures that interest them to the class. It is fun for children to dress up as book characters when giving a report.

Enriching the Lesson

Have the children use clay to make models of the symbols in the border on pages 138–139. Most of these symbols are objects that people in various occupations use at work. If the children wish, they may choose to form something that their family members use to help others. After the model is fashioned, each child may display it on a paper on which a sentence is written about how the object is used for helping.

Objective

This lesson helps the children reflect on the story of the Good Samaritan by putting on a play.

Discussing the Prayer Skill

Read aloud the text at the top of page 140. Tell the children that today they are going to think about the story of the Good Samaritan by putting on a play. Acting out Bible stories is a good way to remember what happened in the story.

Singing a Song

Using the melody of "Jingle Bells," teach the following words.

Those who care,
Those who care,
Those who care each day.
Oh, what joy they give to us
As they care for us each day!

Those who care,
Those who care,
Those who care each day.
Oh, what joy they give to us
As they care for us each day!

Gathering to Reflect by Putting on a Play

After the children have learned the song, have them form a line and process to the prayer area. Invite them to sit on the floor or on the reading chairs and give them a few moments to get ready to pray. After they have quieted themselves, set the stage for a reflection on the Bible story by saying the following prayer.

Dear Jesus, you have asked us to care for others. Sometimes it is hard, as it was for the two men in the story of the Good Samaritan. It was hard for the Samaritan, too, but he went out of his way to help the stranger. Help us think of your way of love as we act out a play about the Good Samaritan.

Then invite the children to put on the play that the children prepared on Day 2 and practiced throughout the week. When they have finished, encourage the children to think about the play for a minute. Close the prayer by having the children sing the song again.

140

Praying with a Play

There are many ways to think over the stories from the Bible.
We can act out the story.
Putting on a play helps us remember the story.
We can imagine what happened and what people said.

You might want to put on a play about the Good Samaritan.

140 Prayer

Praying by Putting On a Play The prayer skill is the continuation of the skill of reflecting on a Scripture story. Praying with plays has a long tradition in our Church, from the days of the medieval miracle plays to the passion plays still common today, especially in the Hispanic community. Plays allow us to enter into an event by participating in it on a kinesthetic level.

🍎 Teaching Tips

Distribute a worksheet headed *Be a Good Samaritan*. Direct the children to draw on the paper the outlines of six hearts. Encourage the children to take the worksheets home and to color in a heart each time they do something to help someone. Tell the children that each time they care for someone, they are acting as Jesus wants us to act and are being Good Samaritans or good neighbors.

Chapter Review

Activity

Choose one of the objects.
Tell how you can use it to be a good neighbor.

1. In Jesus' story, who acted like a good neighbor?

The Good Samaritan

2. Who teaches us to care for others?

Jesus

Jesus says, "Love one another as I love you." Based on John 15:12

3. Talk about how you can help other people.

Completing an Activity

Use the activity on page 141 to review the learning of Chapter 11. After reading the top of page 141, invite volunteers to choose one of the pictured objects and tell how they would use it to be a Good Samaritan. Praise the children for their caring and for their creative imaginations.

Answering Questions

Read aloud the first two questions and ask volunteers to respond. Direct the children to print the answers in their texts. Encourage all the children to participate in the discussion of the third question. Be supportive of each child who responds.

Reading the Scripture Verse

Ask the children to read the Scripture verse after you. It is good to end the lesson by reflecting on the word of God. If you wish, you may have the children memorize this verse.

CURRICULUM CONNECTION

Handwriting A short Scripture verse on Day 5 highlights a main idea of the chapter. Print it on the chalkboard for the children to copy. Invite the children to make Scripture booklets and add to them each week. In addition, you might choose one of the children's papers each week to put in a class book to use for morning prayer. Each day a child may read a verse chosen from the class book.

Enriching the Lesson

Help the children memorize this poem:

If you sometimes feel
Lonely, sad, or blue,
I know a way to help.
I know what to do.

We can sit and talk
or maybe run and play.
I can make you smile
because I care this way.

Ask the children if they have done any of the things mentioned in the poem.

141

12 Jesus Teaches Us to Pray

Objectives

To help the children

■ Recognize the importance of prayer in Jesus' life and in their own lives.

■ Become familiar with The Lord's Prayer.

■ Understand that they each can pray to God in their own way.

■ Understand the meaning of The Lord's Prayer.

■ Pray The Lord's Prayer with a thankful spirit and review the chapter.

Chapter Outline

	Step 1 Learning About Our Lives	**Step 2** Learning About Our Faith	**Step 3** Learning How to Live Our Faith
Day 1	■ Talk about prayer. ■ Study pictures. ■ Read a poem. *ABOUT 7 MINUTES*	■ Respond to a Bible illustration. ■ Learn more about Jesus and prayer. *ABOUT 8 MINUTES*	■ Complete an activity on prayer. ■ Find places to pray. ■ Make a bulletin board. ■ Share a poem with God. *ABOUT 15 MINUTES*
Day 2	■ Discuss a picture. *ABOUT 5 MINUTES*	■ Read a Bible story. ■ Respond to a Bible illustration. ■ Review the vocabulary. ■ Present the doctrine. *ABOUT 10 MINUTES*	■ Use the bulletin board to discuss prayer. ■ Pray The Lord's Prayer. ■ Review the lesson. *ABOUT 15 MINUTES*
Day 3	■ Learn names for God. *ABOUT 7 MINUTES*	■ Learn from Jesus. *ABOUT 10 MINUTES*	■ Write a prayer. ■ Use the children's prayers. *ABOUT 13 MINUTES*
Day 4	■ Study a map. *ABOUT 6 MINUTES*	■ Use the illustrations. ■ Discover who prays The Lord's Prayer. *ABOUT 9 MINUTES*	■ Complete an activity. ■ Think about forgiveness. ■ Share forgiveness during prayer time. *ABOUT 15 MINUTES*
Day 5	**Prayer** Add movements to accompany a prayer; sing a song; and pray The Lord's Prayer. **Review** Complete an activity; answer the questions; read a Scripture verse.		

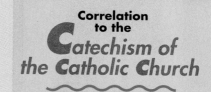

Correlation
to the
Catechism of
the Catholic Church

Paragraphs
520, 2607

Plan Ahead

	Preparing Your Class	**Materials Needed**
Day 1	For Step 3, cut out the letters: *We like to talk and listen to God in our favorite places.* Prepare a space for a bulletin board.	■ drawing paper ■ empty bulletin board ■ letters for sentence
Day 2	For Step 1, find a picture of a child and a father talking lovingly and prepare a conversation that they might be having.	■ picture of a child and a father talking together ■ bulletin board from Day 1
Day 3	If possible, for Step 1, provide names for God in several languages. Practice the American Sign Language for *God,* shown on page 146.	
Day 4	For Step 1, locate on a state map the city in which your school is located.	■ map of your state ■ map of your city
Day 5	Prepare to teach a chant for The Lord's Prayer. Plan a procession route to the prayer area.	■ bulletin board from Day 1

Additional Resources

As you plan this chapter, consider using the following materials from The Resourceful Teacher Package.

■ *Classroom Activity Sheets 12* and *12a*

■ *Family Activity Sheets 12* and *12a*

■ *Chapter 12 Test*

■ *Prayers for Every Day*

■ *Projects: Grade 1*

In preparing the students for the Sunday readings, you may wish to use Silver Burdett Ginn's *Getting Ready For Sunday* student and teacher materials.

BOOKS FOR THE JOURNEY

The Lord's Prayer. Ingrid Shelton. Concordia, 1982. The Our Father is explained in verse.

What Can I Say to You, God? Elspeth Campbell Murphy. David C. Cook, 1980. This book is a child's attempt to figure out how to talk with God.

MORE BOOKS FOR THE JOURNEY

Sunday's Children. "Morning Prayer," p. 56; "Table Prayer," p. 58; "Evening Prayer," p. 60. James Bitney. Resources Publications, 1986. Prayer poems are provided for special moments in the day.

The Way to Start the Day. Byrd Baylor. Charles Scribner's Sons, 1978. This book introduces children to people all over the world who are praying at different times, in different ways, and for different reasons.

REDUCED CLASSROOM ACTIVITIES

Name _____

Jesus Teaches Us to Pray

Match the prayer parts with the pictures.

Our Father, who art in heaven,
hallowed be thy name;
thy kingdom come;
thy will be done
on earth as it is in heaven.

Give us this day our daily bread;
and forgive us our trespasses
as we forgive those
who trespass against us;

and lead us not into temptation,
but deliver us from evil.   Amen.

To the Teacher: This activity presents the meaning of the words to the Lord's Prayer.

Chapter 12   Jesus Teaches Us to Pray   THIS IS OUR FAITH 1   **12**

Name _____

A Prayer Banner

1. Color the banner.
2. Cut along the outside heavy black lines.
3. Put the banner where you will see it every day.

To the Teacher: This activity emphasizes that we can pray always and everywhere.

12a   THIS IS OUR FAITH 1   Chapter 12   Jesus Teaches Us to Pray

PRAYING IS LOVING

We learn to pray to the extent that we have learned to love. An ability to love grows out of our personal experience of God's love. Our prayer experience deepens as our awareness of God's dynamic presence becomes more real. Our encounter with God in prayer is a loving dialogue. It can be a celebration of God's goodness, a plea for what we need, or a grieving for what we are experiencing. When we pray, God celebrates and grieves and rejoices with us.

For the Jesus of the Gospels, prayer was as natural as breathing. His prayer showed a unique intimacy with God, his Father. Jesus' continual awareness of the Father's loving presence gave purpose to Jesus' life and to his prayer.

Finding his prayerfulness attractive, the apostles asked Jesus to teach them to pray. In response, he gave them the Our Father, The Lord's Prayer as a model.

When we say this prayer, we express trust in God as a loving Father whom we revere. We voice thanks and hope that God's love, joy, peace, truth, justice, and mercy may transform our hearts and the whole world. In the Our Father, we ask that God satisfy the hungers of our body and our spirit. What do we need? We need food and clothing, shelter and warmth, love and security. When we pray that God will give us our daily bread, we are praying for all these things.

In the Our Father, we also admit our failings and ask forgiveness, and we admit that God's forgiveness is dependent on our forgiving others. Lastly, we request strength to meet all the experiences of our life.

TEACHING CHILDREN TO PRAY

Your goal is to initiate the children into a life of prayer. The special qualities of childhood can be catalysts for this process. Singing, dancing, and playing all are ways for children to pray. You can both encourage and learn from their spontaneity in prayer. Keep in mind that the example of your own reverential attitude toward all prayer conveys to the children a sense of the power of this dialogue with God.

As members of the Catholic Church, children learn the traditional prayers treasured by countless generations of faithful believers. This experience helps them develop a sense of belonging to Jesus' family of friends. When properly presented, these prayers can foster the natural prayerfulness of children.

Please note that although The Lord's Prayer is simple and direct, as Jesus intended, the venerable language can confuse children. Explain the words and the phrases clearly and simply. Go over the prayer again and again, helping the children memorize it and learn its meaning.

Objective

This lesson helps the children recognize the importance of prayer in the life of Jesus and in their own lives.

Step 1/INTRODUCTION

Learning About Our Lives

Talking About Prayer

Read aloud the chapter title and the question in the margin on page 142. Encourage all the children to participate in the discussion of their favorite ways of praying. With the children recall the definition of prayer they learned in Chapter 8: *Prayer is talking and listening to God.* Print the definition on the chalkboard. Remind the children that, just as they are learning to pray, Jesus learned to pray as he was growing up.

Studying Pictures

Direct the children's attention to the pictures on page 142. Then read the text above the pictures and encourage the children to respond to the question. In the first picture the children are praying together with musical instruments, praising God who speaks to us through the Bible. Talk about the quiet and reverence the child in the second picture is showing and discuss her posture. Stress that when people pray, they become quiet inside and their bodies show that they are talking and listening to God. Invite the children to suggest what each of the people in these pictures might be saying to God.

Reading a Poem

Call the children's attention to the poem at the bottom of page 142. Read it aloud as the children follow along in their books. Invite their comments on the poem. Then repeat it and invite the children to read each line with you.

Step 2/DEVELOPMENT

Learning About Our Faith

Responding to a Bible Illustration

Direct the children's attention to the illustration on page 143. Ask the following questions.

142

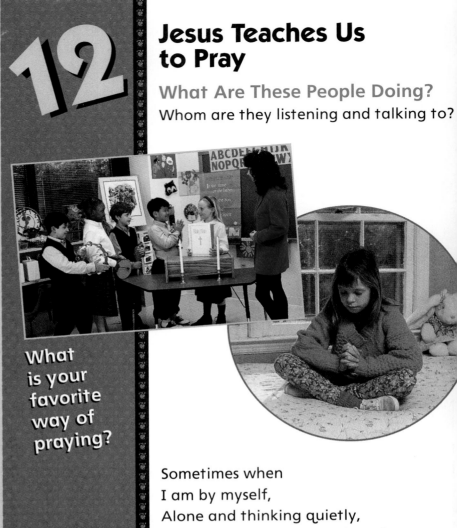

12 Jesus Teaches Us to Pray

What Are These People Doing?

Whom are they listening and talking to?

What is your favorite way of praying?

142   Prayer

Sometimes when
I am by myself,
Alone and thinking quietly,
I talk to God, my special friend,
Or listen as God talks to me.

🍎 Teaching Tips

In THIS IS OUR FAITH, Grade 1, prayer is taught throughout each lesson, and various prayer experiences are provided. In Chapter 8 the lessons focus intensely on prayer, and Chapter 12 returns to the theme, deepening and expanding upon it. This pacing allows the previous learning to mature and then be reviewed and fortified. Observe the children's ability to express their understanding of prayer to see if reteaching is needed.

Focus on

Jesus and Prayer   According to the *Catechism of the Catholic Church,* "When Jesus prays he is already teaching us how to pray. His prayer to his Father is the theological path (the path of faith, hope, and charity) of our prayer to God. But the Gospel also gives us Jesus' explicit teaching on prayer. Like a wise teacher he takes hold of us where we are and leads us progressively toward the Father" (#2607).

Jesus Prayed

When Jesus was a child, he prayed.
After Jesus grew up, he still prayed.
He prayed all alone in the (desert.)
He prayed in the (hills) and while walking.
He prayed when he was happy or sad.
He prayed with his friends.
He prayed in the (Temple) in Jerusalem.

Activity

Where did Jesus pray?
Circle the answers in the story.

143   Prayer

- What is Jesus doing? (*He is praying.*)
- Whom is Jesus talking and listening to? (*God*)
- What do you think Jesus might be saying? (*Answers will vary.*)
- Why do grown-ups need to pray just as children do? (*Answers will vary, but everyone needs to be able to talk to God.*)

Learning More About Jesus and Prayer

Direct the children to the text at the top of page 143. Read aloud "Jesus Prayed." Afterward invite the children to share their thoughts on why Jesus prayed. (*Jesus loved God the Father and wanted to talk and listen to his Father often.*)

Step 3/CONCLUSION

Learning How to Live Our Faith

Completing an Activity on Prayer

Read the activity at the bottom of page 143. Invite the children to circle all the places where Jesus prayed.

Finding Places to Pray

Share with the children your own favorite places of prayer. Ask them where they like to pray and list their answers on the chalkboard. Invite them to explain why they like to pray in these places. Emphasize that the most important thing is that they talk and listen to God with love and attention.

Making a Bulletin Board About Praying

Invite the children to draw pictures of themselves praying in their favorite places. When they have finished, gather them around an empty bulletin board. Cut out the letters: *We like to talk and listen to God in our favorite places.* Give each child a letter to hold and tack up the letters and their pictures. Talk about how the sentence applies to their drawings.

Sharing a Poem with God

As the children are gathered around the bulletin board, tell them that God likes to listen to them when they read poems. Then read aloud the poem on page 142 and invite the children to read each line after you. Afterward, praise their reading and tell them that God must be very proud of them.

143

DAY 2
SCRIPTURE/DOCTRINE

Objective

This lesson helps the children become familiar with The Lord's Prayer.

Step 1/INTRODUCTION

Learning About Our Lives

Discussing a Picture

Show the children a picture of a child and a father talking together. Tell the children a story about the picture, including a conversation the father and the child might be having. Then, ask the children how the child might feel when he or she talks with a parent and the parent listens carefully. Talk with the children about similar experiences they have had.

After the discussion recall that when they pray, they have a conversation with God our Father who always listens to them very carefully. Tell the children that today they are going to learn a prayer they can say to God, their heavenly Father.

Step 2/DEVELOPMENT

Learning About Our Faith

Reading a Bible Story

Talk with the children about the love Jesus felt for his Father, and about how Jesus loved to talk and to listen to God the Father in prayer. Then read aloud The Lord's Prayer on pages 144–145. Ask the following questions.

■ Why, do you think, did the friends of Jesus want him to teach them to pray? (*Answers will vary.*)

■ Have you heard this prayer before? Where? (*Perhaps they have heard it at Mass.*)

■ What do we call this prayer? (*The Our Father or The Lord's Prayer*)

Explain that because Jesus is God's Son, we call him Lord and that The Lord's Prayer is Jesus' prayer.

Responding to a Bible Illustration

Direct the children's attention to the illustration on pages 144–145. Encourage the children to close their eyes and imagine they are with Jesus on a hillside. Ask them to imagine all

144

The Lord's Prayer

Jesus' friends often saw him pray.
They knew he liked to talk
and listen to God, his Father.

One day, Jesus' friends said,
"Please, Jesus, teach us how to pray."
So Jesus taught them this prayer.

144 Scripture

Focus on

Bread During the time of Jesus, people made bread from wheat or barley mixed with olive oil and yeast, except at Passover when no yeast was used. The loaves were round and somewhat flat, as pita is today. Bakers did not use bread pans, as we do. Instead they spread the dough directly onto the flat surface of the oven. You might want to obtain some pita for the class to try.

Our Father, who art in heaven,
  hallowed be thy name;
thy kingdom come;
thy will be done on earth—
  as it is in **heaven**.
Give us this day our daily bread;
and forgive us our trespasses
  as we forgive those
  who **trespass** against us;
and lead us not into temptation,
  but deliver us from evil.
Amen.

Based on Matthew 6:9-13

New Words

hallowed	Hallowed means holy.
heaven	Heaven is being happy with God forever.
trespass	Trespass means to hurt someone.

We Believe

Jesus prayed and teaches us to pray.

Scripture 145

Enriching the Lesson

If the children need help in understanding The Lord's Prayer, explain it phrase by phrase. You will find a complete explanation of this prayer in *Our Catholic Heritage,* page 352.

---

they can hear, see, smell, touch and taste as they listen to Jesus. Then invite the children to open their eyes and to share their imaginings. Finally, ask them what Jesus was saying.

Reviewing the Vocabulary

Point to the New Words section on page 145. Ask the children to repeat the words *hallowed, heaven,* and *trespass* and their definitions. Go back to The Lord's Prayer on page 145 and use the definitions of *hallowed* and *trespass* to help them better understand the prayer.

Presenting the Doctrine

Read aloud the We Believe section on page 145, which summarizes the chapter's doctrine. Ask the children to repeat the sentence.

Step 3/CONCLUSION

Learning How to Live Our Faith

Using the Bulletin Board to Discuss Prayer

Gather the children around the bulletin board that they decorated on Day 1. Ask volunteers to point to their drawings and to explain where they are praying in the pictures. After each volunteer shares, ask the child if he or she could pray The Lord's Prayer in this favorite place. Help the children understand that they can pray the Our Father anywhere and at any time.

Praying The Lord's Prayer

While the children are gathered around the bulletin board, pray The Lord's Prayer together. (If they do not know the prayer, invite the children to repeat it after you as you read it line by line.)

Reviewing the Lesson

To review the lesson, ask the following questions.

■ What is the name of the prayer Jesus taught his friends? (*The Our Father or The Lord's Prayer*)

■ When we ask that God the Father's name be hallowed, what do we mean? (*That God the Father's name is holy*)

■ When we trespass against others, what do we do? (*We do something to hurt them.*)

145

DOCTRINE/PRAYER

Objective

This lesson helps the children understand they can pray to God in their own way.

Step 1/INTRODUCTION

Learning About Our Lives

Learning Names for God

Direct the children to the activity at the top of page 146. Invite the children's comments on the illustration. Then read the text and help the children understand that in every language, people have a name for God. Help the children pronounce the words on the pennants. Invite the children to circle the pennant that shows the word *God* in a language they can speak or would like to learn. Then encourage them to do the American Sign Language gestures with you.

Invite the children to use whatever languages they know to say the word *God*. If they know words for God not shown on page 146, print their words on the chalkboard and invite the children to teach these words to the class.

Step 2/DEVELOPMENT

Learning About Our Faith

Learning from Jesus

Direct the children's attention to the title "God Our Father" at the bottom of page 146. Before reading the text, encourage volunteers to share all that they have learned from Jesus about God and about prayer. Then read the text. Afterward ask the following questions.

- What prayer did Jesus teach us? (*The Our Father*)
- Why did Jesus say "Our Father" instead of "My Father"? (*Jesus wants us to know that God, his Father, is our Father, too.*)
- What does Jesus want you to remember? (*That God loves you and everyone else*)

 Activity

The words below mean "God" in different languages. Circle the pictures that show the word "God" in a language you can speak or would like to learn.

God Our Father

Jesus, the Son of God, prayed.
Jesus taught all of us to pray.
He taught us to say "Our Father."
Why did Jesus say "Our Father"
instead of "My Father?"

Jesus wants us to know that
God is our Father, too.
Jesus wants us to remember that
God loves everyone.

 **Cultural Awareness**

Invite the children to say any prayers that they know in a language other than English. Help the children understand that people everywhere pray to God in their own languages. If one of the children knows a simple prayer such as the Sign of the Cross in another language, ask the child to lead the class in praying it for several days at a specific time, such as before lunch.

Focus on

God, Our Father   Jesus spoke Aramaic and when addressing his heavenly father called God by the Aramaic word *abba* which means "Daddy." It is an informal rather than a formal, reserved greeting. When Jesus taught his disciples to pray, he invited them to use this familiar word to address God the Father, too. By doing so, Jesus underlined to all those who belonged to his family of friends and followers the familial relationship they now shared with God the Father, because of their relationship with Jesus, the Son of God.

Activity

Circle one group of words in each line.
Make up a prayer to say to God.

God	Our Father	Our Creator
You give me	You care for	You created
my friends	my family	the world
with love.	always.	because you are so good.

Write your prayer on the lines below.

_____

- -

_____

- -

_____

- -

_____

- -

_____

Enriching the Lesson

Invite the children to think of simple prayers for various needs. Suggest that they can pray to ask God's blessing on someone, to express sorrow for hurting someone, to thank God for something, or to praise God for being so holy, good, and caring. Print on the chalkboard a few prayers the children compose and invite the children to choose one prayer to copy to use at home as they wish.

Step 3/CONCLUSION

Learning How to Live Our Faith

Writing a Prayer

Read the directions to the activity at the top of page 147. Check to be sure that the children understand that they are to circle one of the three phrases in each line. Then they are to print their prayer. For example one of many possibilities might read: *Our Father, you give me my family with love.*

Using the Children's Prayers

Have the children bring their books and gather in the prayer area. When the children are quiet, invite volunteers to read the prayers they composed on page 147. After the first person has prayed, ask if anyone has a different prayer. There is a large possibility of different prayers from this exercise.

DAY 4
PRAYER

Objective

This lesson helps the children understand the meaning of The Lord's Prayer.

Step 1/INTRODUCTION

Learning About Our Lives

Studying a Map

Show the children a map of their state. Ask if anyone can point out your town or city. Tell the children that Christians live everywhere in their state. As you point to and pronounce the names of cities and towns around the state, ask the children if Christians live there and encourage them to respond with a resounding yes!

Step 2/DEVELOPMENT

Learning About Our Faith

Using Illustrations

Direct the children's attention to the illustration on page 148. Point out the map of the world. Point to North America and to where your city or town would roughly be on the map. Then invite the children's comments on what the map is showing them. Tell the children that each of the people in the illustration is a Christian. Ask them what prayer they think the people are praying. (*Answers will vary. If no one mentions The Lord's Prayer, do so yourself.*)

Discovering Who Prays The Lord's Prayer

Read the text "Praying Jesus' Prayer" on page 148. Ask the following questions.

■ Where do Christians live? (*Everywhere*)

■ What prayer do they all pray? (*The Lord's Prayer*)

■ Who gave us this prayer? (*Jesus*)

Look at the map and identify the various continents and the people who are praying The Lord's Prayer. (*A girl in the United States, a man in South America, an African woman, a Russian European, and a Chinese man.*)

Praying Jesus' Prayer

We Christians live everywhere.
All of us pray The Lord's Prayer.
Look at the map and the pictures.
See how Christians everywhere
pray The Lord's Prayer.

148 Prayer

Teaching Tips

In this session the children will be looking at maps. The skills used are taught in major first-grade social studies books. The purpose of the maps is to help the children visualize the religious teaching of the lesson—Christians everywhere pray The Lord's Prayer. Focus on this concept, rather than map skills.

CURRICULUM CONNECTION

Social Studies Have a map of the city or town in which your school is located and invite the children to tell you or a teacher's aide their addresses. Look up each street on the map index. When you locate a child's address on the map, put a cross by it. Tell the children that these crosses represent places where Christians live. Ask the children which Christians live at these addresses and help them realize that they are the Christians who dot the map with crosses.

Activity

What does The Lord's Prayer mean?

1. Our Father, who art in heaven

Who is "Our Father"?

God

2. Give us this day our daily bread

What does this mean?

Circle the correct picture. All three pictures may possibly be circled.

3. And forgive us our trespasses as we forgive those who trespass against us

Show what it means by putting an **X** by the correct picture.

  X

Learning How to Live Our Faith

Completing an Activity on The Lord's Prayer

Read aloud the question at the top of page 149. Help the children understand that in The Lord's Prayer, Jesus tells them how to live as caring children of God.

Then ask the children to read aloud with you the first numbered phrase in the activity. Next, read aloud to the children the question underneath it. After volunteers have answered, tell the children to print the word *God* in their books. Go through the next numbered phrase in the same manner.

Thinking About Forgiveness

Have the children look at the pictures near the third phrase on page 149. Ask how the girls look in the left picture (angry, miserable, unhappy) and then ask how they look in the right picture (happy, at peace, like friends). Ask the children to read the words about forgiveness from The Lord's Prayer and to put an **X** by the correct picture. Point out that when they say this part of The Lord's Prayer, they are asking God the Father to forgive them in the same way that they forgive others.

Sharing Forgiveness During Prayer

Gather the children in the prayer area. When they are quiet, recall with them the part of the Our Father that talks about forgiveness. Encourage them to forgive others in their hearts as Jesus taught. Ask them to close their eyes and to think about someone who has hurt them. Encourage each child to whisper a prayer asking God the Father to forgive and bless the person. Then have the children join hands and say this special part of The Lord's Prayer together.

Teaching Tips

When teaching the phrase in The Lord's Prayer *Give us this day our daily bread,* children generally think of food. This is natural to literal minded six-year-olds. Help the children expand their understanding of this term to include our daily need for clothes, shelter, education, people who love us, and toys to play with.

Enriching the Lesson

Make a prayer poster of the Our Father. Paste a picture of Jesus at the top of a large piece of newsprint. Cut out the letters of each word of the prayer from the same color paper. Give each child the letters of a word or two to decorate. Outline the letters on the poster, so the children will know where to paste them. Have the children paste the letters on the poster. Post the prayer.

Objective

This lesson helps the children pray the Our Father with a thankful spirit.

Adding Movement to Prayer

Direct the children's attention to page 150 and explain that this page shows movements they can add to the Our Father as they pray it. Then divide the class into two groups and ask the groups to alternate saying the first four phrases of the prayer and then join together on the last phrase. Encourage them to do the accompanying movements when they recite the prayer. Tell the children that they will use Jesus' prayer and these movements in their prayer service today.

Sing a Song About Prayer

Teach the children a melody for The Lord's Prayer. Use a chant, such as the one by Carry Landry (*in Young People's Glory and Praise*, OCP), an echo version of The Lord's Prayer, or any version sung frequently in parish worship.

Praying the Our Father with Movement

Gather in the prayer area. When the children are ready, pray the Our Father with the movements the children learned on page 150. Conclude the prayer service by inviting the children to sing their song.

Praying with Actions

Our Father,
who art in heaven,
hallowed be thy name;

thy kingdom come;
thy will be done on earth
as it is in heaven.

Give us this day
our daily bread;

and forgive us our trespasses
as we forgive those
who trespass against us;

and lead us not
into temptation,
but deliver us from evil.
Amen

150   Prayer

CURRICULUM CONNECTION

Music   Teach the children the following words to the melody "Twinkle, Twinkle, Little Star."

God our Father, we love you.
So we say this prayer to you.
Jesus told us we should pray
Each and every single day.
God our Father, we love you.
So we say this prayer to you.

Teaching Tips

Catholics sometimes hold hands while praying The Lord's Prayer. Ask the children if they have ever seen people doing this at Mass. Holding hands signifies that we are in the same family with God our Father. Take the children to church and stand around the altar, holding hands as they pray or sing the Our Father. Or have the children pray it as an action prayer.

Chapter Review

Activity

1. When we pray The Lord's Prayer, we know God cares for us.

   God asks us to _____pray_____ for others.

2. We know God forgives us.

   God asks us to _____forgive_____ others.

1. What prayer did Jesus teach us?

   The Lord's Prayer

2. Whom do we pray to?

   Our Father

Keep on praying with a thankful heart.
Based on Colossians 4:2

3. Talk about times when you pray The Lord's Prayer.

Review   151

Completing an Activity

Use the activity on page 151 to review Chapter 12. Read the copy at the top of the page. Then invite the children to fill in the blanks.

Tell the children that each time they go to Mass they say the prayer that Jesus taught us. Tell them about the part of the Mass when they pray The Lord's Prayer with their families and the priest, and encourage the children to participate wholeheartedly and reverently in this prayer the next time they celebrate Mass. You may wish to refer to "About the Mass" in *Our Catholic Heritage* on page 327.

Answering the Questions

Read aloud the first two questions and ask volunteers to respond. Direct the children to print the answers in their texts. Encourage all the children to participate in the discussion of the third question. Be supportive of each child who responds.

Reading the Scripture Verse

Ask the children to read the Scripture verse after you. Reflecting on the word of God is a good way to end the lesson. If you wish, you may have the children memorize this verse.

Focus on

Praying with Actions   Praying with actions helps the children give meaning to the words they are saying. This action may seem simple and childlike, but Catholics have a profound tradition of mixing actions and words in our sacramental system. As an example, the pouring of baptismal water signifies a dying and rebirth through water, the source of life. Actions give meaning to words of worship. For little children, actions can add an extra depth of meaning to words because the action brings concreteness to the message.

Enriching the Lesson

For each pair of children, write The Lord's Prayer on five cards, with one phrase on each card. (See *Our Catholic Heritage*, page 352 for the five phrases.) Scramble each set of cards and place each set in an envelope. Then divide the class into pairs, distribute the envelopes, and invite each pair to put the cards in order. Then invite them to look at the cards while reciting the prayer together reverently.

Using the Unit Organizer

Completing a graphic organizer such as a chart or table can help students organize the information that has been presented in the unit. Graphic Organizers enable students to visualize their thinking and recognize relationships among ideas. This will give students the opportunity to understand more completely the materials they have been studying.

With the children look at the banner above the mobile on page 152. This banner states the theme of the unit. Then direct the children to the four objects on the mobile. Each part of the mobile is a main idea in a chapter of the unit. Invite the children to trace over the letters within each object. When the children finish, invite them to talk about ways they can care for living things, love one another, care for the needy, and pray The Lord's Prayer. Help the children understand that these are ways that Christians live their lives.

Looking Back: Self-Assessment

To help the children assess what they have learned ask these or similar questions.

- What did you learn in this unit that you think you will always remember?
- Which was your favorite Scripture story in this unit?
- What did you like most about it?
- What activity in this unit did you most enjoy? Why?

Unit **3** Organizer

Jesus Teaches Us

To __Care__ for other living things.

To __Love__ one another.

To __Care__ for people.

To __Pray__ The Lord's Prayer.

152 Unit Organizer

Unit **3** Review

Write an X by the true sentences.

1. __X__ Jesus teaches us about God.

2. _____ God does not care about us.

3. _____ God cares more about flowers
than about people.

4. __X__ We can always thank God.

Think about the story "Jesus
Cares for a Sick Woman."

Talk about these questions.

1. How did Jesus show
he cared for the woman?

2. How does Jesus show
he cares for us?

3. What does Jesus want
us to do for each other?

Reviewing the Unit

The purpose of the Unit Review is to reinforce concepts presented in the preceding four chapters. After explaining the directions, give the children sufficient time to complete the pages. Answer any questions the children might have.

Testing

After the children have completed the Unit Review, you may wish to distribute copies of the Unit 3 Test from the Test Booklet in The Resourceful Teacher Package.

Optional Unit Project

Help the children recall that God cares for all creation—the plants, animals, and especially us. Explain that the children can give the happy message of God's care to other people. Tell the children to make big, beautiful drawings of colorful flowers and birds. Help them print on each drawing the message *God Cares Even More For You!* Encourage the children to give their drawings to someone who might need this happy message to brighten his or her day. Suggest that the children send the drawings to a nursing home or a hospital, or give them to a relative or neighbor who might be lonely.

Think about the story "The Good Samaritan."

Circle the correct answer.

1. Jesus teaches us to care for people. (YES) NO

2. The Samaritan helped the man who was robbed. (YES) NO

3. We should act like the leader of the people. YES (NO)

4. Only our parents can help people. YES (NO)

Circle the correct word to complete each sentence.

1. Jesus taught us The _____ Prayer.
   (Lord's)   Brother's

2. "Hallowed" means _____.
   happy   (holy)

3. "Trespass" means to _____.
   (hurt someone)   help someone

LETTING OTHERS KNOW MY FEELINGS

How I choose to share my feelings can be hurtful to myself or others.

Activity

Is the feeling shared in a helpful or hurtful way?

Circle **OK** if the picture shows a helpful way to share feelings.

Circle **NOT OK** if the picture shows a way that is hurtful.

Day to Day   155

Objective

To help the children appreciate that while all feelings are acceptable, how one chooses to express feelings might not be acceptable.

Considering Ways Feelings Are Hurtful

Tell the children that all of our feelings are good and are gifts from God but that sometimes we choose to express them in ways that are hurtful to ourselves and others. Read aloud the opening statement on page 155. Discuss how expressing a feeling can be hurtful. Explore ways our bodies can be hurt, such as by pinching, or our feelings can be hurt, such as by someone saying something mean to us.

Completing the Activity

Recall with the children how we recognize feelings (by using body and voice clues—by looking and listening.) Ask the children to identify the feelings being expressed in each of the four pictures. Invite the children to circle *OK* if the feeling is being shared in a helpful way or to circle *NOT OK* if the feeling is being expressed in a hurtful way.

Discussing the Activity

Discuss the children's answers using the following questions.

- Which pictures show feelings expressed in helpful, acceptable ways? (*1 and 4*)
- Which pictures show feelings expressed in a hurtful way? (*2 and 3*)
- Is it wrong to be angry? (*No, it is not the anger that is hurtful, but the way the anger is expressed.*)
- How might the character showing anger express this feeling in a helpful way? (*Walk away until calm, tell the other character that he is angry and why, ask for what he wants in a pleasant tone of voice, ask for help*)
- How might the character feeling sadness express this in a helpful way? (*Tell a grown-up how he feels, share his feeling with a friend, ask for help in solving the problem that is making him feel sad.*)

Lesson continues on page 156.

Teaching Tips

The children may have difficulty recognizing the third picture on page 155 as hurtful. Explain that sharing feelings can be an important part of helping ourselves feel better when we're sad, lonely or upset. Keeping such feelings to ourselves might be hurtful to us.

Drawing a Picture

Invite the children to draw on page 156 a picture of themselves expressing a feeling in a positive way. Before beginning the drawing, explore with the children the different feelings they might choose to draw and list feeling words on the board.

Using the Following Jesus Section

Read aloud the Following Jesus section. Ask for volunteers to say prayers asking Jesus to help the children to express their feelings in ways that are helpful, not hurtful.

Follow-Up Activities

Conduct end-of-day discussions to help the children identify the feelings they have experienced during the day and the ways they had expressed these feelings. You might choose to share your own observations at this time. Problem situations that arose between students may be discussed, with time spent generating more helpful ways to express feelings and recognition for helpful expressions of feelings could also be given.

Activity

Draw a picture that shows you letting others know your feelings.

Following Jesus

Jesus loves me and calls me to be a loving person. One way I can show love is by sharing my feelings in a way that is helpful, not hurtful, to myself or others.

Teaching Tips

While teaching this session, you may wish to use the following book.

The Hurt by Tedi Doleski, (Paulist Press) is a helpful resource for conveying the concept of emotional hurt to children of this age.

Teaching Tips

If any child's drawing shows a hurtful expression of feelings, ask the child if this is OK or NOT OK. Then ask the children to identify a more helpful expression. Comment to the children that sometimes it takes more effort to respond in a helpful way than in a hurtful way.

OPENING DOORS
A Take-Home Magazine™

Growing Closer

IT IS IMPORTANT for every Christian to *know* The Lord's Prayer by heart. It is just as important to *understand* the meaning of the memorized words. Take some time with your family to talk about this common Christian prayer and what some of the phrases mean to each of you. As a family, try rewriting the prayer *in your own words*.

Prayer is one way we show our love and concern for others. "Please pray for me" is a special way of asking others to care for us. Perhaps your family has a special need for prayer at this time, or perhaps you are aware of another's need to be remembered in your prayer. Consider how your family can use prayer as a real way of expressing your caring concern for one another and for others.

Looking Ahead

In Unit 4, your child will be guided to experience belonging to the community of Jesus' friends. Few things are as important to a child's development as a Christian than to feel at home within a Christian community. Usually the child enters into this community through the Christian family. At Baptism the family and parish celebrate the entry of their new member. In this unit your child will learn about the sacrament of Baptism and recall his or her own experience of being welcomed into the community.

8

© Silver Burdett Ginn Inc.

Opening Doors ～～～

Sending the Magazine Home

As you complete Unit 3 with your class, assist the children in carefully removing *Opening Doors: A Take-Home Magazine* (two pages) from their texts by separating the magazine from the book along the perforations. Demonstrate how to fold the two magazine pages to form an eight-page booklet. Ask the children to take the magazines home and encourage their families to read them with the children and participate in the suggested activities.

The Lord's Prayer

The Peaceable Kingdom (Isaiah 11:6–7)

For those who continue to ask, "Lord, teach us to pray" (Luke 11:1), the prayer that Jesus taught his disciples is a worthwhile place to start.

It was seeing Jesus in prayer, in communion with his Father, that moved the disciples to ask how they also might pray. Jesus responded willingly to the disciples' request. When he taught the disciples to pray, Jesus used an ancient formula called a *kaddish*. Both he and the disciples would have been familiar with this form of prayer since childhood. The structure of the prayer includes:

- praise to God
- prayer for the coming of the kingdom
- petitions for God's blessings and forgiveness

Like a kaddish, prayed during the Jewish synagogue service, the Our Father is a community prayer.

Catholics pray the Lord's Prayer each Sunday at Mass. It is in the spirit of unity that in many Catholic parishes, the community joins hands when praying the Lord's Prayer. When we pray this prayer, we are united not only with each other but also with Orthodox Christians, Protestants, Jews, and all those who proclaim God as Father and who pray for the coming of the kingdom.

---

these dedicated religious baked the bricks needed to house the infirm themselves.

The Saint Vincent De Paul Society, a group of laymen who operate at the parish level, was first organized in America in 1845 to provide food, clothing, and fuel for the sick and the poor. The society also founded homes for destitute boys.

American Catholics responded to other social problems as well.

In the 1870s the Industrial Revolution was in full gear, and the Christian Brothers responded by founding schools to teach boys industrial trade skills. Between 1870 and 1900, the Little Sisters of the Poor opened 34 homes for the aged, the Sisters of the Good Shepherd established homes for delinquent women, and the Sisters of Charity founded homes for abandoned infants and unwed mothers.

Since the early 1900s, Catholics have built and staffed many organizations to benefit the destitute. Today men and women of the Church have vowed to continue to be leaders of the social services as long as poverty and social inequity exists. As an example, Catholic Charities, a national organization, has set as its goals the elimination of the causes of poverty as well as the continued ministry to those in need. Religious orders are engaged in ever new and imaginative projects to help abused women, the aged, prisoners, and the homeless. Catholics continue to heed the words of Jesus: . . . "whatever you did for one of these least brothers of mine, you did for me" (Matthew 25:40).

Catholic Charitable Institutions in the 1990s	
Catholic hospitals	640
Dispensaries	206
Convalescent homes	667
Child welfare centers	239
Nurseries	496
Social service centers	1803
Saint Vincent De Paul societies	4700

7

At Mass, we conclude the Lord's Prayer by saying,
"For the kingdom, the power, and the glory are yours, now and forever."

Praying for the coming of the kingdom is an important petition in the Lord's Prayer. As Christians we believe that Jesus came to bring God's kingdom. Once Jesus was asked if he was the promised one who had come to establish the kingdom. He replied, "The blind regain their sight, the lame walk, lepers are cleansed, the deaf hear, the dead are raised, and the poor have the good news proclaimed to them" (Matthew 11:3-5). Jesus painted a word picture to affirm that he had come to bring about God's kingdom. It is a good image to keep in mind as we pray,

"Thy kingdom come.
thy will be done on earth as it is in heaven."

The prayer that Jesus taught us unites us with him in working to bring God's kingdom of love, peace, and justice to our world.

3

Give us this day our daily bread.

A CARING CHURCH

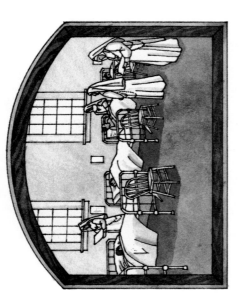

I n religion class, your child is learning how God cares for us and how Jesus wants us to care for others. The Church is presented as people who try to care about others as Jesus did. American Catholics took this message to heart and dedicated themselves and their resources to works of mercy.

Catholic social action took hold in the late 1800s. Nursing for the poor was badly needed at the time of the great epidemics, and religious women and men (such as the Alexian Brothers, a community of male nurses) were among the first to meet the crisis. Many times

6

THE PRAYER JESUS TAUGHT US

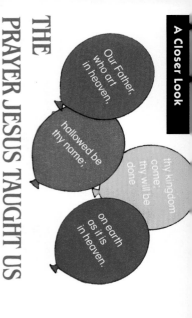

Our Father, who art in heaven.

hallowed be thy name;

thy kingdom come; thy will be done

on earth as it is in heaven.

The Lord's Prayer or Our Father is one prayer all Christians share. Help your child learn this important prayer of our faith by working through the activity on these pages, by praying it often at home, and by praying it with the Catholic Christian community gathered together at Mass.

Give us this day our daily bread;

and forgive us our trespasses

as we forgive those who trespass against us;

and lead us not into temptation,

but deliver us from evil.

Amen.

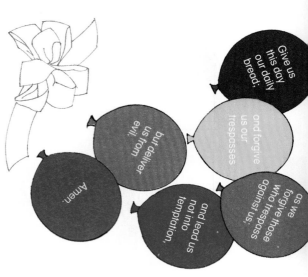

As your child learns each phrase, draw a string to the balloon. Decorate the ribbon when you have learned the whole prayer.

The next time you go to Mass, hold hands with the person next to you as you pray The Lord's Prayer.

4

5

At Mass I pray many prayers.
I pray prayers of thanks and praise.
I pray prayers of forgiveness.
I pray for God's help, too.

At Mass I pray the prayer Jesus taught us.
It is called The Lord's Prayer.
I can pray The Lord's Prayer everywhere!

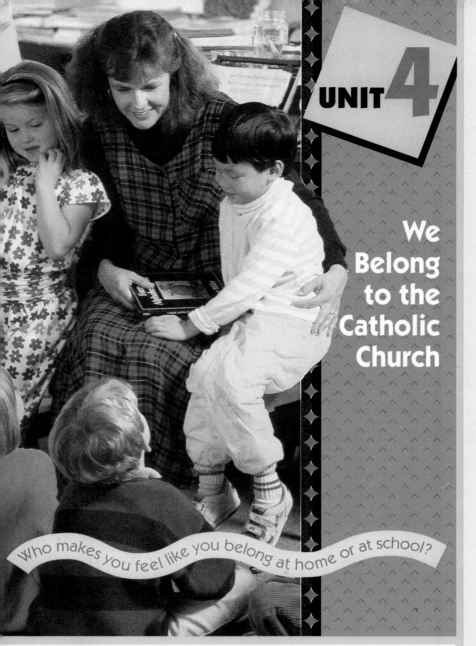

UNIT 4

We Belong to the Catholic Church

Who makes you feel like you belong at home or at school?

Unit Aim

To help the children identify themselves as Catholics, whose central celebration is the Mass.

Doctrinal Summaries

CHAPTER 13
We are friends and followers of Jesus. We call ourselves Christians.

CHAPTER 14
At Baptism we celebrate becoming a member of the family of Jesus. We celebrate our new life as a friend of Jesus.

CHAPTER 15
Christians gather together in groups called Churches. We belong to the Catholic Church. It is the Church where we are at home with our Christian family.

CHAPTER 16
At Mass, Jesus shares a meal with us. Jesus gives himself to us at Mass.

Note:

As you prepare to teach this unit, you may wish to refer to the reference section *Our Catholic Heritage,* beginning on page 327. Additional resources for Unit 4 include a Unit Test and a Family Letter as well as a video and selections from the THIS IS OUR FAITH Music Program. You might also find it helpful to preview *Saints and Other Holy People* and *Prayer Celebrations* for possibilities to enhance the unit.

Introducing the UNIT

Read the unit-focus question aloud and invite the children's responses. Direct attention to the title of Unit 4. Tell the children that in this unit they will learn what it means to belong to the Catholic Church.

New Words

Christian
Christ
sacrament
Baptism
godparents
Church
church
Mass
Eucharist

We Are Christians

Objectives ~~~~~~

To help the children

■ Recognize that as Christians they are friends and followers of Jesus.

■ Value friendship, especially the friendship of Jesus.

■ Discover ways in which Christians follow Jesus' example.

■ Understand that their friendship with Jesus leads them to act in special ways.

■ Pray for others as Jesus did and review the chapter.

Chapter Outline ~~~~~~

	Step 1 Learning About Our Lives	**Step 2** Learning About Our Faith	**Step 3** Learning How to Live Our Faith
Day 1	■ Make up stories. ■ Use the text. *ABOUT 8 MINUTES*	■ Learn from a picture. ■ Work in the text. ■ Complete activities. ■ Review the new words/doctrine. *ABOUT 12 MINUTES*	■ Assemble letters into words. ■ Play Follow the Leader. ■ Gather for prayer. *ABOUT 10 MINUTES*
Day 2	■ Talk about making new friends. *ABOUT 5 MINUTES*	■ Listen to a Bible story. ■ Act out the story. *ABOUT 12 MINUTES*	■ Complete an activity. ■ Create a bulletin board. ■ Use the bulletin board for prayer. *ABOUT 13 MINUTES*
Day 3	■ Recall the learning of Day 2. ■ Follow Jesus. *ABOUT 10 MINUTES*	■ Read the text. ■ Respond to Bible illustrations. ■ Complete an activity. *ABOUT 8 MINUTES*	■ Act out the story of Christian fellowship. ■ Gather for prayer. *ABOUT 12 MINUTES*
Day 4	■ Learn about friendship. ■ Read a poem. ■ Complete an activity. *ABOUT 10 MINUTES*	■ Learn the signs of a Christian. *ABOUT 9 MINUTES*	■ Review words. ■ Make up actions for the poem. ■ Pray with a poem. *ABOUT 11 MINUTES*

Day 5   **Prayer**   Read the text; prepare to process; and pray for others.
           Review   Use the bulletin board to review the chapter; complete an activity; answer the questions; and read a Scripture verse.

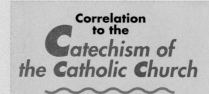

**Correlation
to the
Catechism of
the Catholic Church**

Paragraphs
818, 1267, 1694

Plan Ahead ~~~~~~~~~

	Preparing Your Class	**Materials Needed**
Day 1	For Step 3, cut out nine squares of construction paper per child. On each square, print one letter of the word *Christian.* Put each set into an envelope.	■ a small envelope for each child ■ set of prepared letters for each child
Day 2	For Step 3, think of ways the children can be friends of Jesus. Cut out the letters: *We Christians follow our friend, Jesus Christ.*	■ drawing paper ■ empty bulletin board ■ cut-out letters for a sentence ■ thumbtacks or staples
Day 3	For Step 1, have ready the bulletin board from Day 2.	■ bulletin board from Day 2
Day 4	For Step 3, be prepared to suggest gestures and body movements the children might use for their poem.	
Day 5	Consider what movements you will use to lead the children in the procession.	■ bulletin board from Day 2 ■ musical instruments (optional)

Additional Resources

As you plan this chapter, consider using the following materials from The Resourceful Teacher Package.

■ *Classroom Activity Sheets 13 and 13a*

■ *Family Activity Sheets 13 and 13a*

■ *Chapter 13 Test*

■ *Prayers for Every Day*

■ *Projects: Grade 1*

In preparing the students for the Sunday readings, you may wish to use Silver Burdett Ginn's *Getting Ready For Sunday* student and teacher materials.

Books for the Journey

Best Friends. Selected by Lee Bennett Hopkins. Harper & Row, 1986. These poems joyfully capture what it means to be friends.

Yo! Yes! Chris Raschka. Orchard Books, 1993. This book creatively tells the story of two children—one who needs a friend and another who offers friendship.

More Books for the Journey

My Friend John. Charlotte Zolotow. Harper & Row, 1968. This description of a friendship between two boys reveals what is essential in a good relationship.

Gregory and Mr. Grump. Marcia Leonard. Silver Press, a division of Silver Burdett Press, Inc., 1990. Gregory's first venture into gardening poses some mysterious questions and wins him an unlikely friend in the process.

Reduced Classroom Activities

Name _____

We Are Christians

1. Look at the names on the computer screen.
2. Find the right name to finish each sentence.
3. Write that word in the blank.

CHRIST
ANDREW
JESUS
CHRISTIANS

1. Andrew _____ was a friend of Jesus.

2. Christ _____ is another name for Jesus.

3. I am a friend of Jesus _____

4. We are Christians _____ .

To the Teacher: This activity follows the Scripture story "Making Friends with Jesus."

Chapter 13   We Are Christians   This Is Our Faith 1   **13**

Name _____

Friends and Followers of Jesus

1. Color only those badges below that Christians would wear.
2. Cut along the heavy black lines of these badges.
3. Choose one of these badges to wear.
4. Give another of these badges to a friend and follower of Jesus.

I fight with friends.

I am selfish.

I help others.

To the Teacher: This activity will help the children identify the marks of Christians.

13a   This Is Our Faith 1   Chapter 13   We Are Christians

Background for the Teacher

FOLLOWING JESUS

Jesus' invitation reaches out to those who listen and respond. It is a call to live a life centered on God. Given the opportunity, Jesus will transform us into the vision God has for each of us.

Jesus' message is about relationships. Again and again, the Scriptures show us that Jesus lived his life for others. He had many followers who shared his daily life and ministry. Together they walked the dusty roads, talked into the night, told jokes, slept under the stars, went fishing, and threw out their nets. These were Jesus' disciples. They followed him throughout his ministry and then taught others how to follow Jesus' example. Other followers, including Mary of Magdala and the women of Galilee, formed a supportive network. Jesus' friends formed the core of the communities that arose after his ascension.

UNITY IN COMMUNITY

Jesus calls us together as a community of believers. We know that to accept the God proclaimed by Jesus is to accept a certain way of living. The full expression of our humanity takes place in our loving interaction with others. We are one with Christ, and we accept the God he proclaims when we are one with other Christians.

The early Christians understood this and sought to be known by their love for one another. Daily, they practiced the Corporal Works of Mercy that Jesus stressed in his story of the final judgment (Matthew 25:31–40).

HOW CHILDREN LEARN

The movement in this unit flows from an appreciation of the necessity and joy of friendship to the development of a sense of Christian community. In Chapter 13, the children name and talk about their friends; they talk about making new friends just as Andrew does in the Gospel story of this lesson. The children's understanding of friendship is based on their own experiences of it.

In your teaching, reiterate that Jesus is a good friend, someone with whom the children can share the stories of their life. The children will respond to him as a friend when he is presented to them as the one who loves them. In this lesson you help the children begin to realize that being Christian, a follower of Jesus, involves loving. Love begets love. So it is with the Trinity; so it is with the followers of Jesus.

Objective

This lesson helps the children recognize that as Christians they are friends and followers of Jesus.

Step 1/INTRODUCTION

Learning About Our Lives

Making Up Stories

Read aloud the question in the margin of page 162. Invite the children to name things they like to do with their friends. Direct the children's attention to the photograph on page 162. Invite volunteers to make up a story about the friendship between the two children.

Using the Text

Read aloud "Sharing with Friends" on page 162. Then explain the directions for the activity. Have the children circle the sentences that tell what they share with their friends. Ask volunteers to share friendship experiences.

or...

Invite the children to close their eyes and see themselves with a friend, sharing, playing, and telling how they feel.

Step 2/DEVELOPMENT

Learning About Our Faith

Learning from a Picture

Direct the children's attention to the picture of Jesus on page 163. Help the children note the kindness in Jesus' smile. Encourage the children to pick a color that reminds them of friendship and use this to color Jesus' clothes.

Working in the Text

Read aloud "Jesus Our Friend" on page 163. Print on the chalkboard: _friend, friends, Christ, Christians, followers of Jesus._ Ask the children to circle the words on page 163.

Encourage volunteers to make up a story using these words. One volunteer can use a word, a second volunteer can add to the story by using another word, and so on.

162

13

We Are Christians

Sharing with Friends

It is good to have friends.
You tell stories to friends.
You tell friends how you feel.
You share with your friends.

Activity

What do you share with your friends?
Read the sentences below.
Then circle the sentences that tell
what you share with your friends.

I share toys with my friends.
I share food with my friends.
I share happy times with my friends.
I share what scares me with my friends.
I share secrets with my friends.

What are some things you do with your friends?

Focus on

Friendship To help the children explore friendship experiences, invite them to pantomime something friends do together such as building a snowman, skating, playing ball, swimming, playing a board game, eating ice cream, riding bikes, playing with trucks in the sand pile, riding swings, or talking on the phone. Divide the class into pairs. Call on a pair to do the first pantomime. Invite the first child who guesses correctly to perform next with his or her partner.

Jesus Our Friend

Jesus is our special friend.
We follow his example.
We care for others and try to
be a friend as Jesus showed us.

Another name for Jesus is **Christ**.
The friends of Jesus share this name.
We are called **Christians**.
We Christians are the friends and
followers of Jesus.

Trace over the letters
to complete the sentence.

I am a  Christian

New Words

Christ The name Christ means that "Jesus was sent by God to help all people."

Christian A Christian is a friend and follower of Jesus Christ.

We Believe

We are the friends and followers of Jesus. We call ourselves Christians.

Doctrine 163

Enriching the Lesson

Print the following sentences on the chalkboard or on posterboard: *A friend is special. A friend is someone who is _____.* Invite the children to brainstorm words that describe a friend. *(Possible responses may include kind, fun to be with, happy, caring, loving.)* Finally, assign responses to different volunteers and encourage them to pantomime ways in which friends show these qualities.

Completing an Activity

Have the children turn to page 163 and trace the letters in the text. As a group, have the children read aloud the statement "I am a Christian."

Reviewing the Vocabulary

Point to the New Words on page 163. Ask the children to repeat the words *Christian* and *Christ* and their definitions.

Presenting the Doctrine

Read aloud the We Believe section on page 163, which summarizes the chapter's doctrine. Ask the children to repeat the two sentences after you.

Step 3/CONCLUSION

Learning How to Live Our Faith

Assembling Letters

Give each child one of the sets of letters you prepared before class. Ask the children to assemble the letters that spell another name for Jesus (*Christ*). When everyone has finished, have the children say the name Christ together. Ask them to add the remaining letters to spell the word for a follower of Christ (*Christian*).

Playing Follow the Leader

Ask the children if they have ever played the game of Follow the Leader. Select a volunteer to be the leader and to lead the children in a series of actions. If time permits, play the game more than once so that several children can lead.

Afterward, talk with the children about how Christians follow their friend Jesus and do loving things for others just as Jesus did.

Gathering for Prayer

Gather the children in the prayer area. Tell them that today they are going to praise God with their bodies. Ask them to imitate each prayerful gesture you make. When they are quiet, begin the prayer by raising your arms toward the ceiling. Then bring your arms down and around in front of you and clasp your hands in a prayerful gesture. Next, cross your forearms over your chest and bow your head. Repeat the sequence for the children to follow.

Making Friends with Jesus

One afternoon Andrew saw Jesus walking down the road to town. Andrew wanted to be Jesus' friend, so he hurried to catch up with Jesus.

Behind him, Jesus heard Andrew's footsteps. He stopped, looked around, and saw Andrew. "What are you looking for?" Jesus asked.

Because Andrew wanted to get to know Jesus better, he asked, "Where are you staying?"

164   Scripture

DAY 2
SCRIPTURE

Objective
This lesson helps the children value friendship, especially the friendship of Jesus.

Step 1/INTRODUCTION
Learning About Our Lives

Talking About Making New Friends
Call on volunteers to describe their experiences of making new friends. Use the following questions to help the children share their stories (Answers will vary).

■ How did you meet your new friend?

■ Where did you meet your friend?

■ What are some things you and your friend have fun doing together?

■ Have you ever gone to your friend's home?

■ Has your friend ever come to your home?

■ What do you do together in one another's homes?

Step 2/DEVELOPMENT
Learning About Our Faith

Listening to a Bible Story
Encourage the children to look at the pictures on pages 164–165 while you read aloud "Making Friends with Jesus." Read the story, using different voices for Jesus and Andrew. After reading the story, point to the illustrations, one by one, and invite volunteers to tell the part of the story that the picture illustrates. Comment on the look of eagerness on Andrew's face as he rushes to catch up with Jesus, on the kind look on Jesus' face as he invites Andrew to follow him, on how comfortable the two friends look as they spend the afternoon together.

Acting Out the Story
Invite the volunteers to act out the Bible story. Encourage them to be creative when they get to the part in which Jesus and Andrew talk and laugh together. Ask the class to think about what they would share with a new friend. Afterward, invite the children in the audience to share what they might talk to Jesus about.

164

CURRICULUM CONNECTION

Language Arts Give each child three sheets of 8 1/2" × 11" paper folded in half to make a storybook. Invite the children to think of any stories they know about their friend Jesus. Have the children print their stories in their booklets and illustrate them. Encourage the children to print the title *Stories About Jesus* on the front page. Provide time for the children to share their work. Encourage them to take their booklets home.

Focus on

Common Baptism The *Catechism of the Catholic Church* states, ". . . From the baptismal fonts is born the one People of God of the New Covenant, which transcends all the natural or human limits of nations, cultures, races and sexes: 'For by one Spirit we were all baptized into one body.' ". . . All who have been justified by faith in Baptism are incorporated into Christ; they therefore have the right to be called Christians. . ." (#1267, 818).

"Come and you will see," Jesus said.

Jesus and Andrew walked to Jesus' home.
They spent the rest of the day together.
They liked one another a lot.
Jesus and Andrew became good friends.

Based on John 1: 35–39

Activity

Jesus is Andrew's friend,
and Jesus is my friend, too.
This is one way Jesus is my friend.

_____

- -

_____

_____

- -

_____

Enriching the Lesson

Divide the class into small groups. Invite one group to act out the Bible story on pages 164–165 with you. Playing the part of Jesus, pretend that you are taking a walk. Tell the group to stand together, talking about what they have heard about you (Jesus). Turn and say each child's name and the words *Come, follow me.* Lead the group into a circle and have them sit around you. Tell them that you (Jesus) love and care for each of them and want them to be your special friends. Repeat the role-play with each group.

or...

Instead of assigning roles and acting out the story, invite the whole class to perform the following movements.

- Stand and walk fast as Andrew might have done when trying to catch up with Jesus.
- Turn and look as Jesus might have done when stopping to look at Andrew.

When the children have completed these movements have them choose a partner to do the following ones.

- Walk off chatting as Jesus and Andrew would have done.
- Sit chatting as Jesus and Andrew might have. (Use the children's desks as a table.)

Step 3/CONCLUSION

Learning How to Live Our Faith

Completing an Activity

Read the text at the bottom of page 165 and brainstorm with the children some ways they can be friends with Jesus and follow his example. Invite the children to print on the lines provided one way they can be friends with Jesus. Emphasize that the children can talk to Jesus and share with him their thoughts, dreams, and disappointments and that when they do this they are being a friend to Jesus, who loves to hear their stories and their joys.

Creating a Bulletin Board

Encourage the children to draw pictures of themselves following Jesus' example. Pin the children's pictures on an empty bulletin board. Have letters cut out for the following sentence: *We Christians follow our friend, Jesus Christ.* Give each child a letter to hold and ask the children to help you tack them up. Talk about how the sentence applies to the drawings.

Using the Bulletin Board for Prayer

As the children are gathered around the bulletin board, invite them to pray. Teach the children the following response: *Thank you, God, for giving us Jesus as our special friend.* Invite volunteers to explain their pictures to the group and to God. After each volunteer shares, invite the children to pray the response.

165

Objective

This lesson helps the children discover ways in which Christians follow Jesus' example.

Step 1/INTRODUCTION

Learning About Our Lives

Recalling the Learning of Day 2

Gather the children around the bulletin board they made on Day 2. Invite volunteers to comment on their pictures and to explain how the drawings show them being Christians and following Jesus.

Following Jesus

Recall the game Follow the Leader. Have the children look at page 166 and find the name of the special leader they follow. Then invite the children to recall some of the things Jesus did for others. Finally, ask the children what Jesus would want his followers to do in the following situations.

- Janie was running to catch up with Travis on the way to school. She fell down and scraped her knee and began to cry.

- Teddy started school in the middle of the first grade. He is in Jeff's class, but Teddy is too shy to make friends.

- A TV news show says that many homeless people in the city do not have blankets for the cold night.

- A food store puts a big barrel by the exit door with a sign that says: Food for the Hungry.

Step 2/DEVELOPMENT

Learning About Our Faith

Reading the Text

Read aloud "Love One Another" on page 166 and ask these questions.

- Who are some of Jesus' friends? (*Peter, Andrew, Martha, Mary, and Lazarus*)

- What did Jesus tell his friends? (*"If you are my friends, you will love one another."*)

Love One Another

Besides Andrew, Jesus had other friends.
Peter, Andrew's brother, was
a friend of Jesus, too.
Some of his other friends were Mary,
Martha, and Lazarus, their brother.
They liked Jesus to come to their house.

Jesus told all his friends something
important, "If you are my friends,
you will love one another."

Based on John 13:35

166   Morality

CURRICULUM CONNECTION

Art   Display a large sheet of newsprint and print in the middle of it the phrase *A Christian is.* . . . Ask the children to think of words that describe a Christian (happy, kind, forgiving, generous, friendly). Print these on the newsprint, leaving room to paste pictures. Distribute magazines and have the children find and cut out pictures illustrating these qualities. Invite the children to paste their pictures next to the words. Post the newsprint in a prominent place.

Teaching Tips

When working with instances of moral decision-making, have the children think of as many ideas as possible of how to help someone. Elicit practical solutions to people's needs. Because there may be more than one way to solve each problem, have the children think of many possible solutions.

The friends of Jesus did try to love one another.

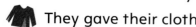 They gave their clothes to keep people warm.

They cooked bread for hungry people.

They helped sick people get better.

They shared their money with poor people.

There is a symbol in front of each sentence above. Draw the symbol in the box by the picture that matches the sentence.

- What did Jesus' friends do to show their love? (*They helped the sick, fed the hungry, clothed the naked, and gave to the poor.*)
- When we love people, whom are we following or acting like? (*Jesus*)

Responding to Bible Illustrations

Direct the children's attention to the illustrations on page 167. Point to each illustration and invite a volunteer to tell a story about the picture.

Completing an Activity

Read the directions to the activity and invite the children to match the illustrations to the correct sentences in the text. Discuss their choices.

Step 3/CONCLUSION

Learning How to Live Our Faith

Acting Out the Story of Christian Fellowship

Invite the children to put on a play and act out the stories about the Christian love shown in the illustrations. Assign the following roles: sick people, hungry people, cold people, poor people, and various Christians. Encourage the children to develop dialogue and to imagine how the people felt before and after the Christians shared their love with them.

or...

Invite the children to draw "before and after" pictures. Each child may choose a sick, hungry, cold, or poor person to draw. On one side of the paper, encourage the children to draw the way the person might have felt before being helped by the Christians and on the other side how the person felt after being helped by the Christians.

Gathering for Prayer

Gather the children in a semicircle in the prayer corner. When they are quiet, teach them the following response: *Thank you, God, for my friend Jesus.* When they know the response, ask one of the children to come and stand before you. Then say the following: *(Name of child), you are a Christian. You follow Jesus Christ. Jesus is your special friend.* After the first child prays the response, have him or her return to the semicircle; then call another child. When you have addressed all the children, invite them to pray the response together.

Teaching Tips

Provide props for the children's play in Step 2 of the lesson plan. Then arrange for the children to present their play to another class or to their parents and friends at a special time.

Enriching the Lesson

Collect pictures of people helping one another. Divide the class into groups and give each group a picture. The children may dramatize the situation. In this way, they can apply what they are learning to the present day.

167

DAY 4

DOCTRINE

Objective

This lesson helps the children understand that their friendship with Jesus leads them to act in special ways.

Step 1/INTRODUCTION

Learning About Our Lives

Learning About Friendship from Illustrations

Invite the children to look at the pictures on page 168. Invite volunteers to talk about times they have done fun things with their friends.

Reading a Poem

Read aloud the poem entitled "Acting Like Friends" on page 168. Divide the class into three groups and assign a stanza to each group. Invite the groups to read their stanzas out loud. Then ask the following questions.

- Why is it fun to play with a friend? (*Answers will vary.*)
- Why do you need friends to laugh and share with? (*Answers will vary.*)

Completing an Activity

Read the directions for the activity at the bottom of page 168. Encourage volunteers to select an illustration and tell a story about it.

Step 2/DEVELOPMENT

Learning About Our Faith

Learning the Signs of a Christian

Read aloud the title "Acting Like Jesus" on page 169. Read aloud the text next to each picture and use the following questions to guide a discussion about things Christians do that show they are followers of Jesus.

- What is the special sign of Christians that is shown in the first picture? (*The cross*)
- Where do we often see this sign? (*In church, at home, in school*)
- How are the children in the next picture caring for our world? (*Picking up trash*)

168

Acting like Friends

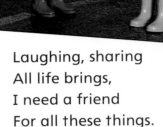

When there's playing
To be done,
I need a friend
To make it fun.

When there's work
I have to do,
It's always easy
When there's two.

Laughing, sharing
All life brings,
I need a friend
For all these things.

Activity

Give names to the children in the pictures who are acting like friends.
Tell stories about them.

168 Doctrine

CURRICULUM CONNECTION

Language Arts Pass out writing paper to the children and invite them to write one thing about their best friend and draw a picture of him or her. To get them started, ask: "What makes your friend special?" Offer assistance with spelling as needed. When the children have completed their work, invite volunteers to share what they have written.

Acting like Jesus

We Christians are the friends and followers of Jesus. Here are some things Christians do.

▲ We use the cross as a sign of Jesus' love for us.

▼ We care about the world.

▲ We care especially about people.

▲ We respect and read the Bible.

◄ We pray The Lord's Prayer.

Doctrine   169

★ ★ ★
Enriching the Lesson

Before class, cut out a cardboard cross, about 8" × 4," for each child. During the session, give each child some paste and a handful of small scraps of construction paper or fabric in a variety of colors. Invite the children to paste their scraps onto their crosses to make mosaics.

- What are some other things you can do as a Christian to show that you care about God's world? (*Answers will vary.*)
- What are the children in the next picture doing? (*Hugging one another and showing love*)
- What are some ways you as a Christian can show love for others? (*Answers will vary.*)
- What do the last few pictures show us about what Christians do? (*They read the Bible, go to church, and pray.*)

If there is a crucifix in your room, point to it and then make the Sign of the Cross with the children. Tell them that today they will use this Christian sign when they pray.

Step 3/CONCLUSION

Learning How to Live Our Faith

Reviewing Words

Print the following terms on the chalkboard or flash cards: *friends, Christ, Christians, Andrew, the cross, caring, helping, sharing, praying, followers, Jesus, the Son of God.* Ask volunteers to each choose a term and share with their classmates one thing they have learned about the term this year.

Making Up Actions for the Poem

Direct the children's attention back to the poem on page 168. Read it aloud again. Ask the children to form their three groups from Step 1. Encourage the children to practice saying their stanzas and develop body movements and gestures for their stanzas. Offer suggestions as needed. Tell the children that they will use their poem in prayer today.

Praying with a Poem

Gather the children in the prayer area and have them stand in their three groups. Then begin to pray by telling God that the children are going to say a poem today. Invite each group to perform its stanza for God. When the three groups have prayed, invite volunteers to say to God whatever they wish to about friendship. End the prayer by praying the Sign of the Cross with the children.

169

Objective

This lesson helps the children pray for others as Jesus prayed.

Reading the Text

Read the text under the title "Praying for Others." Ask the children who are some people they could pray for today. Invite the children to draw them in the space provided.

Preparing to Process to the Prayer Area

Teach the children the response *God, we are Christians, we pray for others just as Jesus did.* Ask the children to put their books on their desks. Tell the children they will return to their desks to pray. Finally, announce that you are going to pretend to be Jesus and are going to lead them in a game Follow the Leader. Ask them to follow you as you process around the room.

Praying for Others

Play instrumental music during the procession. Lead the children around the room. As you lead them, dance a step or two, clap your hands, or raise your arms in praise. When the music stops, lead the children to their seats.

Invite the children to sing a song about being a follower of Jesus. Then invite the children to hold their books open to page 170 and tell God about the person whose picture they have drawn. After each child prays, the others pray the response. Conclude the prayer by having the children sing the song again. Or have musical instruments available and encourage the children to praise God in different ways—by playing their musical instruments, by dancing, or by clapping their hands.

Praying for Others

Jesus prays for everyone because he loves us all.
As the friends and followers of Jesus,
we can pray for others, too.

We can pray for
- sick people,
- hungry people,
- poor people,
- people who need clothing.

Activity

Draw a picture of the people you will pray for today.

170   Prayer

CURRICULUM CONNECTION

Music   Teach the children the following words to the melody "The More We Get Together."

The more we follow Jesus,
Yes Jesus, Oh Jesus.
The more we follow Jesus,
The happier we'll be.
For he is our leader
And leads us in his ways.
The more we follow Jesus,
The happier we'll be.

Focus on

Praying for Others   This is a formal introduction to the Christian practice of praying for others. No doubt the children have been saying prayers such as "God bless Mommy," "God bless Daddy," God bless Susan" for several years. We want to add to the act of praying for others the dimension that Christians do this when they gather together. This prayer skill also introduces them to pray for people when they are sick, hungry, poor, or in need of clothing.

Chapter Review

Choose a word to complete each sentence.

Christians <u>l</u> <u>love</u> one another.

Christians <u>h</u> <u>help</u> others.

Christians <u>s</u> <u>share</u> with people.

Christians <u>p</u> <u>pray</u> .

1. What name do Jesus' friends and followers call themselves?

Christians

2. What is another name for Jesus?

Christ

3. Talk about what we can do to show that we are Jesus' friends and followers.

> Jesus says,
> "You are my friends."
> Based on John 15:14

Teaching Tips

There are several drawing opportunities in this book. Art is, of course, an excellent way for young children to express themselves, since they lack writing skills. When making a picture, allow the children to choose the medium they prefer. When they do so the child accepts a certain amount of responsibility to enjoy the activity. They might cut out construction paper to glue down, find pictures or objects to paste, or paint with watercolors.

Enriching the Lesson

Read to the children *The Giving Tree* by Shel Silverstein (Harper & Row). Show the pictures as you read. Then use the following questions to discuss the book.

- Do you think the tree was a good friend to the boy? In what way?

- Was the boy a good friend to the tree? Why or why not?

- If so, what way does the tree remind us of Jesus?

- In what ways can you be like the giving tree?

Using the Bulletin Board from Day 2 to Review

Gather the children around the bulletin board they assembled on Day 2. Using their drawings, review the learning of the week. Invite the children to talk about how Christians follow their friend and leader Jesus Christ. As the children share, invite them to talk about ways Christians show that they are followers of Christ. Stress that Christians act like Jesus because they love one another, help people in need, share with people, and pray.

Finally, give each child his or her bulletin-board drawing. Encourage the children to take their drawings home, post them in a prominent place, and use them as reminders of how they try to follow Jesus.

Completing an Activity

Read the text at the top of the page and have the children complete each sentence. Tell them that the first letter of each word is already in the space. Afterward, invite their comments on the actions of Christians who follow Jesus' example.

Answering the Questions

Read aloud the first two questions and ask volunteers to respond. Direct the children to print the answers in their texts. Encourage all the children to participate in the discussion of the third question. Be supportive of each child who responds.

Reading the Scripture Verse

End the session by reflecting on a Scripture verse. Have the children read it after you. If you wish, you may also have the children memorize this verse.

14 We Welcome New Christians at Baptism

Objectives

To help the children

■ Recognize that they became a member of the family of Jesus at Baptism.

■ Become acquainted with the rite of Baptism.

■ Recognize the special elements of Christian Baptism.

■ Reflect on Baptism, especially their own.

■ Ask the saints to help them live like Jesus and review the chapter.

Chapter Outline

	Step 1 **Learning About Our Lives**	**Step 2** **Learning About Our Faith**	**Step 3** **Learning How to Live Our Faith**
Day 1	■ Introduce Chapter 14. ■ Read the text. *ABOUT 10 MINUTES*	■ Prepare to talk about Baptism. ■ Work in the text. ■ Review new words/doctrine. ■ Study the picture. *ABOUT 10 MINUTES*	■ Draw a baptismal celebration. ■ Create a bulletin board. ■ Use the bulletin board for prayer. *ABOUT 10 MINUTES*
Day 2	■ Review Day 1. ■ Study a baptismal display. *ABOUT 10 MINUTES*	■ Listen to a baptismal story. ■ Complete an activity. ■ Review the new words. *ABOUT 10 MINUTES*	■ Renew baptismal promises. *ABOUT 10 MINUTES*
Day 3	■ Recall the learning of Days 1 and 2. ■ Complete an activity. *ABOUT 10 MINUTES*	■ Review the sacrament of Baptism. ■ Complete a rebus activity. *ABOUT 10 MINUTES*	■ Draw a picture about being Christian. ■ Gather for prayer. *ABOUT 10 MINUTES*
Day 4	■ Review a bulletin board from Day 1. ■ Complete an activity. *ABOUT 10 MINUTES*	■ Read the text. ■ Explain holy water. *ABOUT 10 MINUTES*	■ Prepare an action prayer. ■ Gather for prayer. *ABOUT 10 MINUTES*
Day 5	**Prayer** Read the text; prepare to process; and ask the saints to pray for us. **Review** Use the bulletin board to review the chapter; complete an activity; answer the questions; and read the Scripture verse.		

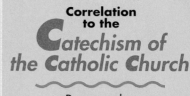
Plan Ahead

	Preparing Your Class	**Materials Needed**
Day 1	For Step 2, bring in a doll. For Step 3, cut out: *Baptism made us members of Jesus' family.* Provide bulletin board space.	■ drawing paper ■ empty bulletin board ■ cut-out letters for a sentence ■ thumbtacks or staples ■ doll
Day 2	For Step 1, display a candle, baptismal shell, white robe, crucifix, Bible, baptismal certificate, some oil, and water. For Step 3, have a candle and some holy water.	■ Baptism objects: candle, baptismal shell, water, white robe, Bible, and oil ■ Holy water ■ candle and holy water
Day 3	For the prayer in Step 3, consider how you will show your happiness at being a member of Jesus' family.	■ Baptism objects: Bible, water, cruet of oil, baptismal robe, candle
Day 4	Read over the session to prepare the lesson.	■ bulletin board from Day 1 ■ holy water font ■ holy water
Day 5	Consider gestures and movements you will use to lead the children in a procession. Use the bulletin board from Day 1.	■ musical instruments: cymbals, drums, whistles, spoons, and so on (optional)

Additional Resources

As you plan this chapter, consider using the following materials from The Resourceful Teacher Package.

■ *Classroom Activity Sheets 14* and *14a*

■ *Family Activity Sheets 14* and *14a*

■ *Chapter 14 Test*

■ *Prayers for Every Day*

■ *Projects: Grade 1*

In preparing the students for the Sunday readings, you may wish to use Silver Burdett Ginn's *Getting Ready For Sunday* student and teacher materials.

BOOKS FOR THE JOURNEY

On the Day You Were Born. Debra Frasier. Harcourt, Brace, Jovanovich, 1991. This book reveals the natural world giving a loving welcome to each member of the human family at birth.

It's My Birthday, God. Elspeth Campbell Smith. David C. Cook, 1993. This book is a prayer about birthdays and being older.

MORE BOOKS FOR THE JOURNEY

Some Birthday! Patricia Polacco. Simon & Schuster, 1991. A delightfully different kind of birthday is celebrated in this book.

The Random House Book of Poetry. "If We Didn't Have Birthdays," p. 126, Dr. Seuss. Selected by Jack Prelutsky. Random House, 1983. In a delightful way, this poem tells how important birthdays are.

REDUCED CLASSROOM ACTIVITIES

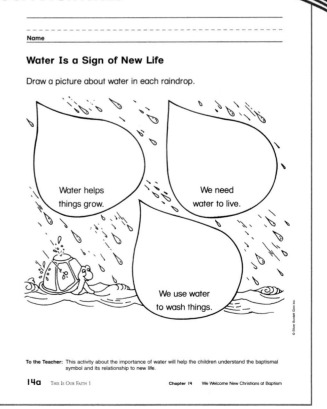

Name _____

We Welcome New Christians at Baptism

Trace each word below in a different color.
The priest said these words when he baptized you.

I baptize you
in the name of the Father
and of the Son,
and of the Holy Spirit.

To the Teacher: This activity follows the story "Rosa's Baptism."

Chapter 14   We Welcome New Christians at Baptism   THIS IS OUR FAITH 1   **14**

Name _____

Water Is a Sign of New Life

Draw a picture about water in each raindrop.

Water helps things grow.

We need water to live.

We use water to wash things.

To the Teacher: This activity about the importance of water will help the children understand the baptismal symbol and its relationship to new life.

14a   THIS IS OUR FAITH 1   Chapter 14   We Welcome New Christians at Baptism

THE SACRAMENTS

The sacraments celebrate our union with Jesus through the action of the Holy Spirit. These seven rituals celebrate significant events in our Christian lives. Through the sacrament of Baptism, we become Christians, followers and friends of Christ Jesus. Saint Paul summarized the theology of Baptism when he wrote: "God our savior . . . saved us through the bath of rebirth and renewal by the holy Spirit, whom he richly poured out on us through Jesus Christ our savior, so that we might be justified by his grace and become heirs in hope of eternal life" (Titus 3:4–7).

NEW LIFE IN CHRIST JESUS

By accepting our baptism into Jesus' death and resurrection, we affirm the gift of our faith. In the baptism of an infant, this affirmation is made through parents and godparents. Saint Paul explained to the early Christians at Colossae that "you were buried with [Christ] in baptism, in which you were raised to life with him through faith in the power of God, who raised him from the dead" (Colossians 2:12). The symbols of Baptism signify our new life in Christ Jesus. Water is cleansing and life-sustaining; oil signifies strength and healing; the lighted candle symbolizes Christ, whose light of goodness dispels the darkness of sin.

CHILDREN AND BAPTISM

Roman Catholics are ordinarily baptized as infants. The Catholic Church calls parents to share their faith with their children and to help them mature in the Christian life. To grow in faith, a child needs the example and guidance of adults. Today the role of parents as prime educators and exemplars of Christian living is emphasized in the sacrament of Baptism. At the same time, the supportive role of the entire Christian community is also made clear. The Church encourages adult Catholics to examine seriously the commitment made at Baptism to respond to Christ's invitation to love one another.

In the initial presentation of Baptism in Chapter 14, you help the children recognize their membership in Jesus' family. They celebrate their birth into this family through the sacrament of Baptism. You help them become familiar with the rite of Baptism and with the symbols of the sacrament.

Present this chapter festively, for it celebrates both their birthdays and their baptismal days. If at all possible, end the chapter with a party to celebrate the very being of the children: They *are*—and they are *Christians*.

DAY 1
DOCTRINE

Objective

This lesson helps the children recognize that they become a member of the family of Jesus through the sacrament of Baptism.

Step 1/INTRODUCTION

Learning About Our Lives

Introducing Chapter 14

Read aloud the question in the margin of page 172 and encourage the children's response. Ask them to look at the photograph and talk about why birthday parties are so much fun. Invite the children to share stories about their birthday celebrations.

Reading the Text

Read aloud "Celebrating Being Alive" on page 172. Invite the children to read what people mean to let you know by honoring you at birthday parties (the words in quotations).

Step 2/DEVELOPMENT

Learning About Our Faith

Preparing to Talk About Baptism

Tell the children that Christians celebrate both the day they were born into their families and the day they became part of Jesus' family. Ask the children if anyone knows the name of the celebration that made them members of Jesus' family. If no one mentions the sacrament of Baptism, explain that they became part of Jesus' family when they were baptized and that on that day, they first became Christians. Recall with the children that a Christian is a follower and a friend of Christ, which is another name we call Jesus.

Working in the Text

Read aloud "A Member of the Family of Jesus" on page 173. Encourage the children to share any stories they have heard about their own baptism or the baptism of someone else. Ask the children to underline in the text the words that Jesus spoke about Baptism. Read these words aloud with the children. Tell them that these important words are in the Bible.

172

We Welcome New Christians at Baptism

How does your family celebrate birthdays?

Celebrating Being Alive

Birthdays celebrate our being alive.
Our families and friends are glad we are alive and belong to them.

Sometimes our family and friends give birthday parties for us.
They are saying, "You are special."
"Thank God you are in our family."
"Thank God you are our friend."

172   Doctrine

CURRICULUM CONNECTION

Language Arts Invite the children to bring in photographs of one of their birthday parties or of themselves as infants. Give each child three sheets of 8 1/2" × 11" paper folded in half to make a storybook about his or her birthday. Provide tape so that the children can tape their photographs in the booklets. Have the children print *The Celebration of My Birth* on the title page and encourage them to write the story of their favorite birthday. Have the children take their booklets home.

Focus on

The Words of Baptism Jesus' commissioning of the disciples to baptize all people and the words of the sacrament of Baptism have similarities. Write both of these statements on the board and have volunteers underline the similar words in one color chalk. You will find the words of the sacrament on page 174.

A Member of the Family of Jesus

Baptism is a sacrament.
A **sacrament** is a celebration of
Jesus' love and God's presence.
Baptism celebrates our new
life with Jesus.

We live our new life with
all other Christians.
Through **Baptism**, they
become our brothers and sisters.
Together we are the family of Jesus.

Jesus said to his followers, "Baptize all people
in the name of the Father, and of the Son, and
of the Holy Spirit."

Based on Matthew 28:19

New Words

✦ **sacrament** A sacrament is a
  celebration of Jesus' love
  and of God's presence.

✦ **Baptism** Baptism is a celebration
  of our new life with Jesus
  and his friends.

We Believe

At Baptism we
celebrate becoming a
member of the
family of Jesus. We
celebrate our new
life as brothers and
sisters of Jesus.

Doctrine   173

Teaching Tips

When using a doll to demonstrate
the pouring of water at Baptism,
remember that there are three pour-
ings, one at the mention of each of
the persons of the Trinity. The symbolism of water recalls God's
intervening on behalf of God's people—the escape of the Hebrews
through the sea and the gushing of
water in the desert during the exo-
dus. Water is a sign of power and
force, among other things.

Enriching the Lesson

Prepare a chart or calendar with the
children's baptismal dates listed.
These dates are usually on their
permanent records because baptismal certificates are usually part of
the documentation needed for
enrollment. If you do not have the
dates recorded, you can acquire
them from your parish office. Be
sure to get the dates for any children baptized in a Christian Church
other than Catholic.

Reviewing the Vocabulary

Point to the New Words box on page 173. Ask
the children to repeat the words *sacrament* and
Baptism and their definitions.

Presenting the Doctrine

On page 173, read aloud the We Believe
section, which summarizes the chapter's
doctrine. Ask the children to repeat the
sentences after you.

Studying a Picture

Direct the children's attention to the picture of
Baptism on page 173. Have the children
examine the picture carefully to notice the
pouring of water onto the head of the person
being baptized. Tell the children that the
celebrant pours the water and says, "(Name), I
baptize you in the name of the Father, and of
the Son, and of the Holy Spirit." Demonstrate
this by using a doll over whose head you pour
water. You may have volunteers repeat this
action while the class says the words.

Step 3/CONCLUSION

Learning How to Live Our Faith

Drawing a Baptismal Celebration

Print on the board the words of a baptismal
certificate and have the children copy them,
decorating the paper with a picture of
themselves being baptized. At this time,
concentrate on the pouring of the water. The
next session will develop the other actions of
the sacrament.

Creating a Bulletin Board

Have the children bring their pictures to an
empty bulletin board and pin up the pictures.
Cut out: *Baptism made us members of Jesus'
family.* Give each child a letter to hold and ask
the children to help you tack up the letters. Talk
about how the sentence applies to their
drawings.

Using the Bulletin Board for Prayer

As the children are gathered around the bulletin
board, invite them to pray. Teach the children
the following response: *Thank you, God, for our
birthdays and for our baptismal days.* Then,
invite volunteers to explain their drawings. After
each volunteer shares, invite the children's
response.

DAY 2
PRAYER

Objective

This lesson helps the children become acquainted with the rite of Baptism.

Step 1/INTRODUCTION

Learning About Our Lives

Reviewing Day 1

Gather the children around the bulletin board they assembled on Day 1. Read the words and ask the children what these words mean to them. Then invite volunteers to comment on their drawings and the ways that they illustrate the bulletin board sentence.

Studying a Baptismal Display

Gather the children around the display you set up before class. Point out that the display is of objects used at Baptism (a candle, a shell for pouring water, a white robe, oil, a crucifix, water, and a Bible or the *Lectionary*). Invite volunteers to name as many of the objects as they can. Identify items the children do not recognize.

Step 2/DEVELOPMENT

Learning About Our Faith

Listening to a Baptismal Story

Encourage the children to look at the pictures on pages 174–175 while you read aloud "Rosa's Baptism." Afterward, point to the illustrations, one by one, and invite volunteers to tell the part of the story that the picture illustrates. Finally, ask the following questions.

- Who is holding Rosa? (*Her mother*)
- Where is Rosa's father? (*He is standing beside Rosa's mother.*)
- Where are Rosa's godparents? (*Standing behind her parents*)
- Why do you think everyone claps for Rosa? (*Answers will vary, but clapping is a sign that all the people are happy that Rosa is now a member of the Christian family.*)

174

Rosa's Baptism

1. Father Alberto and other members of San Jose Church welcome Rosa. Father Alberto and Rosa's parents and **godparents** make the Sign of the Cross on Rosa's forehead.

2. Father Alberto reads a story about Jesus from the Bible. Everyone prays for little Rosa. They promise to help Rosa know, love, and trust God.

3. Father Alberto pours water over Rosa's head three times. He says, "I baptize you, Rosa, in the name of the Father, and of the Son, and of the Holy Spirit."

4. Father Alberto marks Rosa's head with blessed oil.

5. Rosa receives a white robe. Father Alberto prays that she will grow to be like Jesus.

174   Prauer

CURRICULUM CONNECTION

Drama   Divide the class into three groups: four children in Group 1, five children in Group 2, and the remaining children in Group 3. Group 1 dramatizes the preparations made by Rosa's parents and godparents for the baptism. Group 2 portrays Rosa's parents, godparents, and the priest at Rosa's baptism. Group 3 depicts the happiness of Rosa's family and friends at the church as they celebrate Rosa's baptism.

Focus on

Effects of Baptism   According to the *Catechism of the Catholic Church*, "The different effects of Baptism are signified by the perceptible elements of the sacramental rite. Immersion in water symbolizes not only death and purification, but also regeneration and renewal. Thus the two principal effects are purification from sins and new birth in the Holy Spirit" (#1262).

6. Rosa's father lights a candle from the Easter candle. It reminds everyone of Jesus, the Light of the World.

7. The members of San Jose Church stand and clap to welcome Rosa into the family of Jesus.

Activity

On the lines below, write your godparents' names. They help you live as a friend of Jesus.

_____

_____

_____

_____

New Word

◆
◆
◆ **godparents** Godparents are people who help
◆   us grow as friends and followers
◆   of Jesus.
◆

Prayer 175

Enriching the Lesson

Prepare a paper baptismal robe for each child to wear. Fold large sheets of white paper in half and cut out shield shapes. At the top of each "robe," cut out a half circle as an opening for the child's head. Review the giving of the robe at Baptism on page 174 of the text. Then have the children print the word *Christian* on their robes. The children may wear their robes while completing Chapter 14.

Completing an Activity

Read the directions to the activity on page 175 and have the children write the names of their godparents on the lines provided.

Reviewing the New Words

Point to the New Word box on page 175. Ask the children to repeat the word *godparents* and the definition after you.

Step 3/CONCLUSION

Learning How to Live Our Faith

Renewing Baptismal Promises

Gather the children in the prayer area. When they are quiet, tell them that today they will renew the promises made for them at their baptisms. Talk briefly about what a promise is. Then teach the children the following response: *We do.* Next, show them the candle and holy water you brought to the prayer area. Finally, lead them in a renewal of their baptismal promises.

Teacher:	Do you promise to try to do what is good?
Children:	We do.
Teacher:	Do you believe in God?
Children:	We do.
Teacher:	Do you believe in Jesus, God's Son?
Children:	We do.
Teacher:	Do you promise to love Jesus and to try to be like him?
Children:	We do.

Light a candle (if fire laws permit) and hold it high. Then say: *Jesus said, "I am the light of the world. No follower of mine shall ever walk in darkness; he or she shall possess the light of life"* (based on John 8:12).

Invite the children to come toward you in pairs. When they stand before you, encourage each child to make the Sign of the Cross on his or her partner's forehead with holy water.

175

DAY 3
DOCTRINE

Objective
This lesson helps the children recognize some of the elements of Christian Baptism.

Step 1/INTRODUCTION

Learning About Our Lives

Recalling the Learning of Days 1 and 2
Encourage volunteers to talk about the differences between a birthday party and a baptismal celebration. As the children share, stress that on their birthdays they celebrate God's gift of life and becoming part of their families; at their baptism, they celebrate becoming members of Jesus' family.

Completing an Activity
Read aloud the directions to the activity at the top of page 176. Encourage the children to circle the pictures of things that are usually part of their birthday celebrations. Afterward, discuss with the children how they use these items at birthday parties. Encourage the children to talk about other things they do to celebrate their birthdays. (For example, they might have a special family meal, watch movies or videos of earlier birthdays, or record their height on a wall).

Step 2/DEVELOPMENT

Learning About Our Faith

Reviewing the Sacrament of Baptism
Have the children turn back to pages 174–175 of the text. Invite volunteers to point to and explain the various things the priest used at Rosa's baptism (baptismal font, Bible, water, oil, white baptismal robe, lighted candle). Encourage the children to explain how the items were used.

Completing a Rebus Baptismal Activity
Read "Special Signs of Baptism" on page 176. Invite the children to say aloud at the appropriate time the word each rebus symbol represents. Afterward, show the children the actual objects (Bible or *Lectionary*, water, cruet of oil, baptismal robe, candle) and invite them to touch the objects.

176

 Activity

Many things can be signs that we are celebrating a birthday.
Circle the things that are usually part of your birthday celebration.

Special Signs of Baptism

Catholics use many signs to celebrate the sacrament of Baptism.

Here is what happened at your Baptism.

There was a reading from the .

The priest poured on your head.

The priest marked your head with .

You were dressed in a white .

Your parents lighted a from the Easter  .

CURRICULUM CONNECTION

Art Make celebration buttons. Give each child a 5" circle of colored posterboard. Invite the children to print on their buttons the following sentence: *I became a Christian through Baptism.* Then encourage the children to decorate their buttons with symbols of Baptism, such as a cross, a candle, or water. Help the children use tape or pins to attach their buttons to their clothing.

Activity

Finish this picture.
Make it a picture of yourself.

I am a Christian!

My Christian name is

_____

\- .

Learning How to Live Our Faith

Drawing a Picture About Being a Christian

Direct the children's attention to the activity on page 177. Read the text and invite the children to draw themselves as a Christian and a member of Jesus' family. Have them print their Christian names on the lines provided. Encourage the children to share their pictures. If some of the drawings show smiling children, comment that celebrating becoming a Christian at Baptism is a happy event.

Gathering for Prayer

Invite the children to gather in the prayer area. When they are quiet, teach the following response: *Amen! Alleluia! We are Christians.* Then encourage volunteers to use gestures and body movements to show God how happy they are to be members of Jesus' family. Show your own happiness by singing or dancing, or by crossing your arms over your chest, bowing your head, and thanking God for the gift of life and the gift of being a Christian. After each volunteer prays with song, dance, words, or body movements, invite the rest of the children to pray their responses.

🍎 Teaching Tips

Encourage each child to ask his or her family members if they have any photographs, movies, or videos of their baptism. Encourage the children to look at these reminders of their baptism. Then on Day 4 or Day 5, provide time for the children to talk about their baptism. At that time, emphasize how happy their families must have been to celebrate the children's baptism with them.

DAY 4
DOCTRINE

Objective

This lesson helps the children reflect on the sacrament of Baptism, especially the celebration of their own baptism.

Step 1/INTRODUCTION

Learning About Our Lives

Reviewing the Bulletin Board from Day 1

Gather the children around the bulletin board they decorated on Day 1. Help them realize that today they know more about their baptism than they did on Day 1. Ask the children what they would now add to their pictures if they were to draw them over. Tell them that today they will get a chance to draw another baptism picture.

Completing an Activity

Read the directions to the activity on page 178. Encourage the children to draw a picture about something new they learned about their baptism. Afterward, invite the children to share their work with the class.

Step 2/DEVELOPMENT

Learning About Our Faith

Reading the Text

Direct the children's attention to "Holy Water" at the bottom of page 178. Read aloud the text and then ask the following questions.

- Where do we find holy water? (*At the entrance to the church*)
- When was this water poured over our heads? (*At our baptism*)
- What prayer do we say with holy water? (*The Sign of the Cross*)
- When we sign ourselves with holy water, what do we remember? (*We remember our friend Jesus and our baptism into the Christian family.*)
- When did we use holy water this week? (*In the prayer service on Day 2*)

178

---

ctivity

It is good to think about our own Baptism.
Draw what you imagine your Baptism was like.

Holy Water

We can make the Sign of the Cross with holy water. It reminds us that the priest poured water over our heads at Baptism. It reminds us of our new life with Jesus.

178   Doctrine

Focus on

The Rite of Baptism   If possible, sometime during Chapter 14, invite a priest or deacon to demonstrate a baptism. Note that this is best done in church at the baptismal font. If a priest or deacon is not able to do this, obtain a copy of the *Rite of Baptism* and read appropriate sections of it to the children. Ask your parish priest for a copy of this rite from the *Rites of Catholics* (New York, NY., Pueblo Publishing Company).

Celebrating Baptism

The sacrament of Baptism celebrates
our becoming friends with Jesus.
We remember our Christian family.

We are baptized.

We become Christians.

The followers of Jesus
welcome us.

God is our Father.

Jesus is our brother.

We are all brothers
and sisters.

Doctrine 179

Explaining Holy Water

If possible take the children to church to see the holy water font. In many churches, people bless themselves with water from the baptismal font in the gathering area. They remind themselves of their baptism and of the fact that they are followers of Jesus.

Step 3/CONCLUSION

Learning How to Live Our Faith

Preparing an Action Prayer

Read aloud the text under "Celebrating Baptism" on page 179. Then point to each illustration and read the sentence it illustrates. Invite the children to stand and to practice the gestures. Tell them that they will pray today using these gestures.

Gathering for Prayer

Invite the children to bring their books and gather in a semicircle in the prayer area. Place some holy water on the prayer table. Tell the children that today they will pray by acting out the story of Baptism as shown on page 179. When they are quiet and ready, read the first line of the prayer on page 179—*We are baptized*. Then invite the children, one by one, to take some holy water and to bless themselves with the Sign of the Cross. To help them, first do this yourself. When all the children have blessed themselves as a reminder of their baptism, encourage them to use the gestures shown in the book as you continue to read the rest of the prayer aloud.

PRAYER/REVIEW

Objective

This lesson helps the children celebrate their baptism by asking the saints to help them live like Jesus.

Reading the Text

Read "Praying a Litany" on page 180. During the discussion, emphasize that the friends of Jesus who are with God, the saints, did good things for others as Jesus asked them to. Tell the children that they will use a litany of saints when they pray today.

Preparing to Process to the Prayer Area

Tell the children that today they are going to ask the saints to pray to God for them. Teach the children the following response: *Pray to God for us.*

Then provide them with musical instruments. Explain to them that they can sing a song and play their musical instruments as they process. Or encourage the children to dance, clap their hands, or raise their arms in praise as they process and sing their song.

Praying with the Saints

Process to the prayer area and pray the litany on page 180. Invite the children to respond after each invocation to a saint. After praying the litany printed in the text, invite volunteers to add to it by naming people they know who are with God in heaven, such as a grandparent. The other members of the class may respond: *Pray to God for us.* Conclude the prayer by having the children sing the song again. Or encourage them to praise God by playing their musical instruments, dancing, or clapping their hands.

180

Mary

Joseph

Peter

Andrew

Martha

Praying a Litany

At Baptism the priest asks our parents, "What name do you give this child?" Then our parents tell the priest our name. They almost always give us a saint's name.

Saints are people who love God very much. They spend their lives doing good things for others. Now they live with God in heaven. They can ask God to help us.

Here is a way to ask the saints to help us. This kind of prayer is called a litany.

Leader: Mother Mary,
    All: Pray to God for us.
Leader: Saint Joseph,
    All: Pray to God for us.
Leader: Peter and Andrew,
    All: Pray to God for us.
Leader: Martha, Mary, and Lazarus,
    All: Pray to God for us.

Lazarus

Mary

180 Prayer

Praying a Litany Today's prayer skill is twofold. It formally introduces the children to the litany as a prayer form. A litany is a repeated response to a variety of verses. Today's prayer also teaches the idea that others in the community—namely, the saints in heaven—can and will pray for us all.

🍎 Teaching Tips

Learning a Song About Baptism Teach the children a song to sing as they process to the prayer corner. Use the following words to the melody "Frère Jacques".

We are members of a family.
Yes, we are!
Yes, we are!
Jesus is our brother!
Jesus is our brother!
Christians now!
Christians now!

Chapter Review

Activity

Circle what you can see at Baptism.

1. Whose family do we join at Baptism?

   The family of Jesus

2. What do we call the celebration of becoming a member of the family of Jesus?

   Baptism

3. Talk about what it means to be in the family of Jesus.

> Love each other like brothers and sisters.
> **Based on Romans 12:10**

Review 181

Using the Bulletin Board from Day 1 to Review

Use the bulletin board decorated on Day 1 to review the chapter. Invite the children to talk about how they became members of Jesus' family. Have the children recall what the name *Christian* means. Talk about their friend and leader, Jesus Christ, and stress that as followers of Jesus Christ, they want to do the loving and caring things he did. As the children share, invite them to talk about ways Christians show that they are followers of Christ.

Finally, give each child his or her bulletin-board drawing and encourage the children to take their drawings home, post them in a prominent place, and use them as reminders of their baptism.

Completing an Activity

Use the activity on page 181 to review the learning of Chapter 14. Read the text at the top of the page. Then direct the children's attention to the illustrations. Invite the children to circle the items they might see at a baptism. Afterward, encourage them to talk about their selections.

Answering the Questions

Read aloud the first two questions and ask volunteers to respond. Direct the children to print the answers in their texts. Encourage all the children to participate in the discussion of the third question. Be supportive of each child who responds.

Reading a Scripture Verse

End the session by reading the Scripture verse on page 181. Have the children repeat it after you. If you wish, the children may memorize this verse.

★ Enriching the Lesson ★

To help the children feel proud of themselves and their efforts to follow Jesus, have a simple party to celebrate their baptism. Teach them the round "Rejoice in the Lord Always" (*Young People's Glory and Praise,* OCP). Distribute balloons; if you made baptismal robes for the children, invite the children to wear them. Have the children sit on the floor in a circle and sing the round. Provide a simple, healthy snack.

15 We Are Catholics

Objectives ~~~~~

To help the children

- Recognize the Church as the family of Jesus' friends and followers.
- Appreciate the Church as a special family to which they belong.
- Learn the meaning of *church* and become familiar with the objects in it.
- Deepen their understanding of how Catholic Christians act like Jesus.
- Express their belief in the constant presence of Jesus with his Church.

Chapter Outline ~~~~~~~

	Step 1 Learning About Our Lives	**Step 2** Learning About Our Faith	**Step 3** Learning How to Live Our Faith
Day 1	■ Introduce Chapter 15. ■ Examine photographs. ■ Read a poem. ■ Act out the poem. *ABOUT 10 MINUTES*	■ Examine photographs. ■ Read the text. ■ Review the new words. ■ Present the doctrine. *ABOUT 10 MINUTES*	■ Draw a church. ■ Create a bulletin board. ■ Use the bulletin board for prayer. *ABOUT 10 MINUTES*
Day 2	■ Review Day 1. ■ Read a story about belonging to a family. ■ Complete an activity. *ABOUT 10 MINUTES*	■ Learn more about the members of the Christian Church. ■ Draw a packed bag. *ABOUT 10 MINUTES*	■ Write and pray a prayer. *ABOUT 10 MINUTES*
Day 3	■ Recall Days 1 and 2. ■ Learn another meaning of *church*. ■ Talk about a Catholic church. *ABOUT 10 MINUTES*	■ Respond to the text and illustrations. *ABOUT 10 MINUTES*	■ Make prayer cards. ■ Gather for prayer. *ABOUT 10 MINUTES*
Day 4	■ Brainstorm ways that the Church acts like Jesus. *ABOUT 10 MINUTES*	■ Complete an activity. ■ Study magazine pictures. *ABOUT 10 MINUTES*	■ Complete a church activity. ■ Gather for prayer. *ABOUT 10 MINUTES*
Day 5	**Prayer** Read the text and pray with Jesus. **Review** Review the learning of the week by using the bulletin board; complete an activity; answer the questions; and read the Scripture verse.		

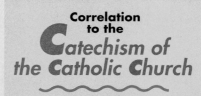
Plan Ahead ~~~~~~~~~

	Preparing Your Class	**Materials Needed**
Day 1	For Step 1, suggest gestures for the poem. For Step 3, cut out the letters for *We belong to the Catholic Church* for the bulletin board.	■ drawing paper ■ empty bulletin board ■ cut-out letters for a sentence ■ thumbtack/staples
Day 2	Read over the session before teaching it. If you plan to use any Teaching Option, make preparations and collect the materials.	■ sheets of 8 1/2" × 11" paper folded in half (two per child)
Day 3	Read over the session before teaching it. Arrange to visit the parish church for Step 3.	■ posterboard cut into 2 1/2" × 7" pieces (one per child)
Day 4	For Step 2, collect an array of magazine pictures that show people in need of help.	■ magazine and newspaper pictures ■ holy water
Day 5	Find a picture of Jesus that will appeal to the sensibilities of six-year-olds.	■ picture of Jesus

Additional Resources

As you plan this chapter, consider using the following materials from The Resourceful Teacher Package.

■ *Classroom Activity Sheets 15* and *15a*

■ *Family Activity Sheets 15* and *15a*

■ *Chapter 15 Test*

■ *Prayers for Every Day*

■ *Projects: Grade 1*

In preparing the students for the Sunday readings, you may wish to use Silver Burdett Ginn's *Getting Ready for Sunday* student and teacher materials.

BOOKS FOR THE JOURNEY

Home. Edited by Michael J. Rosen. HarperCollins, 1992. This book celebrates the places, things, and people that make up a home.

A House Is A House for Me. Mary Ann Hoberman. Viking Press, 1978. Lists in rhyme tell that a house is for animals, things, and people.

MORE BOOKS FOR THE JOURNEY

Experience Jesus Today. "Your House," p. 159. Charles Singer & Albert Hari. Oregon Catholic Press, 1993. This prayer helps us reflect on the church as a building which can be home to the children of this earth.

A Child's First Catholic Dictionary. Richard W. Dyches & Thomas Mustachio. Ave Maria Press, 1994. Definitions, images, words, and beliefs explain what it means to be Catholic.

REDUCED CLASSROOM ACTIVITIES

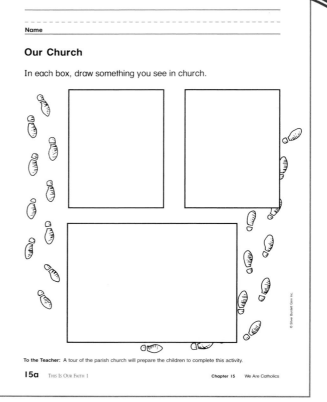

Name _____

We Are Catholics

Draw yourself as a member of the family of Jesus.
Color the words on the banner.

To the Teacher: This activity follows the story "Where We Belong."

Chapter 15   We Are Catholics   This Is Our Faith 1   **15**

Name _____

Our Church

In each box, draw something you see in church.

To the Teacher: A tour of the parish church will prepare the children to complete this activity.

15a   This Is Our Faith 1   Chapter 15   We Are Catholics

THE CHURCH

The Church's unique relationship with Christ Jesus makes the Church both a sign and an instrument of God's union with humanity. This sign and instrument extends to the unity of Christians with one another. The Church community, which has accepted Christ's invitation to unity and worship, is a divine mystery, beyond our full comprehension. That the Church continues, year in and year out, gathering people to God is part of that mystery and is a sign of the presence of the Spirit of Jesus.

Church members are led by the Holy Spirit in their faith journey. God calls the Church to be a sign of the reign of God's love and peace in the world. The Spirit sanctifies the Church, purifies it, and breathes life into it. Through the actions of the Spirit, all Christians gather in the name of Jesus. As the Church, we Christians minister to others, witness the grace of God, and mediate that grace, proclaiming the good news of God's love for everyone in Christ Jesus.

FOR ALL PEOPLE

The Church is catholic or universal. Jesus commissioned his disciples to spread the good news of God's unending and unconditional love to all nations. All cultures can integrate the Gospel message, for Jesus' proclamation touches all that is human in us. Catholics, united under the leadership of the pope and the bishops, affirm life in all its forms. Through our local parish communities, we grow in our identity as Catholics and live our call to universal love.

MEANINGS OF CHURCH

Most six-year-olds will associate the word *church* simply with a building. In this chapter, you have the opportunity to broaden the children's understanding of this word to include all of Jesus' family of believers. You will help the children recognize that they belong to their own families and to the family of Jesus called Christians.

You will also assist the children in recognizing that the place where the Christian community gathers to celebrate the love of God and the presence of Jesus in our midst is called a church. Thus, they learn that the word *church* means both "place" and "people."

In Chapter 15 you will also introduce the children to the Christian Church to which they belong. You name this Church as Catholic. Keep the explanation of the word *Catholic* uncomplicated. The goal of this lesson is simple: to enable the children to identify themselves as Christians who are at home in the Catholic Church.

Objective

This lesson helps the children recognize the Church as the family of Jesus' friends and followers.

Step 1/INTRODUCTION

Learning About Our Lives

Introducing Chapter 15

Invite the children to name the places requested in the margin of page 182. If they do not understand the word *belong*, explain that the word means "feel at home" or "feeling loved and cared for."

Examining Photographs

Ask the following questions about the photographs on page 182.

Do you think the people in this picture feel they belong together? How do you know? (*Answers will vary.*)

Reading a Poem

Read aloud the poem "My Home" on page 182. Afterward discuss the three stanzas of the poem. Ask the children how family members might help one another feel that they belong to the family. Encourage responses such as helping one another, speaking kindly, laughing, playing, sharing, and working together.

Acting Out the Poem

Reread the poem on page 182. Then divide the children into three groups and assign each group one of the stanzas of the poem. Invite the children to brainstorm and select appropriate gestures for their stanzas. When the children are ready, reread the poem as the groups perform their gestures.

or ...

Encourage the children to show photos of their families doing various activities. Let the children tell how what they did helped them feel that they belong to their families. Help them decide what stanza of the poem the picture might go with and have them hold up the photograph at the appropriate time as you reread the poem.

182

Name some places where you feel that you belong.

We Are Catholics

My Home

Inside my home
Lives a family
Of people who
Belong to me.

Inside my home
We laugh and play,
Eat and help,
And read and pray.

Inside my home
We're taught to share
And care for people
everywhere.

Cultural Awareness

Show a globe to the children. Tell them that the Catholic family is very large. Point out different parts of the world and explain that there are Catholic Christians living in all these places. Help the children value their membership in this worldwide community. Invite them to pray for their sisters and brothers in Christ Jesus throughout the world.

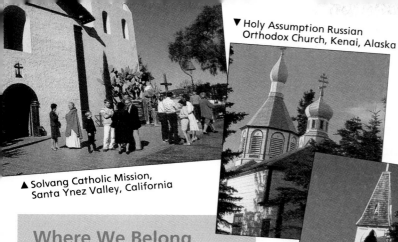

▲ Solvang Catholic Mission, Santa Ynez Valley, California

▼ Holy Assumption Russian Orthodox Church, Kenai, Alaska

Where We Belong

We belong to our families.
As friends and followers
of Jesus, we also belong
to his Christian family.
We gather in groups called
Churches.
The Church we belong to is
called the **Catholic Church**.

▲ St. Paul's Episcopal Church, Port Townsend, Washington

New Words

★
★ Church   We belong to the Catholic
★   Church.
★
★

We Believe

Christians gather
in groups called
**Churches. We
belong to the
Catholic Church.**

 **CURRICULUM CONNECTION**

Language Arts   Help the children write thank-you letters to their families. Print the following letter in correct form on the chalkboard or duplicate it for the children to fill in.

Dear _____,
Thank you for making our house a home by _____.
I love you,
_____.

Encourage the children to give the letters to their families.

Learning About Our Faith

Examining Photographs

Read aloud the captions for the photographs on page 183. Then invite the children to talk about churches they have visited and to tell what they noticed that was the same as or different from their parish church.

Reading the Text

Invite the children to follow along silently as you read aloud "Where We Belong" on page 183. Emphasize that the children belong to two families—their own family and the family of Jesus' friends and followers. Reread the text, leaving out the words *Jesus, Christian family, Churches*, and *Catholic Church*. When you come to these words, ask the children to say the missing words and to underline them.

Reviewing the New Words

Point to the New Words box on page 183. Ask the children to repeat the word *Church* and its definition.

Presenting the Doctrine

Read aloud the We Believe section on page 183, which summarizes the chapter's doctrine. Ask the children to repeat the sentences.

Step 3/CONCLUSION

Learning How to Live Our Faith

Drawing a Church

Distribute drawing paper and invite the children to draw pictures of their parish church. Encourage them to include in the picture as many details as they can remember.

Creating a Bulletin Board

Help the children pin on an empty bulletin board their drawings and the letters: *We belong to the Catholic Church*. Talk about how the sentence applies to their drawings.

Using the Bulletin Board for Prayer

Still gathered around the bulletin board, teach the children the following response: *Thank you, God, for our Catholic Church*. Ask volunteers to explain their drawings and invite the children to pray the response.

183

Objective

This lesson helps the children appreciate the Church as a special family to which they belong.

Step 1/INTRODUCTION

Learning About Our Lives

Reviewing Day 1

To review part of the learning of Day 1, invite the children to brainstorm the meaning of the word *belong*. Then ask volunteers to list the two families they belong to. (Their own family and the family of Jesus' friends and followers).

Reading a Story About Belonging to a Family

Before reading aloud "Belonging to Our Catholic Family" on page 185, ask the children to listen carefully to find out how Allie knows she belongs to her family. Read one paragraph at a time and have the children find the part that tells that Allie likes belonging to her family. Ask the children what clues in the paragraph tell this.

- Paragraph 1: Allie senses that she belongs as her mother helps her get ready for school. She feels close to her mother.

- Paragraph 2: Allie enjoys walking with her father. They do it every day, and Allie feels sure about her father's feelings for her.

- Paragraph 3: Allie laughs with her brother. She likes the closeness of driving with him to school.

Completing an Activity

Read aloud the directions to the activity on page 184. Encourage the children to write a sentence that tells one thing their family members do that creates feelings of belonging to a happy family.

184

Allie's Family Shares Love

Allie's mother helps her get ready for school.
Her mother helps her be happy in the Johnson family.

Allie and her father walk the dog each evening.
Then Allie enjoys belonging to the Johnsons.

Her brother Johnny tells her jokes on the way to school. When they laugh, she loves belonging to her family.

Activity

Write something your family members do to let you know that they love you.

_____

- -

_____

Focus on

Belonging Belonging is a basic psychological actuality. First-grade children feel that the family and all it entails is very much a part of themselves. This viewpoint is expressed in their language: "My mommy, my daddy, my nana, my house, my dog, my baby, my toys, my yard." Helping the children articulate their experiences of belonging to their families helps them better understand the Church.

Focus on

Family The papal document *Familiaris Consortio* states that the family is the fundamental school of Christian love. Acceptance and support of one another is rudimentary to such love. These practices generate feelings of belonging. Therefore, using the metaphor of the family of Jesus' friends and followers to describe the Church helps the children realize the similarities between the Christian family and the Church.

Belonging to Our Catholic Family

At Sunday Mass, the Johnson family
says hello to Father Mike.
The Johnsons know many of the
other people at Mass, too.
Knowing so many people helps
Allie's family feel they
belong to Saint John Church.

Allie's mom helps pack bags of baby
clothes for mothers who need them.
Allie comes along to help pack.
She puts a teddy bear in each bag.
Allie likes to help others.
It is fun to pack bags with the
grown-ups and other children.
It helps make her feel that she
belongs to Saint John Church.

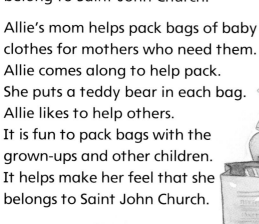

Doctrine 185

★ ★ ★ Enriching the Lesson ★

Encourage the children to make storybooks to show that they belong to their families. Then give each child two sheets of 8 1/2" × 11" paper folded in half. Have the children draw pictures that illustrate important times they shared with their parents and other family members. Encourage the children to write at least one sentence for each illustration. Have them print the title *I Belong to My Family* on the front page.

Step 2/DEVELOPMENT

Learning About Our Faith

Learning About Members of the Christian Church

Tell the children that the family of Jesus' friends and followers do special things together. These activities show that the people belong to the family of Jesus, the Church. Help the children understand that the first vignette on page 185 shows the Catholic family gathered for Mass. Include in your discussion the warm welcome the family of Jesus welcomes extends to all people.

Then read aloud the second vignette (paragraph 2) on page 185 while the children look at the illustration. Ask the following questions.

- What are Allie, her mother, and friends doing at Saint John Church? (*Packing bags of baby clothes*)
- Why are these Christians packing baby clothes? (*Some other mothers need things for their babies.*)
- How does helping pack the bags make Allie feel? (*That she belongs*)
- How do you think helping at church would make you feel? Have you ever helped at church? (*Answers will vary.*)

Drawing a Packed Bag

Invite the children to draw a plastic, see-through bag (have them outline a bag) and draw in the things they would like to give to a poor baby. Or they might cut out construction paper items. Either paste them in the shape of the outline or put them inside a real bag.

or . . .

Invite the children to bring in items they might give to a family who needs baby things—well-maintained toys, clean but used baby clothes, balls, picture books, baby food, and so forth.

Step 3/CONCLUSION

Learning How to Live Our Faith

Writing and Praying a Prayer

With the children, compose a prayer asking God's blessing on all Christians. Print the prayer on a large sheet of newsprint for the prayer area. Then gather the children in the prayer area and invite the class to pray their prayer.

185

DAY 3
DOCTRINE

Objective
This lesson helps the children understand the meaning of *church* as "the place where Christians come together to pray" and familiarizes the children with the objects in it.

Step 1/INTRODUCTION

Learning About Our Lives

Recalling the Learning of Days 1 and 2
Encourage volunteers to talk about how they know they belong to their families. Then ask the children what other special family they belong to. (The family of Jesus' friends and followers)

Learning Another Meaning of *Church*
Remind the children that on Day 1 and Day 2 they learned that the Church is the family of Jesus' friends and followers. Tell them that the word *church* also means "the place where Christians gather to pray."

Talking About a Catholic Church
Invite the children to recall the times they have been in their parish church. Ask them what special things people do in their church and what special things they have seen there. (Do not have them open their books.) Use this time to discover just what the children know about the roles various parishioners play in the liturgy and about the special objects that are used during Mass.

Step 2/DEVELOPMENT

Learning About Our Faith

Responding to the Text and Illustrations
Ask the children to open their books to pages 186–187. Then tell the children that these pages are about what Allie Johnson sees when she goes to church on Sunday. Read aloud "In Our Catholic Church," inviting volunteers to point to the pictures and explain the various special people and things they have seen at church.

Invite volunteers to use the illustrations to tell a story about Allie at church.

In Our Catholic Church

Here is another meaning of the word <u>church</u>.
A **church** is a special place where Christians come together to pray.

Allie and the her family go to Saint John Catholic Church. They see and hear many things.

Allie genuflects.

Soon a boy or a girl lights the candles.

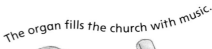
The organ fills the church with music.

Then the priest, the servers, and the reader walk down the aisle. All the people stand and sing.

CURRICULUM CONNECTION

Art Take the children to church and point out the stained-glass windows. Explain the meaning of the pictures and symbols on the windows. Invite the children to make stained-glass windows. Provide each child with a sheet of black construction paper, paste, and an envelope full of small pieces of colored construction paper. Encourage the children to paste their small pieces of paper to their black background to make stained-glass windows.

We begin our Mass with a song.

The reader puts the book with the Bible stories on the lectern.

The priest bows before the altar. He kisses it.

With the priest, the people make the Sign of the Cross.

Activity

Put an **X** by all the things you see in your church. Then talk about other things you see at church.

New Word

✦ **church** A church is a special place where Christians come together to pray.

Doctrine 187

CURRICULUM CONNECTION

Art If the children began work on church dioramas (art Curriculum Connection, Day 2), provide time for them to continue their work. Encourage the children to place inside their dioramas some of the objects they would see in church: a baptismal font, an altar, cross, candles, statues, and so on. They may make stand-up construction paper objects or draw flat one-dimensional ones to cut and paste on the "walls" of the inside of the shoe box.

Enriching the Lesson

Take the children on a tour of the parish church. Walk around the church and invite the children to comment on the objects they have studied in class. During the tour, allow the children to see these objects up close and to touch them. If a priest is available, he may show the children the liturgical vestments and the sacred vessels—the chalice and paten. While at church, invite the children to pray for all Catholic Christians.

---

or ...

Invite the group to engage in the movements illustrated on pages 186–187. Genuflect; pretend to play the organ; to light the candles; read the Bible; process to the altar (walk around the room); sing a song; and make the Sign of the Cross. Have the children stand by their seats to do these movements, but give them plenty of room.

Step 3/CONCLUSION

Learning How to Live Our Faith

Making Prayer Cards

Give each child a 2 1/2" × 7" piece of posterboard. Have the children work together to compose a short prayer thanking God for the people who make up the Church and for the place where Christians meet to worship God. As an example you might pray something like the following: *Thank you God for _____ Church and all the people who gather here.* Print the prayer on the chalkboard and invite the children to copy it onto their cards. Encourage the children to decorate their cards with a picture of something within their parish church, such as a cross, an altar, the Bible, a candle, an organ, and so forth.

Gathering for Prayer

Invite the children to bring their prayer cards to the prayer area or the parish church, if it is available. When they are quiet, ask the children to read their prayer from their prayer cards. End the session with a song.

DAY 4
MORALITY

Objective
This lesson helps the children deepen their understanding of how Catholic Christians act like Jesus.

Step 1/INTRODUCTION

Learning About Our Lives

Brainstorm Ways the Church Acts Like Jesus

Recall that the word *church* has two meanings: "place" and "people." Explain to the children that the family of Jesus does many things to act like Jesus. Brainstorm some of the things the children know that Jesus did. Write their responses on the chalkboard.

Work with the children until they have thought of each of the following categories.

- Jesus loves all people.
- He healed sick people.
- He taught people about God.
- He helped people who needed assistance.

Step 2/DEVELOPMENT

Learning About Our Faith

Completing an Activity

Read the top of pages 188–189 aloud to the children. Help them understand that the basic mission of the Christian people is to love Jesus and all people. Do each section of the activity with the children. Note that the numbers of each section are the same color and that they match the color surrounding the picture that goes with that particular section. Read the sentences in each set describing the three things that the Christian community does and then discuss these activities with the children. Then have the children circle the number of the sentence that matches the picture.

Studying Magazine Pictures

Show the children some magazine and newspaper pictures of people in need. Encourage volunteers to say how their Church could help each of the people in the photographs. Help the children see that the

Activity

Catholics, like other Christians, are called by God to love Jesus and all other people. Here are some things Catholics do.

Circle the number in each set of sentences that tells what is happening in the picture.

1. Followers of Jesus feed the hungry.
2. Followers of Jesus visit the sick.
3. Followers of Jesus study the Bible.

1. Catholics help to buy a van to pick up people who cannot drive anymore.
2. Catholics have a square dance to help everyone become better friends.
3. Some Catholics teach in the Catholic school.

188   Morality

CURRICULUM CONNECTION

Art   If the children began to work on their church dioramas on Day 2 (see the art Curriculum Connection, Day 2), provide time for them to continue their work today. Consider having them make dioramas of the parish hall showing what Christians do there: Conduct bake sales to raise money for those who need help, have soup kitchens for the hungry, provide places for the needy to sleep, run Bible classes, and so on.

Focus on

Diversity   According to the *Catechism of the Catholic Church* ". . . the rich variety of ecclesiastical disciplines, liturgical rites, and theological and spiritual heritages proper to local churches 'unified in a common effort, shows all the more resplendently the catholicity of the unidivided Church'" (#835).

1. Some Catholics take Holy Communion to people who cannot get to Mass.
2. Some of the family of Jesus sing in the choir.
3. Men and women read from the book of Bible stories at church.

Activity

We Belong to the Catholic Church

The name of our parish is

_____

- -

_____ .

Church is all of them acting together as friends and followers of Jesus. Stress that the children belong to the Church.

Step 3/CONCLUSION

Learning How to Live Our Faith

Completing a Church Activity

Direct the children's attention to the illustration on the bottom of page 189. Read the words of the illustration. Then read aloud the sentence below the illustration. Ask the children the name of their parish and print it on the chalkboard, being sure that if the children are from various parishes, you list each name. Invite the children to write it on the line provided.

Gathering for Prayer

Invite the children to gather in a semicircle in the prayer area. Place the holy water on the prayer table. Tell the children that today they will pray by blessing themselves with holy water and then pantomiming for God some ways that Christians can act like Jesus.

Invite volunteers, one by one, to take some holy water to bless themselves with the Sign of the Cross and pray by pantomiming a loving action for God.

Enriching the Lesson

Art Make banners with the words *We belong to the Catholic Church* on them. Use large pieces of newsprint and felt-tip markers. Or cut letters out of felt and glue them to felt or cloth backgrounds. Encourage the children to decorate their banners with Christian symbols (candles, the Bible, holy oil, water, the cross). When the children complete their work, hang the banners in a prominent place.

Objective

This lesson helps the children express their belief in the constant presence of Jesus with his Church.

Reading the Text

Direct the children to the text "Praying with Jesus" on page 190. Ask the children to read aloud what Jesus said in paragraph 1 and to underline these words. Next, talk about paragraph 2. Assure the children that whenever they pray, Jesus is always with them. Tell them that whenever the family of Jesus gathers together, Jesus is present, too.

Show the children a picture of Jesus and remind them that they belong to the family of Jesus' friends and followers. Then place this picture on the table in the prayer area.

Praying with Jesus

Process with the children into the prayer area. Invite the children to sing a song about the Church—praying. Then pick up the picture of Jesus from the prayer table and pray this litany.

Teacher: When we pray, Jesus is with us.

Children: We are the Church.

Teacher: When we do caring things for others, Jesus is with us.

Children: We are the Church.

Teacher: When we pray for others, Jesus is with us.

Children: We are the Church.

Teacher: When we help others, Jesus is with us.

Children: We are the Church.

Teacher: When we gather together to do good, Jesus is with us.

Children: We are the Church.

All: Amen.

190

Praying With Jesus

One day Jesus said something very important to his friends and followers. "Where people come together in my name, I am there with them," he told them.

Based on Matthew 18:20

What did Jesus mean?
When we gather with other Catholics, Jesus is with us.
We belong to the Church, the family of Jesus.
We pray with Jesus to God the Father.

190 Prayer

CURRICULUM CONNECTION

Music Use the following words to the melody "Looby Loo."

Here we all come to pray.
Here we all come to pray.
Here we all come to pray,
For all the people on earth.
We say our prayers each day.
We say our prayers each day.
We ask our God to bless us all
And help us follow Christ.

Teaching Tips

To help the children deepen their belief in God's love for them, play the song "God Is Our Father" from the album *Hi, God* by Rev. Carey Landry,(OCP).

Chapter Review

Activity

You belong to the Catholic Church.
Circle all the things you see in church.

1. To which Christian Church do we belong?

   the Catholic Church

2. What word means both a group of Christians and the place where they gather?

   church

3. Talk about what you like best about your church.

> Jesus says, "Where people come together in my name, I am there with them."
> **Based on**
> **Matthew 18:20**

CURRICULUM CONNECTION

Praying with Jesus The teaching introduced in today's session is an important one, for it helps the children understand that when Christians are gathered together, Jesus is with them. If they pray, Jesus prays with them. If they join together to help others, Jesus is there with them. If they join together to get to know one another better, Jesus is with his friends and followers. This is an important prayer skill.

Focus on

Art Continue working on the dioramas of the church (Curriculum Connection, Day 2). Provide either a long piece of paper or a cloth sheet to serve as a backdrop on which the children can draw clouds, trees, and birds. Supply paper on which to set the dioramas and have the children draw streets on the paper. The children can place trucks and cars brought from home on these roads. Display their work for the rest of the school to view.

Using the Bulletin Board from Day 1 to Review

Gather the children around the bulletin board they assembled on Day 1. Using their drawings, review the learning of the week. Invite the children to talk about their church. Recall that the word *church* has two meanings: "place" and "people." Ask the children which meaning of the word is illustrated by their drawings. (The answer could include both meanings if the children have shown both a building and people gathered in it.)

Completing an Activity

Use the activity on page 191 to review the learning of Chapter 15. Read the text at the top of the page. Then direct the children's attention to the illustrations. Invite the children to circle every picture that helps them know that they belong to the Catholic Church. Afterward, encourage them to talk about their selections. (Accept all the answers as correct.)

Answering the Questions

Read aloud the first two questions and ask volunteers to respond. Direct the children to print the answers in their texts. Encourage all the children to participate in the discussion of the third question. Be supportive of each child who responds.

Reading the Scripture Verse

Read the Scripture verse with the children. Ask the children to repeat it after you. If you wish the children may memorize this verse.

We Come Together for Mass

Objectives ~~~~~

To help the children
- Appreciate the Mass as the special meal they share with Jesus.
- Understand what Jesus did and said at the Last Supper.
- Understand that they hear God's word at Mass.
- Learn some of the special words associated with Mass.
- Pray with Jesus, say "Amen" to God's love, and review the chapter.

Chapter Outline ~~~~~~~

	Step 1 **Learning About Our Lives**	**Step 2** **Learning About Our Faith**	**Step 3** **Learning How to Live Our Faith**
Day 1	■ Introduce Chapter 16. ■ Examine various meals. *ABOUT 7 MINUTES*	■ Read the text. ■ Recall the Mass. ■ Review the new words. *ABOUT 10 MINUTES*	■ Draw a picture of Mass. ■ Create a bulletin board. ■ Use the bulletin board for prayer. *ABOUT 13 MINUTES*
Day 2	■ Look for pictures of a meal. *ABOUT 10 MINUTES*	■ Read and discuss a Bible story. ■ Eat bread and grapes. ■ Present the doctrine. *ABOUT 12 MINUTES*	■ Remember Jesus. ■ Complete an activity. ■ Pray with Jesus. *ABOUT 8 MINUTES*
Day 3	■ Read the text. ■ Do a choral reading. ■ Complete an activity. *ABOUT 10 MINUTES*	■ Read the text. ■ Think about the conversation at the Last Supper. *ABOUT 10 MINUTES*	■ Complete an activity. ■ Listen to a story about Jesus. *ABOUT 10 MINUTES*
Day 4	■ Review the story of Salvatore and Grandma. ■ Read the text. *ABOUT 10 MINUTES*	■ Respond to an illustration. ■ Read the text. *ABOUT 10 MINUTES*	■ Assemble at the altar. *ABOUT 10 MINUTES*

Day 5 **Prayer** Complete an activity; learn a song; prepare to pray; and pray with Jesus.
Review Think over the main ideas of the chapter by using the bulletin board from Day 1; complete an activity; answer the questions; and read the Scripture verse.

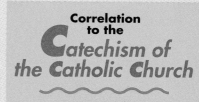

Plan Ahead ～～～～～～～

	Preparing Your Class	**Materials Needed**
Day 1	For Step 3, cut out the letters for *Catholics have a special meal called the Mass* and prepare a space for a bulletin board display.	■ drawing paper ■ empty bulletin board ■ cut-out letters for a sentence ■ thumbtacks/stapler
Day 2	For Step 2, have enough bread and grape juice for all the children.	■ newspapers and magazines ■ glue, construction paper ■ pita or pocket bread ■ bunch of red grapes ■ grape juice/cups
Day 3	For Step 3 plan a trip to the altar in your parish church or set up a make-believe altar in your room and put the appropriate objects on it for the Mass.	■ altar objects: cloth, crucifix, candles, a Bible (*the Lectionary*), hosts, a chalice (optional)
Day 4	Read the session in preparation for class. If you plan to use the Teaching Option, make preparations and collect materials.	■ large sheet of drawing paper
Day 5	Learn the melody for "Kum Ba Yah." If you plan to use the Teaching Option, make preparations and collect materials.	■ bulletin board from Day 1

Additional Resources

As you plan this chapter, consider using the following materials from The Resourceful Teacher Package.

■ *Classroom Activity Sheets 16* and *16a.*

■ *Family Activity Sheets 16* and *16a*

■ *Chapter 16 Test*

■ *Prayers for Every Day*

■ *Projects: Grade 1*

In preparing the students for the Sunday readings, you may wish to use Silver Burdett Ginn's *Getting Ready for Sunday* student and teacher material.

BOOKS FOR THE JOURNEY

Sunday's Children. "For Bread," p. 30; "Prayer for Sunday Morning," p. 52. James Bitney. Resources Publications, 1986. These prayer poems speak to what we do on Sunday at Mass.

The Golden Goose. The Brothers Grimm. Silver Burdett Ginn, 1985. Blessings come when food is shared.

MORE BOOKS FOR THE JOURNEY

Praise God. Gunvor Edwards and Joan Brown. The Liturgical Press, 1994. This Mass book is designed for children.

Sunday Morning. Gail Ramshaw. Liturgy Training Publications, 1993. This book helps children understand and appreciate all the actions of the liturgy, the things Christians do when they worship together on Sunday.

REDUCED CLASSROOM ACTIVITIES

Name

We Come Together for Mass

Our families share meals together.
At Mass, Jesus shares a special meal with us.

1. Color the pictures.
2. Cut along the heavy black lines.

To the Teacher: This two-page activity will help the children understand the importance of the Liturgy of the Word and the Liturgy of the Eucharist. This activity is continued on page 16a.

Name

The Mass Is a Special Meal

Glue the pictures you have cut onto the box where they belong.

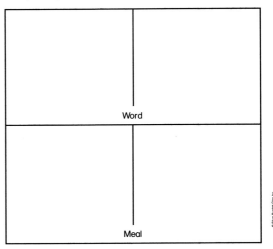

My Family Celebrates	The Church Celebrates
Word	
Meal	

Background for the Teacher

THE EUCHARIST

The Eucharist is the heart of Christian life. A view of the Mass as a community meal enhances our appreciation of the eucharistic liturgy.

In the time of Jesus the sharing of a meal signified peace, trust, and unity. At the Last Supper, Jesus chose the setting of a meal, with its literal and symbolic meanings, to give of himself most fully to his friends and followers.

THE LAST SUPPER

On the night before he died, Jesus ate the ritual seder with his apostles. At this symbolic meal, the Jewish people commemorate their deliverance from slavery in Egypt; they thank God for this great wonder. During a seder meal, Jesus shared bread and wine with his followers and instructed them, "Do this in memory of me" (Luke 22:19).

After God raised Jesus from death, his followers came to realize that each time they shared bread and wine as Jesus asked them, he was present with them. The sharing of this sacred meal they called the Eucharist.

THE PRESENCE OF JESUS CHRIST

In addition to the presence of Christ Jesus in the Eucharist, the Second Vatican Council speaks of the presence of Christ in the word of God spoken in the Scriptures. Christ is also present in the priest who presides at Mass and in the community who gather in his name.

THE CHILDREN AND THE MASS

Chapter 16 presents the Mass to the children in the context of a shared meal. Help everyone in your classroom recognize that when family and friends gather, they share love by talking together, laughing together, and sharing their stories.

Chapter 16 focuses on praying, eating, and talking together. Just as Jesus and his friends talked with one another at the Last Supper, so the children talk and listen to God during the Liturgy of the Word.

Just as Jesus gave himself as food to his friends, so he continues to give himself to his followers during the Liturgy of the Eucharist. This chapter will help make this experience more real to the children.

Explain simply that Jesus is present under the appearance of bread and the wine at Mass, and that through this food and drink, Catholic Christians remember Jesus as he asked them to do.

DAY 1
DOCTRINE

Objective

This lesson helps the children appreciate the Mass as the special meal they share with Jesus.

Step 1/INTRODUCTION

Learning About Our Lives

Introducing Chapter 16

Read aloud the question in the margin of page 192 and encourage the children's responses. Encourage volunteers to tell stories about their family meals. You might ask them what they like to eat with their families. Explain that at meals families often share stories about what they have been doing or tell each other things.

Examining Various Meals

Invite the children to look at the family photographs on pages 192–193. Then ask the following questions, all of which call for varied answers.

- What foods are the families in the pictures eating?
- What do you think they are talking about?
- What differences do you notice among these meals? What similarities?
- If you had your choice, which meal would you like to be a part of?

Step 2/DEVELOPMENT

Learning About Our Faith ✝

Reading the Text

Remind the children that their families are members of the family of Jesus. Tell them that the Catholic family has a special meal we all eat together. Then invite them to read page 193 to find out more about this meal. Invite the children to follow along silently as you read aloud "Catholics Celebrate the Mass." Emphasize that Jesus' family gathers in churches for this meal. Then reread the text, leaving out the words *Catholic Christian, meal, Mass,* and *Eucharist.* When you come to these words, ask the children to say aloud the missing words and to underline them.

16 We Come Together for Mass

What is the best thing that happens when your family gathers together to eat a meal?

192 Doctrine

Cultural Awareness

The photographs on pages 192–193 show a variety of very acceptable behaviors and customs associated with eating in different places throughout the world. Help the children observe that some people sit on mats instead of chairs. Other people sometimes eat from a common bowl. Some people eat with chopsticks, some with silverware, and some with their hands. All are correct ways of eating among these people.

CURRICULUM CONNECTION

Art Make napkin rings and place mats for the children's family to use at their meals. For the place mats, give each child enough sheets of colored construction paper for each family member. Have the children make colorful borders and print in the center of the mat, *Thank you, God, for* _____ (name of family member). For napkin rings, give the children strips of construction paper to decorate, one for each family member. Staple the ends together to form rings.

Catholics Celebrate the Mass

Families share meals together.

The Catholic family shares a meal, too.

We call this meal the **Mass** or the **Eucharist.**

Jesus shares this special meal with us.

New Words

Mass	The Mass is a special meal Jesus shares with us.
Eucharist	The Eucharist is another name for the Mass.

Doctrine 193

Recalling the Mass

Invite volunteers to talk about what Catholics do at their special meal in church. Encourage them to remember the singing, genuflecting, praying, receiving communion, giving the sign of peace, and so on. After the volunteers share their impressions, invite the other children to add to the discussion.

or...

Refer to Silver Burdett Ginn's Big Books: *We Celebrate the Mass* or *We Celebrate the Sacraments* to show the children pictures of the bread and wine, the altar which is our table, the sacred vessels, such as the chalice, the paten, and the ciborium. Point out the many members of the Catholic family gathered for this meal.

Reviewing the New Words

Point to the New Word box on page 193. Ask the children to repeat the words *Mass* and *Eucharist* and their definitions.

Step 3/CONCLUSION

Learning How to Live Our Faith

Drawing a Picture of Mass

Invite the children to draw pictures of the Mass, or the Eucharist, at their parish church. Encourage them to put as many details in their pictures as they can remember. As the children work, go around the room and talk about what happens at Mass: the readings, the communion, the singing, the kiss of peace, and so on.

Creating a Bulletin Board

Have the children bring their pictures and gather around an empty bulletin board. Pin the children's pictures on the board. Have letters cut out for: *Catholics have a special meal called the Mass.* Give each child a letter to hold as you tack up the sentence. Talk about how the sentence applies to their drawings.

Using the Bulletin Board for Prayer

As the children are gathered around the bulletin board, invite them to pray. Teach the following response: *Thank you, God, for the meal we share at Mass.* Invite volunteers to explain their drawings to the group and to God. After each volunteer shares, invite the children's response.

Focus on

Manners When discussing meals, talk about manners. Stress using silverware and a napkin and saying *please* and *thank you.* Explain that manners make a meal more pleasant for everyone. Then ask the children to give examples of the manners people use at church: sitting quietly, taking part in the prayers and the singing, and so on. Point out that manners make celebrating the Eucharist more pleasant and loving.

Enriching the Lesson

To help the children appreciate the fellowship of a meal, share a meal in the cafeteria or in your classroom. You might serve slices of bread and butter, milk (check the children's records for lactose intolerance), a bowl of some kind of pasta with red sauce, and gelatin or cookies for dessert. As the children eat, lead them in a conversation to show that during a meal the people share common interests.

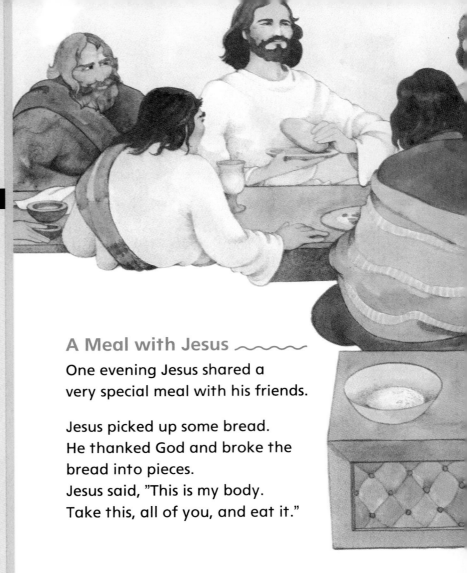

DAY 2

SCRIPTURE/DOCTRINE

Objective

This lesson helps the children understand what Jesus did and said at the Last Supper.

Step 1 /INTRODUCTION

Learning About Our Lives

Looking for Pictures of a Meal

Provide the children with magazines to find and to cut out pictures of people sharing meals. (Or put the children in groups with the assignment of finding one picture per group.)

Distribute glue and/or tape and construction paper and invite the children to mount one of their pictures on construction paper. Invite volunteers to create stories about their pictures. Post them in a prominent place in the classroom and ask the children to brainstorm a general title to put with the pictures. Help them make it up, cut and post the letters.

or...

Use family photos of meals the children brought to class and glued onto construction paper. These can be any meal-type picture, such as a gathering around the kitchen table, a Thanksgiving meal, a wedding banquet, a birthday party, or a picnic. Discuss the pictures and hang them up.

Step 2 /DEVELOPMENT

Learning About Our Faith

Reading and Discussing a Bible Story

Encourage the children to look at the illustration on pages 194-195 as you read "A Meal with Jesus." Pause at each paragraph and use the following suggestions.

■ Paragraph 1: Talk about the friendship Jesus shared with his disciples and what they might have talked about at their meal.

■ Paragraph 2: Emphasize Jesus' words when he broke bread with his disciples.

■ Paragraph 3: Emphasize Jesus' words when he gave the cup of wine to his disciples.

A Meal with Jesus

One evening Jesus shared a very special meal with his friends.

Jesus picked up some bread.
He thanked God and broke the bread into pieces.
Jesus said, "This is my body.
Take this, all of you, and eat it."

194   Scripture

 **CURRICULUM CONNECTION**

Music   If it is available, you might invite the children to listen to the song "Friends All Gather 'Round" by Carey Landry on the record *Bloom Where You're Planted* (OCP).

 *Focus on*

Eucharistic Sacrifice   The *Catechism of the Catholic Church* states, "At the Last Supper, on the night he was betrayed, our Savior instituted the Eucharistic sacrifice of his Body and Blood. This he did in order to perpetuate the sacrifice of the cross throughout the ages until he should come again, and so to entrust to his beloved Spouse, the Church, a memorial of his death and resurrection. . ." (#1323).

194

Next, Jesus picked up a cup of wine.
He thanked God for it and gave it to
his friends.
"Take this and drink from it.
This is my blood," Jesus said.
"Do this to remember me."

Based on 1 Corinthians 11: 23–25

Activity

What did Jesus tell his friends to do?
Trace Jesus' words.

Do this to
remember me.

We Believe

The Mass is a
special meal
with Jesus.
Jesus gives
himself to us
at Mass.

Doctrine   195

Enriching the Lesson

Act out the Last Supper. Place on the
table pita or pocket bread, a pitcher
of grape juice, and paper cups. Ask
the children to sit around the table.
Break up the play into two parts: (1)
The friends of Jesus gather around
the table and enjoy each other, the
meal, and the conversation. (2) Then
act out the breaking and giving of
bread and the sharing of the cup. As
part of the dramatization, give bread
to eat and grape juice to drink.

Eating Bread and Grapes

Give the children a piece of pita and some
purple grape juice. Show them a bunch of
grapes and explain that the juice came from
fruit like these. Help them understand that wine
does, too. Emphasize that this food is like the
bread and wine that Jesus and his friends had at
their special supper. Then invite the children to
enjoy the food.

Presenting the Doctrine

Read aloud the We Believe section on page
195, which summarizes the chapter's doctrine.
Ask the children to repeat the sentences after
you.

Step 3 /CONCLUSION

Learning How to Live Our Faith

Remembering Jesus

Reread the last two lines of Paragraph 3 of the
story "A Meal with Jesus" on pages 194–195.
Tell the children that Jesus wanted to be
remembered by the people he loved. Ask what
wonderful things they remember about Jesus.
Encourage them to tell the stories they
remember. Finally, point out that each time we
celebrate Mass we remember the great love
Jesus has for all people. Tell the children that
we especially remember what Jesus did and
said at the Last Supper.

Completing an Activity

Read the directions to the activity at the bottom
of page 195 and encourage the children to find
and circle in the biblical story what food and
drink Jesus shared with his friends and then to
write their answers on the lines provided.

Praying with Jesus

Gather the children in the prayer area. When
they are quiet, teach them the following
response: *We remember you, Jesus.* Invite
volunteers to tell short stories about Jesus.
Encourage the other children to pray their
response.

Objective

This lesson helps the children understand that they hear God's word at Mass.

Step 1/INTRODUCTION

Learning About Our Lives

Reading the Text

Direct the children's attention to "Remembering Special Words" on page 196. Before reading the text, invite the children to look at the picture as you set the scene of the story. To do this, tell the children that Salvatore had a special friendship with his grandmother.

■ Salvatore sometimes stayed overnight with Grandma.

■ She cooked him a special meal and they sat talking at the table for a long time while she told him how she felt about him.

■ Salvatore remembered the wonderful things that Grandma said.

Afterward, read aloud the story.

Doing a Choral Reading

Have four volunteers each read one special thing that Grandma said about Salvatore. Then divide the class into four groups, assigning one of Grandma's lines to each group. Work with each group so that the children read their line with the same emotion as Grandma probably said it to Salvatore. Then have a choral reading of "Remembering Special Words." Choose a good reader to read the first four lines and have each group speak its assigned line with expression.

Completing an Activity

Read aloud the directions to the activity on page 196. Encourage the children to think of some special words that someone said to them and print them on the line .

Step 2/DEVELOPMENT

Learning About Our Faith +

Reading the Text

Read aloud the story "Remembering Jesus' Words" on page 197. Discuss with the children

Remembering Special Words

When Salvatore thinks of Grandma, he remembers her stories and hugs.
He also remembers the special words she said to him when she was cooking.
    "What a big boy you are!"
    "What a good reader you are!"
    "What a fast ball player you are!"
    "I love you!"

ctivity

Write some wonderful words you remember special people saying to you.

_____

- -

_____

 ***Cultural Awareness***

Since the Catholic Christian family is made up of people from all over the world, provide, from time to time, a snack of traditional ethnic foods. You might include Irish soda bread; Italian pasta; Polish sausage and cabbage soup; Mexican foods, such as tacos and tamales; and African-American foods, such as hopping John (black-eyed peas and rice cooked with sausage), sweet-potato pie, and corn bread. Offer a prayer of thanks for the wonderful people and foods.

 **CURRICULUM CONNECTION**

Art Distribute drawing paper and invite the children to draw a special meal they have had with their family. You might suggest a meal to celebrate a birthday or a holiday, such as Easter, Thanksgiving, or Christmas. Encourage the children to draw special family foods and the decorated table. After the children have completed their work, invite them to share their drawings with the group and to tell the story of the meal.

Remembering Jesus' Words

At Mass, God speaks to us through
the words of the Bible.
We listen to the reader read
God's word of love.

The priest says, "The Lord be with you."
We answer, "And also with you."

Then the priest reads a story of Jesus.
The story tells us about how much
Jesus loves and cares for us.
We can love him back in our daily life.

Activity

Trace the words that tell you
Jesus is always with us.

The Lord be

And also

Doctrine 197

Teaching Tips

When discussing the possible conversation at the Last Supper, use page 16 of the Big Book *We Celebrate God's Word* to show a picture of the Last Supper or turn to pages 194–195 of the children's book.

CURRICULUM CONNECTION

Art Tape a large sheet of newsprint to the wall. Draw a line down the middle and sketch a Bible on one side and bread and a chalice on the other. Explain that the Mass has two important parts: one part centers around the Bible, God's word; the other centers around the Body and Blood that Jesus gives us in the Eucharist.

---

that Jesus speaks to us at our special meal, the Mass, through the words of the Bible. Ask the following questions.

- How does God speak to us at Mass? (*Through Bible stories found in The Lectionary*)
- What is the woman in the picture doing? (*Reading Bible stories* in The Lectionary *at Mass*)
- Who reads the story of Jesus? (*The priest or deacon*)
- What does the story of Jesus tell us? (*How much Jesus loves us; how Jesus helps people; how to be good*)
- What does the priest say to remind us that Jesus is with us as we listen to God's word of love?(*The Lord be with you.*)

Thinking About the Conversation at the Last Supper

Talk with the children about Jesus and his friends gathering for a special meal together. Ask the children to think of some of the things they might have talked about. The friends of Jesus knew the stories of Jesus because they heard him tell them. They knew what Jesus did because many times they were there with him. They may have talked about some of these things at Jesus' special meal.

Tell the children that we can listen to these important stories, too, at our special meal with Jesus, the Mass or Eucharist.

Step 3/CONCLUSION

Learning How to Live Our Faith

Completing an Activity

Read the directions to the activity on page 197. After the children have completed the activity, practice the response several times to use in this session's prayer.

Listening to a Story About Jesus

Take the children to church, if possible, to listen to a story about Jesus. Process to the church singing a song. From the lectern, read the story of the Last Supper. Ask the children to tell any of their favorite stories about Jesus. Remind the children that we hear all of these stories at the Mass, or Eucharist, throughout the year.

DAY 4
DOCTRINE

Objective

This lesson helps the children learn some of the special words associated with Mass.

Step 1/INTRODUCTION

Learning About Our Lives

Reviewing the Story of Salvatore and Grandma

To recall the learning of Day 3, ask the following questions.

- How do you know that Salvatore and his grandmother are happy? (*Answers will vary.*)

- How do you know that they love one another? (*Answers will vary.*)

- What special things do you think Salvatore might be saying to Grandma? (*Answers will vary.*)

Reading the Text

Before having the children open their books, ask them if they think the story of Salvatore and Grandma has a happy ending. Then read the first sentence. Discuss how Salvatore might have felt when Grandma moved away. Then continue reading the story. To discuss the story, ask the following questions.

- What did Salvatore remember about Grandma? (*Her hugs, her stories, and her cooking*)

- What wonderful thing happened? (*Grandma got on a plane and came to visit Salvatore.*)

- What did Grandma do for Salvatore and his family? (*Cooked them a delicious spaghetti meal*)

- What did Salvatore say was the best part of the meal with Grandma? (*Grandma was with them.*)

- Did the story of Salvatore and Grandma have a happy ending? Why? (*Answers will vary.*)

Remembering Grandma

Salvatore misses Grandma who moved away last year. But he remembers her hugs, her stories, and her cooking.

Then something happened. Grandma got on a plane. She came to visit Salvatore.

Salvatore's father took him to the airport to pick up Grandma. As she hugged Salvatore, she said, "I will cook all your favorite foods."

That night Grandma cooked spaghetti for supper. "This is better than any spaghetti I remember," he said. "But Grandma, do you know what the best part of this meal is? You are with us!"

198   Doctrine

CURRICULUM CONNECTION

Language Arts Give each child three sheets of 8 1/2" × 11" paper folded in half to make a storybook about the special food, special people, and special words in their lives. Invite the children to think of stories about these special people, foods, and words. Encourage the children to print and illustrate their story in their booklets. Have them print on the front page of their book the title *My Special Memories*. Afterward, provide time for the children to share their work. Then encourage the children to take their booklets home.

198

Remembering Jesus

The Mass is our special meal with Jesus.
We remember what he said and did at
the special meal he ate with his friends.
The priest does what Jesus did.
The priest says what Jesus said.
"This is my body.
This is my blood,"
says Father Williams.

At Mass, Jesus gives us the Bread of Life.
With this bread we remember Jesus.
When we eat this bread, Jesus is with us.
As friends of Jesus, we share in Jesus' life.

Doctrine 199

Learning About Our Faith

Responding to an Illustration

Direct the children's attention to the illustrations
on page 199. Encourage the children to tell
what they see in the pictures and help them
recognize these pictures as our special Catholic
meal, the Mass, or Eucharist. Comment on the
altar (our special table), the chalice and paten
(special vessels for the meal), and people
receiving Holy Communion (Jesus present
under the appearance of bread and wine).

Reading the Text

Read aloud "Remembering Jesus" on page
199. Have the children find the words that
Father Williams said. ("This is my body. This is
my blood.") Tell the children they are the same
words that Jesus said when he ate the special
meal we call the Last Supper. Help the children
to underline these special words.

Step 3/CONCLUSION

Learning How to Live Our Faith

Assembling at the Altar

Invite the children to assemble around the altar
in church, if possible. Once there, allow time for
the children to settle in. Then remind them that
this is where the priest says, "This is my body.
This is my blood." Then ask the children to hold
hands and pray together The Lord's Prayer.

Objective

This lesson helps the children pray with Jesus and say "Amen" to God's love.

Completing an Activity

Direct the children to the text "Praying Amen" on page 200. Read the text and invite the children's comments. Then read the directions at the bottom of the page. Invite the children to decorate the "Amen" on page 200 with colors that show how they feel when they pray "Amen" at Mass. Go around the room as the children work and praise their efforts.

Learning a Song About the Mass

Teach the children a song to sing about the Mass as they process to the prayer corner. Use the following words to the melody "Kum Ba Yah."

We remember, Lord.

Yes we do!

We remember, Lord.

Yes we do!

We remember, Lord.

Yes we do!

O Lord, you are love.

Preparing to Pray

Tell the children that today they are going to the prayer area to pray with Jesus. Tell them that their response will be a great *Amen!* Check to be sure that the children understand that the word *Amen* means "Yes." Encourage the children to sing the song as they process.

Praying with Jesus

Process with the children. After they are quiet, recall that Jesus is with them when they pray.

Pray, one at a time, the four sentences on page 200 that begin with the words *Yes, God.* Invite the children to respond with a great Amen after you pray each sentence. Conclude the prayer by having the children sing the song again.

200

Praying Amen

At Mass we pray with Jesus. With him, we say "Amen."

Amen means "Yes!"
"Yes, God, I love you."
"Yes, God, I trust you."
"Yes, God, I want to help you care for the world."
"Yes, God, I thank you for your love."

Activity

Color the letters to show how you feel when you pray "Amen" at Mass.

200 Prayer

Amen To know the meaning of the word *Amen* is part of the skill of praying it. It is a simple but repeated response at the Mass, or Eucharist, and it is common practice to end Christian prayers with an Amen. Teach the children a simple Amen so they can sing it at Mass. Help them understand it says "Yes" to Jesus' love for us.

Chapter Review

Activity

Circle the words that are about the Mass.

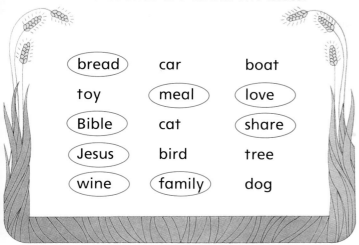

(bread)   car   boat

toy   (meal)   (love)

(Bible)   cat   (share)

(Jesus)   bird   tree

(wine)   (family)   dog

1. What do we call the special meal Jesus shares with us?

the Mass

Jesus says,
"I am the
Bread of
Life."
Based on John
6:35

2. Who gives himself to us at Mass?

Jesus

3. Talk about what you hear, see, and do at Mass.

Enriching the Lesson

Plan a class Mass. If possible, have the priest work with you. Choose from among the following liturgical skills the children may have acquired over the year: singing hymns, processing to the altar and gathering around it, responding to the prayers, reading some simple passages from a children's Bible, bringing up the offertory gifts, and exchanging a sign of peace.

Reviewing with a Bulletin Board

Gather the children around the bulletin board they assembled on Day 1. Using their drawings, review the learning of the week. Invite the children to talk about the special meals in their life and the special meal that Catholic Christians call the Mass. Review the Last Supper story from Day 2 and the words Jesus used when he asked his friends and followers to remember him in the breaking of the bread and the sharing of the cup.

After concluding the discussion, give the children their drawings to take home. Encourage the children to post their drawings in a special place where they can see them and remember Jesus' love for them.

Completing an Activity

Use the activity on page 201 to review the learning of Chapter 16. Read the text at the top of the page. Then direct the children's attention to the words in the frame of wheat. Read all the words aloud. Then invite the children to circle all the words that are about the Mass. Afterward, the children can talk about their selections.

Answering the Questions

Read aloud the first two questions and ask volunteers to respond. Direct the children to print the answers in their texts. Encourage all the children to participate in the discussion of the third question. Be supportive of each child who responds.

Reading the Scripture Verse

Read the Scripture verse aloud to the children. If you wish you may have the children memorize this verse.

End-of-unit pages include a Unit Organizer; Unit Review; Day to Day: Skills for Christian Living; and Opening Doors: A Take-Home Magazine.

Using the Unit Organizer

Completing a graphic organizer such as a chart or table can help students to organize the information that has been presented in the unit. Organizers can enable students to visualize their thinking and recognize relationships among ideas. This skill gives students the opportunity to understand more completely the material they have been studying.

To help the children think about this unit, ask them to read the unit theme: To identify themselves as Catholics, whose central celebration is the Mass. Invite the children to focus on the church and name their parish church. Then help them to remember that the word *Church* also means the friends of Jesus. Have them find and circle the name of the sacrament when we became friends of Jesus. Have them find and circle the name of the special meal Catholics celebrate together with one another and most importantly with Jesus.

Looking Back: Self-Assessment

To help the children assess what they have learned ask these or similar questions.

1. Which picture in this unit did you like best? What did you like about it?

2. What did you learn in this unit that you will remember when you go to church?

3. Which activity in this unit did you most enjoy? Why?

UNIT **4** ORGANIZER

Fill in the blanks.

WE BELONG TO THE CHURCH

WE WELCOME NEW CHRISTIANS AT _____

WE COME TOGETHER FOR _____

202 **Unit Organizer**

202

Review

Circle the correct answer.

1. We are Catholic Christians. (Yes) No

2. The word <u>church</u> has one meaning. Yes (No)

3. Our church has an altar. (Yes) No

4. Jesus is with us as the Bread of Life. (Yes) No

Circle the word that best completes the sentence.

1. At _____ we become part of Jesus' family.

   Mass   (Baptism)

2. The word <u>Church</u> means a group of _____.

   (Christians)   homes

3. The word <u>church</u> also means a special _____.

   person   (place)

4. Jesus shares a special meal with us at _____.

   (Mass)   Baptism

Reviewing the Unit

The purpose of the Unit Review is to reinforce concepts presented in the preceding four chapters and to check how well the children understand these concepts. After explaining the directions, give the children sufficient time to complete the review. Answer any questions the children might have.

Optional Testing

After the children have completed the Unit Review, you may wish to distribute copies of the Unit 4 Test from the Test booklet in the Resourceful Teacher Package.

Optional Unit Project

1. Give the children two sheets of art paper and crayons or felt-tip markers. Help the children recall some of the things commonly seen in a Catholic church. Then tell them to draw a picture of the outside of their parish church on the other sheet. After the children have completed both drawings, encourage them to share their pictures with others. Remind them that the word *church* also refers to the people who are members of God's family.

2. Invite each child to make a banner to be hung in his or her parish church, classroom, or home. Explain that the banner will remind everyone that the word *church* makes us think of God's people and of the home of God's people. The banner can be made of material such as felt or burlap, or of construction paper. Before class, cut out a set of letters for each child. The letters should spell out: *Church is people, church is home.* Give each child a piece of background material, a set of letters, and paste. Help the children spell out the message. Encourage them to decorate their banners, using other bits of material or colored paper you may have available to them.

UNIT 4 REVIEW

Fill in the first letter of each picture.

1. __c__ ar   2. __a__ pple   3. __t__ ent

4. __h__ at   5. __o__ wl   6. __l__ ine

7. __i__ ce   8. __c__ ar

The first letters form a new word.

Write the new word to finish the message.

Our Church home is the _____ Church.

Catholic

TELLING OTHERS HOW I FEEL

I FEEL HAPPY WHEN YOU SHARE WITH ME!

Boots and Zip
share toys.
They share
fun times playing.
Boots and Zip
share feelings.

Activity

Pretend you are Boots and use "I-feel talk."
Tell how you feel about sharing with Zip.

I feel _____ when _____

Day to Day 205

Teaching Tips

Prepare a few role-plays about situations based on feelings, when the role-play actors are finished performing, ask the following questions.

■ What is happening in the situation?

■ Is there a problem?

■ Who needs to tell about feelings?

Select volunteers for the role-playing. Consider writing the "I Feel Talk" formula on the board as a help for the role-play actors. (I feel _____, when _____.)

Day to Day

Objective

To help increase the children's ability to express feelings verbally.

Sharing Feelings

Read aloud the story on page 205. Then ask the children to name some feelings they think Boots and Zip might share with each other. Accept a variety of responses. Tell the children that today's lesson is about sharing feelings.

Introducing I Feel Talk

Ask the children to pretend that they are Boots. Have them write in the spaces provided how Boots feels when he shares with Zip. Emphasize that when we tell someone how we feel we need to include both the feeling and the reason why we feel that way. Write on the board, *I feel _____, when _____.*

Lesson continues on page 206.

205

Choosing Feelings We Like

Read aloud the feeling words on page 206. Ask for volunteers to share times when they have experienced these emotions. Next, have the children circle the feelings they would most like to have.

Role-Plays Telling About Feelings

Ask for volunteers to enact the following situations, using "I Feel Talk." The audience should look and listen for feeling clues.

- A line forms and one person cuts in front of another.
- A little boy keeps messing up his sister's room. She yells at him to get out, and the little boy runs to tell his mother that his sister is being mean.
- A classmate keeps talking to you while you are trying to do your work.
- You are invited to a friend's birthday party. Your father asks you why you have that big smile on your face.

Discussing the Role-Plays

Use the following questions to guide discussion after each role-play.

- How did the character feel during this situation? How could you tell?
- Did (name of actor) use "I Feel Talk?"
- Who can remember what he or she said?
- What happened after he or she told about what was being felt?

Concluding the Lesson

Discuss with the children why it is a good idea to tell others how we feel.

- Sharing positive feelings spreads happiness.
- Sharing sad or upset feelings tells others that we may need help.
- Sometimes others may not be able to tell how we are feeling.

Using the Following Jesus Section

Read aloud the statements in the Following Jesus section. Invite the children to repeat the prayer after you.

Follow-Up Activitiy

Create a display with the "I Feel Talk" sentences that the children have written to a remind them to use the "I Feel" technique.

206

 Activity

Circle the feeling that you would most like to have!

Happy　　**Sad**　　Mad　　Proud　　Surprised

FOLLOWING JESUS

I can share my feelings with Jesus when I pray.

 A Prayer

Jesus, I feel happy when my mom gives me a hug.
I feel sad when others won't let me play.
I feel joy when I help a friend.
I feel peaceful when you are near.

🍎 **Teaching Tips**

The children may or may not be able to demonstrate "I Feel Talk" during their role-plays. Use the discussion time after the role-play to explore why using "I Feel Talk" might be difficult. After discussing the role-plays, have the same or different actors perform the role-plays again.

OPENING DOORS
A Take-Home Magazine™

Growing Closer

THINK ABOUT MASS in your parish. As a family, consider the questions below.

Which of the Masses in your parish is your favorite?

What is your favorite gospel story?

What is your favorite song or hymn?

What is your favorite part of the Mass?

If you could change one thing about the Mass, what would it be?

TO FEEL WELCOME is a need we all understand. With your family, discuss how you as a Catholic family welcome friends, family members, and strangers to your home. Talk about ways your family may consider improving the hospitality already present in your home.

Looking Ahead

In Unit 5 your child will learn that Jesus promised to send his followers the Holy Spirit as a helper and guide. The Spirit would be with them, helping them to be united as brothers and sisters. The Spirit would strengthen them, helping them live caring, just, peaceful, and happy lives. Jesus fulfilled his promise of sending his Spirit after his death and resurrection. That same Spirit is still at work in our hearts and in our communities.

8

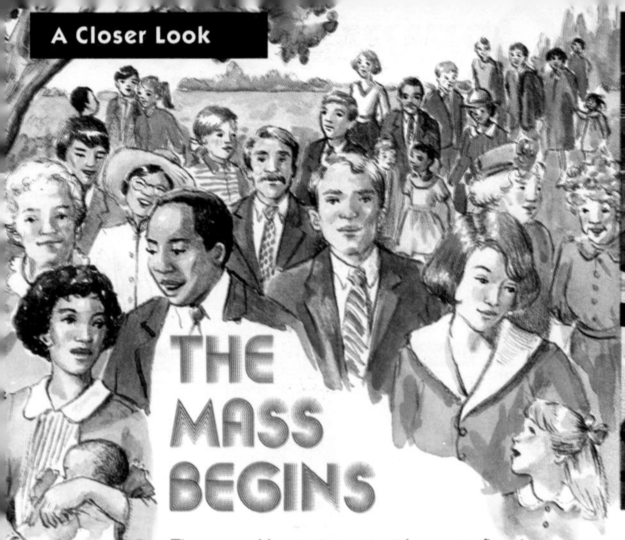

2

THE MASS BEGINS

They assemble: young men and women, first time parents sharing the care of the baby; the nuns who serve the parish; the elderly who walk perkily up to the front pews, obviously comfortable in their environs; and the young who cluster in bunches with their friends. This is the Christian community gathering for Sunday Mass.

The importance of this assembled group cannot be overestimated. They are the community of Jesus' followers and he is present with them. "For where two or three are gathered together in my name, there am I in the midst of them," Jesus said (Matthew 18:20).

Dutch and Belgian families gather around bonfires on Holy Saturday night, set off firecrackers, and ring bells. Children believe the joyful sound of the bells brings their colorful Easter eggs.

Hungarians paint their Easter eggs red to commemorate Christ's blood shed on Good Friday. Throughout Hungary, ruby-colored shells hanging from the branches of Easter trees can be seen.

Austrians bake special yeast breads for Easter. *Osterstollen*, a raisin, braided bread and *Butterküchen*, dotted with butter, sugar, and cinnamon, are favorites.

What foods and customs do you enjoy at Easter? Perhaps, you would like to revive some of your family's ethnic traditions.

7

208

The presence of Jesus in the eucharistic celebration is discussed by the bishops in the documents of the Second Vatican Council. There they reiterate the reality of Jesus' presence under the appearance of the bread and wine and emphasize his presence when the Scripture readings are proclaimed. Furthermore, the bishops clearly state that Jesus is present with his gathered community at Mass.

As the Mass begins, the community of Jesus stands and sings the gathering song. Giving us a common focus, this song merges our individual thoughts and feelings as we prepare to celebrate our common faith. The song also sets the theme for the Mass. If the tone of the Mass is one of jubilation, the gathering hymn is jubilant, too; if the character of the celebration is more reflective, the song expresses this mood.

Then the priest greets us with these words:

"The grace of our Lord Jesus Christ and the love of God and the fellowship of the Holy Spirit be with you all."

These words remind us that we begin the Mass with the Holy Trinity active within the community of Jesus.

Aware that we are in God's presence, we become more and more conscious of our faults. Thus we pause to admit our sinfulness and rely on God's mercy.

Confident of God's forgiveness, our hearts are ready to praise God in the beautiful hymn of the *Gloria.*

> Lord God, heavenly King,
> almighty God and Father,
>   we worship you, we give you thanks,
>   we praise you for your glory.

With these sentiments of praise and thanksgiving in our hearts, the community joins with the priest as he prays the Opening Prayer, and the Mass begins. We are open to hear the word of the "Holy One, the Most High Jesus Christ," in the Scriptures, and we are ready to celebrate the Eucharist.

3

Each Easter season, magazines beguile us with glossy pages of artistically decorated eggs, ethnic recipes, and native folk costumes. These are the traditions and customs of our immigrant ancestors that continue to intrigue so many of us. A few such customs are listed below.

EASTER TRADITIONS

Swedish children write Easter letters to say *Glad Pask,* which means "Happy Easter." Of course, their delightful childish drawings add to the charm of the cards. On the night before Easter, they drop these greeting cards off at the homes of their friends and relatives. This night routinely ends with fireworks to light the night, reminiscent of the bright light of the resurrection.

Polish families make table centerpieces consisting of a sugared lamb resting on green leaves. Around the lamb are dishes of cold roast pork, sausage, salads, sweetmeats, and brightly colored hard-boiled eggs, called *pisanki.* According to legend, when Mary Magdalene went to the tomb of Jesus, she took some hard-boiled eggs to eat. When she saw the risen Christ, the eggs were miraculously painted in rainbow colors.

Irish families enjoy sunrise services on Easter morning. For breakfast, they feast on eggs and "golden bread," which is similar to French toast. Many communities hold dance competitions on Easter Sunday as an occasion for the townsfolk to spend the day together, certainly appropriate for the community of Jesus.

6

Catholics Gather

Your child has probably experienced Sunday Mass. Now discover together the significance of the Gathering Rite that brings us together as members of one family and prepares us to celebrate the Liturgy of the Word and the Liturgy of the Eucharist. Then help your child complete the activity that follows.

Read Along

I go to Mass on Sunday. At Mass I celebrate belonging to the family of Jesus.

Sometimes people at the church door welcome my family. They welcome other families, too.

When the Mass begins, the song leader helps me to sing a happy song. I remember that Jesus is with us. I remember that we belong to him and to each other.

Now I am ready to listen to stories from the Bible. Now I am ready to celebrate Jesus in the Eucharist.

4

Unscramble the letters. You will discover something important about going to Mass!

suseJ   si   ihwt   su   ta   sasM

_____

_____

_____

The next time you go to Mass remember to thank Jesus for making you a member of his special family.

5

The Holy Spirit Helps Us

Whom do you ask for help?

Unit Aim

To help the children learn that Jesus gives us the Holy Spirit to be with us and to help us.

Doctrinal Summaries

CHAPTER 17

The Holy Spirit is the Spirit of God whom Jesus gives us to be with us and to help us.

CHAPTER 18

Jesus helps us when we are afraid. He gives us the Holy Spirit to help us be brave.

CHAPTER 19

God is always ready to forgive us. Jesus brings us God's forgiveness and peace. Jesus gives us the Holy Spirit to help us live peacefully together.

CHAPTER 20

God wants us to be happy. Jesus gives us the Holy Spirit who gives us joy.

Note:

As you prepare to teach this unit, you might wish to refer to the We Believe reference section beginning on page 327. Additional resources for Unit 5 include a Unit Test and a Family Letter as well as a video and selections from the THIS IS OUR FAITH Music Program. You might also find it helpful to preview *Saints and Other Holy People* and *Prayer Celebrations* for possibilities to enhance the unit.

Introducing the UNIT

Direct the children's attention to the photograph on page 211. Ask the children to tell what is happening in the picture. Ask, "What is the child learning to do?" Then read aloud the unit-focus question. Give each child an opportunity to respond. When the children have finished, read with them the Unit 5 title. Help them understand that in this unit they will learn that Jesus gives us the Holy Spirit to help us.

New Words

Holy Spirit
gospel
forgiveness
Galilee

Jesus Gives Us the Holy Spirit

Objectives

To help the children

- Appreciate the Holy Spirit as a gift from Jesus.
- Learn the story of Jesus giving the gift of the Holy Spirit to his followers.
- Appreciate the help we receive from the Holy Spirit.
- Understand that the Holy Spirit helps them act like Jesus.
- Pray with the aid of a banner and review the chapter.

Chapter Outline

	Step 1 **Learning About Our Lives**	Step 2 **Learning About Our Faith**	Step 3 **Learning How to Live Our Faith**
Day 1	■ Talk about loneliness. ■ Use pictures to tell stories. *ABOUT 6 MINUTES*	■ Read page 212. ■ Create a bulletin board. ■ Read page 213. ■ Present new words/doctrine. *ABOUT 14 MINUTES*	■ Draw Jesus. ■ Use the bulletin board for prayer. *ABOUT 10 MINUTES*
Day 2	■ Play a game. *ABOUT 10 MINUTES*	■ Listen to a Bible story. ■ Talk about gifts. ■ Complete an activity. *ABOUT 10 MINUTES*	■ Use colors that remind us of the happiness the Holy Spirit brings. ■ Gather for prayer. *ABOUT 10 MINUTES*
Day 3	■ Recall the learning of Day 2. ■ Respond to paper-plate faces. *ABOUT 10 MINUTES*	■ Read the text. *ABOUT 10 MINUTES*	■ Read a poem. ■ Use the poem for prayer. *ABOUT 10 MINUTES*
Day 4	■ Remember Jesus. ■ Act out Bible stories. *ABOUT 10 MINUTES*	■ Read the text. *ABOUT 10 MINUTES*	■ Write a prayer. ■ Complete an activity. ■ Gather to pray. *ABOUT 10 MINUTES*
Day 5	**Prayer** Read the text; make a banner; prepare to pray; and pray to the Holy Spirit. **Review** Use the bulletin board to review; complete an activity; answer the questions; and read a Scripture verse.		

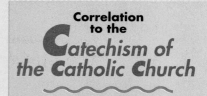
Plan Ahead

	Preparing Your Class	**Materials Needed**
Day 1	For Step 2, cut out the letters for *Jesus gives us the Holy Spirit* and prepare a space for a bulletin board display.	■ drawing paper ■ an empty bulletin board ■ cut-out letters for a sentence ■ thumbtacks/staples
Day 2	For Step 3, prepare various places in the room to post the children's art work. If you plan to use any Teaching Option, make preparations and collect materials.	■ a ball ■ drawing paper ■ a place to post the children's drawings
Day 3	For Step 1, make four paper-plate faces to represent happiness, sadness, anger, and fear. If you plan to use a Teaching Option, collect the materials you will need.	■ bulletin board from Day 1 ■ four paper-plate faces
Day 4	Read over the lesson prior to class. If you plan to use a Teaching Option, collect the materials you will need.	
Day 5	Read over the lesson prior to class. If you plan to use a Teaching Option, collect the materials you will need.	■ bulletin board from Day 1 ■ musical instruments (optional)

Additional Resources

As you plan this chapter, consider using the following materials from The Resourceful Teacher Package.

■ *Classroom Activity Sheets 17* and *17a*

■ *Family Activity Sheets 17* and *17a*

■ *Chapter 17 Test*

■ *Prayers for Every Day*

■ *Projects: Grade 1*

In preparing the students for the Sunday readings, you may wish to use Silver Burdett Ginn's *Getting Ready For Sunday* student and teacher materials.

BOOKS FOR THE JOURNEY

Apt. 3. Ezra Jack Keats. Macmillan, 1986. This is a story of how music fulfills a need in two boys and friendship fulfills a need in a blind man.

Everett Anderson's Goodbye. Lucille Clifton. Holt, Rinehart & Winston, 1988. This is a story about a child who gradually accepts the death of his father.

MORE BOOKS FOR THE JOURNEY

The Good Stepmother. Marquerita Rudolph. Simon & Schuster, 1992. This is a once-upon-a-time story that shows how a little princess finds the one person to meet her needs.

When Stars Come Out. L. J. Sattgast. Questar Publishers, 1994. These bedtime psalms speak of God's loving presence.

REDUCED CLASSROOM ACTIVITIES

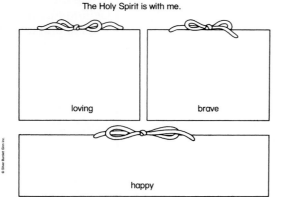

Name _____

Jesus Gives Us the Holy Spirit

1. Read the poem.
2. In the boxes draw yourself being loving, brave, and happy with the help of the Holy Spirit.

> The Holy Spirit helps me be
> A loving, brave, and happy me.
> The Holy Spirit is the key,
> The Holy Spirit is with me.

loving

brave

happy

To the Teacher: This activity follows the Scripture story "The Gift of the Holy Spirit."

Chapter 17   Jesus Gives Us the Holy Spirit   This Is Our Faith 1   **17**

Name _____

We Can Help Each Other

Because the Holy Spirit is with us, we help each other. Make a thank-you neck chain for someone who helps you.

1. Cut out the strips.
2. Glue them together to form links in a chain.
3. Use the pattern to make more links for your neck chain.

| THANK |
| YOU |
| FOR |
| HELPING |
| ME |
| |
| |

To the Teacher: This activity will help the children realize that it is the Holy Spirit who enables us to help others.

17a   This Is Our Faith 1   Chapter 17   Jesus Gives Us the Holy Spirit

THE TRINITY

The mystery of the Blessed Trinity is central to our faith. Jesus revealed God as Father, himself as Son, and the Holy Spirit as God's dynamic presence with us. At the Last Supper, Jesus promised to send the Holy Spirit to be with his followers. After Jesus' death, the disciples hid in the upper room from the same authorities that crucified Jesus. There Jesus appeared to them after God the Father raised him from the dead. He greeted his disciples with the words, "Peace be with you." Jesus breathed on them and said, "Receive the Holy Spirit" (John 20:19, 22).

RELEASING THE SPIRIT

The resurrection of Jesus released the power of the Holy Spirit. Before Jesus ascended to his Father, he told his disciples that they would be baptized with the Holy Spirit in fulfillment of God's promise. Jesus said, "You will receive power when the holy Spirit comes upon you; and you will be my witnesses…to the ends of the earth" (Acts 1:8). The second chapter of Acts describes the coming of the Holy Spirit. Filled with the Spirit of God, the apostles emerged from that room in Jerusalem as inspired and empowered evangelizers.

GIFTS OF THE SPIRIT

In his letter to the Galatians, Saint Paul urged the early Christians to live by the Spirit, who gives love, joy, peace, patience, kindness, goodness, gentleness, and self-control. These gifts of the Spirit are the hallmarks of a Christian life. The Holy Spirit helps us act like Jesus, with strength of character, compassion, empathy, and love for others. The Holy Spirit also helps us pray as Jesus prayed. Thus, we come to know God more intimately and discover the mysteries at the heart of God's deep love for us.

THE HOLY SPIRIT AND THE CHILDREN

In Chapter 17 you introduce the Holy Spirit. This chapter lays a foundation for the children to begin to understand the mystery of the Blessed Trinity. The children can become more aware of the constant presence of God in themselves and in the world.

Chapter 17 is the introductory lesson to this unit. Its message is simple: Jesus shows us the way to live. He also gives us the gift of the Spirit to help us live our Christian vocations. The chapter identifies those actions of the Holy Spirit that six-year-old children can understand, such as helping them to be brave and strong, working with them to forgive others, and filling them with joy and happiness.

Objective

This lesson helps the children appreciate the Holy Spirit as a gift from Jesus.

Step 1/INTRODUCTION

Learning About Our Lives

Talking About Loneliness

Read aloud the chapter title and the question in the margin of page 212. Invite the children to name things that make them happy.

Explain that the word *lonely* means "sad from being without friends or those who love you; feeling all alone." Ask the children if they ever feel lonely. Invite volunteers to pantomime facial and body language that says, "I'm lonely." Then ask them what helped them overcome their feelings of loneliness.

Using Pictures to Tell Stories

Invite the children to look at the pictures on page 212 and ask the following questions.

- How does the person look? feel?
- Why do you think he/she might feel that way?
- Who do you think might help the person to feel less lonely?

Ask volunteers to tell stories with a happy ending about the pictures.

Step 2/DEVELOPMENT

Learning About Our Faith

Reading Page 212

Recall that Jesus had special friends whom he wanted to be happy. Read aloud page 212 and help the children understand that Jesus gave us the Holy Spirit so that we would be happy and not feel lonely.

Creating a Bulletin Board

Distribute drawing paper and ask the children to draw a vertical line down the middle of their papers. Invite them to draw themselves being lonely on one side and feeling happy on the other side. Tell the children to draw signs of the Holy Spirit on the happy side.

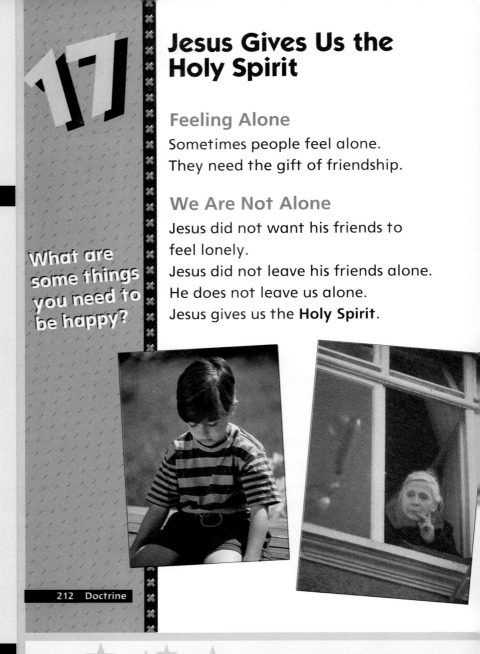

Jesus Gives Us the Holy Spirit

What are some things you need to be happy?

Feeling Alone

Sometimes people feel alone.
They need the gift of friendship.

We Are Not Alone

Jesus did not want his friends to feel lonely.
Jesus did not leave his friends alone.
He does not leave us alone.
Jesus gives us the **Holy Spirit**.

212 Doctrine

★ Enriching the Lesson ★

Ask the children to name some lonely persons whom they might help. (For example, they might mention a new child in school who has no friends or an older neighbor who lives alone.) Encourage the children to help at least one person whom they know is lonely.

🍎 Teaching Tips

In this lesson it is suggested that the children draw signs of the Holy Spirit. Tell the children that since we cannot see God the Holy Spirit, Christians have used signs to signify the Spirit's presence. One sign is breath because the Scripture says that God the Father breathed life into Adam. Christians believe this symbolism is a reference to the Spirit operative at creation.

The Gift from Jesus

The Holy Spirit is God, who is always with us to help us. One of the most important things we need is help to live like Jesus.

The Holy Spirit helps us live like Jesus.
The Holy Spirit helps us be strong and brave, happy and joyful as Jesus was.
The Holy Spirit helps us forgive others and be at peace as Jesus was.

Activity

Draw a picture of something good Jesus did.

New Word

✖ **Holy Spirit** The Holy Spirit is God.

We Believe

The Holy Spirit is God. Jesus gives us the Holy Spirit to be with us and to help us.

Doctrine 213

Enriching the Lesson

Invite the children to make a group collage. On a large sheet of poster paper, print the following heading: *The Holy Spirit helps us be happy.* Then distribute magazines and newspapers, scissors, and glue or paste. Encourage the children to find and cut out pictures of people who look happy. Direct the children to paste their pictures around the heading on the poster paper. Have the children add decorations to the collage and then hang it up.

Afterward, have the children bring their pictures and gather around an empty bulletin board. Pin up the children's pictures and the letters of the sentence: *Jesus gives us the Holy Spirit.* Afterward, talk about what the sentence means and how it applies to their drawings.

Reading Page 213

Invite the children to listen to find out what the Holy Spirit does for us as you read aloud the first paragraph. Discuss the following questions with the children.

- Who is the Holy Spirit? (*God*)
- Why did Jesus give us the Holy Spirit? (*To help us*)
- What is one important thing the Holy Spirit helps us do? (*To live as Jesus showed us to live*)

In the next paragraph, have the children find three ways the Holy Spirit helps us act so that we can live as Jesus showed us. Help them find and circle the words *happy* and *joyful*, *brave* and *strong*, and *peace*.

Reviewing the Vocabulary

Point to the New Word section on page 213. Ask the children to repeat the word *Holy Spirit* and its definition.

Presenting the Doctrine

Read aloud the We Believe section on page 213, which summarizes the chapter's doctrine.

Step 3/CONCLUSION

Learning How to Live Our Faith

Drawing Jesus

Read the directions to the activity on page 213. Invite the children to think of a time when Jesus was full of joy, brave and full of strength, or bringing peace to others. Invite the children to choose a story that reminds them of one of these actions of Jesus and to draw it in the space provided. Tell the children that the Holy Spirit helps us to live this way, too.

Using the Bulletin Board for Prayer

Gather the children around the bulletin board and teach the following response: *Thank you, Jesus, for the Holy Spirit.* Invite volunteers to explain their drawings. After each sharing, invite the children's responses.

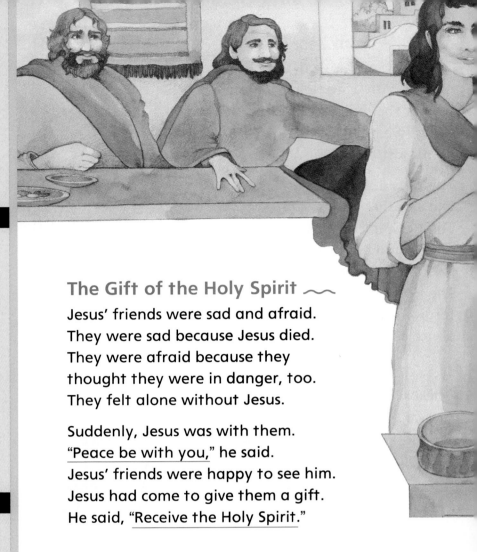

Objective

This lesson helps the children learn the story of Jesus giving the gift of the Holy Spirit to his followers.

Step 1/INTRODUCTION

Learning About Our Lives

Playing a Game

Play a game called "I miss you." Invite the children to sit in a circle with you. Then toss a ball to one of the children and invite that child to tell a story about a time when he or she missed someone. (Perhaps it was a friend who moved away, a sibling who went off to school, or a parent who went on a business trip.) Encourage the children to include in their stories how they felt about these persons leaving. Afterward, invite the child with the ball to toss it to another child.

Step 2/DEVELOPMENT

Learning About Our Faith

Listening to a Bible Story

Encourage the children to look at the picture on pages 214–215 while you read aloud "The Gift of the Holy Spirit."

To check the children's comprehension of the story, ask questions like the following.

- How did the friends of Jesus feel at the beginning of the story? (*Sad and afraid because Jesus had died and they thought they would never see him again*)

- How did they feel when Jesus appeared to them? (*Answers will vary.*)
  Explain that Jesus' friends were in a room with locked doors. After Jesus rose from the dead, he could go anywhere he wanted.

- What did Jesus say when he appeared to them? (*Peace be with you.*)

- What gift did Jesus give his friends? (*The Holy Spirit*)

- How did his friends feel then? (*Brave and happy*)

The Gift of the Holy Spirit

Jesus' friends were sad and afraid.
They were sad because Jesus died.
They were afraid because they
thought they were in danger, too.
They felt alone without Jesus.

Suddenly, Jesus was with them.
"Peace be with you," he said.
Jesus' friends were happy to see him.
Jesus had come to give them a gift.
He said, "Receive the Holy Spirit."

CURRICULUM CONNECTION

Handwriting In this lesson, the children are asked to circle the words Jesus said when he appeared to his friends after he rose from the dead:
Peace be with you.
Receive the Holy Spirit.
You may wish to put these words on the board and have the children copy them as a handwriting activity.

Enriching the Lesson

To focus on the gift aspect of the Holy Spirit, prepare a small surprise gift for each child in your classroom. At the beginning of today's class, give one gift to each child and invite the children to open their gifts. Afterward, encourage the children to share how they felt when they got their surprise gifts. Ask them what colors they would use to show their happiness over the surprise.

Jesus' friends felt comforted.
They felt less afraid.
The Holy Spirit was with them.

Based on John 19:22

Activity

Underline the words Jesus said in the story.
Copy the words below.

Peace be with you.

Receive the Holy Spirit.

Enriching the Lesson

Invite the children to act out the Bible story on pages 214–215. Encourage volunteers to be creative at the beginning of the story when the friends of Jesus are sad and afraid. Invite them to make up dialogue to represent these feelings. Also encourage them to make up dialogue for the end of the story when the friends of Jesus feel happy and brave. Provide time for the volunteers to prepare and present the play.

Talking About Gifts

Ask the children to explain the meaning of *gift*. Emphasize the following about gift–giving.

- Someone gives us a gift to show that he or she loves us.
- We are grateful for the gifts we receive.
- We can share with others by giving them gifts.
- Jesus shows his love for us by giving us the gift of the Holy Spirit.
- The Holy Spirit gives us the gifts of peace, love, joy, strength, and prayer.

Completing an Activity

Read the directions to the activity with the children and help them find the words that Jesus said to his friends.

Step 3/CONCLUSION

Learning How to Live Our Faith

Drawing with Colors That Remind Us of the Happiness the Holy Spirit Gives

Invite the children to choose a color or several colors that help them feel happy. Remind the children that the friends of Jesus felt happy when Jesus gave them the gift of the Holy Spirit. Encourage the children to draw big gift boxes on their papers and to decorate them with the color or colors that show the happiness they feel when they think of the Holy Spirit. Afterward, post these drawings around the room and refer to them during the following weeks. Suggest that the children remember the presence of the Holy Spirit whenever they see the color(s).

Gathering for Prayer

Invite the children to gather with you in the prayer area. Teach the children the following response: *God the Holy Spirit makes us happy!* Then tell the children that today they are going to use their bodies to show God how happy the gift of the Holy Spirit makes them feel. Invite volunteers to demonstrate a happy gesture or body movement (For example: a jump, a dance step, a twirl). Encourage the rest of the children to imitate the movements. Then invite the children to pray the response together.

DAY 3
DOCTRINE

Objective

This lesson helps the children appreciate the help we receive from the Holy Spirit.

Step 1/INTRODUCTION

Learning About Our Lives

Recalling the Learning of Day 2

Reexamine the illustration accompanying the Bible story on pages 214–215. Remark about the happy expressions on the faces of Jesus' friends and followers. Engage the children in a conversation about the happiness the Holy Spirit brings them.

Responding to Paper-Plate Faces

Show the children the fearful, sad, and angry paper–plate faces that you made before class. Using questions like the following, discuss each face individually.

- What feeling is on this face? (*Answers will vary.*)
- Have you ever felt like this? (*Answers will vary.*)
- How do others know when you are sad? afraid? angry? (*Answers will vary.*)
- Who can show us how a body and a face look when a person feels sad? afraid? angry? (*Volunteers will demonstrate this.*)
- What might a person who feels like this need to be happy? (*Answers will vary.*)

Finally, show the children the happy paper-plate face and ask them what might have made this person happy.

To conclude, hold up the paper-plate faces, one by one, starting with the sad face and ending with the happy one. As you hold up each plate, ask the children if this is how they feel when they think about the Holy Spirit. (Most likely the children will say no to the first three plates and yes to the happy face.) When they have responded to all four plate faces, ask the children why the Holy Spirit helps them to feel happy. (Because the Holy Spirit loves them and wants them to be happy.)

216

The Holy Spirit, Our Helper

When we are baptized, people give us gifts.
They give us crosses, medals, and other things.

At our Baptism, Jesus gives us a gift, too.
Jesus gives us the Holy Spirit.

Jesus gives us the Holy Spirit to be our helper.
What does the Holy Spirit help us to do?

Based on Galatians 5:22

216 Scripture

 **CURRICULUM CONNECTION**

Art Invite the children to make faces of themselves that show how they feel after receiving the help of the Holy Spirit. Provide paper plates, crayons or felt-tip markers, paste, and various colors of cut yarn. Ask the children to print their names at the tops of their plates. Then post them in the classroom. Or provide clay and invite the children to mold their faces to show how they feel about receiving the Holy Spirit.

 **Teaching Tips**

When discussing the poem on page 217, you might want to work with the following vocabulary. 1) *Strengthened*—Lead the children to recognize that the Holy Spirit helps us when we are afraid, when we need help, or when we are asked to do something hard. 2) *We are free*— Help the children value the fact that the Holy Spirit is with us to guide us in acting like Jesus, that we can act as we want.

The Holy Spirit Is Always with Us!

At Baptism we receive the Holy Spirit.
We can trust the Holy Spirit to be with us
and to help us.

We are children
Who are happy.
We are children
Who are sad.

Sometimes we may
Choose good things.
Sometimes we may
Choose bad.

But wherever
There are children,
God is watching
Lovingly.

In God's Spirit
We are strengthened.
In God's Spirit
We are free.

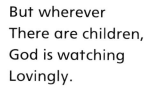

Doctrine 217

Cultural Awareness

Make a mural based on the third verse of the poem on page 127. Remind the children that God loves everyone. Ask your first graders to draw the children of the world. Have one child draw Jesus watching over them in a loving matter. Ask another to draw the world. As they draw, have them think of Jesus who gives them the Holy Spirit to help them. If possible, use crayons that match skin tones of people of different races throughout the world. Brainstorm a title.

Learning About Our Faith

Reading the Text

Ask the children if they know when we received the Holy Spirit. Read aloud the first two paragraphs of "The Holy Spirit, Our Helper" on page 216. Talk about the children's baptisms and the gift of the Holy Spirit.

Direct the children's attention to the third paragraph and read it aloud. Then look at each illustration and talk about the fact that the Holy Spirit helps us to do the following actions.

- Love—How is the little boy showing love? (*Kissing his dad good night*) How has the Holy Spirit helped you to show love? (*Answers will vary.*)

- Be happy—Do you like to dance? What are some other things you do when you are happy? (*Answers will vary.*)

- Be gentle—Do you have a pet? In what ways are you kind to your pet? Can you give an example of being courteous, calm, mild, or gentle toward others? (*Being polite, speaking in a calm voice rather than shouting, and so on*)

- Think before you act—When is it a good idea to think before you act? (*Answers will vary.*)

- Be patient—How did you feel when you had to wait in line, perhaps at the movies or at the store? (*Answers will vary.*) Who will help you be patient? (*The Holy Spirit*) How does a patient person act (*Calmly, not complaining, not running around*)

Step 3/CONCLUSION

Learning How to Live Our Faith

Reading a Poem

Read "The Holy Spirit Is Always with Us!" on page 217, verse by verse, pausing to allow the children to imitate the gestures shown in the illustrations. Finally, read the poem several times until the children know the gestures.

Using the Poem for Prayer

Gather the children in the prayer corner. When they are quiet read the poem as the children pray with gestures.

To Live Like Jesus

We want to live as
Jesus showed us.
How did Jesus act?
Jesus was very brave
and kind.
He was peaceful
and forgiving.
He was full of joy.
He was a friend
to everyone.
Who will help us
act like Jesus?

ctivity

Write a prayer to ask the Holy Spirit
to help you act like Jesus.

Dear Holy Spirit,

SCRIPTURE/MORALITY

Objective

This lesson helps the children understand that the Holy Spirit helps them act like Jesus.

Step 1/INTRODUCTION

Learning About Our Lives

Remembering Jesus

Invite volunteers to share stories they remember about Jesus. Encourage them to talk about times when he was brave, kind, peaceful, filled with joy, helpful, or friendly. If they need help in getting started, encourage them to flip through their religion books, look for illustrations that show Jesus, and then recall Bible stories connected to these illustrations.

Acting Out Bible Stories

After volunteers have concluded their stories about Jesus, divide the class into groups and have the children choose one of the above stories to act out. Provide time for the children to prepare and present their role-plays. After each presentation, encourage the "audience" to tell what the story told them about Jesus. Then ask them how they can act as Jesus did.

Step 2/DEVELOPMENT

Learning About Our Faith

Reading the Text

Direct the children's attention to the illustration at the top of page 218. Ask the children to identify Jesus (the one in white). Then read the text under "To Live Like Jesus." Invite volunteers to answer the question: *Who will give us help us so we can act like Jesus?* Help the children remember that the Holy Spirit helps them act like Jesus.

218

 **CURRICULUM CONNECTION**

Language Arts To help the children think of ways to act as Jesus has shown us, invite volunteers to choose partners and to present skits that show someone in need and someone helping that person. After each presentation, ask the volunteers to name a way the Holy Spirit helped the person care for the person in need.

 *Focus on*

Holy Spirit The *Catechism of the Catholic Church* states, "By this power of the Spirit, God's children can bear much fruit. He who has grafted us onto the true vine will make us bear 'the fruit of the Spirit: . . . love, joy, peace, patience, kindness, goodness, faithfulness, gentleness, self-control,' 'We live by the Spirit'; the more we renounce ourselves, the more we 'walk by the Spirit'" (#736).

Activity

Who acted like Jesus to help each person?
Look at the pictures on the left.
Match them with a picture on the right.
Write the correct letter in each box.

Learning How to Live Our Faith

Writing a Prayer

Have the children think of ways that they could act like Jesus today. They may refer to page 218 for help with their choices. Then invite the children to compose prayers in which they ask the Holy Spirit to help them be like Jesus in this particular way.

Completing an Activity

Direct the children's attention to the activity on page 219. Read the directions with them and encourage them to match the pictures. Discuss the pictures with the children.

Gathering to Pray

Before inviting the children to the prayer corner, choose a few volunteers to read their prayers on page 218 as part of today's prayer experience. These children will need to take their books. Invite the children to process to the prayer corner. Begin the prayer experience with a moment of silence. Then ask for volunteers to read their prayers. After each prayer, the group may say, *Come, Holy Spirit.* Invite the children to chant the response as they process back to their seats.

Enriching the Lesson

Encourage the children to think of someone who acts like Jesus. Give each child a sheet of paper. Invite the children to write thank-you notes. For example: *Dear Mom, Thank you for feeding me this week when I was hungry and for smiling at me when I told you stories.* They might decorate their notes with ribbons, glue-ons, sequins, and so forth. Provide envelopes for the children to carry the message home.

DAY 5
PRAYER/REVIEW

Objective

This lesson provides an opportunity for the children to pray to the Holy Spirit with the aid of a banner.

Reading the Text

Read "Praying to the Holy Spirit" on page 220. Brainstorm with the children ways they would like the Holy Spirit to help them (to be brave, to have courage, to be helpful, to have joy, to be happy, and so on). Stress that when we act in these ways, we are acting as Jesus showed us. On the chalkboard, print the brainstorming suggestions.

Making a Banner

Tell the children that they will make a banner asking for the Holy Spirit's help to live like Jesus. Ask each child to study the list of actions on the chalkboard and to choose one that he or she wants the Holy Spirit's help to do. Provide a large sheet of shelf paper. Write *Holy Spirit, help us . . .* on the banner and invite each child to add a request.

Preparing to Pray

Tell the children that today they are going to ask the Holy Spirit for help to act like Jesus. Teach them the following response, which they will use in their prayer: *Come, Holy Spirit.* Choose some children to carry the banner into the gathering place. Some children may march in front of the banner playing musical (rhythm) instruments, while the remaining children sing a song.

Praying to the Holy Spirit

Process with the children. Hang the banner in a prearranged spot. Pray the petition *Holy Spirit, help us...* which is written on the banner. Invite each child to point to his or her request and to pray it aloud. The group should respond, *Come Holy Spirit!* Conclude the prayer session by having the children sing a song and play their rhythm instruments.

Praying to the Holy Spirit

We can pray to God the Holy Spirit.

Make a banner like the one here.

Print the name of an action you want the Holy Spirit to help you with.

Decorate your banner.

220 Prayer

Focus on

Praying with a Banner For today's prayer, the children will use a banner. Banners often display inspirational sayings and can be an aid to praying. A community banner, such as the one the children made in this lesson, has the added benefit of conveying how others in the group need help from the Spirit. It witnesses to our common reliance on God. Displaying it may evoke prayer in the children whenever they glance at it.

Chapter Review

The Holy Spirit helps us to act like Jesus.
Circle the ways you can act like Jesus.

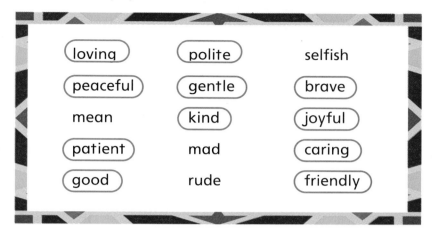

(loving)	(polite)	selfish
(peaceful)	(gentle)	(brave)
mean	(kind)	(joyful)
(patient)	mad	(caring)
(good)	rude	(friendly)

1. Whom did Jesus give his friends to help them?

the Holy Spirit

2. Why does Jesus give us the Holy Spirit?

**Jesus says,
"The Holy Spirit
is with you."**
Based on John 14:16–17

to help us

3. Talk about ways in which the Holy Spirit helps you act like Jesus.

CURRICULUM CONNECTION

Music Teach the children a song about the Holy Spirit or use the following words to the melody of "Jingle Bells."

Spirit please,
Spirit please,
Spirit send me help.
Help me now,
So I can act
As Jesus always did.
(Repeat the verse.)

Enriching the Lesson

Have the children write an open letter to the Holy Spirit. To begin, tape up a piece of paper large enough for each child to write on. Line the paper so the children can write on it. On the paper, print your school's name and address, the date, and the salutation *Dear Holy Spirit.* Then invite each child to write one thing he or she would like to say to the Holy Spirit. When everyone has contributed, read the completed letter and ask all the children to sign their names.

Using the Bulletin Board from Day 1 to Review

Gather the children around the bulletin board they assembled on Day 1. Using their drawings, review the learning of the week. Invite the children to talk about how Jesus gives them the Holy Spirit who helps them act like Jesus. Encourage the children to tell stories about the way Jesus acted and about the ways they have acted like him. Stress that Christians act like Jesus when they love one another, help others, share, and pray.

Finally, give each child his or her bulletin-board drawing and encourage the children to take their drawings home, post them in a place they will notice them each day, and use them as reminders of the Holy Spirit's gifts.

Completing an Activity

Use the activity on page 221 to review the learning of Chapter 17. Read the directions at the top of the page. Then read the list with the children. Note that some of the actions are ways that Jesus wants them to act and some are not. Encourage the children to circle all the ways they can act like Jesus.

Answering the Questions

Invite volunteers to read aloud the first two questions and then ask the children to respond. Direct the children to print the answers in their texts. Encourage all the children to participate in the discussion of the third question. Be supportive of each child who responds.

Reading the Scripture Verse

Ask the children to read the Scripture verse after you. Reflecting on the word of God is a good way to end the lesson. If you wish, you may have the children memorize this verse.

18 The Holy Spirit Gives Us Strength

Objectives

To help the children

- Learn that the Holy Spirit offers them courage when they are afraid.
- Understand that they may be afraid but that Jesus is always with them.
- Recognize that the Holy Spirit helps them when they are afraid.
- Understand that when they help others, the Holy Spirit is with them.
- Use a poster as an aid to prayer and review the chapter.

Chapter Outline

	Step 1 Learning About Our Lives	Step 2 Learning About Our Faith	Step 3  Learning How to Live Our Faith
Day 1	■ Review the learning of Chapter 17. ■ Introduce Chapter 18. ■ Respond to the pictures. *ABOUT 10 MINUTES*	■ Learn how to ask the Holy Spirit for help. ■ Present the doctrine. *ABOUT 10 MINUTES*	■ Complete an activity. ■ Pray using a picture. *ABOUT 10 MINUTES*
Day 2	■ Review Day 1. ■ Talk about storms. *ABOUT 10 MINUTES*	■ Listen to a Bible story. ■ Discuss the Bible story. ■ Dramatize the Bible story. *ABOUT 10 MINUTES*	■ Introduce the Good News. ■ Review the vocabulary. ■ Gather for prayer. *ABOUT 10 MINUTES*
Day 3	■ Read the children's book. ■ Complete an activity. ■ Dramatize being afraid and getting help. *ABOUT 10 MINUTES*	■ Learn how the Spirit helps. ■ Draw pictures of the Holy Spirit helping. ■ Create a bulletin board. *ABOUT 10 MINUTES*	■ Complete an activity. ■ Use the bulletin board for prayer. *ABOUT 10 MINUTES*
Day 4	■ Review the bulletin board from Day 3. ■ Complete an activity. *ABOUT 10 MINUTES*	■ Look at photographs and read the text. ■ Learn a prayer. *ABOUT 10 MINUTES*	■ Talk about helping others be brave. ■ Complete an activity. ■ Gather for prayer. *ABOUT 10 MINUTES*
Day 5	**Prayer** Think about being brave; decorate a poster; and pray to the Holy Spirit. **Review** Review the chapter; complete an activity; answer the questions; and read a Scripture verse.		

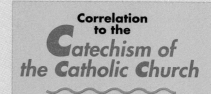

Correlation
to the
**Catechism of
the Catholic Church**

Paragraphs
729, 743

Plan Ahead ～～～～～～

	Preparing Your Class	**Materials Needed**
Day 1	Read the lesson plan before teaching the lesson. If you plan to use any Teaching Option, make preparations and collect materials.	
Day 2	Read the lesson plan before teaching the lesson. If you plan to use any Teaching Option, make preparations and collect materials.	
Day 3	Cut out *The Holy Spirit helps us be brave.* For Step 3, print each of the following words on a separate piece of construction paper: *do, afraid, be, not.*	■ drawing paper/bulletin board ■ cut-out letters for sentence ■ four sheets of colored construction paper
Day 4	Read over the lesson. If you plan to use the Teaching Options, collect the materials.	■ bulletin board from Day 3
Day 5	Prepare an example from your life of a time you were brave. Share it with the children.	

Additional Resources

As you plan this chapter, consider using the following materials from The Resourceful Teacher Package.

■ *Classroom Activity Sheets 18* and *18a*

■ *Family Activity Sheets 18* and *18a*

■ *Chapter* 18 *Test*

■ *Prayers for Every Day*

■ *Projects: Grade 1*

In preparing the children for the Sunday readings, you may wish to use Silver Burdett Ginn's *Getting Ready for Sunday* student and teacher materials.

Books For The Journey

God Is Always with Me. Helen Caswell. Abingdon Press, 1989. This book shows children that even though everything changes, God's love is always with them.

The Little Boat That Almost Sank. Mary Warren. Concordia, 1965. The storm at sea story is told in rhyme.

More Books For The Journey

Sam, Bangs, and Moonshine. Evaline Ness. Holt, Rhinehart & Winston, 1966. Through a painful experience brought on by herself, Sam learns an important lesson.

Sometimes I Get Scared. Elspeth Campbell Murphy. David C. Cook, 1980. A child associates a good shepherd with God's care, protection, and presence during scary times.

Reduced Classroom Activities

Name

The Holy Spirit Gives Us Strength

1. Read the sentences on pages 18 and 18a.
2. Choose two pictures to finish each sentence.
3. Paste the pictures in the boxes.

> To have a strong body, I _____.
>
>

To the Teacher: This two-page activity follows the Scripture story "A Terrible Storm."

Chapter 18   The Holy Spirit Gives Us Strength   This Is Our Faith 1   **18**

Name

> To have a strong spirit, I _____.
>
>
>

18a   This Is Our Faith 1   Chapter 18   The Holy Spirit Gives Us Strength

Background for the Teacher

THE POWER OF THE PRESENCE OF JESUS

On the first Easter evening, Jesus told his friends, "Fear not, I am with you." This promise and other stories from the Gospels that show Jesus' ability to calm fears and to impart courage and strength have always comforted Christians.

Chapter 18 presents the Gospel story of the storm at sea. In this story, Jesus responds to the disciples' pleas for help. Terrified, they beseech him to save them. Jesus, so unafraid that he sleeps in the bow of the boat, awakens and commands the winds and the waves to be still and silent, to be at peace as he is at peace. This story dramatically shows that the presence of Jesus brings strength and calm and gladness. What Jesus did for the terrified disciples in the sinking fishing boat, he does for us in our times of crisis.

CHILDHOOD FEARS

Children experience various kinds of fears. Some are realistic; others are imaginary. Some fears derive from physical realities, such as sickness. Others stem from changes in relationships, such as those caused by death or divorce. Still other fears are psychological, such as the fear of speaking out in a group. Allowing children the opportunity to acknowledge and discuss fears will help them understand that most fears can be made manageable.

OVERCOMING FEARS

Present Jesus as caring and strong, someone who knows our fears and sends us the Holy Spirit to give us strength. Guide the children in appreciating the fact that assistance often arrives through the protection of others. Help them understand that the Holy Spirit also works through them when they support others who are fearful. The activities of this chapter will help the children identify experiences in which the Holy Spirit acts. Encourage the children to pray when they are fearful. Prayer provides the comfort of God's fortifying presence.

Objective

This lesson helps the children learn that the Holy Spirit offers them courage when they are afraid.

Step 1/INTRODUCTION

Learning About Our Lives

Reviewing the Learning of Chapter 17

Help the children review that the Holy Spirit, who was first given them at Baptism, is here to keep them now. Then encourage the children to show how they feel when they think about the Spirit. Explain one way that the Spirit helps them is to give them courage when they are afraid.

Introducing Chapter 18

Read aloud the question in the margin of page 222 and encourage volunteers to tell stories about times when they were scared. After each story, ask the volunteer to use his or her face and body to show how being scared felt.

Responding to the Pictures

Direct the children's attention to "Sometimes We're Afraid" on page 222. Ask the children who can help the children in the pictures to not be afraid (The Holy Spirit or someone the Holy Spirit sends).

Next, read the question at the bottom of page 222: What are you afraid of? Invite the children's responses and print them on the chalkboard. Leave these responses on the board until the end of class.

Finally, tell the children that everyone feels afraid sometimes. Emphasize that this is nothing to be ashamed of. Ask the children to name those who help, protect, or care for them when they are scared. Tell that today they are going to learn about someone special who loves them very much and helps them.

222

18 The Holy Spirit Gives Us Strength

Sometimes We're Afraid

Mike had a scary dream.

Kim is afraid of lightning.

Ruth is afraid of the dark.

Tell about a time when you were afraid. What frightened you?

222 Doctrine

Jim is afraid of spiders.
What are you afraid of ?

 CURRICULUM CONNECTION

Music If possible, play the song "I Whistle a Happy Tune" from *The King and I.* Teach the children the melody and the words and invite them to talk about how whistling a happy tune could help them when they are scared.

Activity

Draw a picture in the space of someone helping you when you are afraid.

Come, Holy Spirit, Help Us

Jesus helps us when we are afraid. He gives us the Holy Spirit to help us be brave.

When we are afraid, we can pray, "Come, Holy Spirit, help us be brave."

We Believe

Jesus helps us when we are afraid. He gives us the Holy Spirit to help us be brave.

Doctrine 223

Enriching the Lesson

Using the list of fears from Step 1, point out that many people fear these things. Help the children understand that both real things and imaginary things cause fear. Have the children put a check next to the fears that are caused by imaginary things, such as ghosts, monsters, and bad dreams. Help the children realize that these things cannot hurt them. But be careful not to discount the real fears the children may feel when they dream about these things or think they see them.

Learning How to Ask the Spirit for Help

Direct the children's attention to "Come, Holy Spirit, Help Us" on page 223. Read the text to the children. Ask the children to circle the words of the prayer they can say to the Holy Spirit when they are scared. Say these words out loud with them several times until the children are familiar with the prayer.

Presenting the Doctrine

Read aloud the We Believe section on page 223, which summarizes the chapter's doctrine. Ask the children to repeat the two sentences after you.

Step 3/CONCLUSION

Learning How to Live Our Faith

Completing an Activity

Read the directions to the activity on page 223. Point out the list of scary things on the chalkboard and encourage the children to recall times when they were scared and someone helped or protected them. Invite the children to draw a picture of someone helping them when they were scared.

Praying Using a Picture

Gather the children in the prayer area. When they are quiet, recall the prayer they learned today: *Come, Holy Spirit, help us be brave.* Then invite the children to share their drawings. Invite volunteers to name one thing that they are scared of. After each response, encourage the children to pray their class response.

DAY 2
SCRIPTURE

Objective

This lesson helps the children understand that they may be afraid at times but that Jesus is always with them.

Step 1/INTRODUCTION

Learning About Our Lives

Reviewing Day 1

Invite the children to talk about their fears. Then ask them who can help and protect them when they are fearful. If no one mentions the Holy Spirit, do so. Then announce that the children are going to hear a Bible story about a time the followers of Jesus were afraid during a storm.

Talking About Storms

Ask the children if they have ever been in a big storm. Share any experiences with storms that you may have had. Then, encourage volunteers to tell about their experiences and to describe how they felt during and after the storm.

Step 2/DEVELOPMENT

Learning About Our Faith

Listening to a Bible Story

Encourage the children to look at the pictures on pages 224–225 while you read aloud "A Terrible Storm." Emphasize the dialogue and the feelings of Jesus' friends. Show Jesus' compassion and command over nature.

Discussing the Bible Story

To help the children understand the story, ask the following questions.

- What do you think Jesus and his friends were doing in the boat? (*Probably fishing*)
- What was Jesus doing when the storm blew up? (*Sleeping*)
- What did the storm do to the boat? (*Waves smashed against the boat; water splashed over the deck.*)
- What did the friends of Jesus yell when the boat began to sink? (*Jesus, help us! We will all drown!*)
- How do you think they felt? (*Afraid*)

224

A Terrible Storm

One day Jesus and his friends were in a fishing boat.
A storm came up suddenly.
Jesus was asleep.
The wind whistled and whipped up the waves.
Water splashed into the boat.
The boat began to sink.

"Jesus, help us!" shouted his friends.
"We will all drown!"

Jesus woke up.
"Why are you so afraid?" he asked.
"I am with you."

224 Scripture

🍎 Teaching Tips

When discussing storms with the children you might want to talk about a storm from literature. Ask if any of the children have ever seen the movie "The Wizard of Oz." Recall the terrible storm in the beginning of the movie and talk about how Dorothy reacted to the storm.

Jesus stood up in the boat.
He faced the wind and the waves.
"Be still!" Jesus shouted. "Be calm!"
The wind and the waves became
calm and still.
Jesus' friends were no longer afraid.
They were glad Jesus was with them.

Based on Luke 8:22–25

This is a story from the **Gospel** of Luke.
The gospel is the good news of Jesus
found in the Bible.

ctivity

What is the good news of Jesus?
Find the words and circle them.

New Word

gospel The gospel is the good news of Jesus
found in the Bible.

🍎 Teaching Tips

To extend the understanding of the word *gospel,* write it on the chalkboard. Then show the children some of the places where they can find the word in the Bible. (For example: the Gospel of Matthew, Mark, Luke, John) Ask the children if they have ever heard the word spoken at Mass. Then read the definition of *gospel* on page 225 of the children's text.

- How would you have felt? (*Answers will vary.*)
- What did Jesus say to his friends when they woke him up? (*Why are you so afraid? I am with you.*)
- Then what did Jesus do? (*He calmed the wind and the waves.*)
- How did his friends feel then? (*Unafraid, glad*)
- How do you think you would have felt if you had been in the boat with Jesus? (*Answers will vary.*)

Dramatizing the Bible Story

Invite the children to dramatize the story of the storm at sea. Have volunteers take the parts of Jesus and his followers. Provide a few moments for the children to reread the story and suggest that they use several chairs as their boat. Explain to the children that they can make up more dialogue for the story. Invite the rest of the children to sit in a semicircle to watch the dramatization.

Step 3/CONCLUSION

Learning How to Live Our Faith

Introducing the Good News

Direct the children's attention to the two lines beneath the illustration on page 225. Read this copy to them. Encourage the children to find and circle the good news in today's Bible story. Help them understand the good news that Jesus will always be with his followers, so we need not be afraid.

Reviewing the Vocabulary

Point to the New Word section on page 225. Ask the children to repeat the word *gospel* and its definition.

Gathering for Prayer

Gather the children in the prayer area. When they are quiet, teach them the following response: *Jesus, I believe that you are always with me because you have given me your Spirit.* Invite volunteers, one by one, to tell God about today's Bible story. They might tell God how they feel about the story or they might relate parts of the story. After each volunteer responds, invite the children to pray the response.

225

DAY 3
DOCTRINE

Objective

This lesson helps the children recognize that the Holy Spirit helps them when they are afraid.

Step 1/INTRODUCTION

Learning About Our Lives

Reading the Children's Book

Read, one by one, the three stories under the heading "Help When We Are Scared" on page 226. After reading each paragraph, provide time for the children to respond to the questions.

Completing an Activity

Direct the children's attention to the activity at the bottom of page 226 and read the two questions there. Invite volunteers to tell about things they have to do that scare them. Then ask the volunteers to tell who helps them when they are afraid. Have the children write their responses on the lines provided.

Dramatizing Being Afraid and Getting Help

Invite volunteers to choose partners and to act out two scenes in a story: (1) being afraid of something they have to do (2) asking and receiving help from someone. Provide time for the dramatizations and encourage the rest of the children to respond with questions, comments, and applause.

Step 2/DEVELOPMENT

Learning About Our Faith

Learning How the Spirit Helps

Read the text "The Holy Spirit Helps Us" on page 227. Stress the last three lines of the text. Then ask questions like the following.

- What gift has Jesus given us? (*The gift of the Holy Spirit*)

- Who helps us when we are afraid? (*The Holy Spirit*)

- How does the Holy Spirit sometimes help us? (*By giving us people who take care of us and protect us*)

226

Help When We Are Scared

Timothy had a test to take.
He had to spell ten words.
He was worried.
Who could help him?

Bena had to act in a play.
She had to remember
all the words.
She was nervous.
Who could help her?

Kim had a bad fever.
He had to get a flu shot.
He was scared.
Who could help him?

ctivity

What makes you worry?
Who gives you strength
when you are afraid?

 **CURRICULUM CONNECTION**

Language Arts Make a copy of the following prayer for each child: *Holy Spirit, help me with your courage and your strength when _____.* Distribute the copies and invite the children to complete the prayers by describing times when they especially need the Holy Spirit's help. Afterward, invite volunteers to share their prayers and encourage the children to take their prayers home and to post them so that they can remember that the Holy Spirit is always with them.

Teaching Tips

When discussing page 226, bear in mind that some children will have few or no anxieties about these happenings. But all of them will be able to identify with the children in the vignettes and empathize with them. The vignettes allow you to show it is natural to be a little worried now and then and might help children in your class express their own worries more freely.

The Holy Spirit Helps Us

Jesus gives us the Holy Spirit to help us when we are afraid. Sometimes the Holy Spirit helps us by giving us people who take care of us.

Activity

Put the words in order to find the good news. Write it in a sentence.

Do not be afraid.

Doctrine 227

Focus on

Fear This is an emotion we feel when confronted by someone or something we judge as harmful. So fear can help us protect ourselves. There are some fears we overcome through the experience of learning the "harm" is not really so bad. In this lesson, all the "scary" topics fit into this category. Some children may be afraid of things which other children pronounce as non-fearful. Learning that others are not afraid may help the child who scares more easily.

Focus on

The Help of the Spirit Christians believe that the Holy Spirit guides and inspires us, igniting our imaginations, enlightening our minds, and motivating our wills. This is direct intervention on the part of the Spirit. In addition God stirs others to aid us. Those who respond to the promptings of the Spirit are moved to act in our best interests.

Drawing Pictures of the Holy Spirit Helping

Distribute drawing paper and ask the children to draw a vertical line down the middle of their papers. Then invite them to draw on the left side a picture of themselves being afraid of something they have to do. Encourage them to draw on the right side how the Holy Spirit helps them when they are afraid. Remind the children that sometimes the Spirit helps them directly. Suggest they draw a symbol of the Spirit, such as a breath of air or the wind blowing. Also encourage them to consider that the Holy Spirit gives them people to protect and to take care of them when they are afraid.

Creating a Bulletin Board

Have the letters cut out for the following sentence: *The Holy Spirit helps us be brave.* When the children have completed their drawings, they may help you assemble the bulletin board. Gather the children at an empty bulletin board. Give each child a letter from the above sentence and have them hand you a letter as you pin the sentence on the board. Then have them hand you their pictures.

Step 3/CONCLUSION

Learning How to Live Our Faith

Completing an Activity

Give each of four volunteers one of the four word cards you prepared before class. Ask them to hold up the words (*do, afraid, be, not*). Call for other volunteers to rearrange the words to say "Do not be afraid." Then direct the children to the activity at the bottom of page 227.

Using the Bulletin Board for Prayer

Gather the children around the bulletin board. When they are quiet, teach them the response *Come, Holy Spirit, help us when we are afraid.* Then invite volunteers to explain their bulletin-board drawings to the group and to God. After each volunteer shares, invite the children's responses.

Objective

This lesson helps the children understand that when they help others, the Holy Spirit is with them.

Step 1/INTRODUCTION

Learning About Our Lives

Reviewing the Bulletin Board from Day 3

Gather the children around the bulletin board they assembled on Day 3. Invite the children to read the sentence on the bulletin board: *The Holy Spirit helps us be brave.* Then encourage volunteers to point out their drawings and to explain them. As the children share, stress that when people help other people, the Holy Spirit is with them.

Completing an Activity

Direct the children's attention to the activity on page 228. Read the text. Before beginning the activity, check to be sure that the children understand that sometimes the Spirit helps people who are frightened by sending people to help them. Then invite volunteers to tell stories about the photographs on page 228. After each child tells his or her story, ask questions like the following.

- Whom might the person who was afraid pray to? (*The Holy Spirit*)

- What might the person who was afraid ask for? (*For help*)

- How might the Holy Spirit help? (*The Holy Spirit could send someone to help the fearful person.*)

Step 2/DEVELOPMENT

Learning About Our Faith

Looking at Photographs and Reading the Text

Direct the children's attention to the photographs on page 229. Encourage volunteers to tell what is happening in these pictures. Then read the page out loud. Explain to the children that the words and the pictures are saying the same thing: the Holy Spirit helps people help others.

Activity

Look at these pictures.
Some of the people are afraid.
They ask the Holy Spirit to help them.
Whom has the Holy Spirit sent to help?

CURRICULUM CONNECTION

Art   Make Holy Spirit prayer cards. Distribute a lined pastel index card to each child. Then invite the children to copy the following prayer onto their cards: *Come, Holy Spirit, help us to help others.* Suggest that the children decorate their prayer cards with colors that help them remember that the Spirit is always with them. If possible, cover the completed cards with clear adhesive plastic and round off the corners.

Come, Spirit of Love

God wants us to help people who are afraid.
The Holy Spirit helps us use our minds and hearts to help others.

Activity

Think about how you can help someone to be brave.
Whom will you help?

_____

- -

_____

What will you do?

_____

- -

_____

Morality   229

Focus on

The Work of the Spirit   The objective of this lesson aims at exploring ways for the children to assist, through the prompting of the Holy Spirit, those who are nervous, upset, or afraid. The Spirit prepares us through grace to take on the way of Christ. Paragraph 743 of the *Catechism of the Catholic Church* confirms this: ". . . whenever God sends his Son, he always sends his Spirit; their mission is conjoined and inseparable."

Learning a Prayer

Teach the children the prayer: *Come, Holy Spirit, help me to help others.* Say this prayer aloud with the children several times until they have become familiar with it. Tell them that they will pray this prayer today.

Step 3/CONCLUSION

Learning How to Live Our Faith

Talking About Helping Others Be Brave

Remind the children that the Holy Spirit guides people to help one another. Read the following situations aloud, one at a time. Ask for volunteers to tell how someone might help the children in the stories.

- Juan is a new boy in school. Because he is so shy, Juan is afraid to introduce himself to anyone.

- Amy won't ride her bike without training wheels. She is afraid that she will fall and hurt herself.

- Sharlene doesn't give any answers in class because she is afraid that she will make a mistake and that the other children will laugh at her.

- Charles will not go to bed unless his mother leaves a light on in his room. He is afraid of the dark.

Completing an Activity

Direct the children's attention to the activity at the bottom of page 229. Then invite the children to print the names of the persons they would like to help and how they would do it. As the children work, go around the room and offer help with spelling.

Gathering for Prayer

Ask the children to bring their religion books to the prayer area. When they are quiet, recall the prayer they learned in Step 2: *Come, Holy Spirit, help me to help others.* Then ask volunteers, one by one, to read from their books (page 229) to tell God about people they want to help and about how they will help them. After each volunteer shares, invite the children to pray their response.

Objective

This lesson helps the children use the poster as an aid to prayer.

Thinking About Being Brave

Tell the children that sometimes helping others takes courage and bravery. If possible, use an example from your own life to illustrate this. Then invite volunteers to tell stories about people they would like to help and about how this would require courage on the children's part. Explain to the children that they can use these stories in their prayer today.

Decorating a Poster

Direct the children's attention to "Praying with a Poster" on page 230. Invite the children to think about how they feel about the Holy Spirit for a moment. Then invite them to decorate the poster.

Praying to the Holy Spirit

Process with the children. After they have all bowed reverently to the Bible, encourage them to raise their arms in praise. Next, invite them to sing a song to the Holy Spirit. Teach the children the following response: *Come, Holy Spirit, and make me brave.*

Then invite volunteers to tell about people they want to help and about why helping them requires courage and bravery. After each volunteer responds, invite the children to pray their invocation to the Holy Spirit. Conclude the prayer by having the children sing a song again.

230

Praying with a Poster

We can hang up posters to remind us of God the Holy Spirit.
Decorate the poster below.

230 Prayer

CURRICULUM CONNECTION

Music   Teach the following words to the melody "Kum Ba Yah."

Make me brave today,
Spirit, please.
Make me brave today,
Spirit, please.
Make me brave today,
Spirit, please.
Please now
Make me brave.

Chapter Review

Cross out all the G letters to find the message.
Copy the message below.

GGGCOMEGGGHOLYGGGSPIRITGGG
GGHELPGGMEGGGGBEGGGBRAVEGG

Come Holy Spirit,

help me be brave.

1. How does Jesus help us when we are afraid?

Jesus gives us the Holy Spirit.

2. What do we call the good news of Jesus?

the gospel

3. Talk about ways the Holy Spirit helps you to be brave and strong.

> Jesus says, "Do not be afraid. I will send you the Holy Spirit."
> Based on John 14:16–18

Focus on

Praying with a Poster In this chapter the children pray with a prayer aid—a poster. Posters can be used to summarize important ideas, and when they are hung, they can remind the children of those thoughts. When the children decorate their own posters, as they do in this lesson, they reflect on the meanings behind the ideas displayed on the posters. Be sure to hang the posters for a time so that the children can ruminate about the ideas.

Using the Bulletin Board from Day 3 to Review

Gather the children around the bulletin board they assembled on Day 3. Using their drawings, review the learning of Days 1–3. Invite the children to talk about how the Holy Spirit helps them when they are afraid. Stress that one way the Holy Spirit helps us is by sending people who will care for them and protect them. Then review the learning of Day 4 by asking the children whom they can help with the aid of the Holy Spirit. Stress that the Holy Spirit is with them when they help others.

Finally, give each child his or her bulletin-board drawing and encourage the children to take their drawings home, post them in a place they notice each day, and use them as reminders of the presence of the Holy Spirit in their lives.

Completing an Activity

Use the activity on page 231 to review the learning of Chapter 18. Read the text at the top of the page. Encourage the children to cross out all the *G* letters to find the prayer: *Come, Holy Spirit, help me be brave.* Next, invite them to copy the prayer on the lines in the middle of page 231. Encourage the children to say this prayer often.

Answering the Questions

Read aloud the first two questions and ask volunteers to respond. Direct the children to print the answers in their texts. Encourage all the children to participate in the discussion of the third question. Be supportive of each child who responds.

Reading a Scripture Verse

Ask the children to read the Scripture verse after you. Reflecting on the word of God is a good way to end the lesson. If you wish, you may have the children memorize this verse.

19 The Holy Spirit Gives Us Peace

Objectives

To help the children

- Understand that God always forgives them and wants them to forgive others.
- Learn a Bible story about Jesus' love, forgiveness, and compassion.
- Learn to use words of forgiveness and sorrow.
- Discover that they can be peacemakers.
- Pray to become peacemakers and review the chapter.

Chapter Outline

	Step 1 **Learning About Our Lives**	**Step 2** **Learning About Our Faith**	**Step 3** **Learning How to Live Our Faith**
Day 1	■ Tell stories about making up. ■ Respond to a poem. *ABOUT 10 MINUTES*	■ Find someone who will help. ■ Review the vocabulary. *ABOUT 10 MINUTES*	■ Complete a prayer. ■ Dramatize ways to respond to hurt and anger. ■ Gather for prayer. *ABOUT 10 MINUTES*
Day 2	■ Review Day 1. *ABOUT 10 MINUTES*	■ Listen to a Bible story. ■ Discuss the Bible story. *ABOUT 10 MINUTES*	■ Complete an activity. ■ Discuss hurt and angry feelings. ■ Gather for prayer. *ABOUT 10 MINUTES*
Day 3	■ Review Day 2. ■ Complete a forgiveness activity. *ABOUT 10 MINUTES*	■ Learn that the Spirit helps. ■ Complete an activity. ■ Present the doctrine. *ABOUT 10 MINUTES*	■ Role-play forgiveness. ■ Make a peace chain. ■ Pray using the peace chain. *ABOUT 10 MINUTES*
Day 4	■ Share experiences of hurt or anger. ■ Read peacemaking stories. ■ Dramatize the stories. *ABOUT 10 MINUTES*	■ Study a photograph about peacemaking. ■ Read the text. *ABOUT 10 MINUTES*	■ Complete an activity. ■ Gather for prayer. *ABOUT 10 MINUTES*
Day 5	**Prayer** Read the text; make pennants; and gather to pray. **Review** Use the peace booklets from Day 4; complete an activity; answer the questions; and read a Scripture verse.		

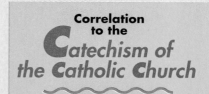

Correlation
to the
**Catechism of
the Catholic Church**

Paragraphs
736, 1441, 1832

Plan Ahead ∿∿∿∿∿

	Preparing Your Class	**Materials Needed**
Day 1	Read the lesson plan before teaching this lesson. If you plan to use any Teaching Option, make preparations and collect materials.	
Day 2	For Step 3, collect an array of magazine and newspaper pictures that show people who look hurt or angry.	■ an array of magazine and newspaper pictures
Day 3	For Step 3, prepare strips of colored construction paper that the children can print on and make into a chain.	■ strips of colored construction paper (one or two per child) ■ paste or stapler and staples
Day 4	For Step 3, make a booklet for each child by folding three sheets of drawing paper together.	■ three sheets of drawing paper per child
Day 5	Read the lesson plan before teaching this lesson. If you plan to use any Teaching Option, make preparations and collect materials.	■ story booklets from Day 4

Additional Resources

As you plan this chapter, consider using the following materials from The Resourceful Teacher Package.

■ *Classroom Activity Sheets 19* and *19a*

■ *Family Activity Sheets 19* and *19a*

■ *Chapter 19 Test*

■ *Prayers for Every Day*

■ *Projects: Grade 1*

You may wish to refer to the following Big Book.

■ *We Celebrate God's Word,* page 14

In preparing the children for the Sunday readings, you may wish to use Silver Burdett Ginn's *Getting Ready for Sunday* student and teacher materials.

BOOKS FOR THE JOURNEY

The Hating Book. Charlotte Zolotow. Harper Collins, 1989. A misunderstanding between friends is finally cleared up, and they become friends again.

Zacchaeus Meets the Savior. Neal Boehlke. Concordia, 1980. The story of Zacchaeus is told in rhyme.

MORE BOOKS FOR THE JOURNEY.

Anytime Prayers. Madeleine L'Engle. Harold Shaw Publishers, 1994. A book in which a section titled "When Bad Things Happen" contains prayers for forgiveness.

The Children's Illustrated Bible. "The Small Man in the Big Tree," pages 62–63. Retold by Selina Hastings. Dorling Kindersley, 1994. The story of Zacchaeus is presented.

REDUCED CLASSROOM ACTIVITIES

Name

The Holy Spirit Gives Us Peace

1. Decorate the doorknob marker.
2. Cut along the heavy black lines.
3. Hang the marker on the doorknob of your room.

A peacemaker lives here!

To the Teacher: This activity emphasizes the importance of forgiving others and asking for forgiveness. Reproduce this page on stiff paper.

Chapter 19   The Holy Spirit Gives Us Peace   THIS IS OUR FAITH 1   **19**

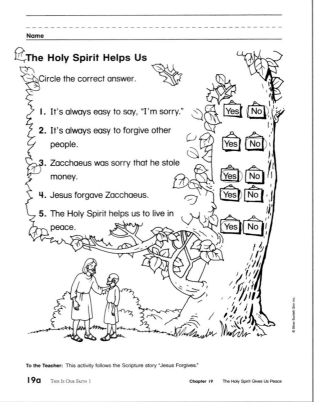

Name

The Holy Spirit Helps Us

Circle the correct answer.

1. It's always easy to say, "I'm sorry."   Yes No

2. It's always easy to forgive other people.   Yes No

3. Zacchaeus was sorry that he stole money.   Yes No

4. Jesus forgave Zacchaeus.   Yes No

5. The Holy Spirit helps us to live in peace.   Yes No

To the Teacher: This activity follows the Scripture story "Jesus Forgives."

19a   THIS IS OUR FAITH 1   Chapter 19   The Holy Spirit Gives Us Peace

231c Chapter Organizer

LOVE FREES US

God's love brings us into wholeness and holiness. This unconditional love is ever present to us, no more so than when we need forgiveness. Jesus has taught us that he came not for the just but for sinners, for all of us who know the pain of hurting others. We know this pain because we have been hurt ourselves.

Yet still, in moments of stress and anger and anguish, we hurt a fellow human being. If we are in touch with that deep center of ourselves where God dwells, then we can hear God's voice: "Make peace. Say you are sorry." And if the person we have hurt is in tune with the message of the Gospels, then he or she hears God's voice: "Make peace. Say that you forgive."

LOVE EMPOWERS US

Jesus left us a legacy of forgiveness. He had come to proclaim God's love for everyone. By his death, Jesus showed that God's love embraces and encompasses the totality of forgiveness.

In every appearance of the resurrected Lord recorded in Scripture, Jesus greeted the disciples with the words "Peace be with you." Jesus offers us peace in the gift of the Holy Spirit. This gift empowers us to forgive one another.

CHILDREN AND PEACEMAKING

Children have the experiences of being hurt and of retaliating in kind. Seven-year-olds can learn that they can choose to hurt or not to hurt. For those times when the children in your classroom choose wrongly, you can assure them that all people make wrong choices at times but that God understands this and loves them even when they make mistakes.

Help the children learn to seek forgiveness by being forgiving yourself. Help them learn to express sorrow by saying "I'm sorry" to them whenever you make an obvious mistake or have hurt someone inadvertently.

In Chapter 19, the story of Zacchaeus, the dishonest tax collector, helps the children understand that Jesus forgave anyone who was sorry. Help them learn that Jesus understands how difficult seeking or bestowing forgiveness is and that he sends the Holy Spirit to help them. Encourage the children to pray to the Spirit for forgiveness and for the courage to forgive.

Objective

This lesson helps the children understand that God is always ready to forgive them and wants them to forgive others.

Step 1/INTRODUCTION

Learning About Our Lives

Telling Stories About Making Up

Read aloud the question in the margin of page 232 and encourage volunteers to tell stories about times they have made up after hurting someone or after being hurt by someone. After each story, ask volunteers (the child who told the story may want to do this) to use their faces and bodies to show how they felt before and after making up. Compliment the children on their stories and their expressions.

Responding to a Poem

Direct the children's attention to "Staying Friends" on page 232. Invite the children to comment on the illustrations.

- Read the first verse and ask the children to find the clue in the illustration in the upper right corner as to what the boy might have wanted to win. (*A race perhaps. Answers will vary.*)

- Focus on the back to back postures and pouting faces of the children in the illustration to the left. Ask whether the children look as though they are friends. Discuss why the children are not friendly. (*The girl said the boy could not win the race and he became angry.*)

- Read the second verse to find out what other unfriendly thing happened. (*The boy walked away, making matters even worse.*)

- Discuss the feelings the boy had. (*He was sad and missed his friend.*)

- Ask the children how they think the girl felt. (*Answers will vary.*)

- Discuss what the children in the poem did to make up. (*The children acted friendly. One gave a gift, and the other acted friendly upon receiving it.*)

232

19 The Holy Spirit Gives Us Peace

Staying Friends

My friend told me I could not win
When I thought I could.
So then I did not try as hard
As I usually would.

I told her I was mad at her,
And then I walked away.
But now I'm feeling very sad.
I miss her when I play.

Sometimes we hurt each other,
Not really meaning to.
But we can always make things right
By the kind things that we do.

What are some ways to make up and be at peace after hurting someone or being hurt?

232 Doctrine

🍎 Teaching Tips

When teaching about forgiveness, ask the children to raise their hands if they have ever been hurt. (Raise your hand, too.) Then talk about the difference between being hurt physically and having hurt feelings. Help the children understand that having hurt feelings can hurt very much. Ask the children to share experiences of hurt feelings. Talk with the children about how they came to peace with the persons who hurt their feelings.

Focus on

Feelings According to Silver Burdett Ginn's *Fully Alive*, the following can be said about ways that young children can begin to manage their feelings. When discussing being hurt, children often mean that their feelings are hurt. Primary-grade children begin to describe their feelings and to understand that other people have feelings that may be different from their own. They also begin to distinguish between feelings and actions and that they cannot always act on their feelings alone. This information can help you guide discussions in a more meaningful way for the children.

God Forgives Us

God always wants to forgive us.
God's **forgiveness** brings us peace and happiness.
Jesus brings us God's forgiveness.

Activity

Jesus gives us the Spirit of peace.

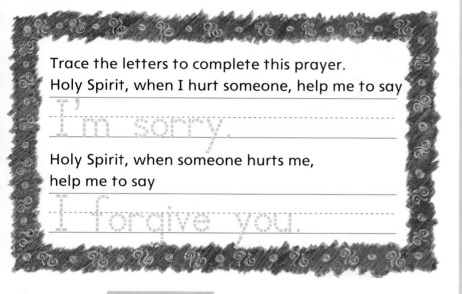

Trace the letters to complete this prayer.
Holy Spirit, when I hurt someone, help me to say

I'm sorry.

Holy Spirit, when someone hurts me,
help me to say

I forgive you.

New Word

✖ **forgiveness** Forgiveness means excusing or
✖   pardoning someone.
✖
✖

Doctrine 233

★ Enriching the Lesson ★

Pray this litany with the children.
Leader: Spirit of peace, sometimes we hurt other people.
Response: Come, Holy Spirit, give us peace.
Leader: When we hurt others, we want to say that we are sorry. Help us do that.
Response
Leader: Spirit of peace, sometimes people hurt our feelings.
Response
Leader: When other people hurt our feelings we want to forgive them. Help us do that.
Response

★ Enriching the Lesson ★

Make prayer cards, using the prayer on page 233. Print the prayer on a piece of paper and duplicate a copy for each child. Invite the children to decorate the cards with all the colors and symbols that make them think of the help the Holy Spirit has given them. Help the children tape the prayers inside their desks or notebooks. Remind the children to say their prayer to the Holy Spirit whenever they make someone feel bad or whenever someone makes them feel bad.

Step 2/DEVELOPMENT

Learning About Our Faith

Finding Someone Who Will Help

Read aloud "God Forgives Us" at the top of page 233. Ask the children to find and circle the words *forgive* and *forgiveness* in the text. Next, ask them to circle the words *Spirit of peace*. Talk to the children about how Jesus is always ready to forgive us and how wonderful this is. Tell them that Jesus not only forgives us but gives us the Spirit to help us forgive those who have hurt us and to ask for forgiveness from those we have hurt.

Reviewing the Vocabulary

Point to the New Word section on page 233. Ask the children to repeat the word *forgiveness* and its definition.

Step 3/CONCLUSION

Learning How to Live Our Faith

Completing a Prayer

Direct the children to the activity on page 233. Read the directions and invite the children to trace over the letters to complete a prayer to the Holy Spirit. Pray it out loud with them.

Dramatizing Ways to Respond to Hurt and Anger

To help the children become aware that they can choose to forgive and to ask forgiveness, discuss the following situations with them and invite volunteers to act out each situation. Ask the volunteers to show how they would respond.

- Someone bumps into you in the store.
- A friend insults you because he or she is angry about something you did.
- You tell a lie about someone and hurt his or her feelings.
- A friend will not let you play when he or she is playing with someone else.

Gathering for Prayer

Ask the children to bring their religion books (or prayer cards—see Enriching the Lesson) with them to the prayer area. When they are quiet, invite them to hold up their books (or prayer cards) and to pray the prayer they completed on page 233.

DAY 2
SCRIPTURE

Objective

This lesson helps the children learn about Jesus' love, compassion, and readiness to forgive.

Step 1/INTRODUCTION

Learning About Our Lives

Reviewing Day 1

Invite the children to talk about times they have been hurt or have hurt others. Then ask them who can help them forgive and ask for forgiveness. If no one mentions the Holy Spirit, tell the children that they can always pray to the Holy Spirit for help in seeking forgiveness and in forgiving. Finally, announce that today they are going to hear a Bible story about a time when Jesus forgave someone.

Step 2/DEVELOPMENT

Learning About Our Faith

Listening to a Bible Story

Encourage the children to look at the picture on pages 234–235 while you read aloud "Jesus Forgives." Read the story with great feeling, gesturing as you read. Emphasize the dialogue and, if possible, use different voices for Jesus and for Zacchaeus. In reading the story focus on Jesus' compassion, love, and readiness to forgive.

Discussing the Bible Story

To help the children understand the story, ask questions like the following.

- How did Zacchaeus hurt others? (*He stole from them.*)

- Why did he do this? (*So that he could be rich*)

- Why did Zacchaeus climb a tree? (*He was short, and he wanted to see Jesus.*)

- What did Jesus say to Zacchaeus? (*Come down, Zacchaeus. Take me to your house.*)

- Why were some people angry with Jesus? (*They thought Jesus should not be nice to someone who stole from others.*)

- What did Zacchaeus tell Jesus? (*I'll give back all I stole. I'm very sorry.*)

234

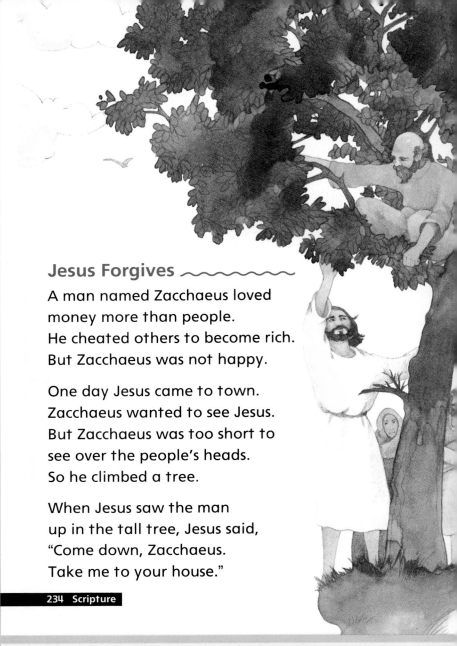

Jesus Forgives

A man named Zacchaeus loved money more than people.
He cheated others to become rich.
But Zacchaeus was not happy.

One day Jesus came to town.
Zacchaeus wanted to see Jesus.
But Zacchaeus was too short to see over the people's heads.
So he climbed a tree.

When Jesus saw the man up in the tall tree, Jesus said, "Come down, Zacchaeus. Take me to your house."

234 Scripture

Teaching Tips

When teaching about forgiveness, recall The Lord's Prayer. Pray it with the children and ask them to listen carefully to the words that have to do with forgiveness. After praying, print the following words on the chalkboard: *Forgive us our trespasses as we forgive those who trespass against us.* Recall the meaning of *trespass* (to hurt someone). Remind the children that in this prayer they ask God to forgive them in the same way that they forgive others.

Teaching Tips

Children are very literal minded. They tend to think of hurts as those things that are physically painful–a boo-boo cured by a bandage, the more colorful the better. To help expand their understanding, interchange the word *hurt* with the expressions "make someone feel bad" or "hurt someone's feelings."

This made some people angry because they thought Zacchaeus did bad things.
But Jesus was kind to Zacchaeus.

"I'll pay back all the money I took from people," Zacchaeus told Jesus. "I am very sorry."
"God's forgiveness has come to you, Zacchaeus," Jesus said. "Be at peace."

Based on Luke 19:1–10

Activity

1. Zacchaeus said, "I'll pay back all I took from people."
   What else did Zacchaeus say?
   Circle his words and print them here.

   I am very sorry.

2. Jesus told Zacchaeus, "God's forgiveness has come to you."
   What else did Jesus say?
   Circle Jesus' words and print them here.

   Be at peace.

Scripture 235

CURRICULUM CONNECTION

Language Arts Invite the children to dramatize the story of Zacchaeus. Have volunteers take the parts of Jesus, Zacchaeus, and the townspeople. Provide a few moments for the children to reread the story and suggest that they use a chair or a desk as the tree. Explain to the children that they can make up more dialogue for the story. Invite the rest of the children to be part of the crowd of people.

Teaching Tips

When teaching the Bible story, you might compare Zacchaeus to a person in the children's neighborhood who is left out by others because of something he or she has done to anger them. Recall that Christians are followers of Jesus. Ask what Jesus might do in such a neighborhood situation. Stress that Jesus would do the same thing he did for Zacchaeus. He would forgive the person because Jesus loves him or her.

- What did Jesus do? (*He forgave Zacchaeus.*)
- Why do you think Jesus did this? (*Jesus loves us all and is always ready to forgive us.*)

In this discussion, emphasize that Jesus is always ready to forgive, but we must be sorry.

Step 3/CONCLUSION

Learning How to Live Our Faith

Completing an Activity

Direct the children's attention to the activity at the bottom of page 235. Read number 1 with the children and encourage them to find, to circle the words Zacchaeus said, and to print them on the line provided. Next, read number 2 and have the children circle Jesus' words and write them on the appropriate line.

Discussing Hurt and Angry Feelings

Give volunteers magazine and newspaper pictures of people who look hurt or who look angry with one another. Using questions like the following, invite volunteers to describe the feelings of the people in their pictures.

- How do you think this person feels? (*Bad, unhappy, sad, and other emotions*)
- Why might this person be hurt? angry? (*Answers will vary.*)
- Have you ever felt this way? What did you want to happen so that you would not feel hurt? angry? (*Answers will vary.*)
- What might the person in the picture need to be happier? (*Perhaps the person needs forgiveness, or to be friends with someone he or she had an argument with.*)

Gathering for Prayer

Have the children bring their magazine and newspaper pictures to the prayer area. When they are quiet, teach them the following response: *Spirit of God, please help us to act like Jesus.* Encourage the children to share with God and their classmates brief stories about their magazine or newspaper pictures. After each story, encourage the children to pray the response.

DAY 3
DOCTRINE

Objective
This lesson helps the children learn to use words of forgiveness and sorrow.

Step 1/INTRODUCTION
Learning About Our Lives

Reviewing Day 2
Invite the children to retell the story of Jesus and Zacchaeus. Ask the children what words Zacchaeus used to show that he was sorry for stealing. Ask what words Jesus used to show that he forgave Zacchaeus.

Completing a Forgiveness Activity
Direct the children to the activity at the top of page 236. Encourage the children to circle all the sentences they use when they make up with someone they have hurt.

Next, encourage the children to share their reasons for circling some of the sentences and for not circling others. Talk about why some of the sentences would bring peace, while other sentences could not do so.

Step 2/DEVELOPMENT
Learning About Our Faith

Learning that the Spirit Helps
Read aloud "Come, Spirit of God" on page 236. Talk to the children about the ideas that Jesus gave us the Holy Spirit to help us make up. Pray the prayer with the class.

Completing an Activity
Have the children look at the two illustrations on page 237. Read the directions to the activity and encourage the children to tell what they think will happen next between the people in the pictures. Stress that the people can choose to make peace and that the Holy Spirit will help them do that. Elicit from the children the words the people might use to make up.

236

 Activity

Circle all the words that you might use to make up with someone you have hurt.

> "I'm sorry."
>
> "You're mean."
>
> "I didn't mean to hurt you."
>
> "I'll try never to do that again."
>
> "I don't like you."
>
> "Please forgive me."
>
> "I'll never play with you again!"
>
> "You will always be my friend."

Come, Spirit of God
Sometimes we hurt others.
Sometimes they hurt us.
Jesus gives us the gift of the Holy Spirit.
We can ask the Holy Spirit to help us make up.
We can be at peace with others.

🍎 Teaching Tips

When teaching this lesson, it would be good to make a few distinctions for the children. Help the children understand that sometimes people hurt others without meaning to and that sometimes they hurt others on purpose. Ask for volunteers to give examples of both and to tell stories about accidental hurting and purposeful hurting. Explain that when people hurt them, they can make the decision to hurt back or to forgive. Tell the children that the Holy Spirit will help them forgive.

Focus on
Fruits of the Spirit The *Catechism of the Catholic Church* states, "The *fruits* of the Spirit are perfections that the Holy Spirit forms in us as the first fruits of eternal glory. The tradition of the Church lists twelve of them: 'charity, joy, peace, patience, kindness, goodness, generosity, gentleness, faithfulness, modesty, self-control, chastity'" (#1832).

Activity

Look at the pictures.
Tell a story about them.
What do you think
is happening?
What do you think
will happen next?

How can the Holy Spirit
help these people?
How can the people
make up and be at peace?

We Believe

Jesus brings us God's
forgiveness and peace.
Jesus gives us the
Holy Spirit to help
us live peacefully
together.

Doctrine 237

Presenting the Doctrine

Read aloud the We Believe section on page 237, which summarizes the chapter's doctrine. Ask the children to repeat the two sentences after you.

Step 3/CONCLUSION

Learning How to Live Our Faith

Role-Playing Forgiveness

Ask for volunteers to role-play the following situations and to make up their own dialogue and happy endings.

■ Peggy asks Fran to play with her. Fran says she can't because she has to visit her grandmother. But when Peggy walks past Fran's house, she sees Fran playing with another friend.

■ Tom's brother and sister are arguing about who will be first in the game. Tom's dad comes into the room and tells them to put the game away because they are arguing.

After the role-plays have been presented, ask the children to identify some of the dialogue they thought helped the people make peace.

Making a Peace Chain

Direct the children's attention back to the sentences they circled at the top of page 236. Then give each child one or two strips of colored construction paper. Invite the children to choose one of the peacemaking sentences from page 236 and to print it on their construction-paper strips. When the children have completed their work, help the children staple or paste all their strips together to make paper chains.

Praying with the Peace Chain

Gather the children in the prayer area. Have them stand in a circle, holding their peace chain. Ask the children to close their eyes and to think of things they have done for which they are sorry. After a minute or two, encourage the children to open their eyes and say, "I am sorry." Then ask all the children to respond with "I forgive you."

DAY 4
MORALITY/PRAYER

Objective

This lesson helps the children discover that they can be peacemakers.

Step 1/INTRODUCTION

Learning About Our Lives

Sharing Experiences of Hurt or Anger

Recall some of the language we can use to ask for forgiveness and to make up with our friends and family.

Next, ask the children who can help them make peace. If no one mentions the Holy Spirit, do so.

Reading Peacemaking Stories

Direct the children's attention to the activity on page 238. Read the sentence under the heading and then invite the children to look at the words and actions in the border and to explain how these words and actions bring peace when people are hurt.

Next, read the three stories on page 238. After reading the question at the end of each paragraph, invite volunteers to tell how the main characters in the stories can make peace with the persons they have hurt.

Dramatizing the Peacemaking Stories

Invite volunteers to act out the peacemaking stories. Encourage them to show how the main character in each story hurts someone and then makes peace. Suggest that they refer to the sentences they have learned about asking for forgiveness and making up. Tell the children that sometimes our actions show that we want to make up and be at peace.

Step 2/DEVELOPMENT

Learning About Our Faith

Studying a Photograph

Direct the children's attention to the photograph at the top of page 239. Invite their comments on what is taking place between the people in the picture. Ask if they have ever seen this happen before. Help them remember that this is the Sign of Peace that Catholics give one another at Mass.

238

Activity

Circle what to say and do to make peace.

Margaret stole Luis' cupcake.
Now Luis is hungry.
What can Margaret do to make peace?

"I'm sorry I lied."

Sam said Lein took his spelling paper.
Then Sam found his paper in his desk.
What can Sam do to make peace?

"Please take my snack."

Amy pushed Johnny on the playground.
Johnny dropped his candy in the sand.
What can Amy do to make peace?

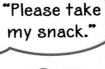

HUG

"Let's be friends again."

"Forgive me."

"Will you play with me?"

"Here's my piece of candy."

Shake Hands

Invite your friend to your house.

238 Morality

Teaching Tips

When teaching the Sign of Peace explain that since the Mass is a time of love and sharing, Catholics at Mass want to be at peace with God, themselves, and each other. Using the picture on page 239, point out that during the Eucharist the priest invites the people to share a sign of peace. Tell the children that they can use many gestures to show peace: they can shake hands, hug, kiss, or greet others in a happy and peaceful way. Stress that when we do these things we are praying that God's peace be with the people.

A Sign of Peace

At Mass, Catholics give one
another a sign of peace.
We ask the Holy Spirit to help
make us peacemakers.
We ask the Spirit of God
to help us forgive.
We ask the Holy Spirit
to help us say, "I'm sorry."

Activity

Make a storybook about a child
who hurts someone and is forgiven.
Write the title of your book here.

_____
- -
_____
_____
- -
_____

Prayer 239

Focus on

The Sign of Peace The *Sacramentary* which is the official Mass book used by the priest during the celebration of the Eucharist does not describe the sign of peace given by the community members to each other. Rather it says to exchange a sign of peace according to local custom. Community members may shake hands, hug, or wish each other peace in a variety of ways. All are acceptable.

Reading the Text

Read aloud "A Sign of Peace" on page 239. Direct the children's attention to the photo and explain that we exchange a sign of peace at Mass. Teach the children the sign of peace by having each child turn to his or her neighbor and shake hands, saying, "The Peace of Christ be with you." If in your parish, you express this exchange of peace differently, teach it that way. Practice it several times with the children.

Read the next paragraph and talk to the children about the peace God wants us to have in our every day life.

Step 3/CONCLUSION

Learning How to Live Our Faith

Completing an Activity

Read the directions for the activity at the bottom of page 239. Then distribute three sheets of drawing paper (folded in half) to each child. To help the children get started on their storybooks, invite volunteers to tell stories about someone hurting someone else and then making peace. When all the children have an idea for a story, encourage them to print and draw their stories in their storybooks and to create covers for them.

Gathering for Prayer

After the children have completed their storybooks, ask them to bring them to the prayer area. Invite volunteers to read their peacemaking stories to God. When they have shared their stories, encourage the children to exchange a sign of peace with those on either side of them.

Collect the booklets for use on Day 5.

239

Objective

This lesson gives the children an opportunity to pray to be peacemakers.

Reading the Text

Direct the children's attention to page 240. Read aloud "Praying for Peace." Emphasize that today they are going to think about what makes peace and pray to the Holy Spirit for peace.

Ask the following questions to help the children reflect on the prayer.

- What important thought can you remember whenever you are upset because someone has hurt you? (*God made me special.*)

- To make peace with others, what important thought must you remember about them? (*They are special, too.*)

Making Pennants

On a sheet of 11 x 17 inch construction paper, outline a triangle to be used as a pennant. Draw the word *peace* in boxed letters in the center of the triangular shape. Give each child a duplicated copy and invite them to color in the word. Then distribute a stick or a new unsharpened pencil to each child and demonstrate curling the larger end of the pennant around it. Help the children secure their pennant to the stick with tape or a staple.

Gathering to Pray

Invite the children to process to the prayer area, waving their peace pennants. They may sing a peace song if you wish. When the children are gathered, ask them to repeat the prayer on page 240 after you. When they have completed the prayer, ask them to describe how we can be gentle to others. Then close the session with a song or instrumental that the children can move to as they process back to their seats, waving their pennants.

Praying for Peace

The Holy Spirit helps us make peace. We can pray to be children of peace.

Dear God,
You made me special.
Help me remember that when someone hurts me, I am your special child.
Fill my heart with your peace.

Show me that other people are special, too.
Help me show them your gentle peace.
Amen.

240 Prayer

Praying for Peace This prayer skill invites the children to pray for peace. (1) Being a peacemaker is a day-by-day, one-step-at-a-time process that begins with a respect for self based on God's unique creation of each of us. (2) We pray to respect others, recalling that God made each of these people special, too. When we respect others, cooperation, friendship, and peace can develop. (3) As children of peace, we ask the Spirit to help us spread peace—specifically by our gentleness.

CURRICULUM CONNECTION

Music Teach the children a song to sing as they process to the prayer corner. Use the following words to the melody "If You're Happy and You Know It."

If you're sorry and you know it,
Say the words, (I'm sorry.)
If you're sorry and you know it,
Say the words, (I'm sorry.)
If you're sorry and you know it,
Then your face will surely show it.
If you're sorry and you know it,
Say the words, (I'm sorry.)

Chapter Review

We can make peace with others.
Put the pictures in 1, 2, and 3 order to show forgiveness.

1. Whom did Jesus give us to help live peacefully together?

the Holy Spirit

2. What word means to excuse or pardon?

forgive

3. Talk about what the Holy Spirit can help us do after we hurt someone or after someone hurts us.

> Forgive others
> the way
> the Lord
> forgives you.
> **Based on Colossians 3:13**

Review 241

Using the Peace Booklets to Review

Distribute the booklets the children made on Day 4. Use these storybooks to review the learning of Chapter 19. Invite the children to share their stories with their classmates. After each sharing, talk about how the Holy Spirit helps people when they want to make peace. Stress that the Holy Spirit helps them to use the words of sorrow or forgiveness.

Finally, encourage the children to take their booklets home, post them in a place they notice each day, and use them as reminders that they can be peacemakers.

Completing an Activity

Use the activity on page 241 to review the learning of Chapter 19. Read the text at the top of the page. Then encourage the children to put the three pictures in the proper sequence to tell a story about peacemaking. Next, invite volunteers to use the pictures to tell a peacemaking story.

Answering the Questions

Read aloud the first two questions and ask volunteers to respond. Direct the children to print the answers in their texts. Encourage all the children to participate in the discussion of the third question. Be supportive of each child who responds.

Reading the Scripture Verse

Ask the children to read the Scripture verse after you. Reflecting on the word of God is a good way to end the lesson. If you wish, you may have the children memorize this verse.

🍎 Teaching Tips

To help the children understand that Catholics try to be peacemakers, plan a class Mass. If possible, have your pastor work with you in preparing a special children's liturgy that stresses peacemaking. Use the hymns the children have already learned and provide opportunities for the children to be as involved as possible, such as processing to the altar, responding to the prayers, singing, reading from *The Children's Lectionary*, bringing up the offertory gifts, sitting in the front of the church, and exchanging the sign of peace.

20 The Holy Spirit Gives Us Joy

Objectives

To help the Children

- Understand that the Holy Spirit helps them to be joyful and happy.
- Discover that because Jesus is with them, the Spirit of joy is too.
- Deepen their understanding that the Holy Spirit can turn sadness into joy.
- Recognize that they can share the Spirit of joy with others.
- Learn the Glory Be to the Father and review the chapter.

Chapter Outline

	Step 1 Learning About Our Lives	Step 2 Learning About Our Faith	Step 3 Learning How to Live Our Faith
Day 1	■ Review Chapters 17–19. ■ Introduce Chapter 20. ■ Use the pictures. ■ Complete an activity. *ABOUT 12 MINUTES*	■ Read the text. ■ Present the doctrine. *ABOUT 8 MINUTES*	■ Draw pictures of joy. ■ Create a bulletin board. ■ Use the bulletin board for prayer. *ABOUT 10 MINUTES*
Day 2	■ Talk about fishing/picnicking. ■ Study the illustrations. *ABOUT 5 MINUTES*	■ Review the vocabulary. ■ Listen to the Bible story. ■ Discuss the Bible story. ■ Dramatize the Bible story. *ABOUT 15 MINUTES*	■ Discuss the learning from the Bible story. ■ Gather for prayer. *ABOUT 10 MINUTES*
Day 3	■ Respond to a joyful photograph. ■ Read a poem about happiness. ■ Act out the poem. *ABOUT 10 MINUTES*	■ Learn how the Spirit turns sadness into joy. ■ Complete an activity. *ABOUT 10 MINUTES*	■ Make story mobiles. ■ Gather for prayer. *ABOUT 10 MINUTES*
Day 4	■ Review the learning of Day 3. *ABOUT 5 MINUTES*	■ Use the text. ■ Read a Bible story. ■ Complete an activity. *ABOUT 13 MINUTES*	■ Think about being happy. ■ Draw a picture. ■ Gather for prayer. *ABOUT 12 MINUTES*

Day 5   **Prayer**   Work with the prayer skill; trace the letters of a prayer; and pray the Glory Be.
          Review   Use the bulletin board from Day 1 to review the learning of Chapter 20; complete an activity; answer the questions; and read the Scripture verse.

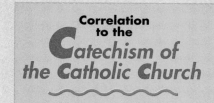

Correlation
to the
**Catechism of
the Catholic Church**

Paragraphs
736, 1832

Plan Ahead ~~~~~~~~

	Preparing Your Class	**Materials Needed**
Day 1	For Step 3, cut out the letters for *The Holy Spirit, help us be happy and joyful* and prepare a space for a bulletin board display.	■ drawing paper ■ empty bulletin board ■ cut-out letters /staples ■ tagboard
Day 2	Read the lesson plan before teaching the lesson. If you plan to use any Teaching Option, make preparations and collect materials.	
Day 3	For Step 1, consider gestures and body movements the children might use for the poem on page 246.	
Day 4	Read the lesson plan before teaching the lesson. If you plan to use any Teaching Option, make preparations and collect materials.	■ drawing paper
Day 5	For the prayer, be prepared to tell the children about all the gifts the Holy Spirit has given you and about how these gifts help you act like Jesus.	■ bulletin board from Day 1

Additional Resources

As you plan this chapter, consider using the following materials from The Resourceful Teacher Package.

■ *Classroom Activity Sheets 20* and *20 a*

■ *Family Activity Sheets 20* and *20a*

■ *Chapter 20 Test*

■ *Prayers for Every Day*

■ *Projects: Grade 1*

In preparing the children for the Sunday readings, you may wish to use Silver Burdett Ginn's *Getting Ready for Sunday* student and teacher materials.

BOOKS FOR THE JOURNEY

Something Special for Me. Vera B. Williams. William Morrow, 1983. The joy of finally finding the perfect thing for your birthday—something that will also bring joy to others.

Ty's One-Man Band. Mildred Pitts Walker. Scholastic, 1984. The story of a man who uses the simplest of instruments to bring music and joy to a village.

MORE BOOKS FOR THE JOURNEY

Experience Jesus Today. "On the Lake Shore," pages 214-215. Charles Singer & Albert Hari. Oregon Catholic Press, 1993. The story of the seashore breakfast retold.

Ben's Trumpet. Rachel Isadora. Greenwillow Books, 1979. A trumpeter sees in a child what others miss and gives him what he needs.

REDUCED CLASSROOM ACTIVITIES

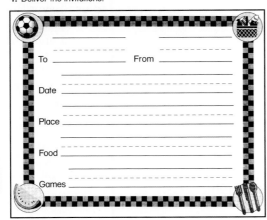

Name

The Holy Spirit Gives Us Joy

The Holy Spirit helps us make others happy.

1. Plan a picnic for your family and friends.
2. Fill out the invitation below.
3. Cut along the heavy black lines.
4. Deliver the invitations.

To _____ From _____

Date _____

Place _____

Food _____

Games _____

To the Teacher: This activity follows the Scripture story "A Dark Night and a Bright Morning."

Chapter 20   The Holy Spirit Gives Us Joy   THIS IS OUR FAITH 1   **20**

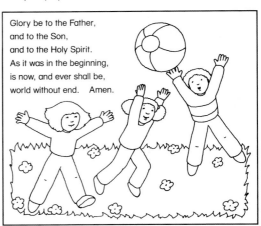

Name

A Prayer of Catholic Christians

1. Color the picture.
2. Cut along the heavy black lines.
3. Put your prayer picture where you will see it every day.
4. Say the prayer often.

Glory be to the Father,
and to the Son,
and to the Holy Spirit.
As it was in the beginning,
is now, and ever shall be,
world without end.   Amen.

To the Teacher: This activity reinforces the words of the Glory Be to the Father prayer.

20a   THIS IS OUR FAITH 1   Chapter 20   The Holy Spirit Gives Us Joy

CHRISTIAN JOY

God calls Christians to be joyful. Our joy comes from our confidence in God's promises of unconditional love and faithfulness. As we undertake the journey of life, we encounter suffering, pain, fear, and hurt—all the daily experiences that wear away at our spirits. But despite this, we can remain hopeful, for Jesus came to give us the gift of abundant life. The Holy Spirit can make us whole and holy, helping us act like Jesus.

As Jesus' compassion and empathy, friendliness and forgiveness, understanding and joy grow within us, we become the whole and holy persons whom God wills us to be. If we experience life as a journey that leads to good, then we learn to trust the power of God's love. We learn to embrace the example Jesus has set for us. We learn to rejoice in the presence of God's Spirit.

JESUS' JOY

Because of his joyous response to God and to others, Jesus attracted people to himself. The writer of John's Gospel described Jesus as hoping that his joy may be ours and that our joy may be complete (Based on John 15:11). After God raised him from the dead, Jesus shared the Holy Spirit— that Spirit of love that flows between God the Father and Jesus, the Son of God—with his Apostles. The Spirit's presence filled them with joy. In fact, the people of Jerusalem and Galilee who saw Jesus' disciples after he ascended to the love of his Father were quick to note the joyfulness of the early Christians.

We too can experience joy, especially in our relationships. The more we share joy, the more fully we receive it. The gift of the Holy Spirit is a gift that grows and deepens within us. As the Spirit expands within us, through our loving actions, we become more like Jesus.

CHILDHOOD JOY

Most children are joyful and find delight in simple experiences. You need to appreciate their natural playfulness and understand that it can enhance their learning, for play is childhood's avenue of self-discovery and exploration. Whenever possible, allow the children to respond playfully to what you are teaching. In this way, you will make learning in your classroom more enjoyable and meaningful.

Chapter 20 can leave the children with a joyful feeling of having learned what being a friend of Jesus means. If the children come to a fuller realization that God longs for their life to be good and their days happy, they will have come a long way in developing a philosophy that will see them through all the days of their life.

DAY 1
DOCTRINE

Objective
This lesson helps the children understand that the Holy Spirit helps them to be joyful and happy.

Step 1/INTRODUCTION

Learning About Our Lives

Reviewing Chapters 17–19
To review the unit thus far, ask the children to open their books to Unit 5 beginning on page 211, and find the following Scripture stories.

- Find the story of the time that Jesus said, "Peace be with you. Receive the Holy Spirit" (*Pages 214–215*).
- Find the picture of the time that Jesus said to his friends, "Why are you afraid? I am with you" (*Pages 223–224*).
- Find the picture of the story in which Jesus said, "God's forgiveness has come to you. Be at Peace" (*Pages 234–235*).

Introducing Chapter 20
Read aloud the question in the margin of page 242. Encourage volunteers to tell stories about their favorite fun times.

or...

Tell the children you are going to read a list of things that go either with being joyous and having fun or with not being particularly happy. Instruct the children to stand up when they hear a joyous thing and to sit down when they hear something that is not fun. Ask them to sit down to begin the game. Then read the following activities: *hearing music, dancing, fighting with your friends, sharing your toys, watching a favorite TV show, laughing, crying, spilling your milk, eating your favorite meal, and getting mail.*

Using the Pictures
Ask a volunteer to read aloud the paragraph under the title "Joy! Joy! Joy!" Direct the children's attention to the pictures on pages 242–243. Ask the class what the children in the photographs are doing (*Jumping rope, riding cars, playing jacks, leapfrog, cat's cradle, and a circle game*) Then ask the question in the

242

20 The Holy Spirit Gives Us Joy

Joy! Joy! Joy!
Make up stories about the children in the pictures.
What are they doing to be happy?

What are your favorite fun times?

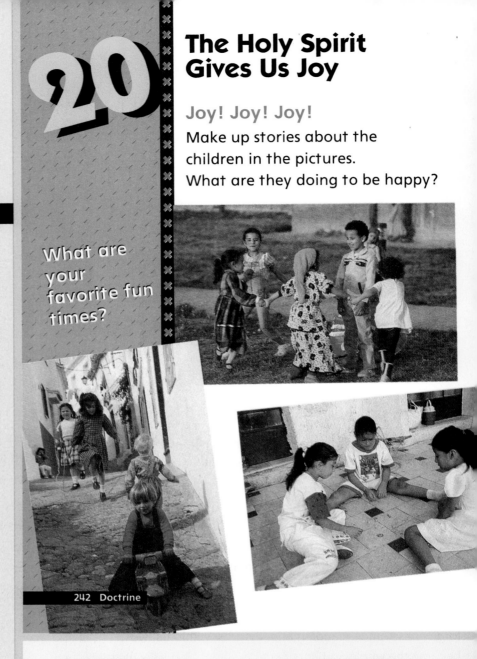

242 Doctrine

Cultural Awareness
Study the pictures on pages 242 and 243. Ask the children if they have ever played one or more of the games illustrated in the photographs. Help them appreciate that children from other countries play many of the same games they do.

Teaching Tips
While teaching this lesson, tell the children that there are people whose entire lives reflect the Spirit of joy and happiness. Refer the children to "About the Saints" in the Amen section of their text. For example, Saint Francis of Assisi lived a life of joy. Point out that he always tried to make others happy because he was such a joyous person. Or tell the story of Saint Nicholas who also enjoyed making others happy.

Activity

Who helps to make you happy?
What helps to make you happy?
Print the names of the people and
things that make you happy here.

_____
- -
_____
- -
_____

Come, Spirit of Joy

God wants us to be happy.
So Jesus gives us the gift of
the Holy Spirit.
The Holy Spirit is with us to help
us be happy and joyful.

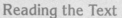

We Believe

God wants us to be
happy.
Jesus gives us the
Holy Spirit.
The Holy Spirit
comes to give us
joy.

Doctrine 243

---

paragraph under the title. Invite volunteers to
tell stories about the pictures and ask them
what feelings the children in the pictures might
have. Emphasize happiness and joy.

Completing an Activity

Direct the children's attention to the activity on
page 243. Read the directions for the activity
and encourage volunteers to share the answers.

Step 2/DEVELOPMENT

Learning About Our Faith

Reading the Text

Ask the children to read "Come, Spirit of Joy"
on page 243 to see what Jesus does to help
make us happy. (Jesus gives us the gift of the
Holy Spirit to help us be happy and joyful.)

Presenting the Doctrine

Read aloud the We Believe section on page
243, which summarizes the chapter's doctrine.
Ask the children to repeat the three sentences
after you.

Step 3/CONCLUSION

Learning How to Live Our Faith

Drawing Pictures of Joy

Distribute drawing paper and invite the children
to draw pictures that show themselves having
fun and being joyful.

Creating a Bulletin Board

Invite the children to gather with their drawings
around an empty bulletin board and pin up the
pictures together with letters for the following
sentence: *The Holy Spirit helps us to be happy
and joyful.* Talk about how the sentence applies
to their drawings.

Using the Bulletin Board for Prayer

Gather the children around the bulletin board
and teach the following response: *Come, Spirit
of joy.* Invite volunteers to explain their
drawings to the group and to God. After each
volunteer shares, invite the children's
responses.

CURRICULUM CONNECTION

Language Arts   Print these words
and phrases on flash cards: *joy, the
Holy Spirit, happiness, good friends,
sharing joy.* Turn them blank side out
and put them on the chalkboard
ledge. Invite the children to choose a
card and use the words in a sentence.

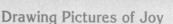

Teaching Tips

Throughout Chapter 20, you might
wish to begin and end each of the
five lessons by inviting the children to
sing "If You're Happy and You Know
It." Consider adding a different action
each day:

Day 1: clap your hands
Day 2: wink your eyes
Day 3: tap your feet
Day 4: turn around
Day 5: jump for joy

Objective

This lesson helps the children discover that because Jesus is always with them the Holy Spirit, who brings joy into their lives, is always with them.

Step 1/INTRODUCTION

Learning About Our Lives

Talking About Fishing or Picnicking

To prepare the children for today's Bible story, ask them to talk about any fishing or picnicking they have done. Then invite volunteers to pantomime getting into a fishing boat, baiting the line, tossing the line in the water, feeling the tug of a fish, pulling in the fish, and holding it up for everyone to admire.

Studying the Illustrations

Then invite the children to look at the illustrations on pages 244–245 and ask them if they see any clues that people were fishing. (The nets, the fish cooking on the stones)

Tell the children that the Bible story on these pages is about a time Jesus' friends went fishing.

Step 2/DEVELOPMENT

Learning About Our Faith

Reviewing the Vocabulary

Point to the New Word section on page 245. Ask the children to repeat the word *Galilee* and the definition after you.

Listening to a Bible Story

Encourage the children to look at the pictures on pages 244 and 245 while a volunteer (a good oral reader) reads aloud "A Dark Night and a Bright Morning."

Discussing the Bible Story

To help the children understand the story, ask questions like the following.

- Why are the friends of Jesus so sad at the beginning of the story? (*They had fished all night and caught nothing.*)

244

A Dark Night and a Bright Morning

Jesus' friends fished all night on the Sea of **Galilee**.
They caught nothing.
They were tired and sad.

In the morning a man on the shore called out to them,
"Try letting your net down on the right side of the boat."

They did what the man said,
and their net was filled with fish!
Their sadness turned to joy.

244 Scripture

CURRICULUM CONNECTION

Language Arts Use the story as a dramatic reading with audience participation. Choose five volunteers to read a paragraph each. The rest of the children can dramatize the story in their seats. For example, suggest the following actions to act out key phrases.

- Fished all night: cast and drag pretend nets
- Caught nothing: shrug and extend their hands in a "what can I tell you" gesture
- Were tired and sad: sigh; flop in their seats with tired expressions

Teaching Tips

When doing a dramatic reading with audience participation, it is not necessary to have the audience dramatize the entire reading. The purpose of the participation for the first graders is to develop a fresh way of hearing a story and to allow all the children to take part. It adds interest without much preparation. While it enhances the reading of the story, it is not meant to be a production.

"It's Jesus!" John shouted with joy.
Peter was so happy that he dived
into the lake and swam to Jesus.

Jesus was on the beach cooking
breakfast for his friends.
They ate bread and fish.
They were so glad to see Jesus.
They enjoyed the food and were
happy being together.

Based on John 21:1–13

Activity

Write one thing that the friends of Jesus did that you
would like to do, too.

_____

- -

_____

New Word

Galilee   Galilee is the area where Jesus
grew up.

Scripture   245

★ ★ ★ Enriching the Lesson ★ ★

Make a joy box. Decorate a shoe
box and its lid. Invite the children to
brainstorm ways they can bring joy
to others. For example, *bring joy to
our school friends by making a
beautiful mural for the hallway, to our
parents by learning a new song to
sing for them, to another class by
inviting them to our dramatization of
a Bible story.* Print these ideas and
others on slips of paper and place
them in the joy box. From time to
time, draw a suggestion from the box
and help the children work together
to follow it.

- What did the man on the shore tell them to
do? (*Let their nets down on the right side of
the boat*)
- Who was the man on shore? (*Jesus*)
- Who recognized him? (*John*)
- What did Peter do to show his happiness?
(*He swam to shore to meet Jesus.*)
- What did Jesus do for his friends when they
came to the shore? (*He cooked bread and
fish.*)
- How do you think Jesus and his friends felt
as they ate breakfast together? (*Happy and
joyful*)
- How do you know that the Spirit of joy was
with the disciples? (*Answers will vary.*)

Explain to the children that the events in this
story happened after Jesus had died and rose
to new life. Stress that the friends of Jesus were
joyful because he was alive.

Dramatizing the Bible Story

Invite the children to role-play the Bible story.
Have volunteers take the parts of Jesus, Peter,
John, and the other disciples. (The remaining
children could represent the boat by joining
hands and sitting in a circle on the floor around
"the disciples.")

Step 3/CONCLUSION

Learning How to Live Our Faith

Discussing the Learning from the Story

Talk with the children about the message of the
Bible story. Emphasize the following points.

- Jesus wanted his friends and all the people
he met to be happy.
- Jesus gives us the Holy Spirit to help us be
happy.
- Jesus gives us the Holy Spirit so that we can
help others be happy, too.

Gathering for Prayer

Gather the children in the prayer area and teach
them the following response: *Thank you, Jesus,
for the Holy Spirit, who gives us joy.* Invite
volunteers, one by one, to tell God about
today's Bible story. After each volunteer
responds or adds to the story, invite the children
to pray their response.

Objective

This lesson helps the children deepen their understanding that the Holy Spirit can turn sadness into joy.

Step 1/INTRODUCTION

Learning About Our Lives

Responding to a Joyful Photograph

Talk about how the children in the photographs on page 246 must feel, stressing the feelings of happiness and joy. Talk about times the children have done things that are fun.

Reading a Poem About Happiness

Read aloud "Happy Times" on page 246 and relate the three stanzas of the poem to the children's lives. To help the children share their experiences, ask the following questions, all of which call for varied answers.

- When you walk outside, what do you see or hear that makes you happy?
- What are some happy things you have done with your family?
- What are some happy things you have done with your good friends?
- What games do you enjoy playing with your friends?

Acting Out the Poem

Divide the class into three groups. Assign each group one of the stanzas of the poem. Then encourage the children to gather in their groups and to brainstorm gestures and body movements they might use as you read their stanzas. Encourage them to practice their gestures.

When the three groups are ready, read each stanza of "Happy Times" and invite each group to add their gestures at the appropriate time.

246

Happy Times

When the sun is shining
And the birds begin to sing,
I like to take a walk outside
And think of happy things.

I think about my family
And the happy days we've spent,
Like the weekend we went camping
And forgot to bring the tent.

I think about my good friends
And the happy things we do,
Like games and races all for fun
And laughing under skies of blue.

CURRICULUM CONNECTION

Art Invite each child to make a cheerful bookmark to give joy to someone. Distribute 2 1/2" × 7" strips of posterboard and crayons or felt-tip markers. Encourage the children to draw smiling faces at the top of their posterboard and to print the following message on it: *Be joyful! God loves you.* Suggest that they put happy colors and symbols around their words. Then encourage the children to deliver their bookmarks as soon as possible.

Helping Others Be Happy

The Holy Spirit helps us live as
Jesus showed us.
Sometimes the Holy Spirit sends
someone to help us.
Sometimes we can be helpers.
The Holy Spirit helps us think of
ways to help others.

Activity

Here is a story of a girl
who needs help.
Mia is very sad.
She tries and tries
to tell time, but it is
too hard for her.
Johnny is good at
telling time.

In the clock, draw
how Johnny can help
Mia be happy.

Morality 247

Step 2/DEVELOPMENT

Learning About Our Faith

Learning How the Spirit Turns Sadness Into Joy

Read aloud the first paragraph of "Helping Others Be Happy" on page 247. Discuss the fact that people are sometimes upset because something is not going well in their lives. Tell the children that the Holy Spirit might ask us to be helpers to turn others' sadness into joy.

Completing an Activity

Direct the children's attention to the activity on page 247. Ask volunteers to identify what it is that upsets Mia. Focus the children's awareness on the cuckoo clock and have the children draw in it a way that Johnny might help Mia. Invite the children to share their solutions to Mia's problem.

Discuss with the children that the Holy Spirit helps us think of ways to help others.

Step 3/CONCLUSION

Learning How to Live Our Faith

Making a Story Mobile

Arrange the children in groups of three and ask them to think of a story about a child having a hard time, such as someone who lost her milk money, heard that a good friend is moving away, or does not know his addition facts. Each group should create a character who thinks of a way to help. Encourage the group to add conversation about the Holy Spirit. The children within each group should decide who will take the responsibility for the picture of the beginning of the story, of the middle, and of the ending. Help the children attach the drawings with string to a hanger to make the mobile.

Gathering for Prayer

Gather the children to pray and teach them the response: *Holy Spirit, guide me to help others.* Invite volunteers to tell the stories of their mobiles to God and the other children. After the volunteers are finished, encourage the children to pray the response.

Objective

This lesson helps the children recognize that they can share the Spirit of joy with others.

Step 1/INTRODUCTION

Learning About Our Lives

Reviewing the Learning of Day 3

To help the children remember that the Holy Spirit turns sadness into joy, ask them to stand and use facial expressions and body postures to answer the following questions. After the children use their bodies to show each action, stress that the Holy Spirit is with them.

■ How do you look when you are sad? happy?

■ How do you walk when you are sad? happy?

■ How do you sit when you are sad? happy?

Step 2/DEVELOPMENT

Learning About Our Faith

Using the Text

Direct the children's attention to the illustration on page 248. Invite a volunteer to read the directions on page 248. Discuss ideas of how Maria's classmates helped her to have a pleasant time at recess. Then have the children write their ideas on the line provided. Finally, ask the children if they think "Spreading Joy" is a good title for this section.

Reading a Bible Story

Direct the children's attention to the illustration on page 249. Tell the children that the woman's name is Martha and that Jesus is helping her to be happier. Ask the children to listen carefully to the story so that they can find out how Jesus is helping Martha be happier. Then read the story to the children and ask the following questions.

■ How did Martha and Mary feel in the story? (*They were happy to see Jesus.*)

■ What did Mary do to show her happiness. (*She sat down and talked to Jesus. She wanted to be with him.*)

■ What did Martha do in the story? (*She went out to get Jesus and his friends something to eat.*)

248

Spreading Joy

Maria has just come to America, and she cannot speak English. On her first day of school, Mrs. Gast taught the children to welcome her. "Bienvenido, Maria," they said.

Finally, it was time for recess. Mrs. Gast wondered, "How will Maria have fun playing with the children? She cannot understand them."

Activity

Write what the children can do at recess to help Maria be happy.

_____

_____

_____

_____

Who is always with us, helping us to live like Jesus?

the Holy Spirit

248 Morality

Cultural Awareness

Talk with the children about other children throughout the world and in their own country who suffer from hunger, sickness, poverty, homelessness, or abandonment. Talk with the children about how they would feel if they were hungry, sick, poor, homeless, or abandoned. Encourage the class to pray for the other children. Also, encourage the children to thank God each day for the happiness in their own lives.

Teaching Tips

When teaching this lesson, some children might be reticent about talking about their own happiness. To help them express themselves, invite the children to make three wishes. They might draw themselves with thought balloons on which they write their wishes. Or cut out thought–balloon shapes they can write their wishes on.

Jesus Spreads Joy

Jesus and some of his friends were out telling people the good news. They were very near to Martha and Mary's house.

Jesus stopped in to visit them. Martha and Mary were happy to see Jesus and his friends.

Everyone sat down and talked. Mary listened to Jesus. She was full of joy.

But Martha was busy cooking for the company. She wanted to be with Jesus, too. "Oh Martha come be with me," said Jesus.

Based on Luke 10:38–42

Activity

What do you think happened next? Act out the story and add your ending.

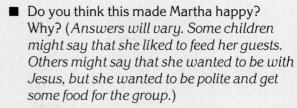

Teaching Tips

When predicting an ending to the story of Martha and Mary, the children might rely on the following clues. The title says Jesus spreads joy. This illustration hints at Jesus inviting the frazzled Martha to be with him. Also, the children, by now, have come to some conclusions about Jesus. Knowing that he wants us all to be happy, they can begin to predict his actions which are constantly kind and good.

Enriching the Lesson

To find ways for the children to spread joy, ask a local hospital or nursing home for the names of patients who have few visitors or little mail. Share these names with the children and invite them to make happy cards to share their joy with these people. If possible, arrange a time for the children to deliver their letters and drawings in person.

- Do you think this made Martha happy? Why? (*Answers will vary. Some children might say that she liked to feed her guests. Others might say that she wanted to be with Jesus, but she wanted to be polite and get some food for the group.*)
- Was Mary being polite by sitting and listening to Jesus instead of helping her sister? (*Yes, it is not nice to leave guests alone if you can help it.*)
- Who especially wanted Martha to enjoy herself? (*Jesus*)

Completing an Activity

Divide the class into groups of five and have the children act out an ending to the story. Before they begin to plan the ending, ask them what clues they have about how it might end.

Step 3/CONCLUSION

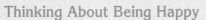

Learning How to Live Our Faith

Thinking About Being Happy

Tell the children that they might have heard the following words when something happy happened. Invite volunteers to share any stories of turning sadness into joy that these words remind them of.

- Thanks for sharing that with me.
- I'm proud to have you as my daughter/son.
- Telling the truth was a brave thing to do. That made me very happy.
- Joe, you just made my day.
- Good job! See, I knew you could do it.

Remind the class that Jesus wants us to be as happy as possible. Encourage the children to pray to the Holy Spirit for help in spreading God's happiness to everyone.

Drawing a Picture

After the discussion, ask the children to draw pictures of times they spread joy. Invite them to title their pictures.

Gathering for Prayer

Ask the children to bring their drawings to the prayer area. Teach the following response: *Come, Holy Spirit, help us spread joy.* Ask the volunteers to share their drawings, telling how they spread God's joy. After each volunteer shares, invite the children to pray the response.

DAY 5
PRAYER/REVIEW

Objective

This lesson helps the children learn the Glory Be to the Father.

Working with the Prayer Skill

Direct the children's attention to page 250 and ask them what the people in the illustration are feeling. Then read the two-line text under the title "Praying the Glory Be." Afterward, stress that Jesus gives them the gift of the Holy Spirit who helps the children feel happy, spreading joy all around them.

Tracing the Letters of a Prayer

Read the direction under the illustration on page 250. Then invite the children to trace the words *Father, Son,* and *Holy Spirit.* Recall for the children how they use these words when they make the Sign of the Cross.

When the children have completed their work, say the prayer with them. Then print on the chalkboard the words *Father, Son,* and *Holy Spirit.* Explain that Christians call Jesus' Father *God the Father.* They call Jesus God's *Son.* And the Spirit of God is called the *Holy Spirit.*

Repeat the three statements you just made, but omit the italicized words and encourage the children to supply each word orally.

Praying the Glory Be to the Father

Process to the prayer area. After the children have gathered, encourage them to quiet themselves. Then invite them to sing a song of joy. Have the children use their religion texts to pray the "Glory Be" from page 250. Conclude by singing the joy song again.

or...

Ask the children to form a line for a procession. Encourage them to sing a song about joy. Weather permitting, process out of doors. Assemble at a designated place and lead them in saying the Glory Be. Return to the class singing the song of joy.

Praying the Glory Be

Christians are full of joy. They believe that God the Father, God the Son, and God the Holy Spirit love them.

Trace the words of a prayer of praise Christians say.

Glory be to the  Father

and to the Son

and to the Holy Spirit.

As it was in the beginning,
   is now, and ever shall be,
     world without end.
       Amen.

250 Prayer

Focus on

The Glory Be The last prayer skill of the regular year's work — the Glory Be — brings together the names of the Father, Son, and Holy Spirit. The children learn this simple but important prayer of praise. It represents the culmination of the year's work — the introduction of the persons of the Trinity to the first graders.

CURRICULUM CONNECTION

Music Teach the children the following words to the melody "Are You Sleeping, Brother John?"

I am joyful.
I am joyful.
Yes, I am.
Yes, I am.
I can spread God's joy.
I can spread God's joy.
Every day,
Every day.

250

Chapter Review

The Holy Spirit helps us live like Jesus. In the box below, draw a picture of a time when the Holy Spirit helped you act like Jesus.

1. Whom does Jesus give us to help us be happy?

the Holy Spirit

2. In the gospel story, who was the man on shore?

Jesus

Jesus says, "I am with you so you can share my joy."
Based on John 15:11

3. Talk about how you can spread joy and help others feel happy.

Teaching Tips

To help the children learn the Glory Be, teach the following gestures.
Glory be to the Father (Open arms wide and raise them)
and to the Son, (Cross hands over the chest)
and to the Holy Spirit. (With hands still crossed, bow forward.)
As it was in the beginning, is now, and ever shall be, world without end. Amen. (Make large circling gestures, bringing hands back across the chest at the "Amen.")

Enriching the Lesson

Encourage the children to do something special to share their joy and happiness with others. (For instance, they could plan a picnic or a party to share with their classmates or with another class. Or they might plan a talent show for their families.)

Using the Bulletin Board from Day 1

Gather the children around the bulletin board they assembled on Day 1. Using their bulletin-board drawings, review the learning of Days 1–4. Encourage the children to talk about how they feel when they think of the gift of the Holy Spirit.

Finally, give each child his or her bulletin-board drawing and encourage the children to take their drawings home, post them in a place they will be noticed each day, and use them as reminders of the presence of the Spirit of joy.

Completing an Activity

Use the activity on page 251 to review the learning of Chapter 20. Read the text at the top of the page. Then invite volunteers to talk about times when the Holy Spirit has helped them act like Jesus. Encourage the children to use the space on page 251 to draw a picture of a time when the Holy Spirit helped them act like Jesus. Afterward, discuss their drawings.

Answering the Questions

Read the first two questions and ask volunteers to respond. Direct the children to print the answers in their texts. Encourage all the children to participate in the discussion of the third question. Be supportive of each child who responds.

Reading a Scripture Verse

Ask the children to read the Scripture verse after you. Reflecting on the word of God is a good way to end the lesson. If you wish, you may have the children memorize this verse.

Using the Unit Organizer

Completing a graphic organizer, such as a chart or table can help the children to organize the information that has been presented in the unit. Organizers can enable the children to visualize their thinking and recognize relationships among ideas. This will give the children the opportunity to understand more completely the materials they have been studying.

Completing the Organizer

The theme of Unit 5 is the Holy Spirit helps us. The children learn that the Holy Spirit is the gift of Jesus to us and helps us to act like Jesus. The Christian behaviors emphasized in this unit are joy, strength, and forgiveness which brings peace.

With the children, look at the illustrations and fill in the blanks by choosing the appropriate words from the three listed.

Looking Back: Self–Assessment

To give the children an opportunity to review the unit on their own terms ask the following questions.

- What chapter in this unit did you find the most interesting? Why?
- What activity did you most enjoy doing?
- What is one thing you want to always remember from this unit?

Unit 5 Organizer

Choose a word to fill in the blank.
The Holy Spirit helps us live as Jesus showed us.
The Holy Spirit helps us . . .

forgive.

be brave.

be full of joy.

Unit **5** Review

Draw a line to match the words with their meanings.

1. Holy Spirit — the good news of Jesus
2. gospel — excusing or pardoning
3. forgiveness — the Spirit of God

Write an **X** before the statements that are true.

1. _____ Jesus does not want us to be sorry for hurting others.
2. _____ Jesus gives us the Holy Spirit to make us sad.
3. __X__ Jesus always forgives us.
4. __X__ The Holy Spirit helps us to live like Jesus.
5. __X__ The Holy Spirit comes to give us God's joy.

Circle the names of three gifts that the Holy Spirit gives to us.

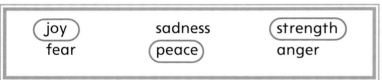

(joy)   sadness   (strength)
fear   (peace)   anger

Reviewing the Unit

The purpose of the Unit Review is to reinforce concepts presented in the preceding four chapters and to check how well the children understand these concepts. After explaining the directions, give the children sufficient time to complete the page. Answer any questions the children might have.

Testing

After the children have completed the Unit Review, you may wish to distribute copies of the Unit 5 Test in The Resourceful Teacher Package.

Project

Before class, cut out magazine pictures that show people using the gifts of the Spirit. Have the children work in groups of three. Give each group a large piece of art paper or posterboard, several magazine pictures, paste, and felt-tip markers. Have the children print the gifts of the Holy Spirit (peace, joy, love, and strength) and choose pictures that show these Christian ways of acting. Invite the children to paste the pictures around each word. Have the children talk about their pictures.

Unit 5 Review

Write the name of the gift Jesus brought to the people in each Bible story.

peace   **joy**   **strength**

1. The friends of Jesus were afraid of the storm.

strength

2. Jesus shared breakfast with his friends.

joy

3. Jesus brought forgiveness to Zacchaeus.

peace

Talk about the questions below.

1. Why is it important to say we are sorry when we hurt other people?

2. Why is it important to forgive people who hurt us?

3. How does the Holy Spirit help us to be happy?

COPING WITH FEELING SAD

Can you tell how the students in this picture are feeling?

Some students in this picture are feeling

_____

----------------------------------- .

Some students in this picture are feeling

_____

----------------------------------- .

Day to Day

Objective

To help the children acquire skills for coping with feelings of sadness.

Using the Illustrations

Ask the children to describe what they think is happening in the picture on page 255 and to tell if they can detect how the children in the picture are feeling. Invite them to make up a story about the picture.

Completing the Activity

Direct the children's attention to the two statements on page 255 about how the children in the picture are feeling. Have them write the appropriate feeling words. (*Happy*, *excited*, or *pleased* would be suitable for those with invitations and, *sad*, *mad*, *disappointed*, or *left out* could be used for those without invitations.)

Discussing the Activity

Use the following questions to guide a discussion about the ways children may help themselves when they have not been invited to a party, and they feel left out.

- Use "I-Feel Talk" to tell someone who will listen how they feel
- Tell Jesus how they feel
- Get busy doing something enjoyable
- Give a hug to a pet, a stuffed animal, a friend or a family member
- Plan a fun activity during the party-time
- Is it wrong to feel sad?

Help the children understand that how we feel is not wrong. Remind them that how we choose to express feelings can be hurtful or helpful. Feeling sad is acceptable, but moping around, being mean to others, or saying unkind words about the person giving the party is not acceptable.

- Have you ever not been invited to a party? How did you feel? What did you do to help yourself feel better?

Lesson continues on page 256.

255

Concluding the Lesson

Ask the children to draw pictures on page 256 of things they could do when they are feeling sad.

Allow time to share pictures and strategies. Help the children decide whether their pictures show helpful or hurtful solutions. Remind them that our feelings change. To feel sad at one moment does not mean that they will always feel sad.

Using the Following Jesus Section

Read with the children the Following Jesus section as a reminder that Jesus is always with them, even when they are sad. Tell the children that through prayer they can ask Jesus to help them feel happy again.

Follow-Up Activity

As a class, have the children write a short prayer that they can say when they are feeling sad. This prayer might include telling Jesus how they feel and why and asking Jesus to help them discover ways to feel happier.

256

Activity

Draw a picture of something you can do when you feel sad.

Following Jesus

Jesus is always with me.
When I'm sad, I can pray to Jesus to help me feel happier.
Write a prayer to tell Jesus your feelings.

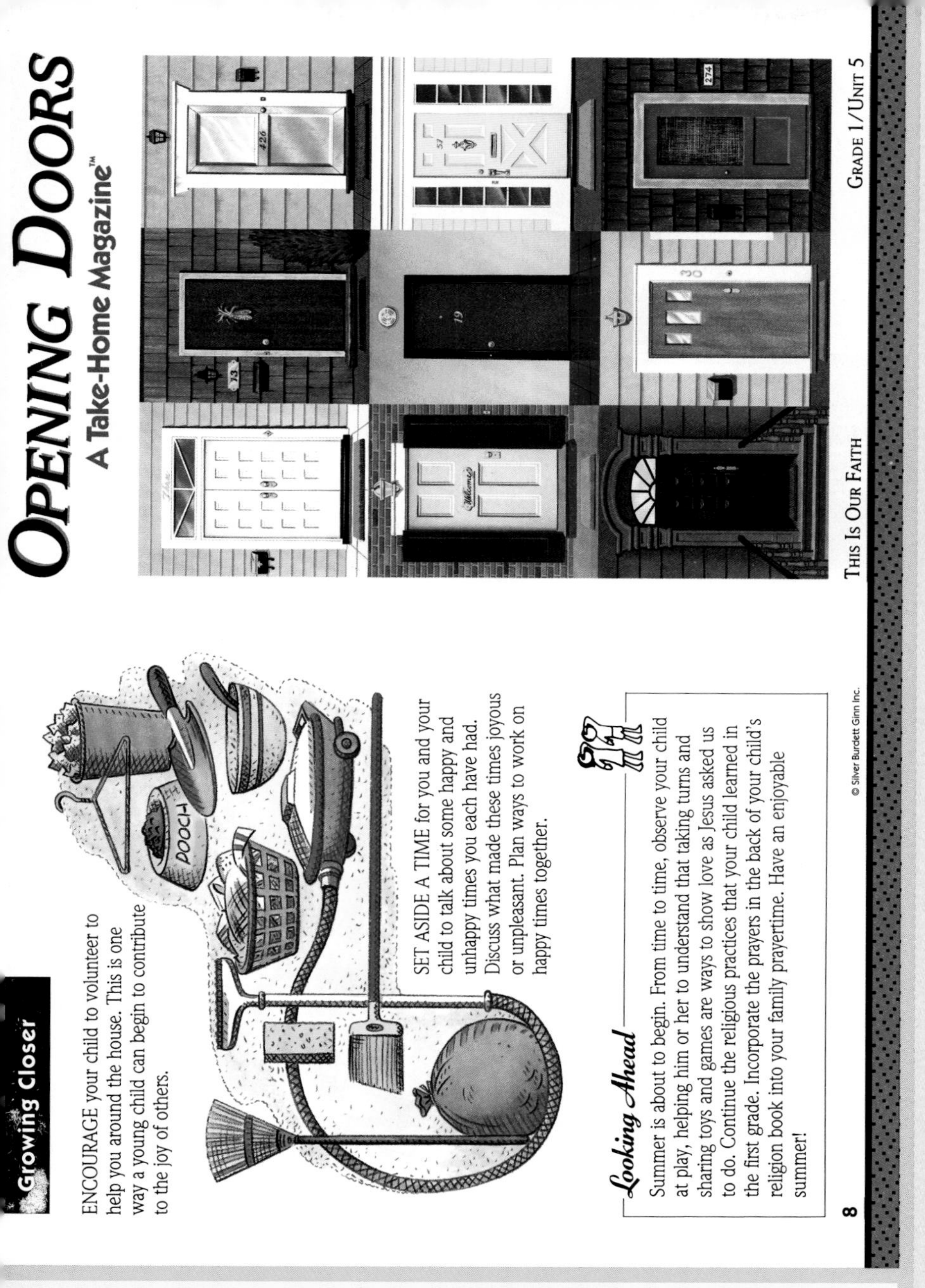

Opening Doors

A Take-Home Magazine™

THIS IS OUR FAITH

Growing Closer

ENCOURAGE your child to volunteer to help you around the house. This is one way a young child can begin to contribute to the joy of others.

SET ASIDE A TIME for you and your child to talk about some happy and unhappy times you each have had. Discuss what made these times joyous or unpleasant. Plan ways to work on happy times together.

Looking Ahead

Summer is about to begin. From time to time, observe your child at play, helping him or her to understand that taking turns and sharing toys and games are ways to show love as Jesus asked us to do. Continue the religious practices that your child learned in the first grade. Incorporate the prayers in the back of your child's religion book into your family prayertime. Have an enjoyable summer!

© Silver Burdett Ginn Inc.

8

Opening Doors

Sending the Magazine Home

As you complete Unit 5 with your class, assist the children in carefully removing *Opening Doors: A Take-Home Magazine* (two pages) from their texts by separating the magazine from the book along the perforations. Demonstrate how to fold the two magazine pages to form an eight-page booklet. Ask the children to take the magazines home and encourage their families to read them and participate in the suggested activities.

THE MASS IS ENDED

Ascension Thursday
(fortieth day after Easter)
This holy day commemorates the ascension of Jesus into heaven which completes his passion, death, and resurrection.

Assumption of Mary
August 15
Since the seventh century, Catholics celebrated the taking of Mary, body and soul, into heaven at the end of her life.

All Saints' Day
November 1
This feast remembers all the saints in heaven, especially those who are not honored on any other day of the year.

The Immaculate Conception
December 8
This day honors Mary who was conceived without original sin.

As you can see, holy days have been added to the Church calendar over the centuries or their dates have been changed. In recent years, the bishops proposed reducing the number of holy days to three. They

suggested retaining either Christmas, the Solemnity of Mary, and the Ascension or Christmas, All Saints' Day, and the Immaculate Conception. If you were polled, for which holy days would you vote?

Holy Days

In former centuries, Church holy days were real *holidays*. People abstained from all work and attended Mass just as they did on Sunday. After Mass, there was often a daylong festival with rich foods, singing, and dancing. Today, holy days are often forgotten as we battle morning traffic, work the late shift, keep appointments, or chauffeur children to after-school activities.

Most of us are familiar with the names and dates of the six holy days of obligation. Did you know, however, that there are really ten holy days observed throughout the universal Church? Each country's bishops have decided upon which of the ten days the local Church will celebrate. The other four holy days observed in some countries other than the United States are: Epiphany, Corpus Christi, the Feast of Saint Joseph, and the Feast of Saints Peter and Paul. In the United States, Catholics celebrate the following six holy days of obligation.

Christmas
December 25
Originally celebrated on January 6, the Feast of the Epiphany, this feast was changed to December 25 to offset pagan sun ceremonies that celebrated the winter solstice.

Solemnity of Mary, Mother of God
January 1
This ancient feast, restored in 1969, honors the Mother of God during the Christmas season.

6

"Then, after singing a hymn, they went out."

Mark 14:26

These are the concluding words of Mark's account of the Last Supper. The disciples had just experienced one of the greatest moments in their relationship with Jesus—the promise that their Master would be present to them each time they gathered at the table. The gospel account doesn't allow us even a glimpse into the disciples' emotions, but we can probably safely assume that the disciples were deeply touched by the supper events and felt closer to Jesus because of it. However, in the hours that followed, some of them doubted Jesus; one betrayed him, one denied him, a few believed and followed him to Calvary. The disciples had met their greatest challenge—to stay faithful to the Master—and many of them failed the test.

Each Sunday, we, too, leave the Mass, the sacred meal by which we celebrate the Lord's Supper. The celebrant commissions us,

"Go in peace to love and serve the Lord."

This is far more than "farewell until we meet again." The word *Mass* means "to send." We believe that when the Mass is ended, it has really just begun. We are sent to carry the message of the gospel into our homes, the workplace, onto the golf courses, and into the beauty salon. This is not always easy, and our good intentions, like those of the disciples, may meet very challenging circumstances.

As we start out for home, we can claim Jesus' promised Spirit as our companion for the journey. God's power strengthens us, guides us, and gladdens each step we take to share faith and life generously with others. When we consider that the Holy Spirit is with us to help us live out the gospel, we can respond to the words of the Dismissal, "Thanks be to God."

3

The Holy Spirit Helps Me

I pray,

Thanks be to God.

This is a picture of how my family will celebrate Jesus this week.

The Dismissal Rite—the ending of the Mass—is the part that challenges us the most. Our celebration is over. How will we live out the celebration until we gather again?

Read these pages with your child. How will you and your family live out the eucharistic celebration during the rest of the week?

Read-Along

At Mass I celebrate Jesus' great love for me.
I thank Jesus for all that he has done for me.
I praise him for the gift of Eucharist.

The Mass is ended.
The priest says,
"Go in peace to love and serve the Lord."

The Holy Spirit will help me love others.
The Holy Spirit will give me strength,
peace, and joy.

The next time you go to Mass, remember to pray aloud the prayer you have just learned.

Celebrating the Journey

Leader Dear God, we like being on a
journey with you.
It is exciting and full of your love.
We thank you for being with us.

Children God is with us always.

Leader Our journey is not over.
It will go on all summer and all
through our lives.
God the Father will be with us.
God the Son will be with us.
God the Holy Spirit will always
help us.

Children God is with us always.

All Amen.

261

Introducing "Celebrating the Journey"

A vital dimension of Christian faith is the celebrations we experience at all the important moments of our lives. "Celebrating the Journey" is a special feature designed to help celebrate the completion of this important phase of the children's faith journey.

Using "Celebrating the Journey"

Plan a special time at the end of the year to use this celebration with your class. Choose a few of the children's favorite songs to sing at various times during the celebration. You may wish to choose a song or acclamation from the THIS IS OUR FAITH Music Program. Allow the children to participate as fully as possible. You may wish to invite others, such as the DRE or principal, the pastor, or the children's families to the celebration. End the celebration with a simple snack.

262

263

Our Church Celebrates Advent

Objectives 〜〜〜〜

- LESSON 1: To help the children understand that Advent signifies waiting for Jesus.
- LESSON 2: To help the children consider the length of the Advent season.
- LESSON 3: To help the children appreciate Advent as a time to prepare for Christmas.
- LESSON 4: To help the children prepare for Christmas by making an Advent chain.

Lesson Outlines 〜〜〜〜〜

	Step 1 Learning About Our Lives	Step 2 Learning About Our Faith	Step 3 Learning How to Live Our Faith
Lesson 1	■ Learn to wait. *ABOUT 5 MINUTES*	■ Discuss Advent waiting. ■ Use the text. *ABOUT 10 MINUTES*	■ Learn about Advent wreaths. ■ Color and write in the text. ■ Pray together. *ABOUT 15 MINUTES*
Lesson 2	■ Count the days of Advent. *ABOUT 10 MINUTES*	■ Read a poem. ■ Learn about Advent candles. *ABOUT 10 MINUTES*	■ Welcome Jesus. ■ Pray together. *ABOUT 10 MINUTES*
Lesson 3	■ Talk about getting ready. *ABOUT 10 MINUTES*	■ Read about Emmanuel. ■ Review Advent traditions. *ABOUT 10 MINUTES*	■ Name preparations for Christmas. ■ Pray together. *ABOUT 10 MINUTES*
Lesson 4	**Project** Prepare for Jesus' birthday and make an Advent chain. **Prayer Service** Prepare for prayer; participate in prayer.		

Plan Ahead

	Preparing Your Class	**Materials Needed**
Lesson 1	Read the lesson plan and prepare to convey to the children the joy of the Advent season. For Step 1, use an egg timer to focus on waiting.	■ hour glass-type egg timer
Lesson 2	Make a large posterboard calendar for this year's Advent season. Mark the Sunday of Advent by drawing the appropriate number of candles in the Sunday squares. Mark Christmas Day with a sticker.	■ poster board ■ Christmas stickers (optional) ■ Advent wreath
Lesson 3	Read through the lesson plan.	■ Advent wreath
Lesson 4	Cut construction paper into 8" x 1" strips, ten to fifteen strips for each child. Make a sample chain to show the children.	■ construction paper in a variety of colors ■ scissors, glue ■ Advent wreath ■ matches (optional—check fire rules)

Additional Resources

As you plan these lessons consider using the following materials from the The Resourceful Teacher Package.

■ *Classroom Activity Sheets* for Advent

■ *Family Activity Sheets* for Advent

■ *Prayers for Every Day*

In preparing the children for the Sunday readings, you may wish to use Silver Burdett Ginn's *Getting Ready for Sunday* student and teacher materials.

REDUCED CLASSROOM ACTIVITIES

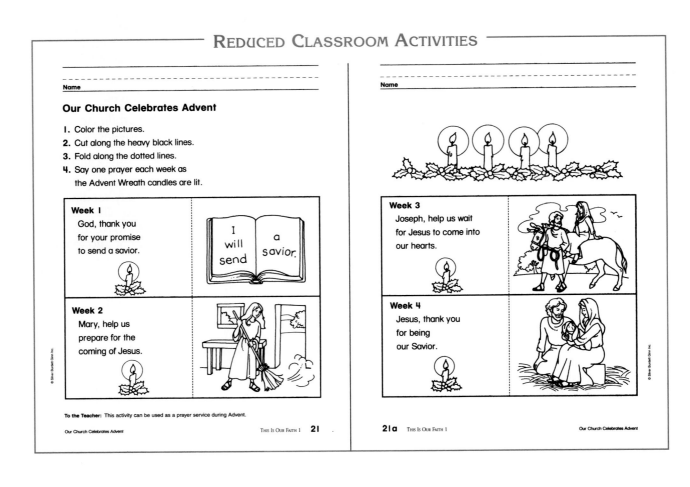

Name

Our Church Celebrates Advent

1. Color the pictures.
2. Cut along the heavy black lines.
3. Fold along the dotted lines.
4. Say one prayer each week as
   the Advent Wreath candles are lit.

Week 1
God, thank you
for your promise
to send a savior.

I will send a savior.

Week 2
Mary, help us
prepare for the
coming of Jesus.

Name

Week 3
Joseph, help us wait
for Jesus to come into
our hearts.

Week 4
Jesus, thank you
for being
our Savior.

To the Teacher: This activity can be used as a prayer service during Advent.

Our Church Celebrates Advent   THIS IS OUR FAITH 1 **21**

21a THIS IS OUR FAITH 1   Our Church Celebrates Advent

Background for the Teacher ~~~~~~

ADVENT

During Advent, Christians focus on three dimensions of time. We look to the past and reflect on how Jesus was born in Bethlehem. We live in the present, preparing our minds and hearts for the celebration of the coming of the Lord into our lives today. And we look to the future with hope, awaiting the Second Coming of Christ—the fulfillment of God's promise. Advent, therefore, is a time of joy, anticipation, and preparation for the comings of Jesus.

WAITING

Children cannot help but look forward to Christmas. It is a time of great excitement and expectation for them. Six-year-old children respond to the commercialism that envelops them during the weeks preceding Christmas. You can build on that response, relating the children's excitement to the longing of Mary for Jesus' birth. Children understand what it means to wait. They have waited for birthdays. They have sat in waiting rooms. They have waited for the school bell to ring or waited for a television program to begin. And they wait for Christmas each year.

PREPARING

All the preparations of the Advent season—baking, shopping, decorating, making an Advent wreath—can serve a dual purpose. These practical activities can be bonded to the children's experience of preparing themselves for the celebration of the birth of Jesus. As you read the student text with the children, invite them to think about and share ways they can prepare to celebrate the birth of Jesus.

Explain that they can make a promise to God. They can promise to share their toys and act lovingly toward each other during Advent. Praise the children as they offer their suggestions for Advent preparations.

LESSON 1

Objective

This lesson helps the children understand that Advent signifies waiting for Jesus.

Step 1/INTRODUCTION

Learning About Our Lives

Learning to Wait

Show the children an egg timer. Ask them how long they think it will take for the sand to sift from the top to the bottom. Have the children put their heads down on their desks and close their eyes. Turn the timer over. Tell the children they can look up when they think the sand has stopped moving. Then guide the children in a discussion.

- Was it hard to wait for the sand to run out?
- Did the time pass slowly or quickly?
- Can you think about some other times in your life when you have had to wait for something?

Have the children talk about how they pass time while waiting. Explain that every year Christians have a special time of waiting—a time called Advent.

Step 2/DEVELOPMENT

Learning About Our Faith

Discussing Advent Waiting

Read aloud the title on page 264. Ask the children if they know what we wait for during Advent (the coming of Jesus).

Using the Text

Read the first two paragraphs on page 264. Encourage the children to discuss how they can prepare for the birth of Jesus. Talk with them about their families' Advent traditions. Ask everyone to read the prayer at the bottom of the page.

264

Our Church Celebrates Advent

A Time of Waiting

God made a promise long ago.
God promised to send Jesus.
The people waited many years
for Jesus, God's Son.
Then God sent Jesus to show us
how to live as children of God.

During **Advent** we wait, too.
We wait for Jesus.
We prepare our minds and
hearts for Christmas.

We pray,
"O Lord Jesus, come! Be with us."

Based on I Corinthians 16:22

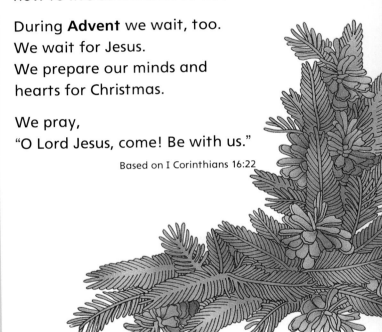

CURRICULUM CONNECTION

Art Have the children make a table cloth or runner for the table on which you will display the Advent wreath in Lesson 2. Spread a large piece of white fabric (a sheet cut to the proper size works well) on the floor or a large table. Direct the children to draw large candles representing themselves on the fabric, using crayons or felt-tip markers. Have them write their names on the candle.

Focus on

Advent The word *Advent* means "coming." Originally, Advent was observed for eight weeks, and like Lent, it was a time of fasting and penance. Pope Saint Gregory the Great at the end of the sixth century changed Advent to four weeks. Today, the themes of joy, anticipation, and hope are associated with Advent.

Activity

1. Color the Advent wreath.

2. Read the words on the candles.

3. Then write the words on the line below.

Learning How to Live Our Faith

Learning About Advent Wreaths

Explain to the children that one symbol of the Advent season is the Advent wreath. Provide the following background: The wreath is a circle to remind us that God's love surrounds us. The flame of the candles tells us that we will shine with God's love. The wreath is often made with evergreen branches to remind us that God's love for us does not change.

Coloring and Writing in the Text

Ask the children to turn to page 265 in their books. Have the children complete the coloring activity. To help them with the correct colors of the candles in the Advent wreath, direct the children to the photograph on page 266. Elicit from the children the colors of the candles, pointing out, if necessary, the rose candle used the third week.

After coloring the wreath, have the children write the words of the Advent prayer in the space provided.

Praying Together

Have the children bring their texts and gather in a circle. Ask the children to join you in praying the prayer they printed on page 265.

LESSON 2

This lesson helps the children consider the length of the Advent season.

Step 1/INTRODUCTION

Learning About Our Lives

Counting the Days of Advent

Display the Advent calendar you prepared earlier and point out the candles marking the four Sundays of Advent. Remind the children of the wreath-coloring activity they did in the previous lesson. Have them recall that the special season when Christians wait and prepare for Christmas is called *Advent.* Count aloud with the children the number of days in this year's Advent season. As each day passes, mark it off on the calendar or have the children take turns putting stickers in the squares as the days pass.

Step 2/DEVELOPMENT

Learning About Our Faith

Reading a Poem

Direct the children's attention to "We Welcome Jesus" on page 266. Ask the children to read the poem aloud with you. Then invite them to stand in a circle and do movements to accompany the poem.

> **Four, three, two, one—**
> (*Hold four fingers up and count them down to one.*)
>
> **Count the weeks 'til Jesus comes.**
> (*Count back up to four.*)
>
> **Each week we add another light,**
> (*Mime lighting a candle.*)
>
> **Our hope for Jesus glowing bright.**
> (*Cup hands in front of body and then extend arms*)
>
> **We pray.**
> (*Fold hands.*)
>
> **We share.**
> (*Turn to right and left with hands held at waist, palms up.*)

266

We Welcome Jesus

Four, three, two, one—
Count the weeks till Jesus comes.
Each week we add another light,
Our hope for Jesus glowing bright.
We pray, we share, we do our part,
To welcome Jesus in our hearts.

The Advent wreath helps us prepare
for Jesus' birthday.
We light a candle and pray together.
Soon all four candles are lighted.

Activity

Draw a picture of yourself during Advent.
Show how you will welcome Jesus.

Trace the letters below that show
you want God to be with us.

Enriching the Lesson

In Chapter 6, the children learned the story of the Annunciation (Luke 1:26–38), or the angel's announcement to Mary that she was to be the mother of Jesus. Using a flannel board, retell this story. Also tell the children a paraphrased version of the angel's announcement to Joseph (Matthew 1:18–24). Help the children appreciate that Mary and Joseph waited for Jesus' birth just as we wait to celebrate Jesus' birthday.

CURRICULUM CONNECTION

Music   Teach the children how to sing the first line of the song "O Come, O Come, Emmanuel" (*This Is Our Faith Music Program Director's Manual,* page 134). Tell the children that the words *and ransom captive Israel* mean that Jesus came to save the people of his land, Israel, and all people. This one line can be sung several times as a three-part round.

We do our part,
(*Place hands on shoulders of children to right and left.*)

To welcome Jesus to our hearts.
(*Place both hands over heart.*)

Learning About Advent Candles

Read the last paragraph on page 266 with the class. Show the children the Advent wreath you brought to class. Refer to the calendar again and help the children understand that each candle stands for one week of the Advent season. Explain that we light a candle each week until all four candles are lit. Display the wreath throughout Advent.

Step 3/CONCLUSION

Learning How to Live Our Faith

Welcoming Jesus

Tell the children that they can get ready to welcome Jesus by praying, sharing, helping, and caring. Recall the prayer the children learned in the previous lesson, *"O Lord Jesus, come! Be with us."* Explain that they can share their love and their anticipation of the coming of Jesus by helping with Advent and Christmas preparations. Encourage the children to think of specific ways they can welcome Jesus. Then have each child draw a picture as indicated on page 267. Afterward, have them share their drawings.

Praying Together

Explain that the word *Emmanuel* means "God is with us." Invite the children to trace the words of the prayer as directed on page 267. Then have everyone say this prayer aloud with you.

LESSON 3

Objective

This lesson helps the children appreciate Advent as a time to prepare for Christmas.

Step 1/INTRODUCTION

Learning About Our Lives

Talking About Getting Ready

Talk with the children about how they get ready to go to bed each evening: brush your teeth, wash up, say your prayers, hang up your clothes, put your dirty clothes in the hamper, watch television, hear or read a bedtime story, and turn out the lights. Explain that these things help us to prepare for bed.

Tell the children that today we will learn how to prepare for something other than bed, namely, Christmas. Explain that during Advent, we prepare for Christmas.

Step 2/DEVELOPMENT

Learning About Our Faith

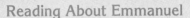

Reading About Emmanuel

Have the children turn to page 268. Read with them "God Be With Us!" Discuss the reading, using the following questions.

- What do we call Jesus? (*Emmanuel*)
- What does the word *Emmanuel* mean? (*God is with us.*)
- Why is Jesus called Emmanuel? (*Because Jesus is God's Son, he is God with us.*)
- What do we prepare for during Advent? (*The coming of Jesus*)
- How do we prepare for Emmanuel? (*By trying to be more loving and kind, by helping others*)
- Why do we wait for Emmanuel with joy? (*Because Jesus is God's greatest gift to us*)

Reviewing Advent Traditions

Help the children recall that we prepare for Christmas by lighting candles on the Advent wreath and praying. Invite the children to name a prayer that we can pray during Advent (O, Lord Jesus, come.)

268

God Be with Us!

Jesus is called **Emmanuel**.
Emmanuel means "God is with us."
We call Jesus "Emmanuel" because
Jesus is God who came to be with us.

During Advent we get ready for Christmas.
We prepare for the coming of Jesus.

We prepare for Emmanuel by trying to be more loving.
We get ready by helping others.

As we prepare for the coming of Emmanuel, we are full of joy.
We wait for Jesus, God's great gift to us.

Teaching Tips

Help the children to appreciate that everything we do in the weeks before Christmas helps us to prepare for the celebration of Jesus' birth. The children are too young to understand the difference between "secular" preparations and "spiritual" preparations. At this age, everything they do adds to their sense of joy and anticipation.

Activity

Put an **X** by the pictures that show how you get ready for Jesus.

We light another candle for each week of waiting.

We prepare a food basket for God's poor.

We get our house ready to celebrate Jesus with us.

We set up a crib to remember what we are waiting for.

Any or all pictures may be chosen according to the children's family customs.

Enriching the Lesson

Distribute drawing materials and invite the children to draw pictures of their families getting ready for Christmas by decorating a Christmas tree together. Give them sequins to glue on their trees as ornaments. Have them print the following message beneath the trees:

"Bless our tree, Jesus.
Bring our family Christmas joy."

Step 3/CONCLUSION

Learning How to Live Our Faith

Naming Preparations for Christmas

Call attention to the pictures on page 269. Discuss how the people in each picture are getting ready for Jesus. Explain to the children that the family in the third picture is getting ready for Christmas by thinking about others. Tell them that the family is making a Christmas food basket for a poor family. Then have the children make an "**X**" on each of the pictures which show how their family gets ready for Jesus.

Praying Together

Have the children repeat the following prayer after you.

Dear Jesus,
Help us prepare for you with joy.
Help us to think of others during Advent.
Help us to remember that you are God's gift to others.
Amen.

LESSON 4

Objectives

This lesson helps the children prepare for Christmas by making an Advent chain.

Preparing for Jesus' Birthday

Recall with the children that in the previous lesson they planned specific actions they could do to prepare for the birthday of Jesus. Read through page 270 with the children and invite them to make Advent chains. Explain that throughout the Advent season they can add a link to their chains each time they carry out their preparation plans or do something to show their love.

Making an Advent Chain

Tell the children that they can start their Advent chains with four links, one link for each of the four weeks of Advent. Distribute to each child four strips of construction paper and glue. Invite the children to print their names on one strip and decorate the others. Consider having the children print on each strip one way to prepare for Christmas—*pray, share, help,* and *care.*

Show the children how to make the first link of their Advent chains by gluing the ends of one strip of paper together to form a circle. Now show the children how to add links by placing another strip of paper through the first link and gluing the ends together. Have the children add the three remaining links to their chains.

Collect the children's chains and display them in an accessible place. Put extra construction-paper strips nearby. Encourage the children to find ways to show their love so they can add to their chains during the Advent season. Just before Christmas, have the children take their chains home.

An Advent Chain

Make an Advent chain.
It will help you prepare for Jesus' birthday.
Each time you do something to show your love, add another link.

1. Your teacher will give you strips of paper, crayons, and glue.

2. On each strip of paper, draw a picture that shows how you care.

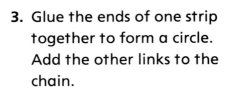

3. Glue the ends of one strip together to form a circle. Add the other links to the chain.

4. At Christmas, put your chain on your Christmas tree.

🍎 Teaching Tips

Reinforce the children's positive actions during Advent with praise and affirmation. Comment on how long their Advent chains are growing. Explain that the good deeds we do help to make Jesus' love grow in the world. Tell them that they are God's helpers, helping prepare the world and their hearts for Jesus.

An Advent Prayer Service

Teacher   We will name the Advent candles.
We will call the first candle promise.
When we light the first candle,
we pray,

Children   O Jesus, you are God's promise to us.

Teacher   We call the second candle hope.
When we light the second candle,
we pray,

Children   O Jesus, we wait in hope for you.

Teacher   The third candle we call joy.
When we light the third candle,
we pray,

Children   O Jesus, you bring joy to the world.

Teacher   The fourth candle we call love.
When we light the fourth candle,
we pray,

Children   O Jesus, you
teach us how
to love.

🍎 Teaching Tips

Conclude your morning prayer each day by repeating the refrain for each week from the prayer service and having the children recite it after you. Reinforce the weekly theme by writing the refrain in large letters with colored chalk on the chalkboard or a poster.

Preparing for the Prayer Service

Display the Advent wreath on a table and plan to gather the children around the wreath to pray part of the prayer service during each week of the Advent season. If safety laws permit, darken the room and light the appropriate candles.

Participating in a Prayer Service

Week One Read aloud the first three lines of the prayer on page 271. Point out the first candle on the Advent wreath. Have the children repeat the name of the first candle. Recall with the children God's promise to send a special person. Ask whom God sent (Jesus). Ask if anyone remembers another name of Jesus (Savior).

Read again the first three lines of the prayer service. Ask the children to read the response aloud. Invite the children to offer a silent prayer of thanks to God for his promise.

Week Two Ask the children to consider why we have hope in Jesus. Explain that Jesus makes us feel hopeful because he is our Savior. Read the prayer of hope on page 271. Ask each child to offer a prayer that begins, *"Jesus, I hope that ...."* Then have the children pray the response: *"Jesus, we wait in hope for you."*

Week Three Teach the children the song "Joy to the World." Invite them to reflect on how they have prepared for Jesus. Mention acts of kindness you have observed the children doing during Advent. You might mention such things as holding a door for someone, sharing crayons, helping another child with his or her work, and so on. Read the prayer of joy on page 271, and have the class read the response: *"O Jesus, you bring joy to the world."* Sing "Joy to the World." Be sure to mention the pink candle which is a sign of joy.

Week Four Discuss with the children ways they can show their love for Jesus. Read the love prayer on page 271. Invite each child in turn to mention the name of someone he or she loves. Conclude by having the children read the response: *"O Jesus, you teach us how to love."*

Our Church Celebrates Christmas

Objectives ~~~~~

- LESSON 1: To help the children understand that we are a part of the gifts we give.
- LESSON 2: To help the children appreciate that at Christmas we celebrate God's gift of Jesus.
- LESSON 3: To help the children appreciate Christmas as a time to share our joy with others.
- LESSON 4: To help the children make a Christmas ornament and celebrate the birth of Jesus in prayer.

Lesson Outlines ~~~~~~~~

	Step 1 Learning About Our Lives	**Step 2** Learning About Our Faith	**Step 3** Learning How to Live Our Faith
Lesson 1	■ Discuss gifts. *ABOUT 5 MINUTES*	■ Read and discuss the text. *ABOUT 5 MINUTES*	■ Make a Christmas card. ■ Receive a gift. ■ Pray together. *ABOUT 20 MINUTES*
Lesson 2	■ Share stories. *ABOUT 5 MINUTES*	■ Discuss preparations. ■ Read and discuss a story. *ABOUT 10 MINUTES*	■ Find hidden words. ■ Make a montage. *ABOUT 15 MINUTES*
Lesson 3	■ Talk about Christmas customs. *ABOUT 10 MINUTES*	■ Read and discuss a story. ■ Find ways to share Christmas joy. *ABOUT 10 MINUTES*	■ Write and color in the text. ■ Pray together. *ABOUT 10 MINUTES*
Lesson 4	**Project** Make a Christmas ornament as a gift for someone they love. **Prayer Service** Plan a Christmas tableau and participate in the prayer service.		

Plan Ahead

	Preparing Your Class	**Materials Needed**
Lesson 1	Gift-wrap a large box containing a small gift for each child. Cut green yarn in 3" pieces. Fold construction paper in half. Draw an outline of a Christmas tree on each sheet. Make a sample card.	■ large gift box/wrapping paper ■ small gift, such as stickers or pencils, for each child ■ construction paper, gummed stars, scissors, glue ■ ten 3" green yarn per child
Lesson 2	To prepare for making a montage, glue a picture of Jesus in the center of a large piece of posterboard.	■ Nativity set or flannel-board figures ■ large piece of posterboard ■ a picture of Jesus ■ magazines, scissors, glue
Lesson 3	Obtain the music and words for the song "Joy to the World."	■ words and melody for "Joy to the World"
Lesson 4	Cut a 48" piece of yarn for each child. Soak the yarn in liquid starch for 15 to 20 minutes. Make a sample ornament. Gather props for the tableau. Obtain the music for "The Little Drummer Boy."	■ liquid starch, yarn, large bowl ■ small balloon for each child ■ long straight pin/clear thread ■ newspapers ■ props for tableau ■ "The Little Drummer Boy"

Additional Resources

As you plan these lessons consider using the following materials from The Resourceful Teacher Package.

■ *Classroom Activity Sheets* for Christmas

■ *Family Activity Sheets* for Christmas

■ *Prayers for Every Day*

You may also wish to refer to the following Big Book

■ *We Celebrate God's Word,* page 5

In preparing the children for the Sunday readings, you may wish to use Silver Burdett Ginn's *Getting Ready for Sunday* student and teacher materials.

Name

Our Church Celebrates Christmas

1. Look at the words in the box.
2. Choose a word to finish each sentence.
3. Write the word below each sentence.

| Jesus | love | Christmas | peace | gift |

1. On ___ we celebrate Jesus' birthday.

Christmas

2. Jesus is our greatest ___ from God.

gift

3. ___ always gives us gifts.

Jesus

4. His gifts to us are ___ and ___ .

peace   love

To the Teacher: This activity will reinforce the concepts presented in "Our Church Celebrates Christmas."

Our Church Celebrates Christmas   THIS IS OUR FAITH 1   **22**

© Silver Burdett Ginn Inc.

Name

Christmas Is a Time for Giving

1. In each box, write the name of a gift that you can share with others.
2. Decorate the boxes.

To the Teacher: Before you help the children with this activity, emphasize the importance of the gifts of time and talent rather than material gifts. You may want to suggest some of these gifts or list on the chalkboard some gifts suggested by the children.

22a   THIS IS OUR FAITH 1   Our Church Celebrates Christmas

© Silver Burdett Ginn Inc.

271c Organizer

GIVING GIFTS

Think about the times you have given a gift to someone. You probably hoped the person would like the gift or wondered if the person needed it. In any case, you sought to make the other person happy through your gift-giving. In real giving, not only do we present an object, but we also share a part of ourselves. We reveal ourselves through the gifts we give.

RECEIVING THE GIFT OF JESUS

In the miracle of the Incarnation, God became man. God, whose eternal love has always sought to make us happy, gave us the greatest gift in Jesus. God's very self was revealed through this gift. God's gift of self to us that empowers us to strive to become like God.

Throughout the life of Jesus, God became revealed even more fully as the One who cares for the needs we all have to be loved, to be forgiven, and to be healed. Christmas celebrates the arrival of Jesus as God's greatest gift to a people in need of such never-ending love.

GIVING LOVE

Children are eager to see what gifts they will find under the tree on Christmas Day. To help them discover the true meaning of Christmas the children will explore what it means to give gifts. Remembering that Jesus, the Son of God, came as God's gift to the world and that He is a gift that God gave all of us with love, the children learn that we, in turn, give love through our gifts at Christmas.

Help the children understand the custom of giving gifts at Christmas by exploring with them the traditions of your own family. Then encourage the children to talk about their family traditions.

In the lessons, you will tell the story of the first Christmas. Remind the children that to listen well, they must be very still. You might display a Nativity scene to help set the Christmas mood.

Objective

This lesson helps the children understand that we are a part of the gifts we give.

Step 1/INTRODUCTION

Learning About Our Lives

Discussing Gifts

Display the large gift-wrapped box. If the children ask about it, explain that it is a gift. Guide the children in a discussion about the box with the following questions. (All answers will vary.)

- Do you enjoy giving gifts?
- Do you like it when others give gifts to you?
- What was the best gift you were ever given? Why?

Step 2/DEVELOPMENT

Learning About Our Faith

Reading and Discussing the Text

Have the children open their books to page 272. Ask them to follow along as you read aloud "A Time for Giving."

Call attention to page 273. Have the children complete the activity. Allow time for the children to talk about the Nativity picture on this page.

Our Church Celebrates Christmas

A Time for Giving

Christmas is the birthday of Jesus.
We give gifts to our family and friends.
They give gifts to us, too.

These gifts remind us of Jesus.
He is our greatest gift from God.
Jesus gives us gifts of love and peace.
We share these gifts with others on Christmas.

We pray, "Glory to God! Peace to all people."

Based on Luke 2:14

272 Christmas: Lesson One

Focus on

The Gloria This hymn which we pray or sing at Mass, begins with the words of the angels' song of praise and joy which the shepherds in Bethlehem heard on the first Christmas (Luke 2:14). The Gloria is not prayed or sung during Advent or Lent. On Christmas Day, after so many weeks of quiet preparation, we join with the angels in praising God:
"Glory to God in the highest, and peace to his people on earth."

Teaching Tips

When teaching page 272, wrap boxes of different sizes in white paper and ribbons. Ask the children: *What gifts does Jesus give us?* Elicit from the children that Jesus gives us love and peace. Write each word on one of the boxes. Then ask the children to name gifts Jesus wants us to share with others (Joy, love, care, friendship, kindness, and so on.) Write each word on a box. Display them in the prayer area.

Activity
Look at the picture.
Write the correct word on the line below
to finish the sentence.

God the Father's greatest gift to us is

Jesus —————————, our Savior.

Learning How to Live Our Faith

Making a Christmas Card
- Show the Christmas-tree card you prepared as a sample.
- Distribute the materials. Each child will need ten pieces of green yarn cut in 3 inch strips, construction paper, glue, and gummed stars).
- Have each child print a personal message on the inside of the card.
- Explain that everyone will make a Christmas card. Show the children how to fold their construction paper to make a card and demonstrate how to score it at the fold to make it lay flat.
- The children should then draw an outline of a large Christmas tree on the front of the card.
- Using your card as a sample, have the children glue the pieces of yarn to the tree outline to simulate pine needles. They may need to trim some of the yarn as they shape the top of the tree.
- Invite the children to decorate their Christmas trees with the gummed stars.

Receiving a Gift
Invite the children to help you open the gift-wrapped box. Distribute the gifts (a small gift such as a pencil or some stickers for each child), wishing each child a merry Christmas. Ask everyone to join in singing "Silent Night."

Praying Together
Gather the children in a circle around you. Ask them to join hands and say a prayer together. Explain that you will begin a sentence and all should respond, *Thank you, God.*

Teacher:	For the gift of Jesus,
All:	Thank you, God.
Teacher:	For Mary and Joseph,
All:	Thank you, God.
Teacher:	For our parents,
All:	Thank you, God.

Teaching Tips
When teaching this lesson, direct the children's attention to the fine art that illustrates this page. Tell the children that many famous artists have painted beautiful pictures of the birth of Jesus and other happenings in his life. Many of these pictures hang in museums where we can see them. Museums have slides made of these famous pictures. In that form they can be reproduced in books for the children to see and enjoy.

LESSON 2

Objective

This lesson helps the children appreciate that at Christmas we celebrate God's gift of Jesus.

Step 1/INTRODUCTION

Learning About Our Lives

Sharing Stories

Invite the children to discuss any stories they may know about the events surrounding their own births or the births of their siblings. (Be sensitive to adopted or foster children.) Ask the following questions.

■ What stories did your mothers or fathers tell you when you were little? (*Answers will vary.*)

■ How did your family get ready for the arrival of your younger brothers or sisters? (*Answers will vary.*)

Have the children list preparations that are often made for the arrival of a baby. Print their suggestions on the chalkboard. (The list might include setting up a crib, purchasing diapers and baby clothes, decorating a room, and thinking about baby names.) Help the children recognize that the arrival of a child (by birth or adoption) is a very special event and that these preparations help a family get ready to welcome the new child.

Step 2/DEVELOPMENT

Learning About Our Faith

Discussing Preparations

Have the children recall that Christians all over the world are preparing to celebrate Christmas, the birthday of Jesus. Ask who first prepared for the birth of Jesus (Mary and Joseph). Tell the children that Joseph may have made a crib and that Mary may have made something to wrap her new baby in. Explain that right before Jesus was born, Mary and Joseph had to go on a trip. The ruler of their country had ordered all people to go to the towns where they were born so that they could be counted. Mary and Joseph had to go to Bethlehem.

274

The First Christmas

Mary and Joseph went to Bethlehem.
The town was crowded with people.
Mary and Joseph had no place to sleep.
They found a barn, and Joseph made a straw bed for Mary.

That night, Jesus was born.
Mary wrapped Jesus in warm clothes.
Joseph found a wooden box and filled it with clean hay.
Joseph used the box as a crib for baby Jesus.
Mary and Joseph watched Jesus sleep.
They rejoiced and thanked God for Jesus.

Based on Luke 2:1–7

Cultural Awareness

Locate the country of Peru on a map. Print the words *Feliz Navidad* on the board and have the children recite these Spanish words for "Merry Christmas." On Christmas Eve at midnight, Peruvians celebrate the "Mass of the Rooster." Legend has it that on the first Christmas, a rooster crowed when Jesus was born. After Mass, children have a contest to see who can sound the most like a rooster.

Find the hidden words. Color them green.
Then color the picture. Jesus is born.

Christmas: Lesson Two   275

Reading and Discussing a Story

Direct the children to turn to page 274. Read "The First Christmas" with the class. Ask the following questions.

- Where did Mary and Joseph go? (*To Bethlehem*)
- Why couldn't they find a place to sleep? (*The inn was all filled up.*)
- Where was Jesus born? (*In a stable*)

Tell the class that the barn where Jesus was born is called a *stable* and the box Jesus slept in is called a *manger,* which was used to feed cows and other large animals.

Have volunteers retell the Nativity story in their own words, using a Nativity set or flannel-board figures.

Step 3/CONCLUSION

Learning How to Live Our Faith

Finding Hidden Words

Have the children complete the hidden word activity on page 275. Help the children recall that Jesus is our greatest gift from God. Emphasize that Mary and Joseph were the first people to thank God for the gift of Jesus and that we remember God's gift each year when we celebrate Christmas, the birthday of Jesus. Encourage each child to offer a silent prayer of thanks for the birth of Jesus.

Making a Montage

Invite the children to make a montage celebrating the birth of Jesus. Provide a supply of magazines and have the children find and cut out pictures of Christmas celebrations. Then ask the children to glue their pictures to a poster which you prepared earlier. This poster might have a large picture of Jesus glued in the center.

Objective

This lesson helps the children appreciate Christmas as a time to share our joy with others.

Step 1/INTRODUCTION

Learning About Our Lives

Talking About Christmas Customs

Invite the children to name some of the things they do with their families on Christmas day. Ask the following questions to stimulate discussion.

- Do you have a special family dinner?
- What does your family eat?
- Do you stay at home or go to someone else's house?
- Who comes to your house?
- Whom do you visit?

Allow time for each of the children to share a story about a family Christmas custom.

Step 2/DEVELOPMENT

Learning About Our Faith

Reading and Discussing a Story

Direct the children to turn to page 276 in their books. Read "A Family Christmas Celebration" with the class. Use these questions to discuss the story.

- What did Dean's family do on Christmas? (*They went to get Grandma at the nursing home.*)

Explain to the children that a nursing home is like a hospital and that it is a place for people to be cared for.

- What did Dean's family do at the nursing home? (*They gave out presents and picked up Grandma.*)
- What was Dean's family celebrating? (*Jesus' birthday on Christmas*)

Finding Ways to Share Christmas Joy

Tell the children that at Christmas, Jesus wants us to share our happiness with others. We do this by showing love in special ways for our families. Point out that Dean's family brought gifts to the nursing home for Grandma's friends.

276

A Family Christmas Celebration

After Christmas Mass, Dean and his dad went to pick up Grandma at the nursing home.

Dean kissed her and said, "We have a fruit basket for the nurses. We have surprises for your friends!" Dad wheeled Grandma around as Dean happily passed out the presents.

When they got home, the family ate a big Christmas dinner. After dinner they gathered around the tree for dessert. It was a beautiful Christmas cake.

★ ★★★ ★
Enriching the Lesson

To help the children appreciate that Jesus asks us to share our joy with others, have them make place mats for a local nursing home, hospital, or shelter. Give out drawing paper and have the children write a Christmas message and draw a Christmas scene. You may want to cover the mats with clear adhesive paper before delivering them.

Then the family gave Grandma her presents and sang Christmas carols. Dean said, "I love Jesus' birthday."

Activity

Here is Dean's family Christmas cake. Print the missing word on the cake. Then decorate the cake.

Happy Birthday

Jesus

Have the children find and underline the words in the text that show that Dean's family shared their joy with others (Picked up Grandma; had a fruit basket for the nurses and surprises for her friends; passed out the presents). Encourage the students to give examples of how we can show love for our families and others on Christmas.

Step 3/CONCLUSION

Learning How to Live Our Faith

Writing and Coloring in the Text

Have the children look at page 277 and tell what they see on this page (a birthday cake). Ask: Whom do you think the birthday cake is for? As the children identify Jesus as the one being honored, praise them for remembering that Christmas is Jesus' birthday. Read the sentence printed on the cake with the class, having them supply the missing word. Instruct the children to print the word *Jesus* on the line provided. Then invite the children to decorate the cake.

Praying Together

To emphasize that Jesus' birth on Christmas brings us happiness and joy, teach the children to sing the first three lines of "Joy to the World." This can be sung as a three-part round.

LESSON 4

Objective

This lesson helps the children honor Jesus by making a Christmas ornament and celebrating the birth of Jesus in prayer.

Preparing for the Project

Cover a work area with newspapers and prepare a drying area for the ornaments. If you invited a parent or aide to help supervise this project, introduce him or her to the children and explain that he or she will be helping them with their ornaments. Ask the children to turn to page 278. Read the project directions and show the children the sample ornament you made earlier.

Making an Ornament

■ Distribute small balloons. (Be sure to have extra balloons in case some break.)

■ Show the children a container of yarn soaked in starch and have each child take a piece of yarn. Demonstrate how to wrap the yarn around the balloon, leaving a few open areas. Offer assistance as necessary.

■ When all the children have finished wrapping yarn around their balloons, place the ornaments aside to dry. (Drying usually takes two to three days. Turn the balloons daily so that they will dry evenly. If the balloons are not drying well, use the low speed on a hand-held hair dryer to speed things up.)

■ When all the ornaments are dry, help each child pop his or her balloon with a straight pin. Show the children how to remove the balloons through the stiffened yarn.

■ Finally, have each child tie a loop of clear thread through the top of the ornament so it can be hung.

■ Suggest that the children give their ornaments to someone they love. Ask to whom they plan to give their ornaments and emphasize that we give gifts in honor of the birth of Jesus.

278

A Christmas Ornament

1. Your teacher will give you a balloon and some wet yarn.

2. Blow up the balloon and tie it tight.

3. Wrap yarn around the balloon so that the balloon is covered with yarn.

4. When the yarn dries, pop the balloon. Now you have a Christmas ornament.

At Christmas we give gifts to spread Jesus' love. To whom will you give your Christmas ornament?

 Teaching Tips

When making ornaments, tell the children that the first tree ornaments were candles. The tradition of the Christmas tree began in Germany. The green branches of the tree were a sign of life. They reminded people that Jesus brings us new life. The flames of light reminded people of the stars that shined over Bethlehem the night Jesus was born.

A Christmas Prayer Service

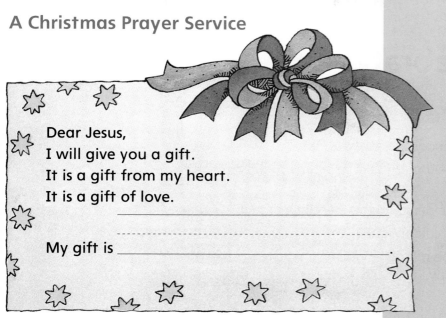

Dear Jesus,
I will give you a gift.
It is a gift from my heart.
It is a gift of love.

_____

My gift is _____.

We pray,
Thank you, God, for Jesus.
Help us to remember
all your gifts.
Help us to give the gift of
ourselves to others.
Glory to God!
Amen.

Christmas: Lesson Five 279

Planning a Christmas Tableau

Begin this section by teaching "Silent Night" found in the THIS IS OUR FAITH MUSIC Program, Grade 1. Tell the children that a tableau of the Christmas story will be part of their prayer. Ask for volunteers to portray Mary and Joseph in the tableau. You will also need two good readers to narrate. Be sure to have a doll (baby Jesus) for the tableau. Direct volunteers to read through the Nativity story on page 274. Assign alternate lines to the narrators and have them mark their lines in their texts. Provide time for practice.

Meanwhile, the remaining children may listen to a recording of the "Little Drummer Boy." Then direct the children to open their books to page 279 and read together the prayer in the decorated gift box. Tell the children that like the little drummer boy, they can give Jesus gifts. Discuss some of the following ideas to help the children determine what gifts they might give.

■ Personal talents such as reciting a poem, or singing a song

■ The gift of love, such as telling Jesus in prayer that you love him

■ Doing something for someone else as a gift for Jesus

Invite the children to print in the space provided what gift they will give to Jesus.

Participating in the Prayer

Have the children gather in the prayer area. Begin the prayer by singing "Silent Night." Remind the children that at Christmas we celebrate the birth of Jesus, God's greatest gift to us. Then have the four volunteers present the Nativity story tableau.

Afterwards encourage the children to share with God and the other children what they want to give as gifts to Jesus. Conclude the session by having the children pray the rest of prayer on page 279.

Enriching the Lesson

As you prepare to pray, use the diagrams below to teach the children how to "say" the words *gift* and *love* in sign language.

Enriching the Lesson

Help the children prepare a manger scene in your classroom. Tell them that we have several names for this scene. We sometimes call it a *Nativity* scene. Explain that the word *Nativity* means "birth." We also call it a *crèche.* Explain that a famous saint called Francis Assissi used real people and animals in his crèche scene. Invite the children to share with one another what their Nativity scenes at home look like and where they display them.

279

Our Church Celebrates Lent

Objectives

- LESSON 1: To help the children choose to follow Jesus.
- LESSON 2: To help the children recognize Lent as a time to become more like Jesus.
- LESSON 3: To help the children understand that Lent is a time to change.
- LESSON 4: To help the children think about how they have acted.
- LESSON 5: To help the children be mindful of following Jesus by making mosaic crosses and praying a litany.

Lesson Outlines

	Step 1 Learning About Our Lives	Step 2 Learning About Our Faith	Step 3 Learning How to Live Our Faith
Lesson 1	■ Discuss symbols. ■ Explain ashes are a symbol. *ABOUT 10 MINUTES*	■ Read and discuss the text. *ABOUT 5 MINUTES*	■ Share ideas. ■ Find a hidden picture. ■ Pray together. *ABOUT 15 MINUTES*
Lesson 2	■ Recall the meaning of Lent. ■ Share experiences. *ABOUT 10 MINUTES*	■ Read and discuss a story. ■ Remember to show love. *ABOUT 10 MINUTES*	■ Learn to be like Jesus. ■ Make Lenten promises. *ABOUT 10 MINUTES*
Lesson 3	■ Mime changes. *ABOUT 10 MINUTES*	■ Sing a Lenten song. ■ Play a word game. ■ Read and discuss the text. *ABOUT 10 MINUTES*	■ Decide how to act during Lent. ■ Pray together. *ABOUT 10 MINUTES*
Lesson 4	■ Answer questions about Lent. *ABOUT 8 MINUTES*	■ Read the text. ■ Listen to a story about Jesus. *ABOUT 12 MINUTES*	■ Think about how we act. ■ Pray a prayer of sorrow. *ABOUT 10 MINUTES*
Lesson 5	**Project** Recall the symbol of Lent and make a cross as a special sign of Lent. **Prayer Service** Learn a song and pray a Lenten litany.		

Plan Ahead

	Preparing Your Class	**Materials Needed**
Lesson 1	Read the lesson plan for this class.	■ drawing paper ■ small United States flag
Lesson 2	Make a scroll from parchment paper. Write on it: I want to be like Jesus. During Lent I will try to be more loving and forgiving.	■ large piece of parchment paper
Lesson 3	Read the lesson plan for this class.	
Lesson 4	Read the lesson plan for this class.	
Lesson 5	Cut poster board crosses 8" X 7" with a 1-1/2" cross beam. Make a sample cross with bits of colored tissue. Inform the presider of the time and place of the prayer service.	■ poster-board crosses ■ scissors; glue ■ colored tissue paper ■ scroll from Lesson 2

Additional Resources

As you plan these lessons consider the following materials from The Resourceful Teacher Package.

■ *Classroom Activity Sheets* for Lent

■ *Family Activity Sheets* for Lent

■ *Prayers for Every Day*

You may wish to refer to the following Big Book.

■ *We Celebrate God's Word*, page 18

In preparing the children for the Sunday readings, you may wish to use Silver Burdett Ginn's *Getting Ready for Sunday* student and teacher materials.

REDUCED CLASSROOM ACTIVITIES

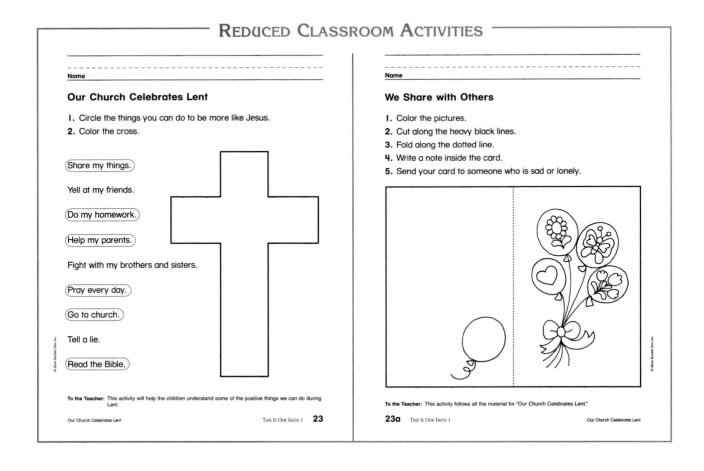

Name

Our Church Celebrates Lent

1. Circle the things you can do to be more like Jesus.
2. Color the cross.

(Share my things.)

Yell at my friends.

(Do my homework.)

(Help my parents.)

Fight with my brothers and sisters.

(Pray every day.)

(Go to church.)

Tell a lie.

(Read the Bible.)

To the Teacher: This activity will help the children understand some of the positive things we can do during Lent.

Our Church Celebrates Lent   THIS IS OUR FAITH 1 **23**

Name

We Share with Others

1. Color the pictures.
2. Cut along the heavy black lines.
3. Fold along the dotted line.
4. Write a note inside the card.
5. Send your card to someone who is sad or lonely.

To the Teacher: This activity follows all the material for "Our Church Celebrates Lent."

23a THIS IS OUR FAITH 1   Our Church Celebrates Lent

Background for the Teacher

LENTEN JOURNEY

Lent can be described as a journey we experience during the forty days preceding Easter. The journey begins on Ash Wednesday, when the Sign of the Cross is traced on our foreheads with blessed ashes. The ashes are a visible sign of our need for repentance.

On Ash Wednesday, we commit ourselves to prayer, penance, and a willingness to put our own desires aside by performing acts of loving service to others. We choose to follow the words of Christ, "Whoever wishes to be my follower must deny his very self, take up his cross each day, and follow in my steps" (Based on Luke 9:23).

GUIDING THE CHILDREN

First graders have limited ability to examine their faults and redirect their behavior. To do this, they need the guidance and example of adults. The children respond best to a positive attitude that helps them focus on the potential they have for doing kind acts and other acts of love. The positive reinforcement you give the children will remind them that their efforts to follow Jesus are appreciated and understood.

SHARING

Whenever you ask the children to share their ideas, work, or past experiences, establish an atmosphere of trust. As an example, when they are drawing you might do so also and show them your drawing. Be sure to compliment the children on their efforts.

As you discuss with the children how to best follow Jesus, consider together small acts they can perform during Lent. Examples might include making peace with a sibling or playmate, sharing toys, helping family members at home, and thinking about others before oneself. Encourage the children to contribute their own ideas.

LESSON 1

Objective

This lesson helps the children choose to follow Jesus.

Step 1/INTRODUCTION

Learning About Our Lives

Discussing Symbols

Distribute the drawing paper and tell the children that they will be drawing symbols. Explain that a symbol is something that stands for something else. Write the word *symbol* on the chalkboard. Have the children repeat the word. To guide the children in a discussion about symbols, draw a crown on the chalkboard and ask the children what it makes them think of (A king or queen). Then point to the flag you brought and ask the children what the flag stands for? (Our country).

Explaining that Ashes Are a Symbol

Explain to the children that ashes are a symbol we use during the season of Lent. Tell them that today we will learn about the meaning of ashes and how the season of Lent helps us to become more like Jesus.

Step 2/DEVELOPMENT

Learning About Our Faith

Reading and Discussing the Text

Read page 280 of the student text aloud while the children follow along silently. Then guide them in a discussion, using the following questions.

- What do we get ready for during Lent? (*Easter*)

- What is the name of the first day of Lent? (*Ash Wednesday*)

- What happens on Ash Wednesday? (*The priest puts ashes on our head in a sign of the cross.*)

- What do we promise to do on Ash Wednesday? (*To try to be more like Jesus.*)

Invite the children to sit in a circle around you. Ask them to listen as you tell them the words of Jesus from the Bible: *"If you want to follow me, you must forget yourself and think of others first"* (Based on Luke 9:23).

280

Our Church Celebrates Lent

The First Day of Lent

We get ready for Easter during Lent.
Ash Wednesday is the first day of Lent.

On **Ash Wednesday,** the priest traces the sign of the cross on our foreheads with ashes.
The ashes remind us to follow Jesus.
We should try to be more like Jesus.

We pray, "I will follow Jesus."

280   Lent: Lesson One

Cultural Awareness

To sharpen the children's awareness of people who are in need within the church and society as a whole, you might suggest that the children do extra chores at home to earn money that can be used to purchase toys or books for a local charity that serves poor families. Or have the children begin assembling small gifts, such as toiletries, puzzle books, and sweets to be used in making Easter baskets for a nursing home.

Activity

Find the hidden picture.
Color each shape with a *.

Learning How to Live Our Faith

Sharing Ideas

Discuss with the children what Jesus' words mean. Help them realize that Jesus wants us to be more like him. Explain that we can do this by trying to let our words and actions show that we are thinking of others, not just ourselves. Help the children understand that this is often hard to do. On Ash Wednesday, we begin to try to follow Jesus more.

Have the children return to their seats. Guide them in a discussion of loving acts they can perform during Lent. Ask each child to tell the act he or she has chosen to perform in order to be more like Jesus. Encourage them to put the action in writing.

Finding a Hidden Picture

Call attention to page 281. Read aloud the directions for the activity. Ask the children to complete the activity, assisting them if necessary. When they have finished, discuss with them the picture that has been revealed (A cross).

Praying Together

Invite the children to pray the following with you *"Jesus, we will follow you."* Encourage them to say the prayer each day during Lent.

Enriching the Lesson

Use a variation of the game "Simon Says" to reinforce some of the loving acts the children might perform during Lent. Invite the children to stand. Direct them to pantomime the following loving acts that Jesus wants us to do:

- Share your toys;
- Be kind to your brothers and sisters;
- Pray for the poor;
- Help your mother at home.

281

LESSON 2

Objective
This lesson helps the children recognize Lent as a time to become more like Jesus.

Step 1/INTRODUCTION

Learning About Our Lives

Recalling the Meaning of Lent
Review the previous lesson with the class. Ask the following questions.

- What is the name of this season of the Church year? (*Lent*)
- What do we call the first day of Lent? (*Ash Wednesday*)
- What happens on Ash Wednesday? (*The priest makes the Sign of the Cross on our foreheads with ashes.*)
- What do the ashes remind us to do? (*To follow Jesus*)

Sharing Experiences
Invite the children to share experiences of playing with friends or siblings. Ask the following questions. (Answers will vary.)

- What do you like to play when you are with your friends, brothers, or sisters?
- What happens when you and your friends want to do different things?
- How do you decide what to do?

Emphasize that although we do not always agree with others, during Lent we try harder than ever to follow Jesus and to treat our family and friends with love.

Step 2/DEVELOPMENT

Learning About Our Faith

Reading and Discussing a Story
Have the children turn to page 282 and follow along as you read "A Time to Become More Like Jesus." Afterwards, use these questions to discuss the story.

- Why were Tim and Amy fighting? (*They both wanted to watch a different TV show.*)
- Why did Tim stop shouting? (*He remembered it was Lent.*)
- Whom was Tim trying to be like? (*Jesus*)

282

A Time to Become More Like Jesus

Tim and Amy were fighting.
Tim wanted to watch one
TV show.
Amy wanted to watch a
different show.
Then Tim remembered
that it was **Lent**.
He remembered that he was trying to be loving and forgiving.
Tim was trying to become more like Jesus.

Activity

How could Tim be like Jesus?
Draw a picture showing what Tim could do.

Teaching Tips

Decorate the prayer area in your classroom with signs of Lent. Drape the prayer table with a purple cloth and explain to the children that the color purple is a sign that we want to change the way we are living by being more loving and forgiving during Lent. Display a large cross on the prayer table.

Activity

Put an **X** next to the pictures that show children trying to be like Jesus.
Then trace the words below.

Jesus says,

" Love one another. "

Based on John 13:34

Enriching the Lesson

Give the children partners and give each pair two sheets of light purple construction paper. Show the children how to trace the outline of one another's footprint on the paper, using a black crayon. Have the children cut their footprints out and print the words "Love one another" on them, along with their names. Tape the footprints to the floor in the prayer area to reinforce that by loving others, we can follow Jesus during Lent.

Encourage the children to suggest ways that Tim could be loving and forgiving. Invite each child to draw on page 282 a picture to show one way Tim could be like Jesus.

Remembering to Show Love

Ask the children to listen as you read these words of Jesus: *"I give you a new commandment: love one another"* (John 13:34). Discuss what these words mean. Help the children realize that during Lent we make special efforts to show our love for others just as Jesus always did.

Step 3/CONCLUSION

Learning How to Live Our Faith

Learning to Be Like Jesus

Read aloud the directions to the activity on page 283. Instruct the children to work independently as they complete the activity. Afterward, invite volunteers to tell a story about each picture. In discussing the pictures that show negative actions, ask how the children in the pictures could try to be more like Jesus. Finally, have the children trace over the words "Love one another" and repeat these words aloud together.

Making Lenten Promises

Gather the children in a circle and show them the scroll you prepared prior to class. Read the words on the scroll: *"I want to become more like Jesus. During Lent I will try to be more loving and forgiving."* Tell the children that as a sign of their willingness to try, they may print their own names on the scroll. Praise each child for being willing to become more like Jesus. Save the scroll for use in Lesson 5.

LESSON 3

Objective

This lesson helps the children understand that Lent is a time to change.

Step 1/INTRODUCTION

Learning About Our Lives

Miming Changes

Have the children pantomime the following pairs of directions: sit, stand; smile, frown; laugh, cry; sleep; wake up. Praise the students for listening so closely to the directions. Then ask them what they had to do to follow each direction. Help them to understand that each time they had to stop what they were doing in order to do something new. Summarize by telling the children that they had to make a change in order to follow the new direction. Explain that in today's lesson, they will learn that Lent is a time to change.

Step 2/DEVELOPMENT

Learning About Our Faith

Singing a Lenten Song

Direct attention to page 284 and read aloud the title "We Follow Jesus." Tell the children that they are going to learn a poem about Lent. Read the poem aloud with the class.

Reading and Discussing the Text

Read with the class the last paragraph on page 284. Ask the following questions.

- How long is Lent? (*Forty days*)
- What can we change during Lent? (*The things that keep us from being like Jesus*)
- What do we ask Jesus during Lent? (*To help us follow him*)

Playing a Word Game

Help the children understand what it means to change by playing a game with them. Say, "During Lent we can change from being selfish to. . ." and have children suggest a word that shows change, such as "sharing." Continue this activity using the following examples: being mean, fighting, yelling, lying, and so on.

We Follow Jesus

Jesus, we will follow you,
Follow you, follow you.
Jesus we will follow you,
All the way to Easter.

Lent is a time to help and share,
A time to pray, a time to love.
We will show our love for you,
All the way to Easter.

Lent lasts all of forty days,
Forty days, forty days.
How will we act for forty days
To show our love for Jesus?

Say your prayers.

Be kind to others.

Make your bed.

284   Lent: Lesson Three

Enriching the Lesson

Carry the memo pad theme out on a large bulletin board in your classroom. Have a number of memo pad pages available for the children to write their names and good deeds on. Tack or staple these on the board. As the pads accumulate, mention how well the students are following Jesus.

Activity

How will you show love during the forty days of Lent?

Finish coloring the memo pad each time you try to be more like Jesus.

Help a friend.

Obey your parents.

Make a get-well card.

Share your toys.

Lent: Lesson Three 285

Deciding How to Act During Lent

Direct attention to the activity on pages 284–285. Tell the children that they will be able to use these pages as they follow Jesus during Lent. Read aloud the directions and have the children read each of the ideas on the signs. Ask them to suggest other ways they can be more like Jesus. Invite them to color in the uncolored parts of the memo pads when they do the Lenten action suggested on the pad. Praise their attempts to follow Jesus.

Praying Together

Have the children bow their heads. Read the words of St. Paul to them: *"Do good and share what you have. God is happy with your good deeds"* (Based on Hebrews 13:16). Then have the students recite together the poem on page 284.

Objective

This lesson helps the children to think about how they have acted.

Step 1/INTRODUCTION

Learning About Our Lives

Answering Questions About Lent

Review the children's understanding of Lent by asking the following questions.

- What do we prepare for during Lent? (*Easter*)

- What is the first day of Lent? (*Ash Wednesday*)

- What is a special sign of Lent? (*The cross*)

- What do we try to do during Lent? (*Try to become more like Jesus; follow Jesus*)

- How can we show our love for Jesus during Lent? (*By being kind; helping others; sharing*)

After discussing the questions, give the children an opportunity to color one or more of the memo pads in their books on pages 284–285, if they have done any of the suggestions. Comment on the children's efforts to show their love for Jesus.

Step 2/DEVELOPMENT

Learning About Our Faith

Reading the Text

Read "Our Journey with Jesus" on page 286 with the children. Direct them to find and circle the word in the text that means that we think more about ourselves than following Jesus (Selfish).

Listening to a Story About Jesus

Have the children sit around you in a circle. Ask them to listen as you tell them a story about Jesus from the Bible.

When Jesus was getting ready to teach people about God, he went to the desert to pray by himself. When he came out of the desert, he told the people, "Be sorry for hurting others! Live my Good News!" (Based on Mark 1:14).

286

Our Journey with Jesus

During Lent we are on a journey
with Jesus.
On our journey to Easter, we think
about how we are living.

Sometimes we do not show
our love for Jesus.
Sometimes we are selfish.
Sometimes we hurt others.
During Lent we think about how to act.

We try to change the things that keep
us from being as loving as Jesus.
Jesus will help us say we are sorry to
the people we have hurt.
He will help us make up and be friends again.

286   Lent: Lesson Four

Focus on

Prayer   This lesson tells the children about Jesus going to the desert to pray in private. It is a good time to foster private spontaneous prayers of love to Jesus among the children. Following Jesus and growing closer to him is accomplished by prayer. Encouraging the addition of private prayer to the children's Lenten practice will help them draw nearer to Jesus.

Looking at How We Live

Let's think about how we act.
Do you need to say, "I'm sorry," and
make up with someone?
Can you say, "I try to love as Jesus asks us"?

I say my prayers every day.

I tell the truth.

I fight with my friends.

I help at home.

I take things that don't belong to me.

I share my toys.

I take care of my things.

I am mean to others.

I say, "I'm sorry," when I hurt others.

I obey my parents and teachers.

Explain to the children that when we act selfishly, we are not showing love as Jesus showed us how to be. During Lent, Jesus wants us to be sorry for our selfish and unloving ways of treating people.

Step 3/CONCLUSION

Learning How to Live Our Faith

Thinking About How We Act

Direct the children to return to their desks. Help the children think about how they have been acting by reading page 287. Read each statement aloud and have the children think quietly to themselves about how they act.

Praying a Prayer of Sorrow

Tell the children that they can tell Jesus they are sorry for the times they hurt someone by acting selfishly. Tell them that Jesus forgives them and helps them remember to live with love. Teach the children the following prayer.

Dear Jesus, I am sorry for being selfish. Help me to be more loving during Lent. Amen.

LESSON 5

Objectives

This lesson helps the children be mindful of following Jesus by making a mosaic cross and by praying a litany.

Recalling the Symbol of Lent

Read aloud with the class "A Special Sign of Lent" on page 288 of the student text. Remind the children that on Ash Wednesday the Sign of the Cross is traced on our foreheads with ashes. Tell the children that these ashes get washed or worn off our foreheads.

Invite them to make a cross that they can keep as a Lenten reminder. Display the sample cross you have made of mosaic-like tissue scarps.

Making a Special Sign of Lent

Distribute the posterboard crosses that you prepared earlier, colored tissue paper, glue and enough newspaper so that each child's workspace will be protected. Instruct the children to tear the tissue paper into small pieces and glue the pieces to the cross. Explain that the pieces of tissue paper can overlap and should cover the entire cross. Encourage the children to use a variety of colors of tissue paper on their crosses.

Move about the room while the children work, assisting them and talking with them about where they will display their crosses at home. Afterward, have the children set the crosses aside to dry.

A Special Sign of Lent

The cross reminds us of Jesus. It helps us remember to be loving and forgiving. Make a cross to remind you to be more like Jesus.

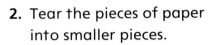

1. Your teacher will give you a paper cross and pieces of colored paper.

2. Tear the pieces of paper into smaller pieces.

3. Paste the pieces all over the paper cross.

4. Share the cross with your family.

CURRICULUM CONNECTION

Language Arts Work with the children to write a Lenten prayer on the chalkboard. Incorporate the following themes into the prayer: following Jesus, trying to become more loving and forgiving, loving one another, being sorry for our sins, and preparing for Easter. After you have completed the prayer, invite the children to copy it neatly on lined paper. Plan to pray it together during your prayer service.

A Prayer Service for Lent

Teacher Jesus, you were kind to others.

Children I will follow you, Jesus.

Teacher Jesus, you show us how to love.

Children I will follow you, Jesus.

Teacher Jesus, you thought of others first.

Children I will follow you, Jesus.

All Help us to follow you, Jesus.
Help us to love one another.
Amen.

Lent: Lesson Six 289

Learning a Song

Teach the children the words to the following song, sung to the tune of "Mary Had a Little Lamb."

Following Jesus
Jesus says, "Come follow me,
"Follow me,
"Follow me."
Jesus says, "Come follow me,
"Follow me through Lent."

Jesus, I will follow you,
Follow you,
Follow you,
Jesus, I will follow you,
Follow you through Lent.

Ask for a volunteer to represent the class by presenting the scroll made in Lesson 2 to the presider during the prayer.

Praying a Lenten Litany

Ask the children to bring their texts and gather in a circle. If you have invited a special presider, have him or her greet the children and lead them in the Sign of the Cross. Ask the children to sing "Following Jesus," which they learned earlier today. Next, have the presider read these words of Jesus:

"If you want to follow me, you must forget yourself and think of others first" (Based on Luke 9:23).

"I give you a new commandment: love one another" (John 13:34).

Ask the presider to talk with the children about ways they can try to follow Jesus during Lent. Then have the children read the responses as you read the prayer on page 289. Invite a volunteer to present the presider with the Lenten scroll as a sign that the children will try to become more like Jesus during Lent. Have the children repeat the closing section of the prayer on page 289.

Teaching Tips

It is a challenge to keep the children focused on the themes developed in this chapter throughout the long weeks of Lent. You can reinforce learning by incorporating the Scripture verses the children have studied into your daily prayers, by having the children recite once a week the prayer you wrote together, by singing the "Following Jesus" song frequently, and by calling attention to the loving and forgiving actions the children demonstrate.

Enriching the Lesson

Call the children forward individually. Sign each of them on the forehead with the Sign of the Cross as you repeat the words of Jesus: *Be sorry for hurting others. Live Jesus' Good News!*

Our Church Celebrates Holy Week

Objectives

■ LESSON 1: To help the children understand that on Passion Sunday we celebrate that Jesus is our humble king.

■ LESSON 2: To help the children prepare to celebrate Holy Thursday, Good Friday, and Holy Saturday.

Lesson Outlines

	Step 1 Learning About Our Lives	**Step 2** Learning About Our Faith	**Step 3** Learning How to Live Our Faith
Lesson 1	■ Greet the children joyfully. ■ Discuss different ways to greet people. *ABOUT 5 MINUTES*	■ Read the text. *ABOUT 10 MINUTES*	■ Show and discuss palm branches. ■ Draw a prayer of praise. ■ Pray together. *ABOUT 15 MINUTES*
Lesson 2	■ Look at a calendar chart. *ABOUT 6 MINUTES*	■ Read the text. *ABOUT 14 MINUTES*	■ Solve a letter puzzle. ■ Talk about Jesus' presence. ■ Pray together. *ABOUT 10 MINUTES*

Plan Ahead

	Preparing Your Class	Materials Needed
Lesson 1	Read through the entire plan before teaching this lesson. If possible, obtain palm branches for the children.	■ palm branches (optional)
Lesson 2	Prepare a Holy Week calendar for this lesson, big enough for the class to see.	■ calendar

Additional Resources

As you plan these lessons consider using the following materials from The Resourceful Teacher Package.

■ *Classroom Activity Sheets* for Holy Week

■ *Family Activity Sheets* for Holy Week

■ *Prayers for Every Day*

In preparing the children for the Sunday readings, you may wish to use Silver Burdett Ginn's *Getting Ready for Sunday* student and teacher materials.

REDUCED CLASSROOM ACTIVITIES

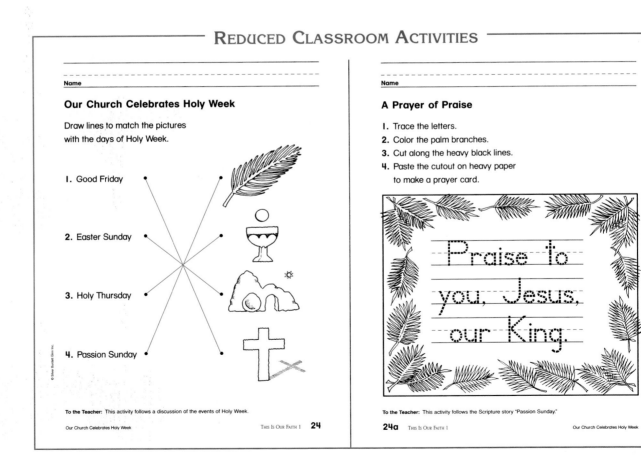

Name

Our Church Celebrates Holy Week

Draw lines to match the pictures
with the days of Holy Week.

1. Good Friday

2. Easter Sunday

3. Holy Thursday

4. Passion Sunday

To the Teacher: This activity follows a discussion of the events of Holy Week.

Our Church Celebrates Holy Week

THIS IS OUR FAITH 1 **24**

Name

A Prayer of Praise

1. Trace the letters.
2. Color the palm branches.
3. Cut along the heavy black lines.
4. Paste the cutout on heavy paper
   to make a prayer card.

Praise to
you, Jesus,
our King.

To the Teacher: This activity follows the Scripture story "Passion Sunday."

24a THIS IS OUR FAITH 1   Our Church Celebrates Holy Week

PASSION SUNDAY

Passion Sunday is the beginning of the most solemn week of the Church year. On Passion Sunday, we celebrate the triumphal entry of Jesus into the city of Jerusalem. As seen in John's gospel, the entry of Jesus into Jerusalem followed the calling of Lazarus back to life and the testimony of witnesses to that event. Word of the teaching of Jesus and of his miracles had spread throughout the city and drew the crowd to him.

Children can easily appreciate the excitement of the crowd that greeted Jesus as he entered Jerusalem. Invite the children to celebrate their love for Jesus by enacting a Passion Sunday procession, encouraging them to add their own prayer to the one given in their texts. They can thank Jesus for the special gifts he gives each of them. The use of palm branches, if available, will help familiarize the children with the Passion Sunday liturgy.

But Passion Sunday is marked by other, less joyful, elements. We know that within a few days, the Christian community will contemplate the meaning of Jesus' arrest and execution. During the Passion Sunday liturgy, we are conscious of the acceptance by Jesus of the suffering and death that were to come to him. Passion Sunday carries the same message for us—that suffering and death are a part of our journey to eternal life.

THE TRIDUUM

In Lesson 2, the children will be introduced to the Triduum as the three most holy days of the year. Lent officially ends on Holy Thursday. The Triduum begins with the evening Mass of the Lord's Supper on Holy Thursday and ends at sunset on Easter Sunday. The celebration of these three days is the high point and climax of the entire liturgical year.

During the Triduum, we celebrate Holy Thursday, Good Friday, and Holy Saturday. On Holy Thursday, we recall the institution of the Eucharist at the Last Supper. Good Friday commemorates Jesus' suffering and death on the cross. On Holy Saturday evening, the Catholic community gathers to celebrate the Easter Vigil. There we rejoice in Jesus' resurrection, initiate new members into our community, renew our Baptismal commitment, and welcome new members to the Lord's table for the first time.

The children will have limited experience of the Church's celebration of the Triduum, for many of them may not participate with their families in the lengthy liturgies that mark Holy Week. Although Masses are not permitted during the day on either Good Friday or Holy Saturday, Liturgy of the Word celebrations and Stations of the Cross services geared to children help them enter into these three sacred days.

LESSON 1

Objective

This lesson helps the children understand that on Passion Sunday we celebrate that Jesus is our king, a king who is humble, not domineering.

Step 1/INTRODUCTION

Learning About Our Lives

Greeting the Children Joyfully

Invite a few volunteers to go quietly out into the hall. Then invite them to come back into the room. As they enter the room, greet each one with joy. You might have cheerful music playing as you do this. Shake each child's hand and lead each one to his or her seat. Have the children welcome each other by clapping as each one is seated.

Discussing Different Ways to Greet People

Ask the following questions about the greetings the children received. (*Answers will vary.*)

- How did you feel when I shook your hand?
- How did you feel when the others clapped for you?

Explain that we can help make people feel welcomed and important in many ways—by shaking hands, waving, or hugging. We can also plan special celebrations to welcome people and to make their visit an important event. Explain that a parade is one such celebration. Have the children talk about parades they may have attended. Explain that the people once greeted Jesus with a special parade.

Step 2/DEVELOPMENT

Learning About Our Faith

Reading the Text

Read page 290 of the student text aloud. Explain that the people were so happy to see Jesus because of all they had heard about him and the miracles he worked. Ask the children to imagine themselves as part of the parade that welcomed Jesus to Jerusalem. Explain that on Passion Sunday we praise and honor Jesus as our loving king.

290

Our Church Celebrates Holy Week

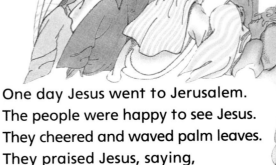

Passion Sunday

One day Jesus went to Jerusalem.
The people were happy to see Jesus.
They cheered and waved palm leaves.
They praised Jesus, saying,
"Blessed is the king who comes in God's name."

Based on Luke 19:28–38

The First Day of Holy Week

Passion Sunday is the first day of Holy Week.
Every year on Passion Sunday, we pray, "Praise to Jesus, our king."

Focus on

Passion Sunday   This is the first day of Holy Week, the most important week of the Church year. The word *passion* means "suffering." During this week, we celebrate Jesus' joyous welcome in Jerusalem, his suffering and death, and his passage from death to new life. Passion Sunday was formerly called "Palm Sunday" because of the palm fronds the citizens waved and laid in Jesus' path as he made his way into the city.

Activity

Finish this prayer by drawing a picture in each box.

Jesus, we praise you

in the morning. ☀	at night. 🌙
Jesus, you are our king. 👑	

Learning How to Live Our Faith

Showing and Discussing Palm Branches

If you have brought in palm branches, show them to the children. Explain that we receive the branches at Mass on Passion Sunday and display them at home as a sign of rejoicing. Stress that they remind us that Jesus is our king and that we can follow Jesus by trying to act like him.

Drawing a Prayer of Praise

Have the children look at page 291. Explain the directions and have the children suggest ways they can show themselves praising Jesus. Then have them use crayons to draw what they suggested in the first two boxes. In the third box, they might draw a symbol, such as a king's crown.

Praying Together

Give each child a palm branch. If you do not have real ones cut some from paper—or if possible take the children outside to cut small branches from trees. Have a procession around the room. Show the children how to march with their palms raised above their heads. As they march, invite the children to join you in repeating joyfully the prayer they illustrated on page 291.

CURRICULUM CONNECTION

Music   Teach the children to sing a lively "Hosanna" and explain that the people of Jerusalem used this word to welcome Jesus into Jerusalem. Write the word *Hosanna* on the chalkboard and tell the children that this word means "Praise be to God!" Give out rhythm instruments for your Holy Week procession and have the children sing "Hosanna" and play the instruments as they march.

LESSON 2

Objective

This lesson helps the children prepare to celebrate Holy Thursday, Good Friday, and Holy Saturday.

Step 1/INTRODUCTION

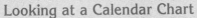

Learning About Our Lives

Looking at a Calendar Chart

Show the children the calendar you prepared for this lesson. Ask them why we use a calendar. Lead them to understand that a calendar helps us to keep track of the days. Tell them that a calendar also helps us to know when important days are celebrated. Ask the children to tell you some of the important days that they think should be written on a calendar. Their responses might include Christmas, Easter, July 4, birthdays, and so forth.

Point to Ash Wednesday and help the children recall that Lent begins on Ash Wednesday. Then point to Passion Sunday and ask the children what they learned about this important day in the previous lesson (Passion Sunday is the first day of Holy Week; we remember that the people in Jerusalem welcomed Jesus like a king.) Show the children the blank calendar squares for Thursday, Friday, and Saturday in Holy Week. Tell the children that they will learn about these special days in today's lesson.

Step 2/DEVELOPMENT

Learning About Our Faith

Reading the Text

Direct the children to turn to page 292 and read "The Holiest Days of the Year" with the class. Discuss the following questions.

- What did Jesus do on the night before he died? (*He shared a special meal with his friends. Tell the children that we remember this special meal at each Mass.*)
- What do we call the day before Jesus died? (*Holy Thursday*)
- What do we remember on Good Friday? (*That Jesus died on the cross*)
- What do we celebrate on Holy Saturday night? (*That Jesus rose from the dead*)

292

The Holiest Days of the Year

When Lent is over, we celebrate the three most important days of the year.

On **Holy Thursday** we celebrate the special meal when Jesus said, "This is my body. This is my blood."

Then Jesus told his friends that he was going to die soon.
But he promised that he would rise from the dead.

After the holy meal, Jesus and his friends went to a garden to pray.
There soldiers came to arrest him.

On **Good Friday** we remember the day Jesus died on the cross.

After Jesus died and was buried, a wonderful thing happened to him.
God the Father raised Jesus to new life.

On **Holy Saturday** night we begin our Easter celebration.
We celebrate Jesus' rising to new life.
We keep celebrating on **Easter Sunday**.

Teaching Tips

When teaching the term *Holy Week,* explain to the children that the word *holy* means "like God." Help the children to appreciate that people who live like Jesus are holy. Explain to the children that Jesus helps us to grow in holiness.

Teaching Tips

When making the calendar, make each space large enough to accommodate the date, the name of the feast, and a symbol. Draw the following symbols.

- Ash Wednesday—a smudge in the sign of the cross
- Passion Sunday—a palm branch
- Holy Thursday—bread and wine
- Good Friday—a cross
- Holy Saturday—the Easter candle.

Activity

During these three holy days, we think of Jesus and the cross.
Starting with the letter "I", copy the colored letters on the line below.
Write what Jesus tells us during these holy days.

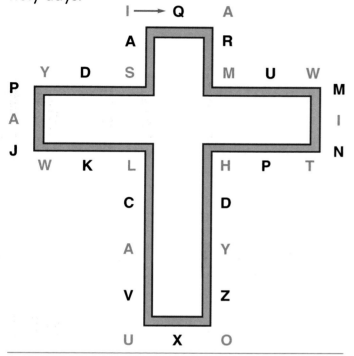

I am with you always.

Explain that we call Good Friday "good" because if Jesus had not died, he could not have risen to new life.

Step 3/CONCLUSION

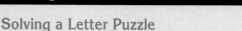

Learning How to Live our Faith

Solving a Letter Puzzle

Explain the directions to the activity on page 293 and have the children complete it. When finished, read the solution aloud together.

Talking About Jesus' Presence

Ask the children to name ways that Jesus is with us today. Responses may include: Jesus is with us

- When we pray
- In the special meal we share at Mass
- In the people who love us
- In the Church community

Praying Together

Invite the children to respond, *Be with us always* to each of the following prayers.

Jesus, you share a special meal with us.
Jesus, you died on the cross.
Jesus, you rose to new life.

Our Church Celebrates Easter

Objectives

- ■ LESSON 1: To help the children recognize the new life of Jesus we celebrate at Easter.
- ■ LESSON 2: To help the children understand some of the ritual celebration of Easter.
- ■ LESSON 3: To help the children understand the events of the first Easter.
- ■ LESSON 4: To help the children share the Easter message and pray a prayer of Easter joy.

Lesson Outlines

	Step 1 Learning About Our Lives	**Step 2** Learning About Our Faith	**Step 3** Learning How to Live Our Faith
Lesson 1	■ Discover new life. ■ Role-play and discuss life cycles. *ABOUT 10 MINUTES*	■ Read the text. *ABOUT 5 MINUTES*	■ Complete words. ■ Pray together. *ABOUT 15 MINUTES*
Lesson 2	■ Share Easter experiences. *ABOUT 5 MINUTES*	■ Read and discuss a story. ■ Remember the presence of Jesus. *ABOUT 10 MINUTES*	■ Complete an activity. ■ Make candles. ■ Pray together. *ABOUT 15 MINUTES*
Lesson 3	■ Review the meaning of Easter. *ABOUT 5 MINUTES*	■ Introduce the play. ■ Read an Easter play. *ABOUT 10 MINUTES*	■ Act out the play. ■ Think about Mary's message. *ABOUT 15 MINUTES*
Lesson 4	**Project** Recall the Easter message; make Easter booklets; and share the Easter message. **Prayer Service** Prepare for the prayer service; participate in a prayer service.		

Plan Ahead

	Preparing Your Class	**Materials Needed**

Lesson 1

Read the lesson plan before teaching this lesson.

- hard boiled egg
- pictures of a cocoon and a butterfly

Lesson 2

Print one letter of the word Easter on each of six poster board squares. For step 3, cut flame shapes out of yellow construction paper, one flame for each child.

- 6 poster board squares
- scissors, tape, felt-tip markers
- paper towel tube for each child
- one piece of white construction paper

Lesson 3

Choose a place to put on the play.

Lesson 4

Read the lesson plan and be ready to help the children make their Easter books. Prepare to lead the prayer service.

- three 4" × 5" pieces of white paper for each child
- stapler
- children's candles from Lesson 2
- large candle/matches (optional)

Additional Resources

As you plan these lessons consider using the following materials from The Resourceful Teacher Package

- *Classroom Activity Sheets* for Easter
- *Family Activity Sheets* for Easter
- *Prayers for Every Day*

You may also wish to refer to the following Big Book.

- *We Celebrate God's Word,* page 19

In preparing the children for the Sunday readings, you may wish to use Silver Burdett Ginn's *Getting Ready for Sunday* student and teacher materials.

Organizer 293b

Name

Our Church Celebrates Easter

Use the code to color the picture.

1	orange	3	yellow	5	blue
2	red	4	green	6	purple

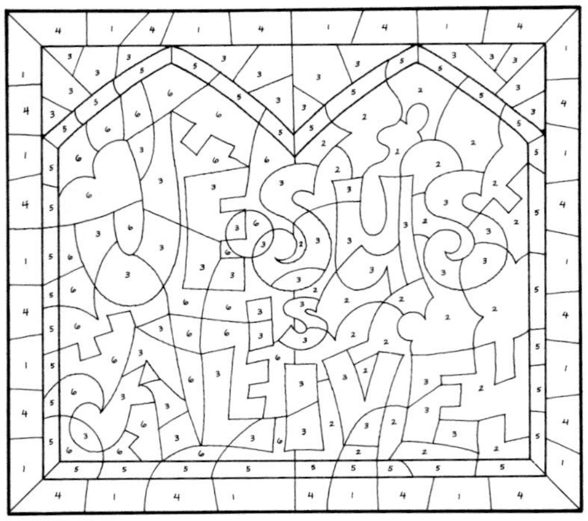

To the Teacher: This activity follows the page "A Time for Joy."

Our Church Celebrates Easter   THIS IS OUR FAITH 1 **25**

Name

We Celebrate New Life

1. Look at the picture stories.
2. Tell what is happening.
3. Color the pictures.

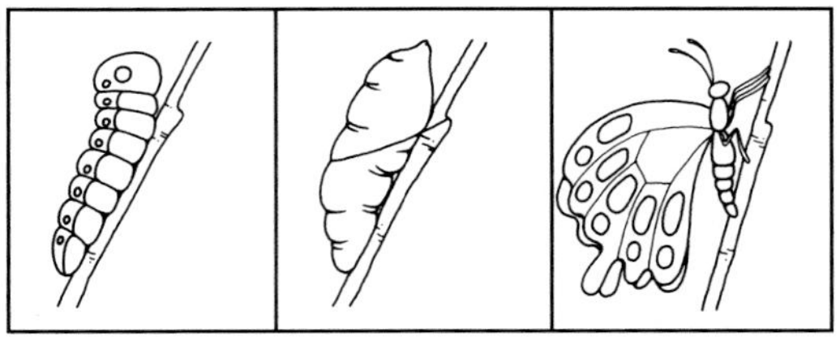

To the Teacher: This activity follows all the material for "Our Church Celebrates Easter."

25a THIS IS OUR FAITH 1   Our Church Celebrates Easter

NEW LIFE IN CHRIST

Easter is the most joyful feast of the Church year. Easter celebrates Christ's victory over sin and death. In his rising to new life, Jesus overcame death in all its forms. In his resurrection, Christ conquered the hold of sin on the world. The Resurrection, the Easter event, brought new life to Jesus. He who lived among us and died on the cross rose as the glorified Christ. Jesus, who touched the lives of those around him through teaching and healing, gave himself to us, through his death, in ultimate humility and love. His resurrection gives us the hope of our own salvation. Together at Mass, we proclaim the Memorial Acclamation:

> *Dying you destroyed our death,*
> *rising you restored our life.*
> *Lord Jesus, come in glory.*

SIGNS OF NEW LIFE

In this lesson, you can help the children understand that the story of Jesus is one of hope and renewal. On Easter, Jesus rose from the dead to new life. The Easter celebration expresses the heart of our faith. It is a time to rejoice in the new life we have received in Jesus.

The paschal candles the children will create are a part of the celebration. They proclaim to others that we are part of the new creation.

In Lesson 1, the life cycle of a butterfly is used to help illustrate the concept of new life. In enacting the role of a caterpillar becoming a butterfly, the children have an opportunity to share in the experience of rising to new life. The role-playing also provides the opportunity for active involvement in the learning process.

Objective

This lesson helps the children recognize the new life of Jesus we celebrate at Easter.

Step 1/INTRODUCTION

Learning About Our Lives

Discovering New Life

Direct the children's attention to the chick and the butterfly on page 295. Talk with them about these signs of new life. Explain that these things change in some way: Baby chicks form inside eggs and a butterfly develops inside a cocoon.

Role-playing and Discussing Life Cycles

Share with the children the life cycle of a butterfly. Have the children enact this process. First provide the following background: A butterfly begins life inside the cocoon. Cocoons are usually found on leaves. Inside the cocoon a caterpillar is changing. A beautiful butterfly is forming. When the butterfly is fully grown, it comes out of the cocoon and flies away.

Have the children sit on the floor and hug their knees, curling themselves tightly into balls, as if they were inside cocoons. Then have them become butterflies. Encourage the children to jump to their feet and flutter about the room.

Ask the children to return to their seats. To summarize, tell the children that the egg and the butterfly are all signs of new life. Explain that at Easter, Jesus rose to new life—a life that he shares with us.

Our Church Celebrates Easter

A Time for Joy

Jesus died.
His friends were very sad.
They buried him in a special place.
Three days later, Jesus' friends visited this special place.

But Jesus' body was not there.
Jesus is alive again.
He is risen.
We continue our celebration of Jesus' new life on Easter Sunday.

On Easter we pray, "Alleluia! Jesus is alive."

Activity

Talk about the pictures and the words.
Write the words on the lines below.

new life

joy

Jesus gives us

new life ---- and ---- joy ----.

Learning About Our Faith

Reading the Text

Ask if anyone has ever had a pet who was lost and was then found. Discuss their feelings when they thought they would never again see the pet. Then talk about how happy they were when the pet returned. Read aloud with the children "A Time for Joy" on page 294. Explain that Jesus now lives in a new way. He shares his life with us today and is with us always.

Step 3/CONCLUSION

Learning How to Live Our Faith

Completing Words

Direct the children's attention to the activity on page 295. After you have discussed with them the pictures and the words, ask them to complete the activity. Remember to praise the children for their printing.

Praying Together

Gather the children in a circle. Invite the children to join you in the following Easter prayer.

Jesus died for us. Alleluia!
Jesus is alive again. Alleluia!

Then invite the children to make up Easter prayers of their own.

Enriching the Lesson

Show the children how to make tissue paper butterflies using multicolored pieces of tissue paper, pipe cleaners, and clip-type clothespins. Before class, cut three pieces of tissue paper for each child using a butterfly pattern. Demonstrate how to gather the tissue together in the middle and fasten with a clothespin. Have the children gently spread the "wings." Then have them wrap the pipe cleaner around the top of the clothespins and twist the ends to form antennae.

295

LESSON 2

Objective

This lesson helps the children understand some of the ritual celebration of Easter.

Step 1/Introduction

Learning About Our Lives

Sharing Easter Experiences

Show the children the six letter cards (E–a–s–t–e–r) you made before class. Invite them to assist you in forming a word with the letters. When the children have identified the word *Easter*, place the cards on the ledge of the chalkboard.

Encourage the class to share stories about their families' Easter traditions. Ask the following questions.

- What do you usually do on Easter morning?
- What does your family have for a special Easter meal?
- What is your favorite part of Easter?

Give each child an opportunity to share an Easter experience. Point out that families celebrate Easter in many different ways and that Catholic Christians celebrate Easter by going to Mass to celebrate that Jesus is alive.

Step 2/Development

Learning About Our Faith

Reading and Discussing a Story

Direct the children to turn to page 296. Invite a volunteer to tell a story about the illustration. Then read "A Sign of New Life" with the class. Discuss the story using these questions.

- In the story what day is it? (*Easter*)
- Where did Tina's family go? (*To Mass*)
- What did Father Mike do? (*Lit the Easter candle*)
- What is the candle a sign of? (*New life*)
- With whom does Jesus share his new life? (*With all of us*)
- Why did everyone sing together (*To praise the Lord*)

296

A Sign of New Life

It was Easter Sunday.
Tina and her family went to Mass.
Father Jim lit the Easter candle.
He said, "This is a sign of new life.
Jesus shares his new life with us."

Later everyone sang together.
They sang, "Alleluia! Alleluia!
Jesus is alive!
Praise to the Lord!"

On Easter we pray,
"Thank you, Jesus for being with us.
Alleluia!"

 ### Cultural Awareness

Share these Easter customs with the class. In Poland, where Pope John Paul II was born, families bring the food they will share on Easter to church to be blessed. They usually do this on Holy Saturday.

Easter is also a time to make special breads. Long ago, people did not eat milk, cheese, meat, or eggs during Lent. On Easter, eating sweet breads made with eggs and sugar was a special way of celebrating Jesus' new life.

Many people like to wear new clothes on Easter. This is a way of saying, "We share in Jesus' new life."

ctivity

onnect the dots and color the picture.
hen trace the word below.

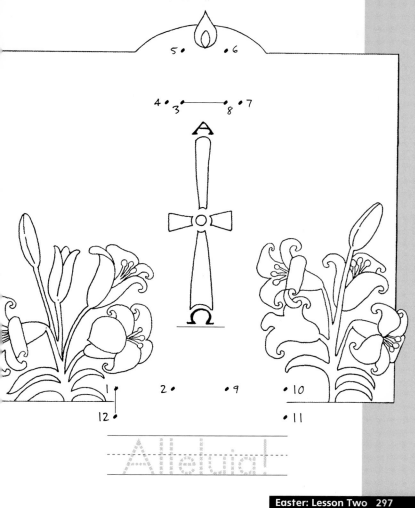

5 •   • 6

4 • 3 •   • 8 • 7

A

Ω

1 •
2 •   • 9   • 10
12 •   • 11

Alleluia!

★ ★★★ ★
Enriching
the Lesson

Visit the church with the children to point out the signs of new life. Call attention to the Easter candle, the lilies that decorate the altar, the banners, and the baptismal font. Tell the children that Easter is a special time for Baptisms. Remind them that when we were baptized, we began to share in Jesus' new life. During the Easter Season, we welcome new members into the Church through the sacrament of Baptism.

Remembering the Presence of Jesus

Remind the children that the Easter candle and our singing are signs of our joy. Then invite them to gather around you to hear a story about Jesus. Use words similar to these:

Jesus was risen. His friends gathered around him. They hugged Jesus and said how glad they were to see him. Then Jesus said to them, "Remember I am with you always" (Based on Matthew 28:20).

Talk with the children about how Jesus is with us today in our friends and family, with us at the Mass, and with us when we pray.

Step 3/Conclusion

Learning How to Live Our Faith

Completing An Activity

Read aloud the directions to the activity on page 297. After the children connect the dots to form a candle, have them color the candle and trace over the word *Alleluia*.

Making Candles

Invite the children to make an Easter candle.

- Distribute paper-towel tubes, small yellow paper flames, and white construction paper.
- Have them decorate their construction paper with pictures of new life and Easter words.
- Demonstrate how to roll the paper around the tube and secure the ends with tape.
- Then ask them to tape the flames to the top of the candle.
- Make sure the children have put their names on their candles.

Praying Together

Have the children bring their paper candles and form a prayer circle. Teach them to sing an Alleluia. Then invite the children to make the Sign of the Cross together and pray the prayer on page 296 after you. Conclude by having them sing the Alleluia they just learned. Collect the children's candles and save them to use during the prayer service in Lesson 4.

LESSON 3

Objective

This lesson helps the children understand the events of the first Easter.

Step 1/INTRODUCTION

Learning About Our Lives

Reviewing the Meaning of Easter

Recall with the children what they have learned about Easter by asking the following questions.

- What happened three days after Jesus was buried? (*He rose from the dead.*)
- What do we call the day Jesus rose from the dead? (*Easter*)
- How do we thank Jesus for sharing his new life with us? (*By praising Jesus; by trying to live as Jesus lived*)

Step 2/DEVELOPMENT

Learning About Our Faith

Introducing the Play

Print the following words and names on the board and explain each one.

- Narrator (*A story-teller*)
- Angel (*A messenger from God*)
- Mary Magdalene (*A friend and follower of Jesus*)
- Tomb (*A place where people are buried*)
- Gardener (*A person who takes care of a garden*)
- Teacher (*A name that Jesus' followers used to describe Jesus*)

Reading an Easter Play

Tell the children that they are going to read a play about the first Easter, when Jesus rose to new life. Instruct the children to turn to page 298 in their texts. Read through the play with the class. Use the questions below for discussion.

- Why was Mary Magdalene crying? (*She thought that Jesus' body had been taken away.*)
- Who did Mary think Jesus was? (*The gardener*)

An Easter Play

Narrator Mary Magdala went to Jesus' tomb, the place he was buried. Jesus was not there, so Mary cried. An angel who was sitting there saw her crying.

Angel "Why are you crying?"

Mary "Someone has taken Jesus away."

Narrator Mary turned and saw a man. She thought he was the gardener. Mary did not know it, but the man was Jesus.

Jesus "Why are you crying? Whom are you looking for?"

Mary "Tell me where Jesus is. I will go there."

Enriching the Lesson

Make an Easter poster with the class. Give the children cut-out paper eggs. Remind the children that eggs are a sign of new life. Invite the children to use crayons to put their names on their eggs and to decorate them. Help them to glue the eggs on a posterboard. Write on the poster: *Thank you, Jesus, for sharing your new life with us.*

Jesus "Mary!"

Narrator Mary looked at the man again.
Now she knew he was Jesus.
Full of joy, Mary ran to him.

Mary "Teacher!"

Narrator Mary saw that Jesus had risen
from the dead.
She rushed to tell Jesus' other
friends.

Mary "I have seen Jesus.
He is alive!"

Based on John 20:11–18

■ What did Mary do after she recognized
Jesus? (*She ran to tell Jesus' other friends
that Jesus had risen from the dead.*)

Step 3/CONCLUSION

Learning How to Live Our Faith

Acting Out the Play

Select volunteers to play the parts of the
narrator, angel, Mary Magdalene, and Jesus.
Have the children practice reading their parts.
Then invite them to act out the play. You may
want to repeat the play several times to give
more of the children an opportunity to
participate.

Thinking About Mary's Message

Ask the children to imagine that they were one
of Jesus' followers on the first Easter. Invite
them to think about how they would feel and
what they would say when Mary Magdalene
brought them the news that Jesus had risen
from the dead. Encourage them to express their
joy and happiness in Jesus' new life.

LESSON 4

Objective

This lesson helps the children share the Easter message and pray a prayer of Easter joy.

Recalling the Easter Message

Recall with the children the joy Jesus' friends felt when they found that he had risen. Ask the children what we celebrate on Easter (Jesus is risen). Discuss the joy we feel on Easter.

Making an Easter Book

Give each of the children three 4" × 5" pieces of white construction paper and crayons or felt-tip markers. Tell them to print "Happy Easter" on one of their pages and then to decorate this page as a cover for their book.

Read page 300 aloud with the children and help them plan what they will draw or print in their books. Talk with the children about writing their prayers to thank Jesus for sharing his new life with them. Make sure that each child has specific ideas in mind. As the children work, move around the room, offering suggestions and assistance where necessary. Afterward, help the children staple their pages together to form books.

Sharing the Easter Message

Invite the children to bring their Easter books and join you in a circle. Encourage them to share what they have drawn and written in their books. Praise their creativity. Ask the children to whom they would like to give their Easter books. Suggest that they give their books to the persons they have chosen. Perhaps, they may want to mail them. If they want to do this, have them ask one of their parents to help them address the envelopes.

An Easter Book

Make an Easter book for someone you love. Tell them, "Jesus is alive! Happy Easter!"

1. Your teacher will give you paper and crayons.

2. Draw a picture of Jesus and his friends.
    Draw pictures of new life.
    Draw a picture of yourself that shows how you feel about Easter.

3. Write a prayer to Jesus thanking him for sharing his new life with you.

4. Your teacher will help you put the pages of your Easter book together.

Enriching the Lesson

Surprise the children with an Easter egg hunt. On small slips of paper write a number of Easter messages, such as: *Jesus is risen for you! Jesus loves you! Jesus is with you always! Jesus shares his new life with you!* Put the messages in brightly-colored plastic eggs. Enlist the help of several parents and, if possible, have the egg hunt outside on the parish grounds. Afterwards, have the children share their Easter messages with one another.

An Easter Prayer Service

All Jesus said, "Remember, I am with you always."

Based on Matthew 28:20

Teacher We love you, Jesus.

Children Your new life shines in us.

Teacher On Easter we remember your love for us.

Children We will try to share your love.

Teacher Jesus, be with us today and every day.

Children Amen.

Easter: Lesson Five 301

★★★ Enriching the Lesson ★★★

Invite the children to think of gestures to accompany each of their responses in the prayer service. Practice words and gestures several times to help the children become familiar with them.

Preparing for the Prayer Service

To get ready for the prayer service, select a volunteer to read the scriptural verse from Matthew found on page 301. Allow time for the volunteer to practice the reading. Prepare a special area for the prayer service. Arrange on a table the candles that the children made in Lesson 2. Place a large candle in the center of the table.

Practice with the class the responses on page 301. Review singing the Alleluia you taught the children in Lesson 2.

Participating in a Prayer Service

Begin the prayer service by having the children make the Sign of the Cross. Next, have the volunteer read the words from Matthew found on page 301. Say:

We have learned that on Easter we celebrate that Jesus is risen. Jesus is alive. He shares his new life with us. (If safety regulations permit, light the candle.) *Jesus asks us to share his new life with others. We can follow the example of Jesus. We can share our life and love with the people we meet.*

Read together the prayer service on page 301. Then call each child forward individually. Ask: *(Name), will you share your life and love with others?* After the child responds affirmatively, present his or her candle and say: *Be a light to others.* Conclude by singing an Alleluia together.

Our Church Honors Saints

Objectives

- **LESSON 1:** To help the children give thanks to God for the love of Saint Joseph, Jesus' foster father, and for the love of our fathers too.
- **LESSON 2:** To help the children understand that their love of God can be expressed through kindness to others.
- **LESSON 3:** To help the children recognize that they can serve God by helping others as Saint Rose of Lima did.
- **LESSON 4:** To help the children remember a particular saint and pray.

Lesson Outlines

	Step 1 Learning About Our Lives	Step 2 Learning About Our Faith	Step 3 Learning How to Live Our Faith
Lesson 1	■ Discuss men in various roles. *ABOUT 5 MINUTES*	■ Listen to a Bible story. ■ Read the text. ■ Connect the dots. *ABOUT 15 MINUTES*	■ Draw Saint Joseph. ■ Pray to Saint Joseph. *ABOUT 10 MINUTES*
Lesson 2	■ Recognize ways to show love. ■ Listen to a poem. *ABOUT 10 MINUTES*	■ Learn about Saint Nicholas. *ABOUT 10 MINUTES*	■ Complete an activity. ■ Pray together. *ABOUT 10 MINUTES*
Lesson 3	■ Discuss nicknames. *ABOUT 5 MINUTES*	■ Read and discuss a story. ■ Trace a prayer. *ABOUT 15 MINUTES*	■ Name ways of imitating Saint Rose. ■ Pray together. *ABOUT 10 MINUTES*
Lesson 4	**Project** Think about a saint and make a diorama showing an event in the life of that saint. **Prayer Service** Prepare to pray and ask Saints Joseph, Nicholas, and Rose to pray for us.		

Plan Ahead

	Preparing Your Class	**Materials Needed**

Lesson 1 — Read through the lesson plan before teaching this lesson. Be prepared to discuss the life of Saint Joseph.

- pictures of men with children and at work
- felt-tip markers
- roll of butcher paper or drawing paper for each child

Lesson 2 — Read through the lesson plan before teaching this lesson. Be prepared to discuss the life of Saint Nicholas.

- pictures of Saint Nicholas

Lesson 3 — Read through the lesson plan before teaching this lesson. Be prepared to discuss the life of Saint Rose.

- drawing paper

Lesson 4 — Read the lesson plan and think about props and ideas for the dioramas.

- shoe box
- construction paper
- paste, glue, scissors
- costumes and props

Additional Resources

As you plan these lessons consider using the following materials from The Resourceful Teacher Package.

- *Classroom Activity Sheets* for Saints
- *Family Activity Sheets* for Saints
- *Prayers for Every Day*

In preparing the children for the Sunday readings, you may wish to use Silver Burdett Ginn's *Getting Ready for Sunday* student and teacher materials.

REDUCED CLASSROOM ACTIVITIES

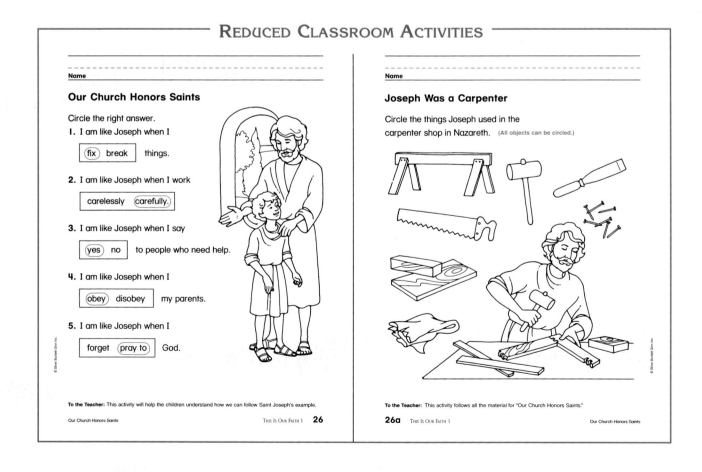

Name _____

Our Church Honors Saints

Circle the right answer.

1. I am like Joseph when I

   (fix) break   things.

2. I am like Joseph when I work

   carelessly   (carefully.)

3. I am like Joseph when I say

   (yes) no   to people who need help.

4. I am like Joseph when I

   (obey) disobey   my parents.

5. I am like Joseph when I

   forget   (pray to)   God.

To the Teacher: This activity will help the children understand how we can follow Saint Joseph's example.

Our Church Honors Saints   THIS IS OUR FAITH 1   **26**

Name _____

Joseph Was a Carpenter

Circle the things Joseph used in the carpenter shop in Nazareth.   (All objects can be circled.)

To the Teacher: This activity follows all the material for "Our Church Honors Saints."

26a   THIS IS OUR FAITH 1   Our Church Honors Saints

Background for the Teacher ∼∼∼∼

SAINT JOSEPH

Biblical references profile Joseph as a good husband, father, and provider. In the expression of very human emotions, Joseph becomes a role model for all of us who care for children. Joseph earned his living as a carpenter. But Joseph had a greater task — to rear the boy, Jesus. Joseph responded to God's word, accepting his responsibility to obey God and help Mary care for Jesus. In order to emphasize that Jesus is truly the Son of God, Joseph is presented as the foster father of Jesus.

SAINT NICHOLAS

This saint has come to be largely associated in children's minds with Santa Claus. However, this lesson is an opportunity to help children recognize Saint Nicholas as a real person who showed his love for God by showing love to other people. Help the children understand that we honor Saint Nicholas in order to remember his example of kindness and generosity.

SAINT ROSE OF LIMA

This saint, the patron of South America, was the first canonized saint of the New World. It is indeed fitting that this first Saint of the Americas should have both Spanish and Inca blood. Saint Rose's life was characterized by tangible expressions of love and care for the neediest people in her community in Lima, Peru in the early 17th century. Born into a large, poor family, Rose helped to support her family with money earned from the sale of home-grown flowers and her gift for embroidery. Through this lesson, the children can be helped to appreciate that in honoring Saint Rose's life, we learn that we can grow in our love of Jesus by showing love and care for others.

LESSON 1

Objective

This lesson helps the children give thanks to God for the love of Saint Joseph, Jesus' foster father and for the love of our fathers, too.

Step 1/INTRODUCTION

Learning About Our Lives

Discussing Men in Various Roles

If you brought pictures of men with children or of men at work, show them to the class. Guide a discussion by encouraging each child to react to each picture. Help the children conclude that the men pictured are fathers.

If you have not brought in pictures, talk with the children about men in various roles. You might discuss men they see during the day such as policemen, teachers, mailmen. Point out that these men might also be fathers. Have the children talk about their fathers or other adults in their lives who assume a parental role. Talk about the work these adults do, the care they give the children, and the good times they share with them.

Step 2/DEVELOPMENT

Learning About Our Faith

Listening to a Bible Story

Have the children sit in a circle around you. Read to them the following adaptation from Scripture (Based on Matthew 1:20–24).

An angel appeared to Joseph in a dream and said, "Mary is going to have a baby. The baby is God's Son. Name the baby Jesus." Joseph obeyed the angel because he trusted God. Joseph took care of Mary while they waited for their baby to be born.

Reading the Text

Have the children return to their seats. Ask them to look at page 302 in the student text. Read the text aloud.

302

Our Church Honors Saints

Saint Joseph

God gave **Joseph** a very special job to do.
Joseph did what God asked him.
He was the husband of Mary and helped her take care of Jesus.

Joseph worked as a carpenter.
His shop was in the Holy Family's home in Nazareth.
He taught Jesus how to make things with wood.

Joseph was a very good man.
He loved Jesus and Mary.
And they loved Joseph very much.

We honor Saint Joseph on March 19 and May 1.
On these days, we pray,
"Saint Joseph, help us lead good lives."

Focus on

Joseph His name means "prosperous," which the children will best understand as "rich." Yet, from all accounts, Joseph was a poor carpenter. Help the children appreciate that Joseph was "rich" in love — love of God and love of family. Thus Lesson 6 of Unit 2, interprets his name as meaning, "God gives more than I can even think of asking for." Joseph, who was of the family of David, enabled Jesus to fulfill the promise that the Savior would come from the House of David.

Activity

Jesus liked to help Joseph.
Connect the dots to find something
Joseph and Jesus made together.
Start at number **1**.
Then color the picture.

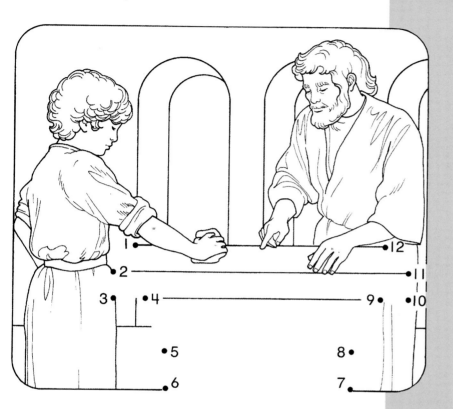

Direct the children's attention to the activity on page 303. Explain the directions and give assistance as necessary.

Step 3/CONCLUSION

Learning How to Live Our Faith

Drawing Saint Joseph

Distribute felt-tip markers. If you have planned to have the children make a mural, have them work in an open area. Explain to the children that they will make a mural showing Saint Joseph acting as both a parent and a carpenter. Have the children draw Joseph working, being with Mary and Jesus, and being alone with Jesus. Or give out drawing paper and have each child draw Saint Joseph in which ever role he or she chooses. Display the finished mural or drawings.

Praying to Saint Joseph

Gather the children into the prayer area and ask them to form a circle. Have them join hands and pray together the following words:

We give you thanks, O God, for those who care for us. They watch over and protect us every day. Saint Joseph, we ask you to love us as you loved Jesus. Help us to learn to love as you did.

Enriching the Lesson

Distribute half-sheets of construction paper. Show the children how to fold the paper to form a card. Invite them to make cards for their fathers or important male figures in their lives. Suggest that the children draw pictures of these persons and write them messages of love and thanks.

303

LESSON 2

Objective

This lesson helps the children understand that their love of God can be expressed through kindness to others.

Step 1/INTRODUCTION

Learning About Our Lives

Recognizing Ways to Show Love

Talk with the children about the people who love them. Ask the following questions. (Answers will vary.)

- Who loves you?
- How do you know when someone loves you?
- What kinds of things do people do to show that they love you?

Point out that the people who love us show their love in many ways. Tell the children that today they will learn about how one special saint showed his love for children.

Listening to a Poem

Show the children several different pictures of Saint Nicholas. Ask if they can name the person in the pictures. They may readily identify Saint Nicholas as Santa Claus. Tell them that Santa Claus brings gifts at Christmas because of the example of Saint Nicholas. Invite the children to open their texts to page 304 and learn more about Saint Nicholas.

Step 2/DEVELOPMENT

Learning About Our Faith

Learning About Saint Nicholas

Read "Saint Nicholas" on page 304 to the class. Afterward, ask these questions and discuss them with the children.

- What did Nicholas do when he was a little boy? (*Shared his toys and food*)
- What did Nicholas do with his money? (*Gave it away*)
- Whom did Nicholas love best? (*God*)
- Whom else did Nicholas love? (*Children*)
- How did Nicholas show his love for children? (*Gave them things they needed, was kind, and helped them*)

304

Saint Nicholas

Little Nicholas shared his toys and food.
When he grew up, he gave all his money away.

Nicholas became a bishop.
He loved God, and he loved children very much.
He helped them and was kind to them.
To help them he sometimes gave them gifts.
People told stories about Saint Nicholas
and his good deeds.

Like Nicholas, they gave gifts to each other.
They shared and helped each other.

We honor Saint Nicholas on December 6.
We pray, "Saint Nicholas, help us to do kind things for others."

Teaching Tips

Point out Nicholas' hat in the illustration on page 304. Tell the children that Nicholas was a bishop. Tell the children that a bishop is a priest who has the special responsibility of leading a group of many parishes. Explain that bishops are given a special hat as a sign of this responsibility. The hat is called a mitre. Write the name of your bishop on the chalkboard and tell the children how your bishop serves the people of your diocese.

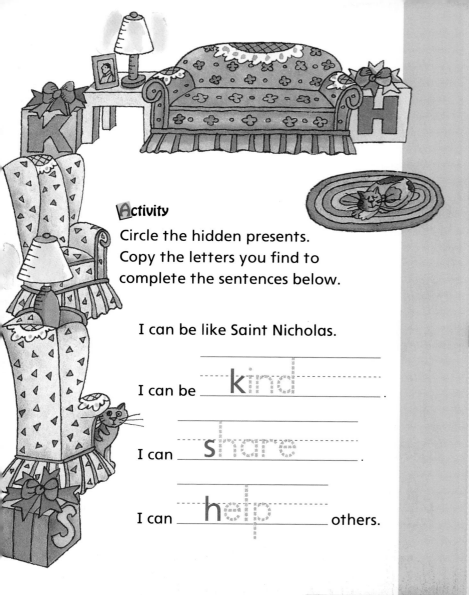

Activity

Circle the hidden presents.
Copy the letters you find to
complete the sentences below.

I can be like Saint Nicholas.

I can be _____kind_____.

I can _____share_____.

I can _____help_____ others.

- Why did people begin to give gifts to others? (*Because Nicholas did*)

Help the children appreciate that we can learn to be generous and kind to others from the story of Saint Nicholas. You may want to tell the children the following legend about Saint Nicholas.

When Nicholas was a little boy, he loved to hear stories about Jesus. His favorite story was about the three men who brought the baby Jesus gifts when he was born. Nicholas decided to be like the three men. He would give gifts to others. He would make the gifts to others his special present to Jesus.

Step 3/CONCLUSION

Learning How to Live Our Faith

Completing an Activity

Direct the children's attention to the activity on page 305. Have the children circle the hidden presents and copy the letters printed on them to form words in the sentences at the bottom of the page. Afterward, have them read the sentences aloud together. Then, discuss how they can be like Saint Nicholas. Ask the following questions.

- How can you be kind?
- What can you share?
- How can you help others?

Praise the students for their ideas and efforts to be like Saint Nicholas.

Praying Together

Close the session by offering this prayer of praise to Saint Nicholas: *We praise you, Saint Nicholas, for being generous and kind to all people, especially children. Help us to follow your example.* Invite the children to respond, *"Amen."*

CURRICULUM CONNECTION

Social Studies Although Saint Nicholas was a bishop in the country we know as Turkey, his feast day is celebrated all over the world, especially in Europe. On the evening of December 5, children in the Netherlands, Switzerland, Germany, and other countries put their shoes outside their doors. When they wake up, they find that they have been filled with fruit and candy. The Dutch have such devotion to Saint Nicholas that they named the first church they built in America after him.

305

Objective

This lesson helps the children recognize that they can serve God by helping others as Saint Rose of Lima did.

Step 1/INTRODUCTION

Learning About Our Lives

Discussing Nicknames

Ask the children if they know what a nickname is. If necessary, explain that a nickname is a name that we use instead of a real name. Offer a few examples to the class, pointing out that Kathy or Katie are two nicknames for Katherine or that someone named Andrew James might be called "A.J." Invite the children to talk about their own nicknames or the nicknames of family and friends. Tell the class that in today's lesson they will learn about a saint who had a nickname.

Step 2/DEVELOPMENT

Learning About Our Faith

Reading and Discussing a Story

Direct the children to turn to page 306 in their texts. Read through the story with the children. Then ask the following questions.

- Why did everyone call Isabel "Rose"? (*People said she was as beautiful as a rose.*)

- How did Rose earn money? (*She grew flowers and sold them.*)

- What did Rose do with the money she earned? (*She helped her family.*)

- How did Rose show her love for God? (*By helping others*)

- Whom did Rose help? (*Sick children, old people, and slaves*)

Explain to the children that long ago, slaves were people who were owned by rich people and that they had no freedom.

Tracing a Prayer

Read the text at the top of page 307. Explain that sewing was another way that Rose earned money to help her family and the sick people she cared for. Direct attention to the activity.

Saint Rose of Lima

Isabel was a beautiful baby. People said that she was as beautiful as a rose. So everyone called her "Rose."

Rose came from a poor family in South America. She grew flowers from tiny seeds. She sold the flowers to earn money to help her family.

Rose showed her love for God by helping others. She made one room in her house into a hospital. She brought sick children and old people to her hospital. Rose helped them get better.

We honor Saint Rose of Lima on August 23. She was the first saint of both North and South America.

306 Saints: Lesson Three

CURRICULUM CONNECTION

Social Studies Using a map locate Peru in South America. Explain that Saint Rose was born in the city of Lima, Peru over 400 years ago. Note that North America, where we live, and South America, where Rose lived, are called the "New World" because long ago, most people who lived far away in Europe did not know there was a North and South America. One day they were sailing and discovered these wonderful lands. They called them the "New World" because the land was new to them.

Activity

Rose liked to sew.
She used a needle and thread
to make pictures and words on cloth.
Color the threads on the cloth below
and find Saint Rose's favorite prayer.

Have the children use crayons to color Saint Rose's prayer. Then read the prayer aloud. Emphasize that we can say this prayer whenever we want to feel closer to Jesus.

Step 3/CONCLUSION

Learning How to Live Our Faith

Naming Ways of Imitating Saint Rose

Ask the children to think of practical things that they can do to imitate Saint Rose by helping others. Encourage them to be specific, naming whom they can help and how they can help.

Praying Together

Gather the children in the prayer area. When they are quiet, have the children fold their hands and bow their heads in prayer. Offer the following prayer.

Thank you, St. Rose, for teaching us to show our love for God by helping others. Help me to grow in Jesus' love.

Invite the children to respond, "*Amen.*"

Enriching the Lesson

Distribute pre-cut squares of fabric or construction paper squares and fabric paint pens to the children. Invite them to draw a picture of a rose on the cloth or paper. Suggest that they keep their rose pictures as a reminder to help others as Saint Rose did.

Objective

This lesson helps the children remember a life of a saint by making a diorama and gives them an opportunity to pray to the saints.

Thinking About A Saint

Write the names of the saints the children studied in this chapter on the board: Joseph, Nicholas, and Rose. Have them copy the name of one saint of their choice on a piece of paper. With the name of the saint in front of them have the children think about a scene from their lives. Ask the following questions to help them picture the saint.

■ Where is your saint?

■ What is your saint wearing?

■ What is your saint doing to show his or her love for God?

■ Is your saint alone or with others?

■ How is your saint helping someone?

Tell the children that today they will make a diorama about the saint and what he or she is doing to show love for God or others.

Making a Diorama

Help the children find the directions on page 308 of their books. Read the directions, one by one, with the children, pausing to complete each step. Ask the children to study the illustrations and demonstrate each step as you make a diorama along with the children. Show them how to form and stand up their characters. You may want to paste additional things on the walls of the box such as a window or a saw. You might even paste some flat furniture or pets or flowers on the wall.

When the dioramas are finished place them on display for all to enjoy. From time to time let each child tell the story of the saint he or she honored with a diorama.

A Diorama

It is fun to make stand-up scenes of a story inside a box.

Make a scene of a story of your favorite saint.

1. Get a box with a lid that comes off.
   A shoe box is good.

2. Think of a story of your favorite saint.
   Where is the saint?
   Who else is there?

3. Make stand-up characters from tagboard.

4. Stand the characters up in the scene.
   Add furniture for an inside scene.
   Add flowers and trees if it is outside.

🍎 Teaching Tips

Gather the children around you and tell them the following story: *One day, Jesus told his followers, "Heaven belongs to the little children"* (Based on Matthew 11:25). Help the children recognize that Jesus wants us to love and care for other people. Talk about how Saint Rose helped other people.

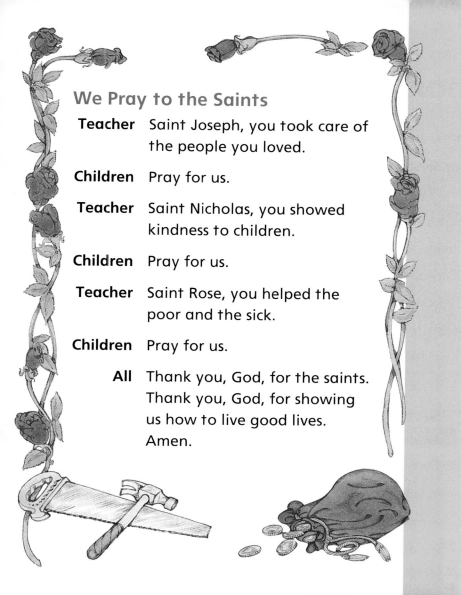

We Pray to the Saints

Teacher Saint Joseph, you took care of the people you loved.

Children Pray for us.

Teacher Saint Nicholas, you showed kindness to children.

Children Pray for us.

Teacher Saint Rose, you helped the poor and the sick.

Children Pray for us.

All Thank you, God, for the saints. Thank you, God, for showing us how to live good lives. Amen.

Saints: Lesson Five   309

Preparing to Pray

Choose three volunteers to be Saints Joseph, Nicholas, and Rose. Have available some costume material and let the volunteers dress up for the prayer service. You might provide a flower or piece of embroidery for Saint Rose to hold, a carpenter's tool for Joseph to carry, and a bishop's mitre for Nicholas to wear. Meanwhile, practice the litany on page 309 with remaining children. When the volunteers have finished dressing up as their saints, invite them to stand in the center of the prayer area.

Gathering to Pray

Invite the class to process to the prayer area with their books. Ask three children to each carry one of the dioramas representing the saints and to lead the procession. These three children may place the dioramas on the prayer table as they enter the prayer area. When all are in their places and are quiet, pray the prayer on page 309 with the class.

Enriching the Lesson

Call attention to the border on page 309. Have the children identify whom the saw and hammer represents (Saint Joseph). Follow the same procedure for the pictures of the bag of coins and the flowers (Nicholas and Rose). Invite the children to draw a small picture on the page that shows Saint Rose of Lima. They might draw a hospital or a picture of Rose helping others.

309

Our Church Honors Mary

Objectives

- **LESSON 1:** To help the children understand the role of Mary in the Church and in our lives.
- **LESSON 2:** To help the children appreciate Mary as part of God's plan for the world.
- **LESSON 3:** To help the children recognize that Catholics honor Mary with the tradition of the May Crowning.

Lesson Outlines

	Step 1 Learning About Our Lives	**Step 2** Learning About Our Faith	**Step 3** Learning How to Live Our Faith 
Lesson 1	■ Draw pictures. ■ Share experiences of Mother's Day. *ABOUT 10 MINUTES*	■ Read and discuss a story. *ABOUT 5 MINUTES*	■ Make a card. ■ Color a picture and trace words. ■ Pray the Hail Mary. *ABOUT 15 MINUTES*
Lesson 2	■ Discuss parents and families. *ABOUT 10 MINUTES*	■ Read and discuss a story. ■ Think about Jesus' family. *ABOUT 10 MINUTES*	■ Complete an activity. ■ Share God's love. ■ Pray together. *ABOUT 10 MINUTES*
Lesson 3	■ Recall facts about Mary. *ABOUT 5 MINUTES*	■ Read and discuss a story. ■ Learn gestures to a prayer. *ABOUT 15 MINUTES*	■ Complete a matching activity. ■ Pray together. *ABOUT 10 MINUTES*

Plan Ahead

	Preparing Your Class	**Materials Needed**
Lesson 1	Fold in half sheets of colored construction paper. Cut 4-1/2" circles from white paper. Cut green construction paper into 6" × 1" strips.	■ construction paper, white circles, and green strips for each child ■ scissors/glue
Lesson 2	Read the lesson plan and collect several pictures of families with children of all ages.	■ pictures of families
Lesson 3	Read the lesson plan before teaching this lesson.	

Additional Resources

As you plan these lessons consider using the following materials from The Resourceful Teacher Package.

■ *Classroom Activity Sheets* for Mary

■ *Family Activity Sheets* for Mary

■ *Prayers for Every Day*

In preparing the children for the Sunday readings, you may wish to use Silver Burdett Ginn's *Getting Ready for Sunday* student and teacher materials.

Name

Our Church Honors Mary

1. Decorate and color the prayer frame.
2. Cut along the heavy black lines.
3. Put the prayer in a place where you will see it every day.
4. Say the prayer often.

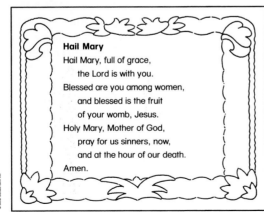

Hail Mary

Hail Mary, full of grace,

   the Lord is with you.

Blessed are you among women,

   and blessed is the fruit

   of your womb, Jesus.

Holy Mary, Mother of God,

   pray for us sinners, now,

   and at the hour of our death.

Amen.

To the Teacher: The activities on pages 27 and 27a follow all the material for "Our Church Honors Mary."

Name

May Is the Month of Mary

1. Connect the dots to finish the picture.
2. Start at number 1.
3. Color the picture.

Activity

Help the children to find their way to Jesus.
Use a yellow crayon.

START

FINISH

Praying and Using the Text

Read aloud the prayer at the bottom of page 316. Have the children stand and repeat the prayer with you. Then encourage the children to suggest ways they can tell everyone about Jesus.

Step 3/CONCLUSION

Learning How to Live Our Faith

Drawing Pictures

Distribute drawing paper and crayons or felt-tip markers. Have the children fold the papers in half. On the top section ask them to draw the three visitors finding Jesus. On the bottom, have them draw themselves doing something to lead others to Jesus. As they draw, you might play a recording of "We Three Kings."

Completing an Activity

Have the children look at page 317 in their texts. Explain the directions and have them complete the activity.

Following the Star

If you have brought in a flashlight and a star-stencil, tape the stencil over the light. Darken the room. Shine the flashlight on the ceiling, slowly sweeping the length of the room with the beam. A star shape will appear on the ceiling.

Focus on

Titles of the Three Men The children may be familiar with the story of the Epiphany. They might also know Jesus' visitors as kings, wise men, or magi. All these titles are true to some degree. The Greek word *magi* means "wise men." The magi probably were from an educated class of Persians who advised kings. What is most important for the children to know is that Jesus' visitors came from foreign lands. They were not Jewish, as Jesus was. This tells us that Jesus came to save all people.

LESSON 2

Objective

This lesson helps the children learn to care for everything God makes.

Step 1/INTRODUCTION

Learning About Our Lives

Discussing Responsibilities

Ask the children to name things they like to do, like playing with toys or watching television. Then ask them to name chores they do each day, such as making their bed or putting toys away. Ask the children what would happen if children did not do their chores? What would happen if parents did not do what they were supposed to? Help the children understand that our lives would be very disorganized if people did not do the things for which they are responsible. Tell them that in today's lesson they will learn about a young boy who only wanted to have fun.

Step 2/DEVELOPMENT

Learning About Our Faith

Reading the Text

Read aloud "St. Francis" on page 318. Discuss the following questions.

- What did Francis like to do when he was young? (*Have fun*)
- What did Francis learn when he was in jail? (*God is more important than fun and money.*)
- How did Francis change his life? (*He gave food and money to the poor; he made friends with animals; he helped people learn about God.*)
- What does St. Francis teach us? (*To care for everyone and everything God makes*)

Listening to a Legend

Gather the children around you and tell them the following story about St. Francis.

The people in town were frightened. At night, they heard a wolf howling. Each night, it sounded as if it was coming closer. The people decided to capture the wolf with big sticks. Francis heard about the plan and said, "Put down your sticks! I will tame the wolf." Then Francis walked bravely into the woods and

318

The Feast Of Saint Francis

Francis' family was very rich.
His family gave him everything he wanted.
Francis was a soldier and was captured.
He was put in jail.
There he thought a lot about God.
He learned that God was more
important than money.

So Francis gave away his beautiful
clothes and dressed like a poor man.
He gave his money to those who needed it.

In his new life, Saint Francis spent a
lot of time talking to Jesus in prayer.

He made many new friends and they
went from town to town, helping people.
Francis loved everyone and called all
people his brothers and sisters.

Focus on

Saint Francis   Born in 1182, Francis died in 1226. He was canonized two years later by Pope Gregory IX, a sign of his impact and reputation as a holy man. An antiphon in the Liturgy of the Hours perfectly characterizes Saint Francis' holiness: "Francis left this earth a poor and lowly man; he enters heaven rich in God's favor, greeted with songs of rejoicing."

rancis made friends with the animals.
He called them his brothers and sisters, too.
rancis teaches us to care for everyone and
everything that God makes.

We celebrate the feast of Saint Francis on
October 4.

We pray, "Loving God, we praise and
hank you for all your gifts."

ctivity

Name a person or thing you can show
are for.

_____

- -

_____

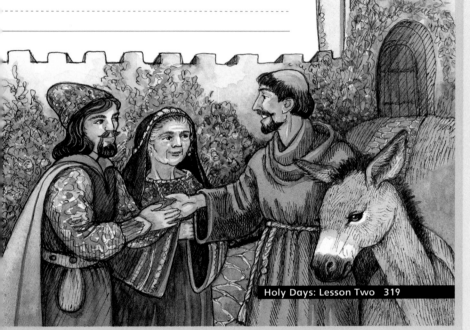

Holy Days: Lesson Two 319

*called softly to the wolf. Soon, Francis and the
wolf came out of the woods together. The wolf
sat at Francis' feet and licked his hand. Francis
said, "This is our brother, Wolf. He is hungry
and lonely. Feed him and be his friend." From
then on, the people cared for their new friend,
the wolf.*

Step 3/CONCLUSION

Learning How to Live Our Faith

Completing an Activity

Explain the directions to the activity on page
319. Invite the children to write the name of
someone or something they can show care for.

Praying Together

Use the children's written answers to pray.
Begin by saying,

*St. Francis, you taught us how to care for all
people and things. We will show care for….*

Have the children read the names they wrote.
After each prayer, invite the class to respond by
reciting the prayer on page 319.

319

LESSON 3

Objective

This lesson helps the children to appreciate Sunday as a holy and special day for Catholics.

Step 1/INTRODUCTION

Learning About Our Lives

Discussing Weekend Activities

Engage the children in a discussion about some of the things they do on an average week-end. Ask them to identify activities they do alone or with friends and others things that they do with their families.

or . . .

Teach the children an action song about the days of the week. Using the melody to "Here We Go 'Round the Mulberry Bush," teach the children the following words.

This is the way we brush our teeth,
Brush our teeth,
Brush our teeth.
This is the way we brush our teeth,
On a Monday morning."

Invite the children to think of an action to accompany the words "go to school." Change the words and actions for each day of the week. For example, "wash my face" on Tuesday, "comb my hair" on Wednesday, "make my bed" on Thursday, and so on. Do not think of words or a gesture for Sunday. Instead, tell the children that they will learn about Sunday in today's lesson. At the conclusion of the lesson, sing the song again, adding "go to Mass" and an action for Sunday.

Step 2/DEVELOPMENT

Learning About Our Faith

Reading the Text

Direct attention to page 320 and read with the class "Sunday." Use the following questions to guide discussion.

■ Where do Jesus' friends go on Sunday? (*We go to Mass. Help the children understand that we can also celebrate with our parish family at Mass on Saturday evening.*)

■ What do we celebrate at Mass? (*Jesus' new resurrected life*)

320

Sunday

Sunday is a holy day.
On Sunday, Catholics go to Mass.
We celebrate Jesus' new life at Mass.
Jesus shares a special meal with us.

On Sunday, God wants us to share happy times with our families.
We can have a picnic, play games, or visit new places.
We can have fun together.

Sunday is a special day because it is God's day.

★ ★ ★ Enriching the Lesson ★

Plan to gather with the children and their families at a Sunday parish Mass in the near future. Have the children make invitations, noting the time and date. Notify the celebrant of your plans and ask to be part of the Entrance Procession or the Presentation of Gifts. Following Mass, have a simple reception for the families to meet one another.

Activity

Look at what families can do on Sunday.
In each picture there is a hidden letter.
Find the letters and write them in the boxes.

What word do the letters make?

Add the word to the sentence below.

Sunday is _holy_____.

■ What does Jesus share with us at Mass? (*A special meal*)

Help the children understand that Sunday is both holy and special. Sunday is holy because we pray with our parish family at Mass. Sunday is also a special time for families to be together. On Sundays, we take time away from work and school to be together and to celebrate our love for one another.

Step 3/CONCLUSION

Learning How to Live Our Faith

Looking at Illustrations

Study the pictures on page 320–321 with the children. Have them identify what the families in each picture are doing. Then ask the children to share some of the things they like to do on Sundays with their families.

Completing the Activity

Explain the directions to the hidden letter activity and have the children copy the letters they find on the lines. Then instruct the children to unscramble the word and print it in the sentence.

Learning a Scripture Verse

Teach the children a Scripture verse about Sundays based on Psalm 118:24: *"This is the day God has made; let us be glad and rejoice."* Have the children repeat this verse after you.

In the Spirit of Jesus

Objectives ~~~~~~

- ■ LESSON 1: To help the children develop an awareness that the people who care for us are signs of hope and to imitate Helen Keller by helping others.

- ■ LESSON 2: To help the children respond to Jesus' example by sharing with others.

Lesson Outlines ~~~~~~~~~~~

	Step 1 **Learning About Our Lives**	**Step 2** **Learning About Our Faith** 	**Step 3** **Learning How to Live Our Faith**
Lesson 1	■ Play a blindfold game. ■ Discuss wearing a blindfold. *ABOUT 10 MINUTES*	■ Read the text. *ABOUT 5 MINUTES*	■ Make a banner. ■ Pray prayers of praise. *ABOUT 15 MINUTES*
Lesson 2	■ Talk about hunger. *ABOUT 10 MINUTES*	■ Read a story. ■ Listen to a story about Jesus. *ABOUT 10 MINUTES*	■ Draw favorite foods. ■ Complete a prayer. *ABOUT 10 MINUTES*

Plan Ahead

	Preparing Your Class	**Materials Needed**

Lesson 1

Before class, prepare felt letters that spell the words *hopeful signs.* Glue these words to a length of fabric to make a banner. From drawing paper, cut out a 5" circle for each child.

- long scarf
- large piece of fabric for banner
- drawing paper
- scissors, glue, felt-tip markers

Lesson 2

Read the lesson plan through before teaching it.

Additional Resources

As you plan these lessons consider using the following materials from The Resourceful Teacher Package.

- *Classroom Activity Sheets* for In the Spirit of Jesus

- *Family Activity Sheets* for In the Spirit of Jesus

- *Prayers for Every Day*

In preparing the children for the Sunday readings, you may wish to use Silver Burdett Ginn's *Getting Ready for Sunday* student and teacher materials.

REDUCED CLASSROOM ACTIVITIES

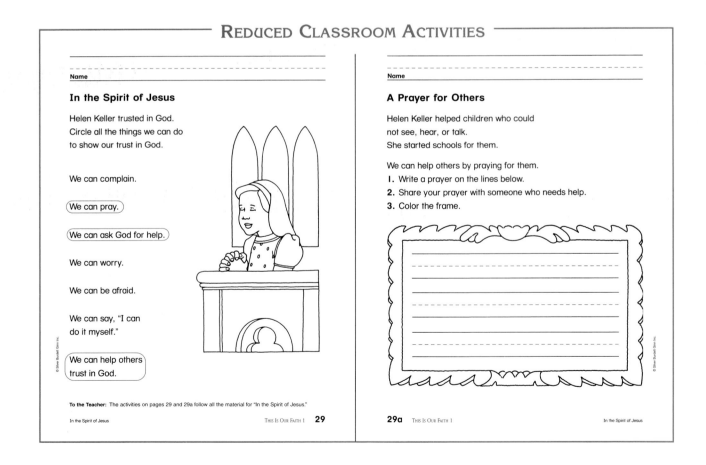

Name

In the Spirit of Jesus

Helen Keller trusted in God.
Circle all the things we can do
to show our trust in God.

We can complain.

(We can pray.)

(We can ask God for help.)

We can worry.

We can be afraid.

We can say, "I can
do it myself."

(We can help others
trust in God.)

To the Teacher: The activities on pages 29 and 29a follow all the material for "In the Spirit of Jesus."

In the Spirit of Jesus   THIS IS OUR FAITH 1   **29**

Name

A Prayer for Others

Helen Keller helped children who could
not see, hear, or talk.
She started schools for them.

We can help others by praying for them.
1. Write a prayer on the lines below.
2. Share your prayer with someone who needs help.
3. Color the frame.

29a   THIS IS OUR FAITH 1   In the Spirit of Jesus

321c Organizer

HELEN KELLER

The story of Helen Keller is one of courage and hope. Anne Sullivan was the willing instrument through which Helen was able to discover these gifts within herself. "The teacher," as Helen called Anne, was able to break through the walls of rejection, fear, and anger that Helen had built around herself. These barriers were replaced by trust and an awareness of the possibilities that life had to offer. Hope was born in Helen Keller.

Hope is the heart of the Old Testament writings. The Israelites longed for a messiah and trusted that the covenant would be kept. Jesus is the fulfillment of that trust. Hope is a virtue in the life of every member of the Christian family. It is expressed as a deep longing for God and for the coming of the reign of God. Hope is trust that all that God has promised will be realized.

Helen Keller is presented in this lesson as a person with traits every Christian can emulate. First graders can easily appreciate the severity of Helen's handicaps and the courage she displayed in overcoming them. They will understand that it was the teacher, Anne Sullivan, who gave Helen reason to hope. In this lesson, you, the teacher, can foster in the children an awareness that God has given us many signs of hope in the people and the world around us. The children can begin to appreciate that God calls us to be a sign of hope and encouragement to each other. The children should understand, though, that Helen Keller was a unique individual and that not everyone can overcome handicaps in the single-minded fashion in which she did. While teaching this lesson, be aware of any children in your class who may have physical disabilities. Focus on Helen's greatest gift to us—her determination to open doors to the handicapped so that they could have the hope of living full and happy lives.

AWARENESS OF OTHERS

In Lesson 2, the children will read about the ministry of a parish food pantry and will come to understand that hunger is a problem that they can help to alleviate. Although your students may be well-fed, they can, to some extent, appreciate what it means to be hungry. This lesson will help them to understand the efforts of the Church community to serve poor people and homeless people by offering the basic necessities of life to those in need. If at all possible, plan to invite the children to donate food or clothing to a food pantry or shelter. Although the children's donations do not come from their own pockets, their contributions are a tangible sign that they realize that God wants us to reach out to those in need. Opportunities such as these serve as a foundation for later works of mercy.

LESSON 1

Objective

This lesson helps the children to develop an awareness that the people who care for us are signs of hope and to imitate Helen Keller by helping others.

Step 1/INTRODUCTION

Learning About Our Lives

Playing a Blindfold Game

Tell the children that they will begin this lesson with a game. Ask for volunteers to be blindfolded. Be mindful of any children who are unwilling to volunteer. Using a long scarf, blindfold the volunteers, one at a time. Have them perform simple tasks—walking across the room or printing a word on the chalkboard.

Discussing Wearing a Blindfold

Talk with the children about the game. Ask the children to explain the difficulties that they had when performing tasks while wearing a blindfold. Guide a discussion by asking the following questions. (*Answers will vary.*)

- Was the game fun to play? Why?
- Would it always be fun to wear a blindfold? Why?

To summarize, tell the children that our world would be very different for us if we could not see. Explain that they will learn about a girl who could not see, hear, or talk, but who taught us something important.

Step 2/DEVELOPMENT

Learning About Our Faith

Reading the Text

Direct attention to page 322 and read the text aloud with the children. Then ask the following questions.

- Why was Helen brave? (*Even though she could not see, hear, or speak, she struggled with the help of her teacher because she wanted to communicate.*)
- How did Helen help others? (*She started special schools for others who could not see, hear, or speak.*)
- What is hope? (*Trust in God*)

322

In the Spirit of Jesus

Helen Keller

Helen Keller could not see, hear, or talk.
But one day a teacher, Anne Sullivan, came to help Helen.
Anne taught Helen to use her hands to sign.

When Helen grew up, she helped children who could not see or hear or talk.
She started special schools for them.

We can be like Helen Keller.
We can help others.

We pray,
"God, let us help others."

 Cultural Awareness

Talk with the children about the ways in which we can help people who are physically impaired in some way. For example, we can read to someone who is blind or help push someone's wheelchair who cannot walk. Lead the children to the recognition that one of the most important ways we can reach out to others is to be a friend to everyone we meet, no matter what challenges they face. Emphasize that everyone wants and deserves our friendship and acceptance.

Activity

Learn the actions for the prayer.
Look at the pictures to help you.
Trace the letters for some of
the words.

Dear God,

Help us always to trust you.

Amen.

Explain to the children that hope means not giving up. Hope is trust. We trust others to care for us, and we trust to help us live.

Have the children say together the prayer at the bottom of page 322.

Step 3/CONCLUSION

Learning How to Live Our Faith

Making a Banner

Make a banner with the children. Show the children the fabric on which you glued the words hopeful signs. Distribute the circles of drawing paper, glue, and felt-tip markers. Have the children draw signs of hope on the circles. Glue their circles to the fabric. Display the banner.

Praying Prayers of Praise

Have the children complete the prayer activity on page 323.

Teaching Tips

Contact a local agency that serves the blind and obtain Braille alphabet cards for the children. These are often free or available at a nominal charge. Note the Braille letters that are used to spell Jesus' name.

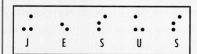

J E S U S

323

LESSON 2

Objective

This lesson helps the children respond to Jesus' example by sharing with others.

Step 1/INTRODUCTION

Learning About Our Lives

Talking About Hunger

Ask the children if they have ever been hungry. Encourage them to share how they feel when they are hungry and what happens when they experience hunger. Lead them to understand that people feel hungry when they skip meals or when they do not eat enough. Remind them that when people are hungry, their stomachs growl and they sometimes get crabby.

Then ask the children if they think that everyone in the world has enough food to eat every day. Help the children to understand that many people in our world are hungry. Tell the children that in today's lesson they will learn how we can help hungry people.

Step 2/DEVELOPMENT

Learning About Our Faith

Reading a Story

Invite the children to turn to page 324 in their texts. Read with the class "The Food Pantry." Discuss the story using the following questions.

- Where did Sister Jean's class go? (*To visit St. Mark's food pantry*)
- What is a food pantry? (*A place for poor families to get food*)
- What did Sister Jean ask the children? (*If they wanted to help feed hungry families*)
- How did the children help? (*They brought food from home to the food pantry.*)
- How were the children trying to be like Jesus? (*They were sharing their food with others.*)

Listening to a Story About Jesus

Tell the children the following story from Scripture (Based on Matthew 25:34–35, 40).

One day, Jesus told his friends a story. "When I come to take you to heaven, I will say: 'My Father blesses you and welcomes you to a new life that never ends! I was hungry, and you fed

324

The Food Pantry

Sister Jean's class visited St. Mark Food Pantry.
Sister Jean said, "Some families have no money for food.
They can get food here."

The pantry was almost empty.
Sister Jean said, "The pantry needs food.
Would you like to help feed hungry families?"

"Yes!" said the boys and girls.

The children asked their parents what food they could bring from home.
They put the food on the pantry shelves.
Sister Jean said, "Thank you for sharing.
I can see that you are trying to be like Jesus."

Enriching the Lesson

If you have a parish or community food pantry, arrange for your class to tour the facility. Or, contact local agencies that collect food for the poor and ask how your class can help in their efforts. Encourage the children to donate needed foods to these agencies. Send home a parent note explaining what foods the children can bring to class.

Activity

What kind of food could you bring
to your parish food pantry?
Draw some of your favorite foods
on the pantry shelves.

Trace the word in the prayer below.
Then say the prayer together.

Dear Jesus, help us to be like you.

Help us to ⎺⎺⎺⎺⎺⎺⎺ with others.

me. I was thirsty and you gave me a drink.' But
the people said, 'Jesus, when did we see that
you were hungry and gave you food? When
did we see that you were thirsty and gave you
a drink?' Jesus answered, 'Whenever you
shared your food and drink with my poor
brothers and sisters, you shared them with me.
Now you will be happy forever in heaven!'"

Help the children to appreciate that when we
show our love for others, we are showing our
love for Jesus.

Step 3/CONCLUSION

Learning How to Live Our Faith

Drawing Favorite Foods

Explain the directions to the first activity on
page 325 and have the children complete it
independently. Afterward, allow time for the
children to share their drawings with the class,
each telling his or her favorite food.

Completing a Prayer

Direct attention to the prayer at the bottom of
the page. Read it aloud and have the children fill
in the missing word. Have the children suggest
ways they can share with others. Encourage
them to follow Jesus' example of caring for
others.

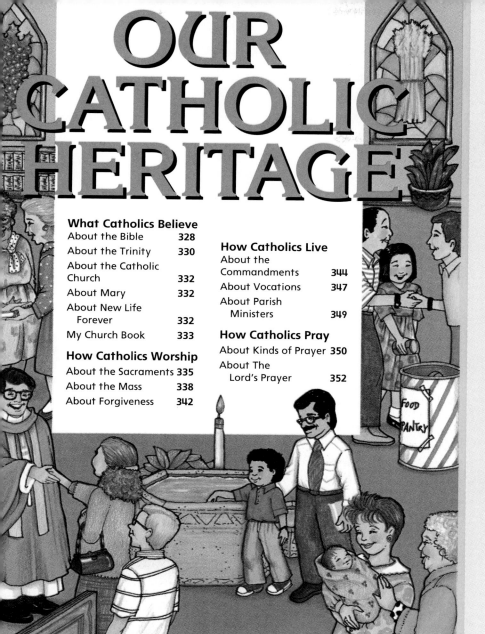

OUR CATHOLIC HERITAGE

Our Catholic Heritage

In June 1994 the *Catechism of the Catholic Church* was published in English and widely distributed throughout the United States. Bishops, pastors, and educators have used the *Catechism* as a basic resource in summarizing Catholic doctrine and for a better understanding of the theological background of the Church's teachings.

In this section, *Our Catholic Heritage,* there is a summary of Catholic belief, which is organized in the same way as the *Catechism*. It is meant as a ready reference for both you and your students to provide in summary fashion the basic teachings of the Catholic Church.

Over the course of the THIS IS OUR FAITH program, the *Our Catholic Heritage* section of each grade level is developmental in nature and planned to complement the information presented in the lesson plans. These pages are most effectively used in conjunction with the student book pages that cover the topics in question.

You may want to read the Apostolic Constitution *Fidei Depositum* and the *Prologue* (paragraphs 1–25). These introduce the *Catechism* and provide a better understanding of its purpose in religious education.

What Catholics Believe

The *Catechism of the Catholic Church,* published in 1994, provides a clear and extensive statement of Catholic doctrine, divided into four parts, or pillars, of our faith. The first, "The Profession of Faith," develops the foundations of our creed, based on sacred Scripture and the tradition of the Church throughout the ages. As a Catholic Christian community, we renew our dedication to these beliefs at Sunday Mass, at Baptism and Confirmation, and during the Easter Vigil. Our recitation of the creed reminds us of our unity in faith with Catholic Christians throughout the world.

About the Bible

TEACHER REFLECTION

Sacred Scripture is a source of nourishment and strength for the Church. The Church has accepted throughout history that the books of both the Old Testament and the New Testament were written under the inspiration of the Holy Spirit. The Church recognizing the importance of biblical scholarship for understanding the Scriptures, encourages us to study the Bible continually to be able to more deeply appreciate the word of God.

You may want to review for yourself the teachings of the Church about the Bible in paragraphs 101–133 in the *Catechism of the Catholic Church.*

STUDENT REVIEW

Read aloud the first paragraph of "About the Bible" on page 328. Using the classroom Bible, show the children that there are many books contained within the Bible. Read aloud the next two paragraphs. Answer any questions the children may have.

Allow them to leaf through a children's picture Bible. Call the children's attention to the map on page 329. Read aloud with the children the names of the cities, starting from the top. Explain that Jesus was born in Bethlehem and grew up in Nazareth. He traveled with Mary and Joseph to Jerusalem on special occasions. When he was grown, he also traveled to Jerusalem with his disciples.

What Catholics Believe

Catholic Christians share many special gifts.
We believe, live, and pray as one family.

ABOUT the Bible

The Bible is a special book about God's love for us.
The Bible has many books.
Each book was written by someone specially chosen by God.

We can read about God's love for us in the Bible.
We can read about Jesus and his followers.
We can also read about how the Holy Spirit helps us.

In the Bible are stories of Jesus and his followers.
The stories tell about the things Jesus said and did.
They tell of the places where Jesus lived and visite
The map on the next page shows some of the plac

The Holy Land

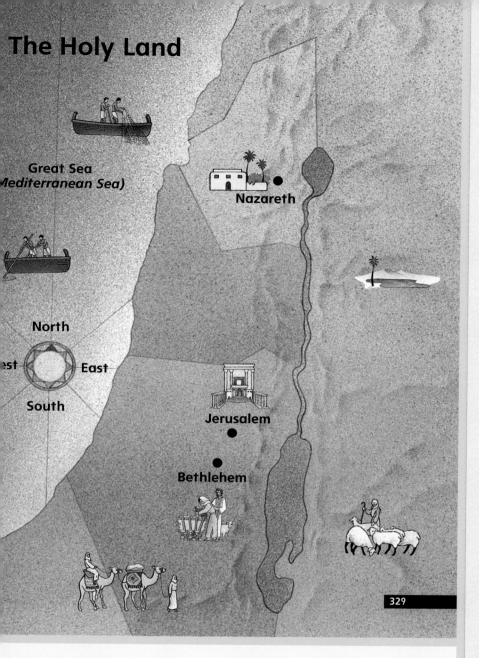

Great Sea
(Mediterranean Sea)

North

West   East

South

Nazareth

Jerusalem

Bethlehem

329

To clarify the children's understanding, answer any questions they may have. Then invite volunteers to take turns showing on the map where Jesus was born, where he grew up, and where he traveled. Have the children repeat each place name aloud as the volunteer points to it.

329

TEACHER REFLECTION

Over the centuries the Church has come to an "understanding" of the Trinity as a result of reflection on the action of God in our lives. We have come to know that God is loving, creative, and redemptive. This revelation of God, in whose image we are made, helps us understand both the meaning of our humanity and our calling to be part of a community. We believe that God reveals the work of the Trinity in the mystery of creation.

You may want to review for yourself the teachings of the Church about creation in paragraphs 279–412 in the *Catechism of the Catholic Church.*

STUDENT REVIEW

Read aloud the section "About the Trinity" on pages 330–331. This section is divided into three parts: one part on God the Father, whom the children know as the Creator; another part about Jesus, God's Son and our friend; and a third section on the Holy Spirit. You may wish to use a specific part for a review as you teach about the Persons of the Trinity, or you may wish to use the whole section at one time.

As you review each section, you might want the children to make summary booklets about each person of the Trinity.

■ For God the Father, have the children draw creation; the Bible; and a picture of Jesus, God's greatest gift to us.

■ For Jesus the children might draw Jesus with the children, Jesus teaching, and the story of Jesus in the garden after the resurrection.

■ For the Holy Spirit the children might draw Jesus saying, "Receive the Holy Spirit" on Easter night in the upper room or a child praying to the Spirit to help him or her in daily life.

ABOUT the Trinity

There is one God.
God is three persons—Father, Son, and Holy Spirit.

We Believe in God

God is our Creator.
God made all things with love.
Everything God made is good.

God speaks to us in the Bible, a special book about God's love.

God loves and cares for us.
God wants us to be happy.
God, our Father, sent us Jesus to help us.

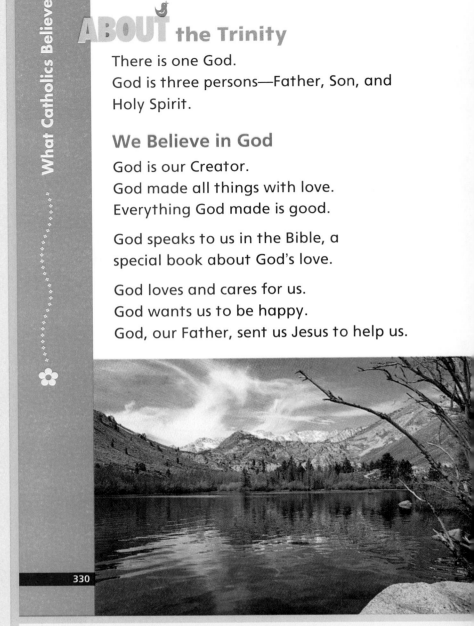

We Believe in Jesus

Jesus is the Son of God.
God the Son became a man.
Jesus is our brother and friend.
He is one of us.

Jesus is our teacher.
Jesus teaches us about God.
God sent Jesus to show us how to love.

Jesus died on the cross and rose
from the dead for us.
Jesus is our **Savior**.
He saves us from sin and death.

Jesus is alive.
He shares new life with us.

We Believe in the Holy Spirit

The Holy Spirit is God.
The Holy Spirit is with us.
The Holy Spirit helps us follow Jesus.
The Holy Spirit gives us gifts to help
us live good lives.

About the Catholic Church

TEACHER REFLECTION

Catholics believe that Jesus established the Church and that the Holy Spirit revealed the Church to the world. We profess in the creed that the Church is one, holy, catholic, and apostolic. We should be able to see and experience these characteristics of the Church in our parishes and throughout the world.

You may want to review the four marks of the Church in paragraphs 813–873 in the *Catechism of the Catholic Church.*

STUDENT REVIEW

Read aloud the section "About the Catholic Church" on page 332. Help the children find the things that Catholics do and then have them draw pictures about these things.

About Mary

TEACHER REFLECTION

With Mary's willingness to be God's servant the incarnation of Jesus Christ began. We honor Mary, the Mother of God, as Mother of the Church because she is a model of holiness for all of us.

You may want to review the teaching of the Church about Mary in paragraphs 963–972 in the *Catechism of the Catholic Church.*

STUDENT REVIEW

Read aloud the section "About Mary" on page 332. Have the children find the sentence that goes best with the illustration. (*God chose Mary to be Jesus' mother.*)

About New Life Forever

Catholics believe in the particular judgment; the realities of heaven, purgatory, and hell; the final judgment; and the Second Coming of Christ.

You may review Church teaching about life everlasting in paragraphs 1020–1050 in the *Catechism of the Catholic Church.*

STUDENT REVIEW

Read aloud "About Life Everlasting" on page 332. Encourage the children to name someone they know in heaven. Ask the children why these people are happy. (*Because they are with God forever*)

ABOUT the Catholic Church

We are **Catholic Christians**.
Catholics celebrate the **sacraments**.
We pray to God and help others.

The pope is the leader of the Catholic Church.
We call the pope our Holy Father.

The Church is the family of Jesus.
We tell the good news about Jesus.

ABOUT Mary

God chose Mary to be Jesus' mother.
Mary loved and trusted God.
Mary is our Mother, too.
Mary loves and cares for us.

ABOUT New Life Forever

Jesus teaches us that if we act with love, we will be happy with God in **heaven**.
Heaven is being happy with God forever.

The cross reminds us
of Jesus, our friend and brother.

Fold

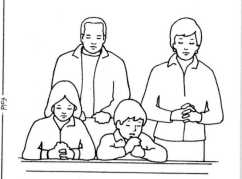

I belong to the
Catholic church.

3

This statue reminds us
of Mary, the mother of Jesus.

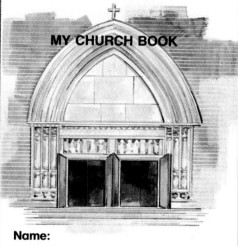

MY CHURCH BOOK

Name:

I

Making the Booklet

Assist the children in making the booklet "My Church Book." Each child will need a pair of scissors, a pencil, and a crayon or a felt-tip marker. You will need a stapler. After the children have separated the pages from their books along the perforations, direct them to cut along the horizontal line indicated by the symbol of a pair of scissors. Direct the children to place the pages on top of each other so that page 1 is on top of page 3. The page numbers should be on the lower right hand corner of both pages. Instruct them to fold the booklet on the fold lines so that page 1 is facing them right side up. Ask the children to make sure that all the pages are in the proper sequence. Staple the books for the children along the fold lines.

Tell the children to print their names on page 1 and the name of their parish church on page 2. Then let the children color the pages of their booklets. After the children have finished coloring, read together the words on each page of the booklet.

This booklet has been designed for the children to use whenever they go to Mass or have an occasion to visit the church. Encourage the children to take their booklets with them on these occasions.

The priest is the parish leader.

4

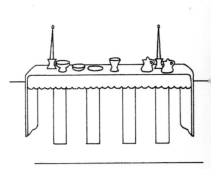

The altar reminds us
of our special
meal with Jesus.

The name of our parish church is

2

The lectern reminds us
that God, our Father,
and Jesus speak to us.

How Catholics Worship

Worship is giving honor and praise to God. We worship God in prayer and the sacraments.

ABOUT the Sacraments

The **seven sacraments** are celebrations of God's love and Jesus' presence.

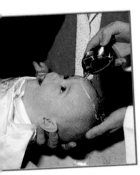

Baptism is a sacrament of welcome into the Church. At Baptism we receive the Holy Spirit. We are baptized with water. The water is a sign that we share Jesus' new life.

At **Confirmation**, we receive the Holy Spirit in a new way. The Holy Spirit helps us tell everyone about Jesus' good news.

335

The liturgical life of the Church is the Catholic Christian community's way of celebrating what we believe. Through the signs of the sacraments and our participation in the liturgical celebrations, we renew our faith and gain an even greater share in the life of grace, God's life in us. Through the sacraments, we are challenged to follow ever more closely the way of Christ, which leads to the realization of God's kingdom.

About the Sacraments

TEACHER REFLECTION

The whole life of the Church revolves around the Eucharist and the other sacraments. In the sacraments we encounter Christ and are enabled to live the life of faith more deeply. The sacraments of initiation—Baptism, Confirmation, and Eucharist—provide the building blocks for Christian life. Through them we are welcomed into the Church and are called to conversion and service.

The sacraments of healing—Reconciliation and Anointing of the Sick—recall the frailty of our human condition. The sacrament of Penance or Reconciliation provides us with an opportunity to acknowledge the reality of sin, to ask for forgiveness, and to begin anew as disciples of Christ. Anointing of the Sick is a source of strength and consolation for those who are ill and those who are caring for them.

The sacraments in service to the community—Matrimony and Holy Orders—celebrate publicly the callings to family life and to ordained ministry in the Church. These vocations are sanctified in the sacramental rites in which we are called to build the Body of Christ through example and service.

You may want to review for yourself the teaching of the Church about the sacraments in Part Two of the *Catechism of the Catholic Church*.

Read aloud the three pages on the sacraments, pausing throughout to find and talk about the pictures of the sacraments. You may wish to use these pages to introduce the children to the names of all seven sacraments when you study the sacrament of Baptism in Chapter 14.

We celebrate the Euchar
or the Mass, when we sh
a special meal with Jesus
In the Eucharist, Jesus
gives himself to us as the
Bread of Life.

In the Sacrament of Reconciliation, we say we are sorry for our sins.

The Anointing of
the Sick brings Je
peace and help to
sick people.

336

In the sacrament of Holy Orders, men become priests and join in Jesus' work in a special way.

The sacrament of Marriage celebrates the love of a man and a woman for each other.

About the Mass

TEACHER REFLECTION

Our celebration of the Mass is the primary source of renewal of our life in Christ. In the Mass we are once again welcomed into the community of the faithful, called to communion with others and service to others, and nourished by the Bread of Life. We are sent forth to exemplify the good news of the gospel in our everyday lives.

You may want to review for yourself the teaching of the Church about the Mass in paragraphs 1322–1405 in the *Catechism of the Catholic Church.*

STUDENT REVIEW

"About the Mass" is placed here as an easy-to-find reference for you and your children. This special feature can be used at appropriate times throughout the year to

- Introduce the Mass.
- Help the children understand the main actions of the Mass—the reading of the Bible and the enactment of the Last Supper.
- Prepare for Mass.

You may wish to extend the use of this section by inviting a parish priest to demonstrate and explain the various vestments and holy objects used at Mass.

How Catholics Worship

ABOUT the Mass

1. Our celebration begins. The priest and other ministers walk down the aisle in a procession. We stand to sing a song.

2. To welcome us the priest says, "The Lord be with you." We answer, "And also with you." We all make the Sign of the Cross.

3. We remember our sins and God's love and forgiveness. The priest prays an opening prayer.

4. We listen to God's word in readings from the Old Testament and the New Testament.

5. In the gospel story, we hear about Jesus' life and teachings.
We stand to welcome Jesus in the gospel.

6. The priest or deacon explains the readings to us in a special talk called a homily.

7. We pray for the Church, for our country, and for all God's people.
We call this prayer the Prayer of the Faithful.

8. We bring gifts to prepare the altar for the meal.
The gifts are the bread and wine.
We always bring ourselves, our most important gift.

9. The priest offers our gift of bread to God.
The priest offers our gift of wine to God.

10. We thank and praise God for all God's blessings, especially for the gift of Jesus.

11. Our gifts of bread and wine become for us the body and blood of Jesus.

12. The priest holds up the body and blood of Jesus. He prays a prayer of praise.
We answer, "Amen!"

13. We pray together the prayer that Jesus taught us, The Lord's Prayer.

14. We offer one another a sign of peace to show that we are all brothers and sisters in Jesus.

15. We come to the table of the Lord to receive Jesus in the Eucharist.

16. We receive God's blessing and answer, "Amen." We sing a song of praise. Then we go in peace to love and serve all people.

About Forgiveness

Teacher Reflection

The grace of the sacrament of Penance or Reconciliation gives us the courage to admit our failures and wrongdoings, to ask for forgiveness, and to renew our dedication to the Christian life. The experience of this sacrament as celebrated in community can give us a better appreciation of the social consequences of sin and the need for reconciliation as a people. Reconciliation makes visible the mercy of our loving God.

You may want to review for yourself the teaching of the Church about Reconciliation in paragraphs 1422–1484 in the *Catechism of the Catholic Church.*

Student Review

"About Forgiveness" is placed here as an easy-to-find reference for you and your children. This special feature can be used at appropriate times throughout the year to

- Help introduce the concept of forgiveness.
- Provide readiness for the sacrament of Reconciliation.

You may wish to use the material in the "About Forgiveness" section in conjunction with Lesson 19.

ABOUT Forgiveness

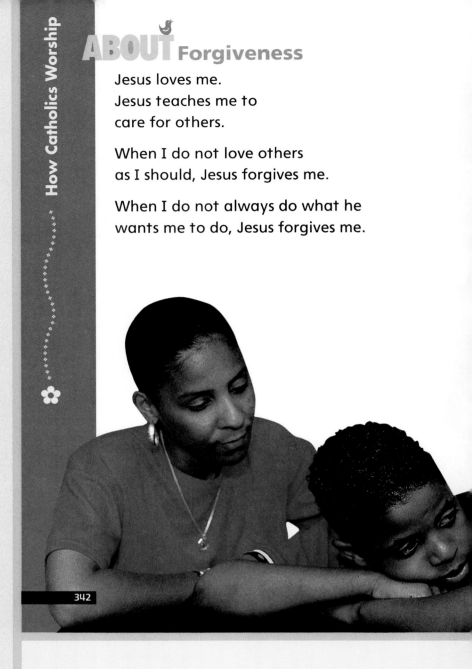

Jesus loves me.
Jesus teaches me to
care for others.

When I do not love others
as I should, Jesus forgives me.

When I do not always do what he
wants me to do, Jesus forgives me.

342

I can pray,

"Jesus, I trust in your love.

I am sorry for all the wrong things I have done.

I am sorry for all the good things I have not done.

Jesus, I want to love you with all my heart."

How Catholics Live

About the Commandments

Morality is faith lived out. To fully understand the demands of Christian morality, we need to recognize that it is based on the limitless love of God and the dignity of every human person as created by God. The focus of Christian morality is not rules but relationships.

TEACHER REFLECTION

As the commandments were first given to the Israelites, so they are proclaimed today to the new people of God and to all men and women of faith. The commandments challenge us to deepen our relationship with God and to see the world around us from God's loving and caring viewpoint. Observing God's commandments is the first step to becoming followers of Christ and thus being called to greater holiness.

You may want to review for yourself the teaching of the Church about the commandments in paragraphs 2052–2557 in the *Catechism of the Catholic Church*.

STUDENT REVIEW

If you chose to use this section, read aloud "About the Commandments" on page 344. Help the children understand that the commandments are divided into ways that we should love God and ways that we should love others and ourselves. You might ask for ten volunteers to stand and to each read one commandment.

How Catholics Live

Jesus teaches us how to live.
He gives us the Holy Spirit and the Church to help us.

The Great Commandment

Jesus said, "You must love God above all things and love your neighbor as yourself" (Based on Mark 12:30-31).

Jesus' **Great Commandment** tells us to show love for God and for our neighbor.

ABOUT the Commandments

We Live God's Laws

We show our love for God.	We believe in God and love God. We use God's name with love. We pray to God every day. We pray with our Church family at Mass.
We show love for our neighbor.	We obey our parents and those who care for us. We care for all living things. We tell the truth. We are careful with other people's things. We share with others and are thankful for God's Gifts.

Jesus' New Commandment

Jesus gave us a new commandment.
He said, "Love one another as I love
you" (Based on John 15:12).

We can love as Jesus loves by being
fair and kind to all people.
We can help others.
We can be forgiving.

345

When we do not act with love, we sin.
Sin is choosing to do something we
know is wrong.

The Holy Spirit Helps Us

We can choose to love or to sin.
The Holy Spirit helps us choose to love.

346

ABOUT Vocations

When we were baptized, we began our new life as Catholic Christians. God calls each of us to help others in a special way.
This is called our **vocation**.

Many Ways of Helping

Here are some ways Catholics can help others.

They can help at Mass by reading, leading the songs, or giving the Bread of Life to people.

They can teach about God and Jesus' message in the gospels.

They can do other things to help too.

About Vocations

TEACHER REFLECTION

Every member of the Christian community is called by God to a particular role in the service of the Church. Although our vocations may be to serve as a priest, a religious or a lay person; as a teacher, missionary, or liturgical minister, we all derive our mission from Baptism into the Church of Christ. Our vocations are strengthened by the Holy Spirit in Confirmation and encouraged by our participation in the Eucharist. Through prayer and our experiences in the Christian community, we are then able to discern God's call to us and commit ourselves to our particular vocations in the Church.

You may want to review for yourself the teaching of the Church about vocations in paragraphs 871–945 in the *Catechism of the Catholic Church*.

STUDENT REVIEW

Invite the children to read the section "About Vocations" on page 347, emphasizing that God calls each of us to help others in special ways. Read aloud "Many Ways of Helping" on page 347. Help the children remember the many ways of helping taught throughout this book or have the children flip through their texts to find pictures of community members helping. (Remind the children that they are members of the community, too.) Encourage the children to note ways that people help at Mass. Then read page 348 with them and learn that priests, deacons, and religious brothers and sisters are Catholic people who are called to serve God in unique ways. Tell the children that when they get older they will discover if God is calling them to these vocations.

Sometimes God calls people to a special way of helping in the Church.
There are priests who lead the parish community.

There are religious brothers and sisters who teach, serve the poor, or help lead the parish.

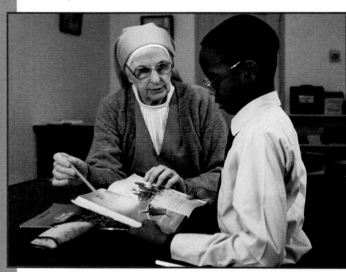

There are deacons who pray with us and help us to care for those in need.

As you get older, you will discover in what special ways God is calling you to be a helper.

People Who Serve the Church

We belong to our parish Church.
At church and school, we see many
people who serve the friends of Jesus.

The priest is
the leader of
the parish
Church.
He celebrates
the Mass and
the sacraments
with the
people.
He cares for God's people.

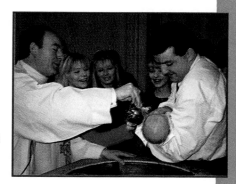

At Mass, we might also see religious
sisters, brothers, and deacons.
They help with the Sunday celebration.

They might also be teachers in the school.
They also lead the friends of Jesus in
caring for others.

God invites all Catholics to take
part in helping others through their
parish Church.

349

TEACHER REFLECTION

In Baptism every Catholic Christian is given the
vocation to participate in service to the Church
community and to further the work of the
Church in the community at large. Most
Catholics are called to serve in their parishes
and neighborhoods and to become models of
service for other parishioners, young and old
alike. This vocation, lived out in the parish, the
workplace, and the community, brings about
the growth of the Church and has the effect of
inspiring others to respond to their own callings
as Christians.

You may want to review for yourself the
teaching of the Church about parish ministry
and other vocations in the Church in
paragraphs 871–945 in the *Catechism of the
Catholic Church.*

STUDENT REVIEW

In the section called "People Who Serve the
Church," the children will look at ways that
Catholics serve. The first graders will focus on
the Catholic event in which they participate
most—the Sunday eucharistic celebration.
There they see the priest celebrating Mass, the
deacon, the lay readers, the eucharistic
ministers, those who bring communion to the
sick, the ushers, and even children who are
altar servers.

Read aloud page 349 with the children. After
finishing the reading, ask the children what
ways they see the community at service during
the Mass. List on the board their responses. You
might have volunteers pantomime the acts of
service they see at Mass and have the other
children guess what is being done.

How Catholics Pray

Prayer is conversation with our loving God and is part of every believer's life and the life of the Church. Daily prayer and devotions, the Liturgy of the Hours, and the Sunday Eucharist all offer ways of celebrating and praising God. Growth in our prayer lives is nourished by taking every opportunity to listen to God and to speak with God as individual believers and as members of the Christian community.

About Kinds of Prayer

TEACHER REFLECTION

There is no preferred way to pray. God leads each person according to his or her needs. In Christian tradition we find three major expressions or models of prayer—vocal prayer, meditation, and contemplation. Vocal prayer can be a recitation of formal prayers that are learned from others or that are part of the liturgy. We can also speak to God in our own words at any time. Meditation engages the mind, imagination, and emotions by focusing on a particular subject (a psalm, a Scripture passage, God's creation, the life of a saint). Contemplative prayer is attentiveness to God. Done in silence, it is active listening to God.

You may want to review for yourself the teaching of the Church about the kinds of prayer in paragraphs 2650–2758 in the *Catechism of the Catholic Church.*

STUDENT REVIEW

Ask for a volunteer to read "How Catholics Pray" on page 350. Then ask the children to find the four ways we pray in "About Kinds of Prayer" on page 350.

Have the children read page 351 and find their favorite time to pray. Then allow the children time to share their preferences aloud.

 How Catholics Pray

Prayer is talking and listening to God. God always hears our prayers.

We can pray alone or with others.

The Mass is our greatest prayer.

ABOUT Kinds of Prayer

We can praise God for our wonderful world.

We can thank God for the gift of our families and friends.

We can ask God to help us live as Jesus taught us.

We can say, "I love you, God."

We can pray in the morning and at bedtime.

We can pray with our families at mealtime.

We can pray in school with our teacher and classmates.

At Sunday Mass, we pray with our families and the whole family of Jesus' friends.

351

TEACHER REFLECTION

The Lord's Prayer teaches us that when we pray we are to be inclusive and mindful of the fact that we are all connected to one another. The Lord's Prayer is the prayer of the community. It also teaches us that first we are to praise and adore God and then petition for our need for nourishment and healing. Since apostolic times this prayer has been considered the most important prayer for the Christian community.

You may want to review for yourself the teaching of the Church about The Lord's Prayer in paragraphs 2759–2869 in the *Catechism of the Catholic Church.*

STUDENT REVIEW

Use this section to teach the meaning of The Lord's Prayer. The children are introduced to The Lord's Prayer in Grade 1, but they need to review the prayer and its meaning constantly. From time to time work with them on a part of this great Christian prayer, concentrating on a phrase or two at a time.

How Catholics Pray

ABOUT The Lord's Prayer

Jesus taught his friends **The Lord's Prayer**. In this special prayer, we honor God. We ask God for the things we need.

Our Father, who art in heaven, hallowed be thy name.

God is our Father. We pray that everyone will remember how good God is.

Thy kingdom come;

Jesus told us about God's kingdom. We pray that everyone will live as Jesus taught us to live.

thy will be done on earth as it is in heaven.

We pray that everyone will obey God's laws.

Give us this day our daily bread;

Our good God cares for us. We pray for our needs and the needs of the poor.

352

and forgive us our trespasses as we forgive those who trespass against us;

We ask God to forgive us for the wrong things we have done.

and lead us not into temptation,

We ask God to help us always to choose what is right.

but deliver us from evil.

We pray that God will protect us from things that may harm us.

Amen.

Our "Amen" says that Jesus' prayer is our prayer, too.

Advent   _____ is four weeks of preparing for Christmas.

angel   An _____ is a messenger and helper from God.

Anointing of the Sick   _____ is a sacrament that brings Jesus' peace and help to sick people.

Ash Wednesday   is the day the priest marks our foreheads with ashes. It is the first day of Lent.

354

Holy Orders ______________________________
is the sacrament in which men become priests.

Baptism ______________________________ is a
celebration of our new life with Jesus and his friends.

Bible The ______________________________ is a special
book about God's love for us.

Christ The name ______________________________
means that "Jesus was sent by God to help all people."

Christian A ______________________________
is a friend and follower of Christ.

Church We belong to the Catholic ______________________________
The word church also means a special place where
Christians come together to pray.

Using the Write-in Glossary

The Write-in Glossary provides a reference for the religious vocabulary introduced in Grade 1.

After you have presented the new words in each chapter (Step 2), you may want to have the children write the new words beside the definitions provided.

Confirmation
_____
is the sacrament in which we receive the Holy Spirit in a special way.

Create
_____
means to make something out of nothing.

Creator
Our _____ is God, who makes everything in the world out of nothing.

Easter
_____
is the celebration of Jesus being raised from the dead.

Emmanuel
_____
means God is with us.

Epiphany
On _____
we celebrate the feast of the wise men who followed the star to find Jesus.

Eucharist

The _____

is the sacrament that celebrates Jesus' special meal.

Forgive

_____

means to excuse or to pardon.

Galilee

_____

is the area where Jesus grew up.

Godparents

_____

are the people who help us grow as friends and followers of Jesus.

Good Friday

_____

is the day we celebrate Jesus' death on the cross.

Good Samaritan

The _____

was a person who cared for someone who needed help.

357

gospel   The _____ is the
good news of Jesus found in the Bible.

Great
Commandment The _____

_____

tells us how to show love for God and our neighbor.

Hallowed   _____ means holy.

Heaven   _____ is being happy
with God forever.

Holy Family   Mary, Joseph, and Jesus are the

_____.

Holy Saturday   _____
night we begin our Easter celebration.

Holy Spirit   The _____
is the Spirit of God.

Holy Thursday   _____
is the day we celebrate the special meal when Jesus
gave us his body and blood to share.

Jesus   _____ is God's Son
and our friend.

Joseph   _____ is the
husband of Mary who helped her raise Jesus.

Lent   _____ is the forty
days we prepare before Easter.

Marriage   The sacrament of _____
celebrates the love of a man and woman.

Mary _____ is the mother
of Jesus and our Mother, too.

Mass The _____ is a special
meal Jesus shares with us.

Nazareth _____
is the town where Jesus lived with Mary and Joseph.

**Passion
Sunday** _____

is the first day of Holy Week.

**Peter and
Andrew** _____

were brothers. They were good friends of Jesus.

Prayer   _____ is listening and
talking to God.

rabbi   When Jesus was a boy a _____
was someone who taught about God and about life.

Reconciliation   The sacrament of _____,
celebrates God's forgiveness.

sacrament   A _____
is a celebration of Jesus' love and God's presence.

saint   A _____
is someone who loves Jesus and others very much. He
or she is a very special follower of Jesus.

Savior   Our _____
is Jesus, the Son of God and our friend. He saves us and
helps us.

361

Sin
_____ is choosing to
do something we know is wrong.

Sunday
_____ is a holy day
when we celebrate Jesus' rising from the dead.

Temple
The _____ was a holy
place in the city of Jerusalem where people prayed
and learned about God.

Trespass
_____ means to hurt
someone.

Trust
_____ means to
believe in someone's love for us.

Worship
_____ means to give
honor and praise to God.

The Resourceful Teacher

INTRODUCTION

Welcome to The Resourceful Teacher section of your Teacher Edition. Like the many other features of THIS IS OUR FAITH, the material in this section is designed to help you be successful in preparing for and teaching your religion class. Here you will find guidelines and practical ideas for teaching and classroom management. This material enlarges on the instructions that accompany each session. Read through these pages thoughtfully as the year begins and turn to them often throughout the year as a source of ideas and of answers to questions that may arise.

The questions that teachers of religion ask—and we have sought them out and heard their inquiries—generally can be divided into three categories.

1. Questions about catechetics and the meaning of faith.

2. Questions about the psychological makeup of the child and the implications for teaching religion.

3. Questions about preparing and conducting a successful religious education class.

Answers to questions in these categories are in the Helps for the Teacher section. In some cases the question-and-answer format is used.

CATECHESIS

Catechesis refers to those actions that help people grow in their personal faith within a community of faith *(National Catechetical Directory, 32–33).*

As a teacher of religion, you should have a clear idea of what you are trying to accomplish with the children in your class. All of us want faith for our children and we know that faith is a gift from God. However, we can do much to help our children grow in faith by helping them grow in knowing, loving, and serving God.

As adult Catholics, we have grown in faith over the years by being part of a community of believers. The children in our religious education classes will also grow in faith through the same interaction with people of faith.

Our first community of faith consists of those people who nurture and care for us in our earliest years. We grow in age and wisdom in our home settings, just as Jesus did. We learn first from people at home about what it means to love others.

This growth in faith continues in the course of our lives as we expand our horizons beyond the home to the school and to the larger community, including the parish. In the parish community, children meet those people who best exemplify what it means to love God and to serve the needs of all people. In the parish, children learn how to pray, worship, and practice the love that Jesus asks of us all.

Part of the children's experience of Church today is your religion class. In fact, it may well be their most significant and meaningful experience in the Catholic Church. Here you have the opportunity to show the youngsters the joy of being a Catholic Christian. You have the God-given chance to help them learn about their Catholic faith. You can help them discover ways in their own lives in which they can make the Catholic faith their own and put it into daily practice. Most of their learning the children acquire in class will be from your example as a faith-filled catechist.

FAITH

In talking about catechesis, we use the words *growing in faith*. But what is faith? As a catechist, you must understand what is meant by faith so that you can help the children grow in their faith.

It is important to remember that the Church understands faith in a twofold way: (1) Faith is that sound doctrine that teaches us about God and that has been passed down in the Church from age to age. (2) Faith is a relationship with God. It is a relationship that we grow in over the years. This growing relationship involves a faith based on believing and trusting in the providential care of God. Faith gives meaning to life and directs our actions in love of God and neighbor.

A major aspect of our relationship with God involves the fact that our faith is the *Catholic* faith. Here we have the heritage and tradition of the Church as it has evolved under the inspiration of the Holy Spirit down through the centuries. Here are the doctrines and principles that have come down to us as our inheritance from past generations of Catholic people. This inheritance includes Bible stories, practices of worship, moral positions, and a wide variety of customs.

THIS IS OUR FAITH aims at helping the children grow in their relationships with God. It also seeks to help the children learn the traditional beliefs and practices of the Catholic Church. In these ways, THIS IS OUR FAITH aims at helping our children know, love, and serve God. It seeks to help the faith of children become "living, conscious, and active, through the light of instruction" (*National Catechetical Directory*, 32).

Catechist

The term *catechist* is the name given to those people in the parish community who seek to help others grow in their Catholic faith through preaching and teaching. Thus, parents are the first catechists a child meets in life. The parish priests are also catechists because they help people know and love God more fully. Teachers of religion are catechists because they instruct children in the doctrines, principles, and customs of the Catholic religion. All catechists should have as their focus the desire to help people grow in their personal relationships with God.

CATECHISM OF THE CATHOLIC CHURCH

The *Catechism of the Catholic Church* is the document that contains the essential and fundamental beliefs of Catholic faith and morals.

It is organized into four parts: The Profession of Faith (what Catholics believe); The Celebration of the Christian Mystery (the Sacraments); Life in Christ (moral teachings); and Christian Prayer, with a concluding section on The Lord's Prayer.

The *Catechism* came about as a result of a recommendation of the bishops, recognizing the need for a compendium of the beliefs of the Church. The document, approved by Pope John Paul II in June 1992, is directed first and foremost to the bishops, who have the primary responsibility for catechesis. It is directed also to those who prepare materials for catechesis, and through them, to all members of the faith.

The *Catechism of the Catholic Church* is the first such compendium of our faith since the Council of Trent and is therefore an important and historic document affecting future catechesis for generations to come.

A correlation of THIS IS OUR FAITH with the *Catechism of the Catholic Church* is available for teachers using the program.

National Catechetical Directory

The primary source for information about catechesis and your role as a religion teacher is the document of the National Conference of Catholic Bishops, titled *Sharing the Light of Faith: National Catechetical Directory for Catholics of the United States*. Approved in the late 1970s by the Bishops of the United States and the Sacred Congregation for the Clergy in Rome, the directory defines the goals and characteristics of quality religious education. The NCD, as it is called, sets forth what should be taught in a comprehensive program and explains how the religious formation of children should be approached.

THIS IS OUR FAITH is built on the foundation of the *National Catechetical Directory*. The program's goals and methods are the same as those that are set forth in the pages of the directory. THIS IS OUR FAITH presents the authentic and complete message of Christ and his Church in a way that is adapted to the learning capacity of the child.

365

PROFILE OF THE FIRST-GRADE CHILD

Anne eagerly took the hand of her Uncle Jim and led him into her first-grade classroom. "This is my desk," she beamed, "and here is my teacher's desk. This is where Wendy sits. She's my friend. I have fun here!"

Uncle Jim was amazed at how much his niece had grown since he had last visited the family. She had become so articulate, with definite preferences for food, friends, music, and television shows. He sensed that Anne's feelings about her school displayed the same joy and curiosity that marked the rest of her life.

As a teacher of six-year-old children, your aim should be to allow room for this enthusiasm for life to be expressed, while setting boundaries of respect and responsibility. The following questions, which come from first-grade teachers, should help in defining more clearly how this can be done. The answers to these questions will give you further insight into the makeup of the six-year-old child.

 I notice that the children in my first-grade class have difficulty sharing with each other. Is this self-centeredness normal?

 Yes. Realize that the experiences of the first-grade child revolve around self. They use the word *my* a great deal, and they sometimes have short emotional fuses when their desires are not fulfilled. You can help by

- Encouraging them to share.
- Being a model of someone who shares.
- Involving them in sharing activities, such as passing out materials for class, using supplies together, and cleaning up together.

 The children in my class seem to lack focus at times. They are interested in the "right now"—paying attention one moment and daydreaming the next. What can I do about this?

 There may not be much you can do except adjust your lesson plan to the situation. The six-year-old child has a short attention span and is easily distracted. Plan your lessons to include

- Activities of short duration, perhaps no more than eight to ten minutes.
- A variety of activities.
- Brief periods of silent reflection or prayer.
- Activities that involve physical movement, such as drawing, singing, or role-playing.
- A review of important points to remember.
- Frequent repetition of directives.

 I tried being logical with these children, and they looked at me with blank faces. What gives?

 Children at six years of age have difficulty thinking back in a logical way as to why something happened. They do not think abstractly. So, as much as possible, involve the children with real objects and experiences. Allow them to use their senses, to handle things, and to taste and smell when appropriate, as part of the classroom experience. Also present one idea at a time and surround it with concrete examples.

I sometime feel insecure about filling my important role as a religion teacher. How can I deal with this feeling?

 First, realize that being a religion teacher is a calling from God, a true vocation within the Christian community. God meant for you to be with these children and the Holy Spirit is with you as you work with the children.

Second, realize that you are not the first, nor will you be the last person, to influence the children's growth in faith. You don't have to do everything; yet you do have the opportunity to do something for these children. Your role, though limited in terms of time, is influential. For some children, contact with you as their religion teacher might be the most significant opportunity that they will have to learn more about the Christian faith. Seize the opportunity as a grace-filled period of time for you and the children.

Third, realize that you have many sources of support around you. Seek out the advice and encouragement of the director of religious education, the priests of the parish, and other teachers of the program. Talk with them about your successes and your problems. But, most of all, pray together.

 How can I help these children grow morally?

 They need to be able to trust you as an adult who will accept them as they are and as someone who genuinely cares for them. Here are some suggestions.

- Be enthusiastic about God's love.
- Be patient, for children develop slowly.
- Assign simple tasks that the children can accomplish.
- When correcting the children, be gentle.
- Appreciate the children's need to feel that they belong to the group. Help them realize that you love them despite their mistakes. Dwell on their good actions.
- Accept the children's feelings of joy, fear, sadness, and anger.
- Help the children discover that Christians are happy people. Make humor and laughter a part of each class whenever possible.
- Appreciate that each child is unique.

 What will help me stay involved?

 Here are some ideas from experienced teachers.

- Know why you are teaching.
- Believe in the contribution you are making.
- Be realistic in your expectations of the children.
- Use your teacher edition with its lesson ideas.
- Develop your own prayer life and read the Scriptures.
- Know what you enjoy about being a religion teacher because this will give you strength and perseverance.
- Keep your sense of humor.

CLASSROOM ENVIRONMENT

Children learn best in an environment that is happy and secure. A healthy classroom environment is one that contains the following characteristics.

First, there is reverence and respect for each individual in the group. The personal worth of each child is stressed when

- The teacher warmly welcomes each child to the session, calling each one by name.

- The teacher treats everyone fairly, showing no favoritism to particular children.

- The teacher praises a child for what he or she may have accomplished.

- The teacher sends home special notes to children who have missed lessons because of sickness.

- The teacher conveys a sense of love and care for each child.

- The teacher enthusiastically responds to the children's ideas.

Second, there is a sense of caring and an atmosphere of cheerfulness with the classroom community. Such an environment is created when

- Children are taught to share with each other.

- Children learn to cooperate as a group to get things done.

- Children are encouraged to praise each other.

- Personal events, such as birthdays and name days, are remembered and celebrated.

- Children are able to speak freely without fear of ridicule.

- Children learn to refrain from making judgments about each other.

Third, a healthy classroom environment is one in which there is a feeling that something of value is being accomplished. The children need to see that they have the opportunity to try new things and gain new skills as part of the experience of religious education. This happens in a practical way when

- Children take part in activities that allow each individual to be successful.

- Children enjoy working together.

- Children have a clear understanding of what is being taught.

- Children have their questions answered in ways that are meaningful.

- Children are presented with a variety of activities.

- Children's prayer lives are cultivated through quiet times for reflection.

- Audiovisual materials are a regular part of the class sessions.

Finally, a healthy classroom environment has a physical setting that is pleasant. Some factors that contribute to a setting conducive to learning are

- A classroom that is arranged in a way that provides the space for activities.

- A cozy and comfortable place with reading chairs, prayer rugs, or cushions that is set aside for prayer and Scripture readings.

- A stand or a table set aside for the enthronement of the Bible.

- A classroom that is made visually appealing through the use of pictures, posters, banners, flowers, and the children's art work.

- Background music used at appropriate times.

DEVELOPING SOCIAL SKILLS

Teaching first-grade children self-discipline means letting them know what is socially acceptable. It also means helping them develop social skills, such as listening well and greeting people properly.

Listening

Explain to the children the steps of listening well.

- Stop whatever you are doing or saying.
- Look at the person who is speaking.
- Hear what the person is saying.

Print the three steps on a chart. Post the chart in the classroom so that the children can be reminded of their responsibility.

You can tell if the children are listening well if they are able to do one of the following.

- Ask questions of the speaker.
- Tell you in their own words what was said.
- Follow directions that are given.

You may wish to explore listening with the children by asking the following questions.

- In what places do you have to listen?
- How do you listen when you watch a movie?
- How do you listen when a parent is talking to you?
- How should you listen in class?

Getting the Children's Attention

Establish a procedure for getting everyone's attention during the session. Some children need to hear something. Others need a visual cue, such as a raised hand. You may want to employ a small bell or noisemaker to get their attention. You may decide simply to give an oral request such as, "I want everyone to stop talking and to listen to me." Experienced teachers find that firmness and directness are the best ways to get attention.

Greeting People

Another social skill children should learn is how to meet adults and new acquaintances. The following model might be used to teach the children this skill.

- Stand in front of the person to be greeted.
- Reach out your right hand.
- Take the hand of the other person and shake it.
- Say to the person, "My name is _____."
- Listen to what the person tells you his or her name is.
- Ask a question or answer a question the person may have.
- End by saying, "It was nice to meet you," or "I enjoyed meeting you."

Using Praise

You will often praise children for what they have said or done. Here are suggestions for making this praise giving effective.

Remember that too much indiscriminate praise makes a child dependent on it. Focus on what the children have accomplished and give praise for specific instances of good work. It's best to provide specific information to children on their competence and the value of their accomplishments. For instance, you might say, "I liked your picture." Here are other examples of effective praise giving.

- "Sue, your answer tells me that you have very special memories of the season of Advent. It makes me happy to learn that your Advent season has been so happy."
- "You were a very good reader. You spoke clearly and loudly enough for even the person in the back row to hear you."
- "Thank you for listening so well to the story that I just read. I noticed that no one spoke when I was talking. You asked questions when you did not understand something. You are good listeners!"

PLANNING

One of the keys to a successful religion class is good planning. This involves taking the time to look ahead. It means being willing to put in work time before class. Such planning is one of the marks of a dedicated and concerned teacher.

There are three special planning times: before the year begins, before each unit, and before actual class time.

Before the Year Begins

Planning starts as soon as you receive copies of THIS IS OUR FAITH. Here are some suggestions for getting started.

- Open to the Contents pages in the student text, noting the major areas of Catholic faith being covered.

- Familiarize yourself with the organization of the book.

- Study the Teacher Edition. The beginning pages of the Teacher Edition provide valuable information on the organization of the program as well as the features of the student text and the Teacher Edition. There you will find a description of the three steps used in every lesson plan. You should become familiar with the features of the student text and this three-step plan.

- Study the Scope and Sequence Chart that also appears in the beginning pages of the Teacher Edition. This will familiarize you with the overall theme of the year as well as with the developmental strands that run through the grade levels.

- Make a program calendar for the year by first determining the number of religion classes you will have. Other activities might include service projects, planning for liturgies, field trips, and so on. Isolate the days on which you will be able to conduct a class using one of the lessons in the student text.

Next, decide what chapters you will cover during the year and on what days these chapters will be presented. Examine the Contents page in the front of your Teacher Edition, noting that there are one introductory lesson, twenty core chapters with five days of lessons each, five unit review lessons, five

Day to Day: Skills for Christian Living lessons and thirty-one lessons in the Amen section, and Our Catholic Heritage, a reference section based on the *Catechism of the Catholic Church*. Each of the sessions is designed to provide you with at least thirty minutes of material.

Before the Unit Begins

Each of the units of THIS IS OUR FAITH has four chapters that have been placed together because they cover related areas of Catholic faith. Become familiar with the overall development of each unit that you are about to begin teaching.

- Notice that in the Teacher Edition there is a page of information that begins each unit. This unit opener contains the unit aim, a doctrinal summary of each chapter, and the vocabulary. Reading the unit opener will give you a preview of the unit.

- For a more detailed overview of the unit, read through the chapters themselves, noting what they are seeking to achieve and the kinds of activities that are suggested.

Before the Class Begins

Experienced teachers have found careful preparation invaluable. Here are some steps they recommend.

- After your religion class is over and you have some time to sit and think, ask yourself how the class went. What was successful? What did the children respond to most? What would you change if you could do the session over? Write down your observations on the pages of your Teacher Edition or in a separate notebook. You will also find this valuable when you teach the same lesson next year.

- Look ahead to the next chapter by turning to its Chapter Organizer in your Teacher Edition. Note the objectives for the chapter.

- Review the Chapter Outline. This gives you an overview of the major activities that make up the lesson plans. Then read through the lesson plans on the pages that follow. Make notes to yourself about what will work with your children and what will need to be altered or supplemented. Make any changes you feel necessary.

- Read the Background for the Teacher section of the Chapter Organizer. This will give you information about the theological content of the chapter as well as notes on the way the topic is approached in the lesson plans.

- Gather any supplies on the Materials Needed list that will not be readily available on the day of class. As you looked through the lesson plan, you had the chance to review the Teacher Option boxes that are a part of every lesson and to decide if you wished to include any of these ideas in the lesson.

- Ask yourself if you really understand what the lesson is trying to accomplish. Think about what you know about the topic and seek additional information if necessary. Pray to the Holy Spirit to guide you in your preparation.

- Finally, take time just before the class to review the lesson outline. Make any necessary changes. Make sure that you have all the materials you will need for the session. Assign an approximate time that you will need to spend on each of the activities in the lesson plan. Mentally rehearse how you will conduct the session.

Try to make this procedure a part of your routine.

What does it mean to adapt the lesson plan to your needs?

Experienced teachers know that the lesson plans that appear in teacher manuals are only suggested ways to teach the chapter. They know their children and the kinds of activities they learn from best. They also know themselves and the ways they teach best in class. Experienced teachers take all of these things into consideration when reviewing a lesson plan. They ask themselves the following kinds of questions.

- What is really possible for me to accomplish in this lesson?

- What will the children be interested in?

- What is in this lesson that will work with my children?

- What do I have in my own experiences, interests, and talents that can complement or enrich this lesson plan?

Experienced teachers will make adjustments to the lesson plans that appear in the teacher edition, based on their answers to the above questions.

Is there anything that I can read during the year that will help me be a better religion teacher?

There are a variety of books and magazines available on becoming a better religion teacher. Two that should be read are *Sharing the Light of Faith: National Catechetical Directory for Catholics of the United States* and *The Creative Catechist* by Janaan Manternach and Carl J. Pfeifer, the authors of THIS IS OUR FAITH. Another helpful resource is the *Program Director's Manual* for THIS IS OUR FAITH.

LEARNING ACTIVITIES

Storytelling

Children love stories. The chapters in THIS IS OUR FAITH contain many stories from the Bible and from contemporary life.

Become totally familiar with each story beforehand. While telling a story, look directly at the children. It is always a good idea to have visuals on hand to illustrate main points, attitudes, or feelings reflected in the story. Keep the storytelling short and simple, interrupting occasionally to ask the children how they would react in similar circumstances. Make sure that you distinguish Bible stories from other kinds of stories.

Drawing

Children do not have the vocabulary or the experience to express themselves in words the way we do as adults. They are able, however, to express themselves through drawing.

In order to use drawing effectively, maintain an atmosphere of order in the classroom. Explain clearly what the children are to do and have all materials ready. An art activity is not a play period. It helps to play appropriate background music.

Be sure that you do not make judgments about the artistic value of the children's drawings. Praise their work; allow them to show their work to others; and ensure that specific insights they have expressed are respected. Above all, do not interpret meanings. Leave that to the individual.

Writing

Writing is a wonderful way for the children to gain insights into themselves and their faith. When we ask the children to write down their thoughts, they are forced to reflect on their ideas and feelings before putting their words on paper. Writing can also bring up concerns and questions from the children that you can relate to your religion lesson.

In the THIS IS OUR FAITH program, such writing activities vary for each grade level. Generally the activities include writing responses to questions, creating stories or poems, or writing personal prayers.

You should seek to create an atmosphere that encourages the children to write with openness and spontaneity. Don't indicate beforehand what you would write or what you expect them to say in their writing. Do not criticize their grammar and spelling, as you might in a language arts class.

Reading

In all the grade levels of THIS IS OUR FAITH, there are stories in the student text, both biblical and contemporary. There is also poetry to be read by the children and each chapter contains some explanation of the teachings of Jesus or of various beliefs of the Catholic Church.

Reading is important because it is the primary way the children gain new information in their religious education class. By reading the text, they are introduced to the vocabulary of the Catholic religion. They learn what the Church believes, and they become familiar with the Scriptures through reading Bible stories and passages.

Listening to the Teacher

Often the notes in the teacher edition will call upon you to explain something to the children, to add information to material in the student text, or to clarify concepts that may be confusing to the children. The key advice in making such explanations is to keep them short and simple and avoid moralizing. Remember that explaining something to children in the form of a lecture has been cited in research as one of the least effective ways of teaching.

Memorizing

Memorization is an essential part of all education, including religious education. Two things should always be kept in mind, however. First, the children should not be required to memorize something they do not understand. Second, the material they memorize should be important or relevant.

In THIS IS OUR FAITH, the children are asked to remember the sections of the chapters called We Believe and New Words. These contain the key doctrinal concepts of the chapters as well as the new vocabulary. You may also want the children to memorize Scripture verses in particular chapters. Various traditional prayers that are valuable for the children to learn are introduced, and others can be found in the Amen section.

Keep in mind that children are usually able to memorize only small amounts of information at any one time. Repetition and the use of memory games are often helpful.

DISCUSSING

Good discussion is an important part of religious education. The children should be able to consider their experiences, their understandings, and their questions about life and about what they have learned.

In planning a discussion, make sure that there is sufficient time. Plan a seating arrangement that lends itself to good discussion. Involve everyone in the group. Keep the discussion moving by asking probing questions. It is important that the children experience a freedom of expression, without fear of censure or ridicule. Make positive comments about their contributions and never allow them to interrupt a child who is speaking.

QUESTIONING

There are four kinds of questions that children will be answering in THIS IS OUR FAITH. These questions can be found on the pages of the student text and in the teacher notes for each chapter.

The children will be asked *fact questions,* in which they are asked to recall information about the Catholic faith. These questions are in the Chapter Review at the end of each chapter. At the end of every four chapters, there is also the Unit Review.

After they have learned the material in the text, the children will be asked *meaning questions.* They will be asked what a particular concept or principle means and how they can put it into practice.

The children will be asked *value questions,* in which they are asked to describe how they feel about what they have learned or what their attitudes are about various aspects of the Catholic faith.

They will also be asked to answer *faith questions,* such as "Why is it sometimes hard for me to do the right thing?" and "What does God want me to do?"

EVALUATING

There is no way of precisely assessing a child's growth in faith because that would involve making a judgment about the relationship of faith between God and the child. There is, however, an opportunity for the religion teacher to evaluate what the children have learned as a result of the class sessions.

Each chapter of THIS IS OUR FAITH contains the opportunity to review with the children the content of the chapter through use of the Chapter Review questions. These appear at the end of each chapter and ask the children to recall the key doctrinal concept of the chapter and any new vocabulary that is introduced in the chapter. The children are also asked to show how they will apply the teaching of the chapter to their daily lives.

At the end of each unit of THIS IS OUR FAITH, there is a two-page review of the unit. This review includes questions on the facts and concepts learned in the previous four chapters. It enables the teacher to evaluate what the students have learned and to give further clarification where needed. The suggested project allows for a practical application of the material taught in the unit.

Often, in the chapters themselves, the children are asked to examine their ideas and attitudes regarding some aspect of their lives or faith. These are fine opportunities for the children to think critically, to reflect on the importance of possessing the Catholic faith, and to form the resolve to search always for deeper meaning in their relationships with God.

PRAYER

Prayer is an important part of each religious education class in THIS IS OUR FAITH. The task of creating an environment for prayer in the classroom is part of your role as a religion teacher. All the children should be able to experience the prayer services and informal prayers and learn the prayer skills that are a part of THIS IS OUR FAITH. The children also should have the opportunity to celebrate the Eucharist during the year, and those who are able to participate in the sacrament of Reconciliation should have the chance to do so. The children should learn firsthand as members of a community of faith and as persons of faith what it means to listen to and talk with God.

The Resourceful Teacher Package supplies you with prayer and liturgy supplements. This packet contains prayer services and ideas for prayer for the entire year. It also provides you with guidelines and helpful hints for planning celebrations with the children.

INVOLVING THE COMMUNITY

Parish Involvement

Earlier in these Helps for the Teacher pages, you read that you perform your role as a religion teacher within the community of faith, that is your parish. You have people around you who also influence the faith development of the children in your class. Involving these people in a partnership with you will do much to help the children grow as Catholic Christians. There are three groups of people to think about when considering this partnership: parents or guardians, priests, and other parishioners.

Involving Parents

- At the beginning of the year, introduce yourself to the parents or guardians of each of the children in your class. You can do this by sending letters home, making friendly phone calls, or inviting the parents or guardians to an open house. Explain what you are going to be teaching the children in their religious education class. Help the parents feel that they are always welcome to talk to you about how their children are doing.

- Make sure that parents or guardians are aware of *Opening Doors: A Take-Home Magazine,* which can be found at the end of each unit in the student text.

- If a child is absent for several classes, call the parents or guardians to let them know how they can help at home.

- Try to keep parents informed about what is happening in the class. Send the children home with assignments to do and ask that they return their work with their parents' or guardians' signatures.

- Ask parents or guardians to help out with the class in a variety of ways. Try to have each parent do something during the year for the class.

- If progress reports are sent home during the year, see them as an opportunity to communicate with the families. Be willing to answer any questions that parents may have.

Involving Priests

The parish priests have a powerful influence on the children in your class. Try to involve the priests in ways other than the celebration of the sacraments of Eucharist and Reconciliation. Invite them to visit your class and to talk about specific topics. Make them feel welcome at all class events by always extending personal invitations.

Involving Parishioners

Challenge yourself to think of ways that you can involve parishioners in your class. Invite people to share their talents and interests with the children. Ask the parish musicians who play for liturgical celebrations to help you bring music to the classroom. Ask the social–service people of the parish to show you ways of involving the children in service activities.

TEACHER'S REFLECTIONS

The Teacher's Reflections section is a special resource. Its purpose is to provide you a basis for reflections on the content of each chapter of THIS IS OUR FAITH.

This section will give you an opportunity to grow in knowledge and faith so that you, in turn, can share that knowledge and faith with your students. As the *National Catechetical Directory* states, "Only men and women of faith can share faith with others, preparing the setting within which people can respond in faith to God's grace" (NCD, 207).

Each reflection consists of a question for each chapter of the text. These questions are intended to be answered after you teach the chapter. There is also space to note what really worked in the chapter or what you would change the next time you teach this chapter.

In addition to the chapter reflections, there are sections for beginning-of-the-year and end-of-the-year entries. You can write your thoughts and concerns as you begin a new year of teaching the good news. And when classes come to a close you can report your general reactions of the entire year along with suggestions for the following year.

Finally, note the "Teacher's Prayer Before Class" below. Pray for guidance and support before teaching your class.

Teacher's Prayer Before Class

Loving God, I am about to share your word with my students. Allow me to awaken in the hearts of my students an awareness of your presence in their lives today. As I share my faith with these children, I ask you to help me

> *bring the good news to them;*

> *proclaim your message of unconditional love to them;*

> *envision ways in which to bring your word into their lives.*

Help me listen to the needs of these children's hearts and respond to them with your gentle and compassionate spirit. I ask this in the name of Jesus, your gift to us. Thank you, gracious God, for calling me to be a teacher who shares your good news. Amen.

BEGINNING OF THE YEAR

How do I feel about teaching the truths of our faith to others this year?

What are my greatest doubts and fears as I begin the year?

What are my greatest strengths as I begin the year?

What do I hope to accomplish by the end of the year?

How do I hope to help my students grow in faith?

CHAPTER 1
How can I help my students discover their special qualities?

CHAPTER 2
How did I help my students see the wonder of God's creation?

CHAPTER 3
How did I make my students aware of the special people in their lives?

CHAPTER 4
How did I introduce my students to Jesus?

CHAPTER 5
What images of the Holy Family did my students take with them?

CHAPTER 6
How did I present the person of Mary to my students?

CHAPTER 7
How did I teach my students to question and answer?

CHAPTER 8
What concepts of prayer did I help my students discover?

CHAPTER 9

How did I help my students realize that God cares for them in a special way?

CHAPTER 10

How did I show my students that Jesus cares for them?

CHAPTER 11

How did I connect the story of the Good Samaritan to the lives of my students?

CHAPTER 12

How did I broaden my students' understanding of prayer?

CHAPTER 13

How did I help my students understand what it means to be a Christian?

CHAPTER 14

How did I help my students understand the meaning of Baptism?

CHAPTER 15

How did I help my students recognize their identities as Catholics?

CHAPTER 16

How did my students see the connection between the Eucharist and a meal?

CHAPTER 17

How did I introduce the Holy Spirit to my students?

ADVENT

How did I help my students be more loving and caring this Advent?

CHAPTER 18

How did I help my students realize that the Holy Spirit can give them strength?

CHRISTMAS

How did I help my students' understanding of Christmas grow this year?

CHAPTER 19

How did I help my students see the value of forgiveness?

LENT

How did I help my students understand the meaning of prayer and Lenten actions during Lent?

CHAPTER 20

How did I share the joy of the Holy Spirit with my students?

EASTER

How did I help my students celebrate a joyous Easter season?

TEACHER'S REFLECTIONS

END OF THE YEAR

How have I changed by teaching the truths of our faith to others this year?

How did I improve my teaching skills this year?

What do I feel I have accomplished this year?

How did I help my students grow in faith?

What could I have done differently?

This Resource Guide provides a list of recommended books, videos, and music recordings for use with the lessons in the student text. The guide follows the organization of the text into five units and the Amen section. The following is an explanation of the formats used in listing the different categories of resource material.

Books Books are listed by title, author or editor, publisher, copyright date, and description. The chapter number or section title in parentheses refers to the place in the student text where the material is recommended for use. For example:

> *I Got Community.* Dale Gottlieb. Holt, 1995. A celebration of various individuals' contributions to the community in first-person narration. (1)

Videos Videos are listed by video title, length, series title if applicable, company, copyright date, description, and student text reference in parentheses. For example:

Zip Your Lip to Gossip. (25 min.) "Wooster Square" series. St. Anthony Messenger Press, 1990. Gossiping and telling things that are not true can hurt others and cause a lot of damage. **(14)**

Music Recordings Recordings are listed by title of the song or selection, title of the record album, company, copyright date, and student text reference in parentheses. For example:

> "Easter Rise Up." *Come Meet Jesus!* Pauline Books & Media, 1991. **(Easter)**

The Resourceful Teacher section ends with a list of frequently used publishers and media companies. An introductory note to this list, on page 390, offers advice about sources and scheduling.

Unit 1

Books

God's World Makes Me Feel So Little. Helen Caswell. Abingdon Press, 1988. This delightful book introduces children to the wonders of God's world and shows them why they are important and precious in God's sight. **(Beginning the Journey)**

Miracles and Me! Christy Keanneally. Paulist Press, 1986. A book of poetry for children that can serve as a resource throughout the year. **(1–4)**

Peter's Song. Carol P. Saul. Simon & Schuster, 1992. A delightful tale about friendship. **(1)**

All the Places to Love. Patricia MacLachan. HarperCollins, 1994. As a woman welcomes her first grandson into the world, she and her family introduce him to the land, the river, and the skies above. **(2)**

Got a Family. Melrose Cooper. Holt, 1993. This picture book tells of the ways that family members can love each other. Young readers will be inspired to make up their own verses about how they are loved. **(2)**

Wonderful Earth! Mick and Nick Inkpen. David C. Cook, 1990. This book celebrates the wonderful variety of plants and animals that God created for planet Earth. It also stresses that human beings are God's divine masterpiece but that they have devastated many of God's other creations. At the end is a plea for better stewardship of the world. **(2)**

My Father's Hands. Sheila McGraw & Peter Cline. Green Tiger Press, 1992. A chronicle of a young boy's childhood as he comes to appreciate how his strengths and values are reflected in his father's hands. **(3)**

Now One Foot, Now the Other. Tomie dePaola. Putnam, 1981. Just as a child needs his grandfather, so too does the grandfather need the grandson. **(3)**

Wilfrid Gordon McDonald Partridge. Mem Fox. Kane/Miller, 1985. Readers will learn that gifts given from the heart are the most precious as they follow Wilfrid in his determination to help his old friend Miss Nancy renew her memories. **(3)**

Best Friends. Steven Kellogg. Dutton, 1986. This book describes friendship through the experiences of two girls before, during, and after a summer's separation. **(4)**

A Gift. Fregosi. Prentice Hall, 1976. This volume delightfully tells the many things a gift might be. **(4)**

You Are Special to Jesus. Annetta Dellinger. Concordia, 1984. Interspersed with Scripture references, this book shows children how special and unique each one of them is to Jesus. It also stresses that Jesus' love is unconditional. **(4)**

Videos

Feeling Good About Me. (16 min.) Sunburst, 1991. This video helps young children build a strong self-image by learning how to create positive experiences and value their own uniqueness. **(1)**

God's Five Gifts. (6 min.) Franciscan, 1992. This video leads children to thank God for their five senses and to recognize how special and unique each person is. **(1)**

No One Quite Like Me or You. (16 min.) Sunburst, 1992. Children learn to accept differences in themselves and others. Emphasizes that we are all as alike as we are different. **(1)**

Our Friends on Wooster Square. Vol. I–III (three 20-min. segments on each tape) Franciscan, 1985. Volume I explores the meaning of being special. Volume II focuses on our creation by God. Volume III considers friendship. **(1–4)**

Creation. (22 min.) "Read-Along Bible Video" series. Treehaus, 1992. An inventive retelling of the Creation story helps children discover that God made the world out of love. **(2)**

Creation. (30 min.) "Sacred Heart Kids Club" series. Don Bosco, 1986. Behind every invention is the inventor, behind every original is the creator who has given generously. In this book the wonder and generosity of God are explored. **(2)**

Creation Celebration Series. (30 min. each tape) Augsburg, 1990. The tapes in this series are "The Amazing Creation Room," "Exploring God's Earth," and "Countdown to Adventure." Set in a Bible context, these tapes explore various aspects of creation. **(2)**

Electric Grandmother. (50 min.) Mass Media Ministries, 1986. A heartwarming tale of love, family, aging, friendship, and hope. **(3)**

My Family, Your Family. (16 min.) Sunburst, 1994. This video illustrates that there are different kinds of families and that a family is dependent on the love its members have for each other. **(3)**

Through Grandpa's Eyes. (20 min.) Franciscan, 1989. Touching on the many ways in which we can communicate, this video brings an awareness of the special gifts others who are "different" bring to us. **(3)**

Getting to Know Jesus. (nine 10-min. segments) Tabor, 1985. Appealing stories of Jesus' life are presented. **(4)**

Hey, Kid! It's Jesus. (25 min.) Shepard, 1987. Through a variety of presentations, viewers find Jesus in their everyday lives. **(4)**

Walking With Jesus. (8 min.) Twenty-Third Publications, 1987. Students follow Jesus' journey to Calvary. This presentation depicts children striving to follow Jesus' loving example. **(4)**

Music Recordings

"Children of the Lord." *Joyful Noises.* Brown-Roa, 1993. **(1,2)**

"Thank You for Being So Good." *Young People's Glory & Praise.* Tape 3. (NALR) North American Liturgy, 1984. **(1, 2)**

"Thank You, God." *Wonderfully Made.* Our Sunday Visitor, 1990. (1, 2)

"God's Circle of Love" and "God Has Made a Family." *Hi God! 3.* (NALR) North American Liturgy, 1986. (3)

"I Have a Family Tree." *Wonderfully Made.* Our Sunday Visitor, 1990. (3)

"I'll Follow Jesus." *Joyful Noises.* Brown-Roa, 1993. (4)

All titles. *Living, Loving and Learning with Jesus.* (NALR) North American Liturgy, 1981. (4)

Unit 2

Books

Jesus Had a Family Just Like Me. Elaine Moore. Concordia, 1987. A little girl contrasts her life with Jesus' life as a child. (5)

Perfect Parents. John Mimmelman. Bridgewater, 1993. Gregory outlines for his mother and father how he thinks perfect parents would treat him. (5)

What Is a Family? Gretchen Super. Twenty-First, 1991. This book about family relationships stresses diversity. Might also use *What Kind of Family Do You Have?* (5–7)

Even If I Did Something Awful. Barbara Shook Hazen. Macmillan, 1992. A child learns that a mother's love is unconditional, no matter what. (6)

On Mother's Lap. Ann H. Scott. Houghton, 1992. This version of the 1972 picture book depicts an Eskimo mother as a symbol of maternal love. (6)

I Love My Daddy Because... Laurel Porter-Gaylord. Dutton, 1991. Reasons for loving one's father are illustrated through both human and animal examples. The companion volume is *I Love My Mommy Because...* (7)

My Dad Is Awesome. Nick Butterworth. Candlewick Press, 1992. A father who is accomplished in everything still takes a bath with a rubber duck. (7)

Why Do You Love Me? Martin Baynton. Greenwillow, 1990. This simple text is about a boy asking his father why he loves him. (7)

Before I Go to Sleep: Bible Stories, Poems, and Prayers for Children. Anne Pilling. Crown, 1991. This book contains religious poems, prayers, and twenty-two stories from the Old and New Testaments. (8)

A Child's Book of Prayers. Linda Yeatman. Workman, 1992. A collection of short stories and poems based on African American spirituals and European and American poems and prayers. (8)

Prayers for Children. Juliet Harmer. Viking, 1990. This month-by-month devotional contains brief poems and short prayers illustrating a child's surroundings. (8)

Videos

Jesus the Son of God. (30 min.) "Our Dwelling Place" series. Don Bosco, 1988. The children on the video learn from the events of Jesus' life that all people are children of God. (5–7)

Mary and Joseph. (25 min.) School-Tec, 1989. This video is a year-round teaching tool that describes Jesus' childhood, family, and development into manhood. (5)

The Wonder of the Boy Jesus. (30 min.) "The Wonder" series. ECU, 1988. A grandfather describes to his grandson the early life of Jesus in Bethlehem and Nazareth and Jesus' experiences at the Sea of Galilee and the River Jordan. (5)

Mary. (30 min.) "Sacred Heart Kids Club" series. Don Bosco, 1986. This video leads to a discussion about Mary, Jesus' mother, and our own mothers. (6)

Mary, Our Friend. (15 min.) Brown-Roa, 1987. Five themes are emphasized: Mary Listens, Mary Shares, The Mother of Jesus, Mary Follows, and Mary Cares. (6)

Getting to Know Jesus. (ten 9 min. segments) Tabor, 1985. Ten appealing stories of Jesus' life are presented in such a way that they capture the imagination of young children. **(7)**

Breaking Through the Roof. (25 min.) "Ben & Eddie" series. Oblate, 1990. Feeling helpless, Eddie prays for an answer to a problem but sees no change. He learns that trust in God is difficult but that God always answers prayers. **(8)**

Traditional Prayers for Children. (40 min.) Paulist Press, 1988. Four 10 min. segments help children understand the Hail Mary, Glory Be, Our Father, and Apostles' Creed. The prayers appear on the screen to help children learn correct wording. **(8)**

Music Recordings

"God's Family." *Joyful Noises.* Brown-Roa, 1993. **(5)**

"We Are the Lord's Own Family." *Colby 2.* Maranatha Music, 1991. **(5)**

"When Jesus Was My Age." *This is Our Faith Music Program, Grade 1.* Silver Burdett & Ginn, 1990. **(5–7)**

"The Mother Song." *Dance, Boatman, Dance.* **(6)**

"Super Mom." *Improvise with Eric Nagler.* **(6)**

"God Is Rich in Mercy." *Hi God! 3.* NALR, 1986. **(7)**

"Wherever I Am, God Is." *Hi God! 3.* NALR, 1986. **(7)**

"Jesus Always Listens." *Joyful Noises.* Brown-Roa, 1993. **(8)**

"Receive Our Prayer." *Hi God! 3.* NALR, 1986. **(8)**

Unit 3

Books

Daddy Makes the Best Spaghetti. Anna Gossnickle Hines. Houghton, 1986. The story of a warm relationship between a father and a son as they spend time together doing things at home. **(9)**

Grandfather's Lovesong. Reeve Lindbergh. Viking, 1993. As a grandfather and grandson roam through the season in a rural setting, the old man describes how much he loves the boy. **(9)**

Where Are You Going, Emma? Jeanne Titherington. Greenwillow, 1988. Emma explores the orchard, but when she thinks she is lost, she is reassured by the sound of her grandfather's voice. **(9)**

Always Gramma. Vaunda M. Nelson. Putnam, 1988. A little girl talks about what she and her grandmother have shared in the face of her grandmother's deterioration. **(10)**

The Magic Fort. Juanita Havill. Houghton, 1991. Kevin takes care of his younger brother when he breaks his arm. **(10)**

Mothers Can't Get Sick. Sylvie Wickstrom. Crown, 1989. When Mama Jones gets sick, all of the family pitches in to show how much they love her. **(10)**

Loop the Loop. Barbara Dugan. Greenwillow, 1992. In this endearing book about intergenerational friendship, Anne visits her old friend Mrs. Simpson, who is now in a nursing home. **(11)**

Sophie and the Sidewalk Man. Stephanie S. Tolan. Macmillan, 1992. Sophie saves money to buy an imported hedgehog and, in the process, learns to share with a homeless man. **(11)**

What Goes Around Comes Around. Sally G. Ward. Doubleday, 1991. Isabel accompanies her grandmother as she makes her rounds bringing food to the needy. **(11)**

A Child's Book of Prayers. Michael Hague. Holt, 1985. This collection of well-known prayers for children has full-page color illustrations. **(12)**

Give Us This Day-The Lord's Prayer. Illus. Tasha Tudor. Putnam, 1989. Children in turn-of-the century New England highlight the lovely paintings that illustrate the words of this prayer. **(12)**

Videos

Care's Chorus. (3 min.) "Sing-Along-Express" series. Vol. 2. Oblate, 1991. This music video focuses on casting all our cares upon God, who always takes care of us. **(9)**

God Keeps His Promises. (30 min.) "Our Dwelling Place" series. Don Bosco, 1988. Through some classic Bible stories, a group of orphans learns that God never forgets his promises. **(9)**

Little Ones Belong to Him. (30 min.) "Gerbert" series. Oblate, 1994. In this big world, sometimes a child can feel very small and unimportant. Gerbert's experience rekindles trust in God's loving care of his children. **(9)**

Choose Life. (30 min.) "Sacred Heart Kids Club" series. St. Anthony Messenger Press, 1988. Children are asked how they treat their pets and others and how they respect life and take care of others. **(10)**

Jesus' Concern for Others. (30 min.) "Our Dwelling Place" series. Don Bosco, 1988. Jesus cared for all people, no matter who they were or what they had done. The healing stories of Jesus are told. **(10)**

Miracles of Jesus. (30 min.) Tabor, 1991. Join Benjamin, the widow's son brought back to life by Jesus, and witness many of Jesus' other miracles of healing and love. **(10)**

Good Samaritan. (25 min.) "Animated Stories from the New Testament" series. Family Entertainment Network, 1989. Children and adults are transported to the Master's feet to see this story unfold. **(11)**

Good Samaritan: A Story About Helping Others. (20 min.) "Adventures in Character Building" series. Oblate, 1990. In this exciting story, Sarah and Miguel learn the true meaning of being kind and helping others. **(11)**

Sammy the Good Neighbor. (8 min.) "Parables for Children" series. Brown-Roa, 1993. Parable of the Good Samaritan. A blue fish is attacked by a shark and lies hurting, while the other creatures pass him by. Finally, Sammy Squid stops to help. **(11)**

Breaking Through the Roof. (25 min.) "Ben & Eddie" series. Oblate, 1990. Encouraged by the faith of others, Eddie trusts in the promises of God. **(12)**

Forgive Us Our Debts. (25 min.) "Animated Stories from the Old Testament" series. Family Entertainment Network, 1991. Combines the parable of forgiveness with the teachings of Jesus to his disciples. **(12)**

Our Father. "Learning My Prayers" series. Piera Paltro. Pauline Books & Media, 1980. **(12)**

Music Recordings

"Raise Your Hands." **THIS IS OUR FAITH Music Program, Grade 1.** Silver Burdett & Ginn, 1990. **(9–12)**

"When the Rain Comes Down." Also found on **When the Rain Comes Down, Daydreamer, Children of the Morning,** and **Wobbi-Do-Wop.** **(9)**

"Wherever I Am, God Is." **Hi God! 3.** NALR, 1986. **(9)**

"Helping Hands." **Wonderfully Made.** Our Sunday Visitor, 1990. **(10)**

"Walk a Mile." **Walk A Mile.** also found on **Big Big World** and **Wobbi-Do-Wop.** **(10)**

"If I Could Give You." **Fingerprints.** Pauline Books & Media, 1990. **(11)**

"Jesus Cares for Everyone." **Come Meet Jesus.** Pauline Books & Media, 1990. **(11)**

"The Our Father." **Young People's Glory & Praise,** Tape IV. NALR, 1984. **(12)**

"Thank You, Lord, for Your Daily Bread." **Tiny Tot Praise 3!** Maranatha, 1992. **(12)**

Books

Friends of Jesus: The Animals Tell Their Story.
Nancy Matthews. Oliver-Nelson, 1991. Various
animals participate in the events of Jesus' life from
his birth to his resurrection. (**13**)

The Magpie's Story. Nick Butterworth. Zondervan,
1988. A magpie vows to stop stealing treasures for his
nest after he sees how the hated Zacchaeus is
reformed by Jesus' love and acceptance. (**13**)

Sit Down. Mary Manz Simon. Concordia, 1991. This
beginning reader with a nineteen-word vocabulary has
a lively account of the Mary and Martha story from
Luke 10:38–42. (**13**)

The Day We Met You. Phoebe Koehler. Macmillan,
1990. This book celebrates the great joy of welcoming
an adopted baby into the family. (**14**)

Mommy Loves Jesus. Catherine Snider. Pauline
Books & Media, 1990. A charmingly illustrated book
that presents parents as the first and best teachers of
faith. Ideal for parent-child sharing. (**14**)

When Joel Comes Home. Susi G. Fowler.
Greenwillow, 1993. A young girl eagerly awaits the
day when the baby her family is adopting finally
arrives. (**14**)

The Church. Carole S. Matthews. Concordia, 1983.
Explains and describes the church as both building
and people. (**15**)

What Is a Family? Gretchen Super. Twenty-First,
1991. This book about family relationships stresses
both the unity and diversity within families. (**15**)

I Can Pray the Mass. Mary Teresa Donze A.S.C.
Liguori, 1990. Explores and explains each part of the
Mass for young children. (**16**)

I Meet Jesus. Jean Vanier. Paulist Press, 1989. Story
of the ways that God has loved us—especially through
his son Jesus. (**16**)

My Massbook. Daughters of St. Paul. Pauline Books &
Media, 1984. A first introduction to the Mass, with
bright, lively illustrations. (**16**)

Videos

Are You My Neighbor? Gourds Must Be Crazy. (15
min.) "Veggie Tales" series. Oblate, 1995. This funny
sci-fi spoof shows kids that loving your neighbor
means appreciating all people. (**13**)

Learn to Follow Jesus. (50-min. segments.) ECU,
1988. Puppets Nanny and Isaiah help teach children
to make their faith alive every day. (**13**)

Selfish Giant. (30 min.) Oblate, 1993. The classic
story retold about a little boy who shows a lively ogre
the joy of sharing and the rewards of caring for others.
(**13**)

Baptism. (30 min.) "Sacred Heart Kids Club" series.
Don Bosco, 1990. Highlights aspects of belonging to
God's family, being part of a joyful community, and
the conversion experience. (**14**)

Brian Was Adopted. (9 min.) "Heart to Heart" series.
St. Anthony Messenger Press, 1993. An eight-year-old
Korean boy is assured of the love of both his adopted
parents and his birth parents by his adopted parents'
words and actions. (**14**)

The Meeting: Eddie Finds a Home. (30 min.) "Ben &
Eddie" series. Oblate, 1990. A director of a youth
center adopts an orphan pup, and together they learn
the true meaning of love, family, and friendship. (**14**)

We Are the Lord's Own Family. (4 min.) "Sing-
Along-Express" series, Vol. 3. Oblate, 1991. A music
video that emphasizes being a part of the family of the
Lord. (**15**)

Amanda Goes to Mass. (9 min.) Twenty-Third
Publications, 1991. Amanda explains her
understanding of what happens when she and her
family worship with their parish family. (**16**)

The Mass & Me. (14 min.) Brown-Roa, 1994.
Discusses the parts of the Mass and how to
participate. Also explores what the Mass really means
to young people. (**16**)

RESOURCE GUIDE

There's So Much to Do—Part II. (20 min.) "The Marvelous Mystery" series. Our Sunday Visitor, 1991. Explores the Liturgy of the Eucharist and emphasizes the basic fact that liturgy is "people work". (**16**)

Music Recordings

"The Together Song." *THIS IS OUR FAITH Music Program, Grade 1.* Silver Burdett & Ginn, 1990. (**13–16**)

"Hup-Two-Three-Four." *Tiny Tot Praise! 1.* Maranatha, 1992. (**13**)

"I Will Follow." *I Like to Be With Jesus.* "Sacred Heart Kids Club Music" series. St. Anthony Messenger Press, 1990. (**13**)

"Blessing Song." *Joyful Noises.* Brown-Roa, 1993. (**14**)

"Welcome to the Family." *Kids' Praise 3.* Maranatha, 1991. (**14**)

"God Is Building a House." *Young People's Glory & Praise.* NALR, 1984. (**15**)

"I Am a Christian." Maranatha Music, 1991. Can be found as a music video on *Sunday Sing-Along Video* or *Sing-Along Express.* (**15**)

"The Best Gift." *Come Meet Jesus.* Pauline Books & Media, 1992. (**16**)

"Jesus, Jesus." *Young People's Glory & Praise.* NALR, 1984. (**16**)

Unit 5

Books

An Angel for Solomon Singer. Cynthia Rylant. Orchard, 1992. A friendly waiter named Angel helps a lonely man escape the dreariness of his life. (**17**)

The Angel Who Forgot. Elisha Bartone. Green Tiger Press, 1992. A mother wishes for an angel to come cure her ill son. But the angel who comes has lost all memory. A dragonfly sent by God reveals to the mother the secret of the amnesia, and she helps the angel recover. (**17**)

Teach Me About the Holy Spirit. L. J. Sattgast, Jane Elkins. Multnomah, 1990. Flora and Flossie are twins who act totally opposite. Flora acts out the fruits of the Holy Spirit in her life; Flossie does not. Soon, Flossie sees the fruit of acting like Flora. (**17**)

Storm in the Night. Mary Stolz. Harper, 1988. A grandfather tells his grandson of the time he was afraid, in order to calm the child's fear of the stormy night. (**18**)

Who's Afraid of the Ghost Train? Frank Rodgers. Harcourt, 1989. Robert uses his imagination to conquer his fears, including riding the carnival ghost train. (**18**)

You're the Scaredy-Cat. Mercer Mayer. Rain Bird, 1991. Two young boys decide to spend the night camping outdoors. (**18**)

Matthew and Tilly. Rebecca C. Jones. Dutton, 1991. Matthew, a white boy, and Tilly, a black girl, resume their close friendship after an argument. (**19**)

My Wicked Stepmother. Norman Leach. Macmillan, 1993. Tom hates his new stepmother, but when he deliberately hurts her and she cries, his hate turns to love. (**19**)

The Terrible Fight. Sharon St. Germaine. Houghton, 1990. After their fight, Becky and Holly realize their friendship is too important to keep them apart. (**19**)

A Cozy Place. Hope Slaughter. Red Hen, 1991. Two girls discover that being in each other's presence makes for a cozy place. (**20**)

The Old Man and the Fiddle. Michael McCurdy. Putnam, 1992. In spite of a fierce storm, an old man continues to play a happy song on his fiddle. (**20**)

The Perfect Spot. Robert J. Blake. Putnam, 1992. A boy and his father spend a happy day together in the woods. (**20**)

Videos

Celebrating the Church Year for Children: Pentecost. (15 min.) "Celebrating the Church Year for Children" series. Paulist Press, 1989. This video shows children the liturgical practices and Christian family practices that convey the spirit of the first Pentecost. (**17**)

Pentecost Passage. (11 min.) "Following Jesus Through the Church Year" series. Twenty-Third Publications, 1990. Krispin experiences the thrill of Pentecost by reenacting it through the followers of Jesus that he encounters. (**17**)

Nightmare: Facing Fear. (30 min.) "Ben & Eddie" series. Oblate, 1990. Eddie is awakened by a nightmare, and Ben calms him with songs and Scripture. Eddie finds strength in Christ. (**18**)

Where's God When I'm Scared? (30 min.) "Veggie Tales" series. Oblate, 1994. Contains two animated fifteen-minute segments that teach children a Bible perspective on handling everyday fears. (**18**)

God Wants Me to Forgive Them. (30 min.) "Veggie Tales" series. Oblate, 1994. Contains two animated fifteen-minute segments that teach children a Bible perspective on forgiveness. (**19**)

I Forgive You. (25 min.) "Our Friends on Wooster Square" series. Franciscan, 1990. Sometimes these words are not easy to say. To forgive means "It's OK, I still like you and want to be your friend, even though I was hurt." (**19**)

Sounds of Peace and Love. (30 min.) "Sacred Heart Kids Club-Christian Morality/Commandments" series. Don Bosco, 1988. The characters can distinguish sounds as Sr. Jane plays them on a cassette. But then she plays real sounds of love from Scripture. (**19**)

Hey Kid! It's Jesus, He's Our Friend. (25 min.) Shepard, 1987. Through a variety of presentations, the viewers find ways to see Jesus in their everyday lives. (**20**)

Our Friends on Wooster Square. Vol. 1. (three 20-min. segments) Franciscan, 1985. Through storytelling, song, and Scripture, children learn about love of God, feelings, and sharing joy. (**20**)

Simon the Lamb. (25 min.) Oblate, 1993. Simon is shunned by the other sheep because he is different. But his differences end up saving the other sheep when a winter storm strands them. He calms their fears, and all are happy. (**20**)

Music Recordings

"Pentecost Prayer." *THIS IS OUR FAITH Music Program, Grade 1.* Silver Burdett & Ginn, 1990. (**17**)

"Everyone Moved By the Spirit." *Young People's Glory & Praise.* NALR, 1984. (**17**)

"Spirit Move." *Young People's Glory & Praise.* NALR, 1984. (**17**)

"Let the Lord Take Your Hand." *Listen to the Maker.* Sacred Heart Kids Club Music. Franciscan, 1990. (**18**)

"My Lord Takes Care of Me." *All God's People Love to Sing.* NALR, 1983. (**18**)

"Love One Another." *Wonderfully Made.* 1990. (**19**)

"Peace to You and Me." *Hi God! 3.* NALR, 1986. (**19**)

"Jump With Joy." *Tiny Tot Praise 2.* Maranatha, 1992. (**20**)

"Make a Joyful Noise." *Joyful Noises.* Brown-Roa, 1993. (**20**)

AMEN

Books

ABC's of Christmas. Francine O'Connor. Liguori, 1992. Recounts traditional well-loved Christmas stories in rhyme and verse. (**Advent/Christmas**)

Hark! A Christmas Sampler. Jane Yolen. Putnam, 1991. This Christmas volume includes original poems and stories, legends, carols, holiday history and traditions, and a Nativity play emphasizing the Christ Child. (**Christmas**)

Tale of Three Trees. Angela Elwell Hunt. Ligouri, 1990. All ages will be delighted by this American folk tale about three trees whose wishes come true in surprising ways. (**Easter/Christmas and so on**)

Easter. Gail Gibbons. Holiday House, 1989. Jesus' life and death are treated briefly but accurately. Traditional Easter symbols and customs and the holy days are explained. (**Lent/Easter**)

I Can Pray With the Saints. "I Can Pray" series. Mary Teresa Donze. Liguori, 1991. Offers a simple biographical sketch of 13 saints, highlighting particular virtues and a prayer to help one imitate their lives. (**Saints**)

Videos

The Gift. (11 min.) Twenty-Third Publications, 1995. A little bug reminds children that the most important gift they can give Jesus at Christmas is love. (**Christmas**)

The Wish That Changed Christmas. (23 min.) Oblate, 1993. Orphaned Ivy has no place to go for the holidays, so she boards a train and a miserable Christmas turns grand when she finds the grandmother she's always wanted. (**Christmas**)

Lenten Lane. (10 min.) "Following Jesus Through the Church Year" series. Twenty-Third Publications, 1990. Krispin travels to Nazareth and Jerusalem and experiences the events of the days preceding Christ's death. (**Lent**)

Easter Lamb. (8 min.) "Read-Along Bible Video" series. Treehaus, 1992. Relates the symbols of Easter to God's unfailing love for all people. (**Easter**)

Mary. (30 min.) "Sacred Heart Kids Club" series. Don Bosco, 1986. The story leads to a discussion about mothers, especially Mary, Jesus' mother and our mother also. (**Mary**)

Special Seasons, Special Days. (20 min.) "Marvelous Mystery" series. Our Sunday Visitor, 1991. Children will learn that the Mass is the center of our Church holy days and that different cultures have different ways of celebrating. (**Holy Days**)

Sam. (25 min.) St. Anthony Messenger Press, 1990. Sam has cerebral palsy and can't do what other children can, but he is not different. This story looks at life from Sam's viewpoint. (**In the Spirit of Jesus**)

Music Recordings

"Jesus Is Coming." *Children of the Mountain.* NALR, 1985. (**Advent**)

"Joseph and Mary Blues." *Mary Christmas.* Pauline Books and Media, 1991. (**Advent**)

"First Christmas Day." *Mary Christmas.* Pauline Books & Media, 1991. (**Christmas**)

"Song of the Stable." *O Holy Night.* Liguori, 1993. (**Christmas**)

"Jesus, Heal Me." *Joyful Noises.* Brown-Roa, 1993. (**Lent**)

"Easter Rise Up." *Come, Meet Jesus.* Pauline Books & Media, 1992. (**Easter**)

"Moms Are Made That Way." *Nightlight.* Pauline Books & Media, 1993. (**Mary**)

"Count It All Joy." *Big Steps for Little Feet.* Pauline Books & Media, 1992. (**In the Spirit of Jesus**)

PUBLISHERS AND MEDIA COMPANIES

Many of the resources listed, beginning on page 381, are available from your school, parish, diocesan, regional, college, or university media center. Inquire there first. If you must seek further, the following partial list of publishers/distributors will be helpful. In all cases in which you plan to use free or rental materials, confirm availability and make arrangements several weeks in advance of your scheduled use. Be sure to preview your selection before showing it to your class.

Abingdon Press
201 8th Ave., S
P.O. Box 801
Nashville, TN 37202-0801
(800) 251-3320

Augsburg Fortress Publishers
426 S. 5th St., Box 1209
Minneapolis, MN 55440
(800) 328-4648

**Bantam Doubleday Dell
Publishing Group, Inc.**
1540 Broadway
New York, NY 10036
(800) 223-6834

BridgeWater Books
(Div. of Troll Assocs.)
100 Corporate Dr.
Mahwah, NJ 07430
(800) 929-8765

Brown-ROA
1665 Embassy West Dr.
Dubuque, IA 52002-2259
(800) 922-7696

Candleflame Productions
5536 N.E. Hassalo
Portland, OR 97213

CCC of America
6000 Campus Circle Dr.
Suite 110
Irving, TX 75063
(800) 935-2222

Concordia Publishing House
3558 S. Jefferson Ave.
St. Louis, MO 63118-3968
(800) 325-3040

David C. Cook Pub. Co.
850 N. Grove Ave.
Elgin, IL 60120
(800) 323-7543

Crown Books for Young Readers
(Div. of Random House)
201 E. 50th St.
New York, NY 10022
(800) 733-3000

Crown Ministries Internat'l
9 Winstone Ln.
Bella Vista, AR 72714
(800) 433-4685

Doubleday & Co., Inc.
See Bantam Doubleday Dell.

Dutton Children's Books
(Div. of Penguin USA)
375 Hudson St.
New York, NY 10014-3657
(212) 366-2000

EcuFilm
810 12th Ave., S
Nashville, TN 37203
(800) 251-4091

E.P. Dutton
See Penguin USA.

Family Entertainment Network
See Nest Entertainment.

Franciscan Communications
See St. Anthony Messenger Press.

Green Tiger Press
See Simon & Schuster Children's.

Greenwillow Books
See William Morrow & Co.

Harcourt Brace & Co.
6277 Sea Harbor Dr.
Orlando, FL 32887
(800) 543-1918

Harper San Francisco
1160 Battery St., 3rd Floor
San Francisco, CA 94111
(415) 477-4444

Harper & Row
See HarperCollins.

HarperCollins Children's Books
See HarperCollins.

HarperCollins Publishers
100 Keystone Industrial Park
Scranton, PA 18512
(800) 242-7737

Holiday House, Inc.
425 Madison Ave.
New York, NY 10017
(212) 688-0085

Henry Holt & Co., Inc.
115 W. 18th St.
New York, NY 10011
(800) 488-5233

Houghton Mifflin Co.
222 Berkeley St.
Boston, MA 02116
(800) 225-3362

Kane/Miller Book Pubs.
P.O. Box 310529
Brooklyn, NY 11231-0529
(718) 624-5120

Liguori Publications
One Liguori Dr.
Liguori, MO 63057-9999
(800) 325-9521

Macmillan Books for Young
  Readers
See Simon & Schuster Children's.

Maranatha Music
31050 Laguna Hills
Laguna Hills, CA 92654

Mass Media Ministries
2116 North Charles St.
Baltimore, MD 21218
(800) 828-8825

William Morrow & Co., Inc.
1350 Ave. of the Americas
New York, NY 10019
(800) 843-9389

Multnomah Bible College &
  Biblical Seminary
8435 NE Glisan St.
Portland, OR 97220
(503) 255-0332

Nest Entertainment
(Family Entertainment Network)
6100 Colwell Blvd.
Irving, TX 75039-9833
(800) 452-4485

(NALR) North American Liturgy
  Resources
See Oregon Catholic Press.

Oblate Media &
  Communications
7315 Manchester Rd.
Maplewood, MO 63143-9914
(800) 233-4629

Oliver-Nelson
(Div. of Thomas Nelson Pubs.)
Nelson Pl. at Elm Hill Pike
Nashville, TN 37214
(800) 251-4000

Orchard Books
See Franklin Watts.

Oregon Catholic Press
5536 NE Hassalo
Portland, OR 97213
(800) 548-8739

Our Sunday Visitor Publishing, Inc.
200 Noll Plaza
Hungtington, IN 46750
(800) 348-2440

Pauline Books & Media
50 St. Paul's Ave.
Boston, MA 02130
(800) 876-4463

Paulist Press
997 MacArthur Blvd.
Mahwah, NJ 07430
(201) 825-7300

Paulist Productions
17575 Pacific Coast Hwy.
Pacific Palisades, CA 90272
(800) 624-8613

Penguin USA
375 Hudson St.
New York, NY 10014
(800) 331-4624

Peter Li Education Group
330 Progress Road
Dayton, OH 45449
(513) 847-5902

Pflaum Press
See Peter Li.

Philomel Books
See Putnam.

Picture Book Studio
See Simon & Schuster Children's.

Pine Point Record Co.
(Div. of Charette/Clark Prod.,
  Inc.)
P.O. Box 901
Windham, ME 04062
(800) 486-0967

Platt & Munk Pubs.
See Putnam.

Prentice-Hall
1 Lake St.
Upper Saddle River, NJ 07458
(800) 947-7700

Priority One Publishing
P.O. Box 869100
Plano, TX 75086-9100
(800) 274-4824

Puffin Books
See Penguin USA.

G.P. Putnam & Sons
200 Madison Ave.
New York, NY 10016
(800) 631-8571

Red Hen Press
P.O. Box 419
Summerland, CA 93067
(805) 969-7058

School-Tech, Inc.
Box 1941
745 State Circle
Ann Arbor, MI 48106
(800) 521-2832

Shepard & Associates
P.O. Box 908
Estes Park, CO 80517
(800) 757-1877

Silver Burdett Ginn
See Simon & Schuster
School Group.

Simon & Schuster Children's
200 Old Tappan Rd.
Old Tappan, NJ 07675
(800) 223-2336

Simon & Schuster School Group
P.O. Box 2649
Columbus, OH 43216
(800) 848-9500

Simon & Schuster Trade
1230 Ave. of the Americas
New York, NY 10020
(212) 698-7000

St. Anthony Messenger Press
(also Franciscan
  Communications)
1615 Republic St.
Cincinnati, OH 45210
(800) 488-0488

Sunburst Communications, Inc.
39 Washington Ave.
Pleasantville, NY 10570
(800) 431-1934

Tabor Publishing
200 E. Bethany Dr.
Allen, TX 75002
(800) 822-6701

Treehaus Communications, Inc.
P.O. Box 249
Loveland, OH 45140
(800) 638-4287

Tudor Publications
3109 Shady Lawn Dr.
Greensboro, NC 27408

Twenty-First Century Books
(Div. of Henry Holt & Co. Inc.)
115 W. 18th St., 6th Floor
New York, NY 10011-4113
(212) 886-9200

Twenty-Third Publications
P.O. Box 180
Mystic, CT 06355
(800) 321-0411

Viking Press
See Penguin USA.

Franklin Watts
(Div. of Grolier Publishing Co.)
Sherman Tpk.
Danbury, CT 06813
(800) 672-6672

Workman Publishing Co., Inc.
708 Broadway
New York, NY 10003
(800) 722-7202

Zondervan Publishing House
5300 Patterson Ave., SE
Grand Rapids, MI 49530
(800) 727-1309

CREDITS
Cover art: Pamela Johnson
Marginalia art: Mee Wha Lee
Helps for the Teacher art: Anni Matsick